T0236827

# Lecture Notes in Computer Science 9759

*Commenced Publication in 1973*
Founding and Former Series Editors:
Gerhard Goos, Juris Hartmanis, and Jan van Leeuwen

More information about this series at http://www.springer.com/series/7409

Klaus Miesenberger · Christian Bühler
Petr Penaz (Eds.)

# Computers Helping People with Special Needs

15th International Conference, ICCHP 2016
Linz, Austria, July 13–15, 2016
Proceedings, Part II

 Springer

*Editors*
Klaus Miesenberger
Institute Integriert Studieren
Universität Linz
Linz
Austria

Christian Bühler
Rehabilitationswissenschaften
Technische Universität Dortmund
Dortmund
Germany

Petr Penaz
Masaryk University
Brno
Czech Republic

ISSN 0302-9743 ISSN 1611-3349 (electronic)
Lecture Notes in Computer Science
ISBN 978-3-319-41266-5 ISBN 978-3-319-41267-2 (eBook)
DOI 10.1007/978-3-319-41267-2

Library of Congress Control Number: 2016943068

LNCS Sublibrary: SL3 – Information Systems and Applications, incl. Internet/Web, and HCI

Printed on acid-free paper

This Springer imprint is published by Springer Nature
The registered company is Springer International Publishing AG Switzerland

# Preface

Twenty-seven years ago, a group of computer science experts from the Austrian Computer Society, led by Prof. Roland Wagner and Prof. A Min Tjoa, started ICCHP conference. Since the first conference in Vienna (Austria) back in 1989, ICCHP has evolved as a unique and one of the few long-term  references of R&D in the field and is evidence of how information and communication technology (ICT), assistive technology (AT), and eAccessibility have been implemented and have significantly contributed to the improvement of the life of people with disabilities. ICCHP had the honor of accompanying and supporting the revolutionary developments of Assistive Technology and eAccessibility over the last decades. It can be proud to serve as a platform for exchange and communication in this context. The UN Convention on the Rights of People with Disabilities (UNCRPD) is the globally accepted reference and expression of the societal transformation toward effective inclusion and participation of all people with disabilities in society. The UNCRPD refers to AT, eAccessibility, eInclusion, and design for all as a precondition and means of support. Exactly these issues are also the core science topics of ICCHP.

ICCHP's scientifically based mission for inclusion and participation in the information society strives for better AT for support, enhancement and restoration of resources of people with disabilities, and compensating limitations of standardized HCI. This mission continues to gain more importance owing to the ongoing ICT revolution (Internet/Web of Things/ubiquitous computing/cloud-based services). The ICT revolution brings along an increased potential for inclusion and participation, but also risks for exclusion and thus the responsibility for implementing eAccessibility. It provokes a growing number of challenging research questions. Old boundaries of concepts dissolve, new approaches and fresh thinking are needed: not only in technical terms but also in legal, social, economic, pedagogic, and other terms. ICCHP is open to all these aspects and invites one to, and provides a platform for, a holistic discussion for improving the lives of people with disabilities in every corner of our world.

ICCHP is proud of its history and to this day it provides one of the few comprehensive and complete collections of scientific work in the field of AT and eAccessibility. All proceedings covering more than 2,300 reviewed articles have been published by Springer in their *Lecture Notes in Computer Science Series*. Since 2006, they have been available online with more than 100,000 (some almost 200,000) downloads of articles. This makes ICCHP a well-recognized reference and a unique source for learning and understanding the theoretical, methodological, and pragmatic specializations of this growing and expanding R&D field.

The proceedings of the 15th edition constitute a collection of high-quality, well-reviewed submissions by scientists, users, practitioners, educators, and policy makers from around the world. Each of the 239 eligible submissions was carefully reviewed by at least by three members of the international Programme Committee composed of

129 experts from all over the world and listed herein. The panel of 18 conference chairs analyzed the review results and prepared the final decisions. Based on this intense and careful analysis, ICCHP 2016 accepted 115 submissions as full papers and 48 as short papers (acceptance rate 59 %). These data provide evidence of the highly competitive process guaranteeing for the scientific quality of the proceedings and the conference.

ICCHP 2016 in Linz hosts high-quality, well-reviewed submissions from scientists, users, practitioners, educators, and policy makers and discussions among more than 500 participants from around the world. In particular ICCHP welcomes young researchers, the next generation of experts in our field, and invites them to contribute to the Young Researchers Consortium as well as to the Coding for a Cause (C4C) competition. "Universal Learning Design" has become a central topic which is taken care of by the Teiresias Center at the Masaryk University Brno. The Roland Wagner ICCHP Award, the C4C Competition, the Young Researchers Consortium, the Summer University on Math, Science, and Statistics for Blind People, and a series of parallel workshops and meetings make ICCHP a unique meeting place to drive AT and eAccessibility forward.

*We welcome the attendees valuable contribution to ICCHP 2016 and encourage them and their colleagues to become regular participants in its most important mission. It is here that research, innovation, and practical endeavors in important topics of AT and eAccessibility come together to be shared, explored, and discussed.*

ICCHP 2016 is proud to be under the patronage of the United Nations Educational, Scientific, and Cultural Organization (UNESCO).

May 2016                                                      Klaus Miesenberger
                                                                      Christian Bühler
                                                                            Petr Penaz

# ICCHP Committees

## General Chair

| | |
|---|---|
| Bühler, C. | TU Dortmund University, FTB, Germany |

## Steering Board

| | |
|---|---|
| Burger, D. | INSERM, France |
| Klaus, J. | Karlsruhe Institute of Technology, Germany |
| Murphy, H.J. | California State University Northridge, USA |
| Suzuki, M. | Kyushu University, Japan |
| Tjoa, A.M. | Technical University of Vienna, Austria |
| Wagner, R. | University of Linz, Austria |

## Publishing Chairs

| | |
|---|---|
| Miesenberger, K. | University of Linz, Austria |
| Penaz, P. | University of Brno, Czech Republic |

## Programme Chairs

| | |
|---|---|
| Archambault, D. | Université Paris 8, France |
| Fels, D. | Ryerson University, Canada |
| Kobayashi, M. | Tsukuba University of Technology, Japan |
| Kouroupetroglou, G. | University of Athens, Greece |
| Manduchi, R. | University of California at Santa Cruz, USA |
| Ramesh, S.K. | CSUN, USA |
| Weber, G. | Technische Universität Dresden, Germany |

## Young Researcher Consortium Chairs

| | |
|---|---|
| Archambault, D. | Université Paris 8, France |
| Fels, D. | Ryerson University, Canada |
| Fitzpatrick, D. | Dublin City University, Ireland |
| Kobayashi, M. | Tsukuba University of Technology, Japan |
| Lam, S. | Project:Possibility, USA |
| Mihailidis, A. | University of Toronto, Canada |
| Morandell, M. | AIT Austrian Institute of Technology GmbH, Austria |
| Pontelli, E. | New Mexico State University, USA |
| Prazak-Aram, B. | AIT Austrian Institute of Technolog GmbH, Austria |
| Weber, G. | Technische Universität Dresden, Germany |
| Zimmermann, G. | Stuttgart Media University, Germany |

## Workshop Chairs

Petz, A.                 University of Linz, Austria
Pühretmair, F.           KI-I, Austria

## International Programme Committee

Abbott, C.               King's College London, UK
Abou-Zahra, S.           W3C Web Accessibility Initiative (WAI), Austria
Abu Doush, I.            Yarmouk University, Jordan
Andrich, R.              Polo Tecnologico Fondazione Don Carlo Gnocchi Onlus,
                         Italy
Arató, A.                KFKI-RMKI, Hungary
Azevedo, L.              Instituto Superior Tecnico, Portugal
Banes                    Qatar Assistive Technology Center, Qatar
Batusic, M.              Fabasoft, Austria
Bernareggi, C.           Università degli Studi di Milano, Italy
Bernier, A.              BrailleNet, France
Bosse, I.                Technische Universität Dortmund, Germany
Bu, J.                   Zhejiang University, China
Chen, W.                 Oslo and Akershus University College
                         of Applied Sciences, Norway
Chorbev, I.              Ss. Cyrill and Methodius University in Skopje, Macedonia
Christensen, L.B.        Sensus, Denmark
Chutimaskul, W.          King Mongkut's University of Technology Thonburi,
                         Thailand
Coughlan. J.             Smith-Kettlewell Eye Research Institute, USA
Craddock, G.             Centre for Excellence in Universal Design, Ireland
Crombie, D.              Utrecht School of the Arts, The Netherlands
Cudd, P.                 University of Sheffield, UK
Darvishy, A.             Züricher Hochschule für Angewandte Wissenschaften,
                         Switzerland
Darzentas, J.            University of the Aegean, Greece
Debevc, M.               University of Maribor, Slovenia
Debeljak, M.             University of Ljubljana, Slovenia
DeRuyter, F.             Duke University Medical Centre, USA
Diaz del Campo, R.       Antarq Tecnosoluciones, Mexico
Draffan, E.A.            University of Southampton, UK
Dupire, J.               CNAM, France
Emiliani, P.L.           Institute of Applied Physics Nello Carrara, Italy
Engelen, J.              Katholieke Universiteit Leuven, Belgium
Galinski, Ch.            InfoTerm, Austria
Gardner, J.              Oregon State University, USA
Hakkinen, M.T.           Educational Testing Service (ETS), USA
Harper, S.               University of Manchester, UK

| | |
|---|---|
| Heimgärtner, R. | Intercultural User Interface Consulting (IUIC), Germany |
| Holone, H. | Østfold University College, Norway |
| Hoogerwerf, E.-J. | AIAS Bologna, Italy |
| Iversen, C.M. | U.S. Department of State, USA |
| Kalinnikova, L. | Pomor State University, Russia |
| Kouropetroglou, Ch. | ALTEC, Greece |
| Kremser, W. | OCG, HSM, Austria |
| Lauruska, V. | Siauliai University, Lithuania |
| Lee, S. | Open Directive, UK |
| Matausch, K. | KI-I, Austria |
| Mayer, Ch. | AIT Austrian Institute of Technology GmbH, Austria |
| Mohamad, Y. | Fraunhofer Institute for Applied Information, Technology, Germany |
| Muratet, M. | INS HEA, France |
| Müller-Putz, G. | TU Graz, Austria |
| Normie, L. | GeronTech - The Israeli Center for Assistive Technology and Ageing, Israel |
| Nussbaum, G. | KI-I, Austria |
| Oku, H. | Kobe Gakuin University, Japan |
| Ono, T. | Tsukuba University of Technology, Japan |
| Oswal, S. | University of Washington, USA |
| Paciello, M. | The Paciello Group, USA |
| Panek, P. | Vienna University of Technology, Austria |
| Paredes, H. | University of Trás-os-Montes e Alto Douro, Portugal |
| Petrie, H. | University of York, UK |
| Poobrasert, O. | Institute of Technology for Persons with Disabilities and Elderly Persons (ITDE), Thailand |
| Raisamo, R. | University of Tampere, Finland |
| Rice, D. | National Disability Authority, Ireland |
| Sanchez, J. | University of Chile, Chile |
| Sik Lányi, C. | University of Pannonia, Hungary |
| Simsik, D. | University of Kosice, Slovakia |
| Sloan, D. | The Paciello Group, UK |
| Snaprud, M. | University of Agder, Norway |
| Stephanidis, C. | University of Crete, FORTH-ICS, Greece |
| Stiefelhagen, R. | Karlsruhe Institut of Technology, Germany |
| Stoeger, B. | University of Linz, Austria |
| Suweda, O. | The Hyogo Institute of Assistive Technology, Japan |
| Teshima, Y. | Chiba Institute of Technology, Japan |
| Takahashi, Y. | Toyo University, Japan |
| Tauber, M. | University of Paderborn, Germany |
| Teixeira, A. | Universidade de Aveiro, Portugal |
| Truck, I. | Université Paris 8, France |
| Velleman, E. | Bartimeus, The Netherlands |
| Vigo, M. | University of Manchester, UK |
| Vigouroux, N. | IRIT Toulouse, France |

| Vlachogiannis, E. | Fraunhofer Institute for Applied Information Technology, Germany |
| Votis, K. | CERTH/ITI, Greece |
| Wada, C. | Kyushu Institute of Technology, Japan |
| Wagner, G. | Upper Austria University of Applied Sciences, Austria |
| Watanabe, T. | University of Niigata, Japan |
| Weber, H. | ITA, University of Kaiserslautern, Germany |
| Whitfield, M. | Ryerson University, Canada |
| Wöß, W. | University of Linz, Austria |
| Yamaguchi, K. | Nihon University, Japan |
| Yeliz Yesilada | Middle East Technical University, Cyprus |

## Organizing Committee

| Bieber, R. (Chair) | CEO, Austrian Computer Society, Austria |
| Feichtenschlager, P. | Integriert Studieren, JKU Linz, Austria |
| Haider, S. | Integriert Studieren, JKU Linz, Austria |
| Heumader, P. | Integriert Studieren, JKU Linz, Austria |
| Jitngernmadan, P. | Integriert Studieren, JKU Linz, Austria |
| Klemen, M.D. | President, Austrian Computer Society, Austria |
| Koutny, R. | Integriert Studieren, JKU Linz, Austria |
| Kremser, W. | WG ICT with/for People with Disabilities, Austrian Computer Society, Austria |
| Miesenberger, K. | Integriert Studieren, JKU Linz, Austria |
| Murillo Morales, T. | Integriert Studieren, JKU Linz, Austria |
| Penaz, P. | Masaryk University Brno (ULD), Czech Republic |
| Petz, A. | Integriert Studieren, JKU Linz, Austria |
| Plhák, J. | Integriert Studieren, JKU Linz, Austria |
| Schult, Ch. | Integriert Studieren, JKU Linz, Austria |
| Wagner, R. | Integriert Studieren, JKU Linz, Austria |

## ICCHP Roland Wagner Award Nomination Committee

| Andras Arato | KFKI Budapest, Hungary |
| Christian Bühler | TU Dortmund, FTB Vollmarstein, Germany |
| Deborah Fels | Ryerson University, Canada |
| Klaus Miesenberger | University of Linz, Austria |
| Wolfgang Zagler | Vienna University of Technology, Austria |

We thank the Austrian Computer Society for announcing and sponsoring the *Roland Wagner Award on Computers Helping People with Special Needs*.

The Austrian Computer Society decided in September 2001 to endow this award in honor of Prof. Roland Wagner, the founder of ICCHP.

The Roland Wagner Award is a biannual award in the range of €3,000. It is handed over at the occasion of ICCHP conferences.

**Award Winners:**

- *Award 7:* Prof. Dr. Art Karshmer (✝ 2015), University of San Francisco, USA and Prof. Dr. Masakazu Suzuki. Kyushu University, Japan, ICCHP 2014 in Paris.
- *Award 6:* The TRACE Centre of the University Wisconsin-Madison, USA, ICCHP 2012 in Linz
- *Award 5:* Harry Murphy Founder, Former Director and Member Advisory Board of the Centre on Disabilities USA and Joachim Klaus, Founder, Former Director of the Study Centre for Blind and Partially Sighted Students at the Karlsruhe Institute of Technology (KIT), Germany, ICCHP 2010 in Vienna
- *Award 4:* George Kersher, Daisy Consortium, ICCHP 2008 in Linz
- Special Award 2006: Roland Traunmüller, University of Linz
- *Award 3:* Larry Scadden, National Science Foundation, ICCHP 2006 in Linz
- *Award 2:* Paul Blenkhorn, University of Manchester, ICCHP 2004 in Paris
- Special Award 2003: A Min Tjoa, Vienna University of Technology on the occasion of his 50th birthday
- *Award 1:* WAI-W3C, ICCHP 2002 in Linz
- Award 0: Prof. Dr. Roland Wagner on the occasion of his 50th birthday, 2001

Once again we thank all those helping to put ICCHP in place and thereby supporting the AT field and a better quality of life for people with disabilities. Special thanks go to all our supporters and sponsors, displayed at: http://www.icchp.org/sponsors.

# Contents – Part II

## Tactile Maps and Map Data for Orientation and Mobility

## Mobility Support for Blind and Partially Sighted People

## The Use of Mobile Devices by Individuals with Special Needs as an Assistive Tool

## Mobility Support for People with Motor and Cognitive Disabilities

## Towards e-Inclusion for People with Intellectual Disabilities

## AT and Inclusion of People with Autism or Dyslexia

## AT and Inclusion of Deaf and Hard of Hearing People

## Accessible Computer Input

**AT and Rehabilitation for People with Motor and Mobility Disabilities**

**HCI, AT and ICT for Blind and Partially Sighted People**

# Contents – Part I

## Technology for Inclusion and Participation

## Mobile Apps and Platforms

## Accessibility of Web and Graphics

## Ambient Assisted Living (AAL) for Aging and Disability

## The Impact of PDF/UA on Accessible PDF

## Standards, Tools and Procedures in Accessible eBook Production

## Accessible eLearning - eLearning for Accessibility/AT

## Inclusive Settings, Pedagogies and Approaches in ICT-Based Learning for Disabled and Non-disabled People

## Digital Games Accessibility

# Environmental Sensing Technologies
# for Visual Impairment

# Environmental Sensing Technologies for Visual Impairment

## Introduction to the Special Thematic Session

Roberto Manduchi[1(✉)] and James Coughlan[2]

[1] Baskin School of Engineering,
University of California, Santa Cruz, USA
manduchi@soe.ucsc.edu
[2] Smith-Kettlewell Eye Research Institute, San Francisco, CA, USA
coughlan@ski.org

**Abstract.** Peoples ability to move around, interact with objects, space and people, and engage in purposeful activities hinges in large part on their visual sense. Tasks such as orienting oneself in a hallway, finding an item at the market, or recognizing a friend from a distance may become difficult or impossible for those who cannot see, or cannot see well. Simple assistive devices may play an important role in supporting activities of daily living for people with visual impairment. For example, people who are blind use simple tools such as a long cane or a dog guide to move safely along a desired path, or a screen reader to access a computer. Persons with low vision often rely on magnifying glasses, telescopes, and screen enlargers to access textual information.

In recent years, the widespread diffusion of smartphones, equipped with accessible interfaces, has spurred a number of innovative technical solutions to some of the problems faced by visually impaired persons. Some of the most successful applications rely on remote sighted helpers for visual interpretation. For example, TapTapSee allows a blind user to take a picture and receive a textual description of the scene content, such as the main visible objects. BeMyEyes uses a FaceTime-like audio/video connection to enable blind users to share the video stream taken with their iPhone or iPad with a remote sighted volunteer, who can answer specific queries, describe what is visible in the video, and also advise the blind user about where to move the camera for a better view. Other models are currently being explored; for example, Aira provides a remote visual interpretation service by professional helpers, who are specifically trained to support blind users in tasks such as navigation, information access, and even people recognition.

These types of crowdsourcing mechanisms have been quite successful for specific tasks. However, crowdsourcing may not be the solution for all types of visual interpretation tasks. For once, video communication requires a good data connection, which is not always available, and can quickly drain the battery of a smartphone. In addition, the time to establish a connection or to receive an answer to a query may be substantial, discouraging frequent use of this technology. Automatic visual analysis by means of computer vision algorithms (executed on the smartphone itself, or on a remote cloud server) is an attractive alternative. Many blind people, for example, use currency reader smartphone apps such as LookTel. Optical character recognition (OCR), a mature technology originally developed for scanned documents, has found its way in mobile apps such as the KNFB Reader or in complete wearable systems such as OrCam. Modern OCR systems can read documents of different types with high accuracy, provided that the blind user can take a good picture (well framed and with enough resolution) of the document. In fact, using a camera without visual feedback can be quite challenging; non-visual interface mechanisms (e.g. audio) are being developed to assist blind users in this process, for example by directing the user to move the camera in a certain direction to get a better view of the document.

There are other powerful environment sensing mechanisms that harness non-visual information. Accessible navigation apps using GPS (e.g., Blindsquare) allow blind pedestrians to localize themselves, follow a route, and discover nearby points of interest. Self-localization can be enhanced by inertial sensors (contained in any modern smartphone or wearable device), which can be used to count steps and determine the users orientation. Another very promising direction is the use of an infrastructure of networked sensors (the Internet of Things). Deployed in the urban environment, these systems can enable a level of awareness that would be difficult to achieve solely with the sensors of a smartphone or other wearable device. For example, Wi-Fi access points placed inside bus vehicles or at bus stations may allow a blind person to access travel-related information, such as understanding which bus just arrived at the stop, or, during a trip, which stop to exit at. iBeacon (Low-Energy Bluetooth) technology is a low-cost approach to indoor localization, which has been deployed (among other places) at the San Francisco international airport. Passive RFID tags may also be employed for short-distance localization, provided that the user carries an RFID reader (e.g., embedded in their long cane).

This Special Thematic Session presents new advances on Environmental Sensing Technologies for Visual Impairment. It includes applications such as scene text detection and OCR with wearable devices; assisted public transportation using Bluetooth Low Energy or Wi-Fi beacons; smartphone apps for outdoor localization; 3-D scene analysis using depth sensors; and augmentation of GIS systems with pedestrian crossing from aerial images. The session builds on a past series of workshops[1] chaired by Coughlan and Manduchi focusing on research into the applications of Environmental Sensing Technologies and computer vision for visual impairment. Like the workshop series that preceded it, this Special Thematic Session is intended to create a forum to forge interdisciplinary links among practitioners in the fields directly related to Environmental Sensing Technologies, including computer vision, wearable sensors, ubiquitous computing, crowdsourcing, man-machine interfaces, and human factors.

---

[1] http://www.ski.org/project/workshop-series-computer-vision-and-sensor-enabled-assistive-technology-visual-impairment.

# Ball Course Detection Function for the Blind Bowling Support System Using a Depth Sensor

Makoto Kobayashi[✉]

Department of Computer Science, Tsukuba University of Technology, Tsukuba, Japan
koba@cs.k.tsukuba-tech.ac.jp

**Abstract.** To realize a blind bowling support system that tells information to a blind player using a voice synthesizer, a function of ball course detection is being developed after implementation of a function of counting remaining pins. The new function detects a position of thrown ball on an area of arrow marks on the bowling lane using a depth sensor. The sensor is connected to a pipe frame that bridged over the lane. Based on the evaluation by a blind bowling player, it can be shown that the function works basically well, although there is still potential to improve its stability.

**Keywords:** Blind bowling · Depth sensor · Depth image · Image processing

## 1 Introduction

Tenpin bowling is one of the popular adapted physical entertainment for the blind people. It is known as a "Blind bowling." The International Blind Sports Federation (IBSA) introduces them in the web page [1] and an official event in the IBSA world games is held [2]. The blind players are classified from B1 class to B3 class depends on the severity of their visual impairment. The B1 class is for totally blind players and they are allowed to touch a 'guide rail' when they throw a ball. The rail is put on the opposite side of their throwing hand and the length of the rail is approximately four meters. It is useful for understanding their standing position and throwing direction. In addition to using the rail, a sighted assistant staff supports the blind players by telling appropriate information. The information includes what the course of throwing ball is, where the hitting point is, and how many pins are left, et cetera. During the bowling game, the blind player tries to control their throwing by these verbal information.

On the other hand, in spite of such an accessible equipment and conditions, blind players would like to play it by themselves without any support by sighted assistants. It is considered as a natural desire. Therefore, to solve the need, a project of developing a Blind Bowling Support System was started in 2013. As a first step of this project, a function of counting the remaining pins was developed [3]. The hardware components are a camera, a computer, and a Bluetooth speaker. The software recognizes when the sweeping rake is coming down by a pattern matching, and it counts remaining pins using difference of brightness values of positions of pins. These positions are manually set in advance. Finally, a synthesized voice reads the results of remaining pins to the player via the Bluetooth speaker.

K. Miesenberger et al. (Eds.): ICCHP 2016, Part II, LNCS 9759, pp. 5–8, 2016.
DOI: 10.1007/978-3-319-41267-2_1

Following the function, as a next step, a new function of detecting a ball course is being developed. In this paper, the evaluation of these systems and results are reported.

## 2  Ball Course Detection Function

The floor of the bowling lane is constructed with long narrow boards and the number of these boards is 39, and in the area of 365 cm from the foul line on the lane, there are seven printed arrow marks on every five boards. In general, information of where the throwing ball goes in the area of these arrow marks is really important for players and sighted assistants tell the information to them. These arrow marks help to determine on what number of the board the ball goes. For example, when it goes on two boards left from the rightest arrow mark, it can be said that the ball goes on the 7th board.

To realize the automatic function of detecting a ball course without sighted assistant, depth sensor (ASUS, Xtion Pro Live) was prepared. The principle of depth measurement is based on the combination of an infrared (IR) camera and a projection of IR light pattern. The IR camera calculates the depth of each pixel by the reflection of the light pattern at different positions. The sensor is connected to a pipe-frame with a clamp arm and the direction of the sensor is to the floor. The pipe-frame is bridged over the area of these arrow marks. Figure 1 shows its overview. The developed software continuously measures the depth of pixels on the horizontal line at the middle of the image and calculates where the nearest point on the line is. When the ball is passed over the measured line, the nearest point represents the center of the ball. The resolution of the depth image is 320 dots by 240 dots and the distance between the sensor and the floor is adjusted as eight dots represents one board, hence dividing the coordinate value of the nearest point by eight makes the number of board where the ball goes on. After the simple calculation, the detected position of the ball is reported by a speech synthesizer via a Bluetooth speaker.

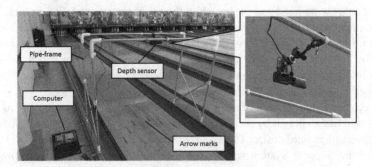

**Fig. 1.** Overview of a ball course detection system. A pipe-frame bridges over an area of arrow marks and a depth sensor is connected the frame to watch the floor of the lane.

## 3 Evaluation of the System by a Blind Bowling Player

As a first evaluation of the developed ball course detection function, the software has checked in the laboratory condition with stable dummy ball and it was clear that it could detect correct position of the ball.

After that, the system was brought to the real bowling alley and a blind player of B1 class tested it in two games. During the test, the ball detection system described above and a remaining pins counting system developed before were running together. Figure 2 shows an alignment of these systems at the bowling alley. These two information comes different speakers to distinguish easily. The timing of output from the ball detection system was adjusted to wait twelve seconds so that it comes after the synthesized voice from the remaining pin counting system.

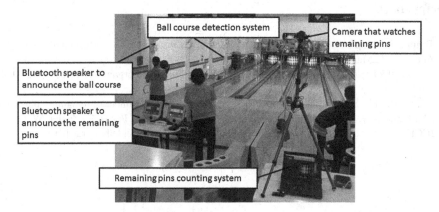

**Fig. 2.** Alignment of a ball course detection system and a remaining pins counting system. The camera of the counting system is put on the right back table. These systems run together and the blind bowling player can get both information after throwing.

As a result, the player threw a ball 40 times including two times strikes and the remaining pins counting system worked perfectly throughout both games. However, it was clear that the ball course detection system has some problem. When the system detects the ball course, the reported result is correct, although there were nine times of no response cases. The rate of correct detection was 77.5 per cent in this case. The main reason of no response case was considered that the ball speed was too fast to detect by only one scanning line. If the position of the ball in captured image frames had been just under the line and just over the line, the system could not detect the ball.

Besides the results, comments from the player was acquired as follows. "Totally, I think the system can help me to understand the situation and I can train my throwing by myself. The remaining pins counting system achieved a practical level. The function of the ball course is not stable but has enough accuracy, even better than real sighted assistant because assistants have some error caused by its viewpoints. And as a next step, I would like to know where the ball hit at first. Please make it in the future."

## 4   Summary and Future Plan

To solve the needs of blind bowling players, a ball detection function for the automatic support system is developed using a depth sensor and evaluate it in a real bowling alley by a blind player. Based on the evaluation by a blind bowling player, it can be shown that the function works basically well, although there is still potential to improve its stability.

As a future plan, the software should be improved not to miss the ball and a more useful function should be implemented based on the comments by blind bowling players.

**Acknowledgements.**   This work was supported by JSPS KAKENHI Grant Number 25350752.

## References

1. Tenpin Bowling - General information. http://www.ibsasport.org/sports/tenpin-bowling/. Accessed 25 Mar 2016
2. Seoul 2015 IBSA World Games. http://www.ibsawg2015seoul.org/en-us. Accessed 25 Jan 2016
3. Kobayashi, M.: Blind bowling support system which detects a number of remaining pins and a ball trajectory. In: Miesenberger, K., Fels, D., Archambault, D., Penaz, P., Zagler, W. (eds.) ICCHP 2014, Part I. LNCS, vol. 8547, pp. 283–288. Springer, Heidelberg (2014)

# Catching the Right Bus - Improvement of Vehicle Communication with Bluetooth Low Energy for Visually Impaired and Blind People

Elmar Krainz[✉], Werner Bischof, Markus Dornhofer, and Johannes Feiner

FH JOANNEUM, Kapfenberg, Austria
{elmar.krainz,werner.bischof,markus.dornhofer,
johannes.feiner}@fh-joanneum.at
http://www.fh-joanneum.at

**Abstract.** Visually impaired and blind people have major difficulties in locating and communicating with public transport vehicles due to their restriction of vision. They must rely on other people's help or technical supports. In this paper we show how direct communication with the bus driver via Bluetooth Low Energy (BLE) is possible. A person with visual restriction is able to send and receive messages via an accessible smartphone app directly to the bus driver. With the help of the suggested system traveling with public transport gets easier and the person's independent mobility is improved.

**Keywords:** Blind · Public transport · Bluetool low energy · Vehicle communication

## 1 Introduction

Independent mobility is an important life issue but when it comes to visually impaired or blind people this implicitness gets a different perspective. In fact, visually impaired or blind people have to rely on public transportation in order to travel from one place to another. However, their journey is often accompanied by several obstacles such as several heavy traffic, noisy environment or indoor navigation at subway stations. Another but rather critical aspect is the restricted communication between a bus driver and a traveler, respectively the public transport systems and a smartphone. Normal-sighted people usually do not have difficulties to look for a bus or tram heading in the right direction, to read departure times from info screens or just signal a bus driver to get a lift. Visually impaired and blind people, however, have major difficulties in communicating and locating their needs due to their Visual restriction.

This research discusses several improvements for the communication between a vehicle and a smartphone to better support visually handicapped people while using public transport. The main contributions are quick communication setups employed by Bluetooth Low Energy (BLE) technology, an optimized user experience for smoother app interactions and finally the use of iOS devices which are quite popular among people suffering from visual impairment.

© Springer International Publishing Switzerland 2016
K. Miesenberger et al. (Eds.): ICCHP 2016, Part II, LNCS 9759, pp. 9–15, 2016.
DOI: 10.1007/978-3-319-41267-2_2

## 2    Related Work

In recent years, there has been substantial research in the support of visually impaired and blind people in terms of public transport. Common problems these people face, are the appropriate routing on footpaths for pedestrians [3,6] the support of orientation and localization within buildings [8,11] as well as the orientation at intersections on heavy traffic roads [4]. These are significant situations demanding general guidance and support, in particular for people with visual impairment [5,9]. In this setting, the communication with vehicles is crucial in order to facilitate independent travelling [2,10]. Last, but not least an interactive, multimodal and intuitive user interface [1,7] is essential for the acceptance of any supporting system.

## 3    Catching the Right Bus

For every person using public transport it is essential to catch the right vehicle. Visually impaired and blind people need help form others or from technical solutions to find the suitable bus or tram. Technical systems need a communication channel from the vehicle directly to the person's device.

### 3.1    Existing System

The previous research project NAVCOM [2] aimed at facilitating the communication between smartphones and public transport vehicles with the use of WLAN. The connection between the internal bus system communication (IBIS system) and a standard smartphone was established via WLAN and relevant information was transmitted wirelessly as shown in Fig. 1.

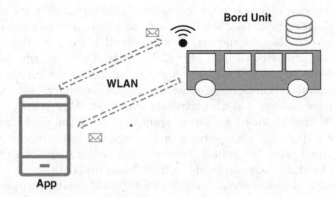

**Fig. 1.** The NAVCOM architecture build on WLAN communication between the public transport vehicles and the smartphones.

Despite its first success, some limitations occurred: Firstly, the time to establish a consistent connection with a bus driving by and a blind person's smartphone took too long. Secondly, the API, needed to program the WLAN components, was not available on the iOS platform.

## 3.2 Improved Approach

In the project at hand, we enhanced the existing NAVCOM system in following ways:

– **Communication with the bus on-board-unit:** BLE (Bluetooth Low Energy) inner workings allow usage of radio frequency signals in a quite different way than WLAN. It can be configured to constantly emit or receive signals without draining batteries. Above all, the connection time of this wireless communication standard is much faster than WLAN, which is crucial in specific traffic situations. It is possible to exchange information even with a bus moving at high speed. Furthermore, this standard is supported by all vendors and allows the usage of various apps on both popular smartphone platforms, iOS and Android.

  Visually impaired and blind people need the following important functions: getting the driver's attention when entering or leaving the bus. So the driver can help to get on/off the bus. If there is just a display of the next station, then the request of the next station is also an important feature. The BLE signal strength can be used to check the distance to the bus, while the entering of the bus (Fig. 2).

  In the future every bus should be accessible. Therefore this has to be defined as a standard. In the serial IBIS system every producer implemented the system in a different way. It was not possible to produce a solution for every customer. Now we have a European standard ITxPT[1] and a German IP-KOM-ÖV standard[2] which work with ethernet network. The European project aim4it[3] focuses on the accessibility of the standard. However it will take 10–20 years that the public transport providers change to the new standard.

– **Navigation:** One of the most essential part for independent traveling of visually impaired people is to choose a viable route without too many obstacles. We optimized route selection by a suitable configuration of an Open Street Map (OSM) routing server, which prefers paths meeting the needs of visually handicapped users' such as finding appropriate pedestrian areas, avoiding roads with heavy traffic or dangerous tracks [3].

  The accuracy of the GPS position can be weak and additional information about the surroundings can improve the navigation. Blind people can verify the route, when the know the side of the wall or the street. Then they also know on which sidewalk of the street they walk. Most of the navigation systems

---

[1] http://itxpt.org.

[2] https://www.vdv.de/ip-kom-oev.aspx.

[3] http://www.ways4all.at/index.php/de/aim4it.

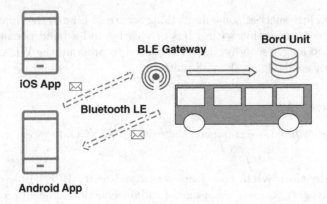

**Fig. 2.** The BLE architecture allows also access to iOS smartphones.

have been developed for outdoor navigation. A two-dimensional model was sufficient for the most cases. There are new challenges in indoor navigation. Especially public traffic stations can be tricky. The stations are distributed over several levels. Here a tree-dimentional model is more appropriate.

However indoor navigation is a difficult task. Some of the designers, try to make it a simple as possible. I.e. the Vienna public transport company use an interesting approach with routing information static texts for every subway station and each platform. Visually impaired users can step through the segments of a route.

– **Accessible User interfaces:** In the last years many users suffering from impaired vision have switched to modern smartphones. The improvements of the built-in accessibility features, such as Android Talkback, allow visually impaired people to use their smartphones for more daily needs. The NAVCOM system – a previous implementation of the authors – allows speech output [7]. In the current phase many further improvements are in development. One example is the user interface which can be replaced with different appearance to support users with different forms of visual restraints, extending and augmenting the built-in accessibility features (see Fig. 3).

## 4    Evaluation

To evaluate the improvements of the supporting system we conducted an empirical study with four visually impaired users. The evaluation was performed in the final project meeting on 15.12.2014 in the area of the public transport station (Praterstern) in Vienna. The testgroup got prepared smartphones (Android based phones with the reinstalled vehicle communication app and enabled screenreader Talkback) and were asked to perform following tasks (see Fig. 4).

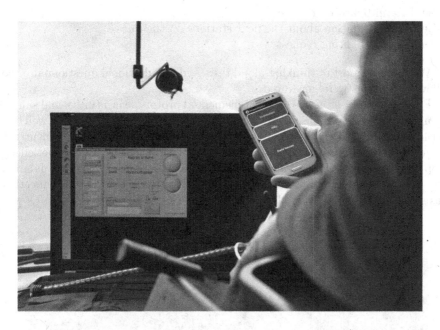

**Fig. 3.** The user interface of the app and the bus driver display.

**Table 1.** Data of user evaluation

| User | Age | Visual impairment | Usage of public transport | Smartphone | Feedback | Suggestion |
|---|---|---|---|---|---|---|
| 1 | 53 | none | daily | iPhone | proof of concept works, but needs improvement | more stability |
| 2 | 57 | blind since age of 9 | daily | 2 PMON | some technical problems | nix |
| 3 | 60 | became blind in the age of 40 | daily | Samsung Galaxy Active | search for available vehicles too long | more information about the next stop |
| 4 | 48 | strong partial visual impairment | rarely | iPhone | connection to vehicle is not reliable, but works great after connection | focus on relaiability of the connection |

– Sending an boarding request
– Getting information about the next stations on the bus
– Sending an alighting request

With the support of thinking-aloud tests and an additional questionnaire the following findings were generated.

Firstly, the user interface of the implemented prototype is intuitive and simple enough to be used even in stressful situations. The communication works well due to the Bluetooth low energy technology. Only in situations with heavy concurrent usage the reliability of the overall system is not sufficient as users experienced drop offs. The test users gave also critical feedback about the systems relaiability. The time to connect to the vehicle was too long, but afterwards the connection was stable (details are available in Table 1).

**Fig. 4.** Test users sending request to bus.

## 5   Conclusion

The proof of concept to use BLE for public transport vehicle communications was successful. According to the statements of the visually-impaired test users, the usage of the smartphone in terms of usefulness and accessibility was feasible. They were able to perform the tasks required in a reasonable time frame. Some problems still occurred with too many simultaneous connections (more than 20). A possible solution for this would be to change to the BLE advertisement mode. This would mitigate overload on the server side and might be worth considering in upcoming versions of the software.

**Acknowledgements.** This work was funded by the Austrian research funding association (FFG) under the scope of the program *Mobility of the Future* within the research project *Ways4me*.

# References

1. Baun, G., Venard, O., Uzan, G., Paumier, A., Cesbron, J.: Le projet rampe: systÈme interactif d'information auditive pour la mobilitÉ des personnes aveugles dans les transports publics. In: Proceedings of the 2nd French-Speaking Conference on Mobility and Ubiquity Computing, UbiMob 2005, pp. 169–176. ACM (2005)
2. Bischof, W., Krajnc, E., Dornhofer, M., Ulm, M.: NAVCOM – WLAN communication between public transport vehicles and smart phones to support visually impaired and blind people. In: Miesenberger, K., Karshmer, A., Penaz, P., Zagler, W. (eds.) ICCHP 2012, Part II. LNCS, vol. 7383, pp. 91–98. Springer, Heidelberg (2012)
3. Dornhofer, M., Bischof, W., Krajnc, E.: Comparison of open source routing services with openstreetmap data for blind pedestrians - pgrouting, opentripplanner and opensourceroutingmaschine. In: Foss4g Europe2014 (2014)
4. Fusco, G., Shen, H., Murali, V., Coughlan, J.M.: Determining a blind pedestrian's location and orientation at traffic intersections. In: Miesenberger, K., Fels, D., Archambault, D., Peňáz, P., Zagler, W. (eds.) ICCHP 2014, Part I. LNCS, vol. 8547, pp. 427–432. Springer, Heidelberg (2014)
5. Koutny, R., Heumader, P., Miesenberger, K.: A mobile guidance platform for public transportation. In: Miesenberger, K., Fels, D., Archambault, D., Peňáz, P., Zagler, W. (eds.) ICCHP 2014, Part II. LNCS, vol. 8548, pp. 58–64. Springer, Heidelberg (2014)
6. Koutny, R., Miesenberger, K.: Pons - mobility assistance on footpaths for public transportation. Stud. Health Technol. Inf. **217**, 440–446 (2015)
7. Krajnc, E., Knoll, M., Feiner, J., Traar, M.: A touch sensitive user interface approach on smartphones for visually impaired and blind persons. In: Holzinger, A., Simonic, K.-M. (eds.) USAB 2011. LNCS, vol. 7058, pp. 585–594. Springer, Heidelberg (2011)
8. Moder, T., Hafner, P., Wieser, M.: Indoor positioning for visually impaired people based on smartphones. In: Miesenberger, K., Fels, D., Archambault, D., Peňáz, P., Zagler, W. (eds.) ICCHP 2014, Part I. LNCS, vol. 8547, pp. 441–444. Springer, Heidelberg (2014)
9. Narzt, W.: Facilitating utilization of public transportation for disabled persons by an open location-based travel information system for mobile devices (viator). In: Proceedings of the 7th International Conference on Mobile Ubiquitous Computing, Systems, Services and Technologies, Porto, Portugal, September 29 – October 3, 2013, UBICOMM 2013, pp. 7–12, September 2013
10. Wang, H.-L., Chen, Y.-P., Rau, C.-L., Chung-Huang, Y.: An interactive wireless communication system for visually impaired people using city bus transport. Int. J. Environ. Res. Public Health **11**(5), 4560–4571 (2014)
11. Zegarra Flores, J., Farcy, R.: Indoor navigation system for the visually impaired using one inertial measurement unit (IMU) and barometer to guide in the subway stations and commercial centers. In: Miesenberger, K., Fels, D., Archambault, D., Peňáz, P., Zagler, W. (eds.) ICCHP 2014, Part I. LNCS, vol. 8547, pp. 411–418. Springer, Heidelberg (2014)

# Navi Rando

## GPS-IMU Smart Phone Application for Helping Visually Impaired People Practicing Hiking

Jesus Zegarra Flores[1(✉)], Laurence Rasseneur[1], Clément Gass[2], and René Farcy[3]

[1] Faculté des Sciences du Sport, Université de Strasbourg,
Strasbourg Cedex, France
{zegarraflores, rassene}@unistra.fr
[2] Point de Vue sur la Ville, Lyon, France
clement.gass@laposte.net
[3] Laboratoire Aimé Cotton, Université Paris Sud, ENS Cachan, CNRS,
Université Paris-Saclay, Orsay Cedex, France
rene.farcy@gmail.com

**Abstract.** The GPS devices adapted for the visually impaired people are used most of the time in urban areas. Additionally, the heading of the GPS is not updated correctly in pedestrian navigation. If the person hesitates at low speed and losses his orientation, he has to walk some tens of meters in order to have updated information. Another technical problem is that the GPS signal can be lost because of bad reception conditions. To reduce the technical problems, the authors propose a GPS-IMU (accelerometers and gyrometers) coupled to a compass app. In our approach, this system is used to give the possibility to the visually impaired people to hike without sighted intervention. The application has two parts; one part to save the GPS coordinates of the path in situ with the corresponding comments and the other part to navigate. The tests were done with three visually impaired (two partially blind people and a fully blind person) experts in the use of the app during the night in 4.65 km road passing from urban areas and rustic paths. The results were presented taking into considerations the rate between the average speed in doing the turnings of the path and the average speed in straight lines. The results are very encouraging because the three visually impaired people arrived to the final destination without any kind of sighted help even in extreme conditions of the tests (the rustic path was not clear enough to be detected with the white cane and the tests were done in a rainy day during the night).

**Keywords:** GPS · IMU · Hiking · Visually impaired person

## 1 Introduction

Currently, most of the GPS devices adapted for the visually impaired people are used in urban areas. For instance: the breeze Human-Ware [1], Kapten Mobility Kapsys [2], GPS application from TeleorionVox [3], etc. In addition, last generation GPS devices are

© Springer International Publishing Switzerland 2016
K. Miesenberger et al. (Eds.): ICCHP 2016, Part II, LNCS 9759, pp. 16–22, 2016.
DOI: 10.1007/978-3-319-41267-2_3

sensible to interferences and the heading is not precise at low speed (pedestrian navigation). If the user hesitates at low speed and loses his orientation, he has to walk with the GPS some tens of meters in order to have an updated heading from the GPS [4]. Additionally, most of the GPS devices are based on routes from the maps; however, in the case of the hiking roads, most of the routes do not exist or if exists they are not voice adapted for the visually impaired people. On the other hand, it is found some investigation in which it is used a voice based descriptive map in order to communicate geographic information with interactive map applications in hiking contexts for elderly people [5].

Nowadays, if a visually impaired person wants to practice hiking, a sighted person guides him. In this case, the visually impaired person holds on to the sighted person's arm or shoulder as they walk along. If the road is narrow, the two persons have to walk in single file when moving.

In order to give the possibility, for the visually impaired people, to hike without sighted intervention, the authors have developed Navi Rando which is an adapted Smart Phone application that uses the information coming not only from the GPS, but also from IMU sensors (accelerometers, gyrometers) and a compass to give guidance instructions. Because of the use of the IMU sensors, the application is able to give the instructions even when the signal GPS is lost. The application has two parts, the application to record a new path or to modify a prerecorded path and the application to navigate.

## 2   Materials

The application to record a path, for making the path accessible to the visually impaired person, allows us to save every GPS coordinates in situ and to give comments related, for example, to the type of the ground ("take path with grassy ground"), or to anticipate and to give the information if there is any danger; for instance: "walk carefully, river on the right of the path", or to clarify if there is any ambiguity in the path; for example, when there is a bifurcation, the comment can be "keep right" or "keep left" in order to take the good path. This information is associated to every GPS point recorded, if it is necessary.

The application to navigate uses the recorded path and gives the vocal information taking into account the body axis direction of the user in the form of "heading" and "distance" to the point, for example: "Point 5, 12 o'clock, 100 m, next point to 3 o'clock", means that the blind person is walking already in the good direction to the GPS coordinates of the point 5 and he has to walk straight during 100 meters, once arriving to the point 5, to going to the point 6, he has to turn right and continue. This information can be given every 10, 15 or 20 s during the navigation. If the blind person is approaching to the point, the distance decreases, moreover, when the person arrives to the current point, the system automatically gives the information to the next point allowing the visually impaired person navigates from point to point. If the GPS signal is lost, the system will take into consideration the information from the IMU sensors in order to continue to give the guidance instructions.

In order to have the two hands free (one hand for using the white cane and the other one for using eventually a walking stick) and to listen the vocal information, the Smart Phone is put inside a pouch on the chest of the person (for example, light blue pouch, Fig. 1).

**Fig. 1.** Visually impaired person hiking using, on the right hand the white cane, on the left hand the hiking stick and the smart phone inside the light blue pouch. (Color figure online)

## 3   Methodology

In order to run the tests, a sighted expert recorded the hiking path of 4.65 km close to the small town of Wingersheim in France with 30 GPS coordinates (see Fig. 2, on the left) giving comments if it was necessary (for example, at the round-about take the second route on the right, take the path with gravel ground, etc.).

**Fig. 2.** On the left, the cartography of the hiking road loop with 4.65 km. On the right, the conditions of the road (grassy ground with puddle).

The path is a loop starting and finishing at a bus station in the small town. The urban area part has about 800 m crossing small streets and a roundabout, the rest of the path is rustic path having grassy ground with puddle (the day of the test was a rainy day) and gravel ground (see Fig. 2 on the right). Three visually impaired (two partially blind people and a fully blind person) testers between 20 and 33 years old from a blind association in Strasbourg agreed to be volunteers of this test.

These three visually impaired persons are experts in the use of the application, the instructions given (with more than 100 km hiking with the application in different kinds of grounds) and the use of the white cane for the hiking. None of the subjects had walked this hiking trail before. As, the hiking tests were done during the night, the first partially blind person (1st subject) still had residual vision during the night, the 2nd subject (partially blind person as well) had full night blindness and the 3rd subject is a fully blind person. Every visually impaired person started from the departure point every 5 min one after the other. The information: duration time, distance walked, GPS trajectory and average speed was collected during the tests with another application working at the same time of the navigation.

## 4 Results

The Table 1 shows the total distance of the trajectory walked and the time taken of the three visually impaired people. The Fig. 3 shows the GPS trajectory of the three visually impaired subjects.

**Table 1.** Total distance and time taken.

| Subjects | Distance of the trajectory done (meters) | Time (minutes) |
|---|---|---|
| 1$^{st}$, partially blind person (cyan line) | 4957 | 54 min 39 s |
| 2$^{nd}$, partially blind person, night blindness (red line) | 5429 | 60 min 1 s |
| 3$^{rd}$, fully blind person (green line) | 5040 | 80 min |

We have also analyzed two parameters, the average speed of the three visually impaired in straight lines with no hesitation (Table 2) and the average speed every time that the subject has changed of direction. During the whole test, there have been thirteen changes of directions that have been called "turnings". In order to calculate the average speed for the turnings, there were taken into account the speeds from 30 m before arriving to the turning until 30 m after passing the turning. The Table 2 shows the average speed in straight segments and Table 3, shows the rate between the average speed of turnings and the average speed of straight segments with every visually impaired person.

Let's consider a good efficiency in turning, (considering the test conditions), when the person does not hesitate much to turn and the rate related to the average speed of the straight segments is more than 70 %. According to Table 3, the authors can point out

**Fig. 3.** GPS trajectories of the three subjects (1st subject in cyan line, 2nd subject in red line and 3rd subject in green line). (Color figure online)

**Table 2.** Average speed in straight segments

| Subjects | (Average speed) Km/h in straight segments |
|----------|-------------------------------------------|
| 1st | 5.3 |
| 2nd | 6.5 |
| 3rd | 3.7 |

**Table 3.** Rate between the average speed of turnings and the average speed of straight segments; NA: Not Applicable.

| Subjects | (Average speed turning)/(average speed Straight segment) | | | | | | | | | | | | |
|----------|---------|-----|-----|-----|-----|-----|-----|-----|-----|------|------|------|------|
| | Turnings | | | | | | | | | | | | |
| | 1st | 2nd | 3rd | 4th | 5th | 6th | 7th | 8th | 9th | 10th | 11th | 12th | 13th |
| 1st | 0.70 | 0.69 | 0.61 | 0.63 | 0.70 | 0.82 | 0.82 | 0.91 | 0.91 | 0.77 | 0.85 | 0.87 | 0.9 |
| 2nd | 0.66 | 0.67 | 0.29 | 0.52 | 0.73 | 0.73 | 0.8 | 0.67 | 0.23 | 0.63 | 0.78 | 0.58 | 0.8 |
| 3rd | 0.64 | 0.42 | NA | NA | 0.74 | 0.64 | 0.96 | 0.85 | 0.82 | 0.77 | 0.98 | 0.85 | 0.6 |

that the first subject did 10 turnings (1st, 5th, 6th, 7th, 8th, 9th, 10th, 11th, 12th, and 13th) with good efficiency and the others with a slightly more hesitation. This can be explained because the 2nd turning is a roundabout and he paid more attention before crossing the streets making him reducing his speed because of the cars and the circulation. The 3rd and 4th were turnings segments with difficulty to walk and also to find with the white cane because of the ground with puddle making him reducing his speed as well.

For the second subject, it can be observed that he did 5 turnings (5th, 6th, 7th, 11th and 13th) with good efficiency, for the rest of the turnings; he had more hesitation being more critically the 3rd and the 9th turning. The decreasing in speed for the 1st and 2nd turning can be explained because he was in the urban area and he paid more attention to cross the streets and the roundabout. The 3rd turning, where the subject went out and deviated completely from the real path because he could not find the path with his white cane due to the rustic ground with puddle. For the 9th turning, he could not either find the path with his white cane and hesitated more, after he stopped for some time, went out the smart phone from the pouch and used the function "finding the current point permanently" which gives just the "heading" and "distance" to the current point and he could arrive to this point and came back to the real path for continuing with the navigation.

The third fully blind subject did 7 turnings (5th, 7th, 8th, 9th, 10th, 11th and 12th) with good efficiency; on the other hand, in the rest of the cases, the most critical turning was the 2nd one because he had to cross a roundabout in the urban area. The 3th and the 4th turning were not considered in the calculus because the person deviated completely from the real path passing for another path and arriving after directly to the 5th turning. During this time of deviation, he was walking slowly and hesitating trying to find a clear path to arrive to the next point.

## 5 Conclusions

Even in extreme conditions; for example, the rustic path was not clear enough to be detected with the white cane, mostly covered with puddle, the test was done in a rainy day (bad GPS reception conditions) and the hiking was during the night, the three visually impaired experts arrived to the final destination using the application without any form of sighted assistance and they were able to understand and get back from their errors.

The first partially blind subject with residual vision during the night did not go out from the path; he was just deviated slightly from the real path. He was the most efficient in doing the turnings compared to the other two subjects. This is explained because of his residual vision, even during the night, he could distinguish in some parts of the road the border of the path. This information in addition to the information coming from the navigation instructions and the white cane confirmed he was in the correct direction.

The second partially sighted subject with night blindness did 5 turnings with good efficiency out of 13, it is due to the fact that he has less experience in full blindness conditions for finding a path with the white cane in turnings. However he was faster in straight segments than the other two subjects. The third fully blind person walked slower but had a good efficiency in turnings compared to the second subject. In addition, he was able to recuperate the route after an alternate path.

We have tested the possibility to save a navigation path file and to use it to give instructions to guide the visually impaired people using Navi Rando in hiking trails. The efficiency of the guiding system seems to be accurate under the following conditions: firstly, the user has to be trained for the use of the white cane in hiking conditions, he needs also to be used to the guidance information "heading" and "distance" and he needs to find his own strategy to navigate using the information coming from the white cane to detect the path, from the GPS and from his own sensorial information.

# References

1. Human breeze. http://store.humanware.com/hus/trekker-breeze-plus-handheld-talking-gps.html
2. Kapten mobility. http://www.kapsys.com/fr/support-produits/kapten-mobility/
3. TéléorionVox. http://www.certam-avh.com/content/telorion-vox-s3
4. Zegarra Flores, J., Farcy, R.: GPS and IMU (inertial measurement unit) as a navigation system for the visually impaired in cities. J. Assist. Technol. 7(1), 47–56 (2013)
5. Laakso, M., et al: User experiences with voice-based descriptive map content in a hiking context, pp. 49–58 (2013)

# Scene Text Detection and Tracking for Wearable Text-to-Speech Translation Camera

Hideaki Goto[1](✉) and Kunqi Liu[2]

[1] Cyberscience Center, Tohoku University, Sendai, Japan
hgot@cc.tohoku.ac.jp
[2] Graduate School of Information Sciences, Tohoku University, Sendai, Japan

**Abstract.** Camera-based character recognition applications equipped with voice synthesizer are useful for the blind to read text messages in the environments. Such applications in the current market and/or similar prototypes under research require users' active reading actions, which hamper other activities. We presented a different approach at ICCHP2014; the user can be passive, while the device actively finds useful text in the scene. Text tracking feature was introduced to avoid duplicate reading of the same text. This report presents an improved system with two key components, scene text detection and tracking, that can handle text in various languages including Japanese/Chinese and resolve some scene analysis problems such as merging of text lines. We have employed the MSER (Maximally Stable Extremal Regions) algorithm to obtain better text images, and developed a new text validation filter. Some technical challenges for future device design are presented as well.

**Keywords:** Reading assistant · Text-to-speech · Scene text recognition · Wearable camera · Text tracking

## 1 Introduction

Several smartphone applications helping the blind read text on documents, goods, and signboards have been released recently. KNFB Reader [1] is a feature-rich application capable of recognizing text in a variety of European languages but Japanese/Chinese/Korean. Amedia Live Reader is specialized for "live reading," in which the text is captured and read aloud on-the-fly, supporting eleven languages including Japanese/Chinese/Korean. Although our product, Grab 'n' Read, is very simple, Windows 10 desktop/Mobile users would find it helpful. These applications and/or similar prototypes under research require users' active reading actions, which hamper other activities. In our earlier report at ICCHP2014 [2], we presented a different approach; the user can be passive, while the device actively finds useful text in the scene and read it aloud. For example, the user just wants to hear prominent text as he/she is walking down the street or corridor. The user probably does not want to hear the same text again and again. We introduced a text tracking feature to avoid duplicate reading of the same text and also to improve the character recognition accuracy.

© Springer International Publishing Switzerland 2016
K. Miesenberger et al. (Eds.): ICCHP 2016, Part II, LNCS 9759, pp. 23–26, 2016.
DOI: 10.1007/978-3-319-41267-2_4

In this report, we present an improved system with two key components, scene text detection and tracking, that can handle text in various languages including Japanese/Chinese and resolve some scene analysis problems such as merging of text lines.

## 2   Improved Scene Text Detection and Tracking

The overall framework is the same as our earlier system [2]. The text detection takes place once every 31 frames, and the text tracking follows. In [2], we were using DCT-based text detection method, which was more tolerant to image blur compared with other methods. However, it is not precise enough without a text validation, and the output coordinates are rough as it is block-based. Stroke Width Transform (SWT) has become popular in recent researches on text detection. However, the performance deteriorates very much with some fonts, especially Mincho (Ming) for example, since SWT assumes the constant stroke width while Mincho fonts contain strokes in various thicknesses.

We have employed the MSER (Maximally Stable Extremal Regions) algorithm [3]. Figure 1 shows the flow of the text region extraction. Connected Components (CC) of black pixels are extracted, and the CC centers are connected to find the Delaunay triangulation. Then, the edges between different objects are filtered out by examining the edge length, color difference between the CCs, CC width ratio, and CC height ratio. As can be seen in (c), the characters within a text line are grouped, while there is no edge connected to other objects.

Finally, a text validation filter is applied to filter out the non-text regions (false positives). We have found that the stroke balance and density of each Kanji character can be used as good features for text validation. Each cluster in Fig. 1(c) is regarded as text region candidate and segmented into character candidate images using projection profile. For each character candidate, the bounding box is partitioned into four even subregions (Fig. 2(a)). The candidate is discarded if the min-max ratio of pixel density exceeds a threshold or if the maximum pixel density exceeds another threshold.

A circle as big as 80 % of the bounding box's short edge, centered at the centroid, is drawn as shown in Fig. 2(b). The candidate is discarded if the pixel density in the circle exceeds a predefined threshold. Our preliminary survey has shown that about 95 % of Kanji characters can be covered by these criteria.

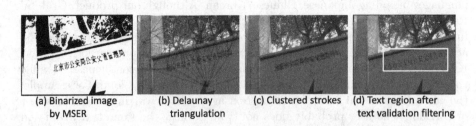

| (a) Binarized image by MSER | (b) Delaunay triangulation | (c) Clustered strokes | (d) Text region after text validation filtering |

**Fig. 1.** Flow of the text region extraction (Color figure online)

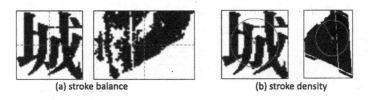

(a) stroke balance                    (b) stroke density

**Fig. 2.** Text validation filter

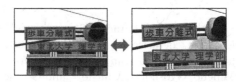

**Fig. 3.** Split and merger of text regions

In [2], we proposed a text tracking method using the Lucaks-Kanade tracker and the SURF (Speeded-Up Robust Features) descriptor [4]. We introduced a cache memory holding some SURF descriptors so the device can remember the text regions temporarily disappeared from the camera's view or hidden by other objects for a certain period of time. Such a framework is effective for continuous text tracking since the camera's view angle is limited to 90° or so even with a wide-view device.

When there are multiple text regions in the scene, we may have situations as shown in Fig. 3 where the text regions merge and split temporarily as the view point changes. In order to track each text correctly and avoid duplicate voice synthesis, the correspondences of the extracted text regions between video frames need to be found. When a text region split into two parts, for example, only one part became the successor and the other part was regarded as a new text in our previous system. In Fig. 4, the TEXT1 region consists of two lines, A and B. If TEXT3 became the successor of TEXT1, the other region TEXT4 was left alone, and the text B got a chance to be read twice or more. This time, we have made some improvements in the SURF-based matching so the system can keep the regions relationship using a graph representation.

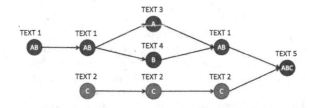

**Fig. 4.** Graph representation of text tracking

**Table 1.** Comparison of text detection methods

|          | Precision (%) | Recall (%) | F-score (%) |
|----------|---------------|------------|-------------|
| Proposed | 63.15         | 83.22      | 71.81       |
| SWT      | 28.99         | 94.70      | 44.39       |

## 3   Experiments

We prepared Japanese and Chinese character datasets, and evaluated the performance of the proposed text detection and validation methods. The Japanese dataset consists of the popular 2,136 Kanji characters. We collected character images in four fonts, Mincho, Gyoshotai, MinchoE, and GothicE, using Microsoft Word. The Chinese dataset consists of the popular 3,500 Hanzi characters. We collected character images in four fonts, SimSun, KaiTi, SimHei, and Dabiao SimSun. The average Recall rates for Japanese and Chinese are 94.57 % and 97.59 %, respectively.

In order to evaluate the text/non-text discrimination performance, we employed MSRA-TD500 (MSRA Text Detection 500 Database) containing Chinese characters, and also created our own dataset consisting of 450 Kanji character images and 2,000 background (non-text) images from the photos taken in Japanese urban areas. Table 1 shows the comparison result with the SWT. The new method can extract Japanese/Chinese text well and is tolerant of the text rotation. The background noise has been effectively reduced.

## 4   Conclusions

We have presented scene text detection and tracking methods that can handle Japanese/Chinese scene text well and yield better performance compared with the popular SWT method. Detailed performance evaluation is included in our future work since the wearable text-to-speech translation camera system is still under development and we have not built a user interface part yet.

A part of this work was supported by the Grant-in-Aid 14–15 in 2014 from the Okawa Foundation in Japan.

## References

1. KNFB Reader. http://www.knfbreader.com/
2. Goto, H., Hoda, T.: Real-time text tracking for text-to-speech translation camera for the blind. In: Miesenberger, K., Fels, D., Archambault, D., Peňáz, P., Zagler, W. (eds.) ICCHP 2014, Part I. LNCS, vol. 8547, pp. 658–661. Springer, Heidelberg (2014)
3. Matas, J., Chum, O., Urban, M., Pajdla, T.: Robust wide-baseline stereo from maximally stable extremal regions. Image Vis. Comput. **22**(10), 761–767 (2002)
4. Bay, H., Ess, A., Tuytelaars, T., van Gool, L.: SURF: speeded up robust features. Comput. Vis. Image Underst. **110**(3), 346–359 (2008)

# Zebra Crossing Detection from Aerial Imagery Across Countries

Daniel Koester[✉], Björn Lunt, and Rainer Stiefelhagen

Karlsruhe Institute of Technology, Karlsruhe, Germany
{daniel.koester,bjoern.lunt,rainer.stiefelhagen}@kit.edu

**Abstract.** We propose a data driven approach to detect zebra crossings in aerial imagery. The system automatically learns an appearance model from available geospatial data for an examined region. HOG as well as LBPH features, in combination with a SVM, yield state of the art detection results on different datasets. We also use this classifier across datasets obtained from different countries, to facilitate detections without requiring any additional geospatial data for that specific region. The approach is capable of searching for further, yet uncharted, zebra crossings in the data. Information gained from this work can be used to generate new zebra crossing databases or improve existing ones, which are especially useful in navigational assistance systems for visually impaired people. We show the usefulness of the proposed approach and plan to use this research as part of a larger guidance system.

**Keywords:** Aerial imagery · Street crossing · Visually impaired

## 1 Introduction

Visually impaired and blind people face a multitude of challenges in many aspects of their daily lives. Among those, outdoor as well as indoor navigation remains a great challenge due to the complexity of their surroundings and interactions with moving obstacles, such as other pedestrians or vehicles. Much needed visual cues are constantly utilized by unimpaired people, to avoid accidents and to not bump into one of the numerous obstacles, and are thus taken for granted. This effect is further amplified by an urban element design that neglects visually impaired peoples' specific needs. Sidewalks are often not equipped with tactile pavings and items such as trash cans, lamp poles, or safety posts are often placed in spatially confusing or free space limiting locations, severely impeding movements by visually impaired people. Street crossings, as well as pedestrian traffic lights, often do not include much needed accessibility features and the general street layout can be very confusing to the visually impaired, e.g., Y-junctions, complicated round-abouts, or temporary construction sites. With respect to accessibility, zebra crossings are amongst the worst offenders, often providing no locational hints at all and only very limited tactile feedback while crossing the street. Furthermore, they provide less certainty and peace of mind compared to formal crossings [1].

K. Miesenberger et al. (Eds.): ICCHP 2016, Part II, LNCS 9759, pp. 27–34, 2016.
DOI: 10.1007/978-3-319-41267-2_5

Today's ubiquitous *Global Navigation Satellite Systems* allow visually impaired people to regain at least some confidence in urban navigation situations. While these can greatly increase mobility, they only provide very high-level navigational information, but can neither warn of obstacles nor supply fine level guidance to the user. Thus, to this day, visually impaired people rely traditionally most on their white cane or a guide dog for these types of information. Furthermore, important geospatial information databases for visually impaired people are often under-utilized or non-existing. Our work therefore tries to improve already existing geospatial databases, such as *OpenStreetMap*[1] (OSM). It's data quality varies a lot as it is collected and edited by volunteers all around the world. Additionally, the specific details of a street crossing, e.g., whether it is equipped with pedestrian traffic lights, is often missing or even incorrect. We plan to use such weekly annotated data in order to create an assistive system that helps visually impaired people cross the street more safely. This work focuses especially on using nearby zebra crossings, as they provide much more safety to visually impaired people compared to just plain crossing the street. Very few specialized navigational assistance systems use such available databases already, e.g., *Trekker Breeze* or *Braille Note GPS*[2], however, these often contain only points of interest or require pre-recorded routes, thus limiting their usefulness. We believe that an increased number and improved quality of available geospatial databases for visually impaired people will aide their usefulness and greatly increase utilization and integration in the near future. Furthermore, such data could be helpful for cars, as they could be made aware of an oncoming zebra crossing and react accordingly.

This work leverages available geospatial data in order to create a training corpus for a data driven approach. We acquire aerial imagery from different sources, such as *Aerowest*[3] or *Google Maps*[4]. The aerial imagery is then pre-processed using information about road locations and directions that are extracted from OSM meta data. This process greatly reduces the considered search space in the aerial imagery, strongly depending on the examined region. We then extract a combination of *Histogram of Oriented Gradients* (HOG) [2] as well as *Local Binary Pattern Histograms* (LBPH) [3] descriptors and train a classical *Support Vector Machine* (SVM) [4] for classification. We also compare it to a line search based approach, using regional data that is similar in appearance, as well as a classifier trained on our own dataset. Furthermore, our resulting classifier is also used to try to detect yet uncharted zebra crossings in the aerial imagery, which were then verified by hand. Our system is widely usable, as it can automatically learn the local appearance of zebra crossing patterns in different countries, which often have different regulations and therefore zebra crossings differ in visual appearance. Finally, our system is capable of creating such a geospatial database for regions where it doesn't yet exist.

---

[1] http://www.openstreetmap.org.
[2] http://www.humanware.com.
[3] http://www.aerowest.de.
[4] http://maps.google.com.

## 2    Related Work

Using aerial imagery of urban areas to create geospatial data has wide applications, e.g., city planning or road detection and analysis [5], and has been studied for a long time [6]. Adding geospatial data to map services [7], specifically the detection of street-level accessibility problems [8] or points of interest for visually impaired people [9,10], has seen lots of interest in recent years.

Detection of zebra crossings from street level scenarios for visually impaired people has already been researched for quite some time. Usually, line detection algorithms are used in combination with other features. Se [11] combines these with intensity variation as well as pose information, to distinguish between zebra crossings and very similar looking staircases. Ahmetovic et al. [12,13] use the position of the horizon obtained through a mobile phone's accelerometer to reduce the search space in combination with their line detection based ZebraRecognizer library. Coughlan et al. [14] and Ivanchenko et al. [15,16] also largely base their work on the same approach, and provide user centered features on top of it.

Zebra crossing detection from aerial imagery was, just recently, first proposed by Ahmetovic et al. [17]. The authors use aerial imagery from Google Maps and download only partitions that actually contain road surface. They achieve this by calculating the distance of the partition's center to the next road using the Google Maps Javascript API and verify zebra crossing candidates with Google Street View panoramas. Their approach uses modified line search algorithms for both detection stages, in the aerial imagery as well as acquired panoramas. This two-step approach is evaluated on a $1.6\,\mathrm{km}^2$ rectangle in a San Francisco neighbourhood. We compare their approach to ours using the same region downloaded from Google Maps and achieve competitive results.

## 3    Methodology

The proposed data driven algorithm is based on available geospatial data and aerial imagery, by providers such as OpenStreetMap, Google Static Maps, or AeroWest. Such aerial imagery providers allow anyone to retrieve images for specific regions – usually only single and rate limited tile-based requests of varying size – that are centered around a user defined longitude and latitude coordinate date. Using OSM meta data from its Overpass API, we acquire the precise positions of road connection points, referred to as nodes, as well as some already labeled zebra crossings. We clean the data to save on computational time, e.g., neglect parking areas, private property, and factory sites, but it is not required. With knowledge gained from this meta data, we download a region of interest's connected and neighbouring parts, focussing on the road surface. We move from node to node in a linear and interpolated fashion, which represent the estimated street locations and acquire the necessary aerial imagery for further processing. Although the meta data's nodes are not always perfectly aligned to the actual road, their observed quality has always proven good enough to capture most, if not all, of the desired road surface.

A sliding window approach that follows the road structure given by the OSM meta data's nodes in the previous step then scans the obtained imagery and saves each window for further processing. This process also aligns it with respect to the road center. This crucial step removes almost any rotational variance of observed zebra crossings, and also drastically reduces the search space and simplifies the classification and detection tasks.

**Fig. 1.** An example of combined aerial imagery and meta data showing a small round-about in a German city. Center lines (blue/bright) often deviate from the ideal position. Zebra crossings (green/dark circles) might be occluded by cars or subject to shadows. Our algorithm uses a sliding window (orange/bright rectangle) along the center lines. Image source: Google. (Color figure online)

Figure 1 shows an example of the combined data with the road center lines, labeled zebra crossings and the sliding window. We use a HOG implementation created by Felzenszwalb et al. [18]. While zebra-crossings are often occluded by shadows and trees or have deteriorated markings, HOG block normalization helps to compensate for such variances. HOG features are suited to this task, because they describe local intensity gradients, i.e., edge directions, which appear quite regular on zebra crossings from an aerial viewpoint. We also compute LBP features on the image window and use their normalized histogram as an input vector for the SVM. Additionally, we also train SVMs with a combined HOG and LBPH feature vector, but the improvements in accuracy and average precision are negligible. We then extract the known zebra crossing locations from the acquired scan windows for a processed region and use HOG and LBPH features with varying parameters to train a SVM. We train linear – much faster to train and test – and *radial based function* (RBF) – yield slightly better results – SVM kernels and compare their results. In a last step, the classification results are clustered using direction information from the sliding window movement as well as distance measures, and these yield our final zebra crossing detections.

After training, we rescan the aerial imagery, or evaluate the classifier on different data, and use the trained SVM to detect zebra crossings, often yielding zebra crossings not present in the meta data. Furthermore, it greatly reduces false positive detections on similar looking structures, e.g., roof tops or staircases, as only actual road surface can be considered by the algorithm.

# 4    Evaluation

We use aerial ortho-imagery, i.e., pixels correlated to precise latitude and longitude locations. It was collected from various urban and rural regions in Germany and sampled from ~10 km of road surface, which contain 3119 zebra-crossings. Any encountered zebra crossings are extracted without regards to the observed image quality. Hence, these contain a great deal of variance: Occlusion from vehicles or trees, deterioration of markings, shadows from nearby trees and buildings, general illumination changes from different daytimes as well as even varying seasons. The resolution varies from 5 to 10 cm per pixel and has to be considered in any pixel-to-coordinate translation.

**Table 1.** Evaluation results on our own dataset (3119 zebra crossings), where *"-lin"* denotes a linear and *"-RBF"* a *radial basis function* SVM kernel, "HOG$^{30\times30}$" is the block size, "LBP$^{17/10}$" are the *radius/neighbour* variation. Numbers given in %.

| Method | Precision | Recall | Accuracy | Avg.-Prec |
|---|---|---|---|---|
| HOG$^{30\times30}$-lin | 74.8 | 93.1 | 92.4 | 94.43 |
| HOG$^{20\times20}$-RBF | 95.2 | 96.2 | **98.9** | 97.99 |
| LBP$^{17/10}$-lin | 99.4 | **97.4** | 98.4 | **99.56** |
| LBP$^{17/10}$-RBF | **99.7** | 97.0 | 98.3 | **99.56** |

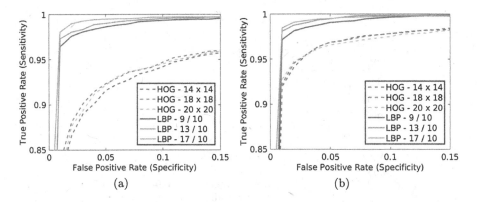

**Fig. 2.** ROC curves for the 5-fold-cross validation on our own dataset: (a) uses a linear SVM kernel, while (b) uses an RBF kernel. Both figures show performance for various HOG block sizes, while LBP parameters are *radius/neighbour* variations. (Color figure online)

We train our algorithm only on a subset of the available data, due to the large number of negative samples, and use data augmentation, i.e., we mirror all positive samples horizontally, vertically, and in combination. Our train and test set for the 5-fold-cross validation then consists of as many positive as randomly chosen negative samples, i.e., ~12500 each, we will consider hard negative mining instead in the future. This augmented and reduced dataset is then used to test different parameter configurations, a process that would otherwise be computationally infeasible when including all negative samples. After testing and subsequently choosing different parameter configurations for LBPH and HOG, as well as fine tuning the SVM's parameters, we compare the classification results in Table 1 and show that our algorithm achieves close to perfect performance. Furthermore, we show $ROC$ curves for some of the different tested HOG and LBPH parameters in Fig. 2 and observe that performance varies only slightly, while LBPH features perform constantly better than HOG features.

**Table 2.** Comparison to Ahmetovic et al. [17] (141 zebra crossings inside a San Francisco rectangle). We report their satellite-data only ( "-SAT"), street-view refinement ( "-SV") and combined results as well as our algorithm trained on surrounding data and a classifier based on our own dataset ( "-PRE"). All numbers given in % and optimized for recall.

|            | Precision | Recall |
|------------|-----------|--------|
| [17]-SAT   | 68.8      | 97.2   |
| [17]-SV    | 97.2      | 97.8   |
| [17]-SAT+SV| 97.2      | 95.0   |
| Ours       | 96.2      | 95.7   |
| Ours-PRE   | 98.9      | 38.4   |

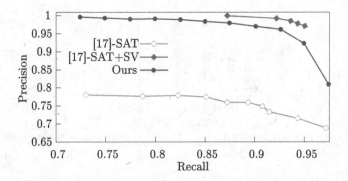

**Fig. 3.** ROC curve for the San Francisco dataset showing Ahmetovic et al.'s [17] performance of individual steps versus our classifier. Original figure taken from [17], updated with our (discretized) data and modified for improved readibility.

In addition to the cross validation, Table 2 and Fig. 3 compare our algorithm to Ahmetovic et al. [17], which tuned their algorithm for maximum recall to minimize the chance of missing any zebra crossings. To make a fair comparison between the different approaches, we download the same San Francisco rectangular region from *Google Maps*. In order to train a SVM with similar data, we manually search for ~250 zebra crossings within the direct neighbourhoods as well as cities close by, as OSM meta data for zebra crossings was not available, a state which we hope to eventually change with our system. Furthermore, we use our pre-trained SVM classifier from our own German dataset for detection purposes and compare the results accordingly.

For ground truth, we had to manually label the rectangle's zebra crossings and count 184 zebra crossings overall: 122 are *"continental crossings"* (typical crossing type found in the U.S. [17]) and 62 that also contain *"transverse markings"* (two additional white perpendicular lines, resulting in a *ladder* like appearance). These numbers differ slightly from Ahmetovic et al. [17], mainly due to us considering *ladder* like zebra crossings as ground truth. We also ignore the 110 plain *"transverse markings"* found on many of the other street crossings, similar to the work we compare to. Detecting these would be a much harder task, as they only consists of 2 parallel lines.

Our data driven algorithm achieves competitive results and even our *across-countries* (Ours-PRE) classifier performs reasonable. It's results might be used further to train a new classifier using it's top and bottom $k$-elements instead of having to manually search for training data, as we had to. Such an approach would allow to generate missing geospatial databases for almost any region.

## 5 Conclusion

We demonstrate a system to improve the general availability and quality of geospatial data, i.e., zebra crossing locations, to be used in navigation and guidance applications for visually impaired people. Our proposed detection algorithm, which learns automatically from provided data, consists of HOG and LBPH features and uses a SVM for classification, achieves state of the art results on our own dataset as well as competitive results on those proposed by other authors. Moreover, we show that our algorithm can perform reasonably well when trained and tested on different data sources, providing a decent cross-dataset performance. Such cross-dataset results might then be used as an intermediate step in order to generate training data for a new generation of classifiers. This process even allows to involve a human to ensure a sufficient training set quality.

It is our belief that the availability of accurate geospatial databases will help foster their integration into products for visually impaired people as well as traditional or autonomous cars, and thus increase the safety on the road. We plan to further investigate our approach, to improve its performance as well as eventually use it in a more complete guidance system for visually impaired people, which not only navigates to the next available street crossing but also helps to safely cross the road. Future research will therefore involve the creation of such a guidance system that detects zebra crossings from a street perspective, recommends the next zebra crossing location using a geospatial database and guides the user towards, as well as safely over, the zebra crossing itself. Finally, studies with visually impaired people will be conducted, as part of a research effort to create a complete guidance solution to be used in urban or rural locations.

# References

1. Matthews, B., Hibberd, D., Carsten, O.: Road and street crossings for blind and partially sighted people: the importance of being certain (2014)
2. Dalal, N., Triggs, B.: Histograms of oriented gradients for human detection. In: IEEE Conference on Computer Vision and Pattern Recognition, pp. 886–893 (2005)
3. Ojala, T., Pietikäinen, M., Mäenpää, T.: Multiresolution gray-scale and rotation invariant texture classification with local binary patterns. IEEE Trans. Pattern Anal. Mach. Intell. **24**(7), 971–987 (2002)
4. Cortes, C., Vapnik, V.: Support-vector networks. Mach. Learn. **20**(3), 273–297 (1995)
5. Hintz, S., Baumgartner, A.: Automatic extraction of urban road networks from multi-view aerial imagery. ISPRS J. Photogrammetry Remote Sens. **58**(1–2), 83–98 (2003)
6. Quam, L.H.: Road tracking and anomaly detection in aerial imagery. In: ARPA Spring 1978 Image Understanding Workshop (1978)
7. Goodchild, M.F.: Citizens as sensors: the world of volunteered geography. GeoJ. **69**(4), 211–221 (2007)
8. Hara, K., Le, V., Froehlich, J.: Combining crowdsourcing and google street view to identify street-level accessibility problems. In: Proceedings of the SIGCHI Conference on Human Factors in Computing Systems, pp. 631–640 (2013)
9. Prasain, S.: Stopfinder: improving the experience of blind public transit riders with crowdsourcing. In: Proceedings of the 15th International ACM SIGACCESS Conference on Computers and Accessibility, pp. 323–324 (2011)
10. Rice, M., Aburizaiza, A., Jacobson, D., Shore, B., Paez, F.: Supporting accessibility for blind and vision-impaired people with a localized gazetteer and open source geotechnology. Trans. GIS **16**(2), 177–190 (2012)
11. Se, S.: Zebra-crossing detection for the partially sighted. In: IEEE Conference on Computer Vision and Pattern Recognition, pp. 211–217 (2000)
12. Ahmetovic, D., Bernareggi, C., Mascetti, S.: Zebralocalizer: identification and localization of pedestrian crossings. In: Proceedings of the International Conference on Human Computer Interaction with Mobile Devices and Services, pp. 275–286 (2011)
13. Ahmetovic, D., Bernareggi, C., Gerino, A., Mascetti, S.: ZebraRecognizer: efficient and precise localization of pedestrian crossings. In: 22nd International Conference on Pattern Recognition (ICPR), pp. 2566–2571 (2014)
14. Coughlan, J., Shen, H.: A fast algorithm for finding crosswalks using figure-ground segmentation. In: Proceedings of 2nd Workshop on Applications of Computer Vision, in Conjunction with ECCV (2006)
15. Ivanchenko, V., Coughlan, J., Shen, H.: Detecting and locating crosswalks using a camera phone. In: IEEE Conference on Computer Vision and Pattern Recognition Workshops (2008)
16. Ivanchenko, V., Coughlan, J.M., Shen, H.: Crosswatch: a camera phone system for orienting visually impaired pedestrians at traffic intersections. In: Miesenberger, K., Klaus, J., Zagler, W.L., Karshmer, A.I. (eds.) ICCHP 2008. LNCS, vol. 5105, pp. 1122–1128. Springer, Heidelberg (2008)
17. Ahmetovic, D., Manduchi, R., Coughlan, J., Mascetti, S.: Zebra crossing spotter: automatic population of spatial databases for increased safety of blind travelers. In: Proceedings of the 17th International ACM SIGACCESS Conference on Computers and Accessibility, pp. 251–258 (2015)
18. Felzenszwalb, P.F., Grishick, R.B., McAllester, D., Ramanan, D.: Object detection with discriminatively trained part based models. IEEE Trans. Pattern Anal. Mach. Intell. **32**(9), 1627–1645 (2009)

# Sound of Vision – 3D Scene Reconstruction from Stereo Vision in an Electronic Travel Aid for the Visually Impaired

Mateusz Owczarek[✉], Piotr Skulimowski, and Pawel Strumillo

Institute of Electronics, Lodz University of Technology, Łódź, Poland
{mateusz.owczarek,piotr.skulimowski,pawel.strumillo}@p.lodz.pl

**Abstract.** The paper presents the preliminary results for the parametrization of 3D scene for sonification purposes in an electronic travel aid (ETA) system being built within the European Union's H2020 Sound of Vision project. The ETA is based on the concept of sensory substitution, in which visual information is transformed into either acoustic or haptic stimuli. In this communication we concentrate on vision-to-audio conversion i.e. employing stereovision for reconstruction of 3D scenes and building a spatial model of the environment for sonification. Two prerequisite approaches for the sonification are proposed. One involves the direct sonification of the so-called "U-disparity" representation of the depth map of the environment, while the other relies on the processing of the depth map to extract obstacles present in the environment and presenting them to the user as auditory icons reflecting specific size and location of the sonified object.

**Keywords:** Electronic Travel Aid · Stereo vision · UV-Disparity · Ground plane detection · Obstacle detection

## 1 Introduction

Numerous solutions for navigation of the blind and visually impaired were proposed over the past few years. Such solutions can be divided into two groups. The first group are assistive applications aimed at supporting the visually impaired in solving specific, usually isolated issues. Very often they use off-the-shelf solutions such as mobile phones or tablets with such examples as text-to-speech applications, image magnifiers, audio description devices, banknote recognizers etc. [1–3]. The second group, referred to as Electronic Travel Aids (ETAs), are systems which aim at enhancing orientation and mobility (O&M) of the blind users. Research work on O&M devices for the visually impaired dates back to the turn of 19th and 20th centuries. First ETA device is attributed to Kazimierz Noiszewski, Polish optician who built Electroftam. This was a device that used light-sensitive selenium cells to convert light energy into sound and tactile stimulations. Another notable attempt was made by Bach-y-Rita in the 1970s who built a system converting images recorded by a video-camera into a pattern of haptic stimulations generated by a matrix of vibrating actuators positioned at the back of the user [4].

© Springer International Publishing Switzerland 2016
K. Miesenberger et al. (Eds.): ICCHP 2016, Part II, LNCS 9759, pp. 35–42, 2016.
DOI: 10.1007/978-3-319-41267-2_6

These devices, however, were bulky and consumed too much power to be practical in use.

In spite of nearly 100 year's effort since first attempts of Noiszewski, none of the solutions has found a wide-spread acceptance among the blind community [5]. That is why research and development studies in this area are being carried out extensively and involve auditory display and/or tactile interfaces [6, 7].

Contemporary, solutions for O&M and ETA for the visually impaired can be subdivided into a number of solutions:

- Simple obstacle detectors – small hand-held devices that sample distance to objects of the environment.
- Navigation and telenavigation systems – employing either GPS (navigation) or establishing wireless connection with a remote guide (telenavigation) to help the blind user in local and global wayfinding tasks in the environment.
- Environment imagers – more complex vision based systems that convert images (or their regions) of the environment into auditory or haptic representations.

Examples of simple obstacle detectors are Ultracane, Laser Cane, Teletact or Miniguide [8].

Examples of the GPS navigation systems for the blind are the American Trekker Breeze by Human Ware and Polish Nawigator by Migraf. Telenavigation systems on the other hand, are still at a prototype technology readiness level and were mainly developed by Brunel University, UK [9] and Lodz University of Technology [10].

Examples of environment imager systems are: the Sonicguide (and its newer version KASPA), the VOICe [11] and similar SVETA [12], Espacio Acustico Virtual [13], and the Sonic Pathfinder [14]. The Sonic Pathfinder was the first environment imager system that processed the sensed data about the environment to limit the amount of information for acoustic presentation. This is an important advance in the approach to ETAs operation since most of the visually impaired users complain about overabundance of auditory information that is used to convey spatial features of the environment. Similar approach was followed in the Naviton project [15]. A pair of camera in a stereovision setting and algorithms for reconstructing 3D structure and building a simplified scene model of the environment were employed.

In this paper we present the preliminary results for the parametrization of 3D scene for sonification purposes – one of the concepts within the Sound of Vision project [6]. The idea behind the project is to create a wearable ETA for assisting the visually impaired individuals by rendering the image of the environment through the auditory display. The device captures the 3D image of the environment, processes it, and presents the relevant information about the environment to the user.

## 2    Image Acquisition and 3D Reconstruction

In order to filter out relevant information that is communicated to the blind user the images of the surrounding environment need to be segmented into disjoint regions that are further classified as ground plane regions and regions representing other objects.

So detected objects are described by a set of geometric parameters. Thus, a specific 3D model of the environment is built for the sonification purposes. Such an approach is novel in comparison to the environmental imager devices outlined in the earlier chapter.

The task of three dimensional scene reconstruction can be considered as a problem of determination of points' coordinates of the objects within the scene. Among the existing reconstruction methods stereovision was chosen due to its simplicity, effectiveness in natural light conditions (passive method), and small size and weight – particularly important in the case of the blind users. What is more, the use of video cameras allows to implement additional, auxiliary image processing algorithms, such as text recognition [3], objects semantic analysis, etc.

The schematic diagram of the proposed method for 3D scene modelling and parametrization is depicted in Fig. 1. It consists of the three key processing steps:

1. Estimation of the ground plane location based on disparity and depth maps.
2. Obstacle detection after background and ground plane removal.
3. Parametric description for each of the detected obstacle.

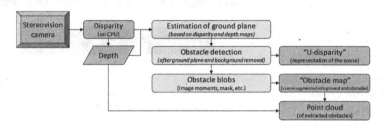

**Fig. 1.** Schematic diagram of the proposed method for 3D scene reconstruction, and ground plane and obstacle detection

For the sake of simplicity, let us assume that images from the stereo vision camera (Fig. 2a) are devoid of geometric distortions and rectified, which is a prerequisite for the calculation of the disparity map. The disparity map in turn is used to convert pixel coordinates from the captured images into world point coordinates in the camera coordinate system, from which depth of the obstacles can be computed [5, 17].

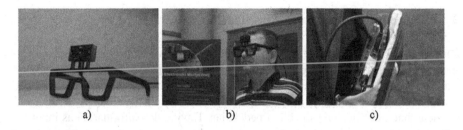

**Fig. 2.** Prototype wearable image acquisition device: (a) Duo MLX stereo vision camera build into a custom-made "glasses" and (b) user wearing them during early tests of the device, while (c) processing unit is held in a backpack

Our broad literature search [2, 7, 16–19] shows that one of the most effective methods for ground plane and obstacle detection, provided that the stereo vision camera is used, are solutions based on the so-called "UV-disparity" representation of the disparity map. The key feature in such an approach is that pixels representing the ground plane are well reproduced in the "V-disparity" map (represented by a distinctive line segment – see Fig. 3d) while obstacles are clearly visible in the "U-disparity" map.

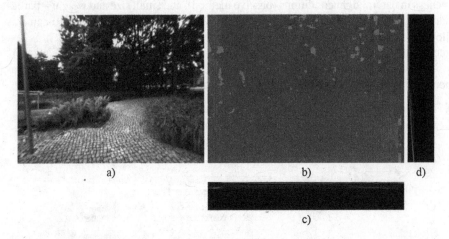

a)                                    b)                              d)

c)

**Fig. 3.** Example test scene: (a) (reference) image as seen by the right camera, (b) disparity image, (c) "U-disparity" and (d) "V-disparity" representations of the disparity map

The line segment in the "V-disparity" representation, which corresponds to the ground plane area, is found using the Hough transform. All the pixels in the disparity map for which the disparity value fits the detected line equation are removed from the disparity map. Those pixels are also taken into consideration while calculating the ground plane equation. In the considered application, there is no need to present the obstacles that are very distant from the observer (more than 8 m). The same applies to the obstacles located high enough above the system user's head.

## 3   Obstacle Detection and Sonification

Further analysis is performed based on the disparity map with all the pixels corresponding to the ground plane, background and those for which distance from the ground plane is greater than the pre-selected value removed. Example of such disparity image is depicted in Fig. 5b. It may be noticed, that it contains only the elements of the environment that may endanger the blind pedestrian. Having this information as input for the next steps, we proposed two approaches, depending on the preferred way of presenting the information about the environment to the user.

### 3.1  Direct Sonification of the "U-Disparity"

One of the ideas is a direct sonification of the "U-disparity" representation, calculated for the disparity map after pre-processing steps. Note that in the "U-disparity" map the obstacles are represented by distinctive line segments (see Fig. 4). What is more, based on the y-coordinate (vertical coordinate) in the "U-disparity" map it is possible to estimate the distance to the face of the nearest obstacle. It is worth mentioning, that such an approach may lead to a simple sonification scheme such as left-to-right scene scanning of the environment.

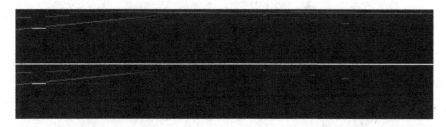

**Fig. 4.** "U-disparity" representation of the reference disparity image (top) and after applying the preprocessing steps described to this point (bottom)

### 3.2  The Concept of the Simplified Sound Icons

The second approach consists of binarization of the earlier processed disparity map (Fig. 5b). This approach was implemented by the contour finding method based on [20]. The aim of this next step is to find the minimum-area bounding rotated rectangles for the detected obstacles (Fig. 5c). Regions of the area below a certain threshold are not taken into account. Results of obstacles detection for two example 3D scenes are shown in Fig. 5d.

Based on the extracted ROIs (Regions of Interest) a set of obstacles' parameters can be calculated. For the sonification purposes we proposed a set of parameters for the detected obstacles that were calculated based on the obstacles regions in color images and the computed disparity (and depth) maps. These parameters are grouped into the following categories: color-related features (e.g. dominant color), depth-related features, disparity-related features, two dimensional features (e.g. area, centroid or image moments, etc.) and three dimensional features (e.g. bounding rectangular cuboid, volume, etc.). Selected parameters will serve as the data source for various scene sonification schemes [21].

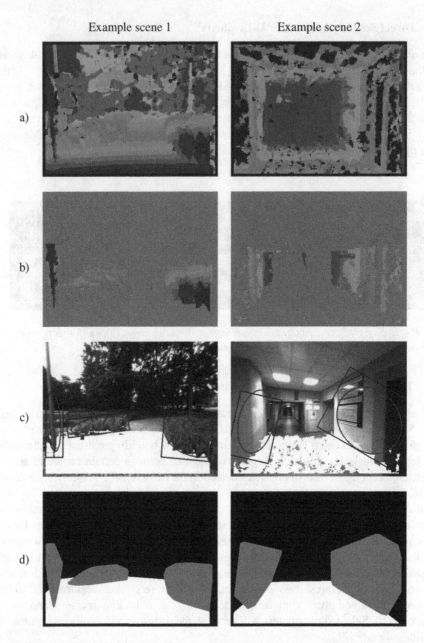

**Fig. 5.** Results of obstacles detection from stereovision images: (a) raw disparity map, (b) result of the processing of the disparity map, (c) minimum-area bounding rotated rectangles outlining the detected obstacles, (d) result segmentation map

## 4    Conclusions

In this study we have undertaken the problem of 3D scene modelling and parametrization from stereo vision. To address this issue, a simple and effective method of detecting obstacles and the ground plane has been developed. It works in real-time, confidently in the outdoor environment and is satisfactory for indoor scenes (we encourage the reader to view our supplementary material, e.g. video sequences, available at http://icchp2016.naviton.pl/). Obstacles can be detected even if the quality of the disparity map is low, provided that the ground plane occupies significant part of the image and is clearly visible. The weakness of this solution is that only significantly large obstacles can be detected for now, as it is very hard to detect small and potentially dangerous obstacles using the stereo vision camera with a short baseline.

**Acknowledgment.**  This work received funding from the European Union's Horizon 2020 research and innovation programme under grant agreement No 643636 "Sound of Vision".

## References

1. Hersh, M., Johnson, M.: Assistive Technology for Visually Impaired and Blind People. Springer, London (2008)
2. Ivanchenko, V., Coughlan J., Huiying, S.: Detecting and locating crosswalks using a camera phone. In: IEEE Conference on Computer Vision and Pattern Recognition (CVPR) Workshop, CVPRW 2008, pp. 1–8, 23–28 June 2008
3. Huiying, S., Coughlan, J.: Reading LCD/LED displays with a camera cell phone. In: IEEE Conference on Computer Vision and Pattern Recognition Workshop, CVPRW 2006, p. 119, 17–22 June 2006
4. Bach-y-Rita, P.: Brain Mechanisms in Sensory Substitution. Academic Press, New York (1972)
5. Strumiłło, P.: Electronic personal navigation systems for the blind and visually impaired (in Polish), Faculty of Electrical, Electronic, Computer and Control Engineering, Lodz University of Technology, Lodz (2012)
6. Sound of Vision: Natural sense of vision through acoustics and haptics. http://www.soundofvision.net/. Accessed 25 Mar 2016
7. Flores, G., Kurniawan, S., Manduchi, R., Martinson, E., Morales, L.M., Sisbot, E.A.: Vibrotactile guidance for wayfinding of blind walkers. IEEE Trans. Haptics 8(3), 306–317 (2015)
8. Dakopoulos, D., Bourbakis, N.G.: Wearable obstacle avoidance electronic travel aids for blind: a Survey. IEEE Trans. Syst. Man Cybern. – Part C: Appl. Rev. 40(1), 25–35 (2010)
9. Garaj, V., Jirawimut, R., Ptasinski, P., Cecelja, F., Balachandran, W.: A system for remote sighted guidance of visually impaired pedestrians. Br. J. Vis. Impairment 21, 55–63 (2003)
10. Barański, P., Strumiłło, P.: Emphatic trials of a teleassistance system for the visually impaired. J. Med. Imaging Health Inf. 5(8), 1640–1651 (2015)
11. vOICe: http://www.seeingwithsound.com. Accessed 25 Mar 2016
12. Balakrishnan, G., Sainarayanan, G., Nagarajan, R., Sazali, Y.: A stereo image processing system for visually impaired. Int. J. Signal Process. 2(3), 136–145 (2006)

13. González-Mora, J., Rodríguez-Hernández, A., Rodríguez-Ramos, L., Díaz-Saco, L., Sosa, N.: Development of a new space perception system for blind people, based on the creation of a virtual acoustic space. In: Mira, J. (ed.) Engineering Applications of Bio-Inspired Artificial Neural Networks. LNCS, vol. 1607, pp. 321–330. Springer, Heidelberg (1999)

14. Heyes, D.: The Sonic pathfinder: a new electronic travel aid. J. Vis. Impairment Blindness **77**, 200–202 (1984)

15. Bujacz, M., Skulimowski, P., Strumillo, P.: Naviton – a prototype mobility aid for auditory presentation of 3D scenes. J. Audio Eng. Soc. **60**(9), 696–708 (2012)

16. Chunlei, Y., Cherfaoui, V., Bonnifait, P.: Evidential occupancy grid mapping with stereovision. In: IEEE Intelligent Vehicles Symposium (IV), pp. 712–717, 28 June 2015 – 1 July 2015. doi:10.1109/IVS.2015.7225768

17. Zhencheng, H., Uchimura, K.: U-V-disparity: an efficient algorithm for stereovision based scene analysis. In: IEEE Intelligent Vehicles Symposium, pp. 48–54, 6–8 June 2005. doi: 10.1109/IVS.2005.1505076

18. Labayrade, R., Aubert, D., Tarel, J.-P.: Real time obstacle detection in stereovision on non flat road geometry through "V-disparity" representation. In: IEEE Intelligent Vehicle Symposium, vol. 2, pp. 646–651, 17–21 June 2002. doi:10.1109/IVS.2002.1188024

19. Zhencheng, H., Lamosa, F., Uchimura, K.: A complete U-V-disparity study for stereovision based 3D driving environment analysis. In: Fifth International Conference on 3-D Digital Imaging and Modeling, pp. 204–211, 13–16 June 2005. doi:10.1109/3DIM.2005.6

20. Suzuki, S., Abe, K.: Topological structural analysis of digitized binary images by border following. Comput. Vis. Graph. Image Process. **30**(1), 32–46 (1985)

21. Bujacz, M., et al.: Sound of vision - spatial audio output and sonification approaches. In: Miesenberger, K., Bühler, C., Penaz, P. (eds.) ICCHP 2016, Part II. LNCS, vol. 9759, pp. 200–207. Springer, Heidelberg (2016)

# Experiments with a Public Transit Assistant for Blind Passengers

German Flores and Roberto Manduchi[✉]

Baskin School of Engineering, University of California, Santa Cruz, USA
{ghflores,manduchi}@soe.ucsc.edu

**Abstract.** Public transportation is key to independence for many blind persons. Unfortunately, in spite of recent accessibility progress, use of public transportation remains challenging without sight. In this contribution, we describe a system that provides enhanced travel-related information access to a blind bus passenger. Users of this system can select a specific bus line and desired destination on a regular Android smartphone or tablet; are notified when the bus arrives; once in the bus, they are informed of its progress during the route; and are given ample advance notice when the bus is approaching their destination. This system was tested with four blind participants in realistic conditions.

**Keywords:** Assistive technology · Public transit · Location-based services

## 1 Introduction

Public transportation has a critical role in the independence of blind travelers [6]. Blind individuals who use public transportation have increased opportunities for education, employment, socialization and leisure. Unfortunately, in spite of significant accessibility advances (in large part resulting from legislation such as the American with Disability Act, or ADA), people who are blind face multiple difficulties when using public transportation [1,10,14]. In particular, access to travel-related information, a main factor contributing to the safety and comfort of public transit passengers, may be challenging without sight. When riding a bus vehicle or a train, one needs to know which bus or train line to take, its departure time, and where to board the vehicle; during the ride, one needs to constantly be aware of the progress made to destination, so as to be ready to exit the vehicle or train car at the desired stop. Some of these tasks (e.g., recognizing an approaching bus) are inherently visual. Others can be facilitated by non-visual (acoustic) means. For example, the ADA mandates that bus vehicles announce stops at transfer points, major intersections, major destinations, stops requested by riders with disability, and in general at frequent enough intervals such that people with visual impairment can orient themselves. In fact, not all stops are announced all the times, and the spoken announcements from the speakers may be difficult to hear by someone with a hearing impairment or in the case of loud

K. Miesenberger et al. (Eds.): ICCHP 2016, Part II, LNCS 9759, pp. 43–50, 2016.
DOI: 10.1007/978-3-319-41267-2_7

ambient noise. In addition, persons who are anxious, unsure, or with some level of cognitive impairment, may need to hear the same announcement time and again [1].

In this contribution, we present a qualitative study with a system (Public Transportation Assistant, or PTA) that was designed to enhance information awareness for blind persons riding a bus vehicle. This system uses WiFi Access Points (AP) placed at bus stations and inside bus vehicles, which communicate with a regular Android smartphone (or, as in our experiments, tablet) carried by the user. This system does not require Internet connection or access to the smartphone's GPS. Bus stop APs provide a passenger who find himself or herself within the AP's WiFi range with information about the bus lines through that stop, timetables, and other types of real-time transit information (e.g. the estimated arrival time of the next bus). The in-vehicle AP communicates the current progress through the route and the stops that are reached by the bus. Users of this system can pre-select a bus line and a destination stop using an accessible interface. They are notified when the desired bus has arrived at their stop; once inside the bus, they receive early warning when the bus is approaching the desired destination. Information is presented to the user in the form of synthetic speech. At any time, users can interrogate the system to hear the latest announcement repeated, as well as any other available information.

We tested our system with four blind participants, who operated it while traveling by bus through a specific route in our campus. Each participant used the PTA system in a very realistic scenario, which involved catching two bus vehicles equipped with an AP, each time selecting a specific destination, and exiting at the correct stop. After the experiment, each tester participated in a semi-structured interview that focused on his or her experience with the public transit system (in particular, any accessibility issues) and on his or her opinion of the system they just tested. These interviews, together with observations from the experiments, shed light on the major problems faced by blind travelers using public transit, and provide a critical assessment of the functionalities of our PTA system.

## 2   Related Work

Improving information access for cognitive or sensorially impaired travelers is the object of active research [1,9]. Other systems and applications for the assistance of blind travelers taking public transportations have been described in the literature. For example, Ubibus [3] was designed to help a blind person catch the correct bus. Likewise, the Bluetooth-based application described in [13] ensures that the user is informed when a bus is arriving at a stop. The Travel Assistance Device (TAD) [2] and the app described by Silva et al. [15] both rely on the GPS in the user's smartphone to determine the user's position and to alert the user when the bus is approaching the desired bus stop. Unlike this previous work, our system is designed from the ground up to assist users throughout the whole travel, from the time they arrive at the initial bus stop until they reach their destination. Hara et al. [10] describe a crowdsourcing approach to building a database with the layout descriptions of bus stop locations. This information can be extremely useful to blind passengers, as also noted in our interviews.

# 3    PTA Technical Description

Our PTA system consists of two major components [7]: WiFi Access Points (APs), deployed inside transit vehicles and at bus stops, and an Android application that runs on Android devices. Each WiFi AP consists of a router that functions as a server and communicates with the Android application. The Android application functions as a client that manages connections, communication and overall user interaction. In addition, the in-vehicle AP communicates with an optional GPS device for positioning. This server-client model allows the system to work with multiple APs and Android devices.

## 3.1    Server

The server component of the system consists of a TP-LINK TL-WR1043ND wireless router reprogrammed with OpenWrt, a Linux-based fully writable file system with a package management software allowing for the creation of custom applications (packages). Two different types of APs were customized and deployed: an in-vehicle AP and a bus stop AP. In-vehicle APs were customized to work inside the bus; bus stop APs were customized to work outdoors. Each AP stores a local repository with the information to be transmitted during each connection request.

The WiFi manager was designed to accept multiple connection requests and facilitate data exchange between the AP and an Android device. For each connection request, the WiFi manager accepts the connection, performs a two-way handshake, and transmits either in-vehicle or bus stop related information to the Android device that requested the information. In-vehicle AP information consists of the bus name, bus route number, and the bus current location. Bus stop AP information consists of the bus stop name, bus stop address, bus route numbers that serve that particular stop, and other information such as timetables.

The GPS manager was designed to receive GPS coordinates from an external GPS module, determine if a given GPS coordinate is within range of a bus stop location, and send to the client the ASCII name of the location that corresponds to the given latitude and longitude coordinates. Since our routers do not have built-in GPS chips, we made use of the GPS chip found in a modern cell phone. A custom Android application was implemented to activate the GPS module in the phone and send periodic GPS coordinate updates to the bus AP at the rate of 1 coordinate per second.

## 3.2　Client

The client component of the system consists of an Android application deployed in a Nexus 7 tablet and designed to incorporate the following modules: WiFi connectivity requests, touch gesture interactions, local database queries, and text-to-speech synthesis. The most important functionality of the system is the reliable management of the scanning, connecting, switching, and disconnecting between bus stop and in-vehicle APs. Connection switches typically occur when the desired bus arrives at a bus stop, in which case the client switches connection from the bus stop AP to the in-vehicle AP. This switch occurs behind the scene – the user is never made aware that a switch occurred. If for any reason the user does not board the desired bus, the client automatically re-connects with the bus stop AP, giving the user the ability to specify a different destination.

The client user interface was designed to effectively communicate relevant information and provide the user with the proper set of instructions and confirmations for the desired task. It uses multi-touch gesture interactions to get user input and text-to-speech synthesis to give verbal feedback. The user interacts with the system in one of two modalities: system-prompted or user-prompted. System-prompted interaction occurs when the user first reaches the transmission range of an AP at a bus stop; after connection with the AP, the user is presented with a structured menu and asked to make a set of selections (such as which bus to take, or which stop to exit at). This is achieved by traversing a list of options using left (next item) or right (previous item) swipes, and selecting the desired item via a single tap. User-prompted interaction occurs when the user taps the screen and holds the finger on the screen for three seconds (tap-and-hold interaction), at which point a main menu is activated.

## 3.3　Application Scenario

In a typical applications scenario of our system, the user would first walk to a bus stop and start the PTA app on his or her smartphone. If the smartphone is within the transmission range of the AP in the bus stop, the application prompts the user to connect to the AP in order to receive transit information. If more than one instrumented bus stops are nearby (for example, two stops facing each other across the street), the application asks the user to select the AP he or she wants to connect to. Upon connection, the application provides information to the user as to the bus lines that go through that stop, and asks the user to select a desired one. Once a selection has been made, the user is again prompted to select a final destination for his or her trip from a list of bus stops that are traversed by the chosen bus line. After the user has selected the destination stop, this initial interaction phase is completed, and the user is instructed to wait for the bus to arrive. While waiting, the user can interrogate the system and ask to hear the remaining estimated time till bus arrival. Once the next bus vehicle of the chosen line arrives, and as soon as the user's smartphone is within WiFi range of the in-vehicle AP, the client software switches connection to this AP, and informs the user of the arrival of the desired bus. The user then enters the bus and finds a seat. The client application, now connected to the in-vehicle AP, receives information about the current bus location, and informs the user about upcoming stops as they are approached by the bus. The user can review the last information produced by the application at any time, and have the application repeat this information multiple times if desired. When the bus is approaching the stop before the final destination, a special announcement is produced; this is specifically designed to give the user ample time for all actions required before exiting the bus (pulling the cord to call the stop, getting up and moving towards the door, etc.). Finally, before the bus reaches the final destination, the user is prompted to get ready to exit the bus. Once the user has left the bus and the bus vehicle has departed, the system disconnects from the bus and puts itself into sleep mode, ready to be awaken when desired and to start the process again.

**Fig. 1.** Blind participants during the user studies.

## 4    Experiment Design

For our experiments, we instrumented three bus stops in our University campus and one bus vehicle. User studies were conducted on an individual basis during February and March of 2015. Four blind participants (Fig. 1) were recruited from the network of acquaintances maintained by the second author (three males and one female, ages: 55–67). Participants were offered the option to use earphones during the tests, rather than listening to the tablet's speaker. Only two participants decided to user earphones.

After a participant had a chance to ask questions about the system and the experiment, he or she was accompanied by the authors to the first instrumented bus stop. The app was then started and the tablet handed to the participant, who was instructed to select a specific final destination, using the system's tap and swipe interface. While waiting for the bus, participants were encouraged to occasionally interrogate the system, asking for the waiting time till bus arrival. Once the bus arrived and the participant received confirmation by the system that this was indeed the desired bus, the participant was accompanied inside the bus, where he or she took a seat in one of the front seats reserved for people with disabilities. During the trip, the participant was informed by the system about each upcoming bus stop. Note that the same information was also announced by the speakers in the bus; however, our participants were able to hear the announcement multiple times, if desired, from the tablet. The participant was asked to pull the cord to call the final stop when he or she determined that the stop was approaching. Once arrived at destination, the participant was accompanied outside the bus, where he or she waited until the system announced that it had disconnected from the bus AP and would go in standby mode. The participant was then accompanied to another instrumented bus stop, located across the street, and asked to wake up the application again (by a tap-and-hold gesture). The whole process was then started again, with a different final destination. The whole test (including waiting for the bus to arrive and traversing the route eastward and westward) took between one and two hours. At the end of the test, each participant participated in a semi-structured interview that was audio recorded.

## 5   Discussion and Conclusions

The experiments and interviews conducted with blind users of our system have brought to light a number of accessibility problems with the public transportation systems, along with possible technological solutions. The participants' shared experience clearly shows that using public transportation can be challenging for people who are blind. Missing the bus or the desired stop are relatively frequent occurrences for blind travelers.

Our PTA system has been designed to provide the following functionalities: (1) Informing the user about the bus lines through a specific stop, timetables, and possibly real-time information; (2) Allowing the user to select a bus line and desired destination stop; (3) Informing the user when the desired bus vehicle arrives at the stop; (4) Providing real-time location information en route, with specific (and possibly customizable) warnings as the bus approaches the final destination. Users of this system can have the system repeat the information as many times as they want, which can be very useful for someone with hearing impairment, in noisy or confusing situations, or when one would benefit to hear the same information repeated multiple times for confirmation. Our main design goal was to provide the user with enhanced information awareness during a bus ride, in hopes that this would make the travel experience safer and more comfortable.

By and large, the system worked as expected, with the exception of a single connectivity problem, and some difficulties by two participants using the tap-and-hold interface. Both issues can be easily resolved, the first one by changing the logic to determine when to announce a connection, the second one by substituting tap-and-hold with another gesture, such as triple-tap. Our participants enjoyed all functionalities offered by the system and generally gave us very encouraging reviews. The main criticism, shared by all participants, was directed at the short advance notice given by the system when the desired bus is arriving at the bus stop. While they considered the bus arrival warning to be a very useful feature, they would prefer that this warning, currently produced a few seconds before the bus pulls in, were given earlier. Unfortunately, by its own nature, the current system is unable to produce a warning at a much earlier time, as connection with the incoming in-vehicle AP is needed before the warning can be generated. Detecting the bus arrival with longer notice would require polling a real-time online bus tracker such as OneBusAway [6] or NextBus.

Our participants also said that they would like the system to help them find the exact location of the bus stop, a functionality that our current technology cannot offer (at best, our system can provide a very approximate estimate of the distance to the Access Point, based on the received signal strength indication or RSSI).

While our system was shown to adequately support all desired functionalities (except for what noted above), other technological solutions are possible. In fact, one main disadvantage of the chosen technology is the need for installation of WiFi Access Points at bus stops and within bus vehicles. In same cases, WiFi APs are already installed, for example on long-haul bus lines. Installation of bus stop with WiFi APs have also been planned in some cities (e.g. San Francisco). In the case of existing APs, it is conceivable that these could be upgraded to offer similar services as our prototype.

Several of the same functionalities offered by our PTA system could be provided by a smartphone app that uses GPS data for localization, and has access to timetables and possibly real time information from the Internet. This solution would not call for any special infrastructure, but it would need good Internet connectivity and GPS signal. (Note that our system does not require Internet connectivity or access to the user's phone's GPS.) In addition, a purely smartphone-based application may not be able to notify the user in real time when the desired bus has arrived at a bus stop. Regardless of the technology ultimately chosen, we believe that our experiments have shown that a personal travel assistant, implemented as a smartphone app, has great potential to improve travel-related information access for blind users, and that our study has highlighted the main functionalities that such a system needs to offer to be really useful to blind travelers.

# References

1. Azenkot, S., Fortuna, E.: Improving public transit usability for blind and deaf-blind people by connecting a Braille display to a smartphone. In: Proceedings of ASSETS 2010, Orlando, FL (2010)
2. Barbeau, S., Labrador, J., Winters, P.L., Perez, H., Georggi, N.L.: The travel assistant device: utilizing GPS-enabled mobile phones to aid transit rides with special needs. In: Proceedings of 15th World Congress on Intelligent Transportation Systems, NY (2008)
3. Banâtre, M., Couderc, P., Pauty, J., Becus, M.: Ubibus: ubiquitous computing to help blind people in public transport. In: Brewster, S., Dunlop, M.D. (eds.) Mobile HCI 2004. LNCS, vol. 3160, pp. 310–314. Springer, Heidelberg (2004)
4. Bohonos, S., Lee, A., Malik, A., Thai, C., Manduchi, R.: Universal real-time navigational assistance (URNA): an urban Bluetooth beacon for the blind. In: Proceeedings of ACM SIGMOBILE International Workshop on Systems and Networking Support for Healthcare and Assisted Living Environments (2007)
5. Cain, A.: Design elements of effective transit information materials. FDOT Final report, November 2004
6. Ferris, B., Watkins, K., Borning, A.: Location-aware tools for improving public transit usability. IEEE Pervasive Comput. **9**(1), 13–19 (2010)
7. Flores, G., Cizdziel, B., Manduchi, R., Obraczka, K., Do, J., Esser, T., Kurniawan, S.: Transit information access for persons with visual or cognitive impairments. In: Miesenberger, K., Fels, D., Archambault, D., Peñáz, P., Zagler, W. (eds.) ICCHP 2014, Part I. LNCS, vol. 8547, pp. 403–410. Springer, Heidelberg (2014)
8. Golledge, R.G., Marston, J.R., Costanzo, C.M.: Attitudes of visually impaired persons toward the use of public transportation. University of California Transportation Center (1997)
9. Guentert, M.: Improving public transit accessibility for blind riders: a train station navigation assistant. In: Proceedings of the 13th International ACM SIGACCESS Conference on Computers and Accessibility (2011)
10. Hara, K., Azenkot, S., Campbell, M., Bennett, C.L., Le, V., Pannella, S., Froehlich, J.E.: Improving public transit accessibility for blind riders by crowdsourcing bus stop landmark locations with Google street view. In: Proceedings of the 15th International ACM SIGACCESS Conference on Computers and Accessibility (2013)
11. Lanzerotti, R.: Blind and low vision priority project. Report from the LightHouse for the Blind and San Francisco Mayors Office on Disability (2007)
12. Lim, J.T.F., Leong, G.H., Kiong, T.K.: Accessible bus system: a bluetooth application. In: Hersh, M.A., Johnson, M.A. (eds.) Assistive Technology for Visually Impaired and Blind People, pp. 363–384. Springer, London (2008)
13. Livingstone-Lee, S.A., Skelton, R.W., Livingston, N.: Transit apps for people with brain injury and other cognitive disabilities: the state of the art. Assistive Technol. **26**(4), 209–218 (2014)
14. Marin-Lamellet, C., Pachiaudi, G., Le Breton-Gadegbeku, B.: Information and orientation needs of blind and partially sighted people in public transportation: Biovam project. Transp. Res. Record: J. Transp. Res. Board **1779**(1), 203–208 (2001)
15. Silva, J., Silva, C., Marcelino, L., Ferreira, R., Pereira, A.: Assistive mobile software for public transportation. In: Proceedings of UBICOMM (2011)

# Tactile Graphics and Models for Blind People and Recognition of Shapes by Touch

# Electromagnetic Microactuator-Array Based Virtual Tactile Display

Zoltan Szabo and Eniko T. Enikov[⊠]

Department of Aerospace and Mechanical Engineering,
The University of Arizona, 1130 N Mountain Ave., Tucson, AZ 85721, USA
{zoltanszabo,enikov}@email.arizona.edu
https://nano.arizona.edu/pages/research.php

**Abstract.** This paper describes the development and evaluation of a novel tactile display assembled from a 4 by 5 array of electromagnetic, voice-coil type micro-actuators. Each actuator is separately controlled and operates at the optimum human tactile recognition vibrating frequency and amplitude as vibrotactile actuators (tactors). As a preprogrammed, meaningful sequence of micro-actuators is actuated, the user recognizes the vibro-tactile pattern on his/her fingertip and identifies it as a single alpha-numeric character. Human subject studies have been conducted where the actuators are vibrating vertically between their resting position and the surface of the involved fingertip in a predefined sequence, which creates the tactile perception of continuous curves. The efficiency analysis by which these curves are identified as characteristic shapes by the subjects shows an average of over 70 % recognition performance.

**Keywords:** Voice-Coil Microactuator · Haptic Phi-Phenomenon · Tactile display

## 1 Introduction

The end of 20th century has been called the information age and it is undeniable information continues to be one of the most valuable assets one can have. In order to obtain or deliver information, multiple platforms, using different technologies, are available. A large number of these methods rely on visual or auditory perception. *Virtual tactile displays* form a separate group, providing information through the sensation of touch, particularly via the excitation of human fingertip. In this paper the development and human subject study based evaluation of an electromagnetic microactuator-array based virtual tactile display is presented.

### 1.1 Application Ideas

The main application area of the presented vibro-tactile display is communication for both sighted and visually-impaired people. By displaying a sequence

© Springer International Publishing Switzerland 2016
K. Miesenberger et al. (Eds.): ICCHP 2016, Part II, LNCS 9759, pp. 53–60, 2016.
DOI: 10.1007/978-3-319-41267-2_8

of characters, one character at a time, the user is able to receive information without engaging auditory or visual senses. The idea can be implemented as a supplementary information delivery method in mobile systems such as cell phones, game consoles, computer accessories (mouse, tablets), etc.

Another application is a dynamic version of the Braille system for visually impaired people. Instead of making the user move the finger over a previously created sequence of static letters, the adjustment of the sequence of excited tactors on the tactile display allows the user to keep the finger at one location. This solution eliminates the need of large devices capable of presenting multiple characters at once. Consequently a small encompassment of the actuators can be attached to other existing devices, such as cell phones. This provides the potential to enter the highly competitive market of portable communication devices as a complimentary instrument.

## 1.2  Existing Solutions

Multiple attempts have been made to create a tactile display that satisfies the human sensation based physiological requirements for successful execution of the previously described ideas. Some solutions are based on electro-mechanical structures of stepper or linear motor driven mechanisms which are normally bulky, not portable, and have a low resolution. A rather static application family of actuators is represented by shape memory alloy wires [1], which are too slow to operate at higher frequencies, and by dielectric elastomer actuators which also prove to be suitable only for non-vibrating or low vibration frequency ranges [2].

Thermo mechanical switches [3] and piezoelectric devices [4] have low energy density thus they are unable to deliver sufficient forces over the range of larger protrusion travel. Most of the aforementioned techniques are large by design or do not provide sufficient force over the displacement of the actuator at the requested frequency.

A promising set of electromagnetic actuators have a $mm$ scale coil and permanent magnet and they are able to produce sufficient amounts of forces [5–7] but their required current is relatively high introducing the effect of overheating under operation which is unacceptable for human use and potentially damages the solenoid wire. The authors of this paper have previously created multiple iterations of voice-coil actuators [8,9] which served as the starting point of development of the presented device.

## 2  Principle of Operation

When a fingertip is exposed to a sequentially activated set of tactile vibrators, the brain perceives the exposure as a continuous curve. This phenomenon is called the *tactile illusion of linear continuity* or *tactile phi phenomenon*. Tactile illusion provides a sensation of a continuous line by sensing only vibrating dots apart from each other along a line or curve. The sequentially activated tactors not only will be perceived as a continuous line, they also create the sensation that the line is moving similarly to what one experiences with *graphestesia*. Graphestesia is the ability to perceive shapes or symbols that are curved by dragging a pen or a pointy tool uninterruptedly across the skin [10]. "Tactile illusion is the connect-the-dots effect version of graphesteasia." [10].

It has been shown that both sighted and visually impaired people are able to perceive symbols based on signals produced by the tactile illusion of linear continuity, without any prior experience or training with using this phenomenon [10,11]. Sighted people normally happen to need a larger number of repetitions to reach proper perception [10]. The existence of tactile illusion motivated the creation and testing of the device presented in this paper.

For the design of such device one must consider the key parameters that define the efficiency of phi-phenomenon based cutaneous sensation. Some of the necessary settings for tactile illusion are 5 ms the *intervibrating point time delay* is the time elapsed between the end of vibration of the last tactor and the beginning of vibration of the next one, 5 *No. of vibrations* is the number of protrusions to the fingertip while activated, 10 ms *solenoid on time* is the time of protrusion per tactor per vibration, 10 ms *solenoid off time* is the time in a vibrating cycle when there is no active protrusion [12].

Another key factor is related to the *spatial acuity of touch*. This is described by the *two point discrimination sense or threshold* which is the smallest distance between two points on the skin at which the excitation of the points still results in the sensation of two separate points of protrusion. When excitation is applied closer to one another than the two point discrimination threshold, the subject will perceive only one point. Previous studies showed that the two point threshold is age dependent [13]. Young people have an average of 1.95 mm, middle age people 2.68 mm and elderly people 5.03 mm as an average two point threshold on their fingertip of their pointing finger. This limitation defines the minimum distance between the tactors on an array to be about 2 mm. Such spacing can provide tactile illusion of alphanumerics when the actuators are arranged into a 5 lines by 4 columns array [12]. From [14] it is known that the minimum necessary force of protrusion is 5–10 mN and the minimum needed protrusion depth is 5 [15] to 11 μm [16].

## 3   Experimental Device

The structural components of the miniaturized version of the actuator presented in [9] are shown in Fig. 1(left). The final coil diameter of 1.893 mm and length of 3 mm are obtained from static electromagnetic numerical analysis in ANSYS. The actuator is able to supply more than 15 mN force over a range of 2.5 mm displacement with a peak of 46.72 mN at 620 μm.

The 4 by 5 assembly of actuators packaged into a cell phone-like design is shown in Fig. 1(right). The 65 × 145 × 14 mm body includes a PCB controlled by an ARM microcontroller and connected to the actuators. The microcontroller provides pulse width modulated signal to each of selectable actuators at a time.

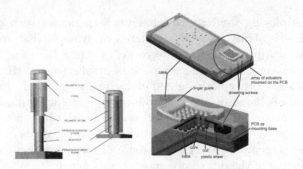

**Fig. 1.** Tactile display device (4 by 5 array of tactors): (left) Structure of the microactuators; (right) Integrated device

## 4  Human Subject Studies

Human subject studies were conducted utilizing the tactile display. The study focuses on the applicability of the device for presenting characters via interaction with the user's fingertip utilizing the tactile illusion. Ten sighted people were gathered and given a brief description of the goal and procedure of the study. The average age of the volunteers is 24 years, ranging from 19 to 31 years. The test included 4 female and 6 male subjects. All the volunteers are right handed, and are free of any previous head traumas, strokes or peripheral nerve injuries. Subject No.5 has been previously exposed to the test device multiple times, while the other 9 had no history whatsoever with experimentation of this kind. During the experiment a predefined sequence of buzzing actuators formed certain characters. The characters and their flow of buzzing is illustrated with numbered arrows in Fig. 2. Some characters, like *1, 7* or *10*, form a *continuous sequence*, while others have *discontinuities* or *jumps. Character ID 3* has 2 jumps, while *Character ID 4* has 1 jump. The time delay between the buzzing of two neighboring dots is identical to the duration of a jump. The number of jumps correlates to the number of distinct curves or lines in a character. *Character ID 4* is made of 2 lines, while *ID 10* is composed of 1.

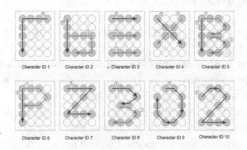

**Fig. 2.** Characters presented on the tactile display

The characters form groups of one digit *numbers*, capital *letters* from the Latin alphabet and other *geometrical shapes* that might represent members of distinct alphabets. The test for every individual consisted of 3 different experiments. The first two experiments were testing the ability to recognize individual characters, while the third investigation asked to recognize a sequence of 3 characters. In every scenario the subject placed his or her right index finger over the array. Once the finger was positioned, the buzzing sequence was launched. The subject then sketched onto a printed sheet what he or she felt. In case the sketched answer was incorrect, the same character was repeated. This continued until the correct character was recognized or until a maximum of 10 attempts, whichever came first.

The human subjects were assigned different sub cases of the three main experiments which provided a control group and a test group to test the underlying hypothesis.

**Experiment 1.** Aims at finding out how many repetitions of exposure are needed to identify the correct individual character. Half the subjects were told the number and order of types of characters (letters, shapes and numbers) while the other half (the control group) was told to be presented by a random mix of these. The *hypothesis* assumes that knowing the type of character helps to recognize the correct answer, since it narrows down the number of possibilities. Analysis of the recorded data over the entire test population shows that every character was identified at least 4 times, while 1 of them is identified 10 times. The number of times each character identified is presented in Fig. 3. Taking the average of these results shows that every character was recognized at an average of 7.5 times. Apparently the hardest *Characters* were *ID. 2, 3* and *4*. All share the features of consisting of straight lines with one or more jumps in the continuity. Since the first two are shapes, it makes it even harder to find out the correct answer due to the extremely large number of possibilities a shape can take. It appears that the jump introduces a loss of reference point, the subjects

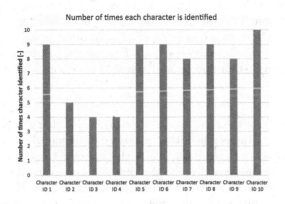

**Fig. 3.** Number of times characters identified

are unable to correctly relate the endpoint of the first line to the beginning point of the second line. As a consequence, for distinguishing between lines with discontinuities and no discontinuities, there should be an obvious sign. Such sign could be a longer pause between the sections.

It is notable that the easiest characters were almost exclusively curved. Besides the simple case of *ID. 1*, all highly recognized characters had curves. One possible explanation for the ease of recognition of such characters could lie in the similarity of buzzing sequence to the dynamics of handwriting.

*Experiment 1 (control group)* shows 4.1 average number of characters recognized, while *test group* only reaches 3.4. This result strongly contradicts the hypothesis. It seems that the knowledge of the category of the character, whether it is a shape, letter or number, rather constrains the subjects to guess instead of freely recognize. Although the statistical possibility of finding the correct answer in case of a number is at least 10 % and increasing by 10 % per every attempt, the subjects have hard time finding the correct answer. The volunteer might feel extra emotional pressure, i.e. extreme increase of arousal, from not being able to recognize the correct character despite the fact that he knows it should be a number out of only 10 options.

The overall average of efficiency per person is 50 %, almost identical that of efficiency per character. A closer look at the standard deviation of the efficiency values reveals that 23 % for the characters and 10 % for the subjects apply. This means that the individual differences in human subjects are less significant when it comes to efficiency measures than that of the characters.

**Experiment 2.** Hypothesizes that repeated exposure to the same characters will improve the recognition efficiency. It is further hypothesized that extra knowledge, i.e. that the characters were already presented, about the characters will improve the recognition efficiency.

The second hypothesis turns out to be correct. When considering the *2.1* and *2.2* experimental cases separately, an average of 65 % with a standard deviation of 27 % is achieved when the subjects are told that the characters have been already presented, while when unaware of this fact, the result is 31 % with 6 % of standard deviation. The results may be explained by the effect of *self-assuring suggestion* coming from hypnosis practice [17]. Another possible explanation is the effect of *learning*. The subjects from *Experiment 2.1* have the chance to associate their previous cutaneous and visual experiences with a known set of characters.

**Experiment 3.** Tests the recognition of 3 consecutive characters, separated by a 2 s pause. The hypothesis states that exposure to previously shown characters will improve character recognition, while the increased number of characters might introduce confusion and reduced ability to keep in mind the full answer. As a final conclusion to *Experiment 3* it is stated that the device is able to reach 63 % character recognition efficiency with a maximum of 32 % word recognition efficiency, which supports the initial hypothesis.

# 5   Conclusions

The overall average character recognition efficiency is 57 % for the characters, while the average character recognition efficiency of the individuals participating in the tests is 55 %. These numbers represent a weighted efficiency i.e. how many more repetitions of exposure to the same character are needed in the population of 10 different characters over all 3 experiments. The average is weighted by the number of repetitions. Finding the character for the first time for every character in all experiments results in 100 % character recognition efficiency. By defining the efficiency in a non-weighted manner, where the maximum efficiency is when the character is found by all volunteers (regardless of the number of repetitions) in all three experiments, an average of 76.28 % is obtained. This means that any character on average is identified 7 out of 10 times. It is notable that specific characters are recognized at an overall of non-weighted 90–100 % with the highest of 91 % weighted efficiency. With the exception of 3 characters, all scenarios are above 70 %. A person with previous exposure to the device achieved a maximum of 77.39 % weighted and 86 % non-weighted level. He was able to identify 86 % of the characters presented to him. It is concluded that the effect of familiarity with the tactile display is significant. For successful use of the device one needs to not only consider the technical aspect of the device itself, but also the training, and the corresponding psychology. It is notable that the characters exposed in all 3 experiments are among the highest efficiency levels. This result gives scientific basis to think that continuous repetition of exposure accompanied by a structured training on using the device might successfully lead to a nearly 100 % efficient device without further hardware modifications.

A major area of future study is the effect of *training*. Pre-test exposure to a specified list of potentially presented characters hypothetically increases the recognition efficiency. Care needs to be taken because associating a tactile sensation to a character can be learned regardless of whether the subject identifies the shape itself. For instance one can feel four dots, and be told it is the letter *P*. The person learns to associate those 4 dots with letter *P*, but this does not say anything about the actual efficiency of the device. Exposure to the list of potential characters also introduces the convention for the flow of buzzing.

An alternative approach could be to observe the handwriting of the subject and implement the flow of writing and shape of letters to the array. This is assumed to improve efficiency.

The conducted human subject studies give confidence in the applicability of the concept of using the tactile illusion via fingertip - display interaction. With additional training and improvements, a new system of communication can be developed with a multitude of applications on the horizon.

# References

1. Taylor, P.M., Moser, A., Creed, A.: A sixty-four element tactile display using shape memory alloy wires. Displays **18**(3), 163–168 (1998)
2. Lee, H.S., et al.: Design analysis and fabrication of arrayed tactile display based on dielectric elastomer actuator. Sens. Actuators A: Phys. **205**, 191–198 (2014)
3. Enikov, E.T., Lazarov, K.V.: Micro-mechanical switch array for meso-scale actuation. Sens. Actuators A: Phys. **121**(1), 282–293 (2005)
4. Vidal-Verd, F., Hafez, M.: Graphical tactile displays for visually-impaired people. IEEE Trans. Neural Syst. Rehabil. Eng. **15**(1), 119–130 (2007)
5. Streque, J., et al.: Elaboration and test of high energy density magnetic micro-actuators for tactile display applications. Procedia Chem. **1**(1), 694–697 (2009)
6. Deng, K., Enikov, E.T., Zhang, H.: Development of a pulsed electromagnetic micro-actuator for 3D tactile displays. In: 2007 IEEE/ASME International Conference on Advanced Intelligent Mechatronics. IEEE (2007)
7. Deng, K., Enikov, E.T.: Design and development of a pulsed electromagnetic micro-actuator for 3D virtual tactile displays. Mechatronics **20**(4), 503–509 (2010)
8. Szabo, Z., Ganji, M., Enikov, E.T.: Development of voice-coil micro-actuator for 3-D virtual tactile displays. In: ASME 2011 International Mechanical Engineering Congress and Exposition. American Society of Mechanical Engineers (2011)
9. Szabo, Z., Enikov, E.T.: Development of wearable micro-actuator array for 3-D virtual tactile displays (2012)
10. Gonzales, G.R.: Symbol recognition produced by points of tactile stimulation: the illusion of linear continuity. Mayo Clin. Proc. **71**(11). Elsevier (1996)
11. Gonzales, G.R., et al.: Tactile illusion-produced number perception in blind and sighted persons. Mayo Clin. Proc. **73**(12). Elsevier (1998)
12. Gonzales, G.R., Gust, G.R., Hughes, K.E.: Fingertip communication: a tactile communication device for a glove. Space Technol. Appl. Int. Forum-2000, **504**(1). AIP Publishing (2000)
13. Stevens, J.C.: Aging and spatial acuity of touch. J. Gerontol. **47**(1), P35–P40 (1992)
14. Pascual-Leone, A., Torres, F.: Plasticity of the sensorimotor cortex representation of the reading finger in Braille readers. Brain **116**(1), 39–52 (1993)
15. Kaczmarek, K.A., et al.: Electrotactile and vibrotactile displays for sensory substitution systems. IEEE Trans. Biomed. Eng. **38**(1), 1–16 (1991)
16. Hatzfeld, C., Kern, T.A.: Engineering Haptic devices
17. Erickson, M.H., Havens, R.A.: The Wisdom of Milton H. Erickson: Hypnosis and Hypnotherapy, vol. 2. Ardent Media, New York (1992)
18. Jeannerod, M.: The Cognitive Neuroscience of Action. Blackwell Publishing, Oxford (1997)

# Empowering Low-Vision Rehabilitation Professionals with "Do-It-Yourself" Methods

Stéphanie Giraud and Christophe Jouffrais[✉]

CNRS, IRIT, University of Toulouse, Toulouse, France
Christophe.Jouffrais@irit.fr

**Abstract.** Teachers and educators working with visually impaired students need to create numerous adapted learning materials that represent maps, shapes, objects, concepts, etc. This process usually relies on tactile document makers. It is time consuming and expensive. Recent "Do-It-Yourself" (DIY) techniques, including 3D printing and low-cost rapid prototyping, may enable to easily and quickly create learning materials that is versatile, interactive and cheap. In this study, we first analyzed the needs of many professionals at an institute for visually impaired children. It appeared that many of the students also present associated behavioral disorders, which has consequences on the design of adapted materials. In a second step, we used a focus group with design probes made with regular or 3D printed objects, and low-cost microcontrollers. At the end of the focus group, we identified four specific scenarios with different teachers and students. We created four low-cost interactive prototypes, and we observed how they were used during learning sessions. In conclusion, DIY methods appear to be a valuable solution for enabling professionals to quickly design new adapted materials or modify existing ones. Furthermore, DIY methods provide a collaborative framework between teachers and visually impaired students, which has a positive impact on their motivation.

**Keywords:** Visual impairment · Do-It-Yourself · Rapid prototyping · 3D printing · Learning materials

## 1 Introduction

Many learning materials used in centers specialized for visually impaired people are adapted or especially designed for this user group. For instance, drawings and charts are made with corkboards or wood. This adaptation depends on the specific needs of each student (residual vision, possible auditory or cognitive impairment, etc.) but also on the needs of each teacher. Each lesson may require tactile representations of visual contents (maps, charts, plots, etc.), but also an update of a previous tactile representation, which is time consuming and may turn to be expensive. In some cases, the appropriate learning materials do not exist or are really too expensive. All these issues result in the lack of adapted materials for visually impaired students. Besides, when too specific, these materials may generate a feeling of being stigmatized by end-users [1].

K. Miesenberger et al. (Eds.): ICCHP 2016, Part II, LNCS 9759, pp. 61–68, 2016.
DOI: 10.1007/978-3-319-41267-2_9

"Do-It-Yourself" (DIY) methods, including 3D printing and low-cost rapid proto-typing, may empower visual impairment specialists to overcome these issues. Indeed, 3D printing enables them to build the physical representations (2.5D maps or plots, 3D models, etc.) that they need. In addition, low-cost prototyping platforms such as Arduino® (Arduino LLC) can be used to include interactive features to these physical representations. In this study, we first observed the needs of visual impairment special-ists. We then introduced a few design probes of low-cost objects printed in 3D and including interactive features. We finally designed four prototypes that were used for teaching, and we observed how they were used. Our general objective was to empower the different specialists in making interactive materials that perfectly fit their own needs, with low-cost technologies.

## 2   3D Printing and Low-Cost Rapid Prototyping: A Solution for Making Adapted Learning Materials

Obviously, 3D printing is a promising method to make physical representations of graphics adapted for children with visual impairment [2–4]. Although computer aided design tools, such as Blender, Rhino, SolidWorks, or AutoCAD are relatively difficult to use [5], many models can be found on websites (see [6]), and the final printing is easy. When necessary, software such as Tinkercad or SketchUp can be used, which are easy to learn [5]. [7] created over ten tactile aids for visually impaired students using laser cutter and 3D printer. They observed that these aids improved the understanding of the class, but also the satisfaction of the participants. [8] also observed the use of 3D printing in three different education settings including individuals with cognitive, motor, and visual impairment. They observed that 3D design and printing encourage STEM (Science, Technology, Engineering, and Math) engagement in students, but also allow the creation of accessible curriculum content by stakeholders. Besides, [6] examined the models found on the online community Thingiverse.com. They listed a large number of models for assistive tools, and they highlighted that many of them were created by the end-users themselves or on behalf of friends. Interestingly, these designers do not have any formal training or expertise. Likewise, [9, 10] listed several examples of materials that were made by non-engineers. They observed that it is efficient to empower non-engineers to create or modify their own materials, and that it increases the adoption process because it provides a better control over design and cost.

In complement to 3D printing, many cheap and small single-board microcontrollers, such as the Touch Board® (Bare Conductive Ltd), Raspberry Pi® (Raspberry Pi foun-dation), Arduino® or Lilypad® (Arduino LLC), allow building interactive physical objects. [11] made an inventory of existing tools, and split them into three categories: microcontrollers, sensor boards, and hacking existing devices. These authors observed that each tool may present a specific benefit (see Table 1). They created the Makey Makey® (JoyLabz LLC), a platform for designing tangible user interfaces, which offers five advantages: 1/Quick start for beginners; 2/Works with any software; 3/Nature-based interfaces; 4/Programming and 5/Soldering not required. Thus, the Makey Makey is designed for a wide range of audiences, from beginners to experts, and encourages creativity. Different studies showed that it facilitates different activities with retired people [12] or with children with disabilities [13]. Other platforms, such as Raspberry Pi, require more skills. However, they embed a processor, a battery, and many input-output connectors, which allows designing mobile applications [14]. On the basis of this overview of rapid prototyping technologies, it appears that makers, according to their skills and objectives, can choose the most appropriate board for their own purposes (see Table 1).

**Table 1.** Characteristics of different tools allowing rapid prototyping (adapted from [11])

| | Quick start for beginners | Works with any software | Nature-based interfaces | Programming not required | Soldering not required |
|---|---|---|---|---|---|
| Touch Board | Yes | | Yes | Yes | Yes |
| Raspberry Pi | | Yes | Yes | | |
| Arduino | | | Yes | | Yes |
| Lilypad | | | Yes | | Yes |
| Makey Makey | Yes | Yes | Yes | Yes | Yes |

## 3 Aims of the Study

Our main objective was to empower professionals at an institute for visually impaired children with DIY tools, in order to create their own learning materials. We relied on 3D printing and microcontrollers to design materials that are cheap, easy to make, and that perfectly fit their needs. We chose the Makey Makey for simplicity, but also the Touch Board because it allows making prototypes without any wire. The institute that we worked with hosts visually impaired children and young adults from three to twenty years old. Some of them present associated auditory impairment, behavioral disorders, or pervasive developmental disorders. Different professionals are with the institute, including qualified teachers and educators, orientation and mobility instructors, as well as tactile document makers.

First, we conducted observations that allowed identifying the needs of the professionals during different lessons. Second, we used design probes (e.g., printed geometrical shapes that were made interactive) with a focus group. Third, we organized practical courses with the professionals based on Makey Makey and Touch Board prototyping. Finally, we co-designed four different prototypes, and we observed how they were used in the classrooms.

## 4 Collaborative Design

In total, four specialized teachers, three educators, two locomotion instructors, one tactile document maker, and twenty-three children aged from eight to twenty years old participated to this study. We carried out non-directive observations in order to understand the needs of the specialists during teaching sessions (see [15]).

### 4.1   Needs Analysis

Obviously, visually impaired students must learn different geographical, mathematical, historical, etc., notions and concepts with restricted or no visual cues. Hence, adaptation of the learning materials is mandatory, and depends on the type of lesson, the level of knowledge, but also on the sensory (visual and auditory) and cognitive abilities of the students. For example, History and Geography teachers must frequently transform visual maps into tactile maps. They mainly use swell paper to make raised-lines maps that include legends in Braille or big characters. These maps quickly get crowded, and they are not sizeable or updatable (cf. Fig. 1A). Thus, for a specific lesson, teachers need numerous maps, which turns to be time-consuming and expensive. In addition, because the children must use different maps with different information contents or scales, it can raise perceptual or cognitive issues.

**Fig. 1.** A. Raised-lines tactile maps used during a Geography lesson. B. Magnets used by orientation and mobility instructors to represent a neighborhood

Orientation and Mobility instructors use to make physical models of geographical areas using various objects, such as magnets or DUPLO® blocks (cf. Fig. 1B). However, the similarity of the objects is an issue for making accurate representations. For instance, within a map of a neighborhood, it is difficult to differentiate roadways from sidewalks. It is also complicated to provide symbolic representations of gigantic elements (e.g. a building or a tower), mostly for cognitively impaired students.

Educators use gamification approaches to design activities in order to raise the engagement and attention of visually impaired children with associated behavioral disorders. For example, children learn shapes (square, circle, rectangle, etc.) by nesting them in the good location, which causes the playback of music. Educators also focus on social links between the children. They try to include these educational objectives within daily activities (meals, toilette, etc.) Thus, they need tools that may improve interaction between the children themselves but also between the children and the environment, and that are usable in many contexts.

### 4.2   Focus Group

Following the observations, we set up three participatory design sessions. The first two sessions aimed at enhancing ideation. We presented regular or 3D printed objects (shapes, miniature vehicles, objects, fruits, etc.), as well as tools for rapid prototyping (Makey Makey and Touch Board), to both the professionals and the students (cf. Fig. 2). Participants were free to play with the set of interactive objects, and imagine scenarios of usage including those or similar objects, according to their own needs. Numerous ideas came out such as: illustrating the concept of electrical power; interactive Braille characters to learn the alphabet; an interactive timeline to learn important periods of the History; a sensory tale that includes touch and sound experiences, etc.

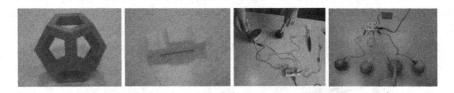

**Fig. 2.** Examples of design probes used with the focus group: printed polygon or car, as well as real objects and fruits

A practical course with Makey Makey and Touch Board platforms was then organized in order to let the professionals make their own prototypes. During the debriefing, all the teachers enjoyed the prototypes, especially because they provide objects with interactive zones. They confirmed having a great interest for rapid prototyping, and explicitly mentioned the fact that they were low-cost and easy to design. DIY tools were considered as empowering, and the participants declared that they will use them to create their own learning materials. Finally, we selected four different prototypes, and we observed how they were used in the classrooms.

## 5    Usage of Prototypes Within the Classrooms

The first scenario involved five visually impaired children from 12 to 18 years old with behavior disorders and pervasive developmental disorders. It aims at encouraging them to eat various fruits that were judged as unpleasant by touch (for example orange or kiwi). Using the Makey Makey and the Scratch software, fruits were connected to a song that each child likes. The prototype really enhanced curiosity and fruit manipulation (see Fig. 3). The children were focused on the activity and frequently smiled and laughed, which is usually quite difficult to get. Finally, some children tasted the fruit, which they always refused to do before.

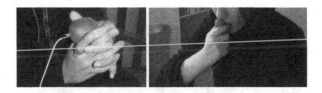

**Fig. 3.** Food diversification activity. A song is played when the kiwi is touched. Some children finally tasted the kiwi

The second scenario aimed at learning the Braille alphabet, and involved an 8 year old visually impaired child with cognitive disorders. The Braille letters were printed and rendered interactive (Touch Board and Arduino). The child chose and recorded the sounds that were played when touching each letter. According to the teacher, the use of the prototype increased engagement and motivation. Actually, the child was looking forward to the next session.

The third scenario was used during a geometry lesson with six visually impaired students from 16 to 18 years old with minor behavioral disorders. Sounds and verbal descriptions providing angle value, length, and width, were triggered when students touched different parts of the geometric shapes (see Fig. 4).

**Fig. 4.** Problem solving with interactive geometric shapes

The fourth scenario involved an 8 years old visually impaired child with cognitive disorders during an orientation and mobility training session. The child had to prepare a journey, and hence had to explore a neighborhood that contains two bridges, one with a railway and another one with a pedestrian path. The instructor considered this layout as very difficult to understand for the children. The prototype represented the whole area with the two bridges (a wood laser-cut bridge and a 3D printed bridge) arranged on a raised-line map. A Touch Board with Arduino software were used to create interactive zones that trigger sounds recorded by the children during a prior walk within the area. There was the sound of a passing train, and the sound of throwing stones into the river (which he often does when he is on the bridge). The child was also free to manipulate a miniature train and a figurine. When the train contacted the wood bridge, the sound of the passing train was played. When the figurine contacted the pedestrian bridge, the sound of stones falling into the water was played. After twenty minutes of lesson (see Fig. 5), the instructor was really satisfied by the prototype, and reported that, on her own opinion, it helped the children understand this difficult neighborhood.

**Fig. 5.** Prototype used for the comprehension of a complex neighborhood during an orientation and mobility training session

# 6 Conclusion

In this study, we observed several professionals of visual impairment working in various contexts and having diverse educational aims. Following these observations, different prototypes were designed using DIY tools, and were used during classes with visually impaired children. Although our final observations need to be completed with more systematic methods, it appears that the DIY method met the needs of the professionals including a high level of customization depending on the students' abilities and the educational aim. The professionals were satisfied because the method is cheap, quick and easy. It is empowering because the prototypes can easily be adapted to other sessions or to a pedagogical progression. [16], using a similar method, showed that rapid prototyping may also complement existing materials.

Importantly, many colleagues of the teachers and educators involved in our study, who were informed about the prototypes, are actually motivated to produce their own materials. For instance, an educator is currently making an interactive shirt with Lilypad boards. When a child wearing the shirt touches his/her elbow, shoulder, breast, etc., a specific sound and description are provided. The objective is to help visually impaired children with severe cognitive disorders to understand their own body, but also improve physical coordination. Altogether, these results highlight the potential of rapid prototyping tools for designing adapted materials.

Besides empowerment of teachers, rapid prototyping is a method that includes children as collaborators - and not only as users - during the design process [17]. For instance, in our case, children were free to choose and record the sounds that were triggered in the prototypes. Regardless of the prototype and the activity that they were involved in, the students were very motivated. They really appreciated being included during the design process. In fact, they want to use the same tools in other classes.

To conclude, "Do-It-Yourself" empowers professionals, but also improves the engagement and the satisfaction of the students. The method may be used in many different ludic and educational contexts (lessons of mobility, orientation, geography, mathematics, engineering, etc.)

**Acknowledgements.** We thank the FIRAH for financial support, as well as the professionals and students of the Institute for Blind Youth of Toulouse (CESDV-IJA), especially Anna Bartolucci, Nathalie Bedouin, Abdel Benabdallah, Anne Lorho and Mounir Sougtani for their collaboration.

# References

1. Bichard, J.-A., Coleman, R., Langdon, P.: Does my stigma look big in this? Considering acceptability and desirability in the inclusive design of technology products. In: Stephanidis, C. (ed.) HCI 2007. LNCS, vol. 4554, pp. 622–631. Springer, Heidelberg (2007)
2. Kim, J., Yeh, T.: Toward 3D-printed movable tactile pictures for children al impairments with visual impairments. In: Proceedings of the CHI 2015, pp. 2815–2824 (2015)

3. Stangl, A., Kim, J., Yeh, T.: 3D printed tactile picture books for children with visual impairments. In: Proceedings of the 2014 Conference on Interaction Design and Children, IDC 2014, pp. 321–324 (2014)
4. Salgado, M., Salmi, A.: Ideas for future museums by the visually impaired. In: Proceedings of the Participatory Design Conference, PDC 2006, pp. 105–108 (2006)
5. Carrington, P., Hosmer, S., Yeh, T., Hurst, A., Kane, S.K.: Like this, but better': supporting novices' design and fabrication of 3D models using existing objects. In: Proceedings of the iConference 2015 (2015)
6. Buehler, E., Branham, S., Ali, A., Chang, J.J., Hofmann, M.K., Hurst, A., Kane, S.K.: Sharing is caring: assistive technology designs on thingiverse. In: Proceedings of the 33rd Annual ACM Conference on Human Factors in Computing Systems, CHI 2015, pp. 525–534 (2015)
7. McDonald, S., Dutterer, J., Abdolrahmani, A., Kane, S.K., Hurst, A.: Tactile aids for visually impaired graphical design education. In: Proceedings of the 16th International ACM SIGACCESS Conference on Computers and Accessibility, ASSETS 2014, pp. 275–276 (2014)
8. Buehler, E., Kane, S.K., Hurst, A.: ABC and 3D: opportunities and obstacles to 3D printing in special education environments. In: Proceedings of the 16th International ACM SIGACCESS Conference on Computers and Accessibility, ASSETS 2014, pp. 107–114 (2014)
9. Hurst, A., Tobias, J.: Empowering individuals with do-it-yourself assistive technology. In: The Proceedings of the 13th International ACM SIGACCESS Conference on Computers and Accessibility, ASSETS 2011, p. 11 (2011)
10. Hurst, A., Kane, S.: Making 'making' accessible. In: Proceedings of the 12th International Conference on Interaction Design and Children, IDC 2013, p. 635 (2013)
11. Silver, J. Rosenbaum, E., Shaw, D.: Makey Makey: improvising tangible and nature-based user interfaces. In: TEI 2012, p. 5 (2012)
12. Rogers, Y., Paay, J., Brereton, M., Vaisutis, K.L., Marsden, G., Vetere, F.: Never too old: engaging retired people inventing the future with MaKey MaKey. In: Proceedings of the 32nd Annual ACM Conference on Human Factors in Computing Systems, CHI 2014, pp. 3913–3922 (2014)
13. Leduc-Mills, B., Dec, J. Schimmel, J.: Evaluating accessibility in fabrication tools for children. In: Proceedings of the 12th International Conference on Interaction Design and Children, IDC 2013, p. 617 (2013)
14. Hamidi, F., Baljko, M., Kunic, T., Feraday, R.: Do-It-Yourself (DIY) assistive technology: a communication board case study. In: Miesenberger, K., Fels, D., Archambault, D., Peňáz, P., Zagler, W. (eds.) ICCHP 2014, Part II. LNCS, vol. 8548, pp. 287–294. Springer, Heidelberg (2014)
15. Ghiglione, R., Matalon, B.: Les enquêtes sociologiques: théories et pratiques. Armand Colin, Paris (1998)
16. Brule, E., Bailly, G., Brock, A., Valentin, F., Denis, G., Jouffrais, C.: MapSense: multi-sensory interactive maps for children living with visual impairments. In: International Conference for Human-Computer Interaction, CHI 2016, p. 10 (2016)
17. Druin, A.: The role of children in the design of new technology. Behav. Inf. Technol. **21**(1), 1–25 (2002)

# Expansion Characteristic of Tactile Symbols on Swell Paper

## Effects of Heat Setting, Position and Area of Tactile Symbols

Takahiro Hashimoto[1] and Tetsuya Watanabe[2(✉)]

[1] Graduate School, University of Niigata, Niigata, Japan
[2] Faculty of Engineering, University of Niigata, Niigata, Japan
t2.nabe@eng.niigata-u.ac.jp

**Abstract.** Swell paper is one method of making tactile graphics. Its expansion heights are affected by several factors. Of them, in this study, we changed three parameters: the heat setting and the position and the size of the tactile images. The expansion heights of the tactile images with various parameters were measured by using a 3D measurement system. As the results, we found the quantitative effects of these parameters on the expansion heights of tactile images.

**Keywords:** Swell paper · Tactile symbol · Blind people

## 1 Introduction

Swell paper is a popular method to create tactile graphics for visually impaired people. It is coated with special microcapsules that swell up when exposed to heat. To produce tactile graphics, images are printed on the swell paper in black ink and then the paper is passed through a machine called a (heat) fuser. The fuser applies heat, which is absorbed by the black areas and causes the microcapsules to swell up.

The degree to which images rise varies due to the heat applied. It is empirically known that not only the heat setting of the fuser but also the position, color (strength) and size of the image changes the heat absorbed: The darker the color is and the larger the image is, the more heat is absorbed, which leads to higher expansion. As for the position of the image on the paper, the expansion is greater for images that are near the center of the paper and less toward the periphery. When passing the paper through the fuser, the part of the sheet that enters the machine first has less expansion than the rest of the sheet. Therefore, an appropriate raising of the images over the entire sheet is difficult to achieve. It has depended on the experience of the person doing the work rather than on any quantitative guidelines [1].

In this study, we made tactile graphics in which those three parameters were varied and measured the height of raised images to clarify the effect of each parameter on expansion. This quantitative data will make the process of creating tactile graphics on swell paper easier for everyone, regardless of experience.

K. Miesenberger et al. (Eds.): ICCHP 2016, Part II, LNCS 9759, pp. 69–76, 2016.
DOI: 10.1007/978-3-319-41267-2_10

## 2    Related Work

One of the authors conducted an experiment on the legibility of braille on swell paper with three different dot diameters [2]. The 3D measurement in the study showed a trend that smaller dots were lower than larger dots.

Cryer, Jones, and Gunn measured heights of 21 different size dots whose diameter varied from 0.70 to 0.145 mm by 0.05 mm [3]. The dot heights varied from the lowest, 0.145 mm, at a diameter of 0.70 mm to the highest, 0.456 mm, at a diameter of 1.65 mm.

These previous studies showed the relationship between dot size and dot height. However, the effect of the heat setting of the fuser or that of the position of the image has not been ever quantitatively explored.

## 3    Effects of Heat Setting

### 3.1    Material

To investigate the effect of heat setting, we made a master drawing that consisted of 50 black dots of 27 pt size (1.7 mm in diameter) arranged in a grid of ten rows and five columns (Fig. 1). This arrangement was chosen because this material was also used to investigate the effect of position on the paper later. The dot size is about the same as the 18 pt (1.68 mm) dots in the braille font provided by Japan Lighthouse [4]. Eighteen pt size of this font was found to be the optimum for tactile reading in the previous study [5].

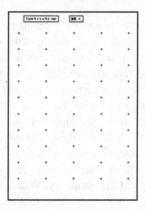

**Fig. 1.**  Master drawing used to measure the effects of the heat setting and position of the image. It consisted of 50 black dots arranged in a grid of ten rows and five columns.

We used a laser printer (MF4680, Canon) to print the drawing on A4 sheets of swell paper (ZY-TEX2, Zychem) and heated them with a fuser (PIAF, Quantum Technology).

The A4 sheets of capsule paper can be fed into the fuser short- or long-side first (Fig. 2). In this investigation, we used the long-side first insertion method.

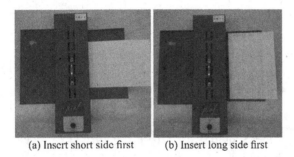

(a) Insert short side first    (b) Insert long side first

**Fig. 2.** Orientation of paper insertion into the fuser.

## 3.2 Heat Setting

The amount of heat applied by PIAF is set by turning the heat control on the top cover. It has a scale from one (minimal heat) to nine (maximum) (see Figs. 2 and 4). A preliminary study in which we measured the dot heights for the different heat settings revealed that setting the control to five or lower on the scale produced dots that were insufficiently high and difficult to measure. We therefore used positions six through nine on the heat control in the present investigation.

## 3.3 Dot Height Measurement

We measured the height of raised dots with a 3D measuring system (VR-3000, Keyence). The highest point from the paper surface was measured for all 50 dots on each sheet (Fig. 3).

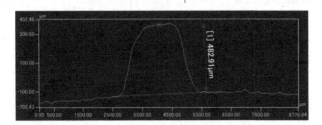

**Fig. 3.** Measurement of dot height with a 3D measuring system

## 3.4 Results

Figure 4 presents the average heights of the dots for each heat setting of the fuser. Because the expansion is slight for dots around the margins of the paper, we exclude the 26 dots around the outside and present the results for the remaining 24 dots in the center. We can see from Fig. 4 that increasing the heat setting increases the expansion. An analysis of variance of these results reveals a significant difference according to the heat setting.

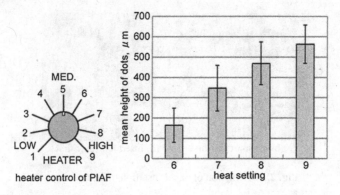

**Fig. 4.** Relationship between heat setting and dot height. In actuality, the fuser, PIAF, does not show these numbers around its heat control.

The dot height for braille specified by the international standard (ISO) is from 0.3 to 0.7 mm [6]. For the dots that we created, the specification was satisfied when the heat setting was seven or higher. We can therefore conclude that a heat setting of seven or above is appropriate for developing braille. This finding is consistent with experience.

## 4    Effects of Position

The variation in dot height with position on the paper for the heat setting of seven is represented by grayscale shades in Fig. 5, where the darker shades indicate higher expansion. We can see that the dot height is low around the edges of the sheet and increases toward the center. The minimum height was 53 μm, which is mostly unreadable by touch, and the maximum was 534 μm, which is readable.

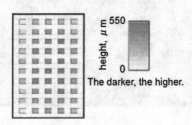

**Fig. 5.** Difference in dot heights according to their position.

Mean dot heights for five columns are presented in Fig. 6. It clearly shows that the dots on the both sides of the paper have less expansion than the dots near the center of the sheet. In addition, Fig. 6 shows that the left part of the sheet, which entered the fuser first, has less expansion than the right part.

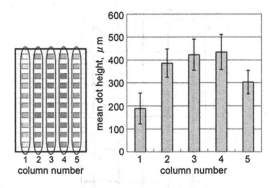

**Fig. 6.** Mean dot height by column.

Mean dot heights for ten rows are presented in Fig. 7. It shows that the dots on the upper and lower ends of the paper have less expansion than the dots near the center of the sheet.

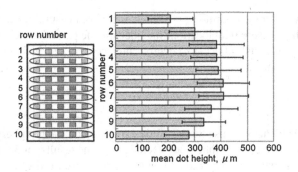

**Fig. 7.** Mean dot height by row.

# 5    Effects of Surface Area

It is known that the larger the surface area of the black printed image, the higher the expansion [1]. When tactile maps are created, main roads are distinguished from other roads by the width of the lines that represent them, so their heights are different, too. Also, we often observed that intersections are higher than the roads. To investigate these differences, we created master drawings of line grids of various line widths.

## 5.1    Material

The master drawing consisted of a grid of five vertical lines and six horizontal lines (Fig. 8). Drawings with line widths of 1, 2 and 4 mm were created. The vertical and horizontal lines were 200 and 290 mm long, respectively. We heated them with the heat setting of 7.

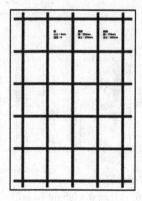

**Fig. 8.** Master drawing used to measure the effects of the size of the image. It consisted of a grid of five vertical lines and six horizontal lines

## 5.2  Line Height Measurement

In the same way as for the dot image, the line height was measured with a 3D measurement system. The measurement locations included 49 line parts (24 horizontal line parts and 25 vertical line parts) adjacent to central intersections and 30 intersections, for a total of 79 measurements.

## 5.3  Results

**Effect of Line Width.**  Because there is little expansion on the periphery of the sheet, the 18 locations around the periphery are excluded and the results for 31 inner locations (16 horizontal line parts and 15 vertical line parts) are presented in Fig. 9. We can see from the figure that expansion is greater for lines that are wider. An analysis of variance for these results indicates that the line width affects the expansion height.

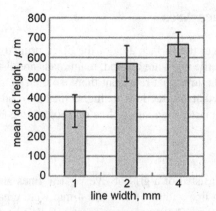

**Fig. 9.**  Relationship between line width and line height.

One tactile graphics guide recommend the use of 1.0 mm line as a major feature [1], its expansion may not be legible enough when heated with the heat setting of 7.

**Comparison of Height between Lines and Intersections.** The heights for the line parts and intersection parts are compared in Fig. 10. The values for the intersections are for the 12 locations that remain after excluding the intersections around the periphery of the sheet. The values for the line parts are for the 17 locations which are between two of the above-stated 12 intersection. We can see from Fig. 10 that the heights for the intersections are larger than for the line parts, even for the same line width. This difference is notable when the lines are thin, 1.0 mm, and is not great when lines are wide, 2.0 to 4.0 mm.

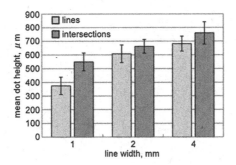

**Fig. 10.** Comparison of the heights of lines and intersections.

# 6  Conclusion

We created tactile graphics on swell paper, varying the heat setting, the position of the tactile symbols on the sheet, and the surface area of the symbols as parameters. Measurements of the height showed the effects of those parameters on the expansion quantitatively. The results provide quantitative recommendation values for these parameters for legible tactile graphics.

Factors other than the three that we report here also affect the expansion. These include the concentration of the printed drawing, the type of printer, and the type of capsule paper. The effects of these factors require future investigation.

**Acknowledgements.** This work was supported by JSPS KAKENHI Grant Number 26350654 and RISTEX, JST.

# References

1. The N.S.W. Tactual and Bold Print Mapping Committee: A Guide for the Production of Tactualand Bold Print Maps, 3rd edn. The N.S.W. Tactual and Bold Print Mapping Committee, Sydney, Australia (2006)
2. Watanabe, T., Oouchi, S.: A study of legible braille patterns of capsule paper. Bull. Natl. Inst. Spec. Educ. **30**, 1–8 (2003)

3. Cryer, H., Jones, C., Gunn, D.: Producing braille on swell paper: a study of braille legibility. Research report 11, RNIB Centre for Accessible Information, Birmingham (2011)
4. Nippon Lighthouse: Braille Font. http://www.eonet.ne.jp/~tecti/tecti/br-font.html
5. Watanabe, T.: Determining the optimum font size for braille on capsule paper. IEICE Trans. Inf. Syst. **E97-D**(8), 2191–2194 (2014)
6. ISO 17049: Accessible design - Application of Braille on Signage, Equipment and Appliances (2013)

# Tactile Identification of Embossed Raised Lines and Raised Squares with Variable Dot Elevation by Persons Who Are Blind

Georgios Kouroupetroglou[1(✉)], Aineias Martos[1],
Nikolaos Papandreou[1], Konstantinos Papadopoulos[2],
Vassilios Argyropoulous[3], and Georgios D. Sideridis[4]

[1] Department of Informatics and Telecommunications,
National and Kapodistrian University of Athens, Athens, Greece
koupe@di.uoa.gr
[2] Department of Educational and Social Policy, University of Macedonia,
Thessaloniki, Greece
[3] Department of Special Education, University of Thessaly, Volos, Greece
[4] Faculty of Primary Education, National and Kapodistrian University of Athens,
Athens, Greece

**Abstract.** We present a study on the identification accuracy of embossed tactile lines and squares in eight dot elevations and two dot densities. The results of correct and misclassified matched stimuli by ten congenitally blind participants are presented in confusion matrixes for the raised-dot lines and squares test stimuli. Moreover, the overall mean response time of the identification task is provided. Participants identify better the lower three dot elevations for both lines and squares on 20 or 10 dpi, with an exception for 20 dpi squares where the highest dot elevation is third in the order of recognition. The application of a multilevel model fitting to the data indicated significant effects for the role of the DOTs (raised dot lines versus raised dot squares) with the raised dot squares being associated with significantly elevated correct responding.

**Keywords:** Embossed braille graphics · Dot elevation · Tactile graphics · Raised dot identification

## 1 Introduction

Most of the current braille embossers incorporate a graphics mode capability. With variations in resolution, the dots can be embossed closer together than when embossing braille text. Some embossers permit a change in height of the dot as well. The implementation of good design techniques for the graphic is imperative when producing embossed graphics. Ladner et al. [1] describe in a systematic way the practices of tactile graphics specialists. The Guidelines and Standards for Tactile Graphics developed by the Braille Authority of North America [2] cover the design principles that must be followed in the production software of embossed graphics and recently have been used to automate the production process [3]. The software for the production of embossed graphics can be: (i) a common drawing software commercially available, such as

K. Miesenberger et al. (Eds.): ICCHP 2016, Part II, LNCS 9759, pp. 77–84, 2016.
DOI: 10.1007/978-3-319-41267-2_11

MS-Office®, CorelDraw®, Adobe Illustrator®, (ii) an open source, application, such as LibreOffice Draw, or (iii) a proprietary/specific graphics software, such as Tactile View®, Picture Braille®, TGD Pro®, and Quick Tac®. As the hardware of the embossers continues to become more sophisticated, further software applications are being developed to produce better raised-dot tactile graphics. There are some benefits of using embossed graphics both for the production process and for the usability by the end user. For example, embossed graphics: (a) can be produced simultaneously with the braille text in the same hard copy sheet and by the same equipment, (b) can be part of a regular braille document, (c) can mix braille text easily during the production), (d) can be produced very quickly and d. Have a much lower cost compared to other common techniques like the stereo-copying technique through the usage of swell paper or/and through the vacuum forming technique (thermoforming) through the usage of plastic sheets. On the other hand, embossed graphics often lack some of the characteristics of tactual readability, there is little variation in height, point symbols are difficult to discern, and the number of textures that can be produced is limited.

Heller [4], after a study with congenitally blind and late-blind individuals, who made tactual matches to tangible embossed shapes, found that touch seems rather poor at the identifying 2D patterns or pictures. He also found that touch has a higher accuracy of surface identification than the vision in finer texture identification. Dot height and dot density are two main variables that dominate the recognition and conceptualization of tactile embossed graphics by individuals with severe visual impairments [5]. Few studies have investigated tactile sensitivity to the elevation (third dimension) of tactile graphics, even though the elevation is a crucial parameter for touch. A study on detection thresholds showed that a single edge can be detected at an elevation of 0.85 μm relative to a flat background [6]. In a study on the amplitude of gratings, participants discriminated elevation differences as small as 2 μm [7]. In addition to elevation, the shape of an edge is important for detecting the tactile feature. Physiological studies show that sharp edges produce higher neural activity in the fingertip receptors than gradually sloping or curved edges [8]. The neural basis of haptic shape perception has been reviewed recently [9] along with a description of how shape information is processed as it ascends the somatosensory neuraxis of primates. Frascara et al. [10] suggested that the tactile height of the symbols should be higher than 0.5 mm at least for area symbols, 1.0 mm for line symbols, and 1.5 mm for point ones. Jehoel et al. [11] studied the tactile elevation perception in blind and sighted participants, and its implications for tactile map creation, using inkjet technology and the TIMP printer [12, 13] with symbols (circles, squares and triangles) printed on matt PVC at six elevations (7, 14, 22, 30, 38 and 47 μm) and five sizes. Shiah et al. [14] found that tactile sensitivity recognition decreased nonlinearly as elevation increased. Skedung et al. [15] found that the human finger tactile discrimination extends to the nanoscale (10 nm).

Braille dot height in national standards and recommendations (not for packaging) vary from 0.25 mm in Sweden up to 1.0 mm in France [16]. International standard Braille dot height for buildings (e.g. elevators) is from 0.6 to 0.9 mm (Tiresias, 2009). A research study [17] on pharmaceutical packaging, concluded in 2008 by the University of Birmingham and RNIB, in cooperation with other European institutions, where dot height in the range of 0.06 to 0.23 mm was studied, found the acceptable height of raised braille dots to be 0.18 mm (67 % of participants definitely recognize text, 27 % probably).

However, while research has shown that elevation influences detection and discrimination thresholds for tactile stimuli, and that the physiological response of fingertip receptors varies with texture, little is known about the influence of these parameters on the identification of embossed stimuli with variable dot height and density. Based on the above considerations, we conducted an experimental study with participants who are blind, to systematically address the identification of embossed tactile lines and squares in various dot elevations.

## 2 Method

Ten congenitally blind volunteers (4 male and 6 female) participated in this study ranged in age from 18 to 44 (mean = 28.1, SD = 9.36). None of the participants had any hearing impairment or other disability. All of them learned to read and write Braille from 4–11 years old (mean = 7.2, SD = 1.99) and still remain active users of the braille code.

Two types of stimuli were used in the experiment: raised-dot lines (7 cm length) and raised-dot squares (2 × 2 cm). All stimuli were produced by a Tiger Braille Embosser (VP200) on free dust paper of 160 g/m$^2$, in two densities (10 dpi and 20 dpi) and in eight elevations of dots, from 0.25 mm to 0.53 mm (each height is numbered from 1 to 8, starting from the lower elevation). The target set includes the same type of stimuli in multiples of 4 for each height (i.e. in total 32 stimuli) in a random order.

The procedure included the following steps: Participants were briefed on the objectives of the study and given verbal instructions at the beginning of the experiment. During the matching phase, participants seated in front of a table were given tactile stimuli of one type and one density. They were asked to touch and feel one test stimulus of a specific height, randomly selected among the 8 elevations, and then to identify, as fast and accurately as possible, the same 4 from the set of the 32 target stimuli placed on the table. The researcher recorded the matching stimuli and the time spent by the participants for the identification. The maximum number of answers was 4 and the maximum allowed identification time was 1 min. Thus, each identification trial ended after the participant announced that he has identified the 4 target stimuli (independently if the matching are correct or not) or after he/she has used up the maximum identification time). This procedure was repeated until all the 8 tactile stimuli of the same type were tested. The task was repeated two times for each type of test stimuli and for each dot density (in total 4 tasks).

## 3 Results

A total of 1.280 responses (10 participants × 32 stimuli for matching × 4 types of test stimuli) were recorded. The identification accuracy and response time of the matching task were examined for each type of test stimuli.

A set of descriptive and then inferential statistical analyses follow in order to ascertain the roles of the type of stimuli (dot lines versus dot squares) and DPI (10 versus 20) on the two dependent variables, (a) correct responding and (b) time need to complete the trials. The confusion matrix for the raised-dot line stimuli in both 10 dpi and 20 dpi are provided in Tables 1 and 2 respectively, showing percentages of correct (diagonal) and misclassified stimuli. The sum in each row is less than 100 % for the cases of no response after the limit of 1 min for each trial. In Tables 3 and 4 we present the confusion matrix for the raised-dot square stimuli in 10 dpi and 20 dpi respectively. We observed that only the stimuli with the lower height in 20 dpi reached an identification accuracy of 100 % in both raised-dot lines and raised-dot squares. Moreover, the identification accuracy decreases with increasing the dot height in all cases.

**Table 1.** Matrixes of matching percentages (%) between test stimuli and target stimuli for the case of raised-dot lines in 10 dpi

| Matched stimuli height (10 dpi) | | | | | | | | |
|---|---|---|---|---|---|---|---|---|
| Test stimulus height (10 dpi) | 1 | 2 | 3 | 4 | 5 | 6 | 7 | 8 |
| 1 | **75,0** | 22,5 | 2,5 | | | | | |
| 2 | 15,0 | **72,5** | 10,0 | | | | | |
| 3 | | 35,0 | **45,0** | 7,5 | | | | |
| 4 | | 12,5 | 17,5 | **20,0** | 5,0 | 15,0 | 10,0 | 5,0 |
| 5 | | 2,5 | 5,0 | 15,0 | **15,0** | 25,0 | 20,0 | 7,5 |
| 6 | | | | 35,0 | 22,5 | **7,5** | 15,0 | 12,5 |
| 7 | | | | 22,5 | 25,0 | 27,5 | **15,0** | 5,0 |
| 8 | | | | 25,0 | 12,5 | 32,5 | 15,0 | **10,0** |

**Table 2.** Matrixes of matching percentages (%) between test stimuli and target stimuli for the case of raised-dot lines in 20 dpi

| Matched stimuli height (20 dpi) | | | | | | | | |
|---|---|---|---|---|---|---|---|---|
| Test stimulus height (20 dpi) | 1 | 2 | 3 | 4 | 5 | 6 | 7 | 8 |
| 1 | **92,5** | 2,5 | | | | | | |
| 2 | 20,0 | **57,5** | 12,5 | 2,5 | | 2,5 | 2,5 | 2,5 |
| 3 | | 12,5 | **40,0** | 20,0 | 7,5 | 2,5 | | |
| 4 | | 2,5 | 35,0 | **27,5** | 15,0 | 7,5 | 10,0 | 2,5 |
| 5 | | | 10,0 | 20,0 | **12,5** | 27,5 | 20,0 | 7,5 |
| 6 | | | 10,0 | 15,0 | 22,5 | **27,5** | 10,0 | 10,0 |
| 7 | | | 2,5 | 10,0 | 27,5 | 25,0 | **15,0** | 15,0 |
| 8 | | | 2,5 | 5,0 | 20,0 | 7,5 | 27,5 | **30,0** |

**Table 3.** Matrixes of matching percentages (%) between test stimuli and target stimuli for the case of raised-dot squares in 10 dpi

| Matched stimuli height (10 dpi) | | | | | | | |
|---|---|---|---|---|---|---|---|
| Test stimulus height (10 dpi) | 1 | 2 | 3 | 4 | 5 | 6 | 7 | 8 |
| 1 | **97,5** | | | | | | | |
| 2 | 2,5 | **82,5** | 5,0 | | | | | |
| 3 | | 42,5 | **40,0** | 2,5 | | | | |
| 4 | | 5,0 | 42,5 | **20,0** | 15,0 | 7,5 | 5,0 | 5,0 |
| 5 | | | 7,5 | 30,0 | **30,0** | 15,0 | 5,0 | 10,0 |
| 6 | | | 12,5 | 30,0 | 15,0 | **12,5** | 15,0 | 12,5 |
| 7 | | | 5,0 | 17,5 | 12,5 | 25,0 | **22,5** | 17,5 |
| 8 | | | | 5,0 | 27,5 | 17,5 | 17,5 | **32,5** |

**Table 4.** Matrixes of matching percentages (%) between test stimuli and target stimuli for the case of raised-dot squares in 20 dpi

| Matched stimuli height (20 dpi) | | | | | | | |
|---|---|---|---|---|---|---|---|
| Test stimulus height (20 dpi) | 1 | 2 | 3 | 4 | 5 | 6 | 7 | 8 |
| 1 | **97,5** | | | | | | | |
| 2 | 25,0 | **52,5** | 7,5 | | | | 5,0 | |
| 3 | | 30,0 | **27,5** | 15,0 | 5,0 | 2,5 | 5,0 | |
| 4 | | 5,0 | 27,5 | **22,5** | 17,5 | 12,5 | 2,5 | 5,0 |
| 5 | | | 12,5 | 22,5 | **25,0** | 12,5 | 10,0 | 15,0 |
| 6 | | | 17,5 | 20,0 | 25,0 | **15,0** | 7,5 | 15,0 |
| 7 | | | 7,5 | 15,0 | 17,5 | 17,5 | **20,0** | 20,0 |
| 8 | | | 2,5 | 7,5 | 12,5 | 12,5 | 17,5 | **47,5** |

Table 5 gives the overall mean response time (MRT) of the identification task, for each height and type of test stimulus, along with its standard deviation (SD) and range (R).

The inferential statistics involved the use of multilevel modeling in which trials were nested within persons [18]. Specifically, the following multilevel model was fitted to the data for each of the dependent variables:

$$Y_{ij(CorrectResponse/Time)} = b_0 + b_1(DOTs) + b_2(DPI) + r_{ij} \tag{1}$$

$$B_0 = u_{0j} \tag{2}$$

with $Y_{ij}$ being responses in the dependent variable (correct response or time) of the person in condition i across all other individuals j. Initially, it was established that ample levels of variance were between individuals to warrant the need for multilevel modeling using the IntraClass Correlation coefficient (ICC) which is estimated as

**Table 5.** The overall mean response time (MRT) of the identification task for each type of test stimulus along with its standard deviation (SD) and range (R)

| Test height | Raised lines 10dpi | | | Raised lines 20dpi | | | Raised squares 10 dpi | | | Raised squares 20 dpi | | |
|---|---|---|---|---|---|---|---|---|---|---|---|---|
| | MRT sec | SD sec | Range sec | MRT sec | SD sec | Range sec | MRT sec | SD sec | Range sec | MRT sec | SD sec | Range sec |
| 1 | 41,0 | 11,0 | 26–57 | 29,0 | 9,9 | 24–52 | 39,0 | 11,2 | 28–59 | 34,3 | 10,3 | 28–53 |
| 2 | 37,0 | 9,5 | 28–55 | 47,5 | 7,6 | 34–60 | 26,6 | 7,9 | 20–47 | 28,5 | 8,7 | 34–59 |
| 3 | 38,8 | 6,6 | 35–58 | 39,5 | 9,3 | 28–60 | 21,9 | 11,3 | 27–54 | 24,8 | 7,1 | 28–50 |
| 4 | 30,9 | 4,7 | 35–50 | 42,7 | 11,4 | 28–60 | 46,6 | 7,7 | 37–58 | 27,4 | 6,3 | 39–58 |
| 5 | 37,3 | 10,8 | 33–59 | 48,8 | 5,5 | 25–58 | 42,5 | 7,7 | 36–60 | 37,4 | 11,4 | 23–59 |
| 6 | 49,8 | 10,0 | 33–60 | 40,9 | 9,3 | 45–60 | 39,2 | 8,3 | 28–55 | 44,5 | 6,6 | 34–57 |
| 7 | 32,3 | 7,2 | 24–50 | 35,3 | 6,1 | 30–50 | 42,1 | 10,1 | 28–58 | 34,0 | 7,3 | 32–55 |
| 8 | 40,7 | 10,9 | 25–59 | 34,2 | 9,4 | 23–55 | 34,7 | 10,9 | 18–53 | 42,0 | 10,9 | 23–57 |

$Var_{Between}/Var_{Between} + Var_{Within}$. The percentages for correct responding and time were 1.7 % and 4.8 %, suggesting the need to model that information further. After fitting the above model to the data, results indicated significant effects for the role of the DOTs (raised dot lines versus raised dot squares) with the latter (raised dot squares) being associated with significantly elevated correct responding (b = 0.206, p = 0.037) and the use of significantly less time (b = −3.206, p = 0.006). The dpi was associated with null effects. Provided that the above coefficients are unstandardized, they are interpreted as the respective change in the dependent variable for a one unit of change in the independent variable (DOTs was coded: 0 = lines, 1 = squares; DPI was coded: 0 = 10 dpi, 1 = 20 dpi). Thus, for example in raised-dot squares (condition coded as 1) the amount of time emitted was −3.206 s, compared to the raised-dot line condition (coded as zero).

The results indicate that the participants identify better the lower three dot elevations for both lines and squares on 20 or 10 dpi, with an exception for 20 dpi squares where the highest dot elevation (level 8) is third in the order of recognition. Participants achieved significantly lower recognition results in all cases for the dot elevation 6, except in the case of lines in 20 dpi.

## 4   Conclusions

We conducted an experimental study to address the identification of embossed tactile lines and squares at eight dot elevations by blind participants. The results indicate low percentages for correct responding and time, suggesting the need to model that information further. Our planned activities include the extension of the current study by including more participants who are blind in order to extract practical implications, such as issues in education, as well as to help the designers to choose suitable design parameters for the tactile rendition of graphics or maps produced using embossed raised dots.

**Acknowledgement.** This research has been undertaken under the project ATMAPS: "Specification of symbols used on audio-tactile maps for individuals with blindness" (Project No. 543316-LLP-1-2013-1-GR-KA3-KA3MP) [www.atmaps.eu] funded with support from the European Commission under the Lifelong Learning Programme. This publication reflects the views only of the authors, and the Commission cannot be held responsible for any use, which may be made of the information contained therein.

# References

1. Ladner, R., Ivory, M., Rao, R., Burgstahler, S., Comden, D., Hahn, S., Renzelmann, M., Krisnandi, S., Ramasamy, M., Slabosky, B., Martin, A., Lacenski, A., Olsen, S., Groce, D.: Automating tactile graphics translation. In: 7th International ACM SIGACCESS Conference on Computers and Accessibility, pp. 150–157. ACM Press, New York (2005)
2. BANA/CBA: Guidelines and Standards for Tactile Graphics. The Braille Authority of North America. http://www.brailleauthority.org
3. Pather, A.B.: The innovative use of vector-based tactile graphics design software to auto-mate the production of raised-line tactile graphics in accordance with BANA's newly adopted guidelines and standards for tactile graphics, 2010. J. Blind. Innov. Res. 4 (2014). doi:http://dx.doi.org/10.5241/4-49
4. Heller, M.A.: Picture and pattern perception in the sighted and the blind: the advantage of the late blind. Perception 18, 379–389 (1989)
5. Krufka, S.E., Barner, K.E.: A user study on tactile graphic generation methods. Behav. Inf. Technol. 25, 297–311 (2006). doi:10.1080/01449290600636694
6. Johansson, R.S., Lamotte, R.H.: Tactile detection thresholds for a single asperity on an otherwise smooth surface. Somatosens. Mot. Res. 1, 21–31 (1983)
7. Nefs, H.T., Kappers, A.M.L., Koenderink, J.J.: Amplitude and spatial-period discrimination in sinusoidal gratings by dynamic touch. Perception 30, 1263–1274 (2001)
8. LaMotte, R.H., Srinivasan, M.A.: Tactile discrimination of shape: responses of slowly adapting mechanoreceptive afferents to a step stroked across the monkey fingerpad. J. Neurosci. 7, 1655–1671 (1987)
9. Yau, J.M., Kim, S.S., Thakur, P.S., Bensmaia, S.J.: Feeling form: the neural basis of haptic shape perception. J. Neurophysiol. (2015). doi:10.1152/jn.00598.2015
10. Frascara, J., Sadler-Takach, B.: The design of tactile map symbols for visually impaired people. Inf. Des. J. 7, 67–75 (1993)
11. Jehoel, S., Sowden, P.T., Ungar, S., Sterr, A.: Tactile elevation perception in blind and sighted participants and its implications for tactile map creation. Hum. Factors 51, 208–223 (2009)
12. McCallum, D., Ungar, S.: An introduction to the use of inkjet for tactile diagram production. Br. J. Vis. Impairment 21, 73–77 (2003)
13. McCallum, D., Ungar, S.: Producing tactile maps using new inkjet technology: an introduction. Cartogr. J. 40, 294–298 (2003)
14. Shiah, Y.J., Chang, F., Tam, W.C.: Recognition of tactile relief by children and adults. Percept. Mot. Skills 113, 727–738 (2001)
15. Skedung, L., Arvidsson, M., Chung, J.Y., Stafford, C., Berglund, B., Rutland, M.: Feeling small: exploring the tactile perception limits. Sci. Rep. 3, 2617 (2013). doi:10.1038/srep02617
16. Tiresias: Scientific & technological Reports: Braille Cell Dimensions. http://www.tiresias.org/research/reports/braille_cell.htm

17. Douglas, G., Weston, A., Whittaker, J., Wilkins, S., Robinson, D.: Braille dot height research: investigation of Braille dot elevation on pharmaceutical products. Final Report, University of Birmingham and RNIB (2008)
18. Raudenbush, S.W., Bryk, A.S.: Hierarchical Linear Models:Applications and Data Analysis Methods. Sage Publications Inc., Thousand Oaks (2002)

# Early Stimulation with Tactile Devices of Visually Impaired Children

María Visitación Hurtado Torres, María Luisa Rodríguez Almendros,
María José Rodríguez Fórtiz, Carlos Rodríguez Domínguez,
and María Bermúdez-Edo[✉]

University of Granada, Granada, Spain
{mhurtado,mlra,mjfortiz,carlosrodriguez,mbe}@ugr.es

**Abstract.** Vision plays an essential role in development, and in recent years our understanding of the close relationship between vision and other areas of development has increased considerably. Touch-system for Visually Impaired Children (TouchVIC) is a Mobile application designed to be used as a support tool in the early stimulation of visually impaired children. It includes nine kinds of different activities for iPad, which are intended to stimulate cognitive, emotional, sensorial and motor aspects; as well as an authoring tool which allows the customization and configuration of exercises in order to adapt them to the child's interests, needs and abilities at all times. It also has options which allow the creation of customized agendas, where activities and evaluation sessions can be sequenced and planned. Another outstanding feature of TouchVic is that it is one of the first Apps of its kind in that it is really inclusive and accessible for professionals or family members who are visually impaired.

**Keywords:** Blind children · Sight impairment · Tablet devices

## 1 Introduction

Any kind of disability in a child constitutes a risk factor that may cause disturbances and disorders in development. During the first years, the functioning can be modified because of neural plasticity and positive reinforcement in environmental actions [10]. Specifically, visually impaired children have limitations in interpreting information and integrating the stimulus received from the exterior in tactile and auditory forms, because they are separated and incomplete [3]. Besides, vision is involved in many adaptive functions that are altered when there is a sight impairment, such as organization of the sleep-wake rhythm, the acquisition of motor skills (gross motor, balance and fine motor skills), cognitive development (attention, memory), spatial awareness, language learning and relationships with other people [4].

Early intervention for visually impaired children consists of a set of psycho-pedagogical, medical and social interventions to improve the children's development in the absence of other disabilities that are specifically related to their visual deficit. It must be done as soon as possible, by an interdisciplinary team coordinated with the family [4].

K. Miesenberger et al. (Eds.): ICCHP 2016, Part II, LNCS 9759, pp. 85–91, 2016.
DOI: 10.1007/978-3-319-41267-2_12

The main aspects in which this intervention works are: auditory and tactile stimulation, motivation, organization and recognition of the child's own body, object recognition (shapes, sounds and locations), object permanence, object finding and spatial orientation [2].

## 2  State of the Art

Technology can be used to make interventions [5], in fact, it can overcome the barriers experienced by disabled people that prevent their full and equal participation in all contexts of life: cultural, social, political, economic and environmental [7]. There are a lot of useful ICT resources that are specifically designed to help people with sight impairment: large screen monitors, screen readers and magnifiers, braille lines and keyboards, etc. However, they are difficult for use by very young children. Only the touchscreen systems can be made accessible to them, improving them with the addition of screen scanning and auditory information (screen reader, synthesis of voice system or a playback of recorded voice) [1]. Besides, applications created for these users require a good design with a well-organized layout, with good contrast and clear, and large size lettering.

We have analyzed 80 applications for tablet devices (Android, iOs and Windows) that could be used by children with visual impairment [11]. The majority of them cannot be used by severely impaired visual people or are intended for adult users because they require good spatial, auditory and motor skills, and previous learning (i.e. the ability to read). Some of them for children have a specific educational focus but this is not integral. Some of them are: Blind Memory, Songify, I love Fireworks, Pekkaboo Barn, Tap-N-See Zoo and My Talking Picture Board. None of them are customizable for children or accessible for visual impaired families or therapists.

Therefore, we suggest the design of an authoring tool, named Touch-VIC, to create activities that enhance the early stimulation therapy given by professionals and family members.

## 3  Methodology

Our team work is interdisciplinary, composed of computer engineers, accessibility experts and specialists in the early education of visually impaired children. Two specialists in this team are blind. The main goal in this project was to design a tool as a complement to the intervention work done by therapists and families. We have followed a user centered methodology to develop the Touch-system for Visually Impaired Children (TouchVIC). It has been conceived and designed following the recommendations of the specialists [6]. They have also tested the different prototypes created during the development. The next subsections describe the main steps of the methodology and their achievements.

# 4  Requirements Specification

The general objective of the project was to develop an application for visually impaired children, on a tactile device, with specific kinds of activities to be customized. The specific requirements were:

- Increase the children's motivation by designing games to interact with images (for children with vision) and sounds to stimulate and reinforce.
- Perform auditory stimulation and ask for the recognition of sounds, songs, voices, silence, etc.
- Help to differentiate the volume or the frequency of a sound.
- Provide parts of a sound (for example a song) to be ordered, or used to compose a new sound.
- Teach concepts related to physical organization and orientation, as spatial relationships.
- Work on object permanence and the location of auditory stimuli.
- Improve auditory and visual memory.
- Provide situations to use the fingers to select or search in the screen positions.
- Work on the reasoning involved in asking for the classification of objects or the association of concepts.
- Support the creation of simple stories with scenarios and characters.
- Teach the basics of Braille.
- Give auditory explanations before and during the performance of an activity.
- Provide auditory reinforcements about hits and fails.
- Improve other cognitive and motor skills such as: coordination of ear-hand, cause-effect, use of language, attention, memory, etc.
- Facilitate the creation and adaptation of activities by the therapists and families, taking into account that they could also be visually impaired.
- Allow the evaluation of each child's progress, taking and showing measures during the performance of activities.

## 4.1  Design

TouchVIC consists of two parts: The App for early stimulation (Child mode), and the authoring tool (Tutor mode).

Nine kinds of activities have been designed taking into account the previous requirements: memory-association, searching, recognition, story-telling, discovering sounds, playing with space, music, classifying, pre-braille. The implemented tool provides a manual that describes them in depth.

The tutoring tool allows the creation/modification of activities that are adapted to each child's needs and interests. Another outstanding feature of TouchVIC is that it is one of the first Apps of its kind in that it is really inclusive and accessible for professionals or family members who are visually impaired.

The App provides templates linked to each kind of activity. The educator can select which resources to use, the appearance of the activities and the difficulty level. In this way the creation and customization of activities is easier.

For each activity the tutor associates concepts (objects, characters or scenarios with sounds and occasionally images) and designs the presentation on the screen (places associated to concepts, order to be presented, etc.). An activity is associated with one child but could be used by others as is or with adaptations. There is a database of concepts that can be used in different activities and by many children. For instance, in the Memory-association activities the screen is divided into paired boxes: 2, 4 or 6. They are selected by pairs, and for each one, a picture, sound or text resource from the concepts list is associated. For users who have still some sight, the content of the boxes can be hidden (Figs. 1 and 2). It trains intentionality, hearing coordination, spatial orientation, language, and listening memory.

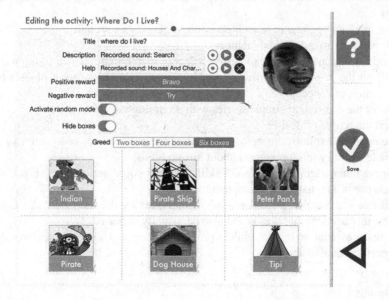

**Fig. 1.** Memory-association design template

The tool for the child offers a list of activities created for him/her that can be selected to be played. The children can explore, touch and play, and receive reinforcements about their performance. While the child is completing the activities, the App makes automatic records of the child's achievements and mistakes, gaming time, and other particular aspects of each activity. Those records are made for individual activities and sessions; and after they are completed, the tutor can add comments and consult the assessments of a particular child.

Each child can also have associated one or more agendas. An agenda is a set of ordered activities to be performed automatically in that order on a specific day of the week, facilitating its use.

**Fig. 2.** Memory-association game in use

## 4.2   Implementation and Testing

The tactile device chosen to implement the application was an iPad because iOs offers more configuration possibilities over accessibility characteristics than other operating systems [8, 9]. TouchVIC can be downloaded for free from the Apple Store. We have created one or two activities of each kind and a lot of content to facilitate its initial use.

The tutoring tool can be used with VoiceOver, but the children's tool plays the stored sounds (recorded or previously synthetized) associated with each activity because they are customized and so more stimulating for the child.

During the implementation, evolutionary prototyping was used. The specialists tested the prototypes to discover faults and validate the requirements. Sometimes the requirements and design were modified in order to get the best activities. One 5 year old blind child participates in testing the activities and her behavior and responses were taken into account (Fig. 3).

The more difficult part to be implemented was the one related to providing accessibility for visually impaired tutors. The specialists in accessibility gave the specifications and helped in the implementation and design details because they were familiar with the iOs accessibility characteristics. Many tests and improvements were performed to get a fully accessible tool.

## 4.3   Scientific and Practical Impact or Contributions to the Field

TouchVIC is the result of a project that was selected to be funded because of its social and educational contributions that are:

**Fig. 3.** Use of Touch-VIC

- Design of a specific app for visually impaired children for their early stimulation.
- Design of an integrated set of kind of activities that improve several auditory and cognitive skills.
- Creation of a tool for tutors, to design customizable activities.
- Provision of accessibility for the tutors.
- Creation of an interdisciplinary team to participate in all the tasks of the life cycle, considering the final users.

Apple knew about this project and asked us to present it in a work journey into ADE Institute 2015 EMEIA (Europe, the Middle East, India and Africa) from Apple Distinguished Educators and Developers who got accepted into the program. It was very well received (particularly the accessibility tool for tutors), and received some suggestions for improvements. We translated the tool into English to present it in this forum and to facilitate its use by more people.

Several organizations and associations are interested in the project and have downloaded the application. Although is a very specific app domain, TouchVIC has been downloaded 282 times in 5 months.

## 5   Conclusions and Future Planned Activities

We have developed an application that can be used to complement the activities carried out in the early stimulation programs for children with visual impairment. TouchVIC integrates activities which are intended to stimulate cognitive, emotional, sensorial and motor aspects; as well as an authoring tool which allows the customization and configuration of exercises in order to adapt them to the child's interests, needs and abilities at all times. It also has options which allow the creation of customized agendas, where activities and evaluation sessions can be sequenced and planned.

Now we are preparing to begin a pilot study that validates our tool and provides suggestions for improvements. Usability tests will also be performed to evaluate the satisfaction of the tutors and the accessibility of the tool.

**Acknowledgements.** The authors would like to thank the Campus of International Excellence Biotic of the University of Granada, the Regional Excellence Project TIC-6600, the collaboration of the ACCEDO group (ONCE) and the accessibility experts of the Macneticos Group, and the users that provided the TouchVIC results detailed in this paper.

# References

1. Berry, B.E., Ignash, S.: Assistive technology: providing independence for individuals with disabilities. Rehabil. Nurs. **28**(1), 6–14 (2003). Wiley Online Library
2. Davidson, P., Harrison, G.: The effectiveness of early intervention for children with visual impairments. In: Guralnick M.J. (ed.) The Effectiveness of Early Intervention, pp. 483–495. Paul H. Brookes Publishing Co., Baltimore (2000)
3. Emerson, R.W., Ashmead, D.: Visual experience and the concept of compensatory spatial hearing abilities. In: Rieser, J.J., Ashmead, D.H., Ebner, F.F., Corn, A.L. (eds.) Blindness and Brain Plasticity in Navigation and Object Perception, pp. 367–380 (2008)
4. Fazzi, E., Signorini, S.G., Bova, S.M., Ondei, P., Bianchi, P.E.: Early intervention in visually impaired children. In: International Congress Series, vol. 1282, pp. 117–121. Elsevier (2005)
5. Fernández-López, A., Rodríguez-Fórtiz, M.J., Rodríguez-Almendros, M.L.: Mobile learning technology based on iOS devices to support students with special education needs. Comput. Educ. **6**, 77–90 (2013)
6. Henry, S.L.: Just Ask: Integrating Accessibility Throughout Design. ET/Lawton, Madison (2007)
7. Hersh, M.: Perception, the eye and assistive technology issues. In: Hersh, M.A., Johnson, M.A. (eds.) Assistive Technology for Visually Impaired and Blind People, pp. 51–101. Springer, London (2008)
8. iOS-Accessiblity Programming Guide For iOS. http://developer.apple.com
9. iOS-Verifying App Accessibility on iOS. http://developer.apple.com
10. Reiser, J.J.: Blindness and Brain Plasticity in Navigation and Object Perception. Taylor & Francis, New York (2008)
11. Torres-Carazo, I., Rodriguez-Fortiz, M.J., Hurtado-Torres, M.V.: Analysis and review of apps and serious games on mobile devices intended for people with visual impairment. In: IEEE 4th International Conference on Serious Games and Applications for Health (2016)

# Experimenting with Tactile Sense
# and Kinesthetic Sense Assisting System
# for Blind Education

Junji Onishi[1]([✉]), Tadahiro Sakai[2], Msatsugu Sakajiri[1], Akihiro Ogata[1],
Takahiro Miura[3], Takuya Handa[4], Nobuyuki Hiruma[4], Toshihiro Shimizu[4],
and Tsukasa Ono[1]

[1] Tsukuba University of Technology, Ibaraki, Japan
`ohnishi@g.tsukuba-tech.ac.jp`, `sakajiri@cs.k.tsukuba-tech.ac.jp`
[2] NHK Engineering System, Tokyo, Japan
`sakai.tadahiro@nes.or.jp`
[3] The University of Tokyo, Tokyo, Japan
[4] NHK Science and Technology Research Laboratories, Tokyo 157-8510, Japan

**Abstract.** In most of cases, communications based on multimedia form
is inaccessible to the visually impaired. Thus, persons lacking eyesight
are eager for a method that can provide them with access to progress in
technology. We consider that the main important key for inclusive education is to real-timely provide materials which a teacher shows in a lesson.
In this study, we present tactile sense and kinesthetic sense assisting system in order to provide figure or graphical information without an any
assistant. This system gives us more effective teaching under inclusive
education system.

**Keywords:** Special education · Visual impaired · Assistive technology · Tactile · Graphical presentation · Information sharing · Inclusive
education

## 1 Introduction

In the absence of the sense of sight, blind individuals mainly rely on their sense
of touch and hearing to access information which is available to sighted people in
visual form. Unfortunately, much of this information may not be amenable to the
sense of touch either because it is presented in two-dimensional form or because
the entities are on a large scale or physically inaccessible precluding tactual
exploration. Though a sighted observer may provide verbal descriptions of these
details but these are usually not sufficient for blind individuals to construct
complete and accurate mental representations of physical entities [1,5].

Various assistive solutions have been developed to address these problems.
Some of them decipher images, real objects and/or scenes and convey audio
descriptions of these either in the form of speech [2–5], via sonication [5,6] or the

---

The original version of this chapter was revised: A new reference is inserted. The
erratum to this chapter is available at 10.1007/978-3-319-41267-2_86

K. Miesenberger et al. (Eds.): ICCHP 2016, Part II, LNCS 9759, pp. 92–99, 2016.
DOI: 10.1007/978-3-319-41267-2_13

descriptions in tactile form either as Braille or by producing tactile images and models. However, this kind of output may be quite slow, tedious and incomplete. Also, the hardware for producing tactile images and models was not easily accessible to the target users [5,7].

On the other hand, according to the Convention on the Rights of Persons with Disabilities, we have to recognize the right of persons with disabilities to education. Then, the equal opportunity is required in the school without discrimination. In realizing this right, we ensure the following terms

- Persons with disabilities are not excluded from the general education system on the basis of disability, and that children with disabilities are not excluded from free and compulsory primary education, or from secondary education, on the basis of disability;
- Persons with disabilities can access an inclusive, quality and free primary education and secondary education on an equal basis with others in the communities in which they live;
- Reasonable accommodation of the individual requirements is provided;
- Persons with disabilities receive the support required, within the general education system, to facilitate their effective education;
- Effective individualized support measures are provided in environments that maximize academic and social development, consistent with the goal of full inclusion.

In order to guarantee equal opportunities to all students, the accessibility of ICT educational tools is worldwide considered a major issue.

Thus, we have developed tactile sense and kinesthetic sense assisting system to present two dimensional figures without any human assistants This can help to provide graphical information to the blind in an inclusive classroom. In addition, any teaching assistants will not be required. This paper presents the evaluation of this system.

## 2    System Overview

### 2.1    System Configuration

The prototype system developed for this paper investigates the method and operation necessary to guide the visually impaired in educational and public facilities. We focused in particular on cost reduction for practical use. Figure 1(a) shows the outer appearance of the system developed for this paper. The system is constructed from products already on the market. This system is constructed of three sections: a haptic device (PHANTOM Omni (manufactured by Sensable), a tactile display device (manufactured by KGS Corp.), and an operation controller. The operation controller controls the content selection and guidance functionalities, and performs calibration to correct the spatial positioning between the tactile display and the haptic guidance display. This system comprises a tactile display that uses raised bumps (texture) and vibration to display the details of the figure, and a haptic guidance display that guides the finger in correspondence to the details in the figure. The information required for each display is defined by a markup language, using XML tags for the tactile/haptic guidance display. The tactile display and haptic guidance operate while sharing the attribute data described in the tags. In other words, by describing the position coordinates and the size of the content to be presented in the tactile display and by determining vibration type, we are able to generate a layout composed of texture and vibration. For haptic guidance, the path and configuration intended by the author is specified through guidance parameters such as guidability, speed/acceleration, height, and order of guidance, in addition to the position information of the object.

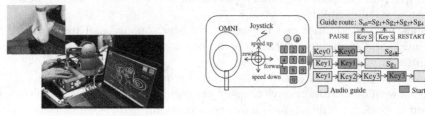

(a) Outline of our system

(b) Operational controller and

outline of the split guidance selection process.

**Fig. 1.** Prop-Tactile presentation system developed by NHK Science & Technology Research Laboratories.

The authoring system contains the following functionalities: a specification of the layout and vibration patterns in the tactile display, the path and configuration for haptic guidance, a rendering function whereby the operation sequence is set through a GUI, and the auto-generation of the XML file for tactile/haptic guidance displays.

## 2.2    Guidance Configuration

Haptic guidance simulates a motion as if someone were teaching the content by guiding the user's finger. Guidance parameters are set for each individual object, but it is possible to express various guidance configurations by combining multiple objects and setting appropriate guidance parameters, such as height and speed for each.

## 2.3    Operation Controller

For the developed system, we considered a user interface (UI) capable of user-directed operations during haptic guidance. The numeric keys 0 to 9 are used during the split guidance selection process. As shown in Fig. 1(b), when the key is pressed once, the voice navigation conveys the contents of the guidance, and the guidance starts when the key is pressed repeatedly. If the user presses another numeric key during guidance, the guidance stops, and the operation returns to the process described above. The key "S" can also be used to stop and restart in the middle of guidance. The joystick can be moved to the left or right during guidance to control the fast forward and reverse functions, while the up/down direction controls changes in speed. This operation allows the user to select the desired guidance sequence and identify the content while reconfirming the path.

On the other hand, this system requires calibration to match the three-dimensional coordinates of the tactile display and haptic guidance system. Therefore, there is an adjustment function that uses the controller joystick to·match the center coordinates of the haptic guidance with the finger positioned at the center of the tactile display. To allow the visually impaired to operate the calibration themselves, the voice guide speaks the procedure and the coordinates near the center needed for adjustment.

## 3   Experimental Evaluation

### 3.1   Experiment Details

**Experimental Outline.** In this experiment, we aimed to show the degree of the system's effectiveness compared with the conventional method of voice guidance and tactile/textural display. The experiment used figures from educational material as targets. The evaluation criteria were based on the system's ability to image the figures and identify object positioning. The effects were confirmed by comparing tables and introspective reports. Figure 2(a) shows the contents used in the evaluation process. The evaluation was based on whether imaging and position recognition were achieved through each of the following methods: voice guidance, textural/vibrating display, and haptic guidance display. Each of these methods was compared to voice guidance with respect to ease of use.

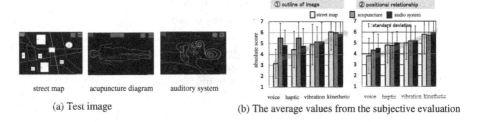

(a) Test image

(b) The average values from the subjective evaluation

**Fig. 2.** Test figure and evaluation result. (Color figure online)

The voice guidance conveyed the details of the figure and object position through speech synthesis. In the tactile display, in addition to a simple textural display, different vibration patterns depicted a portion of the facilities on the street map, the position of meridian points in the acupuncture diagram, and a

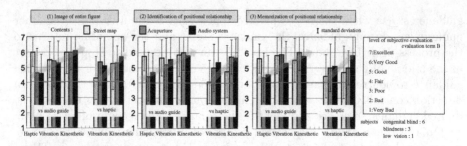

**Fig. 3.** The average values from the subjective evaluation with respect to evaluation detail B. (Color figure online)

part of the auditory system. The haptic guidance system used a tactile (textural and vibrating) display and conducted guidance based on a simulation of teaching by teachers and assistants. During textural/vibrating display and haptic guidance, the audio output spoke only the name of the object when touched. In addition, a link structure allowed the magnification of the acupuncture diagram and auditory system.

**Experimental Design and Evaluation Method.** Table 1 shows the factor and standards used in the experiment, as well as the classification of the subjects. Table 2 shows the evaluation items and details. All visually impaired subjects had experience using tactile graphics. The subjects answered a seven-point subjective evaluation for each display method.

**Table 1.** Experimental factor and standards

| Factor | Standards |
|---|---|
| Display method | 1. Voice guidance |
| | 2. Textural display |
| | 3. Vibrating display |
| | 4. Haptic guidance display |

Subjects: 6 with early blindness, 3 with late blindness, 1 with severe amblyopia
(Students in their 20 s: 7 acupuncture majors, 3 communications majors)

**Experimental Procedure.** This experiment used the procedure below to conduct a subjective evaluation of the four display methods (1–4) listed under the "Factor" column in Table 1. The following content was used during the evaluative process: a street map, a figure of the acupuncture meridian points, and a figure of the auditory system.

1. Listen to the voice guidance twice. Then answer a subjective evaluation of the items cited in evaluation detail A.

**Table 2.** Evaluation items and details

| Evaluation items | (1) Image of the entire figure. |
| --- | --- |
| | (2) Identification of the positional relationship of the objects within the figure (map: facilities, acupuncture: meridian points, auditory system: organs) |
| | (3) Memorization of the object names and positions (only for evaluation detail B) |
| Evaluation details | A. Whether evaluation items (1) and (2) were accomplished by the end of each display method |
| | B. Whether evaluation items (1), (2), and (3) were easier to achieve using a vibrating display/haptic guidance in comparison with a voice guidance/textural display |
| | C. Effectiveness of the display method and system evaluation |

2. Freely explore for 2 min using the textural area of the tactile display. Then answer a subjective evaluation of the items cited in evaluation details A and B.
3. Freely explore for 1 min using the vibration display. Then answer a subjective evaluation as above.
4. Answer a subjective evaluation as above, after using the haptic guidance option.
5. Attempt split haptic guidance and access to the link.
6. Evaluate the system as a whole, and provide an introspective report.

The subjects practiced haptic guidance prior to the experiment. The flow of the experiment and the standards for subjective evaluation were explained to the subjects. They were also given the following instructions:

- With regard to the subjective evaluation, answer the evaluation detail A ("whether the items were accomplished") based on their own judgment at the end of each display method, and answer the evaluation detail B ("whether the items were easier to achieve") based on comparisons: textural display with voice guidance, vibrating display and haptic guidance with both voice guidance and textural display.
- For each display method, focus on the imaging of the figure and the identification of the objects' positions.
- Try to remember the positions and the names of the identified objects.

For evaluation detail A, similar to the procedure, the learning effect was included in the evaluation of the display methods. For evaluation detail B, we tried to evaluate the comparisons between the individual display methods.

## 3.2   Experiment Results and Observations

Figure 2(b) shows the average values from the subjective evaluation with respect to evaluation detail A, for each of the display methods 1–4. Figure 3 shows the average values from the subjective evaluation with respect to evaluation detail B. For each of the evaluation items (1)–(3), the left side of the figure evaluates the textural, vibrating, and haptic guidance displays in contrast to the voice guidance, while the right side evaluates the vibrating and haptic guidance displays in contrast to the textural display.

Figures 2(b) and 3 list the subjective evaluation values by content. In Fig. 2(b), the results for figure imaging rose steadily, similar to the results for the identification of object position, excluding the high evaluation values reported for voice guidance over acupuncture meridian points and the auditory system. The high values seen for this voice guidance are thought to be due to the students' advance knowledge of acupuncture and the hearing system. It is interesting to note that haptic guidance saw an increase of 1–2 ranks in comparison with voice guidance, despite the use of varying content.

Figure 2(b) shows the comparison between the textural display and voice guidance with the vibrating display and haptic guidance. High values were reported for the textural display in the street map for all three evaluation items: (1)–(3). The reason for this is thought to be that the subjects had no advance knowledge of the map, and textural display was easier to understand than voice guidance, which made imaging and position recognition difficult. The vibrating display and haptic guidance were also effective for the map, and saw an increase in evaluation value of about 1.5–2 ranks.

According to the subjective evaluation of the display methods and the entire system after the user was allowed to freely operate split haptic guidance and magnification from the link structure, High evaluation scores were received for both items. In the subjects introspective reports, the following responses were received: "The vibrating displays were effective for complex figures," "It is difficult to understand the tactile graphic by myself, but I could achieve the imaging with guidance, the guidance and vibrations make me feel as if interacting with humans, and During guidance, the machine told me the correct path. I was able to grasp the factors 100 %. The following conclusions can be drawn from the results of evaluation details A, B, and C, and the introspective report:

– The tactile/haptic guidance display methods have a significant effect on voice guidance.
– Haptic guidance also has a significant effect on textural display.
– These methods are highly effective compared with conventional classes, and high evaluation with regard to desired use.

## 4   Conclusion

In this paper, we tested the effectiveness of a prototype graphic display system that uses tactile/haptic guidance, and is intended for use in educational and public facilities.

Using figures found in educational material as targets, we determined the effectiveness of the tactile/haptic guidance display methods in the imaging of figures and identification of object position. We tested the methods through subjective evaluation. The results showed significant effectiveness in comparison with the conventional method of using only voice guidance. Furthermore, haptic guidance showed significant effectiveness in comparison with using only textural display. From the trial, high marks were received for future use in classrooms and desired use. Thus, we confirm the potential of this system to aid the teaching and learning of two-dimensional materials. In the future, we look to carry out further testing in real-world educational settings, and continue development in support of education. We aim for a system construction that helps achieve an inclusive educational environment, allowing for low-cost information dissemination such as real-time information presentation through remote wireless operation. We sincerely hope that this study will contribute to providing the reasonable accommodation required for inclusive education and improving the effectiveness of education.

**Acknowledgments.** This research was supported in both part by the Ministry of Education, Science, Sports and Culture, Grant-in-Aid for Scientific Research (C) 15K04540, 2015, (C) 15K01015, 2015, (B) 26285210, 2015, and Tsukuba University of Technology competitive research grants.

# References

1. Saskatchewan. Department of Learning. Special education unit, teaching students with visual impairments: a guide for the support team: Saskatchewan Learning (2003)
2. Jafri, R., Ali, S., Arabnia, H., Fatima, S.: Computer vision-based object recognition for the visually impaired in an indoors environment: a survey. Vis. Comput. **30**, 1197–1222 (2014)
3. Jafri, R., Ali, S.A.: A multimodal tablet–based application for the visually impaired for detecting and recognizing objects in a home environment. In: Miesenberger, K., Fels, D., Archambault, D., Peňáz, P., Zagler, W. (eds.) ICCHP 2014, Part I. LNCS, vol. 8547, pp. 356–359. Springer, Heidelberg (2014)
4. Jafri, R., Ali, S.A.: A GPS-based personalized pedestrian route recording smartphone application for the blind. In: Stephanidis, C. (ed.) HCI 2014, Part II. CCIS, vol. 435, pp. 232–237. Springer, Heidelberg (2014)
5. Jafri, R., Ali, S.A.: Utilizing 3D printing to assist the blind. In: Proceedings of the 2015 International Conference on Health Informatics and Medical Systems (HIMS 2015), July 27–30, Las Vegas, Nevada, USA, pp. 55–61 (2015)
6. Meijer, P.B.L.: An experimental system for auditory image representations. IEEE Trans. Biomed. Eng. **39**, 112–121 (1992)
7. Neumüller, M., Reichinger, A., Rist, F., Kern, C.: 3D printing for cultural heritage: preservation, accessibility, research and education. In: Ioannides, M., Quak, E. (eds.) 3D Research Challenges in Cultural Heritage. LNCS, vol. 8355, pp. 119–134. Springer, Heidelberg (2014)

# Locating Widgets in Different Tactile Information Visualizations

Denise Prescher[✉] and Gerhard Weber

Institut Für Angewandte Informatik, Technische Universität Dresden,
Dresden, Germany
{denise.prescher,gerhard.weber}@tu-dresden.de

**Abstract.** Large tactile displays demand for novel presentation and
interaction strategies. In this paper, different tactile view types and orientation tools are evaluated with 13 blind users. The study has shown
that the different view types are usable for different tasks. Orientation
can be kept best in view types with Braille output but these are often
not sufficient for graphical tasks. The usage of planar orientation tools,
such as structure region or minimap, need to be trained to allow for an
efficient support of two-dimensional tactual exploration.

**Keywords:** Pin-matrix device · Tactile user interface · Tactile views ·
Blind user · Zooming · Panning · Minimap

## 1 Introduction

Two-dimensional pin-matrix devices provide blind users with much more information at once than conventional Braille displays can do. For instance, BrailleDis
9000 [1] and BrailleDis 7200 [2], developed during the HyperBraille project,
both have a touch-sensitive tactile output area consisting of 120 pins. Therefore,
novel interaction strategies as well as new kinds of tactile output beyond simple Braille text are necessary. The spatial presentation of information can have
a huge impact on the blind user's mental model of a graphical user interface
(GUI), that means how he imagines an interface and its elements.

Although large refreshable tactile displays have been developed for several
years [3], there are hardly any studies on the interaction of visually impaired users
on those devices. Specific tactile graphical applications, such as maps [4], graphic
editors [5–7] or virtual classrooms [8] have been developed and were evaluated
without focusing on the need to locate and identify widgets. One approach, the
usage of tactile scrollbars on a tactile display as a hardware solution was assessed
as useful for reducing errors and task completion time [9]. This suggests that
planar orientation tools can improve interaction on large pin-matrix devices.

In this paper, we evaluate the influence of different tactile information visualizations, called view types in the following, on the completion time for locating
widgets and on the mental model of blind users on the BrailleDis 7200. Furthermore, we describe novel tools to support searching tasks as well as orientation.

© Springer International Publishing Switzerland 2016
K. Miesenberger et al. (Eds.): ICCHP 2016, Part II, LNCS 9759, pp. 100–107, 2016.
DOI: 10.1007/978-3-319-41267-2_14

## 2   The HyperBraille System

To allow blind users an effective interaction on the BrailleDis, a novel screen-reader dealing with two-dimensional user interfaces (called HyperReader) was developed. It provides a multimodal user interface giving access to GUIs and graphical content. The tactile output is managed by the Braille window system which is described in detail in [10]. In the following only a brief summary of the interface setup how it is used in this study is given.

The tactile output area is arranged in five rectangular *regions* whereat each region is responsible for different types of information. At the top the window title is written in Braille. Next to it the current view type is marked. At the bottom some detail information about the focused element is also given as Braille text. In between the body region in which the content of the document is shown is placed. In this setup it is sized 116 × 48 pins. On the left side of the body region the three pin wide structure region is arranged. It provides a fast overview of the content's horizontal structure by marking text lines with specific elements by a single Braille character (e.g. 'r' for radio button or 'g' for graphic).

The content of the body region can be presented in diverse tactile view types (see also [11] and Fig. 1). This allows for exploring the information at different levels of detail and presentation modes. The *operating view* is completely text-based which allows the user to read the content in Braille as if you put multiple conventional Braille displays above each other. Spatial relationships as well as tactile graphical widgets can be explored in addition to Braille in the *symbol view*. The pixel-based *layout view* gives direct access to the graphical representation of a window. As this view is a screenshot of the GUI, text is shown as tactile ink-print. The *outline view* enables a fast overview as the structure of the document is shown as abstract rectangles.

The *minimap* is a special view mode showing the whole small scaled document at once in the body region whereat the current view port (visible content in current view type) is highlighted by a blinking frame of pins. In contrast to those views mentioned above, the minimap is not intended for exploring the content but for providing the overall context. Particularly in large zoom levels of layout-preserving view types, the minimap should help users to maintain an overview of the current position. Irrespective of the view type, the HyperReader provides zooming and panning methods as well as speech output. Tactile *scrollbars* at the right and bottom edge of the body region can help to keep the orientation by indicating the current position within the document by a tactual marker.

## 3   User Study: Locating Widgets

As our HyperReader offers blind people new possibilities in getting information not only as a linear text but also in a spatial manner, the following questions arise:

1. Are the view types necessary to offer the user an efficient operation in different situations?
2. What exploration strategies do subjects use to find special widgets? How helpful is the structure region for that purpose?

3. To what extent can the minimap help to increase the efficiency and accuracy in locating widgets in comparison to the scrollbars?

Answering these questions, a study with 13 blind subjects was conducted (aged from 21 to 51, average age was 32, seven female). Six of them have never worked with the BrailleDis before, five have participated in former tests and, therefore, have a minimum experience and two participants have had some experience with our device for two years.

## 3.1   Procedure

The test was divided in the following four phases: 1. training, 2. search task (find a widget), 3. mental model checking (locate widget in global context), 4. questionnaire.

In the training phase, we first explained the characteristics of the four view types and the regions as well as the interaction techniques, especially zooming, panning and minimap usage. Then we presented all GUI elements occurring in the test on the pin-matrix device and how they look in the different view types. As an important help for the following test, the structure region was introduced in detail. That means, the subject has to know that each row of the pin-matrix device can obtain one or more GUI elements, which are marked with a special letter in the structure region. Therefore, the meaning of the letters had to be learned. As preparation of phase three, orientation on a high resolution embossed print-out was trained on an example.

After the training the two test phases were conducted iteratively as explained in the following. For the test we prepared four comparable GUI dialogs consisting of headings, text blocks, form elements, buttons, images and other standard GUI elements (see Fig. 1). We presented these dialogs in one of the four view types on the BrailleDis 7200 one after another and in random order. The subject then had to identify a special widget within the current dialog, shown in the body region, by using zooming and panning commands. For each dialog we defined four such widgets: (1) activated radio button, (2) image which matches to a short description verbally given to the user (e.g. 'image showing a model airplane')[1], (3) tree item, (4) label of the group box containing the cancel button.

Thus, we have three independent variables (four dialogs, four view types and four widgets). Combining each combination of values of these variables, we have 64 conditions. In order to avoid fatigue effects of the users, we distributed these conditions among all the subjects to have each condition two times. In this manner, subject 1 to 3 had 16 tasks, the others had 8 tasks. For example, we gave one subject dialog 1 in layout view and he had to detect the activated radio button. There was no repetition in these three variables. To illustrate, a subject with eight tasks had each dialog in two different view types (so each view type was used in two tasks) and he had to identify each type of widget in two cases.

We measured the required time for locating the correct widget or canceling the task. In case of success, we provided the subject a tactile print-out of the

---

[1] Note that there are two images in each dialog, both without an alternative text.

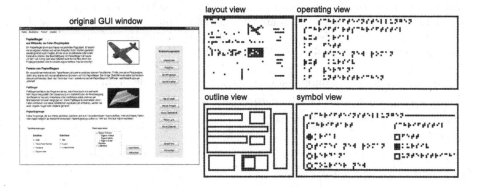

**Fig. 1.** One of the four original GUI dialogs (left) that is shown after filtering on the pin-matrix device. Layout and outline view are both shown in smallest zoom level in this example and, therefore, give an overview over the whole dialog (see middle column). In operating and symbol view (right) only a small part of the dialog is visible (some of the radio buttons and check boxes)

current dialog (high resolution embossed print-out in a size of $42.5\,\mathrm{cm} \times 33.0\,\mathrm{cm}$), whose presentation is comparable to layout view. The new task was to locate the widget within the print-out of the whole dialog by pointing the finger at the top left corner of the widget. To relate the current view port of the pin-matrix device to the GUI's window, the subject could either use the scrollbars as well as the minimap or only the scrollbars. Only in half of the tasks of each subject, the minimap was allowed to use. We measured time as well as the distance to the correct position of the widget's top left corner (offset).

After the test we asked each participant to complete a questionnaire consisting of some rating questions about difficulty of the tasks, several aspects of the view types (orientation, layout, content and distinctness of the GUI elements) as well as the benefit from structure region, scrollbars and minimap. In addition, we also wanted to know which strategies the subjects had applied in finding the widgets on the pin-matrix device and even on the high resolution embossed print-out.

## 3.2   Results and Discussion

The results of locating the different widgets on the pin-matrix device (search task) are shown in Table 1. Thereby, two tasks of one subject (both in layout view) were ignored in the statistics, because the subject canceled these tasks after searching for more than 13 min. As the size of Braille text is fixed, zooming is only available in views without Braille, i.e. layout and outline view.

All widgets were identified in operating view most quickly. Therefore, this simple and text-based view combined with structure region is best suited to locate GUI or text elements. Indeed, the images could only be distinguished in layout view as there was no alternative text or textual description. Furthermore,

**Table 1.** Means and standard deviations under different conditions for completion time required by the 13 participants to locate a widget on the pin-matrix device and for the zoom level in which the widget was located (note: one pixel on the screen corresponds to one pin on the tactile display in a zoom level of 100 %)

| Task condition | Completion time (in seconds) | | Zoom level (in %) | |
|---|---|---|---|---|
| | Mean | Standard deviation | Mean | Standard deviation |
| Average of all tasks | 268.4 | 211.2 | 27.2 | 12.4 |
| Operating view | 117.1 | 72.5 | - | - |
| Symbol view | 238.2 | 153.4 | - | - |
| Layout view | 323.3 | 213.9 | 32.1 | 11.3 |
| Outline view | 378.3 | 256.1 | 22.6 | 11.7 |
| Radio button | 226.7 | 167.1 | 29.1 | 8.9 |
| Image | 207.4 | 132.5 | 19.5 | 11.2 |
| Tree item | 214.3 | 155.8 | 32.1 | 9.7 |
| Group box label | 408.6 | 286.3 | 28.6 | 15.9 |
| With minimap | 257.8 | 229.1 | 27.0 | 10.1 |
| Without minimap | 270.7 | 193.2 | 27.3 | 14.5 |

the layout of a dialog or a document cannot be explored in operating view. Thus, phase three of our test (locate widget in global context) could never be successful in case of this view type.

An ANOVA revealed a significant effect of the view type on the time to complete a search task ($F_{3,56} = 11.887, p < 0.001$). However, paired t-tests[2] show no significant difference on layout and outline view ($t = 0.606, df = 14, p > 0.5$). With regard to the zoom level in which the subjects finished the tasks, there is a significant difference on these two view types ($t = 2.728, df = 14, p < 0.05$). A zoom level at about 30 % seems to be most efficient for layout view because on average subjects were 2.5 times faster than in other zoom levels. In the outline view there could not be found such an optimum zoom level as it depends much more on the size of the searched widget. This can be explained by the fact that small widgets are not visible in small zoom levels as it is known from semantic zooming [12] (details are shown only in higher scales).

The difficulty for each combination of widget type and view type was rated as following[3]: Operating view was seen as being the easiest view type for all widgets except the image for which the layout view was rated best. On average, tasks in operating view were rated the easiest (4.2 of 5), too. Tasks in layout and symbol view were rated as medium difficult (3.2 of 5) and tasks in outline view

---

[2] Only these runs of eight tasks in which the subjects finished all the tasks were considered in the t-tests.

[3] Rating scale was defined as: 0 = not located successfully, 1 = very difficult, 2 = difficult, 3 = medium, 4 = easy, 5 = very easy.

were rated less, but also of medium difficulty (2.7 of 5). The rating confirms the results shown in Table 1.

The average ratings of some other aspects of the view types are shown in Fig. 2. In summary it can be said that orientation can be kept best in view types with Braille output (operating and symbol view) as the content can be understood much easier than in view types without Braille (layout and outline view). Distinctness of the GUI elements is supported by Braille, too. Otherwise, as expected, it is hard to understand the layout in operating view as the user can not identify the real spatial arrangement and relations of the GUI elements. All together, symbol view was rated highest relating to the four analyzed aspects because of its Braille support and its preservation of layout.

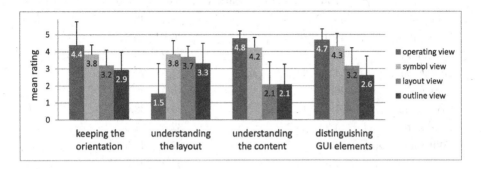

**Fig. 2.** Rating of some aspects of the four view types (scale: 0 = not possible, 1 = very bad to 5 = very good; n = 13; means and standard deviations)

We also asked the participants about their strategy for locating a widget on the pin-matrix device. As introduced in the training phase each user first explored the structure region to determine if there is a need for exploring the current view type in the body region. For covering the whole pin-matrix device most of the subjects (10 of 13) used panning in a more or less structured manner. For orientation scrollbars and minimap were used. Two of the participants stated that they made use of their experience with GUI dialogs to find the position more efficiently. But our measurements did not support this statement.

Eight users stated they created a mental model of the dialog's layout while exploring it on the pin-matrix device. A t-test shows that these subjects who built a mental model[4] had no significant smaller offset ($t = -0.702, df = 48, p = 0.49$) in the global context task, but they are significantly faster in localizing a widget on the embossed print-out than those without a mental model[5] ($t = -2.864, df = 42, p < 0.01$).

Table 2 illustrates the results of the locating task on the high resolution embossed print-out[6]. In about half of the cases (51,3 %), there was no offset.

---

[4] Subjects with mental model: average time = 40.4 s, average offset = 27.5 mm.
[5] Subjects without mental model: average time = 65.9 s, average offset = 37.3 mm.
[6] Note that for the image the task was only executed in layout view.

This indicates subjects could built up a correct mental model about the location of the widget within the dialog. Neither in time ($t = 1.869, df = 13, p = 0.08$) nor in offset ($t = -0.151, df = 13, p = 0.88$) a significant difference can be found between using the minimap or not. Nevertheless, the minimap was rated by the subjects as very helpful (average rating: 2.8 of 3[7]) as well as the structure region (2.9 of 3) and the scrollbars (2.9 of 3).

**Table 2.** Mean completion times and offsets of the 13 participants for locating the position of a widget on the embossed print-out under different conditions

| Task condition | Completion time (in seconds) | | Offset (in millimeters) | |
|---|---|---|---|---|
| | Mean | Standard deviation | Mean | Standard deviation |
| Symbol view | 53.2 | 43.5 | 28.2 | 43.9 |
| Layout view | 48.0 | 30.9 | 30.6 | 63.8 |
| Outline view | 49.8 | 36.1 | 35.2 | 56.5 |
| Radio button | 51.2 | 30.1 | 41.5 | 73.3 |
| Image | 26.7 | 26.7 | 15.9 | 42.0 |
| Tree item | 61.8 | 48.5 | 24.1 | 38.6 |
| Group box label | 44.2 | 25.7 | 32.8 | 53.3 |
| With minimap | 64.9 | 31.2 | 27.9 | 41.5 |
| Without minimap | 42.8 | 36.7 | 33.0 | 61.5 |

### 3.3 Summary

In summary, the study has shown that the different view types can support different tasks on the pin-matrix device. The view type and chosen zoom factor as well as the scrolling position have influence on the time and accuracy of finding widgets. The structure region is very helpful for the user to determine if there is a need for panning or zooming. The minimap is rated as being very helpful, too, although there is no measurable improvement compared to using only the scrollbars. Maybe the usage of a planar orientation help needs more practice to take more advantage of it.

## 4    Conclusion and Outlook

There are some advantages and disadvantages of different tactile view types when searching different kinds of widgets in a dialog window on the BrailleDis 7200 device. Although Braille can support comprehension and distinction of GUI elements, tasks that require for an understanding of the layout or for exploration of graphical content cannot be fulfilled in a text-based view, such as operating

---

[7] Rating scale was defined as: 0 = not helpfully, 1 = a little helpfully, 2 = helpfully, 3 = very helpfully.

view. Thus, it is clear that diverse presentation techniques support interaction on novel two-dimensional pin-matrix devices. Moreover, it is important to train blind users in dealing with spatial exploration and keeping their orientation. Besides, further research of tactile information visualization as well as interaction strategies on large Braille devices is necessary to allow for an efficient work flow.

**Acknowledgements.** We thank all blind participants. The HyperBraille project was sponsored by the German Ministry of Economy and Technology (BMWi) under the grant number 01MT07004.

# References

1. Völkel, T., Weber, G., Baumann, U.: Tactile graphics revised: the novel BrailleDis 9000 pin-matrix device with multitouch input. In: Miesenberger, K., Klaus, J., Zagler, W.L., Karshmer, A.I. (eds.) ICCHP 2008. LNCS, vol. 5105, pp. 835–842. Springer, Heidelberg (2008)
2. Prescher, D.: Redesigning input controls of a touch-sensitive pin-matrix device. In: Zeng, L., Weber, G. (eds.) Proceedings of the International Workshop on Tactile/Haptic User Interfaces for Tabletops and Tablets, CEUR, vol. 1324, pp. 19–24 (2014)
3. Vidal-Verdú, F., Hafez, M.: Graphical tactile displays for visually-impaired people. IEEE Trans. Neural Syst. Rehabil. Eng. **15**(1), 119–130 (2007)
4. Zeng, L., Weber, G.: Audio-haptic browser for a geographical information system. In: Miesenberger, K., Klaus, J., Zagler, W., Karshmer, A. (eds.) ICCHP 2010, Part II. LNCS, vol. 6180, pp. 466–473. Springer, Heidelberg (2010)
5. Albert, P.: Math class: an application for dynamic tactile graphics. In: Miesenberger, K., Klaus, J., Zagler, W.L., Karshmer, A.I. (eds.) ICCHP 2006. LNCS, vol. 4061, pp. 1118–1121. Springer, Heidelberg (2006)
6. Nishi, A., Fukuda, R.: Graphic editor for visually impaired users. In: Miesenberger, K., Klaus, J., Zagler, W.L., Karshmer, A.I. (eds.) ICCHP 2006. LNCS, vol. 4061, pp. 1139–1146. Springer, Heidelberg (2006)
7. Bornschein, J., Prescher, D., Weber, G.: Collaborative creation of digital tactile graphics. In: ASSETS 2015 The 17th International ACM SIGACCESS Conference on Computers and Accessibility, pp. 117–126. ACM, New York (2015)
8. Köhlmann, W., Lucke, U.: Alternative concepts for accessible virtual classrooms for blind users. In: 15th International Conference on Advanced Learning Technologies (ICALT), pp. 413–417. IEEE (2015)
9. Shimada, S., Murase, H., Yamamoto, S., Uchida, Y., Shimojo, M., Shimizu, Y.: Development of directly manipulable tactile graphic system with audio support function. In: Miesenberger, K., Klaus, J., Zagler, W., Karshmer, A. (eds.) ICCHP 2010, Part II. LNCS, vol. 6180, pp. 451–458. Springer, Heidelberg (2010)
10. Prescher, D., Weber, G., Spindler, M.: A tactile windowing system for blind users. In: ASSETS 2010 The 12th International ACM SIGACCESS Conference on Computers and Accessibility, pp. 91–98. ACM, New York (2010)
11. Schiewe, M., Köhlmann, W., Nadig, O., Weber, G.: What you feel is what you get: mapping GUIs on planar tactile displays. In: Stephanidis, C. (ed.) UAHCI 2009, Part II. LNCS, vol. 5615, pp. 564–573. Springer, Heidelberg (2009)
12. Perlin, K., Fox, D.: Pad: an alternative approach to the computer interface. In: SIGGRAPH 1993 20th Annual Conference and Exhibition on Computer Graphics and Interactive Techniques, pp. 57–64. ACM, New York (1993)

# A Concept for Re-useable Interactive Tactile Reliefs

Andreas Reichinger[✉], Anton Fuhrmann, Stefan Maierhofer,
and Werner Purgathofer

VRVis Zentrum für Virtual Reality und Visualisierung Forschungs-GmbH,
Donau-City-Str. 1, 1220 Vienna, Austria
reichinger@vrvis.at
http://www.vrvis.at/projects/ambavis
http://www.ambavis.eu

**Abstract.** We introduce a concept for a relief-printer, a novel production method for tactile reliefs, that allows to reproduce bas-reliefs of several centimeters height difference. In contrast to available methods, this printer will have a much smaller preparation time, and does not consume material nor produce waste, since it is based on a re-usable medium, suitable for temporary printouts. Second, we sketch a concept for the autonomous, interactive exploration of tactile reliefs, in the form of a gesture-controlled audio guide, based on recent depth cameras. Especially the combination of both approaches promises rapid tactile accessibility to 2.5D spatial information in a home or education setting, to on-line resources, or as a kiosk installation in museums.

**Keywords:** (e)Accessibility · Design for all · Blind people · Assistive technology · HCI and Non classical interfaces · Tactile models · 2.5D Reproduction · Interactive audio guide

## 1 Introduction and Related Work

Tactile models are an important tool for blind and visually impaired people to perceive images and objects that are otherwise incomprehensible for them. 3D tactile models (e.g. [8,10]) and 2.5D reliefs (e.g. [5,7]) offer even more possibilities than the more classic raised line drawings and tactile diagrams [2], as depth, 3D shape and surface textures are directly perceivable. However, such tools are more difficult to produce, require complex production machinery, consume material and are therefore more expensive. Further, production time is comparatively long, and once a model is no longer used, it still exists and needs to be stored, or, if no storage space is available, it has to be disposed of.

This is acceptable for permanent exhibitions, where models are presented over a long period and need to be especially durable. It is less acceptable for temporary exhibitions or when a large number of objects need to be made accessible. And, in a home setting, where a user wants to consume a lot of different materials, but only one at a time, it might be completely out of the scope.

© Springer International Publishing Switzerland 2016
K. Miesenberger et al. (Eds.): ICCHP 2016, Part II, LNCS 9759, pp. 108–115, 2016.
DOI: 10.1007/978-3-319-41267-2_15

Therefore, we developed a concept and a first prototype of a novel temporary production method, a relief printer, that does not waste any material, creates the output in a comparatively small amount of time and still in a sufficient quality and size. With such a method, on demand production of touch reliefs will become possible, at home, but also in a museum or school setting.

The second point we target in this work, is the interactive exploration of such reliefs. Touch tools are difficult to understand without proper guidance. Introductory texts to the tactile piece together with the required background information and a description of the depicted objects are important, but often not sufficient. Typically, a blind person is guided by a trained guide who is prepared to answer questions to specific regions, or who can guide the hand to desired locations. But such a guide may not always be present, or a visually impaired person may want to explore the relief in a more autonomous way.

We sketch a concept of a touch-sensitive audio guide, capable of giving location specific information during tactile exploration. This is similar in spirit to a number of already established technologies: The Talking Tactile Tablet [6] operates with raised line graphics on top of a touch-sensitive device; Tooteko [1] is based on NFC tags integrated in 3D models and read by a wearable NFC reader; Talking pen devices[1] sense barely visible printed patterns with an integrated camera; Digital Touch Replicas [12] have touch sensors integrated in haptic exhibits; And, most recently, the colored tactile reliefs of *3DPhotoWorks*[2] feature infrared sensors, embedded at strategic points throughout the tactile art.

In contrast, our proposed method is based on recently developed depth cameras. It does not require sensors to be integrated into the models (as in [1,12] and 3DPhotoWorks) but operates with a depth camera placed over the object and observing the hands. In contrast to the Talking Tactile Tablet [6], it works on arbitrarily formed objects, and not only on thin sheets, and in contrast to talking pen devices it does not require printed patterns, that might be difficult to achieve on curved surfaces. This makes it especially suitable to operate on the introduced relief printer, where sensors cannot be placed inside the medium.

## 2  Conventional Production Methods

Typical production methods for tactile material include swelling paper [2] or Braille embossers in graphics mode[3]. The "Stiftplatte" [9], follows the same idea, but in an interactive form: It uses a technology similar to a Braille display, but arranged in a two-dimensional dense array, as an interactive computer interface. These methods have in common, that there is only a tiny amount of height variation, and therefore no real 3D surfaces are possible. Computer-aided

---

[1] Multiple vendors offer talking pens, like the TalkingPEN (http://www.talkingpen. co.uk), Livescribe (http://www.edlivescribe.com) or Ravensburger tiptoi® (http:// www.tiptoi.com).

[2] 3DPhotoWorks (http://www.3dphotoworks.com) recently created tactile reliefs for the exhibition "Sight Unseen" at the Canadian Museum of Human Rights.

[3] e.g. ViewPlus Braille Printers, http://www.viewplus.com.

production of tactile reliefs, with at least a few centimeters of height variation, is typically performed using subtractive or additive methods [8].

Models created with *subtractive* methods like CNC-milling have a high stability and can be created with a high surface quality. The process produces a large amount of dust, and therefore, a dedicated working place (i.e., a workshop) is required. In addition, a lot of material, energy and operating time is required.

On the other hand, *additive* production methods (widely known under the term 3D printing) offer a much cleaner way of production, suitable to be performed in an office setting. With most processes, no material is wasted, since only the amount of material is used that actually makes up the final output, but, material is still irretrievably used. Production times and costs depend strongly on the method, but are similar or even higher than with subtractive methods, and most methods create unwanted surface artifacts, like steps or ridges that are inherent to the method of material deposition. Further, some methods have a quite small build room, making it difficult to print reliefs of sufficient size.

## 3   Relief Printer Concept

Our idea is inspired by the concept of Ward Fleming's Pin-Art toy [3] (cf. Fig. 2b), which became famous in the 1980s. A large number of pins are arranged in a two-dimensional regular lattice. The pins may be shifted parallel to each other, and their heads form the relief surface of any object that has been pushed into the back of the toy. The relief can be viewed, as long as it is handled carefully to not move the pins by inertia or gravity. If no longer used, the pins can be shifted back, and the toy can be re-used for the next object to be depicted.

The relief printer concept extends this idea by three facets:

1. It is necessary to temporarily fixate the pins in their shifted position, in order to allow the relief to be touched and to be handled without the embossed surface being destroyed.
2. The pins need to be arranged much more closely in order to achieve a higher spatial resolution that is adequate for the resolution of human finger tips.
3. The pins shall be automatically shifted by a computer-controlled machine (the printer), which will allow the cost-efficient, fast, physical realization of digital 3D data.

Since the printing mechanics will be the most complex and expensive part, our concept is to separate the printing mechanics (i.e., the relief *printer*) from the pin array (i.e., the relief *medium*). In this way, multiple low-cost relief media can be used with the same relief printer, similar to a conventional document printer that may be used to print on multiple sheets of paper.

The workflow may be as follows (cf. Fig. 1): (a) The medium is reset by moving the pins into their home position. (b1) The medium is inserted into the printer, the printer shifts the pins according to a digital model. (d) The medium is set to a locked position in which the pins are fixed to withstand touching.

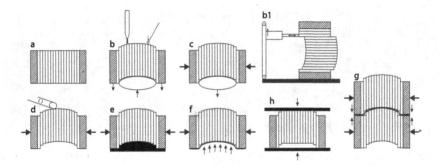

**Fig. 1.** Life cycle and usage possibilities of the relief printer medium (see text)

(h) Once it is no longer used the medium may be set back to the write position, the pins pushed back and the cycle starts again. (b) Alternatively, it can be used to cast an existing object with different tools or compressed air.

Multiple reliefs may be used simultaneously when printed in advance, or one relief may be touched while the other is being printed. It may even be possible to use the medium as a casting mold (e), as die for a press (g), or as die for thermoforming of plastic sheets (f) to create durable reliefs without the need to create a master form as with conventional methods.

## 4   Relief Medium Prototype

The goal of the present work is not a market-ready device, but, as a first phase, a working prototype of the relief medium. Only after a successful evaluation of its usefulness, and a thorough study of its properties, the printer may be developed in a following phase.

In a recent work [4] a real-time changeable relief with 30×30 square pins arranged in an orthogonal lattice with a total of 900 actuators was presented. The pins have a side length of 9.525 mm and an inter-pin spacing of 3.175 mm, giving 12.7 mm per pin, which is way too large for our purpose.

The medium as we envision it, trades resolution for speed. Tactile exploration takes time, and therefore build times of tens of minutes are still acceptable.

Literature using the *grating orientation task* suggest, that the sensor density at the finger tips is at least below 2 mm, and seems to be significantly smaller for blind Braille readers, e.g., 1.04 mm on average of 15 tested blind Braille readers for their self-reported dominant reading finger [11]. These tests however underestimate the actually perceivable resolution, since these are performed with a static, non-moving finger, touching top-down. A moving finger may detect even smaller features, and especially on steep edges, where the side walls of the pins can be felt, jagged lines may appear, which become less apparent with smaller pin sizes. The theoretical optimum is therefore definitely below 1 mm pin diameter, and is more or less dictated by the technical possibilities.

**Fig. 2.** Experiments with an earlier relief from our lab [7]. From left to right: (a) Part of original relief; (b) Embossed in Pin-Art toy; (c) First prototype, 3038 pins, ⌀ 1.75 mm, 89×88 mm, clamped tight and sanded flat; (d) Relief embossed in our first prototype

The need for a high resolution is especially visible in Fig. 2b, where we first tried to approximate a relief with the Pin-Art toy. The average pin distance of 3.27 mm renders the relief almost unrecognizable. This gets even more difficult, as each metal pin is mounted in a guiding hole in which it can wobble side to side. The guiding holes ensure that the pins slide easily and do not influence each other. In our application, this is however not a concern, as long as the printing device ensures the separation during pin movement, for which we already have a concept in mind. Moreover, the guiding holes restrict the achievable resolution, and the separated pins are prone to bend during tactile exploration.

Our solution is a tight arrangement of the pins as depicted in Fig. 2c and d. We use off-the-shelf uncooked cylindrical Spaghetti noodles[4] arranged in the natural hexagonal lattice, arising from the closest packing of circles. Therefore, this arrangement yields the highest attainable information density for a given pin diameter. Once built, the arrangement is stable as each pin is guided and supported by the surrounding pins, and may slide with small force.

However, the arrangement of the pins in an exact lattice is not easily achieved nor maintained. Similar to atoms in a crystal, random arrangement of the light-weight pins leads to lattice defects, e.g., vacant or dislocated pins, stacking faults or grain boundaries between regions of locally rotated lattices, which compromise the stability of the arrangement as some pins at the defects are no longer fully surrounded and are prone to falling out. We solved this by using a frame made from two L-shaped parts held together with rubber bands that exert a sufficient amount of pressure on the arrangement, and manual correction of lattice defects.

Our solution to fix the pins for tactile exploration (cf. Fig. 1d) is to increase the pressure on the frame. It distributes evenly in the lattice and increases the pressure between all pairs of pins, increasing the static friction until an almost hard surface is achieved. We use two clamps to increase the pressure. After sanding the pins to the same length, the same part of the existing relief was embossed (cf. Fig. 2d), with a noticeable increase in surface quality.

---

[4] Spaghetti noodles turned out to be a useful material, being very exact, hard, easy to acquire, low-cost and environmentally friendly, but are a bit brittle and sensitive to moisture and dirt. Further materials should be investigated in the future.

The first prototype already surpassed all expectations in a first evaluation with 7 blind and visually impaired persons. Most of them could get a sense of the depicted shape, but noted the much rougher surface than with the original relief, and the wish for a larger model.

# 5  Touch-Sensitive Audio Guide

As outlined in Sect. 1, we intend to develop a gesture-controlled audio guide, based on optical finger tracking, as no sensors can be integrated into the reconfigurable pin array. The idea is to place a depth camera over the relief, which performs a foreground separation from the static background (desk, relief,...), detects the hands and fingers, and classifies certain gestures. Possibilities are gestures in mid-air for selection of different interaction modes or a menu-like navigation, and gestures on the relief or surrounding objects or buttons like a touch gesture with a single finger in order to trigger location specific audio.

As this part is still work in progress, we comment on our already performed comparison of currently available depth camera sensors, and the selection of the *Intel RealSense F200* as the currently best suitable camera for our purpose.

## 5.1  Requirements on the Tracking Camera

The optimum would be an out-of-the-box solution for articulated finger tracking, on relief surfaces. The working area needs to be at least as large as the relief, plus some surrounding to still detect the full hand when interacting on the borders or outside touch areas. The users will mostly interact near the surface of the relief, but may also perform some gestures above the relief. The track-able working volume should therefore be at least 50×50 cm and 25 cm high, best observed from above or diagonally behind the relief to not disturb the user.

The sensors need to reliably distinguish the fingers from the relief surface, even if the relief is touched. They need to have a small enough error in the depth measurements, and low enough noise to allow reliable separation of the fingers from the background in order to detect touch events. In addition, the spatial resolution of the sensors needs to be high enough to be able to distinguish touch events between the different, often small areas in a tactile relief.

## 5.2  Camera Selection

*Leap Motion*, specifically designed for articulated hand tracking, only works mid-air, and not when the hand is on or near objects.

The *Microsoft Kinect for XBOX 360* and the re-packaged variants *Kinect for Windows, ASUS Xtion, Structure sensor,* and *PrimeSense Carmine 1.08* share the same hardware, and have a rather low effective depth resolution of probably 320×240 pixels or even lower[5], and a minimum distance from the camera of 80 cm.

---

[5] Andreas Reichinger, Kinect Pattern Uncovered. http://azttm.wordpress.com/2011/04/03/kinect-pattern-uncovered. Accessed March 2015.

Together with the required 25 cm high working volume and its wide field-of-view this results in at least 3.5 mm per pixel at the relief distance, quite low for reliable finger detection, even in special *near modes* of newer models. The updated sensor of the *PrimeSense Carmine 1.09* might be better suited, but this device is no longer available after PrimeSense's acquisition by Apple.

Time-of-flight sensors like the *SoftKinetic DS325*, *Creative Senz3D*, *Kinect for Xbox One*, *Kinect for Windows V2*, and various sensors of *pmd Technologies* generally have a larger noise level in the depth measurements. Although this gets better in newer variants, we deem it still too large for our purpose.

*Intel's RealSense* product line has currently two depth sensors, with the *F200* as the near-field model (0.2–1.2 m), featuring full 640×480 resolution, lots of adjustment possibilities and a quite low noise level. In terms of quality and range, the *Intel RealSense F200* seems to be the most suitable device for our purpose on the current market, although the bundled finger tracking solution does not work on surfaces, and we will have to implement our own.

The former company *3Gear Systems* developed an articulated hand tracking software working with different depth cameras, even with the fingers on a planar surface like a desk. However, since their acquisition by *Oculus*, the software is no longer available. On the other hand, fully articulated hand tracking might not be necessary for our purpose, and we will concentrate on a simpler approach.

## 6 Conclusion and Future Work

We developed a concept and presented a first prototype of a novel relief printing method that allows to print temporary tactile reliefs in a relatively short amount of time into an erasable and re-usable relief medium, without wasting any material. This concept is complemented by a touch-sensitive audio guide based on finger tracking with a state-of-the-art depth camera. This may enable or improve the autonomous exploration of printed reliefs or other tactile models. It may help naming and differentiating different parts of the relief, and may enrich the exploration by valuable background information, or targeted guidance.

We believe, that the presented new relief production method can immensely drop the production costs for tactile materials in museums or schools. Institutions may not need to produce tactile materials in advance, but can print the reliefs on demand and may recycle them when no longer needed (e.g. reliefs for pupils for today's topic). It could be implemented as an interactive kiosk in a museum, or allow individuals to afford such a printing device. It can enhance home education for visually impaired people, or may even be useful for various 3D design and visualization studies in a broader context.

Although this work originated from research in the context of blind and visually impaired people, this work may be seen in a broader *design for all* context. Tactile Reliefs and the interactivity may be suitable for people with learning disorders or attention deficiencies, and may be interesting for everyone.

The next steps will be the realization of a larger relief medium with even thinner pins to further increase the resolution, the implementation of the gesture-based audio guide and a formal evaluation to plan further developments.

**Acknowledgments.** This work was performed within the framework of the project Deep Pictures, supported by the Austrian Science Fund (FWF): P24352-N23, and the Erasmus+ project AMBAVis (http://www.ambavis.eu) and has been funded with support from the European Commission. This publication reflects the views only of the authors, and the Commission cannot be held responsible for any use which may be made of the information contained therein. Special thanks to Florian Rist and the Institut für Kunst und Gestaltung of the Vienna University of Technology, and to Thebert Metallbau GmbH (http://www.thebert.at).

# References

1. D'Agnano, F., Balletti, C., Guerra, F., Vernier, P.: Tooteko: a case study of augmented reality for an accessible cultural heritage. Digitization, 3D printing and sensors for an audio-tactile experience. In: The International Archives of Photogrammetry, Remote Sensing and Spatial Information Sciences, vol. XL-5/W4, pp. 207–213 (2015). http://www.int-arch-photogramm-remote-sens-spatial-inf-sci.net/XL-5-W4/
2. Edman, P.K.: Tactile Graphics. American Foundation for the Blind, New York (1992)
3. Fleming, W.: Vertical three-dimensional image screen, US Patent 4,654,989 (1987)
4. Follmer, S., Leithinger, D., Olwal, A., Hogge, A., Ishii, H.: inFORM: dynamic physical affordances and constraints through shape and object actuation. In: Proceedings of the 26th Annual ACM Symposium on User Interface Software and Technology UIST 2013, pp. 417–426 (2013), http://dl.acm.org/citation.cfm?id=2502032
5. Furferi, R., Governi, L., Volpe, Y., Puggelli, L., Vanni, N., Carfagni, M.: From 2D to 2.5D i.e. from painting to tactile model. Graph. Models **76**(6), 706–723 (2014)
6. Landau, S., Gourgey, K.: Development of a talking tactile tablet. Inf. Technol. Disabil. **7**(2) (2001). http://itd.athenpro.org/volume7/number2/tablet.html
7. Reichinger, A., Maierhofer, S., Purgathofer, W.: High-quality tactile paintings. J. Comput. Cult. Herit. **4**(2), 5:1–5:13 (2011)
8. Reichinger, A., Neumüller, M., Rist, F., Maierhofer, S., Purgathofer, W.: Computer-Aided Design of Tactile Models. Taxonomy and Case Studies. In: Miesenberger, K., Karshmer, A., Penaz, P., Zagler, W. (eds.) ICCHP 2012, Part II. LNCS, vol. 7383, pp. 497–504. Springer, Heidelberg (2012)
9. Taras, C., Raschke, M., Schlegel, T., Ertl, T., Prescher, D., Weber, G.: Improving Screen Magnification Using the Hyperbraille Multiview Windowing Technique. In: Miesenberger, K., Klaus, J., Zagler, W., Karshmer, A. (eds.) ICCHP 2010, Part II. LNCS, vol. 6180, pp. 506–512. Springer, Heidelberg (2010)
10. Teshima, Y., Matsuoka, A., Fujiyoshi, M., Ikegami, Y., Kaneko, T., Oouchi, S., Watanabe, Y., Yamazawa, K.: Enlarged Skeleton Models of Plankton for Tactile Teaching. In: Miesenberger, K., Klaus, J., Zagler, W., Karshmer, A. (eds.) ICCHP 2010, Part II. LNCS, vol. 6180, pp. 523–526. Springer, Heidelberg (2010)
11. Van Boven, R.W., Hamilton, R.H., Kauffman, T., Keenan, J.P., Pascual-Leone, A.: Tactile spatial resolution in blind Braille readers. Neurology **54**(12), 2230–2236 (2000)
12. Wing, J.: Ancient hieroglyphics meet cutting-edge technology at Loughborough University. http://www.lboro.ac.uk/service/publicity/news-releases/2012/197_Manchester-Museum.html. Accessed March 2015

# Three-Dimensional Models of Earth for Tactile Learning

Yoshinori Teshima[1]([✉]), Yasunari Watanabe[1], Yohsuke Hosoya[1], Kazuma Sakai[1],
Tsukasa Nakano[2], Akiko Tanaka[2], Toshiaki Aomatsu[3], Tatsuyoshi Tanji[3],
Kenji Yamazawa[4], Yuji Ikegami[4], Mamoru Fujiyoshi[5], Susumu Oouchi[6],
and Takeshi Kaneko[6]

[1] Department of Mechanical Science and Engineering, Chiba Institute of Technology, 2-17-1
Tsudanuma, Narashino, Chiba 275-0016, Japan
yoshinori.teshima@it-chiba.ac.jp

[2] National Institute of Advanced Industrial Science and Technology (AIST), 1-1-1 Higashi,
Tsukuba, Ibaraki 305-8566, Japan
{tsukasa.nakano, akiko-tanaka}@aist.go.jp

[3] Special Needs Education School for the Visually Impaired, University of Tsukuba,
3-27-6 Mejirodai, Bunkyo, Tokyo, 112-0015, Japan
{aomatsu, ttanji}@nsfb.tsukuba.ac.jp

[4] Advanced Manufacturing Team, RIKEN Advanced Science Institute, 2-1 Hirosawa, Wako,
Saitama 351-0198, Japan
{kyama, yikegami}@riken.jp

[5] Universal Design Laboratory for Testing and Education, 3-9-2-611 Hikarigaoka, Nerima,
Tokyo, 179-0072, Japan
fujiyosi@udlte.or.jp

[6] National Institute of Special Needs Education, 5-1-1 Nobi, Yokosuka,
Kanagawa 239-8585, Japan
{oouchi, kaneko}@nise.go.jp

**Abstract.** Three-Dimensional (3D) tactile models of Earth were constructed for
the visually impaired. We utilized exact topography data obtained by planetary
explorations. Therefore, 3D models of Earth by additive manufacturing possess
exact shape of relief on their spherical surfaces. Several improvements were given
to models to suit tactile learning. Experimental results showed that the Earth
models developed in this study by additive manufacturing were useful for tactile
learning of the globe of the visually impaired.

**Keywords:** Tactile 3D model · Additive manufacturing · Topography data ·
Visually impaired people · Globe with exact relief

## 1 Introduction

Blind people can recognize three-dimensional shapes through tactile sensations. Therefore, effective models are useful in tactile learning [1–4].

Standard globes for the sighted persons have no undulations on their spherical
surface. Different countries and the ocean are color-coded on the spherical surface.

© Springer International Publishing Switzerland 2016
K. Miesenberger et al. (Eds.): ICCHP 2016, Part II, LNCS 9759, pp. 116–119, 2016.
DOI: 10.1007/978-3-319-41267-2_16

There are some globes made for the use of the blind. Possibly the oldest three-dimensional relief globe made in the United States stands in the lobby of the Perkins School for the Blind. The diameter of the globe is about 135 cm. American Printing House for the Blind produced two types of tactile globes: one is Relief Globe whose diameter is about 76 cm, and the other is Tactile and Visual Globe which is a standard globe covered with a tactile overlay. Royal National Institute of Blind People produced Tactile Globe whose diameter is about 38 cm. Nippon Charity Kyokai Foundation presented Relief Globe whose diameter is about 50 cm and Sun Kougei Inc. produced Barrier-Free Globe whose diameter is about 32 cm.

These globes have their own feature but we omit the explanation here. There are three relief globes among them. Points to be paid attention to is that they did not utilized exact topography data.

Recently, various additive manufacturing techniques have been developed. We can make a relief globe which reconstructs exact topography data by making use of the additive manufacturing. As one of such examples, Nakano and Tanaka presented a relief globe. They made models of planets in the solar system. Their models involved Venus, Earth, Mars, and Moon. The gradation of colors on the globe corresponds to the elevation of topography [5].

In this study, we developed our relief globes which were modified from the model of Nakano and Tanaka in order to fit the tactile learning by the blind. Further, we assessed the level of understanding of the visually impaired about the positions of both the six continents of the world and Japan.

## 2   Tactile Globes

The diameter of the globe of Nakano and Tanaka was 8 cm. The 1st phase of modification was to change the size of globe. We formed two models whose diameters were 20 cm and 12 cm. We discussed the suitable size for tactile observation among three models, i.e. 20 cm, 12 cm, and 8 cm with a blind person. As the result, the model of the diameter 12 cm was selected. The 12 cm model is suitable for tactile observation by both hands. All diameters of the modified models hereafter are 12 cm.

The 2nd phase of modification was to delete the relief of the bottom of the sea. The above three models have the relief of the bottom of the sea. It is very difficult for the blind to distinguish land from sea when they use such models. In this study, the questions of experiments were about the position of continents. Therefore we deleted the relief of the bottom of the sea.

The procedure for deletion of the relief in the sea is shown below. First, all the value of the elevation of topography was replaced with -3000 m if the value was smaller than zero. Next, the updated elevation data were converted into the STL (STereo Lithography) format, which is the file format used in the additive manufacturing technique. Finally, the model was constructed by using selective laser sintering (material: nylon powder). The obtained model had the sharp step between land and sea, and no relief in the sea.

The 3rd phase of modification was to add the equator, the prime meridian, and the two poles to Model-A2. The following 8 kinds of model were proposed. The equator and the prime meridian were expressed by the belt on Model-B1, B2, B3, and B4. The height of their belt was provided in four stages. The equator and the prime meridian were expressed by the gutter on Model-C1, C2, C3, and C4. The width of their gutter was provided in four stages. The north pole was expressed by a cone. The south pole was expressed by a cylinder. The two poles have common shape to all of eight models.

## 3    Experiments: Investigation of Level of Understanding

Eight subjects which were totally blind persons took part in our experiments, i.e. the investigation of level of understanding. A experimenter explained the positions of both the six continents of the world and Japan to each subject at the beginning of the experiment. This advance explanation was performed with Model-B3.

Next, the subjects were asked to indicate the position of each continents or Japan by their index finger by touching one of the models using both their hands. This examination was performed with four models: Model-B3, Model-C3, Model-A2, and Model-A1.

The experimenter asked each of subjects the following questions:

(Q1)   position of the African continent,
(Q2)   to trace the outline of the African continent,
(Q3)   position of the Antarctic continent,
(Q4)   position of the Australian continent, and
(Q5)   position of Japan.

The experimenter recorded the answering time of respective questions.

Next, the experimenter asked the subject the following questions:

(Q6)   to decide the ranking of four models (B3, C3, A2, A1) along appropriateness for tactile learning,
(Q7)   to decide the ranking of four models (B1, B2, B3, B4) along appropriateness on height of their belt,
(Q8)   to decide the ranking of four models (C1, C2, C3, C4) along appropriateness on width of their gutter, and
(Q9)   the most appropriate model in the questions (7) and (8).

The duration of the experiment was about 30 min per subject.

## 4    Results and Discussions

The best model among these four models was Model-B3 (belt), the second best was Model-C3 (gutter), the third best was Model-A2 (no relief in the sea), and the bottom was Model-A1 (non-modified model). This order altered about Q4 and Q5. It may result in the habituation because the subjects answered same questions on every model.

The ranking of appropriate model for tactile learning among four models (B3, C3, A2, A1). All subjects answered that the best was Model-B3 and the bottom was A1.

The most desirable height of the belt models was Model-B3 (height: 3.3 mm). And Table 5 shows the most desirable width of the gutter models was Model-C2 (width: 3.0 mm) and C3 (width: 5.3 mm).

All subjects answered that the belt models were better than the gutter models. In the case of the gutter model, the width of the gutter deletes topography. Small width is desirable but it is difficult to recognize the gutter of small width. In the case of the belt model, the width of the belt is constant (0.9 mm) and the height of the belt changes.

**Acknowledgements.** This work was partially supported by Grant-in-Aid for Scientific Research (A) (18200049) of Japan Society for the Promotion of Science(JSPS).

# References

1. Teshima, Y.: Three-dimensional tactile models for blind people and recognition of 3D objects by touch: introduction to the special thematic session. In: Miesenberger, K., Klaus, J., Zagler, W., Karshmer, A. (eds.) ICCHP 2010, Part II. LNCS, vol. 6180, pp. 513–514. Springer, Heidelberg (2010)
2. Teshima, Y., Ogawa, T., Fujiyoshi, M., Ikegami, Y., Kaneko, T., Oouchi, S., Watanabe, Y., Yamazawa, K.: Models of mathematically defined curved surfaces for tactile learning. In: Miesenberger, K., Klaus, J., Zagler, W., Karshmer, A. (eds.) ICCHP 2010, Part II. LNCS, vol. 6180, pp. 515–522. Springer, Heidelberg (2010)
3. Teshima, Y., Matsuoka, A., Fujiyoshi, M., Ikegami, Y., Kaneko, T., Oouchi, S., Watanabe, Y., Yamazawa, K.: Enlarged skeleton models of plankton for tactile teaching. In: Miesenberger, K., Klaus, J., Zagler, W., Karshmer, A. (eds.) ICCHP 2010, Part II. LNCS, vol. 6180, pp. 523–526. Springer, Heidelberg (2010)
4. Yamazawa, K., Teshima, Y., Watanabe, Y., Ikegami, Y., Fujiyoshi, M., Oouchi, S., Kaneko, T.: Three-dimensional model fabricated by layered manufacturing for visually handicapped persons to trace heart shape. In: Miesenberger, K., Karshmer, A., Penaz, P., Zagler, W. (eds.) ICCHP 2012, Part II. LNCS, vol. 7383, pp. 505–508. Springer, Heidelberg (2012)
5. Nakano, T., Tanaka, A.: Making Globes of the Planets. The 3rd Science Frontier Tsukuba, November 2004

# Tactile Maps and Map Data for Orientation and Mobility

# Augmented Reality Tactile Map with Hand Gesture Recognition

Ryosuke Ichikari[1], Tenshi Yanagimachi[2], and Takeshi Kurata[1(✉)]

[1] National Institute of Advanced Industrial Science and Technology,
1-1-1 Umezono, Tsukuba, Ibaraki 305-8560, Japan
{r.ichikari,t.kurata}@aist.go.jp
[2] Toyohashi University of Technology, 1-1 Hibarigaoka, Tempaku,
Toyohashi, Aichi 441-8580, Japan
https://unit.aist.go.jp/hiri/seam/aspr/en/index.html

**Abstract.** Paper tactile maps are regarded as a very useful tool for pre-journey learning for visually-impaired people. In order to provide the solution for the perceptual difficulties and the limitation of the amount of contents of the paper tactile maps, we propose the augmented reality (AR) tactile map system. With our AR tactile map, the physical tactile map can be augmented by audio and visual feedbacks which are enlarging/enhancing the focused area and voice over of the POR/POI according to the user's input. As the interface for the AR tactile map, we adopt intuitive user interfaces with hand gesture recognition by using an RGB-D camera. We implemented a prototype according to the requirements determined by the discussion including the visually-impaired people.

**Keywords:** Tactile map · Augmented reality · Gesture interface · RGB-D camera · Walking assistance

## 1 Background

Paper tactile maps are regarded as a very useful tool for pre-journey learning for visually-impaired people. The visually impaired people can review walking routes and surrounding areas by recognizing contents of the tactile maps and their geometrical relations with haptic sense. By integrating with a tracking method of pedestrians [1], they can also tangibly obtain the feedback of walked trajectory for reviewing purpose.

The paper tactile maps are already used by the visually-impaired people to some extent [2]. However, there are many visually-impaired people who don't use the tactile maps because of difficulties for constructing mental image of the contents with haptic sense. Indeed, the tactile maps need a certain level of time and experience for the users to use them very well. There are other problems of the tactile maps. In addition, the contents of the printed tactile map cannot be changed. The amount of contents depends on the resolution of the printing technology and human tactile capability [3].

© Springer International Publishing Switzerland 2016
K. Miesenberger et al. (Eds.): ICCHP 2016, Part II, LNCS 9759, pp. 123–130, 2016.
DOI: 10.1007/978-3-319-41267-2_17

## 2    AR Tactile Map

### 2.1    Tactile Map

There are several types of methodology for producing the paper tactile maps, such as UV offset printing and PIAF (Picture in a flash). UV offset can separately design color of maps and their tactile presentation. The cost for producing tactile map, especially by UV offset printing, is not negligible. There is another problem for designing the tactile map. Technical expertise for designing tactile map is required for deciding which parts in the map should be bumped. TMACS (Tactile Map Automated Creation System) [4] is a system which aims to reduce the barrier for designing tactile maps. We adopt the maps generated by TMACS. In this research, we utilize both types of methodologies for printing tactile map.

### 2.2    Augmentation of the Tactile Map

In order to provide the solution for the perceptual difficulties and the limitation of the amount of contents of the paper tactile maps, we propose the augmented reality (AR) tactile map with hand gesture recognition.

The most common type of AR is visual augmentation with the computer graphics (CG) onto real background image. AR is not limited to the visual augmentation, but it can be applied for audio augmentation [5–7]. With our AR tactile map, the physical tactile map can be augmented by audio and visual feedbacks which are enlarging/enhancing the focused area with voice over of the POR/POI according to the user's input. We also propose intuitive user interface with hand gesture recognition for the interaction with the system.

### 2.3    Requirements for the AR Tactile Map

With interviewing to visually-impaired people, we defined requirements of the system as follows.

– Audio Augmentation to the Tactile Map for Completely Blind People: The most important function is the audio augmentation of the tactile map for completely blind people. According to the focusing points on the tactile map pointed by the user, the proposed system provides information about the focused point by audio playback.
– Enlarging Focused Area in the Map for Low-vision People: Low vision people might perceive appearance of the map if the characters or figures in the images are enlarged. In order to enlarge the contents in the map, we implement zoom-in function with enlarged text annotation. In addition to the image enlargement, other enhancements of the image such as adjusting contrast and colors are required so that low-vision people can perceive the contents.
– Capability to Connect with Walking Navigation Tool and POR/POI database: We plan to use the proposed system with our walking navigation system [8]. POR (Point of Reference) and POI (Point of Interest) are contents of

the navigation system and they are gathered and shared for public. POR is defined as a specific point location which is easily recognized for confirming routes such as characteristic shape and material of ground (steps, stairs, sloop, door), sound/noise, and scent/odor. The AR tactile map is designed as the interface for the navigation system and POR/POI database. The AR tactile map enables the user of the navigation tool to preview the walking route with POR/POI and review walked trajectory on the tactile map with AR augmentation.

- Enabling the Visually Impaired People to Request POR/POI Data Around Specific Area: For the inclusive creation of above described POR/POI database, enabling the visually impaired people to join the activity to collect POR/POI data is desired. In order to enable the visually-impaired people to join the activity, we implemented a function for the visually impaired people to specify the area where they want to obtain POR/POI information.
- Intuitive Controlling Interface for the System: The most intuitive way to control the system is directly touching the tactile map while perceiving the contents of the tactile map. We implemented gesture recognition of the hand gesture when the users touch the tactile map. Functions for pointing and specifying command for operations are both required for the gesture interface of the AR tactile map.
- Enabling Both-hands Touch with the Tactile Map: We often observed that the visually-impaired people touch the tactile map with both hands. Therefore, we aim to design configuration of the system for enabling both-hands touch with the AR tactile map so that the user can use it with the same manner of ordinary tactile maps.

## 3   Implementation

### 3.1   System Configuration

According to the requirements, we implemented a prototype of the system as shown in Fig. 1. The configuration of the software program can be roughly separated into three parts as follows (Fig. 2);

- Main AR Tactile Map Application Part: In the case of current prototype system, the main part of the AR tactile map is implemented on a tablet computer. According to the results of the recognition of the map and calculation of the relative positional relationship in 3D space, audio and visual feedbacks are provided.
- Hand Gesture Recognition Part: In order to specify the focused area on the map by actually touching the tactile map, fingertips are detected when the user hands are close to the map. We adopt an RGB-D camera mounted on the tablet and utilize image processing methods for color and depth images from the RGB-D camera. For the prototype, DepthSense DS325 is used and fixed on the backside of the tablet. In order to realize both hand interactions

**Fig. 1.** Appearance of the prototype system

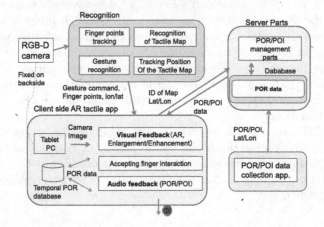

**Fig. 2.** Component of the software configuration

with the system, the current prototype adopts a flexible arm and a smartphone/tablet holder for fixing the tablet and RGB-D camera to the desk. An example of RGB-D image captured by the configuration is shown in Fig. 3.

– Contents Database Server: POR/POI information is managed in the server side. When the main AR tactile application part requests to get POR/POI information by sending the ID of the map and latitude and longitude information of the focused position on the map, the server part sends the POR/POI information according to the request.

### 3.2   Interaction with the Tactile Map

**Extraction of the Hands.** In the prototype, the positional relationship between the tactile map and the RGB-D camera is fixed. Therefore, the background differencing for depth images can be applied for detecting hands.

**Fig. 3.** An RGB-D image for gesture recognition

**Detection of Tapping Gesture.** As the first hand gesture, we adopt tapping gesture with a finger. This gesture is used for obtaining the focused points on the tactile map coordinate. The gesture recognition algorithm distinguishes the intended tapping gesture from other unindented movements of hand when the users are touching of the map. The flow of the algorithm is described as follows.

1. In order to avoid false detection of tapping gesture caused by movements of the hands, the center of mass of the detected hand area is calculated. If the hand area is not moved, gesture recognition of the tapping gesture is carried out.
2. Tapping gesture is recognized by checking time serious variation of each pixel of the depth images. We defined following two states of the finger; (a) finger on the map, (b) finger on the air. These states are recognized by the distance between the hand and the map. Tapping gesture is detected if transitions of the state, state(a) → state(b) → state(a), happened within time windows and the pixels are in the area of the hands.
3. If the number of detected pixels is more than a certain threshold, the tapped point is calculated by means-shift filtering (Fig. 4 red point).

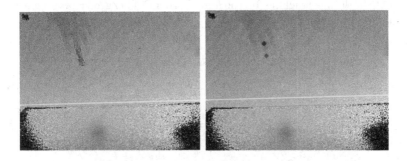

**Fig. 4.** Detection of tapping gesture (Color figure online)

**Detection of Flat Hand Gesture.** The tapping gesture corresponds to "Click" for mouse-based user interface. As the second interface for the system, we implemented Flat Hand Gesture which corresponds to moving the pointer for the mouse-based interface. With the flat hand gesture, areas where user is touching can be obtained continuously in real-time. We use this gesture for real-time sound feedbacks to tell the existence of POR/POI around users' hand when users search before tapping.

**Information Presentation According to the Interaction with Hand Gesture.** The points where user's finger tapped are converted to latitude/longitude to request the server part to send the POR/POI data. When the user tapped the area where POR/POI exists, the tablet PC shows the enlarged image and text whose center is the tapped coordinate. The name of POR/POI data can be played by voice-over at the same time.

**Automatic Detection and Localization of the Tactile Map.** In order to convert the coordinate system from the depth image to world, the coordinate of the four corners of the map are needed to be detected. If multiple tactile maps are used and need to be changed dynamically in applications, automatic identification of the tactile map is required. We implemented automatic identification and tracking of the tactile maps by computer vision technique. The ORB feature point detector and local feature descriptor are used for identifying tactile maps by the RGB image. Mean distances of feature descriptors are compared between the maps for the identification. Corners of the tactile map can be tracked by estimating homography between rectified image templates and input image. At least 4 pairs are required for calculating homography. RANSAC is used for robustly calculating homography matrix. ZNCC (Zero mean normalized cross correlation) is used for verifying the similarity of the contents in the rectangle.

Since the algorithm uses ZNCC and local features, it is tolerant of the brightness changes at some level between input and registered template images. Figure 5 shows an example output of the automatic identification of the tactile map and the tracking of the four corners. The green rectangle shows the estimated outline of the tactile map.

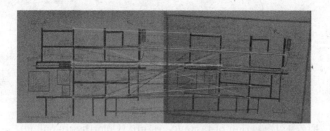

**Fig. 5.** Automatic identification and localization of the tactile map (left: detected template image matched with the input image, right: input image with the matched feature points and outline) (Color figure online)

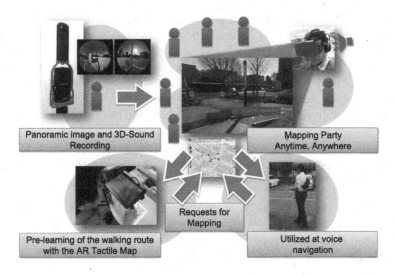

**Fig. 6.** Overview of virtual mapping party

## 4  Conclusion and On-Going Works

In this paper, we proposed the AR tactile map for enhancing physical tactile maps by utilizing audio-visual augmentation. As the gesture interface for the system, we implemented the algorithm for recognizing hand gestures for specifying focused points on the map.

As an on-going work, we have been designing virtual mapping party with pre-recorded omnidirectional images and sound and AR tactile map for gathering POR/POI data as shown in Fig. 6. In the conventional mapping party, such as mapping parties for OpenStreetMap (OSM) data, people come together for creating maps and gathering POI data on site. By contrast, the participants watch video and sound instead of actually going there in the case of virtual mapping party. AR tactile map can be utilized as a communication tool between visually impaired people and sighted people. In particular, the visually impaired people can confirm the POR/POI data collected at the virtual mapping party on the map. Also they can request about area where they need to obtain POR/POI information.

As the first trial of the virtual mapping party, we held the actual workshop on the virtual mapping party at Tokyo. We asked participants to collect POR/POI by experiencing pre-recorded panorama and 3D-sound. For the VR experience of the site, we used HMDs including Oculus Rift, Gear VR, and Google cardboard type attachment for smart-phones based VR experience. We asked them to try the AR tactile map for confirming and requesting POR/POI. After the workshop, we asked them to answer the questionnaire. Here is an excerpt from the participants' comments about the AR tactile map.

- Accuracy of the gesture recognition has a room for improvement.
- Requesting function is good because the it can reflect visually-impaired people's demand.
- Scale size of the map was not fitted. Considering to accuracy of the gesture recognition, the scale size of tactile maps and the density of the distribution of the contents need to be carefully considered.
- It seems to be interesting if the voice recognition can be combined with gesture interface.
- A participant with visual impairment like annotations printed in Braille, but another participant with visual impairment does not like them because they disturbed perception of the shapes of roads and buildings.

According to the participants' comments, the accuracy of the gesture interface needs to be improved. We found the individual difference of the way to touch and tap the tactile map. This seems to be one of the factors of the error. We plan to investigate the solution for this.

**Acknowledgment.** This research is partially supported by JST RISTEX.

# References

1. Kurata, T.: Roles of navigation system in walking with long cane and guide dog. In: CSUN Conference (2014)
2. Ungar, S., et al.: The role of tactile maps in mobility training. Br. J. Vis. Impairment **11**(3), 59–61 (1993)
3. ISO/PRF 19028 Accessible design - Information contents, figuration and display methods of tactile guide maps (Under development)
4. Watanabe, T., Yamaguchi, T., Koda, S., Minatani, K.: Tactile map automated creation system using openstreetmap. In: Miesenberger, K., Fels, D., Archambault, D., Peñáz, P., Zagler, W. (eds.) ICCHP 2014, Part II. LNCS, vol. 8548, pp. 42–49. Springer, Heidelberg (2014)
5. Higa, K., et al.: A two-by-two mixed reality system that merges real and virtual worlds in both audio and visual senses. In: Proceedings of ISMAR 2007, pp. 203–206 (2007)
6. O'Sullivan, L., Picinali, L., Feakes, C., Cawthorne, D.: Audio tactile maps (ATM) system for the exploration of digital heritage buildings by visually-impaired individuals - first prototype and preliminary evaluation. In: Forum Acousticum (2014)
7. Fusco, G., et al.: The tactile graphics helper: providing audio clarification for tactile graphics using machine vision. In: Proceedings of ASSETS 2015 (2015)
8. Okuno, K.: Smartphone-based talking navigation system for walking training. In: CSUN Conference 2015, IND-026 (2015)

# Blind Friendly Maps

## Tactile Maps for the Blind as a Part of the Public Map Portal (Mapy.cz)

Petr Červenka[1(✉)], Karel Břinda[2], Michaela Hanousková[1], Petr Hofman[3], and Radek Seifert[4]

[1] Support Centre for Students with Special Needs, Masaryk University, Brno, Czech Republic
{cervenka,hanouskova}@teiresias.muni.cz
[2] Université Paris-Est Marne-la-Vallée, LIGM, Champs-sur-Marne, France
karel.brinda@univ-mlv.fr
[3] Seznam.cz, a.s., Prague, Czech Republic
Petr.Hofman@firma.seznam.cz
[4] Support Centre ELSA, Czech Technical University in Prague, Prague, Czech Republic
radek.seifert@elsa.cvut.cz

**Abstract.** Blind people can now use maps located at Mapy.cz, thanks to the long-standing joint efforts of the ELSA Center at the Czech Technical University in Prague, the Teiresias Center at Masaryk University, and the company Seznam.cz. Conventional map underlays are automatically adjusted so that they could be read through touch after being printed on microcapsule paper, which opens a whole new perspective in the use of tactile maps. Users may select an area of their choice in the Czech Republic (only within its boundaries, for the time being) and also the production of tactile maps, including the preparation of the map underlays, takes no more than several minutes.

**Keywords:** Tactile map · Tactile perception · Blind people · Web maps accessibility · Automated geodata processing

## 1 Introduction

Acquiring proper spatial knowledge is fundamental for orientation and mobility of blind people and tactile maps are considered to be the most appropriate source of information about space [1]. However, one of the main obstacles to their use by the visually impaired is their problematic accessibility because they are not usually immediately available and updated. Therefore, relief embossing is still a result of demanding manual work and relatively costly and time-consuming procedures.

The idea presented in this paper was born in 2007 when our team was working on ensuring accessibility of the web services provided by the Seznam.cz company. As a result of long-standing efforts, we developed a method of generating maps which are tactile and based on standard visual map underlays. The selected map underlay is consequently converted into a graphic document in conformity with the principles of tactile perception, and it is optimized for technologies using microcapsule paper.

© Springer International Publishing Switzerland 2016
K. Miesenberger et al. (Eds.): ICCHP 2016, Part II, LNCS 9759, pp. 131–138, 2016.
DOI: 10.1007/978-3-319-41267-2_18

Several authors have dealt with the issues of tactile map production over recent years. Watanabe [9] focused on possibilities of printing tactile maps from Open Street Maps source data – individual maps can be generated using the same microencapsulation technology and starting and finishing points may be added while no more explanatory notes are required. Authors have also explored ways of using 3D printing [7], which undoubtedly has its merits, yet is highly demanding in terms of technical equipment and financial resources. Interactive maps with audio-tactile content [4, 6, 8] offer extra convenience. Nevertheless, it was our objective to describe a technological procedure that would be easily accessible to blind users and, at the same time, allow quick generation of updated tactile maps of any area. The result is the public map service www.hapticke.mapy.cz.

## 2    Possibilities and Methods of Automated Tactile Map Production

### 2.1    Points of Departure/Initial Assumptions

When preparing tactile maps, the designer needs to deal with specific issues related particularly to the principles of tactile perception [3, 5]. The designer must:

1. Determine the optimal ratio between the rendered content (maximum of rendered details) and the size of the resulting image (readable through touch), i.e. the **map format** and its **scale**.
2. Reduce significantly the **map content** and select unambiguously individual elements to be shown on the map (point, line and area symbols).
3. Choose a suitable way of **map lettering**.
4. Choose the relief embossing **technology**.

All these aspects significantly influence each other (different technologies enable rendering different number of details) and a suitable compromise needs to be found. In addition, it is necessary to bear in mind other conditions of legibility of the map with regard to the limits of tactile perception. These conditions often include a unified size of Braille characters (offering no possibility of multiple sizes) and the need to maintain sufficient distance between the individual elements of tactile image [1, 2, 5].

The described approach was consistently applied when creating our map key– the Mapnik, a freely accessible map generating interface, was used [10].

### 2.2    Map Scale Selection

The basic map scale was derived from the minimum width of the road which allows the Braille lettering to be rendered in the correct size within its axis. The basic format of the map sheet is the A4 swell paper size.

## 2.3   Rendering and Map Key Generation

The difference between generating standard and tactile maps using the Mapnik program is the unequal use of the configuration file, the so-called map key. The map key defines objects to be chosen from the SQL vector database and determines the order and manner of their rendering. The technical nature also imposes certain limitations applying to the final shape of the map. These can be divided into two groups:

1. Limitations imposed by the employed map generating tool, that is, the aforementioned Mapnik interface, are due to its possibilities of rendering and the set of rules that can be used. For instance, you cannot change the location of an object on the basis of the presence of other objects in its vicinity. This might lead to situations when e.g. a brook disappears under the path running alongside.
2. The second category of limitations are those imposed by the chosen object database. This often results from the fact that the database is primarily created to serve for standard maps rendering, not as a generally accurate representation of all rendered objects. That explains, for instance, why bridges are stored in the database only as a line of both bridge decks which are rendered correctly in the conventional maps, but cannot be used when rendering tactile maps. The distance between them is far too small and their depiction would thus render the neighboring objects worthless.

In addition, it was necessary to select elements to be rendered from a large database, which contains several hundreds elements, and determine an appropriate level of map content generalization. The main method applied was the generalization method of elements classification and simplification, which allows to view the map content in a readable and clearly arranged format suitable for tactile perception (Fig. 1).

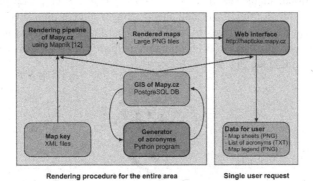

**Fig. 1.**  Development of tactile map rendering from geo-information database

## 2.4   Testing

A user-based testing procedure has been carried out in order to choose fillings that may be unambiguously identified through touch both in isolation and in the context of a real map sheet. Seven blind students, all experienced users of tactile graphics on swell paper, were involved in the testing phase and undertook the assigned tasks. The four types of filling emerged from this testing phase. In the second phase of testing, the testers were given a complete map sheet. This time, the aim was to check whether the identification of line and area symbols was unambiguous and also to examine the whole conception, tactile readability, and clear arrangement of the map sheet.

### 2.5   Map Lettering

To ensure maps are lettered clearly in Braille system, an algorithm was developed. It generates abbreviations of street names and residences so that they are unique in the given area and at the same time intuitive. Explanatory notes of the abbreviations located in the selected area are then exported to an individual text file. It is necessary to ensure sufficient distance of the description from the adjacent drawing; in case an overlap is inevitable, it is imperative to give the description an absolute priority.

### 2.6   Print Technology

We opted for the swell paper technology as it is the most widely available technology of relief embossing in the Czech Republic, which means that users can obtain the generated maps more easily in comparison to other technologies.

## 3   Results

### 3.1   Map Sheet Rendering

Unlike conventional maps available on web-based map servers, map underlays are rendered on individual, predefined map sheets using a unique map sheet designation. The reason is that they are offered to the users as hard (tactile) copy which requires a fixed format. Individual sheets in A4 format render an area of $300 \times 425$ m at an approximate scale of 1:1500 (see Fig. 2).

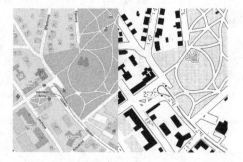

**Fig. 2.**   Example of how an area is displayed on a standard and a tactile map

The content of individual map sheets is based on the same source database as standard maps and has been processed with the same tool, that is, the aforementioned Mapnik

[10]. The indisputable advantage of this practice is that all updates in the database are also immediately reflected in the newly generated tactile maps.

## 3.2  Map Key

**Area Symbols.** All areas were grouped as follows (see also Fig. 3): buildings, water bodies, green areas, industrial areas. Buildings are marked as raised surfaces in their authentic ground plan. Water surfaces are marked using horizontal raster with an indented boundary line. The symbol for green areas applies to all grass and wooded areas; industrial areas are marked using a structured raster with an indented outline.

**Fig. 3.** Example of area symbols

All other areas are rendered without a raster to allow rendering other elements of the map.

**Line Symbols.** Streets and routes are the basic line elements of a tactile map. They are rendered in two different widths; the basic width option is wide enough to allow Braille map lettering (13 mm) while the narrow option (5 mm) is reserved mainly for paths in green areas and streets in high building density areas.

Other line symbols that complete the space and are thus rendered as well are tram lines, railways, and stairs. Other complementary line symbols are stand-alone walls, brooks, and cableways (see Fig. 4).

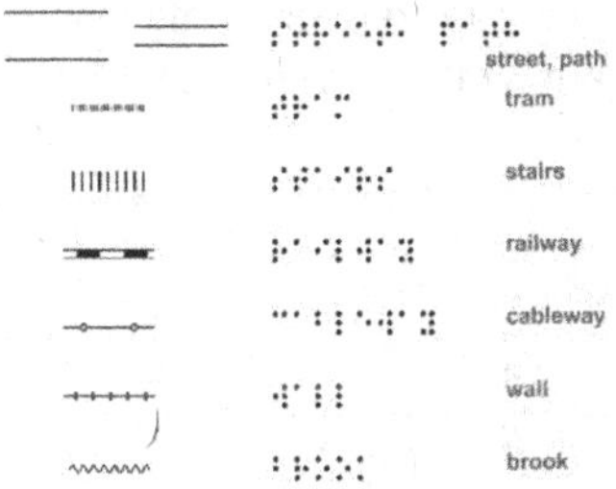

**Fig. 4.** Example of line symbols

**Point Symbols.** Although the database of point symbols offers an inexhaustible number of possible objects, it was necessary, for the sake of comprehensibility and clarity of the rendering, to reduce significantly the point symbols to merely three: tram stops, car parks, and churches located in blocks of houses.

### 3.3  Map Lettering

The map lettering is implemented in two ways in order to allow cooperation between blind and sighted users who cannot read Braille. The streets are lettered in the first place using three letters of their name – they are written in Braille in the street axis. Abbreviations are generated in a manner that prevents repetitions in the selected area.

These descriptions are completed with full names of the streets in light green color. Letterings of the names of squares are produced similarly but four letters are used to aid recognition (see Fig. 5). All abbreviations, together with an explanatory note on full names, are generated into an auxiliary file which is part of the map.

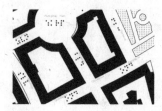

**Fig. 5.**  Example of map lettering (streets are marked using the first three letters of their name in the street axis whereas squares are marked using the first four letters in Braille in the center)

### 3.4  Web Interface

**Map Selection.**  Selecting the map of a given area (or a set of map sheets) does not differ from conventional map browsing, that is, searching for a location by its address, entering the name of the street (displaying the middle of the street), or typing the exact coordinates of the wanted point on the corresponding place of the map portal [12]. After the user has entered the desired location, the site generates a basic map sheet containing the requested location and the user can select the range of print (number of map sheets – see Fig. 6). Blind users may specify the print range using the spreadsheet mode (marking adjacent sheets). The site maintains the continuity between individual sheets to make generating larger maps possible. The map sheets can be complemented by map designation while minimizing interference with the map drawing.

**Fig. 6.**  Example of selecting map sheets for print

In the next step, the user can download the archive with the separate sheets (graphic files in PNG format), the list of abbreviations (a TXT text file), and—in case the user has selected this option—even the map legend in graphic form (a PNG file).

**Map Printing.** As mentioned above, the whole method uses swell paper technology. It is a relatively quick method which uses standard printing in the first stage. The content of the map is printed on a special sheet of paper and, after being processed by a special device equipped with an infrared lamp, the black print elements become embossed in the final stage. Currently we have at our disposal the following devices: the Zy Fuse Heater by the company Zychem and the P.I.A.F. by the company HARPO.

## 4    Discussion

An undeniable advantage of the discussed service is the possibility of generating tactile maps within a short period of time. Its availability contributes to the effective promotion of spatial orientation and development of tactile perception of the blind, while also raising public awareness. Finally, it facilitates the work of educational institutions.

However, two conditions must be met in order to enable a wider use of tactile maps: first, users need to consider them useful; second, they have to be able to interpret correctly the relatively complex map drawing. This requires either having experience with tactile map reading, or resolution and patience to acquire the needed skills.

Technically, it is necessary to consider the possibility of expanding the input geographic data by adding the output text attachments or implementing the content directly into the generated maps.

## 5    Conclusion

The service currently offers continuous view of the entire country, in a scale suitable for rendering urban environments with an emphasis on street network. In the future, we aim to achieve rendering of smaller scales and to increase the range of the rendered territory, as suggested below:

1. Smaller scale map rendering. Recently, we have prepared the map keys for tactile maps in scales of 1:100 000 and 1:50 000 (two basic levels of urban areas maps and a net of roads and railways).
2. A world map. We hope to prepare a basic map of the world using the Open Street Map data integration [11]. This way, we would be able to offer a tactile map of any place in the world (depending only on the OSM data availability).

# References

1. Benzen, B.L.: Orientation aids. In: Welch, R.L., Blash, B.B. (eds.) Foundation of Orientation & Mobility, pp. 291–355. AFB Press, New York (1980)
2. Buzzi, M.C., Buzzi, M., Leporini, B., Martusciello, L.: Making visual maps accessible to the blind. In: Stephanidis, C. (ed.) Universal Access in HCI, Part II, HCII 2011. LNCS, vol. 6766, pp. 271–280. Springer, Heidelberg (2011)
3. Červenka, P.: Maps and orientation plans for the Visually Impaired. Creation and Usage Methods (in Czech). 66 p., AULA, Prague (1999)
4. Ducasse, J., Macé, M., Jouffrais, C.: From open geographical data to tangible maps: improving the accessibility of maps for visually impaired people. In: ISPRS — International Archives of the Photogrammetry, Remote Sensing and Spatial Information Sciences XL- 3/W3, pp. 517–523 (2015)
5. Eriksson, Y., Gunnar, J., Strucel, M.: Tactile maps — Guidelines for the production of maps for the visually impaired. 78 p., The Swedish Library of Talking Books and Braille, Enskede (2003)
6. Miele, J.A.: Talking TMAP: Automated generation of audio-tactile maps using SmithKettlewell's TMAP software. Br. J. Vis. Impairment **24**(2), 93–100 (2006)
7. Taylor, B.T., et al.: TactileMaps.net A Web Interface for Generating Customized 3D–Printable Tactile Maps. ASSETS 2015, pp. 427–428. Lisbon, Portugal (2015)
8. Wang, Z., et al.: Instant tactile–audio map. In: Proceeding of the Eleventh International ACM SIGACCESS Conference on Computers and Accessibility – ASSETS 2009, pp. 43–50. ACM Press, New York, USA (2009)
9. Watanabe, T., Yamaguchi, T., Koda, S., Minatani, K.: Tactile map automated creation system using openstreetmap. In: Miesenberger, K., Fels, D., Archambault, D., Peňáz, P., Zagler, W. (eds.) ICCHP 2014, Part II. LNCS, vol. 8548, pp. 42–49. Springer, Heidelberg (2014)
10. Mapnik. http://mapnik.org
11. Open Street Maps. http://openstreetmap.org
12. Blind Friendly Maps. http://hapticke.mapy.cz

# BlindWeb Maps – An Interactive Web Service for the Selection and Generation of Personalized Audio-Tactile Maps

Timo Götzelmann[1(✉)] and Laura Eichler[2]

[1] Department of Computer Science, Nuremberg Institute of Technology, Nuremberg, Germany
Timo.Goetzelmann@ohm-university.eu
[2] Department of Computer Science, Technical University Dresden, Dresden, Germany
Laura.Eichler@tu-dresden.de

**Abstract.** Tactile maps may contribute to the orientation of blind people or alternatively be used for navigation. In the past, the generation of these maps was a manual task which considerably limited their availability. Nowadays, similar to visual maps, tactile maps can also be generated semi-automatically by tools and web services. The existing approaches enable users to generate maps by entering a specific address or point of interest. This can in principle be done by a blind user. However, these approaches actually show an image of the map on the users display which cannot be read by screen readers. Consequently, the blind user does not know what is on the map before it is printed. Ideally, the map selection process should give the user more information and freedom to select the desired excerpt. This paper introduces a novel web service for blind people to interactively select and automatically generate tactile maps. It adapts the interaction concept for map selection to the requirements of blind users whilst supporting multiple printing technologies. The integrated audio review of the map's contents allows earlier feedback to review if the currently selected map extract corresponds to the desired information need. Changes can be initiated before the map is printed which, especially for 3D printing, saves much time. The user is able to select map features to be included in the tactile map. Furthermore, the map rendering can be adapted to different zoom levels and supports multiple printing technologies. Finally, an evaluation with blind users was used to refine our approach.

**Keywords:** Tactile maps · Audio-tactile · Automated generation · Blind · Interview · Orientation · Worldwide · Accessibility · Embossing · Microcapsular · 3D printing

## 1 Introduction

Tactile maps may contribute to the orientation of blind people or alternatively be used for navigation. In the past, the generation of these maps was a manual task which considerably limited their availability. Nowadays, similar to visual maps, tactile maps can also be generated semi-automatically by tools and web services.

© Springer International Publishing Switzerland 2016
K. Miesenberger et al. (Eds.): ICCHP 2016, Part II, LNCS 9759, pp. 139–145, 2016.
DOI: 10.1007/978-3-319-41267-2_19

Today, physical representations of electronic tactile maps can be produced by a number of different techniques. Up to now, there are three different printing techniques used by automatic map generation systems. *Braille embossers* are used to print Braille text or graphics by punching a series of dots into printer paper. By varying the strength of punches for individual dots, some embossers are able to print different sizes of dots. When this is used in combination with halftone techniques, several height variations can be simulated. Alternatively, a combination of a common printer and a *thermal enhancer (fuser)* can be used. Chemically *treated swell (microcapsular)* paper is printed with monochrome graphics. Subsequently, the fuser heats the black parts above a certain threshold temperature, which causes them to swell. This technique has strengths for printing continuous graphics used in maps, however, in principle only one height level is possible. A recent technology for printing tactile maps are *3D printers*. The most common technique for consumer 3D printing is Fused Decomposition Modelling (FDM). Molten thermo-plastic polymer (e.g., polylactic acid) is deposited by a two dimensionally moving printing head. By sequentially printing multiple layers onto each other, numerous different height levels can be achieved which can be used to topologically group cartographic elements.

This paper introduces a novel web service (http://maps.blindweb.org) for blind people to interactively select and automatically generate tactile maps. In this approach, the resulting tactile maps can be printed by multiple methods.

## 2  Related Work

There have been multiple approaches which address the automatic generation of (audio-) tactile maps. The approach *Talking Tactile Tablet (TTT)* [1] used a frame including a touchpad which was connected to a computer. Embossed tactile sheets could be installed in the frame. After identifying the tactile sheets the user was able to explore the printed graphics and to request additional information at certain points. This system was used by a succeeding approach [2] which could be used by end users to order tactile US maps which were printed automatically by local Braille embossers or third party services: a prototypical system by Wang et al. [3] enabled to generate audio-tactile maps from normal maps designed for sighted people. It utilizes computer vision algorithms to read in labels and map features and creates SVG files including the extracted data. Reproduced tactile maps can be printed using thermal enhancers and subsequently be used along with a touchpad. This technique tackled the issue of limited availability of tactile maps, but was limited to existing printed maps.

The *Tactile Map Automated Creation System (TMACS)* [4] realized an important step towards blind person's mobility by offering a web service which produced street level maps after entering a departure and a destination address. By using a Japanese map database users were able to immediately generate map extracts which could be printed on microcapsular paper. A subsequent approach by Watanabe et al. [5] extended TMACS by using the OpenStreetMap database and provided the first approach which could instantly generate tactile street maps of the whole world. Another approach [6] introduced a process to generate tactile detail maps, which could be instantly printed on swell paper or automatically generated as 3D model for 3D printing. Recently, Taylor et al. [7] sketched another system supporting 3D printers and made suggestions for future improvements.

These approaches enable users to generate maps by entering a specific address or point of interest. This can in principle be done by a blind user. However, these approaches actually *show* an image of the map on the users display which cannot be read by screen readers. Consequently, the blind user does not know what is on the map before it is printed. Ideally, the map selection process should give the user more information and freedom to select the desired excerpt. Map providers for sighted users offer means to (i) enter an address, (ii) review the resulting map extract including details of the map features, (iii) make adjustments to the map extract by panning and zooming and (iv) enable to define individual informational needs of the user. Finally, multiple printing techniques for tactile graphics should be supported.

## 3    Our Approach

We ported our approach [6] to a web service which is online since 2014 and has been used for the evaluation with blind users (see Fig. 1). The aim was to adapt the interaction concept for map selection to the requirements of blind users whilst supporting multiple printing technologies.

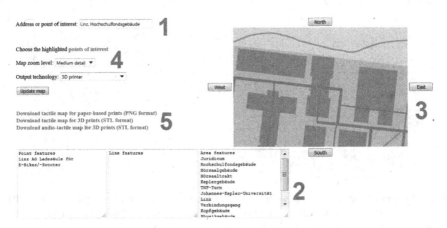

**Fig. 1.** Screenshot of BlindWeb Maps. After entering address (1), included map features (2) can be read by screen readers. The extract can be shifted by directional buttons (3), changes of map features are reported immediately. Map features, zoom level and output technology can be chosen (4) and generated (5) as graphics file or 3D model.

In this approach the user is free to enter either an address or a proper name of a point of his or her interest to immediately generate a tactile map. In order to allow the user to examine the result before the actual printing process, lists of map features included in the map are shown which can be read by usual screen readers. We transferred the prevalent panning of visual maps via mouse interaction to directional buttons which can be used by blind persons with their keyboard. Each shifting action advances the map by 1/3 in the desired cardinal direction. Additionally, the users immediately get feedback about changes of map features caused by panning the map. Another list, accessible by screen readers, informs about map features which are new to the map extract and those which dropped out.

On the one hand, it is crucial to limit the number of elements of tactile maps. On the other hand, it is important to fit the map content to the informational needs of the user. Hence, we developed the functionality for customizable filtering of map features. Users can select (groups of) map features they are interested in in order to adapt the rendering of the map to their needs. Besides usual map features (such as shops, bus stops) special blind specific map features can be highlighted on the map. This includes elements for building entrances, guided traffic lights and tactile paving.

Zooming is realized by offering the selection of multiple detail levels for the maps. In order to realize a reasonable proportion and effective tactile presentation of map contents different rendering styles for each zooming level are used. In principle, our approach can serve the whole range of map zoom levels (i.e., highly detailed map up to world map). Tactile maps have to be generated with their printing technologies in mind – which have differing technical constraints. Similar to the aforementioned zooming, our approach supports individual rendering styles for each technology to adapt the generated maps to the technology's inherent strengths. For example, multiple height levels are only used for 3D printing – for swell paper dotted/hatched textures are used instead (see Fig. 2-left).

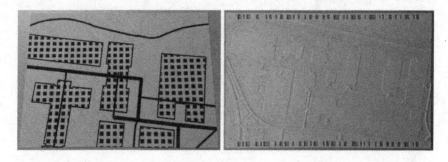

**Fig. 2.** Generated map extract of Johannes-Kepler-University Linz for swell paper prints (left), i.e., automatically adapted to a single height level. 3D printed map including optical markers for optional support of audio-tactile interaction (right).

Technically our approach works as follows: After an address or point of interest is given by the user the web service *OpenStreetMap Nominatim* is used to obtain corresponding GPS coordinates. Next, depending on the zoom level a bounding box is defined and used to request detailed map data from the *OpenStreetMap API* web service. Our web service processes and filters the map data for the requirements of blind users and extracts the textual content of the map features. The map rendering as well as the generation of the 3D models is according to our dedicated approach [6]. Panning the map causes shifting of the bounding box values, selection of another zoom level narrows or widens the bounding box extents. There are individual rendering styles: for (i) different zoom levels and (ii) different printing technologies. All the interaction elements are accessible via shortcuts.

Finally, the user can download the map either as image file for paper bound printing technologies or as 3D model for 3D printers. A medium detailed map covers an area of $422 \times 287$ m (at mid-latitude). The scale is depending on the printed size of the map. For a map of $22,5 \times 15$ cm this is equivalent to a scale of 1:1875. The produced maps are intended to be used as audio-tactile maps in conjunction with a mobile phone (e.g., by [8, 9]). This helps to reduce the tactile complexity by removing Braille labels and limiting the number of symbols and markers.

By using such an interactive approach the user can obtain additional information about map features (such as name and type of it) by pointing at the desired map feature. However, if desired, the user is also able to generate pure tactile maps without elements used for interaction.

## 4  Evaluation

We evaluated a preliminary version of our approach by interviews with blind and visually impaired people in order to obtain suggestions about the selection process as well as the design of automatically produced tactile maps.

### 4.1  Participants

The questionnaire was conducted among 12 visually impaired persons (five female) with an average age of $43.08 \pm 13.43$ years. Seven of the participants were blind since their birth or early childhood, four of them late-blind and one had low vision. Four participants were able to participate in person, the other eight were interviewed by telephone. Except for one all individuals were familiar with the concept of tactile maps, 3D models and reliefs as well as graphics made with a Braille printer. Furthermore, most of them knew tactile maps made with micro capsule paper and deep-drawn foil.

### 4.2  Procedure

After an introduction to the web application and its functionality as well as the result each individual was asked to answer questions about their experience with tactile maps, how they orientate in an unknown area and what they are most interested in to find on a tactile map. They were asked about their own suggestions to improve the web interface as well as the tactile map. Additionally, the face-to-face interviewees were asked to give an opinion about two 3D printed maps made with BlindWeb Maps again with suggestions to improve on the quality and legibility.

### 4.3 Results

The preliminary version included the option to mark the following points of interest as the only point features in the map: pharmacies, doctor's offices, cash dispensers, mail boxes, building entrances and public transport (such as tram or bus stops). To add more useful POIs to the list or eliminate unnecessary elements the interviewed person had the task to assess a map element, including both existing and suggested POIs. Every participant expressed the importance of pedestrian lights (especially with audio signal), which is one of the most relevant components for the orientation of a visually impaired person, right after public transport and building entrances. Restaurants, shops, hotels as well as the already existing POIs were equally marked as interesting and not interesting, which resulted from the individual usage of such a map. To cope with the variety of individual map features we followed the suggestion to sort the elements into categories. The implemented categories were Health, Eat and Drink, Shops and Service, Culture and Entertainment, Nature and Leisure, Traveling, and Accessibility.

Each of the participants mentioned that multiple zoom levels should be supported. 92 % of the interviewees requested more than two zoom levels. We integrated the functionality for the selection of three different zoom levels which uses dedicated map rendering styles.

## 5    Conclusion and Future Work

This paper introduced a novel web service, which enables to generate tactile maps which can be printed by multiple techniques. It focused on the technical approach to provide blind users with a more adequate search process, which allows to review and adjust the map extract. Thus, we transferred interaction techniques known from map web services for sighted users, which are inaccessible to blind users, to more adequate techniques. The audio review of the map's contents allows earlier feedback if the currently selected map extract corresponds to the desired information need. Changes can be initiated before the map is printed which, especially for 3D printing, saves much time.

Based on a comprehensive interview with blind and visually impaired users we evaluated a preliminary version of the web service and initiated multiple changes to better satisfy the user's needs. Accordingly, it is possible to personalize maps by selection of desired points of interest. This may help to compromise between individual informational need of the user and to simultaneously limit the tactile complexity of the map. Additionally, users can choose to highlight map features particularly important to blind people (i.e., building entrances, assisted traffic lights). Finally, to enable both a limited complexity of the tactile map and detailed information on specific map features our approach integrates support for audio tactile maps [8, 9] which allow to interactively request additional information during the exploration of the printed tactile map.

Despite this paper did not focusing on map rendering styles, but instead the interaction concept and its technical approach, this is an important part of our future work. This approach supports multiple zoom levels as well as multiple printing technologies using individual map rendering styles. However, the optimization of automated map rendering styles for blind people at different zoom levels and printing technologies has to be discussed by the scientific community. There is already manifold expertise for automated map rendering at different zoom levels using miscellaneous technologies in the scientific community (e.g., [2, 5]). By collaboration a unified platform for qualitatively high tactile maps available for blind people all over the world can be formed. Thus, this has to be accompanied by a constructive dialogue in a highly international context and verified by further user studies.

# References

1. Landau, S., Wells, L.: Merging tactile sensory input and audio data by means of the talking tactile tablet. In: Proceedings of EuroHaptics 2003, pp. 414–418 (2003)
2. Miele, J.A., Landau, S., Gilden, D.: Talking TMAP: automated generation of audio-tactile maps using Smith-Kettlewell's TMAP software. Br. J. Vis. Impairment **24**, 93–100 (2006)
3. Wang, Z., Li, B., Hedgpeth, T., Haven, T.: Instant tactile-audio map: enabling access to digital maps for people with visual impairment. In: Proceedings of the 11th International ACM SIGACCESS Conference on Computers & Accessibility, pp. 43–50. ACM (2009)
4. Minatani, K., Watanabe, T., Yamaguchi, T., Watanabe, K., Akiyama, J., Miyagi, M., Oouchi, S.: Tactile map automated creation system to enhance the mobility of blind persons–its design concept and evaluation through experiment. In: Miesenberger, K., Klaus, J., Zagler, W., Karshmer, A. (eds.) ICCHP 2010, Part II. LNCS, vol. 6180, pp. 534–540. Springer, Heidelberg (2010)
5. Watanabe, T., Yamaguchi, T., Koda, S., Minatani, K.: Tactile map automated creation system using OpenStreetMap. In: Miesenberger, K., Fels, D., Archambault, D., Peňáz, P., Zagler, W. (eds.) ICCHP 2014, Part II. LNCS, vol. 8548, pp. 42–49. Springer, Heidelberg (2014)
6. Götzelmann, T., Pavkovic, A.: Towards automatically generated tactile detail maps by 3D printers for blind persons. In: Miesenberger, K., Fels, D., Archambault, D., Peňáz, P., Zagler, W. (eds.) ICCHP 2014, Part II. LNCS, vol. 8548, pp. 1–7. Springer, Heidelberg (2014)
7. Taylor, B.T., Dey, A.K., Siewiorek, D.P., Smailagic, A.: TactileMaps.net: a web interface for generating customized 3D-printable tactile maps. In: Proceedings of the 17th International ACM SIGACCESS Conference on Computers & Accessibility, pp. 427–428. ACM (2015)
8. Götzelmann, T., Winkler, K.: SmartTactMaps: a smartphone-based approach to support blind persons in exploring tactile maps. In: Proceedings of the 8th ACM International Conference on Pervasive Technologies Related to Assistive Environments (PETRAE 2015), pp. 2:1–2:8. ACM (2015)
9. Götzelmann, T.: CapMaps: capacitive sensing 3D printed audio-tactile maps. In: Miesenberger, K., Bühler, C., Penaz, P. (eds.) ICCHP 2016, Part II. LNCS, vol. 9759, pp. 144–150. Springer, Heidelberg (2016). doi:10.1007/978-3-319-41267-2_20

# CapMaps

## Capacitive Sensing 3D Printed Audio-Tactile Maps

Timo Götzelmann[✉]

Department of Computer Science, Nuremberg Institute of Technology,
Nuremberg, Germany
`Timo.Goetzelmann@ohm-university.eu`

**Abstract.** Tactile maps can be useful tools for blind people for navigation and orientation tasks. Apart from static maps, there are techniques to augment tactile maps with audio content. They can be used to interact with the map content, to offer extra information and to reduce the tactile complexity of a map. Studies show that audio-tactile maps can be more efficient and satisfying for the user than pure tactile maps without audio feedback. A major challenge of audio-tactile maps is the linkage of tactile elements with audio content and interactivity. This paper introduces a novel approach to link 3D printed tactile maps with mobile devices, such as smartphones and tablets, in a flexible way to enable interactivity and audio-support. By integrating conductive filaments into the printed maps it seamlessly integrates into the 3D printing process. This allows to automatically recognize the tactile map by a single press at its corner. Additionally, the arrangement of the tactile map on the mobile device is flexible and detected automatically which eases the use of these maps. The practicability of this approach is shown by a dedicated feasibility study.

**Keywords:** Tactile maps · Audio-tactile · Blind · Orientation · Worldwide · Accessibility · Tangible user interfaces · 3D printing · Touch screen · Capacitive sensing

## 1 Introduction

Tactile maps can be useful tools for blind people for navigation and orientation tasks. In the latter case, tactile maps can be used to inform about an area beforehand. Alternatively, the consultation of tactile maps in situ may contribute to orientation for blind people. In this context, portability of the map is of particular importance.

In the past, the construction of tactile maps has been a manual task which drastically limited their availability. Today, physical representations of electronic tactile maps can be produced by a number of different techniques. Thermoforming refers to a process of generating a negative template and to deforming thermoplastic foils by heating them and sucking them towards this template with low pressure. This allows reproduction of continuous graphics (cartographic line and area features) with multiple height levels which can be used to topologically group elements. This technology is rather expensive, and the creation of the templates is laborious. Hence, it is uncommon to use this technique for personal use. Tactile embossers punch a series of dots into

© Springer International Publishing Switzerland 2016
K. Miesenberger et al. (Eds.): ICCHP 2016, Part II, LNCS 9759, pp. 146–152, 2016.
DOI: 10.1007/978-3-319-41267-2_20

printer paper. Some embossers are able to vary the strength of punches, which result in different sizes of dots. In combination with halftone techniques, this in principle allows simulation of a smaller number of height levels. Currently, embossers are the optimal choice to print Braille letters. However, the graphical abilities of embossers are limited, since continuous graphics have to be approximated by dots. Additionally, in contrast to thermoforming, the simulation of multiple consecutive height levels is not expedient. Another process enables printing of black and white graphics on chemically treated paper (microcapsular paper/swell paper) by ordinary printers. Subsequently, the printed sheet is heated by a thermal enhancer (also fuser) which elevates black parts of the printed graphics. This technique makes it possible to print complex graphics with continuous elements. However, because only the black parts are elevated by heating, only one height level can be reproduced. Thin lines as well as large black areas can be problematic, because the elevation of these parts can be skewed which may alter the intended tactile sensation. 3D printers are still uncommon, but recently there have been an increasing number of publications which also consider this printing technique. The most common 3D printing technique for the consumer market is Fused Decomposition Modelling (FDM), which is based on the disposition of molten thermoplastic polymers (filaments) which are positioned by a mechanical printing head. Braille letters can also be printed with this technology, but due to its limited printing speed, there are more adequate technologies for this task. On the contrary, its graphical abilities make it possible to print graphics as continuous elements. Even low-cost 3D printers already technically allow numerous high levels with resolutions up to 20 microns (0.02 mm) height difference. This additional level of freedom enables structuration of map features into multiple topological areas which might be used to support their readability. Another advantage is that multiple filaments with different immanent characteristics can be printed into a single, monolithic map, which is utilized in this paper.

Besides static maps, there are techniques to augment tactile maps with audio content. They can be used to interact with the map content, to offer extra information and to reduce the tactile complexity of printed maps. This is particularly important to consider physiological constraints of blind users' tactile sense and to limit the cognitive load whilst reading the map. Such audio-tactile maps can be more efficient and satisfying for the user than pure tactile maps without audio feedback [1]. A major challenge of audio-tactile maps is the linkage of tactile elements with audio content and interactivity. This paper introduces a novel approach to link 3D printed tactile maps with mobile devices, such as smartphones and tablets, in a flexible way to enable interactivity and audio support. By integrating conductive filaments into the printed maps it seamlessly integrates into the 3D printing process.

## 2   Related Work

Accessible audio-tactile maps with physical map representatives for blind people have been addressed with different technologies. Integrated approaches use dedicated hardware to develop highly interactive applications for audio-tactile maps. Zeng et al. introduce multiple approaches which produce interactive tactile maps which can' immediately adapt their appearance on the tactile display (e.g., [4, 5]). Schmitz & Ertl [6] use a tactile display for detailed building plans and outdoor maps which are enriched by text-to-speech (TTS) messages. A major strength of these approaches is the immediate adaptivity of the tactile rendition on the tactile display. However, this technology is very expensive and its portability is limited to desktop usage.

Hybrid approaches use physical tactile maps in combination with computers or mobile devices. The have to store a virtual representation (or at least parts of it) from the physical map which is used to augment the user interaction with the map. These approaches have to solve two additional tasks: (i) the recognition (identification) of the currently used map and (ii) the layout (arrangement) issue to accommodate the physical map with the virtual map data. An approach named Touchplates [7] uses acrylic overlays including visual tags, which can be recognized by tabletops such as Microsoft surface table. It was able to recognize these maps automatically and to determine their arrangement. Its key technology (infrared based diffused illumination) used to recognize the optical markers is built in touch tables which are not portable. Graf [8] carried our experiments with embossed tactile maps and makes several suggestions for linking physical maps with their virtual representatives which are partly used in the following approaches.

The approach Talking Tactile Tablet (TTT) [9] consisted of a frame with a touch sensitive surface which was connected to a computer by a USB interface. Special tactile sheets had to be exactly mounted into this frame which is aligned to three calibration points. In order to recognize the mounted sheet, the user had to touch several points on the tactile sheets. A subsequent approach [10] was to able produce US maps for the TTT automatically by local Braille embossers or third party companies. Wang et al. [11] introduced a prototype system using a touchpad and a computer display to support the exploration of street networks which has been evaluated by blindfolded people. Automatically generated maps could be printed by thermal enhancers and embossers and placed on the touchpad. These tactile maps are were recognized automatically and had to be placed exactly on the touchpad. A common issue of these techniques is the limited portability.

Portability of tactile maps may be advantageous for the spatial understanding of blind users for unfamiliar urban environments [12]. In contrast to the previous approaches the maps by Sennette et al. [13] were applicable to portable devices, such as tablet and smartphones. Using the popular OpenStreetMap database, the map data was edited and enriched by multimedia content, whilst the tactile maps were generated by a thermal enhancer. To use these maps, they had to be aligned exactly with the display's border on the mobile device, the map contents had to be preloaded, since they weren't recognized automatically. Finally, another portable approach [14] based on automatically recognizing 3D printed tactile maps, including multiple height levels by standard smartphones' built-in cameras. Barcodes attached to the upper and lower border of the tactile map encoded the geographic coordinates of the map's area, which allow the application to download the corresponding map data. An optical finger detection analyzed the user's map exploration by their fingers. This approach automatically recognized the map and had weaker constraints to the arrangement of the tactile map. However, this approach only supported one-handed exploration of the map and was sensitive to bad lighting conditions. In the following, this paper introduces a novel approach which automatically recognizes the tactile map by a single press at its corner. Additionally, the arrangement of the tactile map on the mobile device is flexible and detected automatically.

# 3   Approach

Most of the current mobile devices integrate capacitive touch screens, which enable to detect user interaction with the device's display. They localize interaction with the display by load changes caused by touch of a human finger. The touch sensor may be applied onto the display and touched directly by the user (surface capacitance) or be placed underneath an insulating surface (projected capacitance). This indirect technology allows even detection of the proximity of fingers (even through thin materials) and is the most common technology for mobile devices. Usually ten fingers can be detected concurrently. Conductive materials can be used to pass capacitive coupling, which is exploited by tangible user interfaces such as Sketch-a-TUI [15]. This approach allows to sketching conductive wires by a special ink dispenser and thus, to add interactivity to objects placed on capacitive touch screens. These wires have recently also been used [16] with conductive filament which can be deposited at exact positions and 3D printed along with normal (isolating) filament. In this paper we extend this concept to form a capacitive code. By encoding combinations of concurrent touch points in predefined spatially arrangements, both the identification and the arrangement issue (see Sect. 2) can be solved. To do so, a touch of the user on the one side of the 3D printed capacitive code is forked into multiple locations on the display's surface, inducing the detection of multiple concurrent touches. Software analyzes concurrent touches and classifies them into normal touches and specific codes. Thus, the 3D printed tactile map is able to transmit information to the surface by a single touch.

The codes consist of both a conductive and a surrounding isolating part. The conductive part has a flat surface and a set of equidistant cylinders which contact the touch display. In this approach, distances between cylinders are used to encode information. In order to use it for audio-tactile maps, these capacitive codes are attached to the upper left edge of the tactile map (see Fig. 1) which also helps blind users to identify the orientation of the map. They are structured into four cylinders. The first both cylinders contacting the touch surface are located in a certain distance to each other and serve as identification as capacitive code. The remaining cylinders are located in multiples of this distance and encode the corresponding ID of the map. Since the

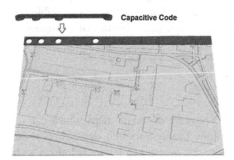
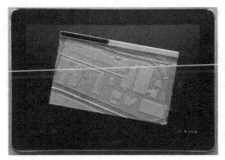

**Fig. 1.** Generated 3D model (left) with conductive element (dark grey) which bifurcates a touch on top to multiple concurrent touches on the touch display - Printed audio-tactile map with 10" tablet fixed by adhesive tape (right).

cylinders are arranged in a straight line alongside the map, the locations of touch points detected by the touch screen are used to compute its degree of skewing.

When the mobile application is started, it waits for the user to place a map on the display and to touch the identification bar at the upper left corner of the map. The map's orientation is determined by the sequence of touch points forked to the touch display. The recognized code allows the software to look up a table containing metadata about this map. Along with the map's ID, its geodetic data of the minimum and maximum coordinates and the physical map size is stored. By using the map's coordinates, the corresponding map contents can be obtained online with OpenStreetMap (OSM) [17] or by a cached version offline. In the latter case, additional annotations and multimedia content can be used in conjunction. Since touches are registered through the thin tactile map the user is able to explore it and to obtain audio information about map features. The user initiates commands by touch gestures (see Sect. 4).

## 4   Feasibility Study

To evaluate our approach, a feasibility study has been conducted. Using an existing approach [18], multiple tactile maps were generated and enriched by capacitive codes by using a free, open-source constructive solid modelling software OpenSCAD [19]. These were printed (see Fig. 1) by a dual-head 3D-printer (Velleman Vertex K8400) utilizing normal PLA (polylactic acid) and conductive filament (Trijexx Conductive). An Android application has been developed which is able to recognize the codes and uses the internal constant for pixel density the measure distances between points and the user interaction with the map. To encode the cylinders contacting the surface, a minimum distance of 5 mm between cylinders has been chosen. Both of the following two cylinders were able to be arranged in five different equidistant positions, which resulted in 25 combinations.

Because of the automatic recognition and detection of the arrangement, the users had to simply fix the map on the display by elastic straps or two short strips of adhesive tape. When the user touched the identification bar, the application first reported the scale of the map. When GPS coordinates were present, subsequently the distance and orientation of the map to the real world was reported. During the tactile exploration of the map, the users were able to obtain information about the map features a double tap (name of feature), a triple tap (type of feature) or a long press (names of surrounding map features).

## 5   Discussion and Future Work

This paper introduced a novel approach for 3D printing of tactile maps which can be recognized and augmented by audio descriptions through mobile devices. For the identification of the maps capacitive markers are used, which can be printed along with map content by our approach in a single turn. Compared to existing approaches of audio-tactile maps using microcapsular paper, this approach allows multiple height levels which can be used encode topological information into maps. CapMaps are recognized by mobile devices, such as tablets and smartphones which utilize capacitive touchscreens by a single touch on the map's corner. The maps do not have to be aligned in a specific way; their alignment is automatically detected by the capacitive markers.

This paper focused on the technical approach of linking physical tactile maps with tablets and smartphones. In our future work, we plan to carry out user studies about the impact and usability of the new possibilities of this approach for a dedicated paper. In particular, we investigate in which way the tactile maps of our portable approach have to be rendered, as well as how the interactive content should be ideally structured to support orientation and navigation tasks on site.

# References

1. Brock, A.M., Truillet, P., Oriola, B., Picard, D., Jouffrais, C.: Interactivity improves usability of geographic maps for visually impaired people. Hum. Comput. Interact. **30**, 156–194 (2015)

2. Poppinga, B., Magnusson, C., Pielot, M., Rassmus-Gröhn, K.: TouchOver map: audio-tactile exploration of interactive maps. In: Proceedings of the 13th International Conference on Human Computer Interaction with Mobile Devices and Services, pp. 545–550. ACM (2011)

3. Su, J., Rosenzweig, A., Goel, A., de Lara, E., Truong, K.N.: Timbremap: enabling the visu-ally-impaired to use maps on touch-enabled devices. In: Proceedings of 12th International Conference on Human Computer Interaction with Mobile Devices and Services, pp. 17–26. ACM (2010)

4. Zeng, L., Miao, M., Weber, G.: Interactive audio-haptic map explorer on a tactile display. Interact. Comput. **27**, 413–429 (2015)

5. Zeng, L., Weber, G.: ATMap: annotated tactile maps for the visually impaired. In: Esposito, A., Esposito, A.M., Vinciarelli, A., Hoffmann, R., Müller, V.C. (eds.) COST 2102. LNCS, vol. 7403, pp. 290–298. Springer, Heidelberg (2012)

6. Schmitz, B., Ertl, T.: Interactively displaying maps on a tactile graphics display. In: SKALID 2012–Spatial Knowledge Acquisition with Limited Information Displays. 13 (2012)

7. Kane, S.K., Morris, M.R., Wobbrock, J.O.: Touchplates: low-cost tactile overlays for visually impaired touch screen users. In: Proceedings of the 15th International ACM SIGACCESS Conference on Computers and Accessibility, p. 22. ACM (2013)

8. Graf, C.: Verbally annotated tactile maps – challenges and approaches. In: Hölscher, C., Shipley, T.F., Olivetti Belardinelli, M., Bateman, J.A., Newcombe, N.S. (eds.) Spatial Cognition VII. LNCS, vol. 6222, pp. 303–318. Springer, Heidelberg (2010)

9. Landau, S., Wells, L.: Merging tactile sensory input and audio data by means of the talking tactile tablet. In: Proceedings of EuroHaptics 2003, pp. 414–418 (2003)

10. Miele, J.A., Landau, S., Gilden, D.: Talking TMAP: automated generation of audio-tactile maps using Smith-Kettlewell's TMAP software. Br. J. Visual Impairment **24**, 93–100 (2006)

11. Wang, Z., Li, B., Hedgpeth, T., Haven, T.: Instant Tactile-audio map: enabling access to digital maps for people with visual impairment. In: Proceedings of the 11th International ACM SIGACCESS Conference on Computers & Accessibility, pp. 43–50. ACM (2009)

12. Espinosa, M., Ungar, S., Ochaíta, E., Blades, M., Spencer, C.: Comparing methods for introducing blind and visually impaired people to unfamiliar urban environments. J. Environ. Psychol. **18**, 277–287 (1998)
13. Senette, C., Buzzi, M.C., Buzzi, M., Leporini, B., Martusciello, L.: Enriching Graphic Maps to Enable Multimodal Interaction by Blind People. In: Stephanidis, C., Antona, M. (eds.) UAHCI 2013, Part I. LNCS, vol. 8009, pp. 576–583. Springer, Heidelberg (2013)
14. Götzelmann, T., Winkler, K.: SmartTactMaps: a smartphone-based approach to support blind persons in exploring tactile maps. In: Proceedings of the 8th ACM International Conference on PErvasive Technologies Related to Assistive Environments (PETRAE 2015), pp. 2:1–2:8. ACM (2015)
15. Wiethoff, A., Schneider, H., Rohs, M., Butz, A., Greenberg, S.: Sketch-a-TUI: low cost prototyping of tangible interactions using cardboard and conductive ink. Proceedings of the Sixth International Conference on Tangible, Embedded and Embodied Interaction, pp. 309–312. ACM, New York (2012)
16. Savage, V., Schmidt, R., Grossman, T., Fitzmaurice, G., Hartmann, B.: A series of tubes: adding interactivity to 3D prints using internal pipes. In: Proceedings of the 27th Annual ACM Symposium on User Interface Software and Technology, pp. 3–12. ACM (2014)
17. Haklay, M., Weber, P.: Openstreetmap: User-generated Street Maps. Pervasive Comput., IEEE. **7**, 12–18 (2008)
18. Götzelmann, T., Pavkovic, A.: Towards automatically generated tactile detail maps by 3D printers for blind persons. In: Miesenberger, K., Fels, D., Archambault, D., Peňáz, P., Zagler, W. (eds.) ICCHP 2014, Part II. LNCS, vol. 8548, pp. 1–7. Springer, Heidelberg (2014)
19. Kintel, M., Wolf, C.: OpenSCAD - The Programmers Solid 3D CAD Modeller, http://www.openscad.org/

# Empirical Study on Quality and Effectiveness of Tactile Maps Using HaptOSM System

Daniel Hänßgen[1]([✉]), Nils Waldt[1], and Gerhard Weber[2]

[1] Faculty II - Mechanical Engineering, University of Applied Sciences
and Arts Hanover, Ricklinger Stadtweg 120, 30459 Hannover, Germany
`daniel.haenssgen@hs-hannover.de`
[2] Department of Computer Science, Technische Universität Dresden,
01062 Dresden, Germany

**Abstract.** This paper covers an empirical study on the quality and effectiveness of tactile maps using the HaptOSM system. HaptOSM is a combination of specialised hardware and software using OpenStreetMap data to create individual tactile maps for blind and visually impaired people. The almost entirely automated manufacturing process makes a single copy per map possible. The study tests the overall quality of HaptOSM tactile maps and compares the suitability of writing film and Braille paper against each other.

**Keywords:** Tactile maps · Blind · Individual · OpenStreetMap · XML · G-Code · CNC · Braille paper · Writing film

## 1 Introduction

The availability of maps to orient oneself in an unknown area is very common today, so moving freely around in public space should be a matter of course for everybody. In contrast, there is only a very limited – and often outdated – choice of haptic maps available for blind and visually impaired people [8]. HaptOSM, shown at the ICCHP 2014 in St. Denis, is a system that addresses this matter [2]. The HaptOSM-software uses OpenStreetMap[1] data along with a couple of parameters and converts them into G-Code [3]. This G-Code is then used to emboss map-data on Braille paper or writing film with a special CNC-Router. It has been found that haptic properties and level of detail on the map are essential concerning the usability of these customized maps. Too little detail makes a map of too little use, but too much detail can render a map also useless, because individual features can no longer be distinguished from each other. This paper shows the methodology applied and early results of an empirical study that was conducted to ensure the quality and versatility of HaptOSM maps.

---

[1] http://www.openstreetmap.org.

© Springer International Publishing Switzerland 2016
K. Miesenberger et al. (Eds.): ICCHP 2016, Part II, LNCS 9759, pp. 153–159, 2016.
DOI: 10.1007/978-3-319-41267-2_21

## 2  State of the Art

Using the OpenStreetMap as data source for tactile maps already showed promising results in the past [10]. The HyperBraille display[2] and embossings from TIGER[3] were used to create tactile information. Other solutions can be found at the corresponding OpenStreetMap wiki-page[4]. Although non of these systems are commercially available yet, there is an online service and a software product by Thinkable[TM] providing tactile maps[5]. The online service called RouteTactile[TM] creates the map data, whereas the software product called TactileView[TM] prints the map using a Braille embosser (e.g. TIGER). The most common manufacturing techniques for tactile information are thermoforming and micro-capsule paper [5,7]. Several studies have already been conducted to compare those two techniques. These papers although came to varying conclusions. While (Ungar et al. [9]) and (Nagel and Coulson [4]) suggested that using micro-capsule paper is the more suitable than thermoforming, other research found no significant difference between the two techniques [6]. (Gardiner and Perkins [1]) showed significant benefits towards thermoforming due to well-designed thermoformed maps offering more constant results than micro-capsule paper.

## 3  Methodology Used

A survey was carried out to get more decent knowledge about the needs and preferences of the target group. Suitable test persons were found using public mailing lists. For example: METTERNICH[6] and OHP[7]. In addition the "Blinden- und Sehbehindertenverband Niedersachsen e. V. (BVN)" (german for "Association of the Blind and Visually Impaired Lower Saxony")[8] was asked for further test persons. 21 test persons aged between 29 and 60 have participated in this study. All survey participants were asked to evaluate two maps on Braille paper[9] and writing film[10] showing identical geographical data. Therefore both materials can be compared against each other.

Figure 1 shows a graphical representation of the tactile map used during the study. On the actual map lines were embossed with about 0.7 mm width and Braille dots with about 1.3 mm diameter. To improve information content and

---

[2] http://www.hyperbraille.de/.

[3] https://viewplus.com/.

[4] http://wiki.openstreetmap.org/wiki/HaptoRender.

[5] http://www.routetactile.com/mapmaker.asp.

[6] http://www.blindzeln.net/mailman/listinfo/metternich.

[7] http://www.as-2.de/mailman/listinfo/ohp.

[8] http://blindenverband.org.

[9] Braille paper is a paper intended to be used with Braille embossers. It has a grammage of $160\,g/m^2$, about twice that of standard paper.

[10] Writing film is an opaque, white, $120\,\mu m$ thick sheet of plastic and must not be confused with drawing film, a transparent sheet of plastic only $45\,\mu m$ thick.

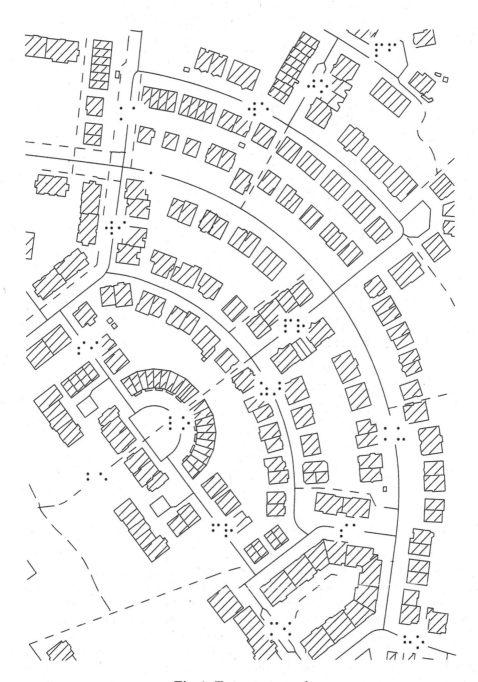

**Fig. 1.** Test map - page 1

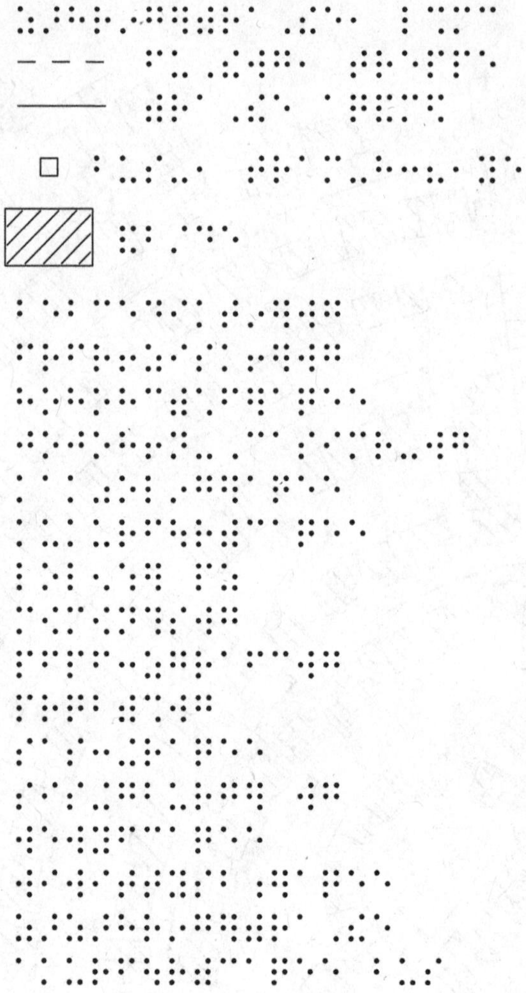

**Fig. 2.** Test map - page 2

clarity the maps had abbreviations for street names and bus stops instead of the full names. A second sheet (Fig. 2) was given with explanations and a legend on how the different elements of the map feel like. The map shows a residential area of Leimen in Baden-Württemberg, Germany on a scale of 1 : 1500. Fortunately non of the test persons knew this area before, thus preventing unequal previous knowledge. The hatched polygons represent buildings. Continuous lines represent streets and dashed lines represent foot paths. Street names are abbreviated using two Braille letters and bus stops are abbreviated using just one Braille letter. The survey was conducted via interviews on telephone, as most of the test persons are located outside of Hanover. The test persons were asked not to examine the maps before the interview to ensure identical initial conditions.

## 4   R&D and Results

The test persons were asked for the following personal data: (a) their current age and the age when they became blind or if they have remaining eye-sight, (b) other disabilities that could influence their sense of touch and (c) their experience with tactile maps. The survey itself consists of a number of questions that had to be answered using a scale of 1 to 10 for both Braille paper and writing film. While 10 means 'no further improvement needed (perfect)' and 1 means 'not usable at all'.

The first question considered the quality of the Braille writing ("How do you evaluate the readability of the Braille writing?"). Second question aimed at the distinguishably of foot path (dashed line) and streets (continuous line) ("How easy do you find it to distinguish between streets and foot paths?"). The third question asked for the quality and choice of the symbols used for bus stops and buildings ("How do you evaluate the readability of the used symbols and do you find the symbols intuitive?"). Table 1 summarizes the results.

**Table 1.** Question results

|  | Writing film | | Braille paper | |
| --- | --- | --- | --- | --- |
|  | Median | $\sigma$ | Median | $\sigma$ |
| Q1: Braille quality | 8 | 1.38 | 6 | 1.91 |
| Q2: foot path/street | 8 | 1.43 | 4 | 2.73 |
| Q3: symbols | 8.5 | 2.02 | 7.5 | 1.69 |

The table shows a significant preference for the writing film concerning Braille text and foot paths or streets. However further investigation on the maps sent to the test persons has shown some unexpected problems. Comparing the used maps with new ones showed significant damage due to the transport. Reduction in embossing strength as well as "wrinkles" that could be misinterpreted as streets were found. Without these faults and if the embossing on Braille paper were as good as on writing film, almost all test persons would have preferred paper, because of the more natural touch of this material. Only two persons said that they preferred writing film, because of its higher durability. Those two were running and hiking and need a waterproof map. So from this point of view there is no clear recommendation for one of these materials used. Assuming both materials would give similar embossing quality, the choice remains to the purpose of the individual. After the questionnaire, all participants chose writing film to make the routing test due to the stronger embossing.

A start point and a destination were given to the test persons. The task was then to find the correct street for that route. The evaluation criterion was the time required to find the requested street name including the time needed to decode the abbreviations for the street names. By looking at the actual data an unexpected relation was shown: The test persons, who said having only little or no experience with maps, were the fastest in finding the correct route. Whereas the test persons, who said having rich experience with maps, were the slowest. Intriguingly this relationship has nothing to do with the age of the persons. This could be explained with the fact, that experienced users look more for all the detail they can get, whereas the novice just try to achieve the task of finding the route (Table 2).

**Table 2.** Routing results

|         | Median | $\sigma$ | min   | max   |
|---------|--------|----------|-------|-------|
| min:sec | 01:42  | 01:28    | 01:06 | 03:33 |

After completing the routing, the test persons had the opportunity to provide an individual opinion. All of them confirmed the high level of usability of HaptOSM maps and expected significant personal advantage by using them. Some of them missed shops and public authorities. The maps could be red at best, when they were put on a flat surface.

## 5  Conclusion and Planned Activities

The results have shown the high potential and demand on tactile maps. Although further improvements are needed. Braille paper maps are clearly preferred due to better sensitivity, but suffer from low durability and high vulnerability to wrinkles. So the main problems connected to paper maps at the moment are too weak embossing and poor protection during transport. Stronger embossing has already been addressed by using an improved embossing machine. Measurements with this new machine look very promising. For better protection during transport the maps will be shipped within an envelope with cardboard back. Also the use of air cushioned envelopes is the object of current investigations.

During the current public beta phase, maps can be ordered from the HaptOSM website (https://haptosm.de). There are no limitation on the region, but language is restricted to German and English (including Braille Grade 1 and Grade 2). A partner handling worldwide marketing and distribution is still searched for.

## References

1. Gardiner, A., Perkins, C.: Best practice guidelines for the design,production and presentation of vacuum formed tactile maps. In: Tactile Book Advancement-Group (TBAG) (2002). http://www.tactilebooks.org/tactileguidelines/page1.htm. Accessed January 2016

2. Hänßgen, D., Waldt, N.: A system creating tactile maps for the blind and visually impaired. In: Proceedings of the Conference Universal Learning Design, vol. 4, pp. 49–56. Brno: Masaryk University, Paris (2014). ISSN 1805–3947
3. LinuxCNC-Team: LinuxCNC documentation (2016). http://linuxcnc.org/docs/2. 7/pdf/LinuxCNC_Documentation.pdf
4. Nagel, D.L.D., Coulson, M.R.C.: Tactual mobility maps / a comparative study. Cartogr.: Int. J. Geogr. Inf. Geovisualization **27**(2), 47–63 (1990). http://dx. doi.org/10.3138/D310-6U13-H13J-H414
5. Perkins, C.: Cartography: progress in tactile mapping. Prog. Hum. Geogr. **26**(4), 521–530 (2002)
6. Pike, E., Blades, M., Spencer, C.: A comparison of two types of tactile maps for blind children. Cartogr.: Int. J. Geogr. Inf. Geovisualization **29**(3–4), 83–88 (1992). http://dx.doi.org/10.3138/RQ41-Q433-8411-7G40
7. Rowell, J., Ungar, S.: A taxonomy for tactile symbols: Creating a useable database for tactile map designers. Cartogr. J. **40**(3), 273–276 (2003). http://dx.doi. org/10.1179/000870403225012998
8. Stehlik, U.: Taktile Medien - Orientierungs - und Informationssysteme. Deutsche Blindenstudienanstalt e.V. (2008)
9. Ungar, S., Jehoel, S., McCallum, D., Rowell, J.: Tactualization of spatial information: towards a perceptual-cognitive approach to tactile map design. In: Proceedings of XXII International Cartographic Conference A Coruña 2005 Proceedings, CD (2005)
10. Zeng, L.: Acquisition of Spatial Environmental Information from Tactile Displays. Ph.D. thesis, Technische Universität Dresden Faculty of Computer Science (2013)

# Specification of Symbols Used in Audio-Tactile Maps for Individuals with Blindness

Konstantinos Papadopoulos[1], Konstantinos Charitakis[1(✉)], Eleni Koustriava[1],
Lefkothea Kartasidou[1], Efstratios Stylianidis[2], Georgios Kouroupetroglou[3],
Suad Sakalli Gumus[4], Karin Müller[5], and Engin Yilmaz[6]

[1] University of Macedonia, Thessaloniki, Greece
kcharitakis@uom.edu.gr
[2] Aristotle University of Thessaloniki, Thessaloniki, Greece
[3] National and Kapodistrian University of Athens, Athens, Greece
[4] Mustafa Kemal University, Antakya, Turkey
[5] Karlsruhe Institute of Technology, Karlsruhe, Germany
[6] Association of Barrier Free Access, Istanbul, Turkey

**Abstract.** The implementation of multisensory environments in the field of map construction for individuals with visual impairments can be a challenging area for both users and designers of orientation and mobility aids. Audio-tactile maps can utilize a large amount of spatial information represented by audio symbols, tactile symbols, audio-tactile symbols (combined) and Braille labels. In regard to audio-tactile maps an important clarification needs to be elaborated and in particular what needs to be carefully examined is the basic query of which information should be presented in haptic mode and which information should be presented in audio or audio-haptic mode. In practice this means that a reasoned process of defining the appropriate symbols for audio-tactile maps should be implemented. The fundamental aim of project "ATMAPS" - Specification of symbols used on Audio-Tactile Maps for individuals with blindness" presented in this paper is the specification of symbols to be used in audio-tactile maps for individuals with blindness.

**Keywords:** Blind · Visual impairment · Audio-tactile map · Audio-tactile symbol

## 1 Introduction

For individuals with visual impairments, the sense of touch is considered as a basic modality for acquiring spatial information [1]. The importance of the tactile aids as tools that provide spatial information is widely acknowledged [2, 3]. Tactile maps are often used by individuals with visual impairments in order to discover to a certain degree new environments in advance [4]. Tactile maps are very useful in education and training of individuals with visual impairments since they can be used as tools for the identification of location, way finding, estimation of distance and formation of cognitive maps [4, 5]. The contribution of tactile maps in formatting new cognitive maps or in reforming the existing ones is very important. Tactile maps can also be an extremely effective tool for

© Springer International Publishing Switzerland 2016
K. Miesenberger et al. (Eds.): ICCHP 2016, Part II, LNCS 9759, pp. 160–167, 2016.
DOI: 10.1007/978-3-319-41267-2_22

representing spatial information for the orientation and mobility (O&M) of individuals with visual impairments [6].

Beyond tactile maps there are several methods to produce accessible maps. Zeng and Weber [7] presented an overview of different type of maps used by individuals with blindness such as printable tactile maps, virtual acoustic maps, virtual tactile maps, augmented paper-based tactile maps or Braille tactile maps, and audio-tactile maps that combine audio with tactile information. All these types of maps differ in their production method, the amount of information and the type of interaction.

Though there are significant benefits on the use of tactile maps, numerous limitations have been pointed out [8, 9]. Multimodal interactive maps, such as audio-tactile maps, appear to be a solution to overcome the challenges that the use of tactile maps has raised [10]. The definition of audio-tactile maps refers to a series of audio-tactile aids [11].

The benefits of tactile maps have been combined in previous studies with those of the verbal aids through the use of technological devices, such as the touchpad devices [12]. Touchpad devices are touch-sensitive pads that offer individuals with visual impairments access to the benefits of tactile maps and verbal aids simultaneously while they explore tactile graphics with their fingers. A tactile map is placed on the device's sensitive pad and the information on the map is associated with the respective points or areas on the pad's surface. The touch sensitive pad reacts to touch events with an audio output (e.g. distinct sound, verbal description, etc.), that corresponds to the respective point or area on the pad.

Later developments allow the use of hardware and software tools for adding audio annotations to tactile maps automatically by loading map data in SVG (Scalable Vector Graphics) format, allowing the automated definition of shapes and text-based information on touchpad devices [13]. Wang, Li, Hedgpeth and Haven [14] proposed a system that automatically created an accessible tactile map augmented with audio descriptions from a single image of a map as an input.

With the latest developments and trends in information technology the use of multi touch devices is widely used for everyday computing. Brock et al. [10] developed an interactive map prototype based on double-tap interaction and was evaluated with great levels of satisfaction by blind users. Their prototype utilized tactile maps placed on multitouch displays combined with audio outputs, instead of using mono touch displays.

Even though there were several attempts on the specification of tactile symbols to be included in tactile maps, there are no previous studies on the specification of symbols to be included in audio-tactile maps. A few types of standardization/specification have been proposed with reference to tactile symbols used in tactile maps. Bundles of tactile symbols were developed such as the Nottingham Map Making Kit [15] as a first attempt for standardization of the tactile map making process and later the Euro-Town Kit [16]. In addition to the attempts for standardization, sets of tactile symbols were proposed [17, 18], while others [19, 20] focused on the limitations of the tactile sense to derive guidelines, based on the symbols' minimum and maximum perceptible dimensions. Picard [21] presented a patent for the design and production of a Visuo-Tactile Atlas focusing on the haptic perception. Lobben & Lawrence [22] proposed a standardization of map symbols for tactile maps produced on microcapsule paper and has been made freely accessible over the internet by the

Braille Authority of North America [23]. Abd Hamid and Edwards [24] gathered information from mobility instructors to specify their requirements.

In the case of audio-tactile maps, in addition to tactile symbols and Braille labels, audio and audio-tactile symbols are used as well. However, there is an important gap regarding the specification of audio and audio-tactile symbols to be included in audio-tactile maps.

The ATMAPS project, titled "Specification of symbols used on Audio-Tactile Maps for individuals with blindness" aims to bridge this gap. The fundamental aim of ATMAPS is the research based specification of audio, tactile and audio-tactile symbols to be used in audio-tactile maps. In the present article, the term audio-tactile map describes the tactile map that can be read with the use of a touchpad device (e.g. IVEO or T3) exclusively. Moreover, among the objectives of the project are to provide specialized training of end users, teachers of individuals with blindness, rehabilitation specialists, O&M trainers as well as designers of O&M aids, on the construction of audio-tactile maps and on the use of touchpad devices (e.g. IVEO).

## 2 Methodology

The specification of symbols to be used in audio-tactile maps (AT-Maps) is going to be implemented through a user-centered approach, where individuals with visual impairments as end-users of AT-Maps will define what information should be incorporated in AT-Maps, in which format the information should be presented and what are the optimal point, linear and areal tactile symbols for the representation of the information on AT-Maps.

The specification of symbols is based on a wide spectrum of AT-Maps. In particular the specification will be connected to: (1) AT-Maps of indoors (inner space of buildings), (2) AT-Maps of neighborhoods/residential areas, (3) AT-Maps of campuses (school, college or university campus), (4) AT-Maps of city centers, (5) AT political, physical, historic, and thematic maps.

The substantiation of the present project is based on the following tasks: (1) Specification of user requirements regarding the information to be included in AT-Maps, (2) Specification of audio-tactile symbols (3) Construction of a multilingual web-based library of audio-tactile symbols, (4) Construction of a political-physical audio-tactile atlas of Europe, and (5) Training activities for end users.

### 2.1 User Requirements

For the user requirements specification a research study was conducted in order to derive the most important information that should be included in different types of AT-Maps. Moreover, the study specified which of the information should be illustrated as tactile symbols, which ones as audio symbols and which ones as audio-tactile symbols. The study was conducted with the participation of individuals with blindness, from the 4 partner countries.

The user requirements specification process was based on the contribution/usefulness/significance of information in regard to: (1) safety during movement of individuals with blindness (e.g. obstacles, stairs etc.), (2) information on the location of services (e.g. public services, schools, shops etc.), (3) way-finding (information to help verify the position of the walker), (4) orientation (e.g. landmarks), and (5) the theme of the map.

The researchers created an initial list of information. The initial list of information was then enriched by suggestions of focus groups conducted in each partner country. The final enriched and sorted list of information for each type of map was then included in a respective questionnaire to be answered by participants with blindness.

The participants were asked to evaluate the information included in the lists based on: (a) the significance of the information in regard to safety, location of services, way finding and orientation during movement, based on a five point Likert scale, (b) the frequency the participants meet the information within their surroundings and the environment they move in, based on a five point Likert scale, and (c) the format the participants prefer the information to be included in the maps (audio, tactile, audio-tactile format).

## 2.2    Specification of Audio-Tactile Symbols

The specification of audio-tactile symbols includes the design, deployment and implementation of evaluation/testing of audio-tactile symbols. In case of AT-Maps a considerable piece of information is presented in auditory modality (e.g. street names, street numbers, different types of information, name of sites, obstacles, etc.). Therefore, what needs to be carefully examined is the basic query of which information should be presented in haptic mode or with Braille labels and which information should be delivered via an audio or audio-haptic mode. In practice this means that a reasoned process of defining the appropriate symbols for AT-Maps should be implemented.

At the moment a research study is conducted in order to evaluate the tactile symbols created. Individuals with visual impairments from the 4 partner countries are participating. The research instruments used in this task are lists of 100 point, 40 linear, and 20 areal tactile symbols created as well as pilot tactile maps that consist of all point, all linear, and all areal tactile symbols created. In this way it will be easy to continuously evaluate and monitor the way the symbols are recognized as stand-alone symbols but also when included in maps. This is considered necessary since many created symbols will be combined and used on the surface of AT-Maps and not individually. The study includes a series of tests conducted in each partner country.

The research study evaluates the legibility (ease of identification) of the tactile symbols, based on different parameters like the time needed for blind individuals to search and identify a specific symbol and the number of errors the participants make until they find the correct ones.

The audio symbols will be verbal descriptions of the listed information derived from the user requirements specification task. The audio output will be produced by text to speech (TTS) software using natural synthesized voices in order to vocalize the listed information.

Statistical analysis will be applied to the data derived from the testing of tactile symbols procedure. The results of the analysis will consist the base on which the specification of symbols will be implemented.

### 2.3 Development of an Electronic Library

A web-based electronic library of audio-tactile symbols will be developed. The organization of the audio-tactile symbols entered in the library will be based on a classification according to their format (audio, tactile, audio-tactile), structure and function. The library of symbols will be searchable with different options for listing the included elements. The tactile symbols will be included in different formats (e.g. vector and raster) and identified in the exact way in order to be reproduced accurately. Each information included in the library will be associated with an audio-tactile symbol. The library will be translated and freely available in English, Greek, German, and Turkish language.

### 2.4 Construction of an Audio-Tactile Atlas of Europe

A political-physical audio-tactile atlas of Europe will be constructed. The procedure for the construction of the tactile atlas includes the following stages: the construction of a digital base map; the generalisation of the graphic forms (in order to be easily readable though active touch); the placement of tactile symbols; the printing of the maps on microcapsule paper using a tactile image enhancer. Finally, audio and audio-tactile symbols, as well as verbal descriptions of thematic information will be included in the political-physical audio-tactile atlas.

### 2.5 Training Activities

Training activities include the training of mentors and training of end-users (individuals with visual impairments). The training of mentors includes the training of individuals who will gain the expertise on the project outcomes in order to be able to train others in their turn and act as mentors for teachers of children with visual impairments, rehabilitation specialists, O&M specialists and designers of O&M aids. The training of end-users is aiming at relaying the new knowledge and skills for end users on the use of AT-Maps and touchpad devices.

## 3   Results

The expected results of the ATMAPS project are going to be: (a) a web based, searchable, multilingual electronic library of audio-tactile symbols, (b) an audio-tactile atlas of Europe, and (c) training material and specialized training activities.

The web based, searchable, multilingual electronic library of audio-tactile symbols will present the specified symbols, the associated information, functional information and guidelines in order to be used in AT-Maps. The users of the developed library will be able to download and use the stored symbols in order to develop their own AT-Maps.

The audio-tactile atlas of Europe will include a variety of spatial information such as coast lines, country boarders, capitals and metropolitan cities, historic cities and regions, islands, mountains, high mountain peaks, rivers, large lakes, etc. Moreover the produced atlas will include thematic information on demographics, culture, history, climate, local products, customs, etc. of each country. In order to represent the above information audio-tactile symbols will be used together with verbal descriptions (mainly synthetic speech) that users can listen to. The maps will be printed in microcapsule paper. The content of audio-tactile atlas will be translated in English, Greek, German, and Turkish languages.

Finally among the expected outcomes of the project will be the produced training material and specialized training activities. It is expected that at least 120 teachers of visually impaired children, rehabilitation specialists, O&M specialists and designers of O&M aids and 100 individuals with blindness will be trained during the training activities in the 4 partner countries (Greece, Germany, Cyprus and Turkey).

Another outcome is expected to be an electronic index of organizations such as associations for the blind, associations of special educators, related governmental and EU organizations all over Europe, in order to provide easy access and categorized information to contact details of organizations for communication purposes to be used from all interested parties. The electronic index will be open and extendible and organizations could be added upon request.

## 4 Discussion

The proposed project brings basic needs, problems and challenges into focus. Although there are already considerable prospects for the development of new tools and aids that are directly connected to the capacities of a touchpad device, scarce AT-Maps and audio-tactile O&M maps/aids have been constructed. Moreover, there is no study designed and substantiated for the specification of symbols that can be used in AT-maps. This inevitably means that audio-tactile symbols currently used for the representation of spatial information, do not follow a series of specifications. In other words, there is not a research-derived, effect-assured, specified "audio-tactile language".

Solving these problems and satisfying the above mentioned needs is a priority since: (1) the AT-Maps constitute a new, pioneering mode of presenting spatial information that is expected soon to be fully incorporated in the education/training and everyday life of individuals with blindness, (2) the O&M aids are necessary for individuals with blindness in their daily life, (3) O&M in space is a prerequisite for the independent living of individuals with blindness, and (4) the specification of symbols will give rise to the production of effective AT-Maps by forming and using a specified unique "audio-tactile language" that will govern the construction of different types of AT-Maps.

Availability of the derived audio-tactile symbols will be accomplished through the developed web-based library of audio-tactile symbols that will be freely available to anyone who might want to construct AT-Maps for educational and training purposes.

However the great value of the proposed project derives not only from its innovative character or the significant improvement in the field of education and training aids for individuals with visual impairments, but also from the radical changes that will probably follow in the field of O&M. These changes concern the design of education curricula, O&M training, and research on the field.

Moreover, new solutions for distance education and training of individuals with visual impairments could arise by the use of multimodal training material.

The development of methods for the training of O&M and rehabilitation specialists, and of teachers will lead to the formation of new domains of O&M training, which in combination with the audio-tactile aids will be spread in Institutions and Unions for individuals with visual impairments.

**Acknowledgements.** The work presented in this paper was conducted in the frames of the ATMAPS project titled "Specification of symbols used on audio-tactile maps for individuals with blindness" under the Lifelong Learning Programme (LLP). The project (543316-LLP-1-2013-1-GR-KA3-KA3MP) has been funded with support from the European Commission. This publication reflects the views only of the authors, and the Commission cannot be held responsible for any use which may be made of the information contained therein.

# References

1. Papadopoulos, K.S.: Automatic transcription of tactile maps. J. Vis. Impairment Blindness **99**(4), 242–245 (2005)
2. Espinosa, M.A., Ochaita, E.: Using tactile maps to improve the practical spatial knowledge of adults who are blind. J. Vi. Impairment Blindness **92**(5), 338–345 (1998)
3. Papadopoulos, K., Livieratos, E., Boutoura, C.: A large scale city atlas for the blind. In: Proceedings of the 20th International Cartographic Conference of ICA, Beijing, China (2001)
4. Papadopoulos, K., Karanikolas, N.: Tactile maps provide location based services for individuals with visual impairments. J. Location Based Servi. **3**(3), 150–164 (2009)
5. Papadopoulos, K., Barouti, M., Charitakis, K.: A university indoors audio-tactile mobility aid for individuals with blindness. In: Miesenberger, K., Fels, D., Archambault, D., Peňáz, P., Zagler, W. (eds.) ICCHP 2014, Part II. LNCS, vol. 8548, pp. 108–115. Springer, Heidelberg (2014)
6. Lawrence, M.M., Lobben, A.K.: The design of tactile thematic symbols. J. Vis. Impairment Blindness **105**(10), 681–691 (2011)
7. Zeng, L., Weber, G.: Accessible maps for the visually impaired. In: Proceedings of IFIP INTERACT 2011 Workshop on ADDW, pp. 54–60. Lisbon, Portugal (2011)
8. Harder, A., Michel, R.: The target-route map: evaluating its usability for visually impaired persons. J. Vis. Impairment Blindness **96**(10), 711–723 (2002)
9. Jacobson, R.D.: Navigating maps with little or no sight: An audio-tactile approach. In: Proceedings of Content Visualization and Intermedia Representations, pp. 95–102. Montréal, Québec, Canada (1998)
10. Brock, A., Truillet, P., Oriola, B., Picard, D., Jouffrais, C.: Design and user satisfaction of interactive maps for visually impaired people. In: Miesenberger, K., Karshmer, A., Penaz, P., Zagler, W. (eds.) ICCHP 2012, Part II. LNCS, vol. 7383, pp. 544–551. Springer, Heidelberg (2012)
11. Brock, A.M.: Interactive Maps for Visually Impaired People: Design, Usability and Spatial Cognition. Doctoral Dissertation. University of Toulouse (2013)

12. Holmes, E., Jansson, G.: A touch tablet enhanced with synthetic speech as a display for visually impaired people's reading of virtual maps. In: Proceedings of CSUN 12th Annual Conference on Technology for People with Disabilities. California State University, LA (1997)
13. Miele, J.A., Landau, S., Gilden, D.: Talking TMAP: Automated generation of audio-tactile maps using Smith-Kettlewell's TMAP software. British J. Vis. Impairment **24**, 93–100 (2006)
14. Wang, Z., Li, B., Hedgpeth, T., Haven, T.: Instant tactile-audio map: enabling access to digital maps for people with visual impairment. In: Proceedings of ASSETS, pp. 43–50. ACM, Pittsburgh (2009)
15. James, G.A., Armstrong, J.D.: Handbook for mobility maps. Blind Mobility Research Unit. Nottingham University, Nottingham (1976)
16. Blindenstudienanstalt, D.: Euro-Town-Kit; Standard Symbols for the Production of Tactile Maps. Deutsches Blindenstudienanstalt, Marburg (1989)
17. Edman, P.K.: Tactile graphics. AFB, NY (1992)
18. Paladugu, D.A., Wang, Z., Li, B.: On presenting audio-tactile maps to visually impaired users for getting directions. In: Proceedings of CHI, pp. 3955–3960. ACM Press, Atlanta (2010)
19. Bris, M.: Rapport « Tactimages & Training », pp. 1–34. Paris, France (1999)
20. Tatham, A.F.: The design of tactile maps: theoretical and practical considerations. In: Proceedings of International Cartographic Association: Mapping the Nations, pp. 157–166. K Rybaczak and M Blakemore, London, UK (1991)
21. Picard, D.: Visuo-tactile atlas. Organisation mondiale de la propriété intellectuelle, France (2012)
22. Lobben, A., Lawrence, M.: The use of environmental features on tactile maps by navigators who are blind. Prof. Geogr. **64**, 95–108 (2012)
23. Braille Authority of North America: Guidelines and standards for tactile graphics. Last retrieved March 2016. http://www.brailleauthority.org/tg/web-manual/index.html
24. Abd Hamid, N.N., Edwards, A.D.: Facilitating route learning using interactive audio-tactile maps for blind and visually impaired people. In: Proceedings of the CHI 2013 Extended Abstracts on Human Factors in Computing Systems, pp. 37–42. ACM, New York (2013)

# User Requirements Regarding Information Included in Audio-Tactile Maps for Individuals with Blindness

Konstantinos Papadopoulos[1], Konstantinos Charitakis[1(✉)],
Lefkothea Kartasidou[1], Georgios Kouroupetroglou[2],
Suad Sakalli Gumus[3], Efstratios Stylianidis[4], Rainer Stiefelhagen[5],
Karin Müller[5], Engin Yilmaz[6], Gerhard Jaworek[5],
Christos Polimeras[7], Utku Sayin[3], Nikolaos Oikonomidis[2],
and Nikolaos Lithoxopoulos[8]

[1] University of Macedonia, Thessaloniki, Greece
kcharitakis@uom.edu.gr
[2] National and Kapodistrian University of Athens, Athens, Greece
[3] Mustafa Kemal University, Antakya, Turkey
[4] Aristotle University of Thessaloniki, Thessaloniki, Greece
[5] Karlsruhe Institute of Technology, Karlsruhe, Germany
[6] Association of Barrier Free Access, Istanbul, Turkey
[7] Panhellenic Association of the Blind, Thessaloniki, Greece
[8] Geoimaging Ltd., Nicosia, Cyprus

**Abstract.** The aim of this study is to investigate the user requirements of young adults with blindness regarding the information to be included/ mapped in two different types of audio-tactile mobility maps: (a) audio-tactile maps of indoors, and (b) audio-tactile maps of campuses. Forty young adults (aged from 18 years to 30 years) with blindness took part in the research. Participants came from four countries: 14 from Greece, 2 from Cyprus, 18 from Turkey, and 6 from Germany. The researchers developed two lists of information to be included in the two types of audio-tactile maps (indoor and campus) respectively. Participants were asked to evaluate the information, regarding: (a) the significance of the information in regard to safety, location of services, way finding and orientation during movement, and (b) the frequency the participants meet the information (within their surrounding and the environment they move in). The first list of information to be evaluated, related to the maps of indoor places consisted of 136 different information, and the second list of information to be evaluated, related to the campus maps consisted of 213 different information. The result of the study is the definition of the most important information that should be included in each one of the two different types of audio-tactile maps. Thus, the findings of the present study will be particularly important for designers of orientation and mobility (O&M) aids for individuals with blindness. Moreover, the findings can be useful for O&M specialists, rehabilitation specialists, and teachers who design and construct O&M aids for their students with blindness.

**Keywords:** Blind · Visual impairment · Audio-tactile map · Audio-tactile symbol

© Springer International Publishing Switzerland 2016
K. Miesenberger et al. (Eds.): ICCHP 2016, Part II, LNCS 9759, pp. 168–175, 2016.
DOI: 10.1007/978-3-319-41267-2_23

# 1   Introduction

Orientation and mobility in unfamiliar environment is a difficult task for individuals with visual impairments. The majority of the researchers that examined spatial performance of individuals with visual impairments and sighted individuals came to the conclusion that visual experience influences decisively spatial behavior [1–3]. Moreover, blindness has a negative impact on the development of blind people's spatial skills [3–5].

Maps constitute an important orientation and mobility aid for individuals with visual impairments and contribute to the handling of their daily problems including autonomy, independence and quality of life [6, 7]. Conventional maps developed for sighted individuals are not accessible for individuals with visual impairments because they contain visual information only [8]. Therefore, individuals with visual impairments often use tactile maps to discover new environments in advance [8] as they find it more helpful for cognitive mapping than direct experience [9].

Espinosa and Ochaita [10] showed that spatial knowledge was better when individuals with visual impairments learned specific routes with the use of tactile maps for cartographic representation than with direct experience or verbal description. The use of tactile maps provides the option to individuals with visual impairments to maintain a stable reference point [11] that enables allocentric coding which leads to better spatial performance and knowledge during spatial learning [2, 12].

In case of audio-tactile maps, information can be represented by tactile graphics, audio symbols, tactile symbols, audio-tactile symbols (combined, e.g. a tactile symbol that when a user touches it, he can hear additional information) and Braille labels. That allows a vast amount of information to be presented in auditory modality. Individuals with visual impairments use touch as the basic modality to acquire spatial information [13] while the audio modality helps them to perceive new information about their surroundings.

Auditory cues in audio-tactile maps as orientation and mobility aids can be either verbal descriptions of spatial layout or landmarks, textual labels [14], suggestions for specific travel situations or routes, or cultural and aesthetic information for particular environments [15]. Because of their sequential nature, verbal descriptions promote incremental structuring and updating of spatial knowledge and contribute to speed and accuracy of map exploration process [14].

Nowadays the benefits of tactile maps can be combined with those of the verbal aids with the use of inexpensive computer peripheral devices, such as touchpads. Touchpad devices are touch-sensitive pads that offer individuals with visual impairments access to the benefits of tactile maps and verbal aids simultaneously while they explore tactile graphics with their fingers. In the present article, the term audio-tactile map describes the tactile map that can be read with the use of a touchpad device (e.g. IVEO or T3) exclusively.

## 2  Study

The aim of the research presented in this article is to investigate the user requirements of young adults with blindness regarding the information to be included/ mapped into two different types of audio-tactile mobility maps: (a) audio-tactile maps of indoors (inner space of buildings), and (b) audio-tactile maps of campuses (school, college or university campus). The result of this research would be the definition of the most important information that should be included in each one of the two different types of audio-tactile maps.

The research is part of a wider study conducted in the frames of the ATMAPS project titled "Specification of symbols used on audio-tactile maps for individuals with blindness" under the Lifelong Learning Programme (LLP).

### 2.1  Participants

Forty young adults with blindness took part in the research. Participants came from four different countries: 14 from Greece, 2 from Cyprus, 18 from Turkey, and 6 from Germany. The sample consisted of 23 (57.5 %) males and 17 (42.5 %) females. The age ranged from 18 years to 30 years (M = 25.48, SD = 3.88). Twenty two participants were blind, 15 had severe visual impairments and 3 were legally blind (visual acuity less than 1/20). The visual impairment was congenital for 22 participants and acquired for the rest 18 participants.

The participants were asked to state the way of their daily movement in their surroundings, by choosing one of the following: (a) with the assistance of a sighted guide, (b) sometimes by myself and sometimes with the assistance of a sighted guide, and (c) by myself, without any assistance. Moreover, the participants were asked to indicate the frequency of their independent movement using a 5-point Likert scale (1 = never, 2 = rarely, 3 = sometimes, 4 = often, 5 = always. Table 1 presents the answers of the participants.

**Table 1.** Ability and frequency of independent movement according to the answers of participants – the scores represent the number of participants in each group.

| | With or without sighted guide | | | Frequency of independent movement | | |
|---|---|---|---|---|---|---|
| | with | with & without | without | sometimes | often | always |
| Participants | 1 | 28 | 11 | 8 | 22 | 10 |

Furthermore the participants were asked to indicate the frequency of use of tactile graphics or pictures using a 5-point Likert scale (1 = never, 2 = rarely, 3 = sometimes, 4 = often, 5 = daily). Regarding the frequency of tactile graphics or pictures use, 6 participants answered never, 10 answered rarely, 14 answered sometimes, 8 answered often and 2 of them answered daily.

## 2.2    Instruments and Procedures

The researchers developed an initial list of information to be included in the two types of audio-tactile maps (indoor and campus). The information included in this initial list was considered to be the most important, based on previous studies and experience of the researchers. The initial list of information was created in English, and translated in three different languages (Greek, German and Turkish). Finally, this list was further enriched by suggestions of focus groups conducted in each partner country (Greece, Germany, Turkey and Cyprus). The participants in the focus groups were individuals with blindness (potential users of the audio-tactile maps), 7 from Greece, 6 from Cyprus, 4 from Germany and 5 from Turkey. The total sample of participants in focus groups consisted of 11 males and 11 females. The age ranged from 23 years to 50 years (M = 34.6). Twenty participants were totally blind or had severe visual impairments and 2 were legally blind (visual acuity less than 1/20). The visual impairment was congenital for 14 participants and acquired for 8 participants.

The final list of information for each type of map was then included in a questionnaire to be answered by individuals with blindness participating in the study. The questionnaire was developed as an accessible text document (.docx file) in order the participants to be able to use screen reading software of their preference to read it. The text document was structured using plain text, 1st level Headings, numbered lists and bulleted lists.

The first part of the questionnaire included the questionnaire instructions in a separate text document with the following sections: (1) short introduction about the ATMAPS project and what audio-tactile maps are, (2) demographic data questions to be filled in by participants, (3) questionnaire purpose, explaining what the purpose of the questionnaire was, (4) instructions on how the participants should evaluate the list of information, (5) questions, three close-ended questions were included (only the 2 questions were analyzed in the present article), and (6) examples on how to answer the questions.

The second part of the questionnaire was included in separate accessible text documents for each different type of map (one for indoors and one for campus respectively). Each questionnaire file included: (1) title of the map type in order the participant to focus on the information related to the particular map type, (2) answering instructions, (3) examples on how to answer the questions, and (4) list of information to be evaluated. The first list of information to be evaluated, related to the maps of indoor places consisted of 136 different information, and the second list of information to be evaluated, related to the campus map consisted of 213 different information.

Participants were asked to evaluate the information, regarding: (a) the significance of the information in regard to safety, location of services, way finding and orientation during movement, based on a five point Likert scale (1 = not significant at all, 2 = somewhat significant, 3 = neutral, 4 = significant, 5 = very significant), (b) the frequency of occurrence of the information (the frequency the participants meet the information within their surrounding and the environment they move in), based on a five point Likert scale (1 = never, 2 = rarely, 3 = sometimes, 4 = often, 5 = very often), and (c) the format (audio, tactile, or audio-tactile) the participants prefer the information to be included in audio-tactile maps. The results of the third question regarding the participants' preference on the format are not included in the present article.

## 3 Results

The means for the information of both questions ("Frequency" of occurrence and "Significance") were calculated. Two different lists of information were created from the participants' answers: (1) a list with the information sorted in descending order starting with the most frequent ones, and (2) a list with the information sorted in descending order starting with those considered being the most significant ones.

Moreover, in order to identify the information that is most important to be included (mapped) in audio-tactile maps, a third list was created containing the information with the higher "Importance factor". The Importance factor was calculated by multiplying Frequency of occurrence with Significance of each information respectively.

Tables 2 and 3 below present the mean scores for the top 20 information reported by the participants for "indoor maps" and "campus maps" respectively, listed from the most important to least important information sorted by Importance factor. Tables 2

**Table 2.** Indoor Maps: most important information sorted by Importance factor

| Information | Importance factor | Frequency | Significance |
|---|---|---|---|
| Toilet or bathroom for men, women, or persons with disabilities | 20.33 | 4.25 (3) | 4.68 (1) |
| Entrance or exit | 20.28 | 4.50 (1) | 4.43 (6) |
| Stairs | 19.50 | 4.25 (2) | 4.50 (2) |
| Dangerous area | 18.15 | 3.90 (10) | 4.45 (5) |
| Elevator | 17.58 | 4.03 (6) | 4.18 (14) |
| Door | 17.48 | 4.10 (4) | 4.05 (23) |
| Floor number | 17.38 | 3.93 (9) | 4.25 (11) |
| Clinic or infirmary or doctor | 17.35 | 3.75 (16) | 4.45 (4) |
| Room number | 17.33 | 3.78 (15) | 4.48 (3) |
| Cafeteria or Coffee shop | 17.30 | 4.05 (5) | 4.08 (20) |
| Steps | 17.05 | 3.93 (7) | 4.03 (24) |
| Library, the room or the service | 16.88 | 3.80 (12) | 4.28 (9) |
| Emergency exit | 16.85 | 3.78 (14) | 4.35 (8) |
| Canteen | 16.80 | 3.93 (8) | 4.00 (26) |
| Reception | 16.80 | 3.73 (17) | 4.40 (7) |
| Dangerous point | 16.65 | 3.73 (21) | 4.10 (18) |
| Hanging obstacle or overhead obstacle | 16.53 | 3.73 (18) | 4.25 (12) |
| Office of the commissioner for the disabled | 16.48 | 3.73 (19) | 4.28 (10) |
| Room | 16.25 | 3.88 (11) | 4.10 (17) |
| Tactile paving for the blind | 16.20 | 3.73 (20) | 4.18 (13) |

and 3 also present the list order of the information based on their frequency and significance scores (see the numbers in parenthesis).

*Note:* The list of the top twenty information sorted by Frequency also includes "Corridor" (13). The list of the top twenty information sorted by Significance also includes "Tactile signpost" (15), "Revolving door" (16), and "Haptic reference point or landmark" (19).

**Table 3.** Campus Maps: most important information sorted by Importance factor

| Information | Importance factor | Frequency | Significance |
|---|---|---|---|
| Bus stop | 21.08 | 4.35 (1) | 4.80 (1) |
| Point of access to public transport, bus stop, metro station | 20.77 | 4.33 (2) | 4.75 (2) |
| Lecture room | 20.15 | 4.25 (3) | 4.58 (8) |
| Student's registry office | 19.63 | 4.13 (5) | 4.70 (3) |
| Lecture theatre | 19.45 | 4.15 (4) | 4.50 (13) |
| Toilet or bathroom for men, women, or people with disabilities | 19.43 | 4.08 (7) | 4.53 (9) |
| Traffic lights | 19.20 | 4.13 (6) | 4.38 (23) |
| Metro station | 19.05 | 4.03 (9) | 4.63 (5) |
| Service center for students | 18.95 | 4.00 (11) | 4.60 (6) |
| Name of faculties of educational institution | 18.55 | 3.95 (13) | 4.45 (16) |
| Library, the room or the service | 18.40 | 4.00 (10) | 4.50 (12) |
| Entrance or exit | 18.35 | 4.08 (8) | 4.23 (35) |
| Room number | 18.28 | 3.95 (12) | 4.40 (21) |
| Taxi station | 18.23 | 3.88 (17) | 4.48 (15) |
| Academic staff offices | 18.03 | 3.93 (14) | 4.48 (14) |
| Intersection, a place where two or more streets meet or cross | 18.03 | 3.90 (16) | 4.40 (20) |
| Office with accessible books | 17.95 | 3.80 (23) | 4.58 (7) |
| Traffic light with audio signals for the Blind | 17.70 | 3.78 (28) | 4.50 (11) |
| Canteen | 17.68 | 3.85 (19) | 4.25 (34) |
| Area name | 17.63 | 3.83 (20) | 4.38 (22) |

*Note:* The list of the top twenty information sorted by Frequency also includes "Stairs" (15) and "Pavement or sidewalk" (18). The list of the top twenty information sorted by Significance also includes "Office of the commissioner for the disabled" (4), "Clinic or infirmary or doctor" (10), "Emergency exit" (17), "Dangerous area" (18), and "Student's office" (19).

## 4  Discussion

The result of the study is the definition of the most important information that should be included in each one of the two different types of audio-tactile maps (indoor and campus). There is no previous study on the definition of user requirements of individuals with blindness regarding the information to be included/ mapped on audio-tactile maps. Thus, the findings of the present study will be particularly important for designers of O&M aids for individuals with blindness. Moreover, the findings can be useful for O&M specialists, rehabilitation specialists, and teachers who design and construct O&M aids for their students with blindness.

The results show that in some cases information is listed in the same order or close enough (see numbers in parenthesis) in terms of frequency and significance (e.g. "toilet or bathroom for men, women, or persons with disabilities", "stairs" for indoor maps, and "bus stop", "point of access to public transport, bus stop, metro station", for campus maps). In other cases, information is listed in different order in terms of frequency and significance (e.g. "door", "steps" for indoor maps, and "traffic lights", "entrance or exit" for campus maps). This indicates that there is information that is considered significant but not met frequently by individuals with blindness in their surroundings and vise versa. However, factors like "frequency" and "significance" of information should be taken into consideration by designers of audio-tactile maps when selecting the symbols to depict information into audio-tactile maps. Thus, the calculation of the "importance factor" seems to be the most effective solution.

The present study investigates the user requirements of young adults with blindness regarding the information to be mapped into audio-tactile maps of indoors and audio-tactile maps of campuses. Future studies could be examining the user requirements of individuals with blindness in a wider range of ages, as well as the user requirements of individuals with blindness for other types of audio-tactile maps, such as for example audio-tactile maps of neighborhoods/residential areas, audio-tactile maps of city centers, geographical audio-tactile maps, and thematic audio-tactile maps. This research is in progress within the ATMAPS project of which the present study is part of.

**Acknowledgements.**  The work presented in this paper was conducted in the frames of the ATMAPS project titled "Specification of symbols used on audio-tactile maps for individuals with blindness" under the Lifelong Learning Programme (LLP). The project (543316-LLP-1-2013-1-GR-KA3-KA3MP) has been funded with support from the European Commission. This publication reflects the views only of the authors, and the Commission cannot be held responsible for any use which may be made of the information contained therein.

## References

1. Papadopoulos, K., Koustriava, E., Kartasidou, L.: The impact of residual vision in spatial skills of individuals with visual impairments. J. Spec. Educ. **45**(2), 118–127 (2011)
2. Papadopoulos, K., Koustriava, E.: The impact of vision in spatial coding. Res. Dev. Disabil. **32**(6), 2084–2091 (2011)

3. Papadopoulos, K., Barouti, M., Charitakis, K.: A university indoors audio-tactile mobility aid for individuals with blindness. In: Miesenberger, K., Fels, D., Archambault, D., Peňáz, P., Zagler, W. (eds.) ICCHP 2014, Part II. LNCS, vol. 8548, pp. 108–115. Springer, Heidelberg (2014)
4. Koustriava, E., Papadopoulos, K.: Mental rotation ability of individuals with visual impairments. J. Vis. Impairment Blindness **104**(9), 570–574 (2010)
5. Koustriava, E., Papadopoulos, K.: Are there relationships among different spatial skills of individuals with blindness? Res. Devel. Disabil. **33**(6), 2164–2176 (2012)
6. Espinosa, M.A., Ungar, S., Ochaita, E., Blades, M., Spencer, C.: Comparing methods for introducing blind and visually impaired people to unfamiliar urban environments. J. Enviro. Psychol. **18**(3), 277–287 (1998)
7. Jacobson, R.D.: Navigating maps with little or no sight: An audio-tactile approach. In: Proceedings of Content Visualization and Intermedia Representations, pp. 95–102. Montréal, Québec, Canada (1998)
8. Papadopoulos, K., Karanikolas, N.: Tactile maps provide location based services for individuals with visual impairments. J. Location Based Serv. **3**(3), 150–164 (2009)
9. Caddeo, P., Fornara, F., Nenci, A.M., Piroddi, A.: Wayfinding tasks in visually impaired people: the role of tactile maps. Cogn. Process. **7**, 168–169 (2006)
10. Espinosa, M.A., Ochaita, E.: Using tactile maps to improve the practical spatial knowledge of adults who are blind. J. Vis. Impairment Blindness **92**(5), 338–345 (1998)
11. Thinus-Blanc, C., Gaunet, F.: Representation of space in blind persons: vision as a spatial sense? Psychol. Bull. **121**(1), 20–42 (1997)
12. Papadopoulos, K., Koustriava, E., Kartasidou, L.: Spatial coding of individuals with visual impairments. J. Spec. Educ. **46**(3), 180–190 (2012)
13. Passini, R., Duprés, A., Langlois, C.: Spatial mobility of the visually handicapped active person: a descriptive study. J. Vis. Impairment Blindnes **80**(8), 904–907 (1986)
14. Habel, C., Kerzel, M., Lohmann, K.: Verbal assistance in tactile map explorations: a case for visual representations and reasoning. In: Proceedings of Visual Representations and Reasoning, pp. 34–41. Atlanta, GA, USA (2010)
15. Bentzen, B.L.: Orientation aids. In: Blasch, B.B., Wiener, W.R., Welsh, R.L. (eds.) Foundations of Orientation and Mobility, 2nd edn, pp. 291–355. AFB Press, New York (1997)

# Mobility Support for Blind and Partially Sighted People

# Obstacle Detection and Avoidance for the Visually Impaired in Indoors Environments Using Google's Project Tango Device

Rabia Jafri[✉] and Marwa Mahmoud Khan

Department of Information Technology, King Saud University, Riyadh, Saudi Arabia
rabia.ksu@gmail.com, marwa_khan-_-@live.com

**Abstract.** A depth-data based obstacle detection and avoidance application for VI users to assist them in navigating independently in previously unmapped indoors environments is presented. The application is being developed for the recently introduced Google Project Tango Tablet Development Kit equipped with a powerful processor (NVIDIA Tegra K1 with 192 CUDA cores) as well as various sensors which allow it track its motion and orientation in 3D space in real-time. Depth data for the area in front of the users, obtained using the tablet's in-built infrared–based depth sensor, is analyzed to detect obstacles and audio-based navigation instructions are provided accordingly. A visual display option is also offered for users with low vision. The aim is to develop a real-time, affordable, aesthetically acceptable, mobile assistive stand-alone application on a cutting-edge device, adopting a user-centered approach, which allows VI users to micro-navigate autonomously in possibly unfamiliar indoor surroundings.

**Keywords:** Visually impaired · Blind · Navigation · Indoors navigation · Obstacle detection · Obstacle avoidance · Google project tango · Depth sensor · Infrared · Assistive technologies

## 1 Introduction

One of the major challenges faced by visually impaired (VI) individuals while navigating independently in indoors environments is detecting and avoiding obstacles or drop-offs in their path. Though a white cane is typically used for this purpose, it has several limitations, such as being highly conspicuous, not being able to detect objects beyond its reach, not sensing obstacles above the waist level and requiring contact with obstacles in order to sense them (which may not be practical - e.g., for detecting people or fragile objects) [1]. Moreover, some VI people, suffering from multiple disabilities, may not have the physical strength or motor skills to use a cane effectively.

This delineates a compelling need to develop technological solutions to assist VI people in detecting and avoiding obstacles in their path. In recent years, infrared-enabled depth sensor-based systems have emerged as some of the most promising solutions for addressing this issue. These systems offer the advantages of being affordable, discreet, noninvasive and unobtrusive (since infrared light is invisible to the naked eye), offering directional information (especially if beacons or tags are placed on obstacles) and being

© Springer International Publishing Switzerland 2016
K. Miesenberger et al. (Eds.): ICCHP 2016, Part II, LNCS 9759, pp. 179–185, 2016.
DOI: 10.1007/978-3-319-41267-2_24

able to operate in the dark or under poor lighting conditions. However, such systems can detect objects only within a certain range and their performance may be negatively impacted by interference from other infrared sources, such as sunlight or fluorescent light.

Moreover, these systems require huge numbers of computations per unit time in order to achieve real-time performance - most mobile platforms currently do not possess powerful enough processors and battery life to support this amount of processing for extended periods of time. Furthermore, prototype devices attempting to combine camera images and depth data to improve the accuracy of the detection tend to have difficulty in precisely synchronizing their various components and sensors with each other. Consequently, currently such systems fall short in terms of accurately localizing the user and providing real-time feedback about obstacles in his path.

The Project Tango Tablet Development Kit [2], recently introduced by Google, is an Android device, equipped with a powerful processor (NVIDIA Tegra K1 with 192 CUDA cores) and various sensors (motion tracking camera, 3D depth sensor, accelerometer, ambient light sensor, barometer, compass, GPS, gyroscope), which allow it not only to track its own movement and orientation through 3D space in real time using computer vision techniques but also enable it to remember areas that it has travelled through and localize the user within those areas to up to an accuracy of a few centimeters. Its integrated infrared based depth sensors also allow it to measure the distance from the device to objects in the real world providing depth data about the objects in the form of point clouds.

We are, therefore, developing an application for the Project Tango tablet to assist VI users in detecting and avoiding obstacles in their path during navigation in an indoors environment. The project is focused on micro-navigation in previously un-mapped surroundings. The application operates by analyzing the depth data for the area in front of the user to detect if any obstacles are present; if so, it provides audio feedback to help him to navigate around them. A visual display option is also offered for users with low vision. Our aim is to exploit two main strengths of the Tango tablet– its ability to provide depth data of the surrounding environment and its capacity for performing computationally expensive operations (the collection and processing of the depth data to extract the obstacles, in the case of our system) in real-time on the device itself without the need to connect to an external server or rapidly draining the battery. Our motivation is to increase the autonomy of VI users by providing them with a real-time mobile assistive stand-alone application on a cutting–edge device which allows them to micro-navigate independently in possibly unfamiliar indoor surroundings.

The rest of the paper is organized as follows: Sect. 2 provides an overview of existing assistive systems for the VI utilizing infrared sensors for obstacle detection and highlights their strengths and limitations. Section 3 describes the proposed application explaining the obstacle detection process and the feedback mechanism. Section 4 concludes the paper and identifies some directions for future work.

# 2   Related Work

Several infrared-based obstacle detection systems for the VI employing infrared tags [3], infrared beacons [3–5] and general thermal input from the environment [6, 7] have been introduced in recent years. These solutions suffer from some inherent limitations originating from the sensor technologies themselves (please refer to the introduction for details). Furthermore, most of these systems require retrofitting the environment with tags and beacons, which is costly, time consuming and limits the use of the system only to previously fitted areas. Nevertheless, some newly emerging sensor technologies (e.g., Microsoft's Kinect [8], Occipital's Structure Sensor [9], and, most recently, Google's Project Tango Tablet Development Kit [2]) are making it possible to exploit infrared light to extract 3D information about the environment without the need to install any equipment in the surroundings. Recent development work on obstacle detection has specially focused on Kinect, either utilizing the data from its depth sensor alone [10–13] or from both its RGB and depth sensors [14, 15]. Since the Kinect sensor module is not designed as a wearable or handheld device, these systems employ makeshift methods for affixing it to various locations on the user's body (e.g., head, chest or waist) resulting in awkward bulky contraptions that are unappealing from an aesthetic perspective and, thus, unlikely to be practically adopted by VI individuals for whom, as confirmed by several studies [16, 17], the cosmetic acceptability of an assistive device is even more important than its utility. Moreover, the processing of the data obtained from the Kinect sensors has to be done on an external server, which introduces some additional constraints and challenges: the user's device has to be connected to a remote system, the inevitable communication overhead may negatively affect the real-time performance and the absence or failure of a network connection would render the system useless (network connectivity is an even more pertinent issue in developing countries where 90 % of the VI population resides [18]).

The Project Tango tablet appears to have a distinct advantage over Kinect in that it is an aesthetically appealing, handheld, mobile device equipped with a powerful processor enabling it to execute computationally intensive code in real-time without the need to connect to a backend server. Moreover, it has several additional embedded sensors and in-built functionalities, which can be utilized for extending and improving the obstacle detection application in the future. Since the tablet has just recently been released in the market and has obvious potential for meeting real-time navigation requirements, there is a compelling need to initiate work to utilize its capabilities for developing navigational aids for the VI. These considerations have motivated us to use this platform for our development work. It should be noted that a few preliminary applications for the Tango tablet have already been proposed for this purpose: The system presented by Anderson [19] collects depth information about the environment, saves it in a chunk-based voxel representation, and generates 3D audio for sonifiction which is relayed to the VI user via headphones to alert him to the presence of obstacles. Wang et al. [20] cluster depth readings of the immediate physical space around the users into different sectors and then analyze the relative and absolute depth of different sectors to establish thresholds to differentiate among obstacles, walls and corners, and ascending and descending staircases. Users are given navigation directions and information about objects using Android's text-to-speech feature. However, both these applications need further development and are yet to be tested with the target users.

## 3    System Design and Architecture

The application is being developed for Google's Project Tango Tablet Development Kit which is an Android-based device. It utilizes the tablet's built-in infrared-based depth sensor to acquire the depth data of the user's surroundings in the form of point clouds. The Project Tango SDK [21] and the OpenCV4Android SDK [22] are used to access the point cloud data and perform the image processing operations, respectively. Pre-recorded audio files are played via an open-ear bone conduction Bluetooth headset for the audio output. Details about the obstacle detection process, the navigation instructions and the optional visual display are provided below.

**Process for Detecting the Obstacles and Determining their Proximity to the User.** The sensitivity of the depth sensor is set so that it detects only the points which are within a range of 2 meters (which is considered to be an appropriate range for detecting obstacles at a normal walking speed). The point cloud scan is obtained from the depth sensors and then converted into a depth image. Some preprocessing operations are performed to remove the noise in the image. The Canny edge detector [23] is used to detect and remove all the edges and a region growing method is used to find all the connected components in the depth image. The largest component in the bottom part of the image is assumed to be the floor and is removed. All the remaining components are considered obstacles.

**Navigation Instructions for Avoiding the Obstacle.** The depth image is divided into three equal columns, where the column in the middle represents the area directly in front of the user. If there are no obstacles in that column, the user can continue walking and no instructions need to be given. However, if an obstacle is detected in that column, the column on the right is checked and if it is obstacle free, the user is told to bear right. If not, the column on the left is checked and if it is obstacle free, the user is instructed to bear left. Otherwise, the user is informed that no clear path can be found in front of him.

The navigation instructions are provided via Bluetooth headphones in either of two formats: As verbal instructions ("bear right", "bear left", "no clear path") or as directional beeps (beeps in right ear for bearing right, beeps in left ear for bearing left, beeps in both ears for no clear path). The user is allowed to choose the format that he prefers.

**Visual Depth Display for Users with Low Vision.** For users with some residual vision, additional guidance is provided by visually displaying the depth information of the obstacles on the tablet's screen so that points in the range of 0–50 cm, 51–100 cm, 101–150 cm and 151–200 cm are displayed in red, orange, yellow and blue, respectively.

For now, we plan to acquire the point cloud scan once every second and provide audio directions accordingly. However, empirical tests would be used to determine if the frequency of acquiring the scans is adequate for detecting and providing feedback about obstacles in real-time. It should be noted that the current design of the user interface for the system is inspired by the review of the literature for existing obstacle detection systems for the VI. However, since the interface design is so vital to the usability and acceptability of the system, we have formulated several research questions related to this and will shortly be conducting a series of semi-structured interviews at local institutions for the VI to gain more insight into the target users' needs and preferences. The results of the interviews would then be used to inform the final design of the application.

## 4  Conclusion and Future Work

A depth-data based real-time obstacle detection and avoidance application for VI users to assist them in autonomous navigation in indoors environments has been described in this paper. The application utilizes the capabilities of the Project Tango Development Kit to provide an aesthetically acceptable, cost-effective, portable, stand-alone solution for this purpose. Adopting a user centered approach, we plan to conduct semi-structured interviews with the target users to inform the interface design and later intend to carry out usability testing for the developed prototype with VI users in order to incorporate their feedback into the system to better adapt it to their needs.

Other directions for future work include the following: Since the RGB cameras on the Tango tablet are synchronized with the depth sensor, hence, in order to compensate for erroneous data and noise in the point cloud scans, we plan to integrate information from the corresponding RGB image of the scene to improve the accuracy of the detection. Also, at present, the system is designed only to detect obstacles but not to identify them. The system will be extended in the future to also recognize frequently encountered obstacles and convey their identities to the user. An option allowing the user to inquire if a particular kind of obstacle is in front of him will also be provided.

We are working in parallel on another application, focusing on macro-navigation, which assists the user in navigating from a specific location to another one in a previously mapped environment utilizing the area learning and motion tracking capabilities of the Tango tablet. The obstacle detection and avoidance system described in this paper would eventually be integrated within this application to meet its micro-navigation requirements.

## References

1. Shoval, S., Ulrich, I., Borenstein, J.: NavBelt and the Guide-Cane [obstacle-avoidance systems for the blind and visually impaired]. Robot. Autom. Mag. IEEE **10**, 9–20 (2003)
2. Google Project Tango. https://www.google.com/atap/project-tango/
3. Ivanchenko, V., Coughlan, J., Gerrey, W., Shen, H.: Computer vision-based clear path guidance for blind wheelchair users. In: Proceedings of the 10th International ACM SIGACCESS Conference on Computers and Accessibility, Halifax, Nova Scotia, Canada, pp. 291–292 (2008)

4. Magatani, K., Sawa, K., Yanashima, K.: Development of the navigation system for the visually impaired by using optical beacons. In: Proceedings of the 23rd Annual International Conference of the IEEE Engineering in Medicine and Biology Society, 2001, vol. 2, pp. 1488–1490 (2001)
5. Harada, T., Kaneko, Y., Hirahara, Y., Yanashima, K., Magatani, K.: Development of the navigation system for visually impaired. In: 26th Annual International Conference of the IEEE Engineering in Medicine and Biology Society, 2004, IEMBS 2004, pp. 4900–4903 (2004)
6. Do, D.H., Riehle, T.H., Solinsky, R., Assadi-Lamouki, P., Hillesheim, C.T., Vu, A.N., Velie, T., Seifert, G.J.: Resolving subjects and measuring observer/subject distances with a thermal tactile imager. In: 30th Annual International Conference of the IEEE Engineering in Medicine and Biology Society, 2008. EMBS 2008, pp. 4302–4305 (2008)
7. Mustapha, B., Zayegh, A., Begg, R.K.: Wireless obstacle detection system for the elderly and visually impaired people. In: 2013 IEEE International Conference on Smart Instrumentation, Measurement and Applications (ICSIMA), pp. 1–5 (2013)
8. Microsoft Kinect. https://dev.windows.com/en-us/kinect
9. Structure Sensor, Occipital Inc. http://structure.io/
10. Zöllner, M., Huber, S., Jetter, H.-C., Reiterer, H.: NAVI– a proof-of-concept of a mobile navigational aid for visually impaired based on the microsoft kinect. In: Campos, P., Graham, N., Jorge, J., Nunes, N., Palanque, P., Winckler, M. (eds.) INTERACT 2011, Part IV. LNCS, vol. 6949, pp. 584–587. Springer, Heidelberg (2011)
11. Filipe, V., Fernandes, F., Fernandes, H., Sousa, A., Paredes, H., Barroso, J.: Blind navigation support system based on microsoft kinect. Procedia Comput. Sci. **14**, 94–101 (2012)
12. Brock, M., Kristensson, P.O.: Supporting blind navigation using depth sensing and sonification. In: Proceedings of the 2013 ACM Conference on Pervasive and Ubiquitous Computing Adjunct Publication, Zurich, Switzerland, pp. 255–258 (2013)
13. Huang, H.-C., Hsieh, C.-T., Yeh, C.-H.: An indoor obstacle detection system using depth information and region growth. Sensors **15**, 27116–27141 (2015)
14. Lee, Y.H., Medioni, G.: Wearable RGBD indoor navigation system for the blind. In: Agapito, L., Bronstein, M.M., Rother, C. (eds.) ECCV 2014 Workshops. LNCS, vol. 8927, pp. 493–508. Springer, Heidelberg (2015)
15. Ribeiro, F., Florencio, D., Chou, P.A., Zhengyou, Z.: Auditory augmented reality: Object sonification for the visually impaired. In: 2012 IEEE 14th International Workshop on Multimedia Signal Processing (MMSP), pp. 319–324 (2012)
16. Golledge, R., Klatzky, R., Loomis, J., Marston, J.: Stated preferences for components of a personal guidance system for nonvisual navigation. J. Vis. Impairment Blindness **98**, 135–147 (2004)
17. Jafri, R., Ali, S.A.: Exploring the potential of eyewear-based wearable display devices for use by the visually impaired. In: Proceedings of the 3rd International Conference on User Science and Engineering (i-USEr 2014), Shah Alam, Malaysia, pp. 119–124 (2014)
18. Visual impairment and blindness: Fact sheet number 282. WHO media center (2012). http://www.who.int/mediacentre/factsheets/fs282/en/
19. Anderson, D.: Navigation for the Visually Impaired Using a Google Tango RGB-D Tablet (2015). http://www.dan.andersen.name/navigation-for-the-visually-impaired-using-a-google-tango-rgb-d-tablet/
20. Tiresias: An app to help visually impaired people navigate easily through unfamiliar buildings. HackDuke 2015 (2015). http://devpost.com/software/tiresias-ie0vum
21. Project Tango SDK. https://developers.google.com/project-tango/downloads#project_tango_sdk_files

22. OpenCV Platforms: Android. http://opencv.org/platforms/android.html
23. Canny, J.F.: A computational approach to edge detection. In: Martin, A.F., Oscar, F. (eds.), Readings in Computer Vision: Issues, Problems, Principles, and Paradigms. Morgan Kaufmann Publishers Inc., pp. 184–203 (1987)

# System Supporting Independent Walking of the Visually Impaired

Mitsuki Nishikiri[1(✉)], Takehiro Sakai[1], Hiroaki Kudo[1], Tetsuya Matsumoto[1], Yoshinori Takeuchi[2], and Noboru Ohnishi[1]

[1] Graduate School of Information Science, Nagoya University, Nagoya, Japan
{nishikiri,sakai,kudo,matsumoto,ohnishi}@ohnishi.m.is.nagoya-u.ac.jp
[2] School of Informatics, Daido University, Nagoya, Japan
ytake@daido-it.ac.jp

**Abstract.** This paper proposes an integrated navigation system that supports the independent walking of the visually impaired. It supports route guidance and adjustments, zebra-crossing detection and guidance, pedestrian traffic signal detection and discrimination, and localization of the entrance doors of the buildings of destinations. This system was implemented on an Android smartphone. As a result of experiments, our system's detection rate for zebra crossings was about 72 % and about 80 % for traffic signals.

**Keywords:** Navigation · Blind · Mobility · Traffic intersection

## 1 Introduction

When the visually impaired walk outdoors, they encounter many challenges, including acquiring information about how to precisely obtain their location, and how to navigate through their environment. From a questionnaire with two blind persons, we identified three specific, critical difficulties that they face: grasping a destination's route, determining the color of pedestrian traffic signals, and localizing the building entrances of destinations. Although many visually impaired people go outside with the assistance of sighted helpers, the visually impaired want the independence to navigate themselves by themselves. To increase their independence, they need supporting systems. Most existing navigation systems are for sighted people and only give vocal route guidance. Obviously, such limited systems fail to provide blind people with information about their current positions and the direction in which they should move. The currently available navigation systems for the visually impaired [1–4] can't fully support the functions needed for independent walking; no integrated navigation system exists.

Therefore, we propose an integrated navigation system that provides the following supports for the independent walking of the visually impaired: route guidance and adjustments, zebra-crossing detection and guidance, pedestrian traffic signal detection and discrimination, and localization of the entrance door of a destination building.

K. Miesenberger et al. (Eds.): ICCHP 2016, Part II, LNCS 9759, pp. 186–189, 2016.
DOI: 10.1007/978-3-319-41267-2_25

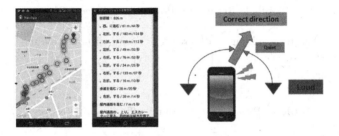

**Fig. 1.** Example of route guidance and Compass function

## 1.1 System Overview

We implemented this system on an Android smartphone, which blind people currently use in their daily lives. This small smartphone includes several sensors that can provide much information needed for realizing this system. Visual information for navigation is obtained by processing images captured by a camera. We use software called "OpenCV for Android" for image processing. Further, considering the accessibility of the visually impaired, we use several free APIs for a voice input interface, voice recognition, and character input with feedback. Using the sensors and APIs, the proposed system provides four functions.

## 1.2 Route Guidance

This function provides to users destination routes that are audibly input. With the "Google Places API", the system obtains the destination's latitude and longitude. Then the "Google Maps Directions API" provides a route from the current location to the destination with behavior descriptions/instructions (e.g., go straight, turn left, turn right) (Fig. 1 Left). Once the guidance starts, the system provides navigation by synthesized voices, e.g., "turn left after walking for 10 m", based on the user's position acquired from the GPS sensor. The system also has a compass function, which provides the direction in which users should move. If users face the wrong direction, they will hear a sound whose amplitude is proportional to the difference between the current direction and the correct direction: the larger the difference, the louder the sound (Fig. 1 Right).

## 1.3 Zebra-Crossing Detection and Guidance

When a user approaches an intersection during a route guidance, the system starts the zebra-crossing detection/guidance function, which locates the zebra crossings and their direction and distance from the current location using images captured by smartphone. The user can take an image of what is directly in front of him without worrying about the smartphone's tilt because it is adjusted by a gyro sensor. To extract the zebra-crossing features, the system converts the obtained images into HSV images and applies a two-dimensional Fourier transform to the converted images. Based on the extracted features, the system

**Table 1.** Result of zebra-crossing detection

| Decision | Image with crossing | Image without crossing |
|---|---|---|
| Crossing | 43 | 1 |
| No crossing | 17 | 26 |

**Table 2.** Result of pedestrian traffic signal detection

| | Red right/LED | Red right/ incandescent bulb | Green right/LED | Green right/ incandescent bulb | total |
|---|---|---|---|---|---|
| Images | 26 | 30 | 26 | 30 | 112 |
| Correct detections | 24 | 22 | 23 | 20 | 89 |
| (detection rate) | (92 %) | (73 %) | (89 %) | (67 %) | (80 %) |

detects the candidate block regions of a zebra crossing in the image. Finally the zebra crossing is determined by the destination's route. Once a zebra crossing is detected, the distance to it from the user's location is estimated. Using the obtained distance, this system provides the direction and the number of footsteps to the zebra crossing.

### 1.4   Pedestrian Traffic Signal Detection

When the user arrives at the zebra crossing's starting point, he captures an image of what is directly in front of him that is matched with templates of the pedestrian traffic signals that were prepared in advance. These templates include images of both the traffic signals of LED and conventional electric bulb types. By template matching, the system detects traffic signals. The traffic signal's color is also recognized by this function. If the pedestrian traffic signal is detected, the traffic signal's color is output.

### 1.5   Entrance of Building Door Detection

When the user arrives near her destination, the system prompts her to take an image of what is in front of her based on the GPS sensor data. With the help of volunteers, the system in advance collects a set of images of the destination's entrance and such information as direction, distance, and types of doors (e.g., automatic or sliding). The system matches the images from the user with each stored image with SIFT features and determines the best matched image and provides the entrance's direction and the distance to it.

## 2   Experimental Result

We conducted three experiments: zebra-crossing detection, pedestrian traffic signal detection, and entrance of a building's door detection. In the zebra-crossing

**Fig. 2.** Experimental result of zebra-crossing detection and pedestrian traffic signal detection (Color figure online)

detection experiment, we used 60 images with a zebra crossing and 27 images without. These images, which were taken by smartphone, were 640*480 pixels (Fig. 2 Left). The zebra-crossing candidate region is surrounded by red lines in the image. Table 1 shows the results of zebra-crossing detection. The detection rate was about 72 % (43/60). Figure 2 (Right) shows an example detection image from the pedestrian traffic signal detection experiment. The pedestrian traffic signal region is surrounded by blue lines in the image's enlarged part (Table 2). We used four image datasets: red traffic signals of LED or incandescent bulb types, and green traffic signals of LED or incandescent bulb types. The total detection rate was about 80 %.

In the experiment that detected a building door's entrance, we created a database and query images of such doors from images captured in advance. The database has 64 images and 96 query images. As a result of matching the queries and the database, the recall ratio was 0.71, and the precision ratio was 0.74.

## 3    Conclusion

We proposed an integrated navigation system that supports the independent walking of the visually impaired and implemented it on a smartphone. Future work will improve its system performance by refining the user-interface and conducting a field test.

## References

1. Walky Talky, Eyes-Free Project. https://code.google.com/p/eyes-free/
2. Intersection Explorer. https://play.google.com/store/apps/details?id=com.google.android.marvin.intersectionexplore
3. Bhargava, B., Angin, P., Duan, L.: A mobile-cloud pedestrian crossing guide for the blind. In: International Conference on Advances in Computing & Communication (2011)
4. Ahmetovic, D., Bernareggi, C., Mascetti, S.: ZebraLocalizer: identification and localization of pedestrian crossings. In: The Conference on Human-Computer Interaction with Mobile Devices and Services, pp. 275–284 (2011)

# Path Planning for a Universal Indoor Navigation System

Elie Kahale[✉], Pierre-Charles Hanse, Valéria Destin, Gérard Uzan,
and Jaime Lopez-Krahe

THIM Laboratory (EA 4004 CHArt), University of Paris 8, 93200 Saint-Denis, France
{elie.kahale,pierre-charles.hanse02,valeria.destin02,gerard.uzan,
jaime.lopez-krahe}@univ-paris8.fr

**Abstract.** Many researches on indoor navigation systems have been done in the last decades. Most of them consider either people without disabilities or a specific type of disabilities. In this paper, we propose a new model based on a universal design concept. Our approach employs a novel method for modeling indoor environment and introduce a new optimization criterion : minimizing the arduousness of the path. This criterion is based on the user's profile and the inherent characteristics of amenities which may affect the displacement of the person. The performance of the proposed methods was tested and validated in a university building through an application for smart-phone.

**Keywords:** Arduousness · Path planning · Indoor navigation · Mobility people with disabilities

## 1 Introduction

Mobility means the possibility of liberally moving, without support of any supplementary person in familiar and unfamiliar scenarios [1]. In fact, people navigating in a new environment often need the help of sighted people to navigate and cognitively map the environment which is time consuming and leads to a lower mobility [2].

Over the past decades numerous indoor navigation systems for people with disabilities have been developed. In [3], the authors propose an indoor navigation system for blind persons. The path planning approach used in that paper provides the shortest path. Other works based on shortest path or even shortest travel time can be found in [4–6].

On another side, the authors in [7] introduce a least hazard criterion to find path for blind people, in which, the suggested path avoid a crossover of a crowded area. A similar work can be found in [8–10].

Furthermore, wheelchair and elderly people cases are considered in [9,11], where the stairs are avoided and the slope of each path is taken into account.

Additional works on indoor navigation systems can be found in the literature [12–14]. Most of these research focus on localization system, while the questions

K. Miesenberger et al. (Eds.): ICCHP 2016, Part II, LNCS 9759, pp. 190–197, 2016.
DOI: 10.1007/978-3-319-41267-2_26

of indoor map modeling and optimal path generation have not been studied enough.

The essential requirements, processes and information needed at each stage of the chain of displacement are introduced in [15] which can be defined by the following five essential components : Safety, Orientation, Localization of the user and his destination, Information and Displacement (please see Table 1).

In this paper we propose a path planning strategy for indoor navigation systems to assist people in their displacement in public-access building, such as large commercial facilities, shopping centers, public spaces, transport facilities, etc. The proposed method must take into account the potential difficulties that users might have and which affect their displacement. In addition, we assume that the environment where the system is deployed must be equipped with sensors enabling the localization of the user, so that the system is able to update the proposed path when the person is lost or an alternative is needed.

The originality of our work is threefold: Firstly, a novel approach employed for modeling indoor environments. Secondly, a new optimization criterion: minimizing the arduousness of the proposed path. Thirdly, The proposed method is based on a universal design concept. In other words, it takes into account the widest possible range of people and addresses the needs of persons with disabilities.

**Table 1.** Travelers needs

| Needs in ... | Characteristics |
| --- | --- |
| ... safety | avoid falling, collisions or straying into a dangerous zone |
| ... orientation | maintain a straight path, turn at the right intersections, memorize and follow a route, determine the direction of the walk, verify intermediate destinations, find or choose an alternative route in case of need |
| ... localization | Ego-localization (where am I?), Allo-localization (What is there around me? Where can I move?) |
| ... information | information on the environment and peripheral activities (tourist attractions, landmarks, shopping facilities, access zones to transport, lines, destinations, routes, schedules, ...) |
| ... displacement | barriers, path accessibility, ... |

## 2   Path Planning Strategy

The path planning is an important component in navigation systems, which can affect the overall performance of the system. The path needs to be planned in such a way to maximize the usability and success rate while minimizing the chance of the user getting lost. A smarter path planning technique needs to consider user's requirements and customize the path accordingly [16]. To this end, we describe the environment through a valued digraph and we use a graph-based approach to determine the route. These two techniques are the subject of the next paragraphs.

## 2.1 Surface Modeling

Note that, in this paper, we employ the notion of surface and not area because we are interested by the large family of paths contained in highly distributive surfaces (e.g. halls, slabs, esplanades, etc.). However, the structure of public-access buildings is composed of multi-levels involving junction elements (e.g. stairs, escalators, elevators, etc.). Each level contains many potential destinations such as shops, cultural spaces, counters, etc. In order to include universal design concept, we consider many amenities as edges, which is not the case in many models. For example, a door can be easily crossed by people without disabilities, difficult to cross by individuals using crutches and impassable by wheelchair users. So, from our point of view, a building consists of a limited number of appropriated amenity classes regarding to paths optimization process which includes *the arduousness criterion* which is developed further.

This modeling can be described through a valued digraph in which the nodes represent walkable surfaces and the edges express junction elements and specified amenities. Moreover, each node of a such digraph is itself a sub-digraph.

To generate the sub-digraphs taking into account the presence of obstacles within walkable surfaces, we use approaches conventionally applied in the field of mobile robotics, in particular, visibility-based method. The defining characteristics of a visibility map are that its nodes share an edge if they are within line of sight of each other, and that all points in the free space are within line of sight of at least one node on the visibility map. The nodes $v_i$ of the visibility graph include the start location, the goal location, and all the vertices of the obstacles. The graph edges $e_{ij}$ are straight-line segments that connect two line-of-sight nodes $v_i$ and $v_j$, i.e.

$$e_{ij} \neq \varnothing \Longleftrightarrow sv_i + (1-s)v_j \in Q_{free} \quad \forall s \in [0,1] \tag{1}$$

where $Q_{free}$ denotes the walkable surfaces.

In order to Construct the visibility graph, we use the Rotational Plane Sweep Algorithm. This approach use a half-line $I$, emanating from the vertex $v$, and a rotational sweep, rotating $I$ from 0 to $2\pi$. The key to this algorithm is to incrementally maintain the set of edges that intersect $I$, sorted in order of increasing distance from $v$. If a vertex $v_i$ is visible to $v$, then it should be added to the visibility graph. For more details please see [17].

## 2.2 User Profile

From the point of view of the french law [21], people with disabilities are classified in six main categories : physical, sensory, mental, psychic, cognitive and multiple impairment. This classification was considered as a basis for the design of dedicated devices.

In this paper, we consider the disability as a set of difficulties to complete a task in interaction with a given environment. The pedestrian movement needs the user's skills of interaction with his physical and social environment, its ability to memories places, to establish connections between networks or to use facilities. In general, there are specific needs of each user according to his capacities. Thus, we determined the 12 potential classes that can characterize the users and have an impact on the computation of an optimal path (Table 2).

**Table 2.** User's profile parameters

| Related to the use of hands | o Trembling or involuntary movements |
| | o Difficult use of hands |
| Related to the displacement | o Supporting stick, crutches, walker |
| | o Stiffness, joint or muscle pains |
| | o Shortness of breath, respiratory or heart problems |
| | o Electric wheelchair |
| | o Manual wheelchair |
| Related to the vision | o Blindness (use of a walking cane) |
| | o Glare, fog, blur, opacity, paleness |
| | o Fragmented, Tunnel or peripheral vision |
| | o Blindness (use of guide dog) |
| | o Difficulty reading |

## 2.3 Optimal Path Algorithm

Remember that the provided path must satisfy the physical capacities of the user and minimize the effort needed to accomplish each step. To take these constraints into account, we propose a new coefficient describing the arduousness associated to each edge in the digraph.

So, after determining the different categories of disabilities and difficulties which may affect the displacement (Sect. 2.2), we have determined the inherent characteristics, which have an impact on the displacement, for each amenity identified as an edge in our modeling. Thus, each edge in our digraph, have two groups of properties: the first one describes the physical constraints of the user, while the second one presents the intrinsic features of the edge. Each element of these properties is represented by a weighting coefficient. Hence, the global arduousness coefficient for a given edge can be expressed as following:

$$\Gamma_{e_i} = \Pi \gamma_{u,e_i} \tag{2}$$

where $\Gamma_{e_i}$ denotes the global arduousness coefficient for the edge $e_i$, and $\gamma_{u,e_i}$ represents a combinatorial characteristics appropriated to the edge and user's profile. Remark that $\gamma_{u,e_i} \in [0,1] \Rightarrow \Gamma_{e_i} \in [0,1]$ that means, an edge having $\Gamma_{e_i} = 0$ is impassable while another one having $\Gamma_{e_i} = 1$ have no constraints.

Generating a route between two points is an operation already applied for the navigation in mobile robots. Several methods of path planning, used in operational research, are proposed in the literature. The most used algorithms are : Dijkstra and A*. Dijkstra algorithm uses a start node and calculates the distance between it and other nodes in the graph iteratively. The iterative process stops when a minimal distance between start and end points is found. Moreover, Dijkstra's algorithm guarantees the optimality of the solution. On the other side, A* algorithm is a derivative from Dijkstra's algorithm. It uses a heuristic function to select next nodes. Thus, it reduces the computational time by reducing the number of calculation to be performed. However, A* algorithm does not guarantee the optimality of the proposed solution [17–20].

Remember that, our objective is to minimize the arduousness (i.e. maximize $\Gamma_{e_i}$). Therefore, replacing the distance by $1/\Gamma_{e_i}$ in Dijkstra's algorithm makes the algorithm able to provide a path with the minimum arduousness cost.

## 3    Simulation Results

In order to validate the performance of the proposed system, we carried out some simulations in a university building. The path planning algorithm was integrated in a Samsung Galaxy S6 (64 bits processor) smart-phone through an application developed in JAVA.

An additional algorithms have been integrated to ensure the robustness of the algorithm facing errors resulting from map data collection. These errors can be summarized in the following two points:

– Data format or unit errors.
– Imprecision in the location of points of interest (some points are even placed in non-walkable surfaces).

Three scenarios were chosen to approve the performance of the system and demonstrate the impact of arduousness coefficient on calculus.

In the first scenario we consider a person without any difficulties. So, the proposed path has no constrained, e.g. it may contain a stair. In fact, even if the arduousness coefficient of an elevator is lower than a stair, the stair will be privileged since the global arduousness coefficient of the proposed path remains inferior to the other possible paths.

While for the second scenario we consider a wheelchair user. Hence, the path is limited and some edge-classes will be eliminated from calculus such that stair, escalator, and even non-accessible door edge-classes.

Finally, in the third scenario we assume that the person is blind and has a shortness of breath. In this case, the path will be constrained and some edge-classes will be privileged regarding others depending on the situation. For example, the case when the person must go from a place to another one located in a floor up, near a staircase and away from the elevator. If the number of floors

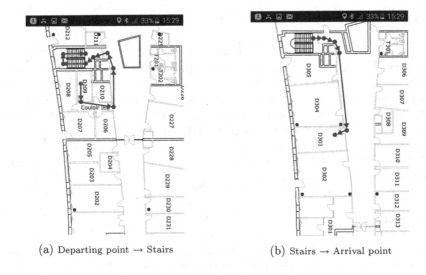

(a) Departing point → Stairs          (b) Stairs → Arrival point

**Fig. 1.** The proposed path for a person without disabilities

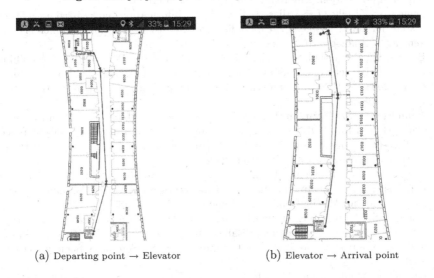

(a) Departing point → Elevator          (b) Elevator → Arrival point

**Fig. 2.** The proposed path for a person with visual impairment and shortness of breath

between the two places is one, the system will suggest the use of the stair. While, when the number of floors is two or higher, the system will privilege the use of the elevator. Note that in this scenario the user combine two types of disabilities. The first and second scenarios are illustrated in the Figs. 1 and 2.

## 4   Conclusion and Future Works

A novel path planning strategy for indoor navigation systems was proposed in this paper. The system is conceived in a universal design concept which takes a large range of human diversity, including physically disabled persons into account. The problem of generating paths in highly distributive surfaces was addressed and a new coefficient describing the arduousness of each step in the path was introduced. Some numerical simulations were carried out to illustrate the performance of the system.

Future works imply to validate the obtained results through experimentation in situ.

## References

1. Lakde, C.K., Prasad, P.S.: Review paper on navigation system for visually impaired people. Int. J. Adv. Res. Comput. Commun. Eng. **4**(1), 166–168 (2015)
2. Passini, R., Proulx, G., Rainville, C.: The spatio-cognitive abilities of the visually impaired population. Environ. Behav. **22**, 91–116 (1990)
3. Duarte, K., Cecílio, J., Sá Silva, J., Furtado, P.: Information and assisted navigation system for blind people. In: Proceedings of the 8th International Conference on Sensing Technology, 2014, Liverpool, UK (2014)
4. Bessho, M., Kobayashi, S., Koshizuka, N., Sakamura, K.: A space-identifying ubiquitous infrastructure and its application for tour-guiding service. In: Proceedings of the 2008 ACM Symposium on Applied Computing, SAC 2008. ACM, Ceará, Brazil (2008)
5. Chumkamon, S., Tuvaphanthaphiphat, P., Keeratiwintakorn, P.: A blind navigation system using RFID for indoor environments. In: 5th International Conference on Electrical Engineering/Electronics, Computer, Telecommunications and Information Technology, Krabi, Thailand (2008)
6. Ding, B., Yuan, H., Jiang, L., Zang, X.: The research on blind navigation system based on RFID. In: International Conference on Wireless Communications, Networking and Mobile Computing, Shanghai, China (2007)
7. Helal, A.S., Moore, S.E., Ramachandran, B.: Drishti: an integrated navigation system for visually impaired and disabled. In: Proceedings of the 5th IEEE International Symposium on Wearable Computers. IEEE Computer Society, Zurich, Switzerland (2001)
8. Kulyukin, V., Gharpure, C., Nicholson, J., Osborne, G.: Robot-assisted wayfinding for the visually impaired in structured indoor environments. Auton. Robots **21**(1), 29–41 (2006)
9. Petrie, H., Johnson, V., Strothotte, T., Raab, A., Fritz, S., Michel, R.: MOBIC: designing a travel aid for blind and elderly people. J. Navig. **49**(1), 45–52 (1996)
10. Tsetsos, V., Anagnostopoulos, C., Kikiras, P., Hadjiefthymiades, S.: Semantically enriched navigation for indoor environments. Int. J. Web Grid Serv. **2**(4), 453–478 (2006)
11. Koide, S., Kato, M.: 3-D human navigation system considering various transition preferences. In: IEEE International Conference on Systems, Man and Cybernetics (2005)

12. Venard, O., Baun, G., Uzan, G.: Experiment and evaluation of the RAMPE interactive auditive information system for the mobility of blind people in public transport. In: International Conference on Intelligent Transport Systems Telecommunications (ITST), Lille, France (2009)
13. Zegarra Flores, J., Farcy, R.: Indoor navigation system for the visually impaired using one inertial measurement unit (IMU) and barometer to guide in the subway stations and commercial centers. In: Miesenberger, K., Fels, D., Archambault, D., Peňáz, P., Zagler, W. (eds.) ICCHP 2014, Part I. LNCS, vol. 8547, pp. 411–418. Springer, Heidelberg (2014)
14. Moder, T., Hafner, P., Wieser, M.: Indoor positioning for visually impaired people based on smartphones. In: Miesenberger, K., Fels, D., Archambault, D., Peňáz, P., Zagler, W. (eds.) ICCHP 2014, Part I. LNCS, vol. 8547, pp. 441–444. Springer, Heidelberg (2014)
15. Uzan, G., M'Ballo, S., Wagstaff, P., Dejeammes, M.: SOLID: a model of the information requirements in transport systems for sensory impaired people. In: Invited presentation, 18th World Congress on Intelligent Transport Systems, Orlando, 16th–20th October 2011
16. Fallaha, N., Apostolopoulosa, I., Bekrisb, K., Folmera, E.: Indoor human navigation systems: a survey. Interact. Comput. **25**(1), 21–33 (2013)
17. Choset, H., Lynch, K., Hutchinson, S., Kantor, G., Burgard, W., Kavraki, L., Thrun, S.: Principles of Robot Motion-Theory, Algorithms, and Implementation. The MIT Press, Cambridge (2005)
18. LaValle, S.M.: Planning Algorithms. Cambridge University Press, Cambridge (2006)
19. Siciliano, B., Sciavicco, L., Villani, L., Oriolo, G.: Robotics: Modelling, Planning and Control. Springer, London (2009)
20. Jungnickel, D.: Graphs, Networks and Algorithms, 4th edn. Springer, London (2013)
21. Law N° 2005–102. https://www.legifrance.gouv.fr/eli/loi/2005/2/11/2005-102/jo/texte

# Supporting Pedestrians with Visual Impairment During Road Crossing: A Mobile Application for Traffic Lights Detection

Sergio Mascetti[1,2(✉)], Dragan Ahmetovic[1], Andrea Gerino[1,2],
Cristian Bernareggi[1,2], Mario Busso[1], and Alessandro Rizzi[1]

[1] EveryWare Lab, Department of Computer Science,
Università degli Studi di Milano, Milan, Italy
sergio.mascetti@unimi.it
[2] EveryWare Technologies, Milano, Italy

**Abstract.** Many traffic lights are still not equipped with acoustic signals. It is possible to recognize the traffic light color from a mobile device, but this requires a technique that is stable under different illumination conditions. This contribution presents *TL-recognizer*, an application that recognizes traffic lights from a mobile device camera. The proposed solution includes a robust setup for image capture as well as an image processing technique. Experimental results give evidence that the proposed solution is practical.

**Keywords:** Blind people · Visual impairments · Mobile device · Smartphones · Traffic lights · Computer vision

## 1 Introduction

Independent mobility involves a number of challenges for people with visual impairment or blindness, including being aware of the presence and the current color of traffic lights. This is particularly challenging when traffic lights are not equipped with acoustic signals. A number of solutions have been proposed in the scientific literature to recognize traffic lights (among others, [1–3]). Existing solutions share a common problem: they use images acquired through the device camera with automatic exposure. With this approach, in conditions of low ambient light (e.g., at night) traffic lights result overexposed while in conditions of high ambient light (e.g., direct sunlight) they are underexposed (see Fig. 1(a)).

This contribution, extracted from our previous work [4], presents *TL-recognizer*, a software module that addresses the above problem with an effective solution: besides image processing and recognition, it proposes a robust setup for image capture that allows to acquire clearly visible traffic light images regardless of ambient light variability due to time and weather. The proposed recognition technique adopting this approach is reliable (full precision and high recall), robust (works in different illumination conditions) and efficient (it can

K. Miesenberger et al. (Eds.): ICCHP 2016, Part II, LNCS 9759, pp. 198–201, 2016.
DOI: 10.1007/978-3-319-41267-2_27

(a)                                    (b)

**Fig. 1.** Image acquisition with automatic exposure and with our technique in different illumination conditions. (a) Acquisition with automatic exposure: high ambient light (left) and low ambient light (right). (b) Acquisition with our technique: high ambient light (left) and low ambient light (right).

run several times a second on commercial smartphones). The experimental evaluation conducted with visual impaired subjects shows that the technique is indeed practical in supporting road crossing.

## 2    The Technique to Recognize Traffic Lights

The recognition process is organized in two main phases: 'input-acquisition' and 'image-processing'. During input-acquisition a frame is captured by the device camera using specifically designed exposure parameters. The overall idea is that, while light conditions during day and night are extremely variable, luminance coming from traffic lights is pretty stable. For this reason, instead of relying on smartphone camera automatic exposure, which balances the mean luminance of every point in the entire image hence possibly resulting in underexposed or overexposed traffic lights, our solution sets a fixed exposition value (EV) chosen among a small group of EVs pre-computed to encompass the luminance variations.

Figure 1(b) shows details of two pictures, each representing a green light in a different illumination conditions. The pictures were acquired with the technique described above and with parameters defined during the experiments (see Sect. 3). From left to right, the two light intensities are: very high (i.e., sunny day at noon), and low (night). These results are examples of the stable acquisition that is guaranteed by our technique, in contrast with what is obtained with automatic exposure (see Fig. 1(a)).

The image-processing phase is aimed at identifying the active optical units (i.e., AOU - the active light in the traffic light), that appear in the image. The overall computation can be logically divided into three steps: extraction, pruning and validation.

During extraction of candidate AOUs for each traffic light color $c$ (i.e., green, yellow and red), *TL-recognizer* identifies a set of image portions, each one representing a candidate AOU. This is achieved by first applying a filter that excludes the pixels with low luminosity values and incompatible hue. The result is a binary image for each color $c$. Then, white regions in binary images are segmented into blocks of contiguous pixels with the technique proposed by Suzuki and Abe [6]. The result is a list of contours, each one composed of a set of points.

In the pruning step the algorithm removes the contours that are too small or too big to represent an AOU. Technically, each contour is assumed to be an AOU (whose size is known) and consequently its distance along the horizontal and vertical axes from the device camera is computed. The AOU is discarded if it is too far (i.e., contour is too small) or too close (i.e., contour is too big) from the user.

Finally, in the validation step, the image portion (the "patch") corresponding to each contour is extracted, rotated and resized to the same size as a template (a different one for each AOU color). The similarity between the two figures (patch and template) is evaluated with the fast normalized cross-correlation technique [7]. The patch is considered to be an active optical unit if the result of the comparison is larger than a given threshold $T$ whose value is defined through empirical evaluation (Sect. 3).

The application outputs the color of the detected traffic light through a multimodal interface: the color is read aloud using speech synthesis, it is visualized by coloring the entire screen of the device, and it is conveyed haptically through specific vibration patterns.

## 3    Parameters Tuning and Experimental Evaluation

The empirical evaluation can be divided into three main sets of experiments: the first and the second are 'computational-based', the third one is 'human-based'. The two 'computational-based' experiments are conducted with the following methodology: images of urban scenarios were recorded, divided into the "tuning" and "evaluation" datasets (see Table 1) and manually annotated with the position and the color of AOUs (if any). Then, *TL-recognizer* is run off-line, and its results are compared with the expected ones.

The first set of experiments is aimed at tuning the parameters. We omit the description due to page limit, details can be found in [4].

The second set of experiments is aimed at assessing the performance of *TL-recognizer* in terms of computation time, precision and recall. The average values are reported in Table 1. We can observe that the results are very similar between the "tuning" and the "evaluation" datasets. This means that, after the parameters tuning process, system performances are stable under different conditions. In both datasets the precision is 1, which means that no traffic light is erroneously recognized. Still, there is a high value for recall, which means that most traffic lights are correctly identified. Finally, the computation time (computed on a Nexus 5 device with Android 5) is in the order of 100 ms, which means that about 10 frames can be processed each second.

Finally, the last set of experiments involved 2 blind subjects and 2 low-visioned subjects (unable to see traffic lights). All subjects have been trained for about one minute on how to use the mobile application implementing *TL-recognizer*. Then, in a real urban intersection, subjects were asked to walk

**Table 1.** Performances of *TL-recognizer*

| Testset | Images | Precision | Recall | Computation time (ms) |
|---|---|---|---|---|
| Tuning | 501 | 1 | 0.85 | 113 |
| Evaluation | 1252 | 1 | 0.81 | 107 . |

towards a crossroad and to determine when it was safe to start crossing in a given direction (straight, left or right) i.e., when a green traffic light appears right after a red one. For each attempt, a supervisor recorded whether the task was successfully completed and took note of any problem or delay in the process. Each subject repeated this task five times.

Overall, all subjects have been able to successfully complete the assigned tasks. The only exception was with the first attempt made by the first subject: since he was pointing the camera too high up and almost towards the sky, the traffic light was always out of the camera field of view. The problem was solved in the following experiments by simply explaining how to correctly point the camera. Note that this problem could also be solved by monitoring the pitch angle of the device and by warning the user if the he/she is pointing too high or too low.

**Acknowledgments.** The work of Andrea Gerino, Cristian Bernareggi and Sergio Mascetti was partially supported by grant "fondo supporto alla ricerca 2015" under project "Assistive technologies on mobile devices". The work of Alessandro Rizzi was partially supported by grant "fondo supporto alla ricerca 2015" under project "Discovering Patterns in Multi-dimensional Data".

# References

1. Kim, Y., Kim, K., Yang, X.: Real time traffic light recognition system for color vision deficiencies. In: Proceedings of the Fourth International Conference of Mechatronics and Automation, pp. 76–81. IEEE Computer Society (2007)
2. Ivanchenko, V., Coughlan, J., Shen, H.: Real-time walk light detection with a mobile phone. In: Miesenberger, K., Klaus, J., Zagler, W., Karshmer, A. (eds.) ICCHP 2010, Part II. LNCS, vol. 6180, pp. 229–234. Springer, Heidelberg (2010)
3. Roters, J., Jiang, X., Rothaus, K.: Recognition of traffic lights in live video streams on mobile devices. Trans. Circuits Syst. Video Technol. **21**(10), 1497–1511 (2011)
4. Mascetti, S., Ahmetovic, D., Gerino, A., Bernareggi, C., Busso, M., Rizzi, A.: Robust traffic lights detection on mobile devices for pedestrians with visual impairment. Comput. Vis. Image Underst. (2015). http://dx.org/10.1016/j.cviu.2015.11.017
5. Technical Committee CEN/TC 226 "Road equipment": European Standard EN 12368:2006 on "traffic control equipment - signal head" (2006)
6. Suzuki, S., Abe, K.: Topological structural analysis of digitized binary images by border following. Int. J. Comput. Vis. Graph. Image Process. **30**(1), 32–46 (1985)
7. Lewis, J.P.: Fast normalized cross-correlation. Int. J. Vis. Interface **10**(1), 120–123 (1995)

# Sound of Vision - Spatial Audio Output and Sonification Approaches

Michal Bujacz[1(✉)], Karol Kropidlowski[1], Gabriel Ivanica[2], Alin Moldoveanu[2],
Charalampos Saitis[3], Adam Csapo[4], György Wersenyi[4], Simone Spagnol[5],
Omar I. Johannesson[5], Runar Unnthorsson[5], Mikolai Rotnicki[6], and Piotr Witek[6]

[1] Institute of Electronics, Lodz University of Technology, Łódź, Poland
michal.bujacz@p.lodz.pl
[2] University POLITEHNICA of Bucharest, Bucharest, Romania
[3] ISI Foundation, Turin, Italy
[4] Széchenyi István University, Győr, Hungary
[5] University of Iceland, Reykjavik, Iceland
[6] Fundacja Instytut Rozwoju Regionalnego, Krakow, Poland

**Abstract.** The paper summarizes a number of audio-related studies conducted by the Sound of Vision consortium, which focuses on the construction of a new prototype electronic travel aid for the blind. Different solutions for spatial audio were compared by testing sound localization accuracy in a number of setups, comparing plain stereo panning with generic and individual HRTFs, as well as testing different types of stereo headphones vs custom designed quadrophonic proximaural headphones. A number of proposed sonification approaches were tested by sighted and blind volunteers for accuracy and efficiency in representing simple virtual environments.

**Keywords:** Electronic travel aid · Spatial audio · HRTF · HRIR · Sonification · Sound model · Sound synthesis

## 1 Introduction

With the XXI century advances in technology, such as embedded devices capable of real time image and audio processing, the possibilities of designing an electronic travel aid for the blind are greater than ever [1]. The main goal of the "Sound of Vision: natural sense of vision through acoustics and haptics" research project funded by the European Commission under the Horizon 2020 framework is to construct and test a wearable device that would convey an auditory and haptic representation of the surrounding environment to a visually impaired person. This paper presents some of the first year's results of the project in terms of audio-related research, especially spatial audio solutions and sonification models.

The overall concept of the Sound of Vision system is creation of an electronic aid for local navigation and obstacle avoidance, similar to a previous Naviton project [2]. The primary method of the environment sensing is stereovision (with possible data fusion from other sensors, e.g. time of flight or accelerometers) [3, 4]. The reconstructed

© Springer International Publishing Switzerland 2016
K. Miesenberger et al. (Eds.): ICCHP 2016, Part II, LNCS 9759, pp. 202–209, 2016.
DOI: 10.1007/978-3-319-41267-2_28

3D scene is processed (reconstruction, segmentation) and output about the detected (or recognized) obstacles is provided through auditory and haptic channels.

## 2   Spatial Audio - State of the Art

Wearable spatial audio technology focuses on the use of Head Related Transfer Functions that enable to artificially alter two channels in a stereo signal to simulate a sound wave's interaction with the human body, especially with the pinna, the head and the torso [5]. This is done by introducing a delay between the stereo channels called Interaural Time Delay (ITD) and filtering each of the channels with an HRTF filter, providing a frequency dependent Interaural Level Difference (ILD). The HRTF filters can be obtained by several methods:

- individual measurement for a specific listener (highest quality method) [4]
- utilizing a generic measurement for an acoustic mannequin (most common method) [6]
- selecting a similar HRTF set from a database of HRTFs from multiple listeners, either perceptually [7] or anthropometrically [8, 9]
- modeling an individualized HRTF based on head and ear shape of the listener, either by sound wave simulations [10] or correlations between HRTF spectra and ear shapes of a large number of listeners [11, 12].

The use of HRTFs alone is frequently insufficient for accurate sound spatialization. Further processing steps, such as headphone equalization, rendering reflections from the environment and head tracking can significantly improve localization accuracy and decrease the chances of common spatial audio problems, such as in-the-head localization or front-back confusions [13]. Also, a number of studies demonstrated that virtual sound localization accuracy can be significantly improved through training [14–16].

The idea of using several speakers on headphones has been used in commercial sets for emulating 5.1 or 7.1 sound systems, but we have found only one occurrence of attempted use for wearable spatial audio, and it was also in the context of an electronic travel aid [17].

## 3   Proposed Spatial Audio Solutions

One of the basic assumptions for the output from the SoV device was that the generated sounds should be perceived as if they originated from the observed environment. This meant the inclusion of some form of spatial audio processing; however, another important requirement was that the sounds should not block natural environmental sounds, which are extremely important for a blind traveler.

Two main approaches were considered - filtering using head related transfer functions (HRTFs, both individualized and generic) with some type of headphones that do not cover the ear channels (e.g. bone conduction or open in-ear headphones) or a custom solution with multiple proximaural speakers that would allow spatialization through amplitude panning.

Special software was prepared for testing of virtual source localization accuracy with various configurations of spatialization (plain stereo panning, generic and individual HRTFs) and output hardware (reference, bone conduction, in-ear, and custom multi-speaker headphones). Ten participants took part in the tests, localizing sound sources in a 5 × 7 grid spaced at 30° (azimuths from −90° to +90° and elevations: −60° to +60°) approximately 100 times in each possible configuration.

The results from the tests were that using individualized HRTFs provided no significant advantage over generic ones (perception of azimuth was actually slightly worse). High quality reference headphones provided the best spatial audio experience; however, at the cost of covering the ears. Bone conduction was a promising alternative; though it showed strongest variance between the test participants (Fig. 1).

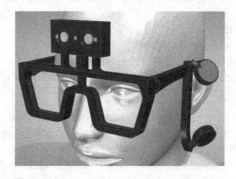

**Fig. 1.** Custom multi-speaker headphones and stereovision camera mount.

The custom headphones were designed and constructed as an alternative to spatial audio generated through the use of head related transfer functions (HRTFs). The 3D model of the headphones was prepared using Solid Edge ST7 software and manufactured using fused deposition modelling (FDM) on a Leapfrog Creator Dual Extruder 3D printer. The headphones included four speakers positioned above and below the ears, all slightly to the front. Amplitude panning was used to position a sound source both in the horizontal and vertical directions (Fig. 2).

The tests of the custom quadrophonic headphones were conducted using a very similar procedure to the HRTF tests. The results were very promising, as both vertical and horizontal localization accuracy was on par with the high quality reference headphones, without the need for HRTF filtering.

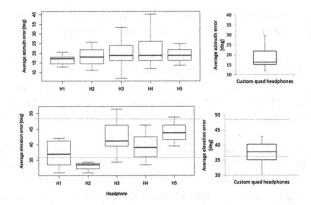

**Fig. 2.** Comparison of off-the-shelf headphones with individualized HRTFs with the custom quadrophonic headphones in terms of average azimuth (top) and elevation (bottom) localization error. H1 – AKG K612 Pro, H2 – Bose QC25, both high quality reference headphones, H3 – Aftershokz M3 bone conduction headphones, H4 – earHero, H5 – Oticon P100 – in-ear air tube headphones. The red lines indicate predicted average errors if the replied either entirely randomly or always pointed to the central sound location.

## 4  Sonification – State of the Art

Recent years have seen the emergence of many electronic systems aimed at aiding the blind [18]. Ranging from popular electronic range sensors [19], through smart phone apps [20, 21], GPS or beacon-based navigation systems [22–24] to a number of research projects aimed at environmental imaging through sensory substitution and virtual acoustics spaces [2], [25].

The sonification [26] in these devices can range from very simple, binary proximity alerts [19], through representing range using musical tones [27], to more complex synthesized sounds, such as clouds of spatially filtered impulses [25].

## 5  Proposed Sonification Approaches

Encoding the 3D visual scene through audio is considered the most important core functionality to be provided by the Sound of Vision project. Finding the most suitable encoding method to provide valuable information about the environment surrounding the user through sound is, thus, a pivotal and challenging task.

The authors decided to explore a number of competing alternatives, dubbed "sound models" in order to identify the most promising sonification solution.

All the tested sonification methods based on a number of common assumptions about the output of the image processing module:

– the observed 3D scene fragment is 90° wide and 5 m in depth
– the 3D scene can be roughly divided into individual objects, described by height and width

- these objects may or may not be continuously tracked from frame to frame
- the objects may be classified as belonging to specific categories (e.g. walls, stairs).

Approaches using the scene depth directly or basing on simplified occupation grids were also considered, however not included in the tests.

All the proposed models also used a similar basic virtual sound source positioning – encoding direction with generic HRTF filtering and distance with loudness.

The four tested sound models were:

Model 1 - Objects as loudspeakers – This model treats each object in the frontal hemisphere as an independent virtual sound source that continuously emits impact sounds, as if the user was striking the white cane on it. The pitch and timbre of the sound resulting from the impact are considered dependent on the object's width and category. The distance between object and user is coded into sound level and repetition rate: the closer the object, the higher the sound level and the more frequent the sound, just like in parking systems.

Model 2 – Time and Frequency division multiplexed scene rendering - The visual field was divided into three 30° wide regions. If a region was empty this was signified by a quiet heartbeat sound. For every object in a region a glissandi was played using granular synthesis such that: the wider the object, the slower and further down the musical scale the glissando went, the taller the object, the coarser was the sound texture.

Model 3 – Depth scanning - A virtual "scanning plane", a surface parallel to the camera view that moves away from the observer through the scene. As the surface intersects scene elements, sound sources originating from the places of intersection are released. Sources correspond to object parameters (distance to loudness and pitch, width to duration, category to instrument type). The model distinguishes two categories of objects – walls (any object with a sufficiently large surface area) and generic obstacles. This model has been previously successfully implemented in the Naviton prototype [2].

Model 4 – Horizontal sweep - A popular approach in many sonification studies (e.g. Navbelt [27]) sometimes referred to as a "piano scan" [28]. The method basically translates distance to pitch in several directions from the observer, making this method suitable for use with unprocessed depth maps or occupancy grids.

The first phase of tests was performed by 10 sighted volunteers, the second phase by 6 blind participants. The tests included such tasks as identifying the position of several obstacles, picking "the odd one out" (an obstacle of different size than others) and choosing a safe route to turn. Some of the scenes were static and in some the observer moved at a constant walking speed. The metrics included reaction times, accuracy, and subjective opinions gathered in surveys with test participants.

Unfortunately, the results of these first tests were inconclusive. In most tasks of the models showed a very significant advantage over the others in accuracy or response times. The testers also had mixed preferences as to the nature of the sounds used. One important conclusion was that testers complained of the lack of continuity of the sounds, i.e. the cyclic auditory "snapshots" of the environment common to all the tested models were a poor method of observing dynamic scene changes.

# 6 Testing Procedures

The tests of the Sound of Vision are conducted with participation of visually impaired testers – blind and partially-sighted, as these groups of end-users are the best experts regarding how the SOV solution is going to meet their needs. What is important in the case of Sound Of Vision, testing is to be interspersed with training, in an approach sometimes called "gamification" [29] – users progress to more difficult tests after completing simpler ones with sufficient efficiency.

So far the tests with blind participants focused on computer simulations for the purpose of selection of sounds for the auditory representation of objects in the environment; however some data was also gathered in real environments, observing travel speeds and patterns while also attempting to collect EEG and other biometric signals [30].

Further testing, introduced by training phases, will include use of virtual environment scenarios, then controlled laboratory environments (e.g. with cardboard obstacles) to finally move on to real-world environment and scenarios (under the care of orientation and mobility specialists). Testers in this phase are going to use the SOV prototype to navigate various indoor and outdoor paths. This will give final confirmation of compliance of the SOV solution with the needs of visually impaired persons.

# 7 Conclusions and Future Work

The conclusions from the spatial audio tests led us away from HRTF-based solutions towards the idea of the custom multi-speaker headphones. Currently two additional aspects are being tested – whether the use of additional speakers (4 per ear) can enhance the perception of spatial audio, e.g. by improving the perception of distance or accuracy of localization, and whether the use of HRTFs in conjunction with the custom headphones produces a significant difference than plain amplitude panning in virtual sound source perception.

From the sonification modes the depth scan shows most promise, though it is clear different approaches seem preferred in different scenarios and further testing is necessary.

**Acknowledgment.** This work received funding from the European Union's Horizon 2020 research and innovation programme under grant agreement No 643636 "Sound of Vision".

# References

1. Strumiłło, P.: Elektroniczne systemy nawigacji osobistej dla niewidomych i słabowidzących [Electronic personal navigation systems for the blind and visually impaired], PŁ, Wydział Elektrotechniki, Elektroniki, Informatyki i Automatyki, Łódź (2012)

2. Bujacz, M., Skulimowski, P., Strumiłło, P.: Naviton - a prototype mobility aid for auditory presentation of 3D scenes. J. Audio Eng. Soc. **60**(9), 696–708 (2012)
3. Skulimowski, P., Strumillo, P.: Obstacle localization in 3D scenes from stereoscopic sequences. In: 15th European Signal Processing Conference EUSIPCO 2007, Poznan, Poland (2007)
4. Owczarek, M., Skulimowski, P., Strumillo, P.: Sound of Vision – 3D scene reconstruction from stereo vision in an electronic travel aid for the visually impaired. In: Computers Helping People with Special Needs. LNCS. Springer, Heidelberg (2016, in press)
5. Dobrucki, A., Plaskota, P., Pruchnicki, P., Pec, M., Bujacz, M., Strumiłło, P.: Measurement system for personalized head-related transfer functions and its verification by virtual source localization trials with visually impaired and sighted individuals. J. Audio Eng. Soc. **58**(9), 724–738 (2010)
6. Gardner, W.G., Martin, K.D.: HRTF measurements of a KEMAR. J. Acoust. Soc. Am. **97**(6), 3907–3908 (1995)
7. Middlebrooks, J.C., Macpherson, E.A., Onsan, Z.A.: Psychophysical customization of directional transfer functions for virtual sound localization. J. Acoust. Soc. Am. **108**(6), 3088–3091 (2000)
8. Geronazzo, M., Spagnol, S., Bedin, A., Avanzini, F.: Enhancing vertical localization with image-guided selection of non-individual head-related transfer functions. In: Proceeding IEEE International Conference Acoustics, Speech and Signal Processing ICASSP 2014, pp. 4496–4500 (2014)
9. Zotkin, D.N., Hwang, J., Duraiswami, R., Davis, L.S.: HRTF personalization using anthropomentric measurements. In: Proceeding IEEE Workshop on Applications of Signal Processing to Audio and Acoustics (WASPAA 2003), pp. 157–160 (2003)
10. Dobrucki, A., Plaskota, P.: Computational modelling of head-related transfer function. Arch. Acoust. **32**, 659–682 (2007)
11. Spagnol, S., Avanzini, F.: Frequency estimation of the first Pinna Notch in head-related transfer functions with a linear anthropometric model. In: Proceeding 18th International Conference Digital Audio Effects (DAFx-2015), pp. 231–236 (2015)
12. Trapenskas, D., Frenne, N., Johansson, Ö.: Relationship between HRTF's and anthropometric data. In: The 29th International Congress and Exhibition on Noise Control Engineering (2000)
13. Wightman, F.L., Kistler, D.J.: Factors affecting the relative salience of sound localization cues. In: Binaural and Spatial Hearing in Real and Virtual Environments, pp. 1–24. Lawrence Erlbaum Associates, Mahwah (1997)
14. Bălan, O., Moldoveanu, A., Moldoveanu, F., Morar, A.: Experiments on training the human localization abilities. In: Proceedings of the 10th International Scientific Conference eLearning and Software for Education, Bucharest (2014)
15. Bălan, O., Moldoveanu, A., Butean, A., Moldoveanu, F., Negoi, I.: Comparative research on sound localization accuracy in the free-field and virtual auditory displays. In: The 11th eLearning and Software for Education Conference - eLSE 2015 (2015)
16. Bălan, O., Moldoveanu, A., Moldoveanu, F., Negoi, I.: The role of perceptual feedback training on sound localization accuracy in audio experiments. In: Proceedings of The 11th International Scientific Conference eLearning and software for Education (2015)
17. Vitek, S., Klima, M., Husnik, L., Spirk, D.: New possibilities for blind people navigation. In: IEEE 2011 International Conference on Applied Electronics (AE), Plisen (2011)
18. Hersh, M., Johnson, M.: Assistive technology for visually impaired and blind people. Springer, London (2008)

19. Farcy, R., Bellik, Y., Locomotion assistance for the blind. In: Keates S., Langdom P., Clarkson P., Robinson P. (eds.) Universal Access and Assistive Technology, pp. 277–284. Springer, London (2002)

20. Manduchi, R., Coughlan, J.M., Ivanchenko, V.: Search strategies of visually impaired persons using a camera phone wayfinding system. In: Miesenberger, K., Klaus, J., Zagler, W.L., Karshmer, A.I. (eds.) ICCHP 2008. LNCS, vol. 5105, pp. 1135–1140. Springer, Heidelberg (2008)

21. Matusiak, K., Skulimowski, P., Strumillo, P.: A mobile phone application for recognizing objects as a personal aid for the visually impaired users. In: Hippe, Z.S., Kulikowski, J.L., Mroczek, T., Wtorek, J. (eds.) Human-Computer Systems Interaction: Backgrounds and Applications 3. Advances in Intelligent Systems and Computing, vol. 300, pp. 201–212. (2014)

22. Skulimowski, P., Korbel, P., Wawrzyniak, P.: POI Explorer - a sonified mobile application aiding the visually impaired in urban navigation In: Proceeding of FedCSIS, ACSIS-Annals of Computer Science and Information Systems, vol. 2, pp. 969–976 (2014)

23. Ferreira, E.J., Navmetro: Preliminary study application of usability assessment methods. In: Human Factors in Design (2013)

24. Mayerhofer, B., Pressl, B., Wieser, M.: ODILIA - a mobility concept for the visually impaired. In: Miesenberger, K., Klaus, J., Zagler, W.L., Karshmer, A.I. (eds.) ICCHP 2008. LNCS, vol. 5105, pp. 1109–1116. Springer, Heidelberg (2008)

25. González-Mora, J., Rodríguez-Hernández, A., Rodríguez-Ramos, L.: Development of a new space perception system for blind people, based on the creation of a virtual acoustic space. In: Mira, J., Sánchez-Andrés, J.V. (eds.) Engineering Applications of Bio-Inspired Artificial Neural Networks, pp. 321–330. Springer, Heidelberg (1999)

26. Hermann, T., Hunt. A., Neuhoff, J.G.: The Sonification Handbook. Logos Verlag, Berlin (2011)

27. Shoval, S., Borenstein, J., Koren, Y.: Auditory guidance with the Navbelt - a computerized travel aid for the blind. IEEE Trans. Syst. Man Cybern. **28**(3), 459–467 (1998)

28. Bujacz, M., Strumiłło, P.: Stereophonic representation of virtual 3D scenes - a simulated mobility aid for the blind. In: Dobrucki, A., Petrovsky, A., Skarbek, W. (eds.) New Trends in Audio and Video, vol. 1, pp. 157–162 (2006)

29. Balan, O., Moldoveanu, A., Moldoveanu, F., Dascalu, M.I.: Audio games- a novel approach towards effective learning in the case of visually-impaired people. In: Proceeding 7th Int. Conference of Education, Research and Innovation, p. 7, Seville (2014)

30. Saitis, C., Kalimeri, K.: Identifying Urban mobility challenges for the visually impaired with mobile monitoring of multimodal biosignals. In: Antona, M., Stephanidis, C. (eds.) Universal Access in Human-Computer Interaction - 10th International Conference, UAHCI 2016, Held as Part of HCI International 2016, Toronto, ON, Canada, 17-22 July 2016, Proceedings. Springer-Verlag, Berlin (2016, in press)

# The Use of Mobile Devices by Individuals with Special Needs as an Assistive Tool

# Mobile Learning for People with Special Needs

## Introduction to the Special Thematic Session

Linda Chmiliar[(✉)]

Athabasca University, Athabasca, Canada
lindac@athabascau.ca

**Abstract.** Ownership and use of mobile devices has become prevalent in recent years and many people have become comfortable with the use of smartphones and tablets on a daily basis. There is growing evidence that portable technology devices are having an impact on people's lives and many people typically use the devices communication and access to social media. Initially, little thought was given to the use of mobile devices for learning. The term "mobile learning" has evolved to refer to: the use of technology that is fully mobile, and the mobility of the users. It also refers to the behavior of the learners as they use the technology to learn and the learning process they engage in. Despite the fact that mobile learning is on the rise, the use of mobile devices as the primary delivery mode for learning activities is still somewhat limited. In addition, the use of mobile devices as a learning tool for people with special needs is an area that is largely unexplored. This paper will provide a short introduction to the use of mobile devices as a learning tool for people with disabilities.

**Keywords:** M-Learning · Disabilities · Special needs · Mobile learning · Mobile devices

## 1 Introduction

Ownership and use of mobile technology devices has expanded considerably over the past decade, and people have become comfortable with the use of devices such as smartphones, tablets, laptops, notebooks, and e-readers on a daily basis. There is growing evidence that portable technology devices are reshaping users' lives in different ways and that mobile devices and wireless technology has resulted in significant changes in how people communicate and live [1]. Typically, mobile technologies are used for communication and access to social media. Initially, little thought was given to the use of mobile devices for learning. Now, the term "mobile learning" has become more evident and the field of mobile learning or m-learning has expanded around the world. The term mobile learning refers to: the use of technology that is fully mobile, and the mobility of the users of the technology while they learn. However, the term mobile learning also refers to activities of the learning process and the behavior of the learners as they use the technology to learn [1]. Despite the growing use of this term and the increase in the use of mobile devices, the use of mobile devices as the primary delivery mode for learning activities is still somewhat limited. In addition, the use of mobile devices as a learning tool for people with special needs is still an area that is largely unexplored. This paper will provide a short introduction to the use of mobile devices as a learning tool for people with disabilities. For the purposes of this paper, the focus will be primarily on hand held devices such as smartphone and tablets.

Today's smart phones and tablets are wireless, portable, and widely available. Due to commercial competitiveness in the industry, there are continual innovations to these devices and constant improvements in features. The design of the devices and the improved features can make the use of mobile devices very attractive for learners with special needs. The iPad and similar tablets are designed so that they can be used as personal computing devices, and many devices have built-in accessibility features that can support people with a variety of special needs. The accessible features allow users to personalize their devices to their individualized needs without having to worry about specific assistive technologies [2]. On the iPad, the intuitive touchscreen interface is quite easy to use, which makes the device accessible to young children with learning difficulties or people with cognitive learning challenges. It is not necessary to learn how to use a separate mouse and cursor before the iPad can be used [3]. The iPad has easily accessible features such as: VoiceOver, a gesture-based screenreader that can help people with visual disabilities; Zoom, that can magnify what is on the screen to help people with low vision; Speak Selection, that provides text-to-speech which can help people with reading disabilities; Dictation, which can help people with written expression difficulties by helping them to express their thoughts; Guided Access, that can help people with attention difficulties; and AssistiveTouch that allows navigation with a single finger, which can help people with motor challenges. There are not as many accessibility features on Android devices. Android devices have a feature called TalkBack that is a gesture-based screen reader. Android devices also have screen magnification and it is possible to obtain an app "Easy Text to Speech" that can provide text-to-speech functionality. Android devices can also provide switch access and Braille support with BrailleBack, an add-on accessibility service.

Smartphones and tablets are seen as being very socially acceptable by the general population and may have appeal for learners with special needs who might prefer to use a device to support their learning that does not have a "social stigma" attached to it. With mobile devices, people with special needs are now using the same digital technology as their peers. This social acceptability and desirability may lead to greater interest in using the device for learning and may also lead to less technology abandonment, a perennial problem in this field. The cost of the devices is also a huge factor. The purchase of traditional assistive technology devices remains unreachable for a large number of people with disabilities, especially in under-developed and developing countries as they tend to be expensive [4]. Comparatively, mobile devices such as smartphones and tablets are more readily available and relatively inexpensive.

There are a multitude of apps available for use with handheld mobile devices. Apps can offer the opportunity for a level the playing field for people with special needs by offering ways to complete tasks in an easy straight forward manner. There are many apps available to support communication that range from simple pointing exercises to complex systems. Apps can also provide access to news, weather reports, and alerts. Apps such as Skype, Facetime, and SMS provide users with alternative methods of communication that don't require a high level of written expression proficiency.

Writing apps can provide learning support such as word processing with word prediction, spell check, word find, and text-to-speech functionality to play back what is written. A number of creation apps can be independently used by learners to produce beautiful books and stories, or videos with minimal technology or writing skill. There are several reading apps that provide text-to-speech functionality that give learners with reading challenges access to course content. Dictionaries and eBooks are also easily accessible. There are many apps for learning skills such as reading the alphabet and words, math skills, social concepts, and even science. These apps can provide interesting, engaging multimedia activities that include verbal, visual, tactile stimuli and responses. For learners for whom learning tasks are often difficult and tedious, learning with apps on the iPad or other tablet may capture their attention and provide motivation. There are also apps that provide learners with special needs access to time management systems, notetaking, graphic organizers, social skill and behavioral supports, and more.

## 2  Conclusion

Given the accessibility features of many mobile devices, and the availability of a multitude of learning and supportive apps, these devices may be able to support and empower people with special needs. The accessibility features give mobile technologies the flexibility and accessibility that may be missing in traditional assistive technologies. The growing development of apps provides many options and solutions to address specific learning needs and challenges. There are a multitude of ways that mobile technologies can help a variety of learners. Research and data regarding the use of mobile devices with people with special needs is emerging and more is needed. The following papers from the ICCHP 2016 15th International Conference on Computers Helping People with Special Needs, help to move the discussion on mobile learning for people with special needs forward. Maria Bermudez-Edo's paper, A Tool to Improve Visual Attention and Acquisition for Low-Functioning People, focuses on a tool developed for children with Autism. Annica Nietzio's paper, Easy Access to Social Media: Introducing the Mediata App, looks at the usability of a specially designed app for individuals with acquired brain-injury. Therese Cummin's paper, Parents' and Teachers Perspectives on using iPads with Students with Developmental Disabilities: Applications for Universal Design for Learning, looks at the use of iPads with students with developmental disabilities. This author, Linda Chmiliar, provided a paper, The iPad Helping Preschool Children with Disabilities in Inclusive Classrooms, that looks at the use of the iPad with young children with a range of disabilities. All four papers provide further information on using mobile technologies to make learning accessible for people with special needs.

# References

1. El-Hussein, M.O., Cronje, J.C.: Defining mobile learning in the higher education. Educ. Technol. Soc. **13**, 12–21 (2010)
2. Fichten, C., Asuncion, J., Scapin, R.: Digital technology, learning, and postsecondary students with disabilities: where we've been and where we're going. J. Postsecondary Educ. Disabil. **27**, 369–379 (2014)
3. Perez, L.: Mobile Devices Empower Students with Special Needs. Education World (2016). http://www.educationworld.com/a_tech/apps-special-needs-disabilities-assistive-technology-students.shtml
4. Ismaili, J., Ibrahimi, E.H.O.: Mobile learning as alternative to assistive technology devices for special needs students. Educ. Inf. Technol. **9**, 1–17 (2016)

# Parents' and Teachers' Perspectives on Using IPads with Students with Developmental Disabilities

## Applications for Universal Design for Learning

Therese M. Cumming[✉] and Iva Strnadová

University of New South Wales, Sydney, Australia
{t.cumming,i.strnadova}@unsw.edu.au

**Abstract.** Cumming, Strnadová, and Singh postulated 2014, that the Universal Design for Learning (UDL) framework promotes "access and inclusion through the development of flexible learning environments comprised of multiple means of representation, engagement and expression". Therefore UDL provides a suitable theoretical framework for research examining use of mobile technology by students with developmental disabilities. This paper details the authors' research work with students, parents, and teachers and their experiences with using mobile technology (specifically iPads) within the UDL framework. It explores the ways that iPads were used to support the learning of students with developmental disabilities, in both general and special education settings. Results, implications for practice and future research are discussed.

**Keywords:** Mobile technology · Universal Design for Learning · Ipad · Developmental disabilities

## 1  Introduction

The Universal Design for Learning (UDL) framework "promotes access and inclusion through the development of flexible learning environments comprised of multiple means of representation, engagement and expression" [1]. Therefore UDL provides a suitable theoretical framework for research examining the use of mobile technology by students with developmental disabilities.

Mobile technology is being utilized at a rapid pace to facilitate the learning of students with developmental disabilities [2–5]. Furthermore, mobile technology has been successfully used to improve students' communication and behaviour [6, 7]. Mobile technology's alignment with (UDL) principles (multiple means of representation, engagement and expression) allows for students' increased access to curriculum and provides an interactive learning environment. However, there are also challenges related to mobile devices, such as affordability [8]. Qualitative research was conducted to determine not only if mobile learning was working as part of a UDL framework for students with disabilities, but also how teachers and parents perceived its ease of implementation, use, and effectiveness.

© Springer International Publishing Switzerland 2016
K. Miesenberger et al. (Eds.): ICCHP 2016, Part II, LNCS 9759, pp. 217–222, 2016.
DOI: 10.1007/978-3-319-41267-2_29

## 2 Methodology

The authors conducted two studies with students with developmental disabilities in New South Wales, Australia that focused on parents' and teachers' perceptions of using iPads with students with developmental disabilities. The first study took place in a Kindergarten to Year 12 (K-12) special school in Sydney, Australia. The parents and teachers of four students with developmental disabilities with high support needs participated in the study. The data analysed for the purpose of this study were: (a) children's annual reports and IEPs, (b) parents' surveys, and (c) teachers' pre- and post-implementation surveys.

The second study took place in a private high school in Sydney, Australia. Four students with developmental disabilities and their five teachers from the Education Support Team (EST) participated in this study. The data analysed for the purpose of this study were: (a) a blog describing the project, with a page for each teacher to document his/her experience, (b) teacher and student video interviews, and (c) a teacher focus group meeting at the conclusion of the project.

The data in both studies were analysed using inductive content analysis approach [8]. The results of both studies were published – see [1, 9]. Applications of using mobile technology, specifically iPads, with students with developmental disabilities within the Universal Design for Learning framework were examined to answer the following questions:

1. What are teachers', parents', and students' overall perceptions of students with developmental disabilities using iPads?
2. How are students using iPads in regard to the UDL framework and principles of representation, engagement, and expression?

## 3 Results

The participating teachers, parents and students in both studies discussed both benefits and challenges experienced by students with developmental disabilities using iPads, and the ways in which iPads allow for the UDL principles of representation, engagement, and expression.

### 3.1 Benefits

The results of the two studies were similar and generally positive. All three groups perceived that the use of mobile technology improved student access to and participation in the curriculum. Students acknowledged the impact of iPads on their learning, positively impacting their literacy skills. They felt that using mobile technology assisted their concentration, and made learning exciting and fun. All of the student participants indicated that if given the choice between completing assignments in a traditional manner or using the iPad, that they would use the iPad. One student participant in study 1 stated, "Probably the iPad because it is much betterer, because you learn more" (M3). Parents felt that iPad integration provided new opportunities for their children to learn.

They felt that this resulted in increased academic skills. The parents also noticed an improvement in their children's communication skills. Some also mentioned that there was noticeable improvement in their child's behaviour, focus and concentration. Importantly, most of the parents suggested that their children demonstrated increased independence and self-determination skills. A parent participant in study 2 was particularly pleased with this outcome, "She will choose which apps she wants to use independently and she works out how to use new apps very quickly" (Parent3). Teachers felt that the technology made it easier to differentiate instruction for each student, and afforded students more capability to access the general education curriculum. The results of data analysis also suggested that teachers and students used iPads for a variety of purposes: (a) to enhance literacy and numeracy, (b) to encourage creativity, new ideas, & skill consolidation, (c) for research, (d) to create social stories, (e) to plan schedules, (f) to get directions while on community excursions, (g) to take photos, (h) to create presentations, (i) to play games, (j) to read books, and (k) to listen to music.

In terms of the UDL framework, communication was an area where all of the groups felt that that employing the iPad to support students was very successful. This is well aligned with providing multiple and diverse means of expression, one of the pillars of the UDL framework [1]. Students were able to use the different iPad applications to express their increased knowledge through presentations, such as using the built in camera and a presentation app for making presentations of how to cook different foods using a recipe. The student participants were also able to participate in a school-wide project by using a photography app, storyboard app, and text to speech software to present their reports at a special ceremony honouring the Jews in concentration camps during WWII. One parent in study 2 described the gains her daughter had made in expression, "Her reading has improved as has her speech because of articulation and spelling-type apps."

The UDL framework encourages teachers to use multiple means of representation to present material to students. The availability of a diverse choice of iPad applications allowed teachers to not only provide information in a variety of ways, but also to individualise the level that the material was presented at for each student. Examples of this included: using an app to teach students Hebrew symbols, using game apps to practice spelling words, sentence formation, identifying parts of speech, and presenting different mathematics and science concepts. Teacher B in study 2 described her experience with individualising instruction: "As a teaching device, I incorporated the iPad during Literacy and Numeracy structured lessons. I have related the students' priorities and goals as well as their interests into the relevant applications."

Another central piece of the UDL framework is to provide multiple means for students to engage with the material being taught [1]. Teachers provided the students with various iPad applications in each subject area to allow students to engage more fully with the material. Teachers perceived that doing this produced an overall improvement in student work, and increased their engagement with assignments. One important example of this was affording students the opportunity to read materials on the iPad, with or without text to speech software. This also allowed for individualising the material, as the application they used allowed students to hear and interact with the text. As one teacher commented:

"The students involved with the study were confident and independent in asking for the iPad, manipulating the iPad to power on/off, pressing the home button, swiping to locate the apps and taking photos. The students were engaged in the alphabet tracing, number tracing, word building, matching letters, matching objects, spelling, counting, addition, puzzles, colouring in, reading, music and cause and effect games and programs."

## 3.2 Challenges

Mobile technology implementation was not without its challenges. Teachers also summarised some of the obstacles they faced during iPad implementation. They could not always find applications that they wanted for certain lessons, particularly materials that were high interest, low level, age appropriate applications, as many of the applications are geared to young children. The teachers in the first study did not receive iPads for their use until the end of the project. This made learning to use the iPads and sharing applications with each other during the school day difficult, as the students were using the devices at those times.

Interestingly, although teachers cited some behaviour problems that occurred as a result of using the iPads (at times students would switch out of the educational app they were using to play games), parents discussed the use of the iPad to improve behaviour at home. All parents in the second study reported using time on the iPad as a behavioural incentive for their child.

Both groups cited the need for professional development, parent training, and collaboration between school and home as important for successful iPad implementation.

Lastly, the teachers were frustrated over their general education counterparts' reluctance to use the devices in their teaching, or even allow the students to use them when attending their classes. They cited lack of time to learn how to use the devices and the lack of availability of devices for all students in the class.

## 4   Implications

The results of this research have the potential to guide others in establishing mobile technology use for students with disabilities as an educational practice within a UDL framework. Based on the results of these two projects, it is recommended that teachers are given time and iPads before the tablets are introduced to the students, in order to allow them to become proficient in using the devices, and to explore applications for specific students and their learning needs. It is important that teachers keep data on each student's use of the iPad and applications, in order to determine whether the students are achieving expected outcomes.

The families of students should be included as partners in the implementation of any mobile technology implementation, in order to provide students with seamless learning and support across environments. Collaborating in this manner also went a long way in improving school-home communication and cooperation. This is in line with the suggestions of Brown [10] that all individuals supporting students' technology use be well versed in the use of the technology, in order to promote full implementation and participation.

Professional development is important in supporting the development of teachers' technological pedagogical knowledge and value of providing opportunities for collaborative work and reflection. Parents should be included in this, as this collaboration is crucial in order to discuss applications, share successes, and problem solve any challenges that arrive.

It is also important to recognise that "keeping up with the technology" and available applications is a continuous process, as the technology is constantly evolving and hundreds of new applications become available daily. Teachers, students, and parents must constantly be on the lookout for applications that can be used to support the teaching and learning needs of their particular classrooms and students. Websites and blogs that review applications can facilitate this, as they are an efficient way for teachers and parents to get an overview of available applications and an idea of which ones to trial.

## 5   Conclusion

The importance of supporting students with developmental disabilities both in and outside of inclusive settings cannot be overlooked. Future studies should include students, their families, and all of the teachers that work with students with disabilities, not just their special education teachers. One of these studies revealed that some general education teachers felt that allowing some students to use the technology while it was not made available to others was unfair. Therefore, implementation in inclusive settings should be studied, looking more closely at how mobile technology can support the learning of all students within the Universal Design for Learning framework.

The response to mobile technology has been very positive globally, especially for use by students with disabilities. Teachers, students, and parents are increasingly expressing their satisfaction with the iPad, as an assistive technology and educational tool. More research in this area is crucial to discover how schools, teachers, and students are effectively using this technology and to provide an evidence base for the educational use of this popular technology.

## References

1. Cumming, T., Strnadová, I., Singh, S.: The use of ipad hand held mobile devices to enhance learning opportunities for students with disabilities: an action research project. Action Res. **12**(2), 150–175 (2014)
2. Gentry, T., Wallace, J., Kvarfordt, C., Lynch, K.: Personal digital assistants as cognitive aids for high school students with autism: results of a community-based trial. J. Vocat. Rehabil. **32**, 101–107 (2010)
3. Cumming, T., Draper Rodriguez, C., Strnadová, I.: Aligning iPad applications with evidence-based practices in inclusive and special education. In: Keengwe, S. (ed.) Pedagogical Applications and Social Effects of Mobile Technology Integration, pp. 55–78. IGI Glob-al, Hershey, PA (2013)
4. Rothschild, B.: Special Tool for Special Needs. Courier Post-Cherry Hill N.J. Retrieved (2011). http://beta.courierpostonline.com

5. Sutherland, E.: Schools expect iPads to outnumber textbooks in next five years. Cult of Mac. Retrieved (2011). http://www.cultofmac.com/127065/schools-expect-ipads-to-outnumber-computers-in-next-five-years-report/
6. Cihak, D., Fahrenkrog, C., Ayres, K., Smith, C.: The use of video modeling via a video ipod and a system of least prompts to improve transitional behavior for students with autism spectrum disorders in the general education classroom. J. Positive Behav. Interv. **12**(2), 103–115 (2010)
7. Kagohara, D., et al.: Behavioral intervention promotes successful use of an ipod-based communication device by an adolescent with autism. Clin. Case Stud. **9**, 328–338 (2010)
8. Elo, S., Kyngäs, H.: The qualitative content analysis process. J. Adv. Nurs. **62**(1), 107–115 (2008)
9. Strnadová, I., Cumming, T., Marquez, E.: Parents' and teachers' experiences with mobile learning for students with high support needs. Spec. Educ. Perspect. **23**, 43–55 (2014)
10. Brown, D.: Some uses of educational and assistive technology for people with disabilities. Comput. Educ. **56**, 1 (2011)

# The iPad Helping Preschool Children with Disabilities in Inclusive Classrooms

Linda Chmiliar[✉]

Athabasca University, Athabasca, Canada
lindac@athabascau.ca

**Abstract.** A review of the literature has revealed that the learning of preschool children with disabilities can be enhanced through play that includes the use of digital technologies. The iPad offers the possibility of exploration in a new way. However, little information exists on how this technology can be utilized effectively. The focus of this study was to look at the use of iPads by preschool children with disabilities participating in an inclusive classroom. The study looked at the learning the children demonstrated across curriculum areas over twenty- one weeks, the apps that the children chose to use, and parent and teacher perceptions on the use of the iPad by the children.

**Keywords:** Preschool · Disabilities · Special needs · iPad · Inclusion

## 1 Introduction

A review of the literature has revealed that learning by preschool children can be enhanced through play and exploration that includes the use of digital technologies. The iPad, with its ease of interaction on the touch screen, thousands of downloadable early learning applications, engaging multimedia capabilities, and reasonable cost is appealing to classroom teachers and parents of preschool children. However, little information exists on how this potential can be utilized effectively with young children with disabilities. The focus of this study was to look at the use of iPads by eight preschool children participating in an inclusive classroom during the afternoon, and looked at the learning the children demonstrated on the iPad over twenty-one weeks, the apps that were used, and parent and teacher perceptions on the use of the iPad by the children.

## 2 Background

Research on new digital technologies such as the iPad and applications with preschool children is slowly emerging. Matthews and Seow [1] looked at the symbolic representation of 12 children ages 2–11 years using electronic paint on tablet computers. The researchers videotaped children drawing with both tablet computers and traditional media. They found that the tablet and stylus-interfaced technology was a superior tool for drawing. Couse and Chen [2] explored the viability of tablet computers in early education by investigating preschool children's ease in acclimating to tablet technology

© Springer International Publishing Switzerland 2016
K. Miesenberger et al. (Eds.): ICCHP 2016, Part II, LNCS 9759, pp. 223–226, 2016.
DOI: 10.1007/978-3-319-41267-2_30

and its effectiveness in engaging them to draw. The teachers reported high child interest in the task and drawings as being above expectation. Chiong and Shuler [3] looked at the use of iPod touch devices with children ages 3 to 7 and found that the children made gains in vocabulary and phonological awareness when using the iPod. Bebell, et al. [4] found that kindergarten children using an iPad had greater gains in literacy learning than those not using tablets. Chmiliar [5, 6] in a series of two pilot studies with preschool children with disabilities, found that young children between the ages of three to five were able to successfully learn to navigate the iPad. In each of the pilot studies, preschool children with a range of disabilities used iPads independently at home over an 8 week period of time. The children demonstrated improvements in many preschool skills at the conclusion of the study.

The focus of this study was to look at the use of iPads by preschool children with disabilities participating in an inclusive classroom. The study looked at: the learning the children demonstrated across curriculum areas over twenty-one weeks; the apps that the children chose to use; and parent and teacher perceptions on the use of the iPad by the children.

## 3    Methodology

The central question for the present research was: What improvement in early learning skills do preschool children with disabilities evidence while using the iPad and early learning apps over a period of 21 weeks?

This research took place in an inclusive preschool program with eight preschool children ages 3 to 5, identified as having disabilities. The children had a range of disabilities including significant speech and language delays, neurological impairments, developmental delay, or behaviors on the autism spectrum. Each child in the study had the iPad to use at home throughout the study and were required to bring the iPad into the classroom each day. The iPads were used in a learning centre in the classroom with all of the children.

This study used a mixed-method approach. First, this study can be seen as participatory action research with the classroom teacher and the researchers working together to understand how to best implement this technology in the inclusive preschool environment. In this research, there were 6 action cycles over a period of 21 weeks. In Cycle I the teacher, children, and parents were introduced to the tool for one week. In each of the remaining cycles, each cycle focused was on a specific area of preschool readiness addressed in the classroom and each cycle lasted 4 weeks. The five focus areas were: drawing, creativity and fine motor skills; tracing and printing; concepts color/shapes; concepts for numeracy; and concepts for literacy.

Second, this study utilized a multiple case study design. Multiple-case design, or collective case design, refers to case study research in which a number of instrumental bounded cases are selected to develop a more in-depth understanding of the phenomena than a single case can provide. Each individual student case consists of a comprehensive description of the student's preschool skills and experience with the iPad and the apps.

# 4    Results

During each of the cycles, data from the informal pre and post assessments was gathered. Across cases, it was evidenced that all of the children in the study demonstrated extensive learning directly related to participation in the apps. For example: in the first cycle, significant changes in ability to complete puzzles and mazes was observed for all of the children in the study. In one case, a three year old girl with a neurological impairment started the 4 weeks not being able to complete even a simple puzzle on the iPad. At the end of the 4 weeks the student was independently completing 32 piece interlocking puzzles. Another example is a four year old boy who was not able to "pinch the pepper" at the beginning of the cycle but was able to successfully pinch many "peppers" in rapid succession at the end of the cycle. During the cycle that focused on literacy one three year old girl learned the majority of the alphabet letters and the sounds of the letters. Another four year old boy learned to read a number of words and combined them into sentences on a very interactive engaging app. Overall, it was observed that each child demonstrated very individual choices as to what appealed to them and it was evident that the greatest learning that occurred for each child was directly related to the apps that they specifically liked and engaged with. All of the children were able to navigate through the apps independently and engaged with all of the apps provided to them during each cycle. It was observed that each child would explore apps where they knew and were comfortable with the content, and alternate this with apps where the content was challenging for them. However, some of the reluctant children engaged with apps more quickly when the app was introduced to them by an adult.

Observations of each child in the home, and the interviews with the parents, produced interesting results. It was observed that most of the children engaged with the iPad and apps for longer periods of time at home and appeared to have a higher level of attention in the home environment. In every case, the parent(s) reported changes in their child's skills they felt were directly related to apps on the iPad. One parent felt that her child's speech and language growth was specifically related to apps on the iPad due to the child's word choices and voice inflection that was similar to the language in the app. In another case, the parent reported that the child had learned a much larger range of shapes on the app than what was being taught in class. In yet another case, the parents were very impressed with how their four year old child was creating her own movies with her toys. In several cases the parents reported that they had observed a sibling engaging with the child, the older sibling leading the child into what they thought were more advanced activities. The iPad use by two of the children had to be monitored carefully by the parents. They felt that the child was too engaged with the iPad. This was a struggle for them as they were witnessing so much learning at home related to use of the iPad.

# 5    Conclusion

This exploratory study is one of a number of small studies aimed at examining the use of the iPad with preschool children with disabilities. Due to the very limited scope of the study and the small number of preschool children involved, there is not yet sufficient evidence to determine the best practices of the use of this tool with this population. However, given the positive results that this study produced, the use of this device as an early learning tool for children with disabilities should be explored further.

Overall, the children were observed to have made significant gains in learning in many areas. In most cases the greatest learning was evidenced when the apps available on the iPad appealed to the unique interests of the child. It is important to provide a number of apps to the children to select from that address the skills and knowledge being focused on. It is also important to provide a range of difficulty in the apps so that the child can review previously learned skills as well as explore new concepts.

# References

1. Matthews, J., Seow, P.: Electronic paint: understanding children's representation through their interactions with digital paint. J. Art Des. **25**, 251–263 (2007)
2. Couse, L., Chen, D.: A tablet computer for young children? exploring its viability for early childhood education. J. Res. Technol. Educ. **3**, 75–98 (2010)
3. Chiong, C., Shuler, C.: Learning: Is there an App for That? Investigations of Young Children's Useage with Mobile Devices and Apps. The Joan Ganz Cooney Center and Sesame Workshop (2010). http://www.joanganzcooneycenter.org/Features-82.html
4. Bebell, D., Dorris, S., Muir, M.: Emerging Results from the nation's First Kindergarten Implementation of iPads (2012). https://s3.amazonaws.com/hacked/Adv2014_Research Sum120216.pdf
5. Chmiliar, L.: The iPad and the preschool child with learning difficulties. J. Technol. Persons Disabil. **1**, 191–200 (2013)
6. Chmiliar, L.: Learning with the iPad in early childhood. In: Miesenberger, K., Fels, D., Archambault, D., Peňáz, P., Zagler, W. (eds.) ICCHP 2014, Part II. LNCS, vol. 8548, pp. 579–582. Springer, Heidelberg (2014)

# Easy Access to Social Media: Introducing the Mediata-App

Christian Bühler, Susanne Dirks, and Annika Nietzio[✉]

Department of Rehabilitation Technology, TU Dortmund University,
Dortmund, Germany
{christian.buehler,susanne.dirks,annika.nietzio}@tu-dortmund.de
http://www.reha-technologie.de

**Abstract.** The MEDIATA app is a mobile application providing easy access to online platforms and social media for persons with acquired brain injury. Special focus is put on communication with friends and family and the use of mainstream social networks and communication platforms. The main functionality of the application can be used without assistance. In this way MEDIATA can enable self-determined use of ICT and increase participation and independence of persons with acquired brain injury. This paper reports the findings from two user requirements studies and the resulting design and implementation of the app.

## 1 Introduction

The Internet plays a substantial role in life; not only in education and the working environment but also for leisure and social activities. People with cognitive and learning disabilities have been excluded from the use of the Internet for a long time. Most web sites and services did not address the accessibility needs of this user group. Additional reasons were lack of training and assistance or simply the unavailability of devices with internet connectivity and assistive technology.

In recent years tablet computers have become widely available. These devices are inexpensive and easy to operate. They offer direct interaction with the content via touch screen or even voice input. The users no longer have to learn to operate mouse or keyboard. However, there are still some challenges caused by complicated (web) content and applications. People with cognitive and learning disabilities often don't have the opportunity to get training and assistance for using the internet in their free time.

The project MEDIATA ("Mediale Teilhabe durch assistive Technologien" – Digital inclusion by assistive technology) works on the improvement of digital inclusion of persons with acquired brain injury. The goal is to support the persons in their use of information and communication technology (ICT) with special focus on communication with friends and family and use of online platforms and social networks. The MEDIATA project is developing a mobile app that provides access to mainstream social networks and communication platforms.

Brain injury can be caused by stroke or brain haemorrhage, diseases such as meningitis, or by accidents with traumatic brain injury. It often affects cognitive

K. Miesenberger et al. (Eds.): ICCHP 2016, Part II, LNCS 9759, pp. 227–233, 2016.
DOI: 10.1007/978-3-319-41267-2_31

functions (memory, attention, language, etc.) and can cause motor impairments such as limited dexterity. It may also result in changes in personality, difficulties with decision making, and loss of communication skills [4].

The MEDIATA project aims to involve users at all stages of research and development. We carried out a literature review and a user study to identify the specific accessibility requirements of the user group. Our goal is to create an application that can be used easily and without assistance; thus enabling self-determined use of ICT and increasing participation and independence of persons with acquired brain injury.

The remainder of this paper is organized as follows: Sect. 2 reviews current accessibility guidelines with special focus on the needs of persons with acquired brain injury. Section 3 reports the findings from the user involvement activities and presents the design of the MEDIATA mobile application. In the concluding section open issues and plans for future research and development are discussed.

## 2    Background: Accessibility Guidelines

The Web Content Accessibility Guidelines (WCAG) developed by W3C/WAI are the widely recognized standard for Web accessibility. The literature review looks into three specific topics which are relevant for the MEDIATA project.

### 2.1    Cognitive Accessibility

Initially the WCAG guidelines focused on technical aspects that are needed to make web content accessible for persons using screen readers or other assistive technology. The needs of people with cognitive or learning disabilities were not addressed in the same way [6]. Currently the W3C Cognitive Accessibility Task Force [11] is working on the definition of new techniques that take into account cognitive accessibility. The diversity of the user group is a big challenge. There are many different variants of cognitive disabilities ranging from mild problems in specific tasks (such as dyslexia or dyscalculia) to severe intellectual disabilities affecting many cognitive functions.

So far only little research has been dedicated to cognitive accessibility. Most of the research and guidelines address persons with learning difficulties. Another user group that is often researched are older people with age-related loss of cognitive capacity [1].

In contrast to the groups mentioned above the user group of MEDIATA used ICT already *before* they acquired their disability. So they may have some knowledge or mental concept that can help them to (re-)learn how to use the devices and apps. To the best of our knowledge specific accessibility requirements for persons with acquired brain injury have not been explored by researchers so far. Research in assistive technology (AT) for persons with acquired brain injury mainly covers special AT devices and does not address strategies how to make mainstream products and services accessible [9].

## 2.2    Accessibility of Mobile Applications

Mobile devices differ from traditional desktop computers with regard to input and output modalities (smaller screen, operation by gestures, no separate keyboard or pointing device). This leads to accessibility problems caused by small buttons, complex gestures, and fast changes of the displayed information [7].

Muskens et al. [5] collected some guidelines for mobile apps for elderly people with mild cognitive impairments and reduced dexterity. The requirements include: reduction of complexity, clear task structure, consistency of information and information arrangement, and rapid and distinct feedback. Further requirements are avoiding distracting elements, and providing enough time.

The *European Telecommunications Standards Institute (ETSI)* recently established a Special Task Force working on "Recommendations to allow people with cognitive disabilities to exploit the potential of mobile technologies" [8]. The task force covers issues such as gestures and voice input as well as areas that are especially challenging for persons with cognitive disabilities, such as understanding written language or user authentication. Mobile devices offer various input modalities which allow traditional authentication methods based on password or PIN codes to be replaced by biometric methods, e.g. fingerprints or face recognition.

## 2.3    Social Networks and Accessibility

Shpigelman and Gil asked persons with cognitive disabilities and learning disabilities about their use of Facebook [10]. The users reported problems with sign up and log in, frequent changes of the user interface that require the users to relearn how to use it, and the understanding of complex language such as terms and conditions. Improvement suggestions included the request for a simple version with reduced complexity.

Another important aspect is reported by Edler and Rath [3]: People with learning disabilities want to use the same social networks and platforms as people without disabilities. There is a strong wish for inclusion. The users don't want a special, protected place. This might require support from assistants and training to increase media literacy.

# 3    Research and Development

## 3.1    Phase 1: User Survey

The user requirements study in MEDIATA was carried out in two phases. In the first phase a quantitative method based on a survey questionnaire ($n = 30$) was applied to study the use of ICT by persons with acquired brain injury. One of the research questions of this phase was: "Are there differences between the wish to use ICT and the actual usage?" In the following, we give only a brief summary of the findings of this phase. Details can be found in [2].

Before their brain injury most participants used ICT and social media. The results of the survey show that the use of ICT and social media decreased after the brain injury was acquired. However the participants still have the wish to use online services such as email, video chat, or social media. The main obstacles are limited availability of suitable devices with internet connection and lack of assistance and training.

### 3.2   Phase 2: Participatory User Study

The second phase of the user requirements study focused on the problems that persons with acquired brain injury encounter when using ICT. The study applied participatory, qualitative methods. Two groups ($n_1 = 6$, $n_2 = 8$) of users were observed and interviewed during the use of different apps on a tablet computer. The main finding of this phase is that the accessibility of commonly used apps is low. Problems occurred in the following areas:

- remembering and entering passwords
- complex user interfaces with several menu levels
- different apps using different interface elements, layout, and gestures for the same task
- pop-ups and ads causing distraction
- reading and understanding complex text

These problems are similar to the ones reported in other studies. For persons with acquired brain injury the main problems are tasks involving memory (such as remembering passwords) and generalization (i.e. recognizing functions that look different in another app). Also distractions often cause problems. If notifications and pop-ups interrupt the current task, the users find it difficult to resume their activity. The notifications themselves can be unsettling because the users can't distinguish relevant from irrelevant information.

### 3.3   Phase 3: Design and Implementation of Mediata App

The design of the MEDIATA app is based on the findings from the previous project phases and the recommendations identified during the background research. The app provides a simplified meta-interface with recognizable features for a set of commonly used social media and communication platforms. The meta-interface can be used to carry out tasks on several social media and communication platforms.

For the first iteration we identified four tasks that occur in many usage scenarios: *login*, *search*, *watch video* and *send message*. More tasks will be added in subsequent iterations.

In the *login* task the amount of user interaction can be reduced significantly. Login details and passwords can be saved on the device. Afterwards the device can be configured the use to method of authentication preferred by the user. This might be a traditional password but can also be a method that does not require remembering words or numbers.

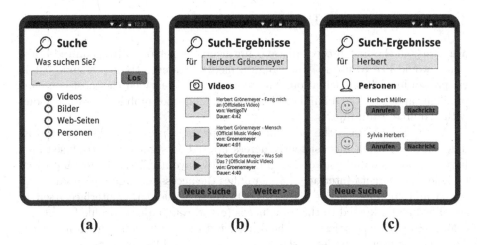

**Fig. 1.** Mock-up design of the search interface

For the *search* task the following elements are needed:

- An input field that is easy to find (always in the same position) and clearly shows that text entry is available.
- Clear verbal instructions – because icons alone might be misleading (e.g. A magnifying glass can mean either "search" or "zoom in".)
- Simplified display of results with reduced number of entries and reduced complexity of each individual entry.

Figure 1 illustrates the design of the search interface. The screen on Fig. (1a) shows a clearly labelled search box. The user can select which type of content should be searched. The options are: videos, images, web pages, and contacts. All types of content are searchable through the same (meta-)interface. The screen of Fig. (1b) shows to search results for videos. The amount of information is reduced. In addition to a still image only the title, the name of the uploader, and the duration are shown. Further information like related content or number of views are removed. If the user searches for contacts, the results are presented in a similar way, as illustrated in Fig. (1c): A picture and the name of the person are shown together with the option to contact that person such as "Call" or "Send message".

The mock-ups will be discussed with persons with acquired brain injury in a focus group setting. Special emphasize will be put on the understandability of the text and interface elements to make sure that the users can recognize the functions of the interface elements occurring on different screens of the app.

The app is implemented as a hybrid app so that it can be made available on different mobile operating systems. We have selected the Ionic development framework. The MEDIATA app connects to the platforms using the official APIs and exposes a selected subset of functionality.

## 4    Conclusion and Planned Activities

The study in the first project phase confirmed that persons with acquired brain injury would like to use ICT and digital media. However there are some barriers preventing full participation. The second study identified the most common problems and collected a number of design guidelines for mobile apps for persons with acquired brain injury.

A major problem is the recognition of repeated tasks that are presented in different ways often inconsistently across apps. Users get easily confused and have difficulties to adjust to changing interface layouts. The MEDIATA project designed a new meta-interface that simplifies the access to commonly used social media and communication platforms. On the one hand the interface itself is simplified and adjusted to the users needs (e.g. through a user profile for setting colour and font properties). On the other hand the interface is a meta-interface. That means: users experience the same interfaces in different apps. There is no need to relearn and remember different ways of carrying out the same task.

The design and implementation of the app are currently ongoing. There will be regular meetings with the user groups to get their feedback on the prototypes and ensure the accessibility of the app. In summer 2016 the app will also be evaluated with a larger group of users.

**Acknowledgements.** The MEDIATA project is supported by Stiftung Bethel, Bethel.regional, and gGmbH *In der Gemeinde leben* Düsseldorf.

## References

1. Arch, A.: WAI Guidelines and Older Web Users: Findings from a Literature Review: Editor's Draft, 11 March 2009. http://www.w3.org/WAI/WAI-AGE/comparative.html. Accessed 26 Jan 2016
2. Dirks, S., Anton, N., Bühler, C.: Förderung der medialen Teilhabe von Menschen mit erworbenen Hirnschädigungen durch assistive Technologien. In: Cunningham, D., Hofstedt, P., Meer, K., Schmitt, I. (eds.) INFORMATIK 2015. Lecture Notes in Informatics (LNI), pp. 1311–1323. Gesellschaft für Informatik (2015)
3. Edler, C., Rath, M.: People with learning disabilities using the iPad as a communication tool - conditions and impact with regard to e-inclusion. In: Miesenberger, K., Fels, D., Archambault, D., Peňáz, P., Zagler, W. (eds.) ICCHP 2014, Part I. LNCS, vol. 8547, pp. 177–180. Springer, Heidelberg (2014)
4. Engström, A.L.L., Lexell, J., Lund, M.L.: Difficulties in using everyday technology after acquired brain injury: a qualitative analysis. Scand. J. Occup. Ther. **17**, 233–243 (2010)
5. Muskens, L., van Lent, R., Vijfvinkel, A., van Cann, P., Shahid, S.: Never too old to use a tablet: designing tablet applications for the cognitively and physically impaired elderly. In: Miesenberger, K., Fels, D., Archambault, D., Peňáz, P., Zagler, W. (eds.) ICCHP 2014, Part I. LNCS, vol. 8547, pp. 391–398. Springer, Heidelberg (2014)

6. Nietzio, A., Naber, D., Bühler, C.: Towards techniques for easy-to-read web content. Procedia Comput. Sci. **27**, 343–349 (2014). 5th International Conference on Software Development and Technologies for Enhancing Accessibility and Fighting Info-exclusion (DSAI 2013)

7. Patch, K., Spellman, J., Wahlbin, K.: Mobile accessibility: How WCAG 2.0 and other W3C/WAI guidelines apply to mobile. In: W3C First Public Working Draft, 26 February 2015. http://www.w3.org/TR/2015/WD-mobile-accessibility-mapping-20150226/. Accessed 26 Jan 2016

8. Pluke, M., et al.: ETSI STF 488: Recommendations to allow people with cognitive disabilities to exploit the potential of mobile technologies (2016). https://portal.etsi.org/STFs/STF_HomePages/STF488/STF488.asp. Accessed 21 Mar 2016

9. Rispoli, M., Machalicek, W., Lang, R.: Assistive technology for people with acquired brain injury. In: Lancioni, G.E., Singh, N.N. (eds.) Assistive Technologies for People with Diverse Abilities. Autism and Child Psychopathology Series. Springer Science+Business Media, New York (2014)

10. Shpigelman, C.-N., Gill, C.J.: How to make online social networks accessible for users with intellectual disability? In: Miesenberger, K., Fels, D., Archambault, D., Peñáz, P., Zagler, W. (eds.) ICCHP 2014, Part I. LNCS, vol. 8547, pp. 471–477. Springer, Heidelberg (2014)

11. W3C: Cognitive and Learning Disabilities Accessibility Task Force (2016). https://www.w3.org/WAI/PF/cognitive-a11y-tf/. Accessed 31 Jan 2016

# A Tool to Improve Visual Attention and the Acquisition of Meaning for Low-Functioning People

María Luisa Rodríguez Almendros, Marcelino Cabrera Cuevas,
Carlos Rodríguez Domínguez, Tomás Ruiz López, María Bermúdez-Edo[✉],
and María José Rodríguez Fórtiz

University of Granada, Granada, Spain
{mlra,mcabrera,carlosrodriguez,tomruiz,mbe,mjfortiz}@ugr.es

**Abstract.** Students with Autism spectrum disorder (ASD) have difficulties in social interaction and communication, social skills and acquisition of knowledge. Individuals affected by low-functioning autism are not able to manage the level of abstraction that the use of language requires. Besides, in the most severe cases they have problems in recognizing representations of objects from the real world. In order to intervene in these aspects, it is necessary to facilitate the learning of the processes of the acquisition of meaning, associating the meanings to signifiers at the visual and verbal levels. We have designed a computer-assisted tool called SIGUEME to enhance the development of the perceptive-visual process and the cognitive-visual process. We have performed a pilot study of the use of SIGUEME by 125 children from Spain, including an evaluation based on pre/ post testing. This study suggests significant improvements in children's attention span.

**Keywords:** Autism spectrum disorder · Low-Functioning autism · Technology-based intervention · Cognitive skills

## 1 Introduction

Autism spectrum disorder (ASD) is a set of complex neurodevelopmental disorders with diverse levels of disability, varying from very mild to very severe. People with ASD are characterized by impairments in social interaction and communication along with restricted, repetitive, and stereotyped patterns of behaviours, interests, and activities [1]. Among the problems that can occur with autism, mental retardation is the most wide-spread.

People affected by low-functioning autism or mental retardation cannot use applications such as alternative and augmentative communicative systems or educational games because they have problems in recognizing the representations of objects from the real world [2] (a representation can be an image, photo, colour picture, B&W picture, silhouette, pictogram, a video of the object in movement, a written word or a video in sign language of an object).

Experts in ASD and educational professionals report the lack of tools to facilitate the learning of the processes of the acquisition of meaning and a low interest from

K. Miesenberger et al. (Eds.): ICCHP 2016, Part II, LNCS 9759, pp. 234–241, 2016.
DOI: 10.1007/978-3-319-41267-2_32

students using traditional materials. In addition, another key factor is that these work methods are followed without adapting their content to motivate each individual child.

In order to intervene in these aspects when working with low-functioning people with ASD we have designed a computer-assisted tool, SIGUEME, composed of six incremental phases. Our main goals are to get the user's attention and help users to generalize from a specific real object. This learning is designed to be systematic, gradual and repetitive. Exercises or games in SIGUEME include different representations to interact with them and to evaluate if the person is recognizing them.

## 2    State of the Art

There are many technological applications to work with ASD mainly in the areas of early diagnosis, language, communication, emotion recognition and social abilities. Several papers [3–5] review the use of computer-based interventions to facilitate the progress of people with ASD. The majority of the analysed interventions are based on the use of textual and graphical representations (pictograms, photos or pictures) that the child must recognize to begin the intervention. Mayer [6] has observed that students with ASD learned and generalized better when the content was presented in multimedia format. Only a few studies have focused on low-functioning children with autism working on symbol or object identification [7–9].

Some deficiencies can be highlighted in the previous reviews: no control group, absence of measures to generalize behaviours, and little robustness of the conclusions about their effectiveness [10]. Besides, these interventions overlook that there is an initial need to get the visual attention of the user [11].

The previous claims support the need to provide a tool to intervene in the learning of the meaning of words, associating the meanings to their significance at visual and verbal levels. The tool should teach how to generalize concepts from videos, photos, pictures and pictograms, accompanied by their verbal labels. The tool should begin by capturing the child's attention, and by maintaining his attention predispose him to learning.

## 3    Method

We have developed an educational software tool to enhance the development of the perception-visual and the cognitive-visual processes in children with low-functioning ASD. We have followed a user-centred development process, where experts in ASD and educational professionals have actively participated in the requirements elicitation, development and evaluation phases. In these phases, we have carried out various activities such as interviews, questionnaires, ethnographic analysis, prototyping, heuristic evaluation, etc. The next subsections describe the steps of the development process followed.

## 3.1   Requirements Elicitation

The main functional and non-functional requirements elicited in this phase are the following:

- Improve visual trace and fixation.
- Improve visual attention to basal stimulation.
- Develop the capacity of observation, using easy images with increasing difficulty.
- Improve the visual attention to representation of objects in videos, photos, drawings and pictograms.
- Enhance the mental representation and the linguistic comprehension with visual images and sounds.
- Develop visual memory.
- Help to understand the cause-effect relationship.
- Associate verbal labels (written and listened) to objects in videos, photos, drawings and pictograms.
- Associate gestures (sign language) to objects.
- Help to identify and classify objects in videos, photos, drawings and pictograms, as well as their verbal labels.
- Facilitate the development of the action-attention process with adults.
- Exercises designed as games.
- Improve the behaviour related to control of stereotypies, loss of attention and hyper-activity, increasing the motivation and interest in the game.
- Customize in order to adapt to the different user's needs and skills.
- Observe and evaluate the child's progress (time to perform the exercises, comparing different sessions of the same phase, etc.).
- Facilitate the child's interaction, using–if it is possible–a touch screen, a mouse or a specific switch.
- Use on different devices (PC, interactive whiteboard, iPad and Android tablets) with different operating systems (Windows, Linux, Android and iOS).
- Help to use the program.
- An Internet connection is not necessary during its use.

## 3.2   Development

Our proposal SIGUEME [12] has been designed following the guidelines and require-ments established by experts and educators consulted in the previous section. In addition, they have also participated in the development phase testing prototypes to validate the requirements and evaluate the usability and accessibility.

SIGUEME offers authoring tools so that teachers, families and therapists can design and personalize the activities, adapting their content, as well as the user interface and interaction. It also includes an evaluation tool to observe graphically the user's progress.

SIGUEME consists of six incremental phases, which range from basal stimulation to the classification of pictograms, photographs and texts, making use of videos, gestures and words (see Fig. 1). The phases are:

- Attention: the student's visual attention is improved by using basal stimuli. This phase presents a serial of animation sequences divided in four blocks of exercises.
- Video: attention is trained through moving images in realistic 3D video sequences.
- Image: abstraction is increased by presenting the same concepts, using 2D photographs.
- Pictures: the equivalence of traits among concepts illustrated on a photo, picture or grey scale silhouette.
- Pictograms: recognition of pictograms and generalization of concepts from previous phases using different activities.
- Games: categorization of representations of objects, taking into account colours, functionality, similarity, etc.

 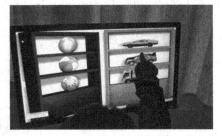

**Fig. 1.**  Using SIGUEME at different phases and on different devices

We have designed SIGUEME considering usability and accessibility according to the following design principles: uncluttered screens (simple images with no distractions if they are not necessary); consistently designed screens (same layouts, icons, titles, etc.); error prevention; visibility of system status; contextual information; help for performing exercises; different types of letters/fonts; different forms of interaction; etc.

The authoring tool is integrated in the same application and allows professionals to customize: (1) content, but with their own initial content, (2) interaction (select one, select two, or drag and drop when matching), (3) presentation: kinds of images to show, to use or not to use sign language, reinforcements (images or sounds), etc. (see Fig. 2, in Spanish). So SIGUEME can be personalized to adjust to the different user's needs and skills, creating a different version of SIGUEME for each user.

The evaluation tool shows graphics about the child's performance and allows comparison of the results of different work sessions of the same or different users (see Fig. 3, in Spanish). It shows time performing and exercise, and occasionally hits and faults, for each phase, exercise, scenario and objects in the selected date.

SIGUEME has been implemented to be used on Android tablets, iPads and PCs (Windows and Linux).

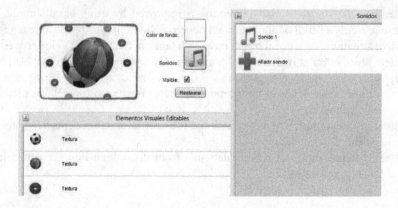

**Fig. 2.** Configuration of a sequence of the Attention phase with the authoring tool of SIGUEME

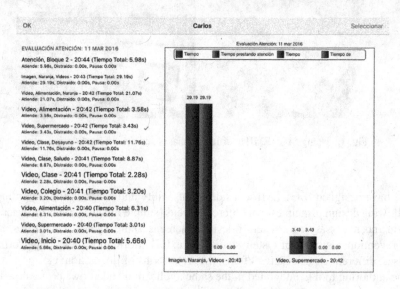

**Fig. 3.** Attention evaluation in the Video phase (Color figure online)

### 3.3 Evaluation

SIGUEME has been tested in a pilot study with 125 children of 18 schools from different cities of Spain. The pilot study involved an Experimental group (87 subjects) and a Control group (38 subjects).

Pre-tests and post-tests to evaluate attention, recognition, association/categorization, interaction and communication were completed before and after the intervention with SIGUEME.

Questionnaires created by experts evaluate the performance of each exercise and the repetitions and the benefits of the tools for educators (usability and adaptability) and students (students' response).

The intervention in the experimental group was performed during 25 sessions of 10–15 min approximately during three months.

## 4    Results

SIGUEME has been developed by a research group of the University of Granada with a special school (Purisima Concepcion Foundation), and it has been funded by Orange Foundation Spain.

The SIGUEME tool is distributed for free on the website (http://proyectosigueme.com) and on app stores (App Store and Google Play).

SIGUEME has received a national award, "Historias de Luz (Stories of Light)", in the education category.

The pilot study results show significant improvements in attention, categorization and interaction with the tool (see Fig. 4).

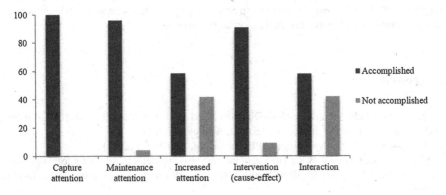

**Fig. 4.**   General use of the application (Color figure online)

In addition, the study also demonstrated that SIGUEME is useful for educators because it allows an incremental adaptability to the user's preferences and specific learning (see Fig. 5).

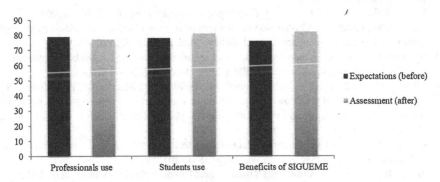

**Fig. 5.**   Assessments of professionals (Color figure online)

## 5    Conclusions and Further Developments

We have developed the SIGUEME application to enhance visual attention and train the acquisition of meaning in people with low-functioning ASD and intellectual disability. This tool also allows users to achieve significant and comprehensive associations between visual elements as representations of reality, and therefore the acquisition of their verbal labels.

SIGUEME is a useful tool to encourage initiation into the use of AACS (Alternative and Augmentative Communication Systems), tools such as PECS (Picture Exchange Communication System) or educational programmes normally used in schools.

Now, we have prepared usability tests to evaluate the satisfaction of professionals and provide suggestions to improve our application. Translation into other languages such as English is one of our future objectives.

**Acknowledgements.**  This project has been funded with support from the Regional Excellence Project TIC-6600 and Orange Foundation, in Spain. We want to thank them and also the schools that collaborated in the study, their professionals and students.

## References

1. American Psychiatric Association: Diagnostic and Statistical Manual of Mental Disorders, 5th edn. American Psychiatric Association, Arlington (2013)
2. Tandon, R.K.: Child Psychology. APH Publishing, New Delhi (2004)
3. Wainer, A.L., Ingersoll, B.R.: The use of innovative computer technology for teaching social communication to individuals with autism spectrum disorders. Res. Autism Spectr. Disord. **5**(1), 96–110 (2011)
4. Ploog, B.O., Schart, A., Nelson, D.: Use of Computer-Assisted Technologies (CAT) to enhance social, communicative, and language development in children with autism spectrum disordes. J. Autism Dev. Disord. **43**(2), 301–322 (2013)
5. Knight, V., McKissick, B.R., Saunders, A.: A review of technology-based interventions to teach academic skill to students with autism spectrum disorder. J. Autism Dev. Disord. **43**(11), 2628–2648 (2013)
6. Mayer, R.E.: Multimedia Learning. Cambrigde University Press, Cambridge (2001)
7. Clark, K.M., Green, G.: Comparison of two procedures for teaching dictated-word/symbol relation to learners with autism. J. Appl. Behav. Anal. **37**, 503–507 (2004)
8. Hetzroni, O., Rubin, C., Konkol, O.: The use of assistive technology for symbol identification by children with Rett syndrome. J. Intellect. Dev. Disabil. **27**, 57–71 (2002)
9. Whalen, C., Moss, D., Ilan, A.B., Vaupel, M., Fielding, P., Macdonald, K., Cernich, S., Symon, J.: Efficacy of teachtowm: basics computer-assisted intervention for the intensive comprehension autism program in Los Angeles unified school district. Autism **14**(3), 179–197 (2010)
10. Whyte, E.M., Smyth, J.M., Scherf, K.S.: Designing serious game interventions for individuals with autism. J. Autism Dev. Disord. **45**, 3820–3831 (2015)
11. Banire, B., Jomhari, N., Ahmad, R.: Visual Hybrid Development Learning System (VHDLS) framework for children with austim. J. Autism Dev. Disord. **45**(10), 3069–3084 (2015)

12. Rodríguez-Fórtiz, M.J., Fernández-López, A., Ruiz-López, T., Rodríguez-Domínguez, C., Cabrera-Cuevas, M., Rodríguez-Almendros, M.L.: Providing adaptations for special education mobile learning. EAI Endorsed Trans. Future Intell. Educ. Environ. **1**(1), 1–12 (2014)

# Mobility Support for People with Motor and Cognitive Disabilities

# A Mobile Travel Companion Based on Open Accessibility Data

Christophe Ponsard[1], Fabrice Estiévenart[1], Valery Ramon[1(✉)],
Alexandre Rosati[2], Emilie Goffin[3], Vincent Snoeck[4], and Stéphanie Hermans[5]

[1] CETIC Research Center, Charleroi, Belgium
valery.ramon@cetic.be
[2] HEPH Condorcet, Mons, Belgium
[3] Access-i, Namur, Belgium
[4] Atingo, Namur, Belgium
[5] ANLH, Brussels, Belgium

**Abstract.** Nowadays, both the quantity and quality of online information about accessibility are improving thanks to the development of Open Data and the use of crowdsourcing. However citizens with reduced mobility still often have to combine multiple sources of information to prepare their trips and can thus hardly do it on the move. The purpose of this paper is to address this problem by proposing a mobile travel companion. On the backend side, a number of available Open Data about public transportation (bus, train, parking) as well as accessibility of public infrastructures are consolidated both from experts and a crowdsourcing initiative. On the user interface side, it demonstrates how to design an end-to-end view on the accessibility information covering both the travel and the visited infrastructures. The interface organisation is compatible with mobile terminals and makes intelligent use of geolocalisation and proximity information. The whole concept is validated on a complete set of data from a major Belgian city.

## 1 Introduction

For all of us, securing the organisation of a journey requires some level of preparation, addressing a number of aspects such as checking about the location of the target place and its availability, selecting one - or a combination of - transportation means, making sure about the global schedule, etc. Many online tools are available to support such tasks, now often in a mobile and contextual way: a mobile query on some infrastructure will reveal its opening hours, propose to display its location on a map and guide you to it.

However such support does not fully answers the needs of people with reduced mobility (PRM) because of accessibility requirements they need to check, both for the target infrastructure (e.g. ability to visit an exhibition in wheelchair) and the transportation means (e.g. is there an accessible bus stop or parking place nearby). Nowadays the online availability of such information is increasing. The main problem is to provide a good support in its consolidation in order to

K. Miesenberger et al. (Eds.): ICCHP 2016, Part II, LNCS 9759, pp. 245–252, 2016.
DOI: 10.1007/978-3-319-41267-2_33

avoid the user to look at multiple sources of information to support his decision making. This increases both the time and complexity to plan a journey and makes it impractical on a mobile terminal. So, in addition to the accessibility barrier, it introduces an extra digital gap for PRM.

Many public organisations have become aware of the importance of publishing their information as Open Data, i.e. free to use, reuse and redistribute [13]. This enables to combine, link and exploit data to support scenarios going beyond the scope of each data owner. Those data might be released by public authorities or result from some form of collective (crowdsourcing) work [11].

This paper aims at giving methodological guidance and advices to successfully deploy a "travel companion" based on such data and that will help PRM to more easily and reliably prepare their trips. Figure 1 presents the staged process which will help answering key questions like: How to identify available Open Data? How to engage data owners to publish their data in open form? How to consolidate data and republish them? How to design an efficient user interface (i.e. mobile, accessible, personalised) based on those data? How to empower disabled users to be part of the process (e.g. through crowdsourcing)?

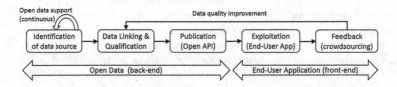

**Fig. 1.** Process and tool support

A concrete case conducted in the French-speaking part of Belgium (more specifically the area of Liège) has driven our work and will also illustrate our approach. The rest of the paper is structured as follows. Section 2 gives a state of the art and challenges in the area of open accessibility data. Section 3 details our methodology sketched in Fig. 1. Section 4 describes how it was implemented and presents its results. Section 5 discusses our contributions and main lessons learned. Finally Sect. 6 draws conclusions and highlights some perspectives.

## 2  State of the Art in Open Accessibility Data

Open Data is based on the key principle that knowledge is open if anyone is free to access, use, modify, and share it – subject, at most, to measures that preserve provenance and openness [13]. Open accessibility data is the data related to the accessibility issues and associated with geographic data (e.g. accessible entrances, toilets, parking,... ). Accessibility data also refer to data that benefit people with special needs [2]. It covers data related to building infrastructures but also to transportation means (schedules, stations, etc.) and also includes geographical and sensor information (e.g. road slopes, presence of potholes, etc.).

Ontologies provide the relevant information structure for structuring a given domain. Ontologies are available for the transportation domain, either with a general purpose like [10] or with more specific goals like information retrieval by passengers [8]. A specific ontology targeting accessibility has been developed by the ASK-IT project [9]. It provides finer grained concepts to capture specific facilities and services for PRM. Specific ontologies for the accessibility of public places have also been developed by different assessment approaches [14] or more recently based on the ISO21542 standard [6]. Defining a single ontology is impractical given it is cross-domain. Although it is a challenging task, it is possible to build such an ontology by mapping and interlinking open accessibility data of different natures [2]. It is then possible to combine datasets which can contain accessibility data at different levels of granularity.

A major problem is to gather datasets large enough in geographic and accessibility coverage, with a good quality level (freshness, precision) and under a mature format, e.g. according to the 5-stars levels of Open Data [16]. For the transportation sector, large datasets containing also accessibility information are now commonly released by companies under Open Data, e.g. for railways or buses. Public authorities are also increasingly proposing platform gathering data in their geographic area (e.g. region, major city). However, the quality level depends on the final data source which can be finer grained (e.g. information about accessible parking data might be missing for cities failing to feed the platform). A complementary source of information is produced by specific organisations specifically collecting accessibility data either using experts and/or relying on crowdsourcing, i.e. relying on a network of users to collect specific feedback about accessibility. Examples of the later approach are *J'accede* (France) [7] or *Wheelmap* (international) [18]. Although the later technique can present quality flaws, the information can be successfully cross-checked between different users and with other sources [11].

Considering our key focus of providing an integrated view on accessibility data, we also reviewed existing work focusing on providing an end-user experience beyond the data. Most work reported in the literature suffers from some limitation such as:

- *restricted focus*: most approaches either focus on building accessibility (e.g. the French [7]) or transportation (e.g. the VIATOR travel companion [12] or the Vienna accessibility augmented map [17]).
- *restricted geographic coverage*: the interface much relies on data and most reported work (including ours at this stage) still remains focused on specific pilots, typically at the city or country level.
- *older work*: some reported work done a few years ago do not fully take into account the high level of availability of data such as maps and travel planning services, the high mobile connectivity of people and the evolution of end-user terminals (smartphones, tablets). However, a number of end-to-end considerations such as the specific barriers (transfers, personalisation, etc.) remain relevant nowadays [15].

## 3   End-to-End Methodology for Open Accessibility Data

Our work was driven by the needs of the CAWAB, an accessibility consortium in Wallonia and quite anchored in our local context. It was carried out in an Agile way. In this section we describe the methodology that we followed and that emerged from our work.

**Table 1.** Inventory of Open data related to accessibility in Wallonia and Brussels

| Provider | Domain | Description | Area | Format | Star | URL |
|---|---|---|---|---|---|---|
| SNCB | Railways | Stations and schedules | Belgium | Custom API | 3 | data.irail.be |
| AWT | Buses | Bus Stops | Wallonia | GTFS | 3 | opendata.awt.be/dataset/tec |
| AWT | Cars | Handicap Parking Spaces | Wallonia | Excel | 2 | opendata.awt.be |
| Brussels City | Cars | Handicap Parking Spaces | Brussels | many | 4 | opendata.bruxelles.be |
| access-i | Buildings | Accessibility information | Wallonia | CSV | 3 | www.access-i.be (private) |
| ANLH | Buildings | Accessibility information | Wallonia Brussels | CSV | 3 | www.anlh.be (private) |
| jaccede | Buildings | Accessibility information | France Belgium | API URI | 4 | www.jaccede.com/fr/a/api-jaccede (key) |

The different steps of the methodology are sketched in Fig. 1 and detailed in the rest of the section. We do not claim it is neither exhaustive nor definitive. It reflects our current level of maturity but is based on the following key evolution principles which are worth stating:

- use a bread-first strategy to quickly cover the whole chain and get users involved. More tricky data sources are considered later.
- engage dialogue both with data owners and end-users (through validation and crowdsourcing feedback channel)
- progressively raise the maturity level of Open Data using the 5-stars levels defined by Tim Berners-Lee [16].
- first ensure coverage of non-overlapping domains before considering consolidation of overlapping datasets

In the rest of this section we detail the different steps and illustrate some relevant aspects of the case study that has driven our work. This case was conducted in the French-speaking part of Belgium and more specifically in the area of Liège, one of its major cities.

**Step 1 - Identification.** In order to identify data, the following categories of data owners need to be investigated and contacted: transportation companies (railways, buses, taxis), public authorities (parking, public places), accessibility associations.

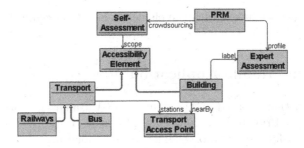

**Fig. 2.** Simplified unifying ontology

A direct look at the website usually quickly reveals the level of maturity and openness. To systematically collect key information, we used a specific template that is illustrated on our case study in Table 1. Identifying the current "star" level of a dataset is important as well as its possible evolution curve. It is always better to push data owners to raise their level because it will ease the later steps.

**Step 2 - Consolidation.** As shown in Table 1, different levels of quality and structuring levels exist. Most data could be made available in structured format although not always in open format (typically Excel files), so ranking at maturity level 2. In order to be usable by our platform, those data were imported, analysed and important semantic metadata like accessibility attributes, GPS coordinates and controlled vocabularies were identified and annotated. A few sources were available at star level 4, with directly addressable resource (URI). Those data can be directly linked. This also removes the need to care about their evolution. Following the approach of [2], we defined a simplified unifying ontology to consolidate transport and building data (see Fig. 2).

**Step 3 - Republication.** A RESTful API is recommended for exposing the gathered Open Data source as a unique semantic endpoint for information about accessibility, transport and geographical databases.

**Step 4 - Exploitation for End-Users.** In order to allow the PRM to access the information, a user interface needs to be developed. Because it should be accessible on the move, this "travel companion" should run on mobile terminal and special care needs to be taken to the ease of navigation. In addition e-accessibility is also required. We focused on some key users stories to locate specific building types in a target area, retrieve accessibility information about them and build an accessible travel to reach them.

**Step 5 - Feedback (Crowdsourcing).** A direct feedback channel from the user is interesting to challenge the currently published data and identify the need to update or improve coverage. The data can then be consolidated in the platform as a dataset linked with the element subject to feedback as described in Fig. 2.

## 4  Resulting Mobile Application

Our implementation is based on the django REST framework for exposing the backend data [3]. Prior to that, imported data were transformed using mETL, an Extract, Transform, Load tool [5]. The database focusing on the area of Liège gathers about 5000 bus stops, 60 train stations, 850 accessible parking places, 20 labelled buildings (by access-i) and 20 crowdsourced places (by J'accede).

**Fig. 3.** Travel companion: map navigation to the building and its accessibility

The end user interface was developed in portable HTML and later bundled for mobile platform using Ionic [4]. It is available online at the following URL: http://accessi.accessible-it.org. Figure 3 shows the navigation screens covering the US1 and US2. PRM can also configure the application to only show information specific to their profile, e.g. for wheelchair or hard-of-hearing.

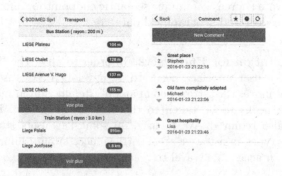

**Fig. 4.** Travel companion: transport and feedback

From the page of a specific building, it is possible to locate the nearest accessible bus stop, railway station or parking places. If the returned results do not fit the needs, the search area can be increased in one touch (US3). An evaluation shortcut is also available on all pages and gathered comments can also be checked as show in Fig. 4.

## 5   Contributions and Lessons Learned

We can summarise our contributions and lessons learned in the development of our travel companion and the backend Open Data framework as follows.

– *Importance of a long term roadmap supported by Open Data.* The process to identify the data, qualify them, engage their owner in a process to open them under the right form requires a lot of time. The proposed methodology proved effective to start and keep a good momentum by making a partial solution available and incrementally improving it while coping with different paces of different data owners. Opening the data generally results in the emergence of new scenarios which make the approach stronger and sustainable.
– *Dealing with overlapping dataset.* At this point, we did not have to cope with overlapping datasets except for the buildings. For those, we chose to preserve the underlying assessment methods (i.e. access-i vs J'accede) by using different colours on the map and distinct user interface components for displaying details. Merging the data is not trivial, not only because it requires to align the methods but also because their nature is different (expert vs crowdsourcing). This will be addressed in our future work.
– *Usability and e-accessibility of the user interface.* A mandatory condition from the PRM side is to propose an interface that will be very easy to use and, of course, which is digitally accessible for all. This is still challenging for mobile applications. In our case, the requirement is not fulfilled due to the presence of a map component and tactile navigation only.
– *IT Development is not the bottleneck.* In our experience, the development part was not slowing down the work. There are lots of powerful tools generally available under Open Source license that efficiently support the consolidation of data and development of portable mobile applications.

## 6   Conclusion and Perspectives

In this paper, we presented our experience in developing a mobile travel companion relying on open accessibility data and providing support both related to the travel and target location. For this purpose, we proposed a methodology combining datasets from different sources and making them accessible to the target audience by supporting mobile terminal and by relying on the geographical context and the user profile.

Although we have carried out this work in the context of our regional accessibility roadmap within the access-i initiative [1], we strongly believe that it could help other organisations or communities to engage in a similar process or improve their on-going work.

Our future work will continue to follow the defined methodology with a focus moving on to the consolidation of overlapping datasets. We will consider the issue related to differences in underlying assessment methods and data quality. We also plan to consider the integration of transportation scheduling using Open Data.

**Acknowledgements.** This work was partly funded by the Walloon Region through the IDEES CO-INNOVATION project. We thanks CAWAB partners for their commitment and for opening their data. Also thanks to *jaccede* for giving us access to their API.

# References

1. Access-i: Information Portal on Accessibility. http://www.access-i.be
2. Ding, C., Wald, M., Wills, G.: Open accessibility data interlinking. In: Miesenberger, K., Fels, D., Archambault, D., Peňáz, P., Zagler, W. (eds.) ICCHP 2014, Part II. LNCS, vol. 8548, pp. 73–80. Springer, Heidelberg (2014)
3. Django Project: The web framework for perfectionists with deadlines. https://www.djangoproject.com
4. Drifty: IONIC Mobile App. Framework (2013). http://ionicframework.com
5. Faludi, B.: Extract, Transform, Load in Python. https://github.com/ceumicrodata/mETL
6. ISO: Building Construction Accessibility and Usability of the Built Environment
7. Jaccede.com: Pour une cité accessible. http://www.jaccede.com
8. Jain, G.V., Jain, S.S., Parida, M.: Public transport ontology for passenger information retrieval. Int. J. Trans. Eng. **2**(2), 131–144 (2014)
9. Kehagias, D., Tsampoulatidis, I.: Ask-it ontological framework. http://www.ask-it.org/ASKIT_dels
10. Lorenz, B., Ohlbach, H.J., Yang, L.: Ontology of Transportation Networks. University of Munich, REWERSE Project, Technical report A1-D4 (2005)
11. Mirri, S. et al.: On combining crowdsourcing, sensing and open data for an accessible smart city. In: Proceedings of the 8th International Conference on Next Generation Mobile Apps, Services and Technologies, pp. 294–299. IEEE Computer Society (2014)
12. Narzt, W., Wasserburger, W.: VIATOR a mobile travel companion for disabled persons. In: 18th International Conference on Urban Planning, Regional Development and Information Society (REAL CORP 2013), January 2013
13. Open Knowledge Foundation: Open Definition. http://opendefinition.org
14. Ponsard, C., Snoeck, V.: Objective accessibility assessment of public infrastructures. In: Miesenberger, K., Klaus, J., Zagler, W.L., Karshmer, A.I. (eds.) ICCHP 2006. LNCS, vol. 4061, pp. 314–321. Springer, Heidelberg (2006)
15. Rehrl, K., Bruntsch, S., Mentz, H.J.: Assisting multimodal travelers: design and prototypical implementation of a personal travel companion. Trans. Intell. Transport. Sys. **8**(1), 31–42 (2007)
16. Berners-Lee, T.: 5-star Deployment Scheme for Open D. http://5stardata.info
17. Voss, H., et al.: Utilizing viennese geographic open government data for better inclusion of mobility-impaired persons. In: European Data Forum (EDF) (2015)
18. Community, W.: Collaborative website about wheelchair accessibility. http://wheelmap.org/en

# Mobility Support for People with Dementia

Reinhard Koutny[✉] and Klaus Miesenberger

Institut Integriert Studieren, University of Linz, Linz, Austria
{reinhard.koutny,klaus.miesenberger}@jku.at

**Abstract.** Mobility support exists for a variety of target groups. Most of these approaches do not consider people with dementia although mobility is crucial to preserve physical abilities and slow down the course of disease. This paper presents an approach which tackles the consequences of dementia on mobility on different levels. The preparation phase gains self-confidence. A smart device based solution informs the traveler and checks if she is in a state of confusion. Stakeholder involvement, like informal and formal caregivers, and an incremental safety net ensure a subtle and effective resolution of situations of confusion.

## 1 Introduction

Mobility is a crucial task for taking part in society and leading an autonomous life. However, many people suffer from limited mobility due to a variety of reasons. People with motor disabilities can often overcome their limitation by using wheelchairs and similar aids. People with visual disabilities and blind people perform mobility trainings for preparation on their daily routes and can choose between numerous assistive technologies and aids. Commonly used aids are for example guide dogs, white canes but also ATs based on smart devices. People with dementia require different means of support because their mobility is not just limited by physical or sensory deficits but people get confused and lost. These situations of confusion need to be addressed, resolved and minimized as good as possible.

## 2 State of the Art

Dementia causes a limitation of mobility due to confusion and equally important due to a lack of self-confidence and anxiety [1], although people with incipient dementia often would have the capabilities to still be mobile. Dementia is progressive and changes mobility over the course of disease [1], which causes them to increasingly rely on external support until a level is reached where independent mobility, due to the risks, is not possible anymore. However, preserving mobility as long as possible is of utmost importance since the course of disease can be demonstrably slowed down, if a human's cognitive abilities still get utilized and challenged is good as possible [2]. Also people with dementia tend to be subject to degradation of physical abilities due to less physical exercise caused by their limited mobility [2, 3]. Nowadays, studies have been undertaken, to evaluate different means of mobility support including technology based approaches [4]. The outcome is still not satisfactory which leads to the conclusion that

© Springer International Publishing Switzerland 2016
K. Miesenberger et al. (Eds.): ICCHP 2016, Part II, LNCS 9759, pp. 253–256, 2016.
DOI: 10.1007/978-3-319-41267-2_34

support needs to be provided on different levels as dementia also affects mobility on different levels. At the University of Linz in cooperation with other partner institutions two projects have been realized aiming at mobility support for people with disabilities but also neglecting people with dementia. However, substantial functionality can be reused from these two projects to tailor mobility support for people with dementia. These projects aimed for support for public transportation for different kinds of target groups. VIATOR [5] focused on a smart devices based approach for public transportation providing holistic support throughout the whole journey, including route planning, management of cancelation and delays, detours, and notifications when to set off for a journey and when to get off a vehicle. PONS [6] focused on the shortcomings of its predecessor VIATOR [5], namely footpaths. Navigation indoors was of concern, as the basis, localization and adequate geographic data was still an issue inside of buildings. Therefore, indoor localization, based on multilateration of BLE beacons in combination with inertial pedestrian navigation was a major goal as well as tools and libraries for accessible location based item creation tailored to the requirements in the context of public transportation. Also, the consortium figured out that there is still a lack of service at public transportation and travelers still have to deal with a lot of distracting side tasks. Exemplary, ticketing as a service was examined and secure contactless ticketing based on BLE was implemented. Even though, a lot of target groups and use cases were considered, people with dementia have different requirements which need to be addressed. To keep people with dementia mobile as long as possible, a combination of measures needs to be applied to support the person during the preparation, during the journey and in a state of confusion.

## 3    Preparation and Virtual Walk-Through

Before the journey, the person needs to prepare for difficulties on the road, find alternative routes for inaccessible parts and gain confidence in his or her own abilities. A virtual walk-through on a PC or smart device can put this into practice using the outcome of PONS and VIATOR. Tools for creation and modification of geographic data enriched with multimedia content including images, videos and voice recordings were developed in PONS. Composition mechanisms for journeys using public transportation including alternative routes according to cancelations and user profiles were developed in VIATOR. Both can be used for the virtual walk-through which offers a user-friendly, Google-Street-View-like [7], preparation for the traveler. The traveler can virtually move forth and back on his or her route, from one waypoint to the next. Waypoints are location based items displayed on a map which can contain pictures, videos and voice recordings in addition to textual information.

## 4    Feedback and Information During the Journey

The same information can be used during the journey and can be accessed at any time. Persons with dementia often recognize on their own that they get confused. Therefore a system which allows the traveler to access temporarily forgotten information at an early stage is preferable and advisable to a system which only detects already lost persons. On the smart device the traveler can retrieve information about general information about the journey, e.g. goal, destination, time of arrival. But also more specific information is available, like information about the next waypoint and the directions. In fact, the user can redo the virtual walk-through to recall the prepared journey. In addition, the user can communicate with the smart device in a natural way and ask questions, like: What was the goal of the journey? What was the destination of the journey? What is the next waypoint? Where am I? Indoor localization, as outcome of PONS, can be used for gapless indoor and outdoor routing.

## 5    Recognition of Confusion

An early detection of a situation of confusion is crucial, to firstly minimize the risks for the person and his or her fellow men and secondly to strengthen the sense of security and self-confidence, which directly influences a person's mobility. Since, till this day, there is no way to directly measure and determine confusion caused by dementia (e.g. via EEG), heuristics need to be applied, which can be derived from behavior and movement patterns. A promising approach is the so called geo-fencing. The person suffering from dementia can travel on the current route or multiple predefined routes. If the person leaves the allowed perimeter or does not walk waypoints in the proper order respectively walks back or remains at the same location for an unusually long duration, the system can conclude that the traveler might be confused and initiate the necessary steps. The project PONS was concerned with indoor localization which provides the basis for continuous routing, indoors and outdoors. On top of localization, automated and semi-automated route creation based on algorithms of SLAM (Simultaneous localization and mapping) [8], Robot Mapping [9, 10] and Map Conflation [11] can be applied. This allows a cost-efficient route creation mechanism.

## 6    Safety Net and Stakeholder Involvement

After detection of a situation of confusion, it needs to be resolved. As confusion is a quite awkward situation for a person, the resolution needs to be as subtle as possible. Therefore, we propose an incremental process, starting with the most subtle measure until the situation is resolved and the person can remember or is taken care of:

1. Actively initiate an automated dialog with the person on the smart device: By means of acoustic and vibration signals the attention of the possibly confused person gets attracted and the dialog gets initiated. The system asks the person about his or her condition and if he or she is confused and knows where to go. In a situation of confusion, the system delivers information about the goal and the destination of the journey or how to get to the next waypoint.
2. Notification of informal caregivers: Friends or family members get informed and are asked to call the potentially confused person to resolve the situation.

3. Notification of formal caregivers: Nursing staff, staff of the Red Cross or bus drivers get informed and are asked to get in touch with the potentially confused person to resolve the situation.

# 7  Conclusion

We have shown in this paper an approach for mobility support for people with dementia. Dementia decreases mobility on different levels. Our approach considers this and proposes support during preparation, during the journey and in situations of confusion. A virtual walk-through prepares the person and helps to gain self-confidence, information about the journey and directions to the next waypoint support the person during the journey. Geo-Fencing and other heuristics related to movement and behavior patterns are used to detect confusion. Finally, an incremental and subtle process is applied to resolve situations of confusion involving stakeholders.

# References

1. Oddy, R.: Alzheimer´s Society: Promoting mobility for people with dementia: a problem-solving approach. Age Concern Books, London (1998)
2. Heyn, P., Abreu, B.C., Ottenbacher, K.J.: The effects of exercise training on elderly persons with cognitive impairment and dementia: a meta-analysis. Arch. Phys. Med. Rehabil. **85**(10), 1694–1704 (2004). Elsevier
3. Pitkälä, K., Savikko, N., Poysti, M., Strandberg, T., Laakkonen, M.-L.: Efficacy of physical exercise intervention on mobility and physical functioning in older people with dementia: a systematic review. Exp. Gerontol. **48**(1), 85–93 (2012). Elsevier
4. Rasquin, S., Willems, C., de Vlieger, S., Geers, R., Soede, M.: The use of technical devices to support outdoor mobility of dementia patients. Technol. Disabil. **19**(23), 113–120 (2007)
5. Koutny, R., Heumader, P., Miesenberger, K.: A mobile guidance platform for public transportation. In: Miesenberger, K., Fels, D., Archambault, D., Peňáz, P., Zagler, W. (eds.) ICCHP 2014, Part II. LNCS, vol. 8548, pp. 58–64. Springer, Heidelberg (2014)
6. Koutny, R., Miesenberger, K.: PONS-mobility assistance on footpaths for public transportation. Stud. Health Technol. Inf. **217**, 440–446 (2015). IOS Press
7. Google Inc.: Google Street View (2016). www.google.at/maps/streetview/
8. Leonard, J.J., Durrant-Whyte, H.F.: Simultaneous map building and localization for an autonomous mobile robot. In: IEEE/RSJ International Workshop on Intelligent Robots and Systems 1991. Intelligence for Mechanical Systems, Proceedings IROS 1991, Osaka, vol. 3, pp. 1442–1447 (1991). doi:10.1109/IROS.1991.174711
9. Nüchter, A.: 3D Robotic Mapping: The Simultaneous Localization and Mapping Problem with Six Degrees of Freedom. Springer Tracts in Advanced Robotics, vol. 52. Springer, Heidelberg (2009)
10. Stachniss, C.: Robotic Mapping and Exploration. Springer Tracts in Advanced Robotics, vol. 55. Springer, Heidelberg (2009)
11. Longley, P., et al.: Geographic Information Systems and Science. Wiley, Hoboken (2010)

# Community Engagement Strategies for Crowdsourcing Accessibility Information

## Paper, Wheelmap-Tags and Mapillary-Walks

Christian Voigt[1(✉)], Susanne Dobner[1], Mireia Ferri[2], Stefan Hahmann[3], and Karsten Gareis[4]

[1] Zentrum für Soziale Innovation, Vienna, Austria
{voigt,dobner}@zsi.at
[2] Polibienestar Research Institute, Valencia, Spain
mireia.ferri@uv.es
[3] University of Heidelberg, Heidelberg, Germany
stefan.hahmann@geog.uni-heidelberg.de
[4] Empirica Gesellschaft für Kommunikations- und Technologieforschung mbH, Bonn, Germany
karsten.gareis@empirica.com

**Abstract.** Social innovations are increasingly being seen as a way of compensating for insufficiencies of both, state and market to create inclusive and accessible environments. In this paper we explore crowdsourcing accessibility information as a form of social innovation, requiring adequate engagement strategies that fit the skills of the intended group of volunteers and ensure the needed levels of data accuracy and reliability. The tools that were used for crowdsourcing included printed maps, mobile apps for collective tagging, blogs for reflection and visualizations of changing mapping statuses.

**Keywords:** Crowdsourcing · Accessibility information · Social innovation

## 1 Introduction

An increasingly aging population as well as a change in awareness of the needs of people with mobility impairments raises the importance of having meaningful information on accessibility to identify accessible places, increase quality of life and guide further policy actions. This challenge is likely to increase, as for example in Vienna 24 % of the whole population will be aged 65 plus by 2030 [1]. In policy debates, social innovation is increasingly being seen as a way of compensating for insufficiencies of both, state and market to create inclusive and accessible environments [2]. Specifically, we define social innovations as "new ideas (products, services and models) that simultaneously meet social needs (more effectively than alternatives) and create new social and collaborative relationships. They are innovations that are not only good for society but also enhance society's capacity to act" [2]. The social innovation format we investigate in this paper is crowdsourcing accessibility information. More concretely, we explore engagement

© Springer International Publishing Switzerland 2016
K. Miesenberger et al. (Eds.): ICCHP 2016, Part II, LNCS 9759, pp. 257–264, 2016.
DOI: 10.1007/978-3-319-41267-2_35

strategies in the context of crowdsourcing accessibility information for and with persons using wheelchairs, walking frames or prams. The tools that were used for crowdsourcing included printed maps, mobile apps for collective tagging, blogs for reflection and visualizations of changing mapping statuses (see http://myaccessible.eu). Engagement is a known and non-trivial challenge for social innovation that need a certain size in order to create the desired improvement, e.g. the usefulness of a map increases with the number of places that include accessibility information. Yet, collective tagging, like any other form of crowdsourcing, needs engagement strategies to keep citizens contributing their time and efforts. Just because a technology allows for mapping anytime and anywhere, it does not follow that people would actually use the technology. Calls for contributions need to strike a balance between communicating the importance of people's involvement and facilitating crowdsourcing conditions in ways that empower mappers, who need to feel comfortable with the task at hand. Gonçalves et al. [3] found evidence that conditions such as 'self-efficacy' and 'creating impact' are crucial for boosting volunteers' involvement. The paper is structured into two parts: (a) a short theory-based introduction of the potential of social and technological innovation for crowdsourcing geo-located accessibility information and (b) an empirical part, including critical reflections on mapping events in three European cities: Elche (Spain), Vienna (Austria) and Heidelberg (Germany). A survey of user expectations about the possibilities and benefits of accessibility mapping will link the volunteering aspects with the use aspects of volunteered information.

## 2    Innovations in Volunteering Geo-located Accessibility Information

### 2.1    Social Innovations

From a theoretical point of view, 'social innovation' is still a quasi concept, meaning that despite a growing body of literature from diverse disciplines, no consolidated or widely accepted definition or framework exists. Many difference in defining social innovations are based on varying interpretations of what is taken as a starting point in the innovation process: a functionalist understanding sees social innovation as a response to a known problem, contrary to a 'transformationalist' understanding that questions initial assumptions about problems and their causes, possibly reframing the problem altogether [4]. Another salient feature of social innovations is their systemic nature, implying that due to their scale, most social innovations need related, complementary innovations. For example, if citizens are to do something about the lack of accessibility in various areas of city's infrastructures, they need to see that national legislation; budgeting and public media develop into the same directions.

### 2.2    Technological Innovations

Maps are enormously effective tools for raising awareness and for influencing people's concept of the place and time they live in [5]. The OpenStreetMap (OSM) project, founded in 2004 at the University College London has the goal to create a free database with geographic information of the entire world. A plethora of spatial data such as roads, buildings, land use areas, or points of interest is entered into the project's database. Likewise, mobile communication in combination with collective approaches to creating digital maps, enable totally new ways for citizens to engage in innovation processes for social inclusion. Sensor-rich and Internet-enabled mobile devices allow citizens to map their environment, using different data formats (e.g. location coordinates, pictures, videos or text) [6].

In the context of this paper, we distinguish between mapping the accessibility of place (buildings, parks, metro stations) and the accessibility of routes (sidewalks, street crossings, slopes). While data completeness in OSM is already quite good for car, bicycle and pedestrian routing applications [7], there are still major gaps concerning the data needed for accessible route planning, including information about sidewalks, dropped kerbs and surface conditions.

## 2.3  User Perspectives

In an overview of research methods in disability studies Goeke and Kubanski [8] have argued persuasively that disability research fails to represent the knowledge and experiences of peoples with disabilities, largely because disability discourse has been dominated by people who have no disabilities themselves and the vast majority of research is conducted by non-disabled researchers. Here traditional research methodologies run the risk of disempowering and disenfranchising people with disabilities by drawing conclusions and making recommendations on their behalf.

To avoid the criticism above, pilot groups in the three cities included people with disabilities in their work and the planning of mapping activities. A complementary data collection instrument was a survey to capture more specific information about user groups and users' expectations. During a period of 12 month (Nov. 2014–Nov. 2015), altogether 61 people responded. Male and female users were almost balanced with 52 % and 48 % respectively. One third of respondents was in the 26- 40 years age group, and overall respondents' age ranged from 16 years to 76 years and older. Half of the respondents had manual wheelchairs (51 %), electrical wheelchairs were used by 38 %. With 2/3 the majority used smartphones, but only 3 % used navigation tools that had been specifically developed for people with mobility impairments. Another question aimed at better understanding how and when people with mobility aids used online navigation tools such as Google Maps, Transport for London, City Mapper or comparable services. Unsurprisingly, except for the group with walking frames, users of smartphones were also using their devices for mobility related planning, primarily during travel but also prior to starting a trip (see Fig. 1).

Looking at usage patterns along the various age groups (Fig. 2), no marked differences are apparent, except for age group 41–55, which had the highest portion of respondents indicating that they would rarely use online navigation services. Survey participants could also indicate how limiting they experienced different types of barriers, an information that could help to acknowledge the importance of different types of accessibility information to be collected during future mapping activities.

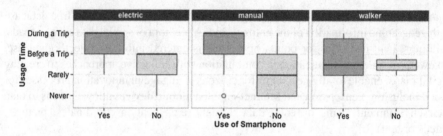

**Fig. 1.** Use of online navigation services grouped by smartphone use and type of mobility aid (n = 61).

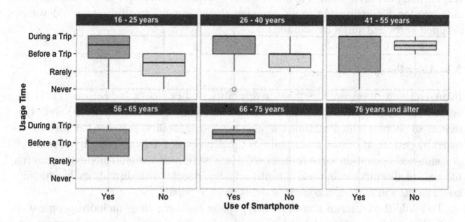

**Fig. 2.** Use of online navigation services grouped by smartphone use and age group (n = 61).

About 3/4 experience cobblestone and sandy surfaces as major barriers, 2/3 struggle with narrow paths and 2/3 indicated that using public transport independently was a challenge. Although 64 % of respondents said that they would travel more with better routing services, they also stated that human support was still more relevant to their travels than navigational support and accessibility information online. In that context it became apparent that a large group (two thirds) needs a travel assistant, at least occasionally. Hence, parents and helpers need technology support too and should be included in the design of future online services.

We also explored the possibility of an online community for people who would like to share mapped routes, their experiences with electronic mapping or their travels in general. About 25 % said they already had shared mobility related information online, but 40 % indicated that they had not yet thought or would not know an adequate platform (23 %). The data presented so far provides some context for the ensuing case discussions. Approaches to crowdsourcing accessibility mapping were quite different in all of the three cities - primarily in terms of who participated in the mapping events, wherefore different engagement strategies were needed.

# 3    Engagement Strategies

## 3.1    Printed Maps in Elche

The group in Elche contacted their city council for support, organized a press conference and workshops to raise awareness about the issues that could be addressed by having more accessibility information at city level. Early 2015, they organized a mapping event with 15 people and mapped more than 100 places in the historical city center. An underlying motivation was also the city's strong interest in accessible tourism, which were to be reflected by the availability of accessible tourist places (e.g. public buildings, cafes, restaurants, and shops) in this area.

The 15 participants included seven wheelchair users, two students, and representatives of Spanish disability rights organizations such as "Sin límites" and "Frater". The mapping event was planned for one hour and mappers split into two groups to map the accessibility of their city center. Afterwards local media and politicians not previously involved in the project reported about the event and showed further interest. However, the objective of involving a greater number of citizens that had no direct relationship with disability had not been achieved. Although further analysis of attitudes and motivations is needed, the political disaffection caused, among other reasons, by the economic situation in Spain may affect participation of citizens in events organized by local governments.

To allow all interested citizens to participate in the event, the organizers printed some maps of the area to tag. The activity proved successful in raising awareness for the topic of accessibility among business owners. They were receptive to advice on topics such as installing a ramp or lowering some of their tables to a height appropriate for wheelchair users (Fig. 3).

**Fig. 3.**  Wheelmap Interface and printed map

An important preparatory step was to increase Elche's coverage in the OpenStreetMap through a pre-mapping event. This meant that 'points of interest' (e.g. the Geo-positions and addresses of public buildings, shops etc.) had to be added to OSM beforehand.

## 3.2  Blogging in Vienna

In Vienna, the mapping group approach a local school, to co-organise a mapping event between September and November 2015. Altogether 39 students took part in the mapping project, including people from the adjacent residential facility, two classes comprising IT students aged between 17–18 years and leather design students, aged between 15–17 years. Students went out in groups of 3–5 to map the accessibility of their surrounding - each group had a wheelchair to borrow (since only one participant was a wheelchair user). The mapping project consisted of three main phases: (1) introduction and mapping, (2) presentation of results and blogging and (3) reflection.

Introduction and active mapping phase: Students were introducing to the Mapping Project at the residential facility and in class before going out in groups to map their surroundings. In addition to the introduction of the tool, each student was given a 'mapping toolkit'. The 'mapping toolkit' included descriptions of how to use the Wheelmap app, a task description and a step-by-step guide through the mapping project (e.g. role descriptions, timelines). The roles included a photographer, a journalist, an expert for accessibility (the person using the wheelchair) and a mapper. Unlike the group in Spain, all students had smartphones and no major issues had been reported in using the mobile mapping application. The mapping phase was planned for two weeks and concluded with a short survey on how the mapping affected their perception of barriers in the city and whether there were any difficulties in doing the mapping.

Presentation of results and blogging: In order to reflect and collect experiences, students met after the active mapping phase and presented their experiences to the others. Four questions were sent to the students beforehand in order to guide their presentations and stimulate discussions. The four questions included: (1) What did you enjoy most about the mapping project?, (2) What did you find most surprising during the mapping action?, (3) What kind of difficulties did you encounter? and (4) How did others react to your mapping activities? Additionally students had the opportunity to publish their blog post on a Wordpress-based Blogging-site.

Reflection: During both the presentations and blog posts students reflected upon their experiences. Generally, some reported commiserating stares from people on the street, while others found it fairly easy to navigate and experienced a lot of readiness from passers-by to help. A challenge for every group was to change the wheelchair driver during the event, as it "felt strange to just get out of the wheelchair on the street" (quote student). After the mapping event, the number of students who indicated that improving accessibility was 'important' or 'very important' increased from 18 to 27. The main two reasons mentioned were their experiences with a wheelchair (23 respondents) and the encounter with physical barriers. However, the survey results also showed that beside recommending topic-related articles to others (28 %) or recommending the Wheelmap app to others (43 %) only 17 % of the students were planning to continue to map the accessibility of places via their Wheelmap app. Hence it might be necessary to distinguish different degrees of engagement, ranging from passive awareness to active awareness (affecting everyday-life dealings with people with disabilities) and proactive awareness (prompting continuous collection of accessibility data).

### 3.3  Mappilary Images in Heidelberg

Unlike the outdoor mapping events in Elche and Vienna, Heidelberg implemented a PC-Lab mapping event. Advantages of Lab-based approach to tagging sidewalks include: many persons can be taught how to map in parallel, internet connection and standard OpenStreetMap map editing toolbox can be made readily available and the success of the event is independent of weather conditions. The main disadvantage, however, is a complex OSM tagging scheme, hard to learn for inexperienced mappers, as the tags require knowledge about specific notation rules and labels, which are not yet supported by guiding templates. Directly using the existing tagging scheme would not be very scalable due to the high training requirements of volunteers. Therefore, Heidelberg is testing an alternative data collection approach, decoupled from the OpenStreetMap tagging process. For this, about 20 students used an online crowdsourcing-platform (http://crowdcrafting.org) in combination with Mapillary (http://mapillary.com), a platform providing openly licensed street level imagery, that can be used by volunteers to identify sidewalks. As a consequence, volunteers only need to identify a sidewalk in the image provided by the Mapillary service (Fig. 4). In combination with the coordinates and the orientation of these images, it will then be possible to automatically translate the volunteers' response into OSM tags on the respective street segments [9].

**Fig. 4.** Crowdsourcing sidewalk information from street level images.

A first test of automatic transfer of the sidewalk information extracted from Mapillary images to OpenStreetMap was based on about 200 classified pictures in the area of Heidelberg indicated that sidewalk information was correct about 89 % of the times, but only 59 % of the existing sidewalks had been identified. This relatively low completeness values indicates that a considerable share of actually existing sidewalks could not be found via this method. The accuracy value of 89 %, however, shows that the current approach produces false positives, which is a bigger problem, since OpenStreetMap requires an accuracy level as close as possible to 100 %, before a set of data is accepted by the OSM community.

## 4  Conclusions

Our paper analyzed three cases of crowdsourcing accessibility information to be incorporated into the OpenStreetMap and subsequently used by online services such as Wheelmap and Openrouteservice. The argument presented was that participant motivation as well as participants' capacity to execute the task effectively were crucial to repeat and scale crowdsourcing activities to a degree where they would generate the data needed to categorise most of a city's accessible places and routes.

Concerning required ICT literacy skills, the three cases presented a range of engagement strategies requiring different degrees of skills and access to technology. Technologies ranged from paper maps in Elche and Apps on Smartphones in Vienna to Image Databases and more advanced OSM Editors in Heidelberg. The underlying idea is to find a technology that fits the skills of the intended group of volunteers and does not interfere with the actual collection of data, while ensuring the needed levels of data accuracy and reliability.

**Acknowledgement.** This research has been supported by cap4access, a project funded by the European Commission in the 7th Framework Program.

# References

1. Statistics Austria: Bevölkerungsstand und – struktur. http://www.statistik.at/web_de/statistiken/menschen_und_gesellschaft/bevoelkerung/index.html
2. Bureau of European Policy Advisers: Empowering people, driving change Social Innovation in the European Union. http://ec.europa.eu/bepa/pdf/publications_pdf/social_innovation.pdf
3. Gonçalves, J., Kostakos, V., Karapanos, E., Barreto, M., Camacho, T., Tomasic, A., Zimmerman, J.: Citizen motivation on the go: the role of psychological empowerment. Interacting with Computers iwt035 (2013)
4. Bekkers, V., Tummers, L., Stuijfzand, B.G., Voorberg, W.: Social innovation in the public sector: an integrative framework. LIPSE Working papers (2013)
5. Crampton, J.W.: Maps as social constructions: power, communication and visualization. Prog. Hum. Geogr. **25**, 235–252 (2001)
6. Kanhere, S.S.: Participatory sensing: crowdsourcing data from mobile smartphones in urban spaces. In: Hota, C., Srimani, P.K. (eds.) ICDCIT 2013. LNCS, vol. 7753, pp. 19–26. Springer, Heidelberg (2013)
7. Neis, P., Zielstra, D., Zipf, A.: The street network evolution of crowdsourced maps: OpenStreetMap in Germany 2007–2011. Future Internet. **4**, 1–21 (2011)
8. Goeke, S., Kubanski, D.: People with disabilities as border crossers in the academic sector-chances for participatory research. In: Forum: Qualitative Social Research. Freie Universität Berlin (2012)
9. Hahmann, S.: Detection of urban street properties using georeferenced images and interpretation from the crowd. In: 1st International Land Use Symposium – ILUS, Dresden, Germany (2015)

# Sharing Real-World Accessibility Conditions Using a Smartphone Application by a Volunteer Group

Takahiro Miura[1]($\boxtimes$), Ken-ichiro Yabu[1], Takeshi Noro[2,3], Tomoko Segawa[4],
Kei Kataoka[4], Akihito Nishimuta[2,3], Masaya Sanmonji[2,3], Atsushi Hiyama[5],
Michitaka Hirose[5], and Tohru Ifukube[6]

[1] Institute of Gerontology, The University of Tokyo, 7-3-1 Hongo,
Bunkyo-ku, Tokyo 113-8656, Japan
miu@iog.u-tokyo.ac.jp, yabu@human.iog.u-tokyo.ac.jp
[2] Graduate School of Engineering, The University of Tokyo, 7-3-1 Hongo,
Bunkyo-ku, Tokyo 113-8656, Japan
[3] Matching Hongo, 4-36-5 Hongo, Bunkyo-ku, Tokyo 113-0033, Japan
[4] Hongo Ikinuki Kôbô, Hongo, Bunkyo-ku, Tokyo 113-0033, Japan
[5] Graduate School of Information Science and Technology, The University of Tokyo,
7-3-1 Hongo, Bunkyo-ku, Tokyo 113-8656, Japan
[6] Institute of Gerontology, The University of Tokyo, 7-3-1 Hongo,
Bunkyo-ku, Tokyo 113-8656, Japan

**Abstract.** Although the rapid progress of real-world accessibility improvements affects the migration pathway of people with mild/severe visual/physical impairments to their destination, up-to-date accessibility information is difficult to obtain quickly because of delays to open information for public and local disclosure. Therefore, it is necessary to develop a comprehensive system that appropriately acquires and arranges scattered accessibility information, and then presents this information intuitively. However, these systems present volunteers with difficulties when they are gathering accessibility conditions and then arranging them. In this work, our goal is to extract the elements that enable accessibility-sharing applications to collect real-world conditions efficiently. Particularly, we developed a smartphone-based application for sharing accessibility conditions and carried out events to share accessibility information in cooperation with a local volunteer group.

**Keywords:** Accessibility information · People with disabilities · Volunteers · Smartphones

## 1 Introduction

Regardless of accessibility development in Japan, visually and physically impaired people continue to experience difficulties in obtaining information about accessible/inaccessible places and routes because of the limited local disclosure of this information. This inconvenient situation is detrimental to the

© Springer International Publishing Switzerland 2016
K. Miesenberger et al. (Eds.): ICCHP 2016, Part II, LNCS 9759, pp. 265–272, 2016.
DOI: 10.1007/978-3-319-41267-2_36

quality of life for people with disabilities because it decreases their opportunities to go outside, which reduces the likelihood of social participation and limits their opportunities for recreation. In addition to older disabled people, young disabled people are affected by the same problem. Therefore, it is necessary to develop a system that allows these people to obtain this information more easily. Furthermore, the issue of trust is important to ensure the continuous use of such a system, as reported by Holone et al. who reported a system that shared accessibility annotations using OpenStreetMap [1].

In Japan, an increasing number of websites and projects are available for sharing accessibility information to support disabled people. The Eco-mo Foundation provides information related to public transportation, particularly inside stations, through *the Station & Terminal Information Search* (i.e., *rakuraku odekakenet*) [2]. Other public administration offices have also developed websites that provide barrier-free information. Network data on walking spaces have also been released experimentally by the Ministry of Land, Infrastructure, and Transportation [3]. Furthermore, the Cabinet Office provides a collection of links to accessibility maps in the prefectural capitals [4]. In the private sector, KDDI provides *EZ Navi Walk*, which makes route information available to users, as a commercial service [5]. However, these websites only cover downtown areas. In addition, they are provided in PDF format, which may make it impossible for mobile phone users to read their accessibility maps. There are so many nonprofit groups that open accessibility conditions in various areas, such as the successful provision of maps of multipurpose restrooms [6].

However, they usually faced the difficulty in gathering accessibility information continually even in the local area and opening a high-quality summary of accessibility conditions because they were tired up with arranging collected information. The decrease of this burden by an information and communication technology (ICT) system can realize their sustainable activities. Moreover, relating maps created by different groups by the ICT system can also decrease the efforts of information retrieval of accessibility route by people with disabilities.

In this study, we propose a social sharing platform that provides accessibility information to people with disabilities and volunteers. We firstly developed a smartphone-based sharing application for accessibility conditions. Then, we primarily carried out an efficiency evaluation of the information collection based on an events to share accessibility information in cooperation with a local volunteer group. The questions explored in this paper are as follows.

1. How can a social platform help users and volunteers to share accessibility information in field assessments?
2. What are the important factors that would enable local volunteers to effectively gather accessibility information and summarize a paper-based accessibility map?

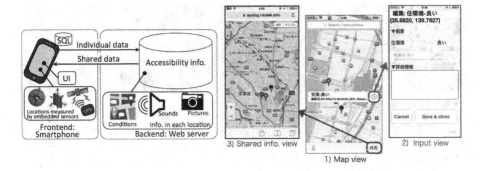

**Fig. 1.** (Left) Structure of our developed system, and (Right) user interface of smartphone application for sharing accessibility conditions (Color figure online)

## 2    Developed Application

### 2.1    System Overview

The left and right parts of Fig. 1 show an overview of the system and interfaces of the developed smartphone application, respectively. We investigated users' behavior in sharing accessibility conditions by designing the system to target and easily share various accessibility conditions. Thus, we implemented a front-end application for a smartphone that is capable of registering subjective and objective evaluations of accessibility conditions after acquiring the locations of information. The users can also log additional information such as environmental sounds and pictures, and details entered by texts. Moreover, we also developed a back-end system as a server application to support the sharing of accessibility information.

### 2.2    Interface

Our developed application shown in the right part of Fig. 1 has three views, namely (1) map view, (2) input view, and (3) shared information view. We employed Xcode 6.3.2 (OS: Mac OS X 10.10.4) and Objective-C as an integrated development environment and programming language. This application is available on iOS devices such as the iPhone or iPad.

The (1) map view is the initial view that displays a map, the current position, and hovering markers that represent accessibility information. The users enter new information and modify it through this view. The markers summarize accessibility conditions using three colors, i.e., red: dangerous/impassable, yellow: caution needed, and blue: safe/passable. The information is classified into two main categories, i.e., subjective and objective information, to facilitate easy information input by sighted volunteers and visually impaired people. The sighted can easily determine the types of assistive systems that are installed, whereas the visually impaired have recognition difficulties and they may sometimes only have a vague impression of their surroundings. Another feature is the

**Fig. 2.** Examples of photos taken during the field assessment by the local volunteer group using our application. From the left, these photos represent an ordinary road, a narrow road with a pavement consisting of bumpy stones, a road with a steep gradient, a historical place of interest (old water well), and mis-paved tactile ground surface indicators, respectively. (Color figure online)

fact that some volunteers may wish to post accessibility information about a particular place to a specific group of people, e.g., some slopes are installed for the conveyance of equipment rather than for wheelchair users.

When the user needs to enter or modify the detailed conditions associated with a marker, they can do this by using the (2) input view that transits from the map view. The input view provides the function to marker selection that combines with reporting brief conditions, taking pictures, recording environmental sounds, entering text inputs, and subjective evaluations using radio buttons and check boxes. The current location was identified based on the global positioning system (GPS). The added or modified entries are accumulated in the SQLite database in the smartphone and can be output in various formats such as JSON or XML.

The users can check shared accessibility information uploaded to the back-end server by the (3) shared information view. The back-end server application is coded in PHP 5.5.9 and the Google Maps JavaScript API v3, has a MySQL database, and runs on Ubuntu Linux 14.04. The display of this view is designed as almost same as the (1) map view.

## 3    Evaluation

We evaluated the application mentioned above and carried out events to share accessibility information in cooperation with a local volunteer group. This evaluation was conducted in a district that includes many steep narrow roads and some historical sightseeing places in Tokyo, Japan. In this district, accessibility conditions for wheelchair users have remained unimproved.

### 3.1    Method

Eight volunteers without disabilities (five males and three females) and two electric wheelchair users participated in the application evaluation. Five of them belonged to a local volunteer group and were familiar with the local geography.

First, the iPhone 5s devices, on which our application was installed, were distributed to the participants, and then we instructed them how to manipulate the application. They were also asked to search and share the accessibility and inaccessibility conditions. At that time, we asked them to take a picture of remarkable conditions and input the detail in text. It took approximately three or four hours to conduct this evaluation.

After this field assessment as illustrated in Fig. 2, the members of the local volunteer group checked the accessibility information and then summarized this as a local sightseeing and accessibility map.

## 3.2  Results and Discussion

The right and left parts in Fig. 3 show an example of shared accessibility conditions and an arranged map created by the local volunteer group. The blue trajectory shown in the left part of Fig. 3 is a passing route plotted based on the GPS locations. In total, they input 70 entries that include steep and narrow slopes and accessible slopes in the vicinity of various sightseeing places, as shown in Fig. 2. The blue, yellow, and red markers with a wheelchair symbol represent accessible, caution-needed, and dangerous locations for wheelchair users. They judged these differences in conditions based on the measured results of a clinometer and subjective impressions by wheelchair users. As a result, forty-one, seven, and seventeen places were judged as being accessible or good, caution-needed, and dangerous locations, respectively. The 41 places indicated by blue markers include not only safe roads, but also historical sightseeing places. According to their comments, they did that because our application cannot add sightseeing-related markers, but only accessibility-related markers. We improved this problem in the next version of the application. On the other hand, 7 yellow and 17 red markers indicate places that only include inaccessible road conditions such as a steep slope and a narrow road with a bumpy surface. Moreover, five other places include multipurpose toilets in facilities such as a local station and a museum; and elevators in the station and a university.

Interestingly, during the field assessment, participants gradually selected their role of specialty; some input accessibility data, some measured the inclination degree by using the clinometer, others mainly checked subjective impressions by wheelchair users. In particular, some participants who were not good at using a smartphone tended to help the wheelchair users to safely ascend and descend steep slopes, and orally reported the subjective impressions from the perspectives of not only wheelchair users but also a support person. At that time, participants who were relatively good smartphone users entered their impressions after inputting the gradient of a road measured by a participant. In the evaluation, the ratio of the participants who engaged in information entry, measurement, and subjective check was almost 1:1:3. The participants who involved with the subjective check reported that they could felt their useful contribution to the activity. This fact indicated that it is necessary to gather people with various characteristics for obtaining various types of subjective and objective

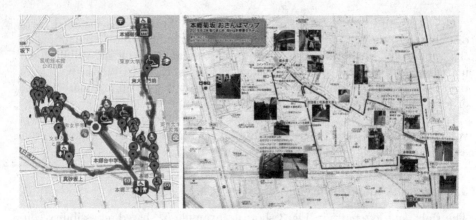

**Fig. 3.** (Left) Example of shared accessibility conditions by one of the participants and (Right) arranged map created by local volunteer group based on the shared accessibility information acquired by the evaluation. Captions are in Japanese. (Color figure online)

accessibility conditions, and giving different roles to them. However, the optimal allocation of human resources will form part of our future work.

According to the comments by the local volunteers who created the map shown in the right part of Fig. 3, they found it easy to check the shared data and create the map by using our application. Previously, they recorded the conditions on printed maps and then faced the difficulty of identifying the illegible memos when they summarized the data as a camera-ready map. Moreover, although they also experienced difficulties checking the dense accessibility information on printed maps, they could adjust the scale of the map to identify the exact positions of data in our smartphone application. However, when there were locations for which many users reported accessibility conditions, the volunteers experienced problems when checking and selecting the data. Thus, it would be necessary to develop a user-friendly interface to allow for easy browsing of dense data of particular locations.

Therefore, we preliminarily implemented the newly editable map shown in Fig. 4 after the evaluation. We aimed to design the map such that it facilitated discussion among members; hence, this map enables users to add or hide textual and pictorial information corresponding to a marker as a draggable balloon. This web-based map was implemented on the back-end server shown in the left part of Fig. 1 and users can access this map from the shared information view shown in the right part of Fig. 1 or from a web browser. Some of the participants in this evaluation commented that this application is as useful to activate their discussion and could easily be used to create a paper-based map. We considered this map as one of the platforms that could not only help citizen science activities but also social innovation activities similar to our study mentioned in this paper.

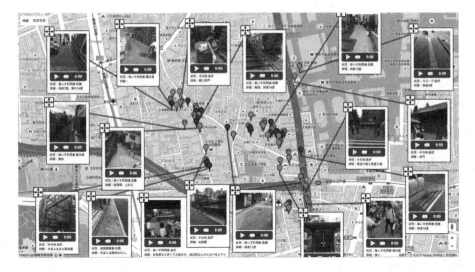

**Fig. 4.** Our implemented editable map that enables users to switch the display/hide state of the balloons corresponding to the markers. This map view was implemented based on the creation procedure and the result of the right part of Fig. 3. Texts in this figure are in Japanese. (Color figure online)

## 4    Conclusion and Future Work

This paper presents an application we developed to assist volunteers to create a local accessibility map. We implemented the application, which enables accessibility conditions to be shared, with its front- and back-end as a smartphone and web server, respectively. We distributed it to a local volunteer group, and then checked the performance of the application, their assessment behavior, and a wrap-up to a paper-based accessibility map. The achievements of our study can be summarized as follows.

- Our application performed well to facilitate the sharing of accessibility information in a field assessment and creating a summarized paper-based map. This is because participants were able to check their shared conditions more easily than with paper-based assessment. In the past, they recorded the conditions on printed maps and then faced the difficulty of identifying the illegible memos once they had to summarize the data as a camera-ready map.
- Excluding application improvement, one of the important factors that was necessary to enable local volunteers to effectively gather accessibility conditions was to determine how to collaborate effectively, especially in the cases that volunteers with different backgrounds participated. In our evaluation, participants gradually selected their role of specialty; some input accessibility data, some measured the inclination degree with the clinometer, and others mainly checked subjective impressions by wheelchair users.
- We tentatively developed a brand-new editable map shown in Fig. 4 based on the comments in the evaluation. This map is characterized by draggable

balloons that can display textual and pictorial information corresponding to a marker. According to the comments by some of the participants, this application was useful to activate their discussion and helpful to easily create a paper-based map.

**Acknowledgement.** This material is based on work funded by a JSPS Grant-in-Aid for Young Scientists (B) #15K16394, the 45th Grants for Social Welfare Activities from the Mitsubishi Foundation #26326, and S-innovation (Strategic Promotion of Innovative Research and Development) funding under Industry Academia Collaborative R&D Programs administered by the Japan Science and Technology Agency (JST). Special thanks are due to the members of the Matching Hongo and the Hongo Ikinuki Kôbô for logistical assistance, and to Miwa Murayama, the members of Collaboration Promotion Section, Civic Affairs Division, Civic Affairs Department, Bunkyo City and the Bunkyo Social Innovation Platform for their great help.

# References

1. Holone, H., Misund, G.: People helping computers helping people: navigation for people with mobility problems by sharing accessibility annotations. In: Miesenberger, K., Klaus, J., Zagler, W.L., Karshmer, A.I. (eds.) ICCHP 2008. LNCS, vol. 5105, pp. 1093–1100. Springer, Heidelberg (2008)
2. Station and terminal information search: rakuraku odekakenet. http://www.ecomo-rakuraku.jp/rakuraku/index?nextpage=TerminalSelectE.html
3. Search system of barrier-free path (2012). http://www.mlit.go.jp/sogoseisaku/soukou/soukou-magazine/1203kensaku.pdf
4. Cabinet office list of barrier-free maps of major cities in each prefecture. http://www8.cao.go.jp/souki/barrier-free/link/bfmapken.html
5. Yamauchi, K., Chen, W., Wei, D.: An intensive survey of 3G mobile phone technologies and applications in Japan. In: The Sixth IEEE International Conference on Computer and Information Technology, CIT 2006, pp. 265–265. IEEE (2006)
6. Maps of multipurpose toilets (this translated title was prepared by the authors). http://wc.m47.jp/

# Development and Evaluation of Navigation System with Voice and Vibration Output Specialized for Persons with Higher Brain Dysfunction

Akihiko Hanafusa[1]($\boxtimes$), Tsuyoshi Nojiri[1], and Tsuyoshi Nakayama[2]

[1] Department of Bio-science and Engineering, Shibaura Institute of Technology,
307 Fukasaku, Minuma-ku, Saitama 337-8570, Japan
hanafusa@shibaura-it.ac.jp
[2] Research Institute, National Rehabilitation Center for Persons with Disabilities,
4-1 Namiki, Tokorozawa, Saitama 359-8555, Japan

**Abstract.** Higher brain dysfunction (HBD) is an umbrella term used for the aftereffects of conditions such as traumatic brain injuries, cerebrovascular disturbances, and encephalitis. Approximately 60 % of persons with HBD lose topographical orientation very easily, which prevents them from walking outdoors without a caregiver. Persons with HBD find existing smartphone navigation applications difficult to master even with extended periods of training; therefore, a smartphone application that can be used by persons with HBD to facilitate independent walking was developed. The new application is simple and easy to use and routes can be specified by caregivers. The system outputs messages via dialogs and voice with vibration, when attention is necessary in cases where the user has arrived at certain sub-goals or has gone off-route. Experiments were conducted with subjects without a disability and HBD subjects to evaluate the effectiveness of the voice and vibration functions. The results showed that the subjects felt that the system was effective and highly usable. However, the average result from the eye mark recorder showed that the viewpoint was concentrated on the smartphone. The result of a second trial conducted with HBD subjects revealed that the average value of time spent observing the device, the number of times the device was observed, and the percentage of time tend to reduce.

**Keywords:** Higher brain dysfunction · Topographical disorientation · Smartphone application · Navigation system

## 1 Introduction

Higher brain dysfunction (HBD) is an umbrella term used for the aftereffects of conditions such as traumatic brain injuries, cerebrovascular disturbances, and encephalitis. It encompasses cognitive dysfunctions such as memory defects, inability to pay attention, and topographical disorientation. Currently, the number of persons with HBD in Japan is approximately 270,000, and it is estimated that 500,000 people have disabilities due to cerebral damage. The results of field surveys conducted have shown that

© Springer International Publishing Switzerland 2016
K. Miesenberger et al. (Eds.): ICCHP 2016, Part II, LNCS 9759, pp. 273–280, 2016.
DOI: 10.1007/978-3-319-41267-2_37

approximately 60 % of persons with HBD lose topographical orientation very easily, which prevents them from walking outdoors without a caregiver [1]. The ownership rate of smartphones by persons with HBD is virtually the same as that of persons without a disability. However, studies have shown that some persons with HBD require a long training period to master existing smartphone navigation applications while others are unable to master such applications even with extended periods of training. This is because the memory impairment and executive function disorders cause HBD patients to experience difficulty in manipulating these applications with many functions. A mobile phone application that supports HBD has been developed in Japan, and the presentation of procedures for activities of daily living (ADL) and schedule applications with alarms are shown to be effective [2]. Similarly, it has been reported that personal digital assistants (PDAs) and electronic aids are effective in assisting persons with HBD with daily living [3, 4]. Navigation and transportation support methods that target dementia patients and persons with intellectual disabilities have also been developed [5–8]. In contrast, very little effort has been directed toward the development of navigation applications specifically for persons with HBD.

A smartphone application that can be used by persons with HBD to facilitate independent walking has been developed [9]. This paper gives an overview of the application and discusses the results of evaluations conducted using persons without a disability and persons with HBD. In the study, particular focus was placed on the voice and vibration functions employed when attention is necessary, as well as an evaluation of their effects using a head mounted eye mark recorder and second time experiments by HBD subjects. Experiments were conducted with the approval of the respective ethics committee of relevant organizations.

## 2 Overview of the Developed System

Studies conducted in stations and trains have shown that persons with HBD experience difficulty in recognizing landmarks and remembering the correct routes to walk. They also have no cognizance of spatial positions. However, it has also been found that directions from staff help them to become cognizant of their errors and correct their routes. Further, because HBD patients have stated that they wish to know whether a chosen route is correct, a system that can present an alert and stimulate corrective action has been developed. The features of the developed system are as follows:

- Simple navigation system that HBD patients can use without a long training period.
- Simple startup process for the user, which only involves choosing a registered route.
- Simple navigation display, in which a red arrow indicates the direction and a heads-up display on the map is rotated automatically to show the direction of movement as always upward.
- Any route containing landmarks can be registered as a sequence of sub-goals (passing points) by the caregiver. Thus, the same safe route is always presented and users are not confused.
- When the user reaches a sub-goal, a message is presented to notify the user of the current position or give a warning. Any message can be registered.

- If the user goes off-route, a message is presented alerting the user that it is necessary to correct the route.

The application was developed using the Android SDK (Google Inc.) and Eclipse (Eclipse Foundation), and tested on Xperia TM GX SO-04D (Sony Corp.) smart-phones. In the developed application, Google Maps Android API v2 is used to display the map. The application has two functions: a route-setting function and a navigation function. The route-setting function is used by the caregiver to register the route, whereas the navigation function is used by persons with HBD. Routes are registered by tapping sub-goals on the map sequentially from start to destination. Sub-goals are numbered and accompanying messages can be stored. Figure 1(a) shows an example of the application display with three registered sub-goals. Using the navigation function shown in Fig. 1(b), registered sub-goals are traced in succession. Further, the current position obtained via GPS and the next sub-goal are connected by a red line to show the direction of movement. In addition, the direction of movement is always set upwards by rotating the map, with the help of a geomagnetic sensor. The function used is called the heads-up function. The indicator shows not only the total and remaining distances, but also the percentage of the total distance walked at the top of the display. When the current position coincides with a set range around the sub-goal, a message "Arrived at sub-goal" is shown in the dialog (Fig. 1(c)). If "OK" is clicked, the next sub-goal is then set as the next target. However, if "Cancel" is clicked, the target sub-goal is not changed. If the distance between the current position and the set route exceeds a specified limit, the message "Going off the route" is displayed as shown in Fig. 1(d).

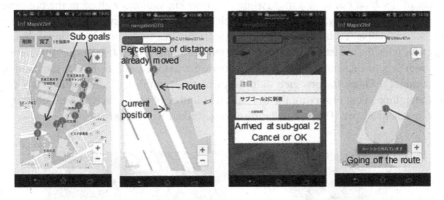

**Fig. 1.** Screenshot of navigation system. (a) Route setting (b) Navigation function (c) Arrive at sub-goal (d) Going off route

## 3 Results and Discussion of Evaluations

### 3.1 Evaluation Using Subjects with HBD

Four subjects with HBD were used to evaluate the system. The subjects walked 300 [m] inside and 500 [m] outside the National Rehabilitation Center following the explanation of the application. Two subjects had no prior experience in using any navigation application. The first one could not use the navigation application because he had difficulty with the tapping task. The second subject who had no navigation application experience was able to reach the goal outside the center with the developed application, whereas he was unable to walk outside even with a paper map. The remaining two subjects with navigation application experience were able to reach the goal with both a paper map and the developed application. Therefore, of the four subjects, three reached the goal without assistance from other persons even though they were using the application for the first time. However, several of the subjects and their caregivers stated that voice or vibration feedback is necessary because gazing at a smartphone while walking is dangerous.

### 3.2    Experiments with Voice and Vibration Output Functions

Considering the opinion of the subjects and their caregivers, voice and vibration outputs were added to notify subjects when they approach sub-goals and when they go off-route. Subsequently, experiments were conducted using ten subjects without a disability and two subjects with HBD. All subjects had experience using other navigation applications. The movement of the viewpoint was measured using the head-mounted eye mark recorder (EMR) NAC EMR-8 (Image Technology Inc.) to determine how long and how many times the viewpoint was on the smartphone (Fig. 2). First, the subjects walked approximately 300 [m] with the voice and vibration output functions enabled. Next, six subjects walked approximately 500 [m] with the functions disabled but with a map, while the other six subjects walked in the opposite direction. Subsequently, the subjects completed Quebec User Evaluation of Satisfaction with assistive Technology (QUEST) questionnaires to evaluate their level of satisfaction with the assistive device and System Usability Scale (SUS) questionnaires. For both sets of questionnaires, higher scores were associated with higher satisfaction and usability. Other factors such as movement time, number of times subjects went off-route, time spent observing the device, and number of times devices were observed were normalized per 100 [m] as the distances walked were different.

**Fig. 2.** Experiments with head-mounted EMR. (a) Head-mounted eye mark recorder (EMR) (b) Viewpoints displayed on the screen.

Figure 3 shows the trajectory of the viewpoint movement of two persons with HBD. The movements associated with the subjects without a disability were the same as that of subject B. The movement of subject A was greater than the movements of other subjects. The movements were not stable and it appeared that the subjects were looking around. Figure 4 shows the distribution of left eye movements in each sampling period of HBD subjects A and B. Here,"improved app." refers to the application that has voice and vibration outputs, whereas "previous app." refers to the application without those functions. Modal class exists in 5 to 10 [deg] for subject A and less than 5 [deg] for subject B. The average movements in the angle of the left eye were 9.21 and 4.80 [deg]. This means that the eyesight of subject B is more fixed compared to that of subject A. Moreover, when the map is used by subject B, the eyesight is fixed mostly.

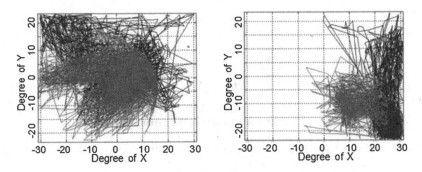

**Fig. 3.** Trajectory of viewpoint movement for the improved application (blue: right, red: left). (a) HBD subject A (b) HBD subject B. (Color figure online)

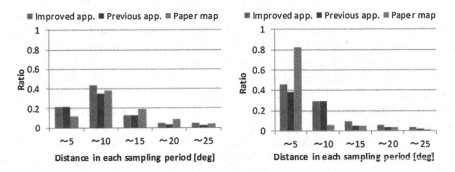

**Fig. 4.** Distribution of left eye movement of HBD subjects. (a) HBD subject A (b) HBD subject B. (Color figure online)

Figure 5 shows average distribution of left eye movement of subjects without a disability. From the result, subjects without a disability tend to fix their eyesights more compared to HBD subjects. Also, there was no significant difference by the used application. Table 1 shows the respective averages for both subjects without a disability and subjects with HBD. The improved application has the highest QUEST and

SUS scores. The results indicate that subjects felt that the application with voice output function was effective and had a higher usability. Furthermore, the opinions of the subjects were positive. However, with the voice and vibration output functions, the number of times the device was observed is smaller, the moving angle of the viewpoint is smaller, and the time spent observing the device is longer, especially for subjects with HBD. These results indicate that the viewpoint was concentrated on the smartphone. This may have resulted from the order of the experiments, in which the improved application was processed first. More experiments with a larger number of subjects with HBD are necessary to confirm the learning effect.

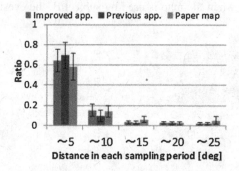

**Fig. 5.** Average distribution of left eye movement of subjects without a disability. (Color figure online)

### 3.3 Second Time Experiments by HBD Subjects

In order to confirm the learning effect, a second experiment was performed with the HBD subjects A, B, C, and D on different days and courses. The application with voice and vibration output functions was used for the second trial. The results of the first and second trials are shown in Table 2. Subject A missed the route almost at the hallway point and was unable to return to the correct route in the second trial. However, the percentage of time spent on the device decreased by half, although the number of times the device was observed increased. Subjects B and D were able to reach the goal in both the first and second trials and the time spent observing the device, number of times the device was observed, and percentage of time spent were all reduced in the second trial. Subject C was also able to reach the goal for the second time, even though the subject failed to reach the goal for the first time. The time spent observing the device and percentage of time spent were also reduced. Subjects A and C could not reach the goal using the map; on the other hand, they could reach the goal by the developed application. In the average column, only success trials are considered. Average value of time spent observing device, number of times the device was observed, and the percentage of time spent were reduced by 19.0 s, 2.2 times, and 26.6 %, respectively. However, there was no significant difference (p < 0.05) by the Mann–Whitney U test because there were only three cases.

**Table 1.** Results of experiments for subjects without a disability and HBD subjects

| | Ten subjects without a disability | | | Two HBD subjects | | |
|---|---|---|---|---|---|---|
| | Improved app. | Previous app. | Paper map | Improved app. | Previous app. | Paper map |
| No. of failure | 0 | 0 | 0 | 0 | 0 | 0 |
| Time necessary for moving [s] | 84.6 | 80.9 | 77.0 | 83.0 | 86.6 | 76.6 |
| Number of times off-route | 0.00 | 0.04 | 0.00 | 0.00 | 0.10 | 0.00 |
| Time spent observing device [s] | 41.4 | 26.3 | 22.2 | 57.2 | 41.1 | 21.9 |
| Number of times device observed | 8.2 | 6.7 | 6.5 | 7.3 | 10.9 | 8.8 |
| Percentage of time spent observing device [%] | 48 | 32 | 28 | 70 | 47 | 28 |
| Average of left eye viewpoint movement [deg] | 7.32 | 8.36 | 7.85 | 7.01 | 10.75 | 8.41 |
| Average of right eye viewpoint movement [deg] | 6.75 | 10.46 | 11.31 | 10.78 | 12.06 | 13.07 |
| QUEST [score] | 4.5 | 4.2 | 3.5 | 3.9 | 3.8 | 3.8 |
| SUS [score] | 83.8 | 74.0 | 62.0 | 87.5 | 83.8 | 63.8 |

**Table 2.** Results of first and second trials by HBD subjects

| | Subject A | | Subject B | | Subject C | | Subject D | | Average[a] | |
|---|---|---|---|---|---|---|---|---|---|---|
| | 1st | 2nd | 1st | 2nd | 1st | 2nd | 1st | 2nd | 1st | 2nd |
| Success(S) or failure(F) | S | F | S | S | F | S | S | S | – | – |
| Time necessary for moving [s] | 77.7 | 125.3 | 83.0 | 90.3 | 114.3 | 106.8 | 94.0 | 70.0 | 84.9 | 89.0 |
| Number of times off-route | 0.0 | 0.1 | 0.0 | 0.0 | 0.0 | 0.2 | 0.0 | 0.0 | 0.0 | 0.1 |
| Time spent observing device [s] | 66.0 | 60.9 | 20.7 | 12.0 | 105.0 | 61.2 | 61.3 | 17.6 | 49.3 | 30.3 |
| Number of times device observed | 9.3 | 14.0 | 4.7 | 2.7 | 7.7 | 11.7 | 15.3 | 8.4 | 9.8 | 7.6 |
| Percentage of time spent observing device [%] | 85 | 49 | 25 | 13 | 92 | 57 | 65 | 25 | 58.3 | 31.7 |

[a]Average of three success cases

# 4  Conclusion

In this study, a navigation system specifically for persons with HBD was developed and evaluated. The developed system is simple and easy to use and routes can be specified by caregivers. The system outputs messages via dialogs and voice with vibration, when attention is necessary in cases where the user has arrived at sub-goals or has gone off-route. Three out of four HBD patients were able to reach their goal even though they were using the application for the first time in the evaluations conducted. Further, a patient who failed to walk outside even with the use of a paper map was able to reach the goal with the aid of the developed system. The results of the first experiments conducted to evaluate the effectiveness of the voice and vibration functions showed that the subjects felt that they were effective and highly usable. However, the average result from the eye mark recorder showed that the viewpoint was concentrated on the smartphone. The result of a second trial conducted with HBD subjects revealed that the average value of time spent observing the device, the number of times the device was observed, and the percentage of time tend to reduce Thus, more experiments and evaluations using a greater number of persons with HBD are necessary in future work.

**Acknowledgments.** The authors are grateful to all persons who cooperated to evaluate the developed system.

# References

1. Nakayama, T.: A survey on the use of ICT among persons with higher brain dysfunctions. IEICE Technical report, **109**(152), 5–10 (2009). (in Japanese)
2. Nakayama, T., Miyaji, Y., et al.: Mobile phone application for supporting persons with higher brain dysfunctions. IEEJ Trans. Electron. Inf. Syst. **130**(3), 394–400 (2010). (in Japanese)
3. Gentry, T., Wallace, J., Kvarford, C., Lynch, K.B.: Personal digital assistants as cognitive aids for individuals with severe traumatic brain injury. Brain Inj. **22**(1), 19–24 (2008)
4. Boman, I.L., Tham, K., Granqvist, A., Bartfai, A., Hemmingsson, H.: Using electronic aids to daily living after acquired brain injury. Disabil. Rehabil. Assistive Technol. **2**(1), 23–33 (2007)
5. Laura, S., Eeva, L., Mari, E.: Wayfinding aid for the elderly with memory disturbances. In: ECIS 2011 Proceedings, 137 (2011)
6. Grierson, L., Zelek, J., Lamd, I., Black, S., Carnahan, H.: Application of a tactile way-finding device to facilitate navigation in persons with dementia. Assistive Technol. Official J. RESNA **23**(2), 108–115 (2011)
7. Chang, Y., Tsai, S., Wang, T.: A context aware handheld wayfinding system for individuals with cognitive impairments. In: Proceedings of the 10th International ACM SIGACCESS Conference on Computers and Accessibility, pp. 27–34 (2008)
8. Davies, D.K., Stock, S.E., Holloway, S., Wehmeyer, M.L.: Evaluating a GPS-based transportation device to support independent bus travel by people with intellectual disability. Intellect. Dev. Disabil. **48**(6), 454–463 (2010)
9. Nojiri, T., Hanafusa, A., Nakayama, T.: Development of navigation system for persons with higher brain dysfunction. Life Support **27**(2), 68–76 (2015). (in Japanese)

# SIMON: Integration of ICT Solutions
# for Mobility and Parking

Alberto Ferreras[1(✉)], José Solaz[1], Eva María Muñoz[2], Manuel Serrano[2],
Antonio Marqués[2], Amparo López[2], and José Laparra[1]

[1] Instituto de Biomecánica de Valencia, Valencia, Spain
alberto.ferreras@ibv.upv.es
[2] ETRA Investigacion y Desarrollo, S.A., Valencia, Spain
emunoz.etraid@grupoetra.com

**Abstract.** Mobility and parking in urban areas are often difficult for people with disabilities. Obstacles include lack of accessible information on routes, transport alternatives and parking availability, as well as fraud in the use of the specific services intended for these citizens. The SIMON project aims to improve this situation through the integration of different ICT solutions, including a new model for the European Parking Card for disable people with contactless technologies to support user unique identification in existing parking areas whilst preserving privacy. SIMON has also developed solutions for mobility including information, navigation and access to restricted areas.

**Keywords:** Mobile application · Multimodal mobility · Parking for mobility impaired people · Urban accessibility

## 1 Introduction

Transportation, mobility and accessibility are extremely important matters for those with disabilities. Some common problems present in urban areas are related to issues like: difficulties for planning and manage trips using both public and transport modes, locate and access to parking facilities or access to certain areas, among others. Initiatives like the Disabled Parking Card (Blue Badge) have tried to facilitate mobility and parking, but they don't ease trip planning and navigation. Fraud and misuse situations are also very important concerns that affect to the disabled card [1]. Fraudulent use of Blue Badges prevents people in genuine need from accessing on-street parking where they need it most.

Several studies have shown the benefits of integrated approaches for the management of urban mobility and parking. Some cities have started to face these issues using innovative technologies that fall into the "Smart City" scope. However, there are still few solutions that can offer an integrated response that take into account the needs and requirements of the mobility impaired citizens [2, 3].

The SIMON project seeks to respond to these challenges. **SIMON (asSIsted Mobility for Older aNd impaired users)** [4] is a demonstrative European project, launched in January 2014, with four large-scale pilots in Madrid, Lisbon, Parma and Reading.

© Springer International Publishing Switzerland 2016
K. Miesenberger et al. (Eds.): ICCHP 2016, Part II, LNCS 9759, pp. 281–284, 2016.
DOI: 10.1007/978-3-319-41267-2_38

## 2   Goals

Two main goals are essential for the SIMON approach:

- Reduction of fraud by demonstrating the use of an ICT-enhanced European Disable Badge for public parking, both on the basis of physical – i.e. smartcards - and virtual access right tokens – i.e. e-access through mobile devices.
- Proposal of specific multimodal navigation solutions for mobility impaired people: the proposal of an urban navigation system starts with the use of open data hubs and pre-existing toolsets that will be populated and exploited with specific features to address the requirements and needs of people with reduced mobility: routes, accessibility information, access, incidents, etc.

## 3   Methodology

The implementation of the project is organised into 4 large phases:

- A **preparation phase** to define the system requirements, the users' needs and the architecture of the different components. This phase included:
  - Definition of the characteristics of the system's users, in terms of their functional capacity as well as their accessibility and usability requirements.
  - Development of the system requirements in terms of functionality, usability and accessibility.
  - Development of the different use cases and scenarios. After an initial definition, the use cases were matched with the reference architecture defined for the system and, subsequently, discussion groups were held with disabled users to validate the proposed flow and decide which situations were priorities.
  - Conceptual design sessions, in which developers and final users participated to define the structure and behavior of the apps and services.
- A **small-scale pilot** for testing the technologies and applications developed. This includes the technological check of the robustness of the ICT services deployed but also usability and accessibility testing with users.
- A **large-scale demonstration phase** which will allow the deployment of SIMON under real conditions in pilot cities: Madrid, Lisbon, Parma and Reading. This large pilot includes both the massive use of the application by citizens, controllers and operators in real conditions, and specific detailed testing with volunteer users (also in real conditions, but with scheduled activities).
- At the end of the project, a **road map** will be implemented for the deployment of the results, which will include transferability, scalability and recommendations on standardization.

Throughout these phases, the design and integration activities are being combined with the direct participation of the groups involved and stakeholders.

## 4    Applications and Services Developed

SIMON system integrates four main services: SIMON SAYS provides the core identity management functions to enable the validation and verification of parking spaces. SIMON BOOKS provides the functions to reserve parking spots and to determine their availability. SIMON OPENS provides the functionality to establish access to urban restricted areas and SIMON ANSWERS provides the functions to enable multi-modal navigation within the target cities. This set of services feed two mobile apps: SIMON LEADS (for citizens) and SIMON CONTROLS (for controllers).

The SIMON LEADS mobile application (Fig. 1a) enables users to navigate through the target cities in a multi-modal fashion that is adapted to their preferences and abilities. The app also interacts with the new model of European Disabled Badge to both ease the authentication of users when they validate in parking spaces and to provide the identification of users when they try to access a restricted urban area (controlled by barriers or cameras for plate recognition).

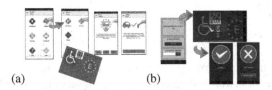

(a)                                     (b)

**Fig. 1.**    SIMON mobile apps: SIMON LEADS (a) and SIMON CONTROLS (b)

SIMON CONTROLS (Fig. 1b) checks whether a user has been validated in the system to make use of a specific parking space or not. In case that the user has not done the validation or has no right to park in that place, the enforcement officer can notify the infraction and act according to the municipality law.

## 5    Validation of the Proposed Solutions

A small scale testing was considered essential for a preliminary assessment, to detect if the ICT services deployed are robust, to validate usability and to obtain a first feedback from users about the fulfilment of SIMON requirements as defined in the initial phase of the project.

During the months of May, June and July 2015 the small scale pilot was carried out at each of the pilot sites with the collaboration of some selected users. A first prototype version of services and applications was available to be tested. Specific procedures were followed in order to assess about the users becoming familiar with the app, learning or understanding the main functionalities and detecting improvable elements.

In general, both applications have been positively assessed (above 3.8 on a scale of 5 points) from utility and usability point of view (Fig. 2).

These results have permitted to refine, adapt and deploy the apps and services at each of the pilot sites.

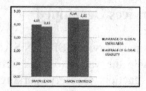

**Fig. 2.** Global assessment of SIMON apps (1: Totally disagree, 5: Totally agree). (Color figure online)

The large-scale pilot began on September 2015 and will be active during one year. Pilots have been designed to form a scalable base for long term deployment. This incremental approach will allow testing all the functionalities and services in terms of usefulness, technical compliance, usability and accessibility. A high number of users are expected (mostly disabled users, relatives and caregivers, but also controllers and other mobility professionals of the municipalities), where the different ICT services as well as the whole system performance will be evaluated and validated.

## 6    Conclusions

SIMON project aims at improving the mobility and parking of disabled citizens by means of better identification systems and the integration of different ICT solutions for information, navigation and accessibility.

During the first stage of the project the system has been defined and the first prototype has been tested in restricted conditions. Actually the system has been implemented in four large scale pilots in Madrid, Lisbon, Parma and Reading. The scalable approach of the pilots will be achieved at two levels. On the one hand, SIMON pilots already consider accessibility as a long-term commitment with full political and institutional backing; on the other, the consortium will produce a Roadmap for deployment at European level, where milestones, barriers and actions to overcome them are identified in order to make SIMON a fully deployed reality within the next decade.

## References

1. Shoup, D.: Ending the abuse of disabled parking placards. Access (39) (2011)
2. Lambrinos, L., Dosis, A.: DisAssist: an internet of things and mobile communications platform for disabled parking space management. In: IEEE Global Communications Conference, GLOBECOM 2013, Atlanta, GA, USA, pp. 2810–2815. IEEE (2013)
3. Blake, D.: Disabled parking: dilemma, fight or flight. Parking News, 243. British Parking Association (2006)
4. SIMON: assisted mobility for older and impaired users. http://simon-project.eu

# Towards e-Inclusion for People
# with Intellectual Disabilities

# Towards e-Inclusion for People with Intellectual Disabilities

## Introduction to the Special Thematic Session

Cordula Edler[(⊠)]

Inbut, Integrative Consulting and Support, Zell unter Aichelberg, Germany
`cordula.edler@t-online.de`

**Abstract.** The needs of persons with various intellectual and learning disabilities (ID) are still underrepresented in the current scientific discussion about accessibility of IT systems, Assistive Technologies, and R&D. The STS Towards e-inclusion for People with Intellectual Disabilities will explore new and innovative ways for e-Inclusion and R&D.

**Keywords:** Persons with various intellectual and learning disabilities (ID) · Assistive technologies · Web accessibility · R&D

## 1 Introduction

Worldwide accessibility of information has increasingly appeared on the policy agendas since the adoption of the UN convention [1] on the rights of people with disabilities.

Information accessibility in general, and web accessibility in particular, by nature also encompass interoperability issues between IT systems and Assistive Technologies (AT). This has led in the past to the predominance of a primarily technical view of accessibility in terms of presentation, navigation and interaction techniques (see W3C/WAI). Also in R&D (research and development) of Assistive Technology (AT) and Web Accessibility for people with disabilities it is the commonly accepted guiding principle, with one exception: Persons with various intellectual and learning disabilities (ID). Till today this target group is barely respected in research and Human computer Interaction (HCI) [2].

## 2 Who is the Target Group?

The target group within this STS are persons with various intellectual and learning disabilities. The organization WebAIM defines the issue as follows: "In loose terms, a person with a cognitive disability has greater difficulty with one or more types of mental tasks than the average person." [3].

The importance of this target group is the significant number of people with cognitive disabilities, as they represent the largest group of disabled people worldwide.

There are for example 4 times more people with cognitive disabilities than blind people, even though the issues of blind people are more likely to be taken care of in terms of general web accessibility [4].

A common problem within this user group is that the potential and abilities of the individual vary a lot, depending on the kind of disability and also from individual to individual. Because of this it is almost impossible to make a general list of problems that is common to all users. Already in 2007, Bernasconi observed: "There are however issues that are more common within all disabilities [5]". We should focus on and deal with these problems, and try to find the best possible solution for all.

## 3   State of the Art

It is however apparent that persons with ID are using more and more IT and AT. But the key challenges in using the Web are not only of a technical nature; often they are a result of insufficient information design and the lack of suitable approaches to build up media competence and – a significant problem – the lack of sufficient personal support and acceptance from family members and/or caregivers [6].

Today most people use digital access devices. In this context accessibility for persons with ID means much more than the ability to read and understand written texts. It is also about the handling of digital devices in typical life situations, the adaptation of these devices to one's own changing needs and preferences, about the design of information accessed via these digital devices, and about the critical and responsible use of the technology and contents, whether self-produced or through web-based access. Many questions in this context still require answers, e.g. how to introduce new technologies to persons with different kinds of learning disabilities, how to find a good balance between trust in and protection of users, which level of media competence can be achieved, and where restrictions or protective measures are still necessary in order to include these persons through ID.

## 4   How can Assistive Technologies, Web Accessibility, R&D for People with ID be Enhanced?

In this STS we will explore new and innovative ways to include persons with intellectual and learning disabilities in the information society and also in R&D of assistive technology with the focus on innovative features and mobile devices.

## References

1. United Nations: Convention on the rights of persons with disabilities. http://www.un.org/disabilities/default.asp?id=150. Accessed 1st April 2016
2. Istenic Starcic, A., Bagon, S.: ICT-supported learning for inclusion of people with special needs: review of seven educational technology journals, 1970-2011. BJET **45**(2), 202–230 (2014)
3. http://webaim.org/articles/cognitive/. Accessed 1st April 2016

4. http://webaim.org/articles/cognitive/conceptualize/. Accessed 1st April 2016
5. Bernasconi, T.: Barrierefreies Internet für Menschen mit geistiger Behinderung. Eine experimentelle Pilotstudie zu technischen Voraussetzungen und partizipativen Auswirkungen. Oldenburg: BIS, p. 67 (2007)
6. Edler, C.: E-Inklusion und Cognitive Accessibility, Menschen mit kognitiven Behinderungen nutzen Tablets im Alltag, in Merz Medien und Erziehung, Jhrg. 59, Nr. 4, München (2015)

# Criteria of Barrier-Free Websites for the Vocational Participation of People with Cognitive Disabilities. An Expert Survey Within the Project "Online-Dabei"

Elena Brinkmann[✉], Lena Bergs[✉], Marie Heide[✉], and Mathilde Niehaus[✉]

Unit of Labour and Vocational Rehabilitation, University of Cologne, Cologne, Germany
online-dabei@uni-koeln.de

**Abstract.** The project "Online-Dabei" contributes to the refinement of user-oriented standards for barrier-free websites for people with cognitive disabilities. In this project, the user-oriented standards prescribed by the German federal ordinance on barrier-free information technology (BITV 2.0) are examined with respect to the needs of people with cognitive disabilities. Results of a pilot study indicate that information needs related to the transition from school to work are crucial for the vocational participation of adults with cognitive disabilities. Follow-up research will specify the requirements for web site design that meets these needs using expert interviews.

**Keywords:** Accessibility · Barrier-free websites · German federal ordinance on barrier-free information technology (BITV 2.0) · Web content accessibility guidelines (WCAG) · People with cognitive disabilities · Expert interview

## 1 Introduction

### 1.1 Background

The world-wide-web in today's society plays a significant role when it comes to information gathering, networking and engaging with others. However, people with cognitive disabilities[1] are prevented by various barriers to use the internet to the full extent, which may impede vocational participation of people with cognitive disabilities. These barriers include technical barriers resulting from low web site usability, material barriers (e.g., having no access to a PC), and content barriers related to unclear content structure and/ or complex language [4].

Previous international studies on website accessibility for people with cognitive disabilities have examined aspects such as website layout (navigation, length of text, use of pictures), comprehensibility of the language used on websites, effects of compensatory tools, and user behavior of people with cognitive disabilities in general.

---

[1] In this paper, the target group is labeled "people with cognitive disabilities". Both the terms "mental retardation" and "learning disability" are discussed controversially because of their stigmatizing character as well as issues of conceptual overlap [1, 2]. The term "people with cognitive difficulties" has also been proposed [3].

© Springer International Publishing Switzerland 2016
K. Miesenberger et al. (Eds.): ICCHP 2016, Part II, LNCS 9759, pp. 289–296, 2016.
DOI: 10.1007/978-3-319-41267-2_39

For instance, Williams and Hennig [5] and Rocha et al. [6] developed specific recommendations for creating websites based on empirical research on aspects of layout (i.g. using image navigation menu; using a fairly large text size; designing a menu layout where all of the entries are clearly visible on the page). Karreman et al. [7] confirmed the importance of easy language on the internet for people with intellectual disabilities. Rink [8] and Maaß [9] critically discussed the specifications of the German federal ordinance on barrier-free information technology (Barrierefreie Informationstechnik-Verordnung, BITV 2.0) [10] regarding easy language, and concluded that the rules for translation into Easy-to-read are formulated to scarce and unspecific.

An evaluation of compensatory tools was provided by Bernasconi [11] and Schaten [12], demonstrating for example that the use of a glossary is helpful for some people with cognitive disabilities because the access to the text and thus transported information has been improved. User behavior of people with cognitive disabilities has been analyzed in the Web 2.0 study of Aktion Mensch [13], concluding that the target group has interest in a competent computer use, but there are still various barriers to use the internet to the full extent. While the topic of website accessibility for people with cognitive disabilities has gained research interest over the past decade, the comparability of previous research findings is limited due to both the definitions of disability and the participants' degrees of disability varying widely between studies.

In summary, improving website accessibility for people with cognitive disabilities provides a challenge due to the multidimensional nature of the barriers involved. User-oriented standards should therefore be developed using both participatory methods and previous research findings [13]. In addition, Van der Geest and Velleman [14] suggest a less product-oriented and more process-oriented procedure during website design in order to improve web accessibility. Moreover, initial findings of "Online Dabei" suggest that the type of information needed by the target group should be considered as well. A survey of young people in the transition from school to work indicated a wide range of requirements. In particular, the participants expressed information needs regarding vocational aptitude and training opportunities [15].

## 1.2   Project Goals

The project "Online Dabei", funded by the German Federal Ministry of Labour and Social Affairs, contributes to the development of user-oriented standards for barrier-free websites for people with cognitive disabilities. The BITV 2.0 [10] serves as a ground rule and was implemented in addition to the international guidelines of the W3 consortium (WCAG 2.0) [16]. It aims to enable people with disabilities to access information technology (BITV 2.0, Paragraph 2), referring to Article 9 of the Convention on the Rights of Persons with Disabilities (CRPD) [17] which claims access to information as a precondition for participation in all aspects of life. In contrast to WCAG 2.0, BITV 2.0 particularly takes into account the needs of people who require Easy-to-read, specifying the information to be provided on the start page in Easy-to-read (BITV 2.0 Paragraph 2 Sect. 3). This includes information about website content, website navigation, and a link to additional information provided in German sign language or Easy-to-read. Accordingly, German government administration authorities are obliged to provide website content in Easy-to-read as stated by BITV 2.0 since March 2014. In addition, requirements for people with cognitive disabilities can be found under priority II of the BITV 2.0 The requirements include that that the web must have content which is: Perceivable, Operable, Understandable. Furthermore, 13 rules in total were developed for translation into Easy-to-read and are available in appendix 2 of BITV 2.0.

One aim of this project is to develop recommendations of about how to include more user-oriented aspects in BITV 2.0 while examining additional technical and linguistic requirements. It has already been criticized that the Ordinance of BITV 2.0 implements only a minimum standard which barely contributes to the participation of people with disabilities [18]. According to the results of a pilot study, the second aim of the project is to examine information needs of people with cognitive disabilities in the process of transition from school to work. Websites are only useful for the target group if they are related to personal issues. The degree to which individual questions about professional matters are answered determines the quality of an information or communication option [15]. To develop tailor-made information and communication, studies which detect the information needs of people with cognitive disabilities in terms of a successful transition from school to work are needed. The development of information services should be in the context of promoting capacity in the sense of empowerment [19] and the vocational participation in accordance with article 27 of the CRPD [17].

In summary, further investigations in terms of expert surveys lead to the following research questions: What specific criteria must be considered in the development of barrier-free websites for people with cognitive disabilities? What kind of information is important for young people with cognitive disabilities to enable the successful transition from school to work?

## 2    Methods

The first part of the project was a pilot study conducting a user-oriented evaluation. The aim of the study was to obtain initial directions for the development of standards and to investigate the information needs of the target group.

The standardized questionnaire, which is used, contained closed and open questions in Easy-to-read and was developed in a participatory manner, i.a., including members of the target group. 138 people with cognitive disabilities and 105 educational professionals had been questioned previously about the best possible structure (e.g. possible answers as text or icons) and design (e.g. font and size). These results were taken under consideration to design a questionnaire for people with cognitive disabilities; the questionnaire for the user-oriented evaluation was developed subsequently.

With this questionnaire in Easy-to-Read a total of 22 websites were evaluated. All websites had topical connection to vocational participation. 17 of these websites are from federal authorities, which adhere to the BITV 2.0 standards. The questionnaire includes the following aspects: Emotional evaluation of content, comprehensibility of content, relevance of content for professional future, recommendation of websites and aspects of layout like number of images and font size.

The websites were tested and evaluated by a sample of adults with cognitive disabilities (N = 754) from four different institutions. People who have a recognized special education or rehabilitation specific needs in accordance with the Volume III and IX of the Social Insurance Code (Fünftes und Neuntes Buch Sozialgesetzbuch – SGB III/IX) took part in the evaluation study. Furthermore, the participants have the goal to be integrated professionally in the open labor market.

Afterwards, the data was analyzed using the SPSS statistics program.

## 3   Results of the Pilot Study

Overall, 68.3 % of the sample group assessed the websites using Easy-to-read positively. The websites were also considered to be well comprehensible by a majority of participants: About 84.5 % of the respondents understood the websites well. There was no significant difference between the comprehensiveness of institutions, more women than men indicate to understood the websites generally better $\chi^2 (1, N = 731) = 4.21, p < 0.05$. The extent of the estimated relevance for the professional future depended on the content of the websites. A wide range existed between the most preferred website (87 %) and the least preferred website (19.2 %). The majority (69.5 %) of all respondents liked the images on the websites. In 63.4 % of cases, images had contributed to the understanding of the text. Furthermore, 76.4 % of the respondents evaluated the font size on the website positively. In their opinion, the font size was appropriate.

About 80 % of respondents use the internet, half of which on a daily basis. The mobile phone is the most popular device for internet usage. The use of the internet depends on the housing situation: Higher media consumption is observed among those who live with their parents than among those who live in a boarding school or in other forms of housing.

Overall, the evaluation of the websites was very positive, but the ratings regarding website accessibility varied between websites indicating differences in accessibility between the websites. Regarding the amount of information provided on the websites, most websites showed information concerning the table of contents and the navigation. The target group criticized a lack of relevant information in a number of cases. For example, one participant stated: "The website is a little bit confusing and there is not enough information about education." Another person indicated that some websites need "more information – e.g. about people with disabilities."

## 4   Discussion and Follow-Up Study

The theoretical considerations and the results of the pilot study have shown the need for developing homogeneous standards concerning web accessibility for people with cognitive disabilities. Moreover, it has been found that the information needs of the target group must be focused on because in the pilot study the participants expressed a desire for more information.

The positive evaluation of existing websites may partly be due to a sample specific response bias in questionnaire surveys [20] which be addressed in a follow-up study.

The follow-up study will continue in the further course examining the requirements for the composition of websites and the assessment of information needs based on expert interviews. Especially important is the participation of members of the target group who also serve as experts. The interviews are carried out by means of semi-standardized questionnaires. To this end, an interview guideline is being developed, which includes both closed and open questions, and so in addition to standardized questions and answers can also accommodate experts' own ideas.

**Interview Guideline.** The interview guidelines will be developed based on the BITV 2.0 criteria as well as on previous research findings, including our own results from the pilot study. In order to meet the target group's specific needs, the conceptual design of the interview guidelines was developed regarding the special needs of people with cognitive disabilities. The increase in participatory research projects in recent years can be utilized increasingly for methodological approaches, in terms of interviewing people with cognitive disabilities [21]. In addition to general test quality criteria, sample-specific response bias, such as acquiescence tendency [22], should be taken into account. People with cognitive disabilities have been found to be particularly prone to systematic response bias in yes-no questions [20, 23, 24], suggesting that this type of question should be avoided in interviews and questionnaires addressing the target group, using multi-level answers (i.e., Likert scaling) instead [25]. Moreover, avoiding complex issues, using communicative validation, and providing an opportunity for respondents to express uncertainty regarding the reply direction may help reduce response bias [20]. Specific pre-test training of participants was also found to reduce response bias in previous research [25, 26]. Based on these methodological considerations, and following recommendations for people with cognitive disabilities [25], the interview guideline will include closed questions using 3-point scale answer options in addition to open questions.

**Participants.** It is essential for the selection of experts to select cases which are particularly important and instructive in regards to the issue at hand. In the present study, the selection of the sample occurs non-probabilistic or intentional. Thereby, a distinction between the type of the sampling and the type of sample composition should be made [27, 28]. In this context a theory-driven design [28] of the sampling is appropriate due to prior results through the pilot study.

The aim of the sample composition is to gain further theoretical knowledge and to ensure heterogeneity of perspectives [28, 29]. Hence, the case selection has gradually taken place during the research process.

The specific criteria for the sample composition are related to the interdisciplinary nature of the subject. Different perspectives from various experts are necessary for the development of standards for barrier-free websites for people with cognitive disabilities. The following groups of experts are taken into account: Individuals with cognitive disabilities as experts acting in their own cause; Computer scientists and digital media designers with specific experience in implementing barrier-free websites; Social education workers and special pedagogues with insight into the living conditions and resources of individuals with cognitive disabilities; Website operators facing the challenge of developing need-oriented and barrier-free websites; People concerned with Easy-to-read such as linguists (both scientists and practitioners).

**Expert Interviews.** The expert interviews will be conducted either face-to-face or by telephone. Advantages of face-to-face interviews include more control of disturbances and unrelated activities during the interview and access to additional (e.g., non-verbal) information. In addition to acoustic information, visual data can be recorded in face-to-face settings [30]. Conducting the interviews in an environment familiar to participants, thereby offering a feeling of security, can be considered an advantage for both face-to-face and telephone settings. Telephone interviews offer a reduction of monetary cost and duration of the interview [30]. All interviews will be recorded and supplemented with short notes from the interviewer. The recorded interviews will then be transcribed and evaluated with the help of the qualitative content analysis in accordance with Mayring [31]. The results will then be compiled and discussed at a subsequent future workshop. Synergy effects should be achieved by the variety of perspectives in the workshop, enfolding new perspectives and collaborations and seeking a consensus [32, 33]. Preceding the workshop, the participants will receive the results of the expert interviews in written form in order to provide a common knowledge base.

The results of the future workshop and the pilot study will be summarized into an action guideline, which will help substantiate and disseminate joint standards and information needs in order to improve the development of barrier-free websites and promote vocational participation of people with cognitive disabilities.

# References

1. van Essen, F.: Soziale Ungleichheit, Bildung und Habitus. Möglichkeitsräume ehemaliger Förderschüler. Springer, Dordrecht (2013)
2. Theunissen, G.: Geistige Behinderung und Lernbehinderung. Zwei inzwischen umstrittene Begriffe in der Diskussion. Geistige Behinderung 47(2), 127–136 (2008)
3. Mensch zuerst – Netzwerk People First Deutschland e. V.: Dafür kämpfen wir: Wir wollen "Menschen mit Lernschwierigkeiten" genannt werden!, http://www.menschzuerst.de/pages/startseite/was-tun-wir/kampf-gegen-den-begriff-geistig-behindert.php
4. Bernasconi, T.: Barrierefreies Internet für Menschen mit geistiger Behinderung. Eine experimentelle Pilotstudie zu technischen Voraussetzungen und partizipativen Auswirkungen. Univ., Diss.–Oldenburg, 2007. BIS-Verl. der Carl-von-Ossietzky-Univ, Oldenburg (2007)
5. Williams, P., Hennig, C.: Optimising web site designs for people with learning disabilities. J. Res. Spec. Educ. Needs (JORSEN) 15(1), 25–36 (2015). doi:10.1111/1471-3802.12034
6. Rocha, T., Bessa, M., Gonçalves, M., Cabral, L., Godinho, F., Peres, E., Reis, M.C., Magalhães, L., Chalmers, A.: The recognition of web pages' hyperlinks by people with intellectual disabilities: an evaluation study. J. Appl. Res. Intellect. Disabil. 25(6), 542–552 (2012). doi:10.1111/j.1468-3148.2012.00700.x
7. Karreman, J., van der Geest, T., Buursink, E.: Accessible website content guidelines for users with intellectual disabilities. J. Appl. Res. Int. Disabil. 20(6), 510–518 (2007). doi: 10.1111/j.1468-3148.2006.00353.x
8. Rink, I.: Nachteilsausgleich im Bereich Hörschädigung. Zur Übersetzung von Mathematikarbeiten in leichte Sprache. Masterarbeit, Universität Hildesheim (2014)

9. Maaß, C.: Leichte Sprache: das Regelbuch. In: Barrierefreie Kommunikation, Teil 1. LIT, Berlin (2015)

10. Bundesministerium der Justiz und für Verbraucherschutz: Verordnung zur Schaffung barrierefreier Informationstechnik nach dem Behindertengleichstellungsgesetz (Barrierefreie-Informationstechnik-Verordnung - BITV 2.0). (2011)

11. Bernasconi, T.: Barrierefreies Internet für Menschen mit geistiger Behinderung - Pädagogische Konsequenzen aus den Ergebnissen einer Pilotstudie. Zeitschrift für Heilpädagogik (8), 300–307 (2009)

12. Schaten, M.: Barrierefreiheit 2.0: ein neuer Ansatz zur verbesserten Zugänglichkeit zu Webinhalten für Menschen mit Lernschwierigkeiten, TU Dortmund (2014)

13. Berger, A., Caspers, T., Croll, J., Hofmann, J., Kubicek, H., Peter, U., Ruth-Janneck, D., Trump, T.: Web 2.0/barrierefrei. Eine Studie zur Nutzung von Web 2.0 Anwendungen durch Menschen mit Behinderung, http://publikationen.aktion-mensch.de/barrierefrei/Studie_Web_2.0.pdf

14. van der Geest, T., Velleman, E.: Easy-to-read meets accessible web in the e-government context. Proc. Comput. Sci. **27**, 327–333 (2014). doi:10.1016/j.procs.2014.02.036

15. Bundesinstitut für Berufsbildung: »Wir müssen Jugendlichen ein breites Spektrum an beruflichen Entwicklungsmöglichkeiten bieten«. Interview mit Professor Dr. Klaus Hurrelmann. Berufsbildung in Wissenschaft und Praxis (1), 8–11 (2014)

16. Caldwell, B., Cooper, M., Reid, L.G., Vanderheiden, G.: Web Content Accessibility Guidelines (WCAG) 2.0. W3C Recommendation 11 December 2008 (2008)

17. Bundesministerium für Arbeit und Soziales: Politik für Menschen mit Behinderung und zum Entschädigungsrecht in der EU, USA und Japan. Ein Überblick, Bonn (2011)

18. Bock, B.: Leichte Texte schreiben. Zur Wirksamkeit von Regellisten Leichter Sprache in verschiedenen Kommunikationsbereichen und im World Wide Web. trans-kom 8(1), 79–102 (2015)

19. Theunissen, G.: Empowerment und Inklusion behinderter Menschen. Eine Einführung in Heilpädagogik und soziale Arbeit, 3rd edn. Lambertus, Freiburg im Breisgau (2013)

20. Finlay, W.M.L., Lyons, E.: Acquiescence in Interviews With People Who Have Mental Retardation. Ment. Retard. **40**(1), 14–29 (2002). doi:10.1352/0047-6765(2002)040<0014:AIIWPW>2.0.CO;2

21. Niediek, I.: Wer nicht fragt, bekommt keine Antworten – Interviewtechniken unter besonderen Bedingungen, http://www.inklusion-online.net/index.php/inklusion-online/article/view/323/275

22. Mummendey, H.D., Grau, I.: Die Fragebogen-Methode. Grundlagen und Anwendung in Persönlichkeits-, Einstellungs- und Selbstkonzeptforschung, 6th edn. Hogrefe Verlag, Göttingen (2014)

23. Heal, L.W., Sigelman, C.K.: Response biases in interviews of individuals with limited mental ability. J. Intellect. Disabil. Res. **30**(4), 331–340 (1995)

24. Matikka, Leena M., Vesala, Hannu T.: Acquiescence in quality-of-life interviews with adults who have mental retardation. Ment. Retard. **35**(2), 75–82 (1997)

25. Fang, J., Fleck, M.P., Green, A., McVilly, K., Hao, Y., Tan, W., Fu, R., Power, M.: The response scale for the intellectual disability module of the WHOQOL: 5-point or 3-point? J. Intellect. Disabil. Res. **55**(6), 537–549 (2011). doi:10.1111/j.1365-2788.2011.01401.x

26. Hartley, S.L., MacLean, W.E.: A review of the reliability and validity of likert-type scales for people with intellectual disability. J. Intellect. Disabil. Res. **50**(11), 813–827 (2006). doi:10.1111/j.1365-2788.2006.00844.x

27. Merkens, H.: Auswahlverfahren, Sampling, Fallkonstruktion. In: Flick, U., Kardorff, E.v.v., Steinke, I. (eds.) Qualitative Forschung. Ein Handbuch. Rororo Rowohlts Enzyklopädie, vol. 55628, 11th edn., pp. 286–299. Rowohlt Taschenbuch Verlag, Reinbek bei Hamburg (2015)

28. Schreier, M.: Qualitative stichprobenkonzepte. In: Naderer, G., Balzer, E. (eds.) Qualitative Marktforschung in Theorie und Praxis. Grundlagen - Methoden – Anwendungen, 2nd edn,

pp. 241–256. Gabler Verlag/Springer Fachmedien Wiesbaden GmbH Wiesbaden, Wiesbaden (2011)

29. Döring, N., Bortz, J.: Forschungsmethoden und Evaluation in den Sozial- und Humanwissenschaften. Springer-Lehrbuch, 5th edn. Springer, Heidelberg (2016)
30. Gläser, J., Laudel, G.: Experteninterviews und qualitative Inhaltsanalyse: als Instrumente rekonstruierender Untersuchungen, 4th edn. VS Verl. für Sozialwiss, Wiesbaden (2010)
31. Mayring, P.: Qualitative Inhaltsanalyse. Grundlagen und Techniken, 12th edn. Beltz Pädagogik. Beltz, Weinheim (2015)
32. Holzbaur, U.: Events nachhaltig gestalten. Grundlagen und Leitfaden für die Konzeption und Umsetzung von Nachhaltigen Events, 1st edn. Springer Gabler, Wiesbaden (2016)
33. Lipp, U., Will, H.: Das große Workshop-Buch: Konzeption, Inszenierung und Moderation von Klausuren, Besprechungen und Seminaren, 7th edn. Beltz Weiterbildung Training. Beltz, Weinheim (2004)

# Easy Reader – or the Importance of Being Understood

Peter Heumader[1(✉)], Cordula Edler[2], Klaus Miesenberger[1], and Andrea Petz[1]

[1] Institut Integriert Studieren, University of Linz, Linz, Austria
{peter.heumader,Klaus.miesenberger,andrea.petz}@jku.at
[2] inbut, Zell unter Aichelberg, Germany
cordula.edler@t-online.de

**Abstract.** With current advancements in technologies like natural language processing engines and image recognition software the development of a tool that would automatically translate content, that is too difficult to understand for the individual person with cognitive disabilities, into an easier to understand, alternative format seems possible. In this paper we want to describe the idea to create a flexible extensible framework that would help people with cognitive disabilities to better understands and navigate web-content.

**Keywords:** People with cognitive disabilities · Web accessibility

## 1 Introduction

Information and communication technologies (ICT) and the internet have become an everyday but at the same time crucial aspect of life and participation. However, for many, web accessibility means a web page that is (technically) accessible for people with sensory and/or manipulation disability, e.g. partially sighted and blind people or people with Ataxia.

Making web content accessible and easy to understand for "the" general audience including users with SPLD or even intellectual disabilities (ID) can be a far greater challenge. Studies [1] have shown that even content like emails and press handouts from companies are too complex to be understood by most people. Reducing the complexity and language level used would increase the potential clientele of the companies, but in most cases would not be enough for people with ID.

According to a research report by the W3C [2], people with ID need adapted content that suits their specific needs, rather than just content with reduced reading complexity. Some concepts to address these issues are:

- Structure: Changing the structure and navigation of content can improve readability and understandability and by this enhance the user experience.
- Layout: Changing font, font size and presentation to improve the readability of the text.
- Linguistic adaptions into easier to understand language. E.g. simplified text, Plain Language or Easy to Read [2].

K. Miesenberger et al. (Eds.): ICCHP 2016, Part II, LNCS 9759, pp. 297–300, 2016.
DOI: 10.1007/978-3-319-41267-2_40

As severity and impact of ID differs from personal prerequisites as well as use cases, there is no general approach to make web content accessible for every person with ID [4]. We want to deal with this issue by creating the basis of an extendable tool that assists people with ID while browsing based on automatic conversion of content into a personalized, optimized and above all understandable individual version.

## 2    State of the Art

The readability of online content got a research focus in recent years. W3C hosted a symposium to explore the needs of people with low vision, dyslexia, and other conditions and situations that impact reading [3]. The symposium defined issues and research context in general by creating a description of text customization and the needs of people with problems with reading and understanding information. By synthesizing and organizing current research results the symposium worked on a guide to integrate specific text customization functionality in mainstream products – resulting in recommendations for future research targeting the understanding and implementation of text customization functionalities more effectively.

Another symposium held by the W3C within the WAI-ACT project from 2012 to 2013 dealt with "Easy to Read on the Web" [2]. The symposium described, defined, and compared the needs of different user groups and outlined them as basic requirements for Plain Language and Easy to Read. Current state of the art in the field of Plain Language and Easy to Read on the Web was analyzed and the emerging recommendations, guidelines, standards, examples, tools, concepts, and ideas were collected. Also attempts were made to integrate Plain Language and Easy to Read into Web accessibility guidelines and standards so that developers and policy makers are able to better understand and address the user needs. Out of this symposium considerable work has been done to provide rules, guidelines and recommendations on how to best address Easy to Read for people with cognitive disabilities.

Besides that the UN Disability Convention (UN CRPD) also calls for the participation of people with disabilities on all issues that affect them directly as a human being which also should take people with ID into account [7].

## 3    Idea

The overall idea is to create a flexible, extendable cloud based framework that assists users with ID while surfing the web by:

- Alternative information (videos, photos, screencasts …) for content that the user does not understand
- Replacement of content that the user does not understand (text with symbols, text in other languages, sign protocols, speech synthesis …)
- Explanations on browser-content that the user does not comprehend
- Changing the layout
- Assisting while reading

The frontend of the framework should be implemented as a browser plugin and will replace content that is not understandable for the user with content that is understandable. The plugin will utilize findings from natural language processing and computational linguistics as well as means for annotation, enrichment, conversion up to a possible automated translation of information (e.g. in Plain Language or Easy to Read) in order to raise the level of self-dependence and keep the amount of personal assistance needed at an absolutely necessary minimum.

The framework should also allow users to change the style of web content. If a certain font, color or font size impairs the user's reading or understanding abilities, the tool proposes changes. Also the user interface of our tool, should automatically adapt to the user's needs and preferences so that it is as intuitive and easy to use as possible. By default the Easy Reader will support a wide spectrum of user interaction paradigms. Next to classical input methods like mouse or keyboard support the tool supports alternative input methods via speech, or gestures recognition and assistive technology.

## 4   First Mockup

Currently a static mockup was developed to test the overall concept. For the mockup a random Wikipedia entry was altered and enriched with some of the core functionality of the easy reader and an initial user interface on the right hand side (see Fig. 1).

**Fig. 1.** EasyReader mockup using an avatar for interaction

The users interface was intentionally placed on the right hand side to not disturb the user while reading the entry. Besides changing the layout and the font size of content users had also the option to hide the entire menu and to change the content in easier to understand formats like Plain Language and Easy2Read (see Fig. 2.). Another option for users was to use a build in speech synthesizer to aid them while reading or watch a video about the content to better understand the content.

**Fig. 2.** EasyReader mockup displaying text in easy to read format

## 5  Conclusion

In this paper we presented the idea of a framework that helps users with cognitive disabilities to understand and to navigate through web content. We proposed architecture for the framework that would be extendable and scalable.

## References

1. Ben, H., Oliver, H., Frank, B.: Wie verständlich kommunizieren Unternehmen der Consumer Electronics-Branche? (2016). URL: http://comlab-ulm.de/_downloads/studien/2014_Studie_ConsumerElectronics_HH.pdf
2. W3C: Research report on easy to read on the web (2016). URL: http://www.w3.org/wai/rd/2012/easy-to-read/note/ED-E2R
3. W3C:TEXT customization for readability online symposium (2014). URL: http://www.w3.org/WAI/RD/2012/text-customization/#organization(DL:29.10.2014)
4. Edler, C.: Tablets on the Coffee Table: ein e-Inclusion-Projekt zur Authentizität- und Identitätsorientierung von Menschen mit kognitiven Behinderungen (2014)
5. United Nations: convention on the rights of persons with disabilities (2016). URL: http://www.un.org/disabilities/default.asp?id=150
6. Hirschberg, M.: Menschenrechtsbasierte Datenerhebung – Schlüssel für gute Behindertenpolitik. In: Anforderungen aus Artikel 31 der UN-BRK. S. 14ff (2012)

# Potentials of Digital Technology for Participation of Special Needs Children in Kindergarten

Isabel Zorn[✉], Jennifer Justino, Alexandra Schneider, and Jennifer Schönenberg

Faculty of Applied Social Sciences, Institute for Media Research and Media Education,
TH Köln, University of Applied Sciences, Cologne, Germany
Isabel.zorn@th-koeln.de

**Abstract.** This paper presents research results from an ethnographical action research study about digital media usage in kindergarten. A case study conducted with a 5 year-old child with CP points out beneficial effects of technological innovations for kindergarten children with special needs. These include not only intended learning about cause-and-effect or visual focusing, but encompass a rise in social interaction among children, extended concentration, reduced boredom, decline of unsocial behavior. It concludes that efforts to rise media literacy among kindergarten educators is needed to exploit digital medias potentials.

**Keywords:** Media literacy · Educational technology · Disability · Touch screen · Digital media

## 1 Introduction

Regular as well as special needs kindergarten education have many objectives in common. Education should support children's development regarding health, communication, and social interaction as well as challenge and assist children to develop their talents and personality [1]. Children with special needs may have greater difficulties in doing so and may need more specific and innovative support. Digital media devices, such as smartphones or tablet computers, are widespread in German house-holds, but 80 % of German children aged two to five have not yet used them [2]. Neither is the usage of digital media common in German kindergarten education, thereby disregarding digital media's great potential for supporting children with special needs, for instance in terms of facilitating interaction with other children.

This paper presents research results from an ethnographical action research study about digital media usage in kindergarten. Using the example of a case study conducted with a 5 year-old child with special needs it points out the beneficial effects of technological innovations for kindergarten children with or without special needs.

### 1.1 State of the Art of Research and Practice

German kindergarten educators are reluctant towards integrating state-of-the-art computing technologies into their education concepts [3], while it is more common to use ICTs in kindergarten in UK and Northern Europe [4–6]. Fear of harming children's

© Springer International Publishing Switzerland 2016
K. Miesenberger et al. (Eds.): ICCHP 2016, Part II, LNCS 9759, pp. 301–304, 2016.
DOI: 10.1007/978-3-319-41267-2_41

development by introducing them to digital media, such as tablet computers or video games, is widespread and nourished by populist reports [e.g. 7]. Scientific literature on using technology for special education is available mostly for school age [8], but perspectives on kindergarten age are rare in German speaking contexts. Literature on technology use for children with special needs can be found in rehabilitation sciences with focus on rehabilitation and compensation, such as augmentative and alternative communication. Here, iPad use by specialists such as therapists, is growing [9, 10]. Potentials of touchscreen games for older people with dementia is a growing research field [11]. Implementing popular technology as integrated aspects of daily kindergarten life for special needs children is rare, although systematic suggestions of activities or educational tablet apps exist [12]. So far little research has been conducted on how to integrate technology into daily life in kindergarten and on how to improve sustainability of tablet related activities in these institutions.

## 2    Methodology

Action research methodology [13] was used in a small field work project, encompassing four children in four kindergartens (age three to five years). Participatory observation of one special need child in each institution was conveyed, field notes were taken and analyzed to identify a child's potentials, challenges and restraints. Analysis revealed that children not only suffer from their health handicap, but also from how their kindergarten environment reacts to them. Based on these results, several interventions with educational use of digital media were designed and tested with each child in their kindergarten setting in an iterative process. Objective of the intervention was to provide educational solutions for the observed challenges. Again, participatory observation was done, field notes were taken and analyzed, failure and successes of interventions were analyzed and adapted until satisfying results could be observed.

## 3    Case Study

Lukas is five years old and has profound multiple disabilities from cerebral palsy, including tetraspastics, motor and mental disability as well as audio and visual impairment. He cannot speak, but screams often. We assume that he screams from boredom. He sits in a wheelchair with his right hand tied to the chair most of the time in order to keep him from scratching and hurting his eye. He is often excluded from playing with his peers and he often sits alone or next to peers without any sort of contact. During many of the regular kindergarten activities that he cannot join he is "parked" in his wheelchair next to some toy hangings in order to provide him with visual "training". In an iterative design process, the Android tablet app "Finger Paint with Sounds" was tested. Lukas dipped his hand into virtual color pots on the touch screen and "painted" on the screen, thereby at the same time producing sounds that are connected to the different colors. This helped him realize his actions and perceive self-efficacy, otherwise mostly perceived through screaming. His eyes were wide open, focusing on the activity more intensely than usual. Concentration span was up to 30 min compared to only five to ten minutes with other games. Usually, during therapies, Lukas moves to a separate room with the therapist, as was the case here, too. One day, the app was played in a room with other children. They soon played together with Lukas, which made his concentration span rise to more than one hour, his eyes focussing both the screen and other children. He laughed. Never during interventions with the app did he scratch his eye or scream.

## 4  Discussion of Scientific and Practical Impact for Media and Early Childhood Education

The case study indicates a rise of interest in playing in a social context, since Lukas' concentration span and interaction were extended. Self-endangering practices were reduced, making it obsolete to use drastic action such as tying a hand to the wheelchair when he engages with interest in the activity. In contrast to more traditional games or paper images offered to Lukas, the advantages of the tablet app are: bright light and contrasts, more easy opportunities for experiencing cause-and-effect. They can thus offer valuable additional (if not more adequate) learning opportunities.

The main finding is that interacting with digital media does not primarily have negative effects on children. In contrast, it can contribute to achieving educational and therapeutical objectives in kindergarten, e.g. developing children's skills and personality, learning about cause-and-effect and self-efficacy and improving joint attention and children's social interactions. Media activities can be played in a group, which was often the actively preferred and most effective (more concentration and interest) scenario for all children in the study. Thus the intervention contributed to children's inclusion and foiled assumptions that playing with digital media will isolate children.

## 5  Conclusion

The potential benefits to overall educational and therapeutical objectives in kindergarten education refute the commonly found argument that using technology is a choice depending on educators' preferences. Instead, usage of digital media is an asset that needs further research. Moreover the development of easy-to-use digital media activities is needed to meet the specific needs of individual children in order to improve their language, health, motoric development, aesthetic education, learning about cause and effects, improving self-efficacy, and technology literacy. Additionally, the deployment of methods to leverage educators' interest and competence in identifying suitable games and applying suitable game-like activities with digital media needs more attention.

# References

1. Ministerium für Familie, Kinder, Jugend, Kultur und Sport NRW, Ministerium für Schule und Weiterbildung NRW (eds.): Bildungsgrundsätze. Mehr Chancen für alle. Grundsätze zur Bildungsförderung für Kinder von 0 bis 10 Jahren in Kindertagesbetreuung und Schulen im Primarbereich in Nordrhein-Westfalen, 1st edn. Verlag Herder, Freiburg (2016)
2. Medienpädagogischer Forschungsverbund Südwest: miniKIM 2014. Kleinkinder und Medien. Basisuntersuchung zum Medienumgang 2- bis 5-Jähriger in Deutschland (2015)
3. Brüggemann, M., Averbeck, I., Breiter, A.: Förderung von Medienkompetenz in Bremer Kindertageseinrichtungen. Bestandsaufnahme und Befragung von Fachkräften in Bremen und Bremerhaven zur frühen Medienbildung, Bremen (2013). http://www.ifib.de/publikationsdateien/Meko-Kita-Sept2013_ifib.pdf
4. Siraj-Blatchford, J., Whitebread, D.: Supporting ICT in the early years: Supporting early learning. Open University Press, Maidenhead (2003)
5. Siraj, I., Siraj-Blatchford, J.: A Guide to Developing the ICT Curriculum for Early Childhood Education. Trentham Books, Stoke on Trent, Sterling (2006)
6. Palme, H.-J.: Coole Klicks. Empfehlenswerte Spiel- und Lernprogramme für kleine Denker mit Migrationshintergrund. Reihe Multimedia. 10. KoPäd Verl, München (2005)
7. Ryall, J.: Surge in 'digital dementia' - Telegraph (2013)
8. Bosse, I.: Keine Bildung ohne Medien! Perspektiven der Geistigbehindertenpädagogik. Teilhabe - die Fachzeitschrift der Lebenshilfe 52(1), 26–32 (2013)
9. Hallbauer, A., Kitzinger, A., (eds.): Unterstützt kommunizieren und lernen mit dem iPad. Loeper, Karlsruhe (2014)
10. Boyd, T.K., Barnett, J.E.H., More, C.M.: Evaluating iPad technology for enhancing communication skills of children with autism spectrum disorders. Interv. Sch. Clinic 51(1), 19–27 (2015). doi:10.1177/1053451215577476
11. Astell, A.J., Malone, B., Williams, G., Hwang, F., Ellis, M.P.: Leveraging everyday technology for people living with dementia: a case study. J. Assistive Technol. 8(4), 164–176 (2014). doi:10.1108/JAT-01-2014-0004
12. Krstoski, I.: UK-App-Blog. Das Blog zum Thema iPad und Unterstützte Kommunikation (UK) (2016)
13. McNiff, J., Whitehead, J.: Action Research: Principles and Practice. Routledge-Falmer, London (2002)

# Reordering Symbols: A Step Towards a Symbol to Arabic Text Translator

Lama Alzaben[⊠], Mike Wald, and E.A. Draffan

School of Electronics and Computer Science, University of Southampton,
Southampton, UK
laa1c13@soton.ac.uk,
{mw,ead}@ecs.soton.ac.uk

**Abstract.** Graphic symbols can be used as an alternative way of communication. Translating from a message composed of symbols to a fluent sentence will enable symbol users to be understood by those who may not be familiar with the use of symbols. Symbol messages may not match the target language in terms of order and syntax. This paper describes an attempt to reorder symbols, based on their labels, to match the target language namely Modern Standard Arabic. An initial experiment has been conducted using a SMT decoder with two n-gram models to reorder words in general then discuss its application to symbols. The output was evaluated using BLEU: an automatic evaluation metric used in machine translation. The average score of the output has improved over the input. Further improvements are suggested and will be carried out in future experiments.

**Keywords:** AAC · Graphic symbols · Statistical machine translation

## 1 Introduction

Graphic symbols can be used as a form of aided Augmentative and Alternative Communication (AAC) for people who are not able to communicate using spoken or written language. Translating a multi-symbol message, composed using an AAC device or application, into a fluent utterance will increase symbol users ability to communicate. The AAC user may not follow the correct word order when composing messages [1]. Thus, symbols within the composed message need to be reordered to match the word order of the target language as a step towards a full symbol to text translation system. The task of reordering is challenging because the input, the multi-symbol message, is in an unknown structure. As a result, various reorderings of symbol labels need to be explored and evaluated to find the best order that matches the target language. The problem of word order mismatch also occurs when translating between natural languages. Unlike graphic symbols, natural languages have a recognised grammar that governs their word order. However, statistical machine translation (SMT) [2,3] does not model the syntax explicitly. Recent SMT implementations (i.e. [7]) use a log-linear model of different features each with a given weight [3]. The SMT decoder

© Springer International Publishing Switzerland 2016
K. Miesenberger et al. (Eds.): ICCHP 2016, Part II, LNCS 9759, pp. 305–309, 2016.
DOI: 10.1007/978-3-319-41267-2_42

explores the space of different arrangements of various translation options using a search algorithm (i.e. beam search) to find the one with the maximum score. The search space is large and it is computationally difficult to fully explore. Different strategies have been used by the SMT decoder to minimise the explored space.

This work demonstrates how an SMT decoder using the log-linear model can be used to correct the order of tokens to match the target language word order (in this case Arabic) as a step towards a full symbol to text translation system.

## 2    Related Work

Some statistical symbol-to-text systems have been proposed. Waller and Jack [9] used a trigram model to predict missing function words and correct words forms. A recent work by Sevens et al. [6] generates Dutch text from a symbol message. Their focus was on finding the textual correspondence of each individual symbol. They used a beam search decoder that used a tri-gram language model. However, both [6,9] assumed an agreement in order between the input and the output. SymbolPath is another symbol to text system [10] where the input is made by drawing a path over selected symbols. It assumes that selected symbols may not be precise in both content and order. It determines the intended syntactic order based on semantic frames that guide the arrangement of words around predicates or verbs. However, generated utterances are limited; the utterance needs to be simple in terms of the number of verbs, actors and modifiers. Also, the fluency of the text has not been evaluated.

## 3    Methodology

The problem of mismatch between symbol order and Arabic word order is approached using a SMT decoder that uses a log-linear model with language models as features, inspired by its success in SMT [3]. SMT [2,3] uses statistical models to score various partial hypothesised translations, incrementally until the most probable full translation is identified. The language model is one of the core models; its role is to ensure a fluent output by lending more probability to observed sequences. The addition of a class language model is suggested by [3], as it may be able to score longer sequences when compared to word language models. A symbol set may be managed and augmented by various information such as their lexical label and POS tags that can be exploited to recover the order of the symbols. Thus, the use of the SMT decoder with a word and part of speech (POS) tags language models is chosen. However, unlike the case in SMT, a symbol label may not correspond to a surface word in a language; lacking additional affixes (i.e. definite article) and inflection marks. Thus, building a language model from a corpus of stems or lemmas is suggested instead of a model of tokenised surface words.

## 4 Experiment

Due to the unavailability of a corpus of multi-symbol messages, experiments abstracted from symbols and measured the ability of the chosen methodology to recover the correct order of the textual tokens using surface and POS n-gram models. The experiment used the SMT Phrasal decoder [7]. Both models were 5-gram language model trained on around 80 % of the sentences in the Corpus of Contemporary Arabic[1]. Tokenising, normalising and POS tagging the training data were undertaken using MADAMIRA [5]. The test set was composed of 521 sentences extracted from examples linked to the selected symbol set[2]. It was preprocessed in a similar manner to the training data and tokens within each sentence were randomly mixed. Since tokens within test set sentences were randomly ordered, the input order was not considered. However, in reality this may not be the case; the input may not be as far from the matching target. Thus, the generated output needs to be as close as possible to the input to preserve the intended meaning.

In this experiment different settings have been compared: using a surface n-gram language model only and one with adding the POS n-gram model against the input. The output was evaluated using BLEU [4] an automatic evaluation metric used in SMT. Average BLEU scores are reported in Table 1.

**Table 1.** Evaluation scores

|   | Exp | BLEU-4 |
|---|---|---|
| 1 | Input | 18.90 |
| 2 | LM | 32.91 |
| 3 | LM and POS-LM | 37.15 |

Results showed that the average BLEU score improved over the input and a further improvement was achieved when adding POS n-gram model with uniform weights. Some further improvements with respect to BLEU scores was achieved when assigning a higher weight to the surface n-gram model which suggests the need for an optimisation algorithm to find the best values for each. The analysis of each sentence shows that only 20 % of the test set sentences have fully matched the reference and 55 % of the whole test set have improved. A possible contributing factor to the worsened sentences is the mismatch between the test set and the training data. The test set was extracted from examples linked to the selected symbol set, which was chosen since they might be closer to the structure of symbol messages than sentences extracted from a general corpus. On the other hand, the training data was composed of text collected from the Web under various topics.

---

[1] http://www.comp.leeds.ac.uk/eric/latifa/research.htm.
[2] http://tawasolsymbols.org/en/home/.

## 5    Conclusion

This work assumes that symbols are labelled with a full-formed word that represents its meaning and some kind of classification that groups these symbols such as their POS. The experiment demonstrates the importance of annotating symbols with additional linguistic information to help in finding the order that matches the target language's word order. The performance of the methodology used depends on how much the corpus used in training matches the domain. Finding a suitable Arabic corpus is a challenge since most available ones are collected from newspapers that are significantly different than conversational utterances. One way to overcome this challenge is by filtering out irrelevant sentences from a large corpus based on their length or their syntactic complexity. Another way might be by constructing a corpus of fictional AAC messages [8].

Further experiments will be carried out with some alterations such as controlling the pruning strategy of the decoder and using another type of language model. Translating symbols into a fluent Arabic utterance rather than a sequence of labels will be explored in future work.

## References

1. Binger, C., Light, J.: The morphology and syntax of individuals who use AAC: research review and implications for effective practice. Augmentative Altern. Commun. **24**(2), 123–138 (2008)
2. Brown, P.F., Pietra, V.J.D., Pietra, S.A.D., Mercer, R.L.: The mathematics of statistical machine translation: parameter estimation. Comput. Linguist. **19**(2), 263–311 (1993)
3. Och, F.J., Ney, H.: The alignment template approach to statistical machine translation. Comput. Linguist. **30**(4), 417–449 (2004)
4. Papineni, K., Roukos, S., Ward, T., Zhu, W.: BLEU: a method for automatic evaluation of machine translation. In: Proceedings of the 40th Annual Meeting on Association for Computational Linguistics, pp. 311–318. Association for Computational Linguistics (2002)
5. Pasha, A., Al-Badrashiny, M., Diab, M., El Kholy, A., Eskander, R., Habash, N., Pooleery, M., Rambow, O., Roth, R.M.: Madamira: a fast, comprehensive tool for morphological analysis and disambiguation of arabic. In: Proceedings of the Language Resources and Evaluation Conference (LREC), Reykjavik, Iceland (2014)
6. Sevens, L., Vandeghinste, V., Schuurman, I., Van Eynde, F.: Natural language generation from pictographs. In: Proceedings of the 15th European Workshop on Natural Language Generation (ENLG), pp. 71–75. Association for Computational Linguistics (2015)
7. Spence Green, D.C., Manning, C.D.: Phrasal: a toolkit for new directions in statistical machine translation. In: ACL 2014, p. 114 (2014)
8. Vertanen, K., Kristensson, P.O.: The imagination of crowds: conversational AAC language modeling using crowdsourcing and large data sources. In: Proceedings of the Conference on Empirical Methods in Natural Language Processing, pp. 700–711. Association for Computational Linguistics (2011)

9. Waller, A., Jack, K.: A predictive blissymbolic to english translation system. In: Proceedings of the Fifth International ACM Conference on Assistive Technologies, pp. 186–191. ACM (2002)

10. Wiegand, K., Patel, R.: SymbolPath: a continuous motion overlay module for icon-based assistive communication. In: Proceedings of the 14th International ACM SIGACCESS Conference on Computers and Accessibility, pp. 209–210. ACM (2012)

# SAMi: An Accessible Web Application Solution for Video Search for People with Intellectual Disabilities

Tânia Rocha[✉], Hugo Paredes, João Barroso, and Maximino Bessa

INESC TEC, Universidade de Trás-os-Montes e Alto Douro, Vila Real, Portugal
{trocha,hparedes,jbarroso,maxbessa}@utad.pt

**Abstract.** In this paper an accessible Web application that uses icons instead of text to performed YouTube video search, called SAMi, is presented. With this iconic interaction Web application (SAMi), we aimed to develop universal access on the Web, by presenting an alternative way of Web search (without using text); to be a starting point for the definition of an accessible interaction metaphor, based on universal design iconography for digital environments; and ultimately, to contribute to the democratization of access to the Web for all users, regardless of the degree of literacy. The main results obtained with the user test evaluation were: first-rate performance, higher satisfaction and total autonomy in their interaction with SAMi.

**Keywords:** Web accessibility · Usability · Web application · Video search · YouTube · Eye tracking · Intellectual disabilities

## 1 Introduction

Since text (usual way to access content on the Internet) limits the autonomous interaction for people with difficulties in reading and writing [1], as a means of intervention to overcome the problem, in this paper, we present an accessible Web application that uses icons instead of text to performed YouTube video search, called SAMi. SAMi works with the Youtube API and for this reason presents all YouTube videos on an alternative accessible interface. Have an important audio feature that helps users in their interaction. Users only have to click on icons (design specifications in [1]) that represent search categories rather than insert a keyword in the search field, facilitating the user-interaction and ultimately give access to a public before excluded of the Web environments.

In this paper it is presented the development and evaluation of the prototype. The paper is structured as follow: in the second section, the background is presented; the third section discusses how SAMi was developed regarding navigation system and structure design; the forth section focus on the validation of the prototype by performing a user evaluation, for that it is specified the participants of this study, the experimental design, the procedure and apparatus used, and the results are analyzed and discussion; in the final section the conclusions and future work are presented.

© Springer International Publishing Switzerland 2016
K. Miesenberger et al. (Eds.): ICCHP 2016, Part II, LNCS 9759, pp. 310–316, 2016.
DOI: 10.1007/978-3-319-41267-2_43

## 2   Background

According to the American Psychiatric Association (APA) in the Diagnostic and Statistical Manual of Mental Disorders, 5th edition (DSM-V), a person with intellectual disability have a condition that affects cognitive functions and their development over time, leading to major learning difficulties which is one of its most recognized and prominent characteristics [2]. Recurrently, this group of people sees the access to the Web constrained because tools and even contents are created without any concern for accessibility or usability [1]. Thus, digital accessibility and usability topics gain significance.

One of major problems found in former studies are the user interfaces used, being the usual input devices (mouse and keyboard), difficult to control and handle because require a steeper learning curve and are not 'user-friendly' [3]. However, we find, in previous studies, that people with intellectual disabilities, without major motor impairments, could interact with keyboards (not autonomously because they need help on the character recognition) and mouse (with some autonomy), but none of them provided actual ease of use regarding this group of users [1]. Another problem found was related with text recognition or input, specifically: text entry (the most problematic difficulties register), text hyperlinks recognition and selection [4, 5], typing and reading of instructions [4]. Despite these problems, our own studies point to an increase in motivation by this group regarding the use of digital environments, but also show us that there are still several barriers to overcome in order to turn it into a truthfully autonomous, satisfactory, valuable user experience [1, 5]. In this context, we performed several studies to compare interaction in digital environments, using the usual interaction metaphor (text) and one based on iconic language [1, 5–7]. With these studies, we learn that text hyperlinks limit the interaction of the target audience. Thus we believe that is a need to develop more solutions for increase effectiveness of people with intellectual disabilities interaction. SAMi intents to be a solution.

## 3   How SAMi Was Developed?

For SAMi' development, the major user interaction difficulty was taking into account: the Keywords input and text content interpretation. It is necessary to overcome the need of using text to interact with Web environments, since the group with intellectual disabilities had many difficulties, due to their reading and writing difficulties, in understanding this type of content (text), as enounced in [8, 9] works. Also, this type of content does not allow that this group can be autonomous in their Web interaction.

Knowing that these users pay much attention to the images [1, 5], we proposed an iconic Web application prototype with Web search functions by using iconic categories and audio help, aiming to facilitate the hyperlink recognition but also as a way of doing Web search. Another important issue was the results presented in the search. These must be interesting content to the audience in question, so we intend to use the Youtube API to return content in videos. Furthermore, the navigation menu was being designed in order to be clear and well-defined so that users do not feel lost, as defined in the work of [10]. Thus, the prototype presented a navigation system which adds visual cues and breadcrumb but other elements that facilitate navigation, such as: a local hierarchical menu with general and advanced searches by categories, bread-crumbs (aid of users with dyslexia and those who interact with screen readers), and also an easy access button to return to the homepage. Also to guarantee the easiness interaction of the navigation system, users need a minimum mouse manipulation (only use left mouse button, without necessity of scrolling), as defined in the work of [4, 9, 11], and totally exclude the keyboard.

The elements designed for the prototype had a function of helping the user to interact with it. So, for that we designed all elements and layouts with a user-centred design approach. However, we provide similar elements that can provide a universal interaction of the prototype. For this, we design elements with double stimuli, such as: audio with text description, animations that combined image and audio description and images with text description, as defined in the work of [12]. In this regard, it is described all elements presented in the prototype. The colors palette was taking in consideration, as advised in the work of [10]. We ensure contrast between the background and icon hyperlinks, as referred by [4] and avoid black text on white background, as suggested by [10]. There, users can select four main colors and we gave mandatory complementary colors. These pairs were defined according to the guidelines for dyslexia [13]. The background color defined with a clear-cut design, avoiding noisy backgrounds that could distract the user. Regarding the graphic elements sizes, we defined that for a good visibility, in a HD monitor, must be between 72 * 72 pixels and 114 * 114 pixels. On the other hand, in some of the existing text content it was used sans-serif fonts, as they are easier to read on screens with low resolution. Specifically, it used bold formatting, avoiding italic and underlined and the typography size was set in ems instead of pixels or percentages [13]. In Fig. 1, the main screen of the prototype can be observed.

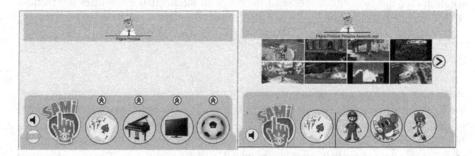

**Fig. 1.** Sami main screen (left) and second screen (right).

At the top, we can see a space reserved for the teacher, being an audio help for users must be in a prominent area. In the middle area, it is the space reserved to presentation of the search results. And in the bottom, it is presented the navigation menu by iconic categories. Following one of Bell guidelines (2009), at the bottom is created a separator to divide the body of the navigation menu function and the background or middle area of search results presentation. To increase search capabilities of the prototype, a solution is presented for advanced search. In detail, users click on the specific category for advanced search and view videos according to their preferences. For each main category search (games, music, movies or sports) there are two more options in the advanced search, as it can be seen in Fig. 1. Also, users can view more results by clicking the right arrows (in the middle area) and to if they wish to click in a video, this pops up and opens in another page on a larger format.

## 4  SAMi's Prototype Validation

After we finish the implementation of we wanted to observe and assess how users perform a search, in order to analyze the level of performance and autonomy that these users can achieve with the proposed prototype. In order to do so, we performed a user test evaluation as specified below.

### 4.1  Participants

Twenty participants were invited to partook in this pilot study (eight women and twelve men), whose ages ranged from 19 to 46 years old. These participants were selected by a special education teacher and a psychologist, according to the average rate of literacy and primary education (coincident with the third grade). Concerning digital abilities, we can say that this group presented the same level of technology experience, as they had been part of a previous project of digital integration [1]. Regarding their intellectual disabilities, the individuals were not associated to only one pathology, but a group of pathologies (for example, fetal alcohol syndrome with dysgraphia). All participants were volunteers and had permission of their parents or tutors to perform the tests.

### 4.2  Experimental Design

The assessment phase lasted for four weeks, about 35 h in total, and approximately half hours per individual. Users had to perform four tasks: task 1 (T1), users must perform a music search; task 2 (T2), users must perform a movies search; task 3 (T3), users must perform a sports search; task 4 (T4), users must perform a games search.

Regarding the assessment criteria, we followed the variables of usability evaluation (effectiveness, efficiency and satisfaction) to assess user performance. As for effectiveness, we registered how many participants performed the tasks without giving up. In efficiency, we registered resources spent to achieve effectiveness: time to perform the task, errors made during the interaction with the Web application and difficulties observed. To record satisfaction, we observed if the participants showed comfort when performing the tasks and if they asked to repeat the tasks.

### 4.3  Procedure and Apparatus

Participants were seated correctly in front of the touch screen in a controlled environment. After explain the aim of the Web search tasks, they started to interact with the prototype. The task ended after the user clicked one a video corresponding to the specified in the task. The evaluator/observer did not help in the interaction. The following material resources were used: a computer (Asus X552C), a touch screen Dell Multi Touch Monitor 54.6 cm (21.5" inches display), and a Logitech M100 optical mouse. Note that the user was seated at a distance not superior to one meter of the touch screen.

## 4.4   Results and Discussion

The results are presented in accordance with the variables of usability evaluation (effectiveness, efficiency and satisfaction). Regarding effectiveness, we observed that every participant finished the four tasks with success and no one wanted to drop out, on the contrary, when the task ended they automatically asked if they could perform another search. This indicates a direct link between effectiveness and satisfaction with the use of the prototype. In efficiency, we registered resources spent to achieve effectiveness: time to perform the task, errors made during the interaction with the Web application and difficulties observed. Concerning the time spent to conclude a task, the average time of conclusion of the task 1 was 58.3 s. The fastest participant took 15 s to conclude the task and the slowest, 171 s. In task 2, the average time was 57.2 s. The fastest took 12 s and the slowest 151 s. Regarding task T3, the average time was 51.6 s. The fastest took 9 s and the slowest 134 s. At last, in task 4, the average time was 47.5 s. The fastest took 5 s and the slowest 114. Note that average time drop decreased after the first interaction with the prototype. Concern difficulties observed, we observed they had some minor problems in the correct control and handling the mouse input device. This fact could have increased some users' task conclusion time. Users did not show difficulties in the recognition of the icons. On average 22 errors were made. In the first task was counted 15, specifically, users clicked continuously in one of the mouse buttons or in the two ate the same time. In the second task, the number decreased to 7 errors. Notice that after the second task, users do not make more errors. Indicating they needed some time to overcome these difficulties and to and perform an effectiveness use of this device. None of these difficulties led to the drop out of the tasks. Another observation made was that after the participants finished the task proposed, they asked to interact with the prototype freely. We register the observations made in this autonomous search time and we found out that, to perform a new search, users chose to click in the search icons instead of clicking in the videos presented in results. After some time, in their third or fourth search they used both search forms. Again they showed great satisfaction with the prototype interaction.

## 5   Conclusions and Future Work

After we performed a usability evaluation (user tests), the results showed that SAMi allowed a good interaction for this specific public because overcome the necessity of writing and reading comprehension abilities for search. This icon search approach has unequivocal results in the inclusion of groups already previously excluded because improved efficiency and effectiveness in performing tasks and provides autonomy search of digital content. Given the positive impact as an effective solution to the inclusion and digital literacy, it is considered appropriate to extend the scope in order to make it universal. In this context, as future work, we intend to expand the number of people to be covered and replicate the same results in order to more digital excluded people can enjoy an accessible interaction with this solution. Thus, we will replicate the results to other groups such as children and the elderly.

**Acknowledgments.** This work is financed by the ERDF – European Regional Development Fund through the Operational Programme for Competitiveness and Internationalisation COMPETE 2020 Programme within project «POCI-01-0145-FEDER-006961» ; by National Funds through the FCT – Fundação para a Ciência e a Tecnologia (Portuguese Foundation for Science and Technology) as part of project UID/EEA/50014/2013; and by the Project "NORTE-01-0145-FEDER-000016" financed by the North Portugal Regional Operational Programme (NORTE 2020), under the PORTUGAL 2020 Partnership Agreement, and through the European Regional Development Fund (ERDF).

# References

1. Rocha, T.: Interaction metaphor for Access to Digital Information an autonomous form for People with Intellectual Disabilities. Ph.D. Thesis. University of Trás-os-Montes e Alto Douro, Vila Real (2014)
2. American Psychological Association - APA: "DSM-V- The Diagnostic and Statistical Manual of Mental Disorders - 5th edn." (2013). http://www.dsm5.org/Pages/Default.aspx
3. Blake, J.: The natural user interface revolution. In: Natural User Interfaces in .NET, pp. 1–43. Manning Publications Co. (2012)
4. Roh, S.: Designing accessible Web-based instruction for all learners: Perspectives of students with disabilities and Web-based instructional personnel in higher education. Doctoral dissertation, Indiana University, USA (2004)
5. Rocha, T., Bessa, M., Gonçalves, M., Cabral, L., Godinho, F., Peres, E., Reis, M., Magalhães, L., Chalmers, A.: The Recognition of Web Pages' Hyperlinks by People with Intellectual Disabilities: An Evaluation Study. J. Appl. Res. Intellect. Disabil. **25**(6), 542–552 (2012). doi:10.1111/j.1468-3148.2012.00700.x
6. Rocha, T.: Accessibility and Usability for people with intellectual disabilities. Master Thesis. University of Trás-os-Montes and Alto Douro (2009)
7. Rocha, T., Carvalho, D., Bessa, M. Reis, S., Magalhães, L.: Usability evaluation of navigation tasks by people with intellectual disabilities: a Google and Sapo comparative study regarding different interaction modalities. DSAI'13 Special Issue on Universal Access in the Information Society Journal - UAIS (accepted for publication)
8. Harrysson, B., Svensk, A., Johansson, G.: How People with Developmental Disabilities Navigate the Internet. British J. Spec. Educ. **31**(3), 138–142 (2016)
9. Small, J., Schallau, P., Brown, K., Ettinger, D., Blanchard, S., Krahn, G.: Web accessibility for people with cognitive disabilities. In: Resna Proceedings (2004)
10. Bell, L.: Web Accessibility: Designing for dyslexia. IM 31020 (2009). http://lindseybell.com/documents/bell_dyslexia.pdf
11. Freeman, E., Clare, L., Savitch, N., Royan, L., Literhland, R., Lindsay, M.: Improving website accessibility for people with early-stage dementia: a preliminary investigation. Aging Mental Health **9**(5), 442–448 (2005)

12. Zarin, R.: Mejla Pictogram 2.0. Institute of Design in Umea, Sweden and Swedish Institute for Special Needs Education (2009). http://216.46.8.72/tmp/v2/images/pictoCom/Final_report_Pictogram2.pdf
13. The British Dyslexia Association- BDA.: Dyslexia Style Guide (1972–2012). http://www.bdadyslexia.org.uk/

# Target Group Questionnaire
# in the "ISG for Competence" Project

Szilvia Paxian[1], Veronika Szücs[1], Shervin Shirmohhamadi[2], Boris Aberšek[3],
Andrean Lazarov[4], Karel Van Isacker[5], and Cecilia Sik-Lanyi[1(✉)]

[1] University of Pannonia, Veszprem, Hungary
{paxian,szucs}@virt.uni-pannon.hu, lanyi@almos.uni-pannon.hu
[2] Istanbul Sehir University, Istanbul, Turkey
drshervin@gmail.com
[3] University of Maribor, Maribor, Slovenia
Boris.Abersek@um.si
[4] ZGURA-M Ltd, Plovdiv, Bulgaria
andrean@marie-curie-bg.org
[5] PhoenixKM, Kortemark, Belgium
karel@phoenixkm.eu

**Abstract.** This paper introduces the "Intelligent Serious Games for Social and Cognitive Competence" project. The aim of these games are to teach youth with disabilities on creativity. The development of interactive mobile games and 3D simulations helps the social integration and personal development of children and youth with disabilities. The project targets to improve the quality of education and trainings to gain more efficiency. To enhance creativity and innovation the project uses serious games and 3D simulations this way teaching and learning becomes interesting, playful, attractive and efficient.

**Keywords:** Serious game · Disabilities · Mobile games

## 1 Introduction

### 1.1 The R&D or Application Idea

"Intelligent Serious Games for Social and Cognitive Competence" (isg4competence) project [1] is a newly started project and supported by ERASMUS + program. The development of interactive mobile games and 3D simulations helps the social integration and personal development of children and youth with disabilities. The main target group of this project are children and youth with disabilities, however, the products created by the project partners can be also used by special education centres, school teachers, trainers and universities with pedagogical, psychological and IT departments.

The common work began with making a questionnaire for the target groups.

K. Miesenberger et al. (Eds.): ICCHP 2016, Part II, LNCS 9759, pp. 317–320, 2016.
DOI: 10.1007/978-3-319-41267-2_44

## 1.2  The State of the Art in This Area

There are several projects which support the development of skills of children and young adults with learning disabilities like GOET [2, 3] DESYODIP [4], T-EST [5], e-SuNET [6]. One of the main goal of these projects is to develop the children's and young adults' different skills, which helps them in starting an independent life. Our project's (isg4competence [1]) goal is to develop desktop and mobile games for the acquisition of basic skills like literacy, numeracy, ICT. To improve the social competence of the children and youth with disabilities the 5 partner countries will design 3D interactive simulations and mobile serious games in a single payer mode. All of the products under the umbrella of "ISG for Competence" project will be available for free.

## 2  The Methodology Used

"ISG for Competence" project runs from September 2015 until August 2018. At the first step in the project there were 4 tasks:

- Defining the methodology to be used for the research, ensuring all stakeholders have been contacted and involved.
- Design of questionnaire for the survey and implementation through offline and online questionnaires.
- Translation of the questionnaire in all partner languages.
- Survey and data collecting 100 respondents to be reached in each country (People with Disabilities (PwDs), NGOs of PwDs, school educators, special education trainers, training providers etc.)
- For this goal a questionnaire was made.

## 3  The R&D Work and Results

The questionnaire contains questions like:

- Target groups (Professionals involved in education, Families, Intermediaries, Training centre, Universities, Policy makers).
- What target group(s) does the responder work with? (selection is allowed for more than one option): Children/youth with mild learning difficulties (dyslexia, dyscalculia, …), Children/youth with mild learning disabilities (ADHD, autism spectrum, Asperger syndrome, etc.), Children/youth with low social skills/deviant behaviour, Children/youth with sensory impairments.
- What pedagogical approaches do you apply to educate/train your target group(s) to acquire (new) cognitive competences?
- In the responder's opinion which of the following cognitive competencies should your students obtain/enhance during their school years (6-18)? Self-esteem and self-confidence, Motivation, Concentration, Managing anxiety, Team working, Communication, Problem solving, Prioritising, Decision making, Creative thinking, Active listening, Other, please specify.

- What are the main barriers which the responder face in order to support the acquisition /enhancement of the following cognitive competencies? (please answer with regards to the specific group of students that you are educating) Self-esteem and self-confidence, Children/youth with mild learning difficulties (dyslexia, dyscalculia, …), Children/youth with mild learning disabilities (ADHD, autism spectrum, Asperger, etc.), Children/youth with low social skills /deviant behaviour, Children/youth with sensory impairments, Motivation.
- Why are existing pedagogical approaches/training materials fail in ensuring that the process of acquisition of cognitive competencies is successful?
- How effective and efficient do you believe ICT educational tools (serious games/ mobile games adjusted to the target groups) can be developed to address these gaps?
- Would the responder like to be involved in the piloting of innovative serious games which supports the acquisition of cognitive competencies?

The evaluation of the answers from every partner countries is in progress. After the evaluation process we will have a statistically relevant data. We will show the results at the conference and the results will be published in the proceedings book.

## 4    The Scientific and Practical Impact or Contributions to the Field

The scientific and practical impact or contributions to the field are multiple. To improve the lifestyle of children and youth with disabilities (mild learning disabilities, sensory impairments, low level social skills, specific learning difficulties -dyslexia, dyspraxia, autism spectrum disorder, ADHD) and to help them tackle the what they can face. To meet the targets so that the basic skills levels could be improved. To encourage progress and to help the children and youth with disabilities in their improvement of learning, social competencies and understanding.

## 5    Conclusion and Planned Activities

Under the umbrella of the "ISG for Competence" project we developed a questionnaire and made a survey. Future plans:

- Qualitative and quantitative analysis of findings (national and comparative).
- Examination of the results of needs analysis to identify the final scenarios for modelling.
- Development of learning content through a curriculum via cooperative development.
- Identification of additional materials and adaptation to materials to deliver curriculum.

**Acknowledgement.**    The Intelligent Serious Games for Social and Cognitive Competence project - 2015-1-TR01-KA201-022247) has been funded with support from the European Commission. The paper and participation in the conference has been supported by "Stiftung Aktion Österreich-Ungarn", project number: 91öu6 (Conference participation AAATE2015-ICCHP2016).

# References

1. isg4competence: Intelligent Serious Games for Social and Cognitive Competence (ERASMUS + 2015-1-TR01-KA201-022247). http://www.isg4competence.eu/
2. GOET: Game on Extra Time (UK/08/LLP-LdV/TOI/163_181). http://goet-project.isrg.org.uk/
3. Lanyi, C.S., Brown, D., Standen, P., Lewis, J., Butkute, V.: Results of user interface evaluation of serious games for students with intellectual disability. Acta Polytech. Hung. **9**(1), 225–245 (2012)
4. DESYODIP: Developing Skills of Young Disabled People (LDV TOI, 2013-1-TR1-LEo05-47575. http://www.desyodip.com/
5. T-EST: Transfer of Employment Support Tools for People with Disabilities (LLP-LDV-TOI-12-AT-00119)
6. e-SuNET: Sustainable Network for the families of disabled people through e-learning (540073-LLP-1-2013-1-CY-GRUNDTVIG-GMP)

# The Development and Evaluation of an Assistance System for Manual Order Picking - Called Pick-by-Projection - with Employees with Cognitive Disabilities

Andreas Baechler[1(✉)], Liane Baechler[2], Sven Autenrieth[1], Peter Kurtz[3], Georg Kruell[1], Thomas Hoerz[1], and Thomas Heidenreich[2]

[1] Mechanical Engineering, University of Applied Sciences, Esslingen, Germany
{andreas.baechler,sven.autenrieth,georg.kruell,
thomas.hoerz}@hs-esslingen.de
[2] Social Work, Health Care and Nursing Sciences, University of Applied Sciences, Esslingen, Germany
{liane.baechler,thomas.heidenreich}@hs-esslingen.de
[3] Working Sciences, University of Technology, Ilmenau, Germany
peter.kurtz@tu-ilmenau.de

**Abstract.** The present paper focuses on conducting research in the field of technical support by assistance systems in order picking for people with cognitive disabilities. One of the goals is to present the prototype of an assistance system for manual order picking (called pick-by-projection), which is the result of an interdisciplinary and user-centered process with and for people with cognitive disabilities. Additionally this paper aims at presenting results of a first evaluation with 24 employees with cognitive disabilities, who were testing pick-by-projection in comparison to three methods of the current state of the art.

**Keywords:** People with cognitive disability · Assistive technology · Order picking · Inclusion

## 1 Introduction

In the following we show the socio-political background, the state of the art and the related work.

### 1.1 Socio-Political Background

Globalization and demographic change in Germany leads to significant changes in the industrial production and the associated logistics. As a result of globalization, the provider market is developing towards a buyer market with personalized products and with goods and information available at all times [1]. This development leads from large-scale bulk goods towards the small-scale shipment of goods in the field of delivery to final customers. Despite this development, often referred to as "atomization of shipment sizes", the customer's requirements for the distribution of goods are increasing. To remain, in spite of these changes, competitive for a global market with low logistic costs,

© Springer International Publishing Switzerland 2016
K. Miesenberger et al. (Eds.): ICCHP 2016, Part II, LNCS 9759, pp. 321–328, 2016.
DOI: 10.1007/978-3-319-41267-2_45

both a high flexibility with a short instruction-, picking- and delivery time, as well as a high throughput and quality is necessary [2]. In this context, the human being with its properties of complex perception, its gripping, touching, hearing and vision, as well as with its cognitive abilities offers suitable conditions, in order to react quickly and flexibly to these changes in the market and the logistics [3].

In the "bottleneck analysis 2013" of the German Federal Ministry for Economic Affairs and Energy the demographic change and the shortage of skilled workers is considered in detail. This lack of junior- and skilled employees means that the needs of the industry in their specific fields of activity can not be covered adequately any longer [4]. In contrast to these developments the increasing economic requirements on sheltered workshops has led to the fact that new pathways in the employment of people with disabilities (particularly into the mainstream labour market) have to be explored.

The efforts for an inclusive design of the mainstream labour market are not only driven by market-related changes, but also politically demanded by the Convention on the Rights of Persons with Disabilities and compulsory regulated in Germany by the Social Code IX with the law to "Rehabilitation and participation of disabled persons" [5, 6]. For these reasons, it is necessary - not only for economic, but also for social aspects - to integrate people with disabilities in industrial environments such as manual order picking [7]. However to make this possible, it is necessary to offer people with disabilities an individual, process-integrated and context-sensitive assistance.

## 1.2  State of the Art

Order picking is defined as a process of collecting items from inventory and transporting them to a specific place. This process reflects the core of today's warehouse logistics. The order picking process is one of the most important manual activities in intra-logistics and industry. As a part of the supply chain it is one of the most labor-intensive and complex sectors [2]. In the last years many innovations were made in the area of order picking (from purely manual solutions to fully automated systems). Despite various developments the manual version remains the most common type in practice [8]. Humans are mostly not replaceable by machines in order picking due to their flexible tactile- and gripping ability, a low level of investment and their cognitive skills [3].

In practice several systems are used to support a normal performance picker by locating the position and picking the correct parts, container and amount. The three most common variants provide the information for the picker in different ways. The required information is provided by an illuminated container indicator (pick-by-light), a paper list (pick-by-paper) and a mobile terminal with display (pick-by-display).

## 1.3  Related Work

Especially in the area of assistive technology for impaired people with cognitive disabilities research is done by Sauer et al. [9]. As part of the "mixed realities" [10] augmented reality is a growing technology, e.g. using it in a medical context during surgeries or as a training tool [11]. Augmented reality is also used in the area of manual order picking, by supporting the picker with the execution information through a head-mounted display [12]. Diverse research activities of Günthner and Rammelmeier [13] demonstrate the influence of data glasses by detecting errors and reducing the error rate. Reif and Guenthner [14] developed and evaluated an augmented reality based picking system, which is called pick-by-vision in an industrial environment. Their research shows that users are faster and make less errors with pick-by-vision, than with a paper pick list. However, the research with head-mounted displays - which illustrates the users' information directly in front of their eyes by data glasses - also shows that several users experienced problems with headaches, orientation and equilibrium.

## 2 Assistance System

The participatory development of the pick-by-projection-system takes place in four stages. The skills and needs of the future operators are focused according to the user-centered development process. In a first step, the "human and machine" interaction are analyzed [15]. With the results presented in this paper, the development, design, production and realization of the hardware is carried out in a second step (see Fig. 1). Parallel, in a third step different instructions with pictograms and a control system are developed, evaluated and selected [16]. In a final step the implementation of the software and the iterative evaluation of the system (in a first step with normal performance people and afterwards with employees with cognitive disabilities) takes place.

**Fig. 1.** Hardware setup of pick-by-projection

## 3 Evaluation

Subsequently, the evaluation with the study design and the various picking methods will be presented.

### 3.1 Study Design

For evaluating the four picking methods (pick-by-paper, pick-by-light, pick-by-display, pick-by-projection), we chose a repeated measures within-subjects design. Due to the high effort for an evaluation with employees with cognitive disabilities, the first investigation for detecting problems, weaknesses and gaining experience was carried out with normal performance people as representatives [17]. The independent variable is the picking method. As dependent variables we capture the error rate, the task completion time (TCT) and the task load of the methods. We used Wizard-of-Oz methods for operating the systems.

### 3.2 Picking Methods

**Pick-by-Light.** For the pick-by-light task, the system was attached below the boxes (Fig. 2). The system included a digital screen, a key and an LED lamp. The flashing of the lamp signals the picking position. The digital display (realized with a picture) shows the quantity of parts to be taken. After removing the parts a button must be pressed to confirm the removal. Afterwards the next picking position is shown by the glowing of the associated lamp.

**Fig. 2.** Experimental setup of pick-by-paper (left), pick-by-light (centre-left), pick-by-display (centre-right) and pick-by-projection (right)

**Pick-by-Paper.** In this picking method a paper picklist is used for specifying the number of parts to be picked, the removal and deposition location of each type of parts and the sequence in which the order has to be completed (Fig. 2). As previously explained the removal and deposition location of the items to be picked are marked with numbers. The paper picklist was created according to an original sample, which is already used in the industry.

**Pick-by-Display.** In this system a cart mounted display with all required information on it is used for the picking process (Fig. 2). Each position of the order is displayed separately on the touchscreen monitor. The display on the monitor visualizes the storage and the deposition location as well as the number of pieces to be removed. After executing the displayed task it must be confirmed on the screen. Afterwards the next task is displayed.

**Pick-by-Projection.** In this method the order picking units are augmented with an assistive system, including projectors, depth cameras and a scale (Figs. 1 and 2). A projected instruction guides the picker through the picking process. An illuminated arrow shows the direction for moving the assistance system to the picking location. After achieving the correct location the amount of parts to be picked is illustrated by a number. Additionally a pictogram indicates the process step that has to be carried out. A scale is integrated into the picking process for checking the correct number of items. Afterwards the visual guidance is given for depositioning parts on the picking trolley by a projector. Every moving step of the picking process is detected and controlled by depth cameras.

# 4   Results

The systems were evaluated with 24 participants (15 male, 9 female), with an age range from 19 to 59 (M = 37.14, SD = 11.50). The sample consisted of 17 participants with cognitive disabilities and seven participants with mental disorders. The majority of the participants showed no order picking experiences and were therefore novices at these four picking methods. Only three participants (12.5 %) had experiences in order picking. The study took approximately 90 min for each participant.

The next sections report the average task completion time, the average error picks and the average task load between all four picking types only with the 17 employees with cognitive disabilities and without the seven participants with psychiatric disorders.

## 4.1   Task Completion Time

The working times of the four conditions were analyzed by a Friedman's analysis of variance by ranks. This test indicates a highly significant difference with $\chi2$ (3) = 15.8, p =.001. The analysis of the 95 % confidence intervals shows that the picking method pick-by-light (M = 334.12 s., SD = 78.90 s.) is significantly faster than the other three picking methods pick-by-display (M = 683.50 s., SD = 194.95 s.), pick-by-paper (M = 715.50 s., SD = 173.66 s.) and pick-by-projection (M = 516.53 s., SD = 289.46 s.) (Fig. 3).

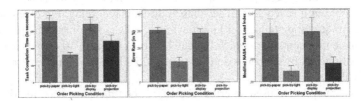

**Fig. 3.** Means and standard deviation of the task completion time (left), error rate (middle) and the score of the modified NASA-TLX (right) for the four picking conditions.

## 4.2   Error Picks

The total number of errors is used to calculate the average error per pick metric. A Friedman's analysis of variance by ranks test revealed a statistically significant differ-ence for error picks between the four different order picking choices ($\chi2$ (3) = 15.00, p =.002). The fewest error picks were made while picking with pick-by-projection

(M = 0.84 %, SD = 2.00 %), followed by the pick-by-light (M = 9.87 %, SD = 7.31 %) and then the pick-by-display method (M = 28.57 %, SD = 5.98 %). The most error picks were made while picking with pick-by-paper (M = 30.36 %, SD = 3.75 %) (Fig. 3).

### 4.3 Task Load

To measure the cognitive load, we used the modified NASA-TLX. Again a Friedman's analysis of variance by ranks test revealed a statistically significant differences between the four different order picking choices ($\chi 2$ (3) = 10.26, p = .016). The participants perceived the task load of the work as the smallest when using the pick-by-light method (M = .27, SD = .32). This was followed by picking with pick-by-projection (M = .28, SD = .28) and the highest task load was reported while picking with pick-by-display (M = 1.10, SD = .68) and pick-by-paper (M = 1.06, SD = .70) (see Fig. 3).

## 5   Discussion

The results of the study show a significant difference for the task completion time between the picking method pick-by-light and the other methods. A reason for these results might be the additional process step for depositioning and picking up a box from the scale in the pick-by-projection condition. Additionally the weighing process takes several seconds, which causes a higher TCT of the pick-by-projection system. Furthermore the participants had the freedom to leave the trolley statically while picking the parts. Only with the pick-by-projection system they had to move the trolley to reach the next position. Almost all participants left the trolley statically while commissioning the order with the three other state of the art systems. This decision saved many seconds compared to moving the trolley for each task.

Most of the errors, which have been made with pick-by-light, pick-by-paper and pick-by-display were removal mistakes. This means that the participants took an entire box instead of picking single parts. This mistake was ranked only with one error in the error detection, but it saved several seconds in the time recording. For example a task for picking 10 single parts takes 30 s on average. If someone performs this task by removing the entire container (which typically holds more than 10 objects asked for), he or she only needs five seconds and thus saves 25 s but only gets one error for the wrong execution.

The assistance system used an error feedback, when mistakes occurred during the task. This additional functionality prevented errors but led to a higher execution time and task load. In addition the Wizard-of-Oz solution required a reaction time of the operator and caused a slight delay in the process execution and thus the TCT. The results reveal that the picking method pick-by-projection induces the lowest error rate and a statistically significant difference between the four order picking choices. For customers and especially for the user group of employees with cognitive disabilities the importance of avoiding errors is greater than reducing the execution time.

Additionally, the results of the average task load show significant differences between the four picking methods. The results indicate a trend of a lower task load while picking with pick-by-light and pick-by-projection. The difference between pick-by-light and pick-by-projection might occur because of the high information content with pick-by-projection. Usually not every person with cognitive disabilities does need such a high information rate with a flashing green bar, a pictogram, an Arabic number and a picture of the parts. To perform an order picking process safely the illustration by a flashing bar and the Arabic number should be enough. This insight also leads to the fact that it is necessary to develop and integrate an adaptiveness into the assistance system.

## 6   Conclusion and Future Work

In this study four different methods for manual order picking methods were described and evaluated. Three of the four picking methods are currently used in the industry (pick-by-light, pick-by-paper, pick-by-display) and represent the current state of the art. The fourth system, pick-by-projection, is a newly developed picking method, which could be useful for the user group of people with cognitive disabilities.

In an evaluation of the four different order picking methods, the task completion time, the error rate and the task load were considered. On the one hand the results show that during an order picking process with the newly developed method the participants make less errors. But on the other hand the error reduction causes an increasing task completion time as well as an elevated task load, compared to pick-by-light.

Given the fact that only 17 subjects with cognitive disabilities were used in this study, more studies using subjects with cognitive disabilities are needed to reveal more differentiated effects and results of the different systems.

In a subsequent study the same procedure will be carried out again with at least 24 employees with cognitive disabilities and an optimized and autonomously functioning assistance system. It can be assumed that in such a study the assistance system leads to a reduced error rate, TCT and task load compared to the other systems.

**Acknowledgements.** This work is part of the project "motionEAP". It is funded by the German Federal Ministry for Economic Affairs and Energy, grant no. 01MT12021E.

## References

1. Günthner, W.A., Schedlbauer, M., Wulz, J.: Augmented reality in der innerbetrieblichen logistik. In: wt Werkstattstechnik-online, S., pp. 363–365 (2004)
2. Hompel, M., Sadowsky, V., Beck, M.: Kommissionierung. Materialflusssysteme 2 – Planung und Berechnung der Kommissionierung in der Logistik. Springer, Berlin (2011)
3. Arnold, D., Furmans, K.: Materialfluss in Logistiksystemen. Springer, Berlin (2009)
4. Bundesministerium für Wirtschaft und Technologie (BMWi): Engpassanalyse 2013. Besondere Betroffenheit in den Berufsfeldern Energie und Elektro sowie Maschinen- und Fahrzeugtechnik. Berlin (2013)
5. Bundesministerium für Arbeit und Soziales: Übereinkommen der Vereinten Nationen über Rechte von Menschen mit Behinderungen. Vom Bundeskabinett beschlossen am 3. Bonn, August 2011

6. Artikel des Sozialgesetzbuches - Neuntes Buch - (SGBIX) Rehabilitation und Teilhabe behinderter Menschen: Sozialgesetzbuch (SGB) Neuntes Buch (IX) – Rehabilitation und Teilhabe behinderter Menschen – (SGB IX) (2001)
7. Bundesministerium für Arbeit und Soziales: Initiative Inklusion. Maßnahmen zur Förderung der Teilhabe schwerbehinderter Menschen am Arbeitsleben auf dem allgemeinen Arbeitsmarkt (2014)
8. Straube, F., Pfohl, H.-C., Günthner, W.A., Dangelmaier, W.: Trends und Strategien in der Logistik: Ein Blick auf die Agenda des Logistik-Managements 2010. Hamburg, Dt. Verkehrs-Verlag (2005)
9. Sauer, A.L., Parks, A., Heyn, P.C.: Assistive technology effects on the employment outcomes for people with cognitive disabilities: a systematic review. Disabil. Rehabil. Assistive Technol. 5(6), 377–391 (2010)
10. Milgram, P., Kishino, F.: A taxonomy of mixed reality visual displays. IEICE Trans. Inf. Syst. **E77-D**, 1321–1329 (1994)
11. Azuma, R.T., et al.: A survey of augmented reality. Presence 6(4), 355–385 (1997)
12. Schwerdtfeger, B., Reif, R., Günthner, W.A.: Pick-by-vision. There is something to pick at the end of the augmented tunnel. Virtual Reality **15**, 213–232 (2011)
13. Günthner, W.A., Rammelmeier, T.: Auf dem Weg zur Null-Fehler-Kommissionierung (2012). http://www.fml.mw.tum.de/fml/images/Publikationen/22012-07AufdemWegzurNull-Fehler-Kommissionierung.pdf
14. Reif, R., Günthner, W.A.: Pick-by-Vision: an augmented reality supported picking system. In: WSCG 2009 Proceedings of the 17th International Conference in Central Europe on Computer Graphics, Visualization and Computer Vision, pp. 57–64 (2009)
15. Baechler, A., Kurtz, P., Hörz, T., Kruell, G., Baechler, L., Autenrieth, S.: About the development of an interactive assistance system for impaired employees in manual order picking. In: PETRA 2015 Proceedings of the 8th International Conference on Pervasive Technologies Related to Assistive Environments (2015)
16. Baechler, A., Baechler, L., Kurtz, P., Heidenreich, T., Hörz, T., Kruell, G.: A study about the comprehensibility of pictograms for Order Picking processes with disabled people and people with altered performance. In: KES-IIMSS 2015, Intelligent Interactive Multimedia Systems and Services, pp. 69–80 (2015)
17. Baechler, A., Baechler, L., Autenrieth, S., Kurtz, P., Hoerz, T., Heidenreich, T., Kruell, G.: A comparative study of an assistance system for manual order picking – called pick-by-projection – with the guiding systems pick-by-paper, pick-by-light and pick-by-display. In: Proceedings of the 49th Annual Hawaii International Conference on System Sciences, January 5-8, 2016, (9 p.). Computer Society Press (2016)

# The Use and Impact of an Assistance System for Supporting Participation in Employment for Individuals with Cognitive Disabilities

Liane Baechler[1]([✉]), Andreas Baechler[2], Markus Funk[3], Sven Autenrieth[2], Georg Kruell[2], Thomas Hoerz[2], and Thomas Heidenreich[1]

[1] Social Work, Health Care and Nursing Sciences, University of Applied Science, Esslingen, Germany
{Liane.baechler,thomas.heidenreich}@hs-esslingen.de
[2] Mechanical Engineering, University of Applied Science, Esslingen, Germany
{andreas.baechler,sven.autenrieth,georg.kruell,
thomas.hoerz}@hs-esslingen.de
[3] Institut for Visualization and Interactive Systems, University of Stuttgart, Stuttgart, Germany
markus.funk@vis.uni-stuttgart.de

**Abstract.** The UN Convention on the Rights of Persons with Disabilities implies an increase in participation in employment for individuals with cognitive disabilities. In this process, assistive technology plays an important role. This paper shows results of how a technical assistance system providing cognitive support can promote participation in the field of employment.

**Keywords:** Assistive technology · Participation · Cognitive disabilities

## 1   Introduction and Socio-Political Background

Since the UN Convention on the Rights of Persons with Disabilities has come into effect, there has been a change in the system of enabling people with cognitive disabilities to participate in working life. Current discussions with the sole demand of inclusion within the open labour market incorporate the danger that many people with cognitive disabilities, who, for various reasons, cannot be well integrated into the world of work, remain completely disregarded. The available assistance system empowers people with severe cognitive disabilities to take part in working life. This is demonstrated through a study in a sheltered workshop, which can also be a viable area for including people with cognitive disabilities into work processes.

## 2   State of the Art and Description of the System

In the area of assistive technology, innovations and changes are needed for people with cognitive disabilities [1]. Previous work shows why particularly people with cognitive disabilities could benefit from an assistance system in assembly operations; thus people with cognitive disabilities are included in the study [2].

K. Miesenberger et al. (Eds.): ICCHP 2016, Part II, LNCS 9759, pp. 329–332, 2016.
DOI: 10.1007/978-3-319-41267-2_46

This paper describes the evaluation of an assistance system of an assistance system for people with cognitive disabilities within a multidisciplinary research project. The employees receive assistance from the system, which provides a memory aid using in-situ projection during the work process. The assistance system consists of a projector, which displays contour visualizations of instructions directly into the worker's field of vision (in-situ) and a depth sensor, which monitors the execution of work activities in order to give context-aware feedback. Employees with cognitive disabilities could thus perform complex assembly processes step by step, as the system recognizes mistakes and instructs subsequent steps only if previous steps have been carried out correctly.

## 3  Design of the Study

Over a period of six weeks, workers with cognitive disabilities produced clamps at a machine (see Fig. 1, left) with the support of the assistance system for one day (see Fig. 1, middle) and with the support of pictorial instructions for one day (see Fig. 1, right), representing the state-of-the-art in the sheltered workshop.

**Fig. 1.** The machine for producing clamps (left). The assistance system using in-situ projection (middle). The pictorial instructions (right).

The assistance system displayed the work steps in-situ, while the pictorial instructions gave printed and numbered images of the order of every work step.

A total of 13 people (seven male and six female; age: M = 39.4; SD = 10.9) participated voluntarily in the study.

Ethical approval for the study was given by the Ethics Committee of the German Psychological Association. Over the entire duration of the study, the participants were accompanied by a qualified educational specialist and a technical specialist. The study included the collection of quantitative data (e.g. workload with the NASA Task Load Index [3] for individuals with cognitive disabilities [4]) as well as qualitative data.

## 4  Results

The quantitative analyses are based on significance tests using the conservative nonparametric Wilcoxon matched-pairs signed rank test.

## 4.1  Task Completion Time

The average time for assembling a clamp with the assistance system was 136.90 s (SD = 34.35), while the average time using the pictorial instructions was 138.61 s (SD = 34.54) (see Fig. 2 left). There were no significant difference between conditions (Z = −.105, p = .917). Number of errors. Workers made an average of 10.09 errors per day (SD = 10.36) while using the assistance system compared to 35.97 errors (SD = 24.01) with the pictorial instructions (see Fig. 2 middle) showing a significant difference between the two instruction types (Z = −3.059, p = .002). Workload. The average workload using the modified NASA-TLX version was 1.23 (SD = .26) while using the assistance system compared to an average workload of 2.88 (SD = .48) when using the pictorial instructions (see Fig. 2 right). Significance testing revealed a significant difference (Z = −3.183, p = .001).

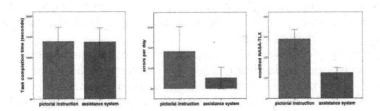

**Fig. 2.** Means and standard deviations of the task completion time (left), error rate (middle) and score of the modified NASA-TLX (right) for pictorial instructions vs. assistance system.

Qualitative data were collected through participant observations and field interviews. The analyses of the transcribed data was done using a coding process based on classic grounded theory methodology [5]. The following core category could be determined and is described by representative quotes.

## 4.2  Empowerment

Observations showed that through the help of the assistance system, people with severe cognitive disabilities were enabled to perform the task. Expert personnel reported being impressed with the performance of the participants while working with the assistance system. The following statement reflects this observation: *"Most of the participants have a very low performance level. Because of this they have difficulties in participating in working life within the sheltered workshop. I am surprised about the effects achieved by the assistance system and what adequate instructions can effect"*. Additionally, observations showed that the participants could work more independently while using the assistance system. The in-situ feedback enabled workers to perform with more self-confidence, because the visual feedback immediately showed them the next work step. Thanks to this, the participants described less mental effort while assembling with the help of the assistance system. The following statement illustrates this: *"With the assistance system I can work more independently. If I forget a work step the assistance system points out that I made an error. So I can eliminate the error by myself. With the light signals it is more fun to work and much less exhausting"*.

## 5   Conclusion

In summary, the results show that using the assistance system had a great benefit for people with cognitive disabilities. For the participants the errors per day and the perceived cognitive workload were significantly lower when using the assistance system while retaining the same TCT. The results show that particularly people with severe limitations who have previously not been able to perform such work activities benefit from the assistance system. The results also show that the assistance system does not speed-up the work task. These effects are in line with the aim of the assistance system to enable participation and not to increase productivity. Further studies will show, whether the number of errors does have an effect on the TCT and thus the assistance system accelerates the assembly process.

The multidisciplinary development and the use of the assistance system complies with the requirements of the right to work by increasing and facilitating access and participation for people with cognitive disabilities in integrated employment, especially in industrial assembly workplaces in mainstream society. This kind of assistive technology can make a considerable contribution to inclusive employment.

**Acknowledgements.** This work is part of the project "motionEAP". It is funded by the German Federal Ministry for Economic Affairs and Energy, grant no. 01MT12021E.

## References

1. Sauer, A.L., Parks, A., Heyn, P.C.: Assistive technology effects on the employment outcomes for people with cognitive disabilities: a systematic review. Disabil. Rehabil. Assistive Technol. 5(6), 377–391 (2010)
2. Bächler, L., Bächler, A., Kölz, M., Hörz, T., Heidenreich, T.: Über die Entwicklung eines prozedural-interaktiven Assistenzsystems für leistungsgeminderte Mitarbeiter in der manuellen Montage. In: Wendemuth, A., Jipp, M., Söffker, D. (eds.) 3. Interdisziplinärer Workshop-Kognitive Systeme: Mensch, Teams, Systeme und Automaten, Beitrag 4. DuEPublico, Magdeburg (2015)
3. Hart, S.G., Staveland, L.E.: Development of NASA-TLX (task load index): results of empirical and theoretical research. Adv. Psychol. 52, 139–183 (1988)
4. Funk, M., Bächler, A., Bächler, L., Korn, O., Krieger, C., Heidenreich, T., Schmidt, A.: Comparing projected in-situ feedback at the manual assembly workplace with impaired workers. In: Proceedings of the 8th International Conference on Pervasive Technologies Related to Assistive Environments. ACM (2015)
5. Corbin, J., Strauss, A.L.: Basics of Qualitative Research: Techniques and Procedures for Developing Grounded Theory. Sage, California (2008)

# AT and Inclusion of People with Autism or Dyslexia

# Internal Validity in Experiments for Typefaces for People with Dyslexia

## A Literature Review

Trenton Schulz[✉]

Norsk Regnesentral – Norwegian Computing Center, Kristen Nygaards hus, Oslo, Norway
trenton.schulz@nr.no

**Abstract.** In recent years, designers claim to have created typefaces that help people with dyslexia, but what evidence supports these claims? We look at studies involving these fonts to see evidence for or against them. The studies try to be scientific, but lack internal validity; i.e., the studies don't eliminate the possibility that something else could explain the result. We provide a short summary of the studies and why they do not provide internal validity.

**Keywords:** Dyslexia · Typeface · Font · Typography · Design

## 1 The Rise of Typefaces for Dyslexia and Their Current State

Many people have problems reading. The Program for the International Assessment of Adult Competencies (PIAAC) found that over one in ten Norwegian adults can be classified as weak readers [2]. Adults in this group suffer from dyslexia or other reading and writing disabilities. To reach weaker readers, experts recommend presenting written information in alternative forms, such as audio or other forms of visualization, but it should also be readable. This means presenting information in easy-to-read language, but it can include basic typographic information, such as the selection of typefaces (popularly called fonts) the size of type, line length, and line spacing.

Since 2000, several fonts have been designed with the goal of aiding people with dyslexia. The dyslexia fonts include Zwijsen Dyslexiefont, Lexia Readable, Slyexiad, Dyslexie, OpenDyslexic, and Moore; this does *not* include fonts that have been recommended by dyslexia organizations. This paper only looks at typefaces that have published studies (Slyexiad, Dyslexie, and OpenDyslexic).

Slyexiad was created by Hillier for his doctoral thesis [9]. The font is based on research on adult dyslexic readers. It's available as a serif and san serif version. Hillier used methods from psychology and user-centered design to create and test the font. His idea was not to use standard typographical design as that targets non-dyslexic readers [7]. The final font has larger letter spacing, larger x-heights, and longer (in comparison to x-height) ascenders and descenders.

Dyslexie (Dutch for dyslexia) was created by Christian Boer as part of his thesis in 2008 [14]. Boer designed his font to make the letters dance less. This includes changes

K. Miesenberger et al. (Eds.): ICCHP 2016, Part II, LNCS 9759, pp. 335–338, 2016.
DOI: 10.1007/978-3-319-41267-2_47

so that the letters do not look the same mirrored, a larger x-height, and more spacing between letters. The font has been updated a few times, and a license is required for educational or commercial purposes, but a style is available free for home use. There are 17 mobile apps and one educational program that use Dyslexie.

Abbie Gonzalez designed OpenDyslexic by modifying Bitstream Vera Sans, a font available under an open source license [5]. Gonzalez created the font because other fonts "have restrictions, or are not affordable," [6]. The font looks similar to Dyslexie, but Gonzalez claims inspiration from Andika, Apple Casual, Lexia Readable, Sassoon, and Comic Sans [6]. OpenDyslexic is popular, and its website includes a long list of applications, books, and devices that incorporate OpenDyslexic.

## 2   Methodology

Mackenzie [11] defines internal validity as how much an effect observed is due to the test condition. Here, could other factors explain the results as easily as the font?

Font properties affect text. For example, a font's x-height contributes most to optical height meaning fonts at the same point size may not appear nor measure the same (e.g. Helvetica and Times). Changing spacing between letters and words also affects how many letters can be on one line. Changing one property may affect another. So, one cannot compare fonts by taking text and only typesetting it at the same point size. The text may look too different and take up different space on the surface. So, it would be difficult to say the typeface that makes the difference or the typesetting.

We looked for attempts to control for the properties of the fonts being compared or offering an alternate explanation based on these properties. For example, if Font A had more character spacing, it might have performed like Font B. If it was available, we looked at stimulus material, like how the type was set. This gave us an idea of the study or experiment trying to keep internal validity, even if there were no mention in the article itself. It also would make it possible to reproduce a study if desired.

## 3   Looking at the Studies

We looked at six studies for internal validity issues. One study [14] was marketing research and didn't compare fonts – it has issues with a placebo effect or post-hoc biases – so we ignore it here. Here is a summary of the remaining studies.

Beier [1] defined readability as "ease of reading in running text" and legibility as "clarity of the individual letters." Hillier evaluated readability and legibility while creating Sylexiad typefaces using people with and without dyslexia [8, 9]. He compares Sylexiad styles against Arial, Times New Roman, and Sassoon Primary. The tests included timing the participants to complete reading a line of text or paragraph, checking comprehension, and asking for preferences. We don't see examples of the stimulus material. Hillier notes in his thesis that dyslexic readers prefer "the more generous spatial aspects associated with Serif Slyexiad and Sylexiad Sans." [9]. Unfortunately, he didn't set Times New Roman or Arial with more letter and word spacing to see the difference. Does Sylexiad make the difference or is it spacing?

De Leeuw [10] compared Dyslexie to Arial. People with and without dyslexia used a version of the Dutch one-minute reading test where single words are presented with the goal of seeing how many words can be read in a minute. De Leeuw found that students with dyslexia make the same *amount* of errors with either font, but they are different *kinds* of errors. For example, using Dyslexie, readers with dyslexia made fewer errors reading vowels compared to Arial. There was no difference in reading speed. The fonts are set to the same optical height (12 point for Dyslexie, 14 point for Arial), but there is no mention of control for letter spacing; Dyslexie has much more space between letters than Arial. Again, it is difficult to know if the effects reported are due to letter spacing or to other features in Dyslexie or Arial.

Rello and Baeza-Yates [13] compared 12 different fonts (nine regular and three italic variants) to find a good font for people with dyslexia. Text was displayed in black on a white background; 14 point; left justified with a line length under 70 characters on a 17-in monitor. An eye-tracker measured the time to read the text and the amount of time the eye rested on an item (eye cycad) before moving to the next. Beyond comparing typefaces, they looked at the difference between serif vs. san-serif and italic vs. regular. Arial had the fastest (average) reading time, Courier had the lowest (average) fixation time, and Verdana was the preferred font. OpenDyslexic was second in reading time, took longer for fixation than many, and preferred least. The eye-tracker adds more data for comparing the fonts, but looking at the sample of the fonts that are included shows a large variation between letter spacing, x-height, and line spacing. Any of these properties might also explain the difference. In addition, Arial was designed to be similar to Helvetica, yet the scores are different. Why this difference? There seems to be more than just the font that is causing the issues.

Pijpker's master's thesis [12] looked at Dyslexie and colored backgrounds. The comparison was against Arial and a colored yellow background. 64 children aged 8 to 12 divided by having dyslexia or not and reading proficiency. Pijpker looked at reading speed and accuracy, and compared the font and color. The results showed color and Dyslexie had some effect on reading speed and preventing errors, but the results are not statistically significant – meaning the results could just be random.

Comfort, Kalichuk, Wenban, and Wasylkiw [4] performed a study comparing Arial and Open Dyslexic with forty college students (half with learning disabilities, half without). They timed how quickly someone read aloud and counted the number of errors made. Results show that while some in the control group and experimental group claimed OpenDyslexic was easier to read, the results say otherwise. Comfort et al. are unsure if reading aloud was the best way to test.

## 4   Conclusion and Future Work

Since these studies do not have internal validity, we have no *solid* scientific evidence if dyslexia fonts help *or* hurt. This implies freedom of choice, but other groups that must be considered when typesetting a document, future app (mobile or desktop), or webpage. It would be nice to measure the effectiveness of a font change, or a better idea why a certain choice works for different reasons.

A way forward may be looking at the strategies people with dyslexia use to cope with reading issues and see if that can be measured. Then, we would have a way of seeing what helps or hurts in type design for this group. Otherwise, a good way to measure readability and performing comparison tests with knowledge of typography may produce the evidence that may answer the question once and for all.

For now, how should people typeset text to reach as many people as possible? It seems that standard typography rules do not harm or hurt either. Guidelines (e.g., Butterick [3]) that give ranges of values can be helpful. When deciding text size, measuring the optical size – preferably on the display where it will be shown – should make the text presentable. Then, you only need to focus on its content.

**Acknowledgements.** Research partially sponsored by *Personalized mobile Learning Arena* (PLA) project from Norwegian Research Council (Project number: 245623).

# References

1. Beier, S.: Typeface Legibility: Towards defining familiarity. The Royal College of Art (2009)
2. Bjørkeng, B.: Ferdigheter i voksenbefolkningen: Resultater fra den internasjonale undersøkelsen om lese- og tallforståelse (PIAAC). Statistisk Sentralbyrå (2013)
3. Butterick, M.: Butterick's Practical Typography (2013). http://practicaltypography.com
4. Comfort, A., et al.: Can a font improve reading? In: CSUN 2014 Conference (2014)
5. Gonzalez, A.: OpenDyslexic—Free OpenSource Dyslexia Font. http://opendyslexic.org/
6. Gonzalez, A.: Related Research—OpenDyslexic. http://opendyslexic.org/about/related-research/
7. Hillier, R.: Sylexiad: a typeface for the adult dyslexic reader. Ultrabold **2**, 36–37 (2007)
8. Hillier, R.: Sylexiad. A typeface for the adult dyslexic reader. J. Writ. Creat. Pract. **1**(3), 275–291 (2008)
9. Hillier, R.A.: A Typeface for the Adult Dyslexic Reader. Anglia Ruskin University, Cambridge (2006)
10. De Leeuw, R.: Special Font For Dyslexia? University of Twente, Enschede (2010)
11. Mackenzie, I.S.: Human-Computer Interaction. An Empirical Research Perspective. Morgan Kaufmann, San Francisco (2013)
12. Pijpker, T.: Reading Performance of Dyslexics with a Special Font and a Colored Background. University of Twente, Enschede (2013)
13. Rello, L., Baeza-Yates, R.: Good fonts for dyslexia. In: Proceedings of the 15th International ACM SIGACCESS Conference on Computers and Accessibility, ASSETS 2013, pp. 1–8. ACM Press (2013)
14. van de Vrught, J., Ossen, A.: Dyslexie Regular Research 2012. Studio Studio Graphic Design, Zeist, The Netherlands (2012)

# Characterization of Programmers
# with Dyslexia

José L. Fuertes[1], Luis F. González[2], and Loïc Martínez[1(✉)]

[1] Universidad Politécnica de Madrid, Madrid, Spain
{jfuertes,loic}@fi.upm.es
[2] Politécnico Colombiano Jaime Isaza Cadavid, Medellín, Colombia
lfgonzaleza@elpoli.edu.co

**Abstract.** Computer programmers with dyslexia can be found in a range of academic and professional scenarios. Dyslexia may have the effect on a computer programmer of degrading the expected results during collaborative software development. These people may perform better using visual programming languages. However, we need to understand what programmers with dyslexia experience in order to be able to come up with possible solutions. We have conducted an analysis of existing literature and a survey on dyslexia and programming. This paper reports the preliminary results based on the data gathered so far and the key characteristics and needs of this group with the aim of defining the profile of computer programmers with dyslexia.

**Keywords:** Dyslexia · Computer programming · Inclusion

## 1 Introduction

Changes in inclusion due to policies such as the Convention on the Rights of Persons with Disabilities [1], make it possible for persons with dyslexia to become computer programmers. Dyslexia is a specific reading disorder, where "Reading comprehension skill, reading word recognition, oral reading skill, and performance of tasks requiring reading may all be affected. Specific developmental disorders of reading are commonly preceded by a history of disorders in speech or language development" [2].

A computer programmer with Dyslexia may have a degraded performance using traditional programming languages and may perform better using visual programming languages. However, we need to understand their profile as programmers in order to come up with possible solutions. So, an analysis of the literature and an electronic survey have been conducted.

## 2 Related Work

There is literature and software applications aimed at helping children with dyslexia. However, dyslexia among software developers has not been much researched, and we have not come across any software tool designed to help computer programmers with dyslexia in the process of creating computer programs.

© Springer International Publishing Switzerland 2016
K. Miesenberger et al. (Eds.): ICCHP 2016, Part II, LNCS 9759, pp. 339–342, 2016.
DOI: 10.1007/978-3-319-41267-2_48

A literature review has identified two relevant studies. The first claims that dyslexic programmers usually come up against a number of difficulties when developing software [3]: remembering code details, sticking to a good code presentation layout, correctly defining variables correctly and being at coding and at debugging… However this group of people have a great capacity for analysis, as usually they have an IQ above the average. The second study describes problems associated with dyslexia in the programming area in higher education [4]. They confirm problems described by [3] and they provide some accessibility guidelines for programmers with dyslexia.

Afterwards, we have identified the characteristics of adults with dyslexia [5]: they may have different learning-related symptoms, which show up as problems with reading, writing, organization, speech or mathematics. They may experience visuospatial difficulties (problems with mathematics, reading, writing and organization), speech sound difficulties (problems with speaking, reading, writing and organization) and correlating difficulties (problems with writing).

## 3 Results of the Survey

We have built a survey to determine the profile of computer programmers with dyslexia. The survey has been answered by Spanish-speaking computer programmers selected by a combination of convenience sampling and purposive snowball sampling. They were inquired sociodemographic, behavioral and programming variables [6].

The sample of 155 programmers had an average age of 22 years (from 20 to 44). 6.5% of all respondents believe that they are dyslexic (n = 10). Of this group 40% con-sider that dyslexia has a negative effect on their programming performance. It is striking that only 20% of these 10 have been professionally diagnosed as being dyslexic, which probably means a lack of awareness and proper treatment of this disability.

Regarding behavioral variables (Table 1), we found that 70% of computer programmers with dyslexia suffer anxiety when programming compared to 37.9% of programmers without dyslexia. Poor concentration does not appear to be a problem in the surveyed sample, as stated by 80% of computer programmers with dyslexia and 68.3% of programmers without dyslexia. However, these data contrast with the 60% of programmers with dyslexia and the 50.3% of programmers without dyslexia that responded that they were easily distracted when studying. On the other hand, 50% of the programmers with and 61.3% of the programmers without dyslexia stated that they do not often suffer mood swings. With respect to depression, 90% of the programmers with and 78.7% of programmers without dyslexia do not suffer from this. 60% of people with dyslexia in contrast to 23.4% of those without dyslexia consider themselves anxious persons. We also observed that 80% of programmers with and 68.3% of programmers without dyslexia do not suffer from insomnia. We found that 50% of programmers with and 55.2% programmers without dyslexia have trouble getting up in the morning.

In regard to programming activity, only 30% (n = 3) of programmers with and 20% (n = 29) of programmers without dyslexia have ever used a visual programming language. We found that 66.6% of programmers with dyslexia state that they make

**Table 1.** Percentages of disagreement with respect to behavioural variables.

| Percentage of disagreement with respect to behavioural variables (n = 155) | PwithD (n = 10) | PwithoutD (n = 145) | p |
|---|---|---|---|
| I often made any number of excuses to get of going to school | 80.0% | 86.2% | 0.030 |
| I now often make excuses to get out of going to work or university | 80.0% | 83.5% | 0.618 |
| I often resort to attention-seeking behaviour | 70.0% | 85.5% | 0.002 |
| I often suffer episodes of irritability | 40.0% | 61.4% | 0.196 |
| I consider myself to be an aggressive person | 80.0% | 83.5% | 0.065 |
| I consider myself to be a withdrawn person | 90.0% | 67.6% | 0.420 |
| I consider myself compulsive person | 50.0% | 55.2% | 0.016 |
| I like to be isolated from others | 60.0% | 62.1% | 0.817 |
| I consider myself hyperactive person | 40.0% | 64.8% | 0.019 |
| I am often unhappy | 50.0% | 71.7% | 0.270 |
| My self-esteem is low | 60.0% | 60.7% | 0.899 |
| I suffer from disordered vision | 70.0% | 95.9% | 0.000 |
| I often suffer from fatigue | 40.0% | 66.2% | 0.143 |

more mistakes programming using a textual language against 33.3% who state that they make more errors using a visual programming language. Table 2 shows the most representative data with respect to programmer preference for, ease of use of and speed using a visual language.

**Table 2.** Characteristics of affinity for visual programming

| Affinity for visual programming (n = 32) | PwithD (n = 3) | PwithoutD (n = 29) | p |
|---|---|---|---|
| I prefer a visual language | 66.7% | 24.1% | 0.746 |
| I find a visual language easier to use | 66.7% | 34.4% | 0.933 |
| I program faster with a visual language | 66.7% | 48.2% | 0.869 |

We have applied a chi-squared test to the variable "Do you think you are dyslexic?" with all the behavioral variables. We found that there is a statistically significant relationship for the variables: behavior to get attention ($p = 0.02$), compulsive behavior ($p = 0.016$), excuses for not going to school ($p = 0.03$), programming hypoactivity disorder ($p = 0.026$), frequent state of isolation in programming ($p = 0.047$), hyperactivity disorder ($p = 0.019$), anxious behavior ($p = 0.01$) and distorted vision ($p = 0.0$).

# 4   Analysis of the Results

The percentage of the sample (6.5%) stating that they believe that they are dyslexic is the range of adult population with dyslexia that goes from 5% to 10% [7].

It is usually considered that adults with dyslexia have obvious symptoms of low self-esteem and no confidence and feel helpless in some life situations [8], but the result for these variables, after applying a chi-squared test, confirm that these emotional variables do not play a role in defining their profile. The percentages related to performance, preference and ease of use of textual programming languages [3] confirm claims that programmers with dyslexia using programming tools with visual or graphic support are 20% better than programmers without dyslexia at developing computer programs. We did find that programmers with dyslexia make fewer mistakes than programmers without dyslexia when using a visual programming language.

## 5   Conclusions and Future Work

The emotional characteristics proposed in [8] to define the profile of adults with dyslexia seem not to be relevant to define the profile of programmers with dyslexia. However, further research is required to explore other variable types.

We have also found that programmers with dyslexia have a preference for visual programming, as also explained in [3], and they claim to make fewer mistakes.

We intend to gather more replies to our survey, by sending it to programmers in other Spanish-speaking countries and to programmers that belong to associations of persons with dyslexia. Then we plan to broaden the spectrum and perform the same study with English-speaking programmers to get a broader understanding of issues.

In the long term, and with the aim of counteracting the performance differences in interactive programming, we propose to design a two-way visual and textual code transformation model. The goal is to develop software on a single interface that interacts between the two codes, providing support for programmers with dyslexia in the process of interacting with their teammates.

## References

1. UN. Convention on the rights of persons with disabilities. United Nations (2006)
2. WHO. ICD-10 international statistical classification of diseases and related health problems, Introduction manual, vol. 2. Malta: World Health Organisation publications (2011)
3. Dixon, M.: Comparative study of disabled vs. non-disabled evaluators in user-testing: dyslexia and first year students learning computer programming. In: Stephanidis, C. (ed.) HCI 2007. LNCS, vol. 4554, pp. 647–656. Springer, Heidelberg (2007)
4. Stienen-Duran, S., George, J.: Supporting dyslexia in the programming classroom. In: 5th International Conference on Software Development and Technologies for Enhancing Accessibility and Fighting Info-Exclusion, Procedia Computer Science, pp. 419-430 (2014)
5. Ingram, T.: The dyslexic child. Pract. **192**, 503–516 (1964)
6. González, L.: Encuesta tesis doctoral "transformación bidireccional de código de software visual y texto, para mitigar los efectos de la dislexia en el desarrollo de software" (2016) (in Spanish). http://oa.upm.es/39155/
7. Everatt, J., Smythe, I., Ocampo, D., Gyarmathy, E.: Issues in the assessment of literacy-related difficulties across language backgrounds: a cross-linguistic comparison. J. Res. Read. **27**, 141–151 (2004)
8. Shaywitz, S.E.: Dyslexia. Sci. Am. **275**(5), 98–104 (1996)

# What Technology for Autism Needs to be Invented? Idea Generation from the Autism Community via the ASC*me*I.T. App

Sarah Parsons[1]([✉]), Nicola Yuill[2], Judith Good[2], Mark Brosnan[3], Lisa Austin[3], Clarence Singleton[3], Benoît Bossavit[4], and Barnabear[5]

[1] University of Southampton, Southampton, UK
S.J.Parsons@soton.ac.uk
[2] University of Sussex, Sussex, UK
{nicolay,J.Good}@sussex.ac.uk
[3] University of Bath, Bath, UK
{M.J.Brosnan,l.austin,C.J.Singleton}@bath.ac.uk
[4] Public University of Navarre, Pamplona, Spain
benoit.bossavit@unavarra.es
[5] Roke Manor Research, Romsey, UK
barnabear2@gmail.com

**Abstract.** In autism and technology research, technologies are often developed by researchers targeting specific social and communication difficulties experienced by individuals with autism. In some technology-based projects, children and adults with autism as well as parents, carers, teachers, and other professionals, are involved as users, informers, and (more rarely) as co-designers. However, much less is known about the views of the autism community about the needs they identify as areas that could be addressed through innovative technological solutions. This paper describes the ASC*me*I.T. project which encourages members of the autism community to download a free app to answer the question: If there was one new technology to help people with autism, what would it be? This project provides a model of e-participation in which people from the autism community are involved from the start so that new developments in digital technologies can be better matched to support the needs of users.

**Keywords:** Autism · Crowdsourcing · e-Participation · Inclusion · Social justice

## 1 Introduction

Increasingly there has been important recognition of the value of involving so-called 'end-users' in the development of technologies through participatory design processes [6]. Not only is such involvement important in terms of ensuring that technologies are more accessible and usable for everyone, including disabled users, but involvement can also be empowering for individuals by enabling their

© Springer International Publishing Switzerland 2016
K. Miesenberger et al. (Eds.): ICCHP 2016, Part II, LNCS 9759, pp. 343–350, 2016.
DOI: 10.1007/978-3-319-41267-2_49

digital and social inclusion [3]. Moreover, the participatory design of technologies has been suggested as an essential principle in ensuring that human-computer interaction as a field of study is more ethical and responsible with regard to innovation [1].

Our interest in this paper is how technologies could be developed better to meet the needs of people with autism and those who support them (including families, teachers, carers, other professionals and practitioners). Internationally, Autism Spectrum Disorder (ASD) is the fastest growing developmental disability [5], creating significant challenges for educational, health and social care services [4,16], as well as for families and individuals (e.g. [7,9,10,12]). The increasing prevalence of autism is recognised as a global health priority [20], with WHO member nations being urged to prioritise the needs of individuals with autism and their families and communities through increasing research in service provision in order to improve available support.

## 2   State of the Art

Technology has an important role to play in this context, with strong interest from the research community especially regarding how technologies can be applied to support the social and communication difficulties that are the core diagnostic features of ASD [14,18,19]. Participatory design of technology is an increasingly important part of this wider context, recognising the unique perspectives and experiences that people with autism, and those who support them, can contribute to the process (e.g. [8]). There are acknowledged challenges involved, not least the thorny issue about who actually makes the decisions about the features of a technology that may or may not get developed [15]. There are also important discussions and recommendations about how methodologies and activities can be planned and structured more effectively to support the communication and interaction needs of children and adults with autism (e.g. [2,13]).

Nevertheless, despite there being more examples of projects that have involved people with autism in participatory design processes focusing on how to develop particular features or content, there is a lack of evidence that people with autism have been involved in the initiation of ideas about which technologies need to be developed in the first place. In other words, assumptions are made about the needs of people with autism and how technology may meet those needs, without first establishing whether those are the right priorities for people with autism and their families. The priorities targeted in research may of course be aligned with the priorities of people with autism, although there is evidence that suggests that substantial caution may be needed in making this assumption. Pellicano et al. [17] found that individuals with autism and their families felt excluded from most research and wanted research to address issues that were of greater importance and relevance to them, namely: education for life skills and services to support a range of needs. By contrast, the bulk of research funding targeted biomedical topics focusing on etiology and treatment.

In technology-based research, it could be that the priorities of members of the autism community are already being addressed. Alternatively, it may be that there are overlooked areas that are important to the autism community but which are not yet being tackled by researchers. Either way, there is a need to find out more about the needs and wishes of people with autism and their families within this context. There is a strong social justice argument for ensuring the stronger representation of stakeholders' views in shaping the research agenda as well as participating more fully in research. The ASC*me*I.T. project provides one way in which this social justice agenda could, at least partially, begin to be achieved.

# 3   The ASC*me*I.T. Project and Methodology

## 3.1   Development of the App

The ASC*me*I.T. project was inspired by Barnabear - a self-described 'Aspie and software engineer'. Barnabear was an invited speaker at our ESRC funded seminar series on 'Innovative technologies for autism: critical reflections on digital bubbles' (http://digitalbubbles.org.uk/). He highlighted the wide variation of needs of people with ASD, and challenged the audience to consider: 'What problem would you want solved and what [technology] would you invent?' This important question led us to develop a project idea based on sourcing suggestions for technology development directly from the autism community.

' We subsequently secured funding from the Universities of Southampton, Bath and Sussex for the project, involving Barnabear as a consultant, to develop an app that allows members of the autism community to answer the question: If there was one new technology to help people with autism, what would it be? The format of the ASC*me*I.T. app was based on a free crowd sourcing community app called 'ifOnly' to encourage people with disabilities to share the problems they encountered in everyday life. The 'ifOnly'app (developed by Austin at the University of Bath), allowed people to record, upload and share videos and audio that demonstrated everyday problems they faced at home.

Two versions of the ASC*me*I.T. app (for Android and iOS) were developed at the University of Bath following iterative development within the research team. At the start of the development process, the app developers reviewed the 'ifOnly' app and developed some wireframes for the initial ASC*me*I.T. idea. These were shared with the project team, and Barnabear provided feedback on the wording of the main question as well as clarity of the information and ease of navigation through the different screens. Users of the app can upload a short video (less than 1 min) that describes their idea and/or email their idea to the project team. Figure 1 shows screenshots from the app, showing the main question and options for making, and submitting, ideas. The apps were made available for free download in July 2015 from the App store (for iOS) and from the Google Play store (for Android). A project website provided further information about the project, including the schools prize draw, and general terms and conditions (see http://ascme-it.org.uk/).

Research Ethics Committees at the Universities of Bath, Southampton and Sussex all reviewed and approved the project.

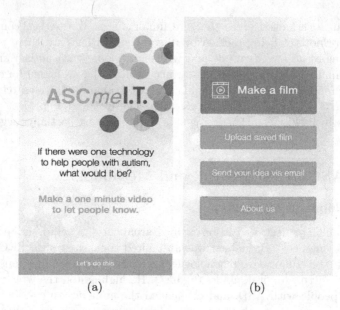

**Fig. 1.** (a) The opening screen of the app with the main question; (b) the screen showing options for submitting ideas

## 3.2    Encouraging Submissions

We have promoted a first 'wave' of the project so far (Sept to Nov 2015), with a specific focus on encouraging schools (teachers, pupils and parents) to submit ideas via the app. We had 30 Raspberry Pi Starter Packs available as free prize draw entries to incentivise school submissions. We visited local schools, put out local press releases about the project (which were picked up by local radio and print media), and utilised our educational and autism specific networks to raise awareness. We have also promoted the project, and the free app, at various practitioner and academic conferences, nationally and internationally.

In response to the first wave of promotion we have had 198 (iOS) and 273 (Android) downloads of the app, with 28 usable ideas submitted via video upload or email, from the UK, US and India. We are currently collating and analysing these ideas and have given 12 Raspberry Pi packs away to school-based entries in the prize draw. We have recently launched a second wave of the project (March to June 2016) to encourage further submissions from schools and colleges, and the autism community more widely. This should allow us to continue to update our picture of the needs being identified by members of the autism community so that we can begin to select and shortlist some of the ideas for further development.

## 3.3    Illustrations of Ideas Submitted so Far

As an illustration of the ideas submitted in the first wave, 16 out of the 28 entries were from school pupils or adults on the autism spectrum. Other submissions, where participants supplied this information, came from friend / associates, parents, or teachers. Ten ideas related to academic subjects and skills, with five of these focusing specifically on Maths, for example:

"I struggle in the area of Maths and I was thinking of a Maths app. On the one side you could have tutorials on how to do different questions and on the other side you could have different kinds of categories that people struggle with, and so maybe you could start with the basics of adding and subtracting and there can be certain questions that would help them"— student with autism.

Eight submissions related to social communication and interaction, covering a range of issues including: bullying, anxiety, facial recognition, making new friends and being supported, asking the right questions, and expressing feelings:

"Having worked with lots of autistic children over the years, although they are all different, obviously one of the things that they do have in common pretty much is social communication problems. So an app that they could use to express how they are feeling would be really useful as a lot of the time, especially when they are frustrated, they haven't got the words to tell you and a Boardmaker symbol doesn't really quite cut it"—teaching assistant.

Other suggestions covered more general issues, such as having a personalised suite of games targeted at the things that an individual feels they need help with; helping individuals with scheduling of daily tasks; and suggestions for the functional organisation of a space. One especially thought-provoking suggestion came from a student with autism who said:

"My idea is ... something that helps people that feel their autism is a curse that would boost their morale. It could contain weblinks to pages explaining autism and pages explaining what it might mean for them, how other people felt with it, and some statistics like 1 in 100 children is autistic. I think that could boost their morale and get them through their social life and their academic life"—student with autism.

Overall, we received an interesting first round of suggestions covering some of the things that we might have expected (e.g. those related to social difficulties) but also some things that may tend to be overlooked in autism technology research, particularly ideas related to academic subjects (cf. [11]).

## 4   Contribution to the Field and Next Steps

The ASCmeI.T. project is unique in aiming to tap into the personal experiences and creativity of people with autism, and their families and teachers, to generate ideas about technological solutions that might help them and benefit others. This is the first opportunity in the UK, as far as we are aware, for people from the autism community to get involved from the start so that new developments in digital technologies for autism can be more closely matched with the identified needs of users. We have a strong foundation upon which we can continue to encourage the submission of ideas during 2016, including working with autism organisations in the UK to promote the app nationally, and with Masters students at our institutions to develop more detailed specifications and/or prototypes for some of the ideas. The aim of the project is to work with some of the ideas submitted to develop them further and bring them closer to reality. The eventual aim is to make individual and social impact with technology ideas generated by the autism community, for the autism community.

We also plan to research whether the issues that people have described in their submissions have digital technology solutions that already exist; looking at the first round of submissions our hunch is that this may well be the case for many of the suggestions. Therefore, it could be that one of the main challenges for users is being able to find existing solutions to the difficulties they identify, rather than those solutions not existing in the first place. Whatever we find out will be of value for the field: we will know more about the issues that people with autism, and those who support them, identify as areas of particular need; we will scope out the feasibility for further development of some of the ideas submitted; we will be able to signpost the autism community to current potential solutions (where these exist); and we aim to work with industry partners to bring some of the ideas to fruition with the goal of making a real difference to the lives of at least some people with autism.

More widely, the methodology of the ASC*me*I.T. project establishes an approach that could be utilised with many other user groups. In this sense, the project provides a model of e-participation that has significant potential. As technologies continue to change at a dramatic pace, and the assistive technology industry undergoes significant change, this model of e-participation offers an accessible, and potentially powerful, way forward in seeking to ensure that concepts for new technology have evolved directly from user preferences and needs. In this way, the market may be more prepared to access and use the final product, with concomitant benefits for designers and companies who wish to seek a better return on their investments.

**Acknowledgements.** The ASC*me*I.T. project is funded via EPSRC Impact Acceleration Account funding at the University of Bath; ESRC Impact Acceleration Account funding at the University of Sussex; and Higher Education Innovation (Enterprise) Funding from the University of Southampton. Many thanks to Bourne Community College, West Sussex, U.K., and to Olivia Barber for their valuable contributions to the project.

# References

1. Abascal, J., Nicolle, C.: Moving towards inclusive design guidelines for socially and ethically aware HCI. Interact. Comput. **17**(5), 484–505 (2005)
2. Benton, L., Johnson, H., Ashwin, E., Brosnan, M., Grawemeyer, B.: Developing IDEAS: supporting children with autism within a participatory design team. In: Proceedings of the SIGCHI Conference on Human Factors in Computing Systems, pp. 2599-2608. ACM, 2012 May
3. Bleumers, L., All, A., Marin, I., Schurmans, D., Van Looy, J., Jacobs, A., Willaert, K., de Grove, F.: A review of the literature and empirical cases. EUR 25652 Joint Research Centre Institute for Prospective Technological Studies. Luxembourg: Publications Office of the European Union. doi:10.2791/36295.
4. Buescher, A.V., Cidav, Z., Knapp, M., Mandell, D.S.: Costs of autism spectrum disorders in the United Kingdom and the United States. JAMA Pediatr. **168**(8), 721–728 (2014)
5. Cimera, R.E., Cowan, R.J.: The costs of services and employment outcomes achieved by adults with autism in the US. Autism **13**(3), 285–302 (2009)
6. Coleman, R., Clarkson, J., Dong, H., Cassim, J.: Design for Inclusivity: A Practical Guide to Accessible, Innovative and User-Centred Design. Gower Publishing Limited, Hampshire (2012)
7. Eaves, L.C., Ho, H.H.: Young adult outcome of autism spectrum disorders. J. Autism Dev. Disord. **38**(4), 739–747 (2008)
8. Frauenberger, C., Good, J., Alcorn, A., Pain, H.: Conversing through and about technologies: design critique as an opportunity to engage children with autism and broaden research (er) perspectives. Int. J. Child-Comput. Interac. **1**(2), 38–49 (2013)
9. Gray, D.E.: 'Everybody just freezes. Everybody is just embarrassed': felt and enacted stigma among parents of children with high functioning autism. Sociol. Health Illn. **24**(6), 734–749 (2002)
10. Hartley, S.L., Barker, E.T., Seltzer, M.M., Floyd, F., Greenberg, J., Orsmond, G., Bolt, D.: The relative risk and timing of divorce in families of children with an autism spectrum disorder. J. Fam. Psychol. **24**(4), 449 (2010)
11. Knight, V., McKissick, B.R., Saunders, A.: A review of technology-based interventions to teach academic skills to students with autism spectrum disorder. J. Autism Dev. Disord. **43**(11), 2628–2648 (2013)
12. Lasgaard, M., Nielsen, A., Eriksen, M.E., Goossens, L.: Loneliness and social support in adolescent boys with autism spectrum disorders. J. Autism Dev. Disord. **40**(2), 218–226 (2010)
13. Millen, L., Cobb, S., Patel, H.: Participatory design approach with children with autism. Int. J. Disabil. Hum. Dev. **10**(4), 289–294 (2011)
14. Parsons, S.: Learning to work together: designing a multi-user virtual reality game for social collaboration and perspective-taking for children with autism. Int. J. Child-Comput. Interact. **6**, 28–38 (2015)
15. Parsons, S., Cobb, S.: Reflections on the role of the 'users': challenges in a multi-disciplinary context of learner-centred design for children on the autism spectrum. Int. J. Res. Method Educ. **37**(4), 421–441 (2014)
16. Parsons, S., Guldberg, K., MacLeod, A., Jones, G., Prunty, A., Balfe, T.: International review of the evidence on best practice in educational provision for children on the autism spectrum. Eur. J. Spec. Needs Educ. **26**(1), 47–63 (2011)

17. Pellicano, E., Dinsmore, A., Charman, T.: What should autism research focus upon? community views and priorities from the United Kingdom. Autism **18**(7), 756–770 (2014)

18. Ploog, B.O., Scharf, A., Nelson, D., Brooks, P.J.: Use of computer-assisted technologies (CAT) to enhance social, communicative, and language development in children with autism spectrum disorders. J. Autism Dev. Disord. **43**(2), 301–322 (2013)

19. Wass, S.V., Porayska-Pomsta, K.: The uses of cognitive training technologies in the treatment of autism spectrum disorders. Autism **18**(8), 851–871 (2014)

20. World Health Assembly (2014) Autism. Sixty-seventh World Health Assembly WHA67.8. Agenda item 13.4, 24th May 2014. http://apps.who.int/gb/ebwha/pdf_files/WHA67/A67_R8-en.pdf?ua=1

# Using Mind Mapping Software to Initiate Writing and Organizing Ideas for Students with SLD and ADHD

Betty Shrieber[✉]

Kibbutzim College of Education Technology and the Arts, Tel-Aviv, Israel
betty.shrieber@smkb.ac.il

**Abstract.** The article is a summary of research conducted in the field of planning functions of postsecondary students with Specific Learning Disabilities (SLD) and/or Attention Deficit Hyperactive Disorder (ADHD). The article provides an overview of the students difficulties initiating writing tasks due to their disabilities. Model of planning functions of students with SLD provides insight into the contribution of motivating factors to initializing four planning functions. The review also presents the advantages of using mind mapping software to initiate writing tasks and organizing ideas for this population. Relevant academic literature shows that use of mind mapping software may assist students with SLD and/ or ADHD to initiate writing tasks, overcome their difficulties in better organize information, and develop learning and cognitive skills.

**Keywords:** Specific Learning Disabilities · Attention Deficit Hyperactive Disorder · Planing functions · Initiation · Motivation · Writing · Mind mapping software · Assistive technology

## 1   Introduction

The investigation of adults with Specific Learning Disabilities (SLD) and Attention Deficit Hyperactive Disorder (ADHD) has been developing rapidly in recent years. There is a growing recognition that SLD persists through the years, continuing to influence adult function not only during academic studies but also later in career and daily life. Compared to adults without SLD, only a small percentage of adults diagnosed with SLD study in higher education institutions [1–3]. While ADHD affects 8–12% of children worldwide [4], just 3–4% of the student population in postsecondary education are diagnosed with ADHD [5].

The current picture indicates that students with SLD or ADHD face academic difficulties throughout their academic life, including executive function (EF) impairment [6–8], poor working memory [7], and planning difficulties [9, 10]. In addition, SLD is understood to be a cross-cultural and chronic condition that typically persists into adulthood, and identified significantly interfere with academic achievement, occupational performance, or activities of daily living that require these academic skills, alone or in any combination.

© Springer International Publishing Switzerland 2016
K. Miesenberger et al. (Eds.): ICCHP 2016, Part II, LNCS 9759, pp. 351–357, 2016.
DOI: 10.1007/978-3-319-41267-2_50

A study identifying the characteristics of postsecondary students with SLD revealed four clusters: verbal LD, working memory, non-verbal LD, and complex LD. Attention-related data in all four clusters were found to be low [10].

However, along with the difficulties these disabilities create, it is also important to look at the successes of this population. Studies examining success of adults with SLD posit that the sense of control over their lives is an essential component of their success [12, 13]. The success attributes identified during this longitudinal project that traces the lives of adults with learning disabilities, included: self-awareness, proactivity, perseverance, appropriate goal setting, and effective use of social support systems [12, 13]. These factors were found as predictive of success also in the acquisition of academic skills. Factors like age, gender, family SES, and IQ revealed non-significant differences between the successful and unsuccessful group [12].

On the other hand, successful adults with learning disabilities report their difficulties lie in lack of organizational ability, setting goals and planning actions. They also express frustration regarding overload of information and processing of problems, in expressing and organizing ideas, and most particularly articulating them on paper [7, 14].

## 2    Organizing and Setting Priorities

Organizing information and determining priorities plays a major role in the planning process. Scholnick et al., [9] present four components that construct order and organization: (1) organization – the ability to represent a planning problem and construct it by order of operations; (2) making distinctions between the constraints and mapping sequence of acts during planning; (3) memory – memory capacity enables the planner to think of several alternatives of planning, and realize the connections between them to consider future planning possibilities; (4) control – taking control is achieved by the three first steps: controlling the sequence of operations required for planning, meeting working memory requirements, and taking into account the constraints of the planning action [9].

Neuropsychological literature associates poor executive functions with difficulties in planning, including decision making, self-regulation, flexible thinking, organizing and managing time, selective attention, and working memory [15–18].

Shrieber and Hetzroni [10] identified three components of the planning process in students with and without SLD (and those with/without ADHD) studying in higher education institutions: motivational factors, planning factors, and the implementation of the planning action.

Motivational factors include "motivation for studying" and "sense of success".

Planning functions include four abilities: (1) organization and prioritization; (2) future planning process; (3) time estimation; (4) learning condition awareness.

The implementation of planning actions includes two functions: decision-making and time management. The study reveals that students with SLD demonstrate lesser abilities compared to students without SLD in planning and implementation functions during learning.

Figure 1 represents the theoretical model of planning functions of students with SLD [10]. This model provides insight into the contribution of motivating factors to initializing the four planning functions. In this study, motivation was found to be the strongest predictor for organizing and setting priorities. In addition, organizing and setting priorities and time estimation were found to be strong predictors of success in time management [19].

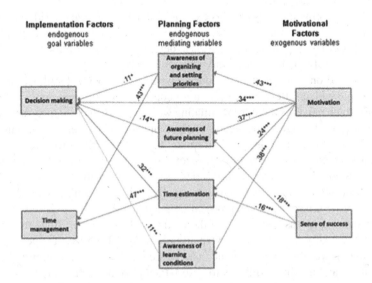

**Fig. 1.** Theoretical model of planning functions [19]

In the view of these findings and additional executive function theories, it is essential to build an effective strategy that helps adults with learning disabilities to set priorities in their day-to-day lives: in their private lives, academic life or as managers, entrepreneurs, or employees in the workplace.

Setting priorities allows people to make the distinction between the essential and incidental. Students with learning disabilities struggle with these functions, finding it difficult to distinguish between major tasks and incidental assignments, or identifying the main theme or topic of written texts [20].

## 3    Difficulties in Initiating Writing Tasks

One of the major difficulties of people with executive function disabilities is the initiation of tasks. [21] Students with SLD also reported significantly higher levels of procrastination. [22] Poor time estimation [10, 19] might explain the difficulties that students with SLD undergo to complete their tasks on time, and might be the explanation for their academic procrastination. Such students will usually wait until the last moment before attempting to complete tasks. Ironically, this inefficient strategy allows them to estimate the exact time they need to spend in order to complete the task on time. The exact time estimation, along with secretion of adrenaline, might cause them to focus on the task and be alert during its execution. Another factor that makes initiation of writing tasks more difficult is overload on working memory, a trait typical of students diagnosed with SLD and ADHD. Deficiencies of working memory during early childhood (from age four) constitute reliable indicators of academic difficulties that later manifest in writing, reading and arithmetic [23].

However, working memory enables carrying out the following: considering of planning alternatives, identifying the connections between them, anticipating future planning needs, and prioritizing existing information to determine the best option for action planning [9, 24] – all of which are necessary to establish order.

The overload on working memory during writing is associated with learning disabilities. People with an attention disorder must cope with background noise, both visual and audio, which prevents them from initiating writing tasks. In order to initiate writing, first they need to distinguish between principal and secondary content, arrange information in logical order, and decide what should be the first written topic.

We can see difficulties in written expression also in students with writing and reading disabilities. Students with writing disabilities struggle with writing and spelling as they overloads working memory; these students usually report an inability to articulate their thoughts in written form and even physical fatigue from the effort required. Also, they find it difficult to process the content of the writing task. Moreover, students with SLD and ADHD typically write with many spelling mistakes. The effort to spell and write correctly overloads their working memory capacity, diverting the entirety of their concentration, and making it difficult to absorb the information presented.

## 4    Mind Mapping Software for Improving Writing Skills

Assistive technology (AT) is a tool for making the learning environment more accessible. It enables individuals with SLD to compensate for reading, organization, memory, and math deficits, enabling them to express themselves at levels commensurate with their intelligence [25–27]. An overview of the research shows that AT has been found to be especially effective for students who have specific reading and writing deficits [28, 29].

There is a range of assistive technology that addresses student needs in all academic areas. Integration of AT in higher education to address the needs of students with disabilities has increased over the last few years. Mind mapping and concept mapping software provide a visual representation of concepts, ideas and information. Use of such programs enables users to present ideas verbally and graphically in a range of fields: economics and accountancy, marketing, education, medicine, art, biology, social sciences, and others [30]. Evidence shows that use of concept mapping and mind mapping software may help all students, and particularly students with SLD, to better organize information, develop high-function cognitive skills, and develop learning and cognitive clarity [31–34].

Mind mapping software, such as Xmind and MindMup, can be used intuitively after brief training. These applications facilitate initiation of writing assignments: students_(add might ) might begin tasks with associative writing of their thoughts and focus on them as main topics. They are then asked to prioritize these topics, arranging them as main categories and subtopics by using the cursor to drag topic headings from one column to the next. Finally, they begin to "layer" the topics by inserting into each category various materials, notes, documents and website materials, and even designing a map with pictures and a nice background.

Xmind software also provides verbal representation along with visual representation (Fig. 2). The verbal cue constitutes outlines of the writing process. At this point, students can begin to write their assignment according to map categories, outlines, and the collected background materials that were thematically categorized.

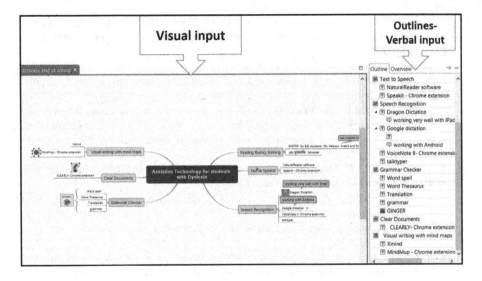

**Fig. 2.** Xmind mind mapping: visual and verbal representation

Students using these maps reported that use of mind mapping is effective, especially when dealing with existing materials, such as preparing for exams or completing class assignments, and proved more effective than previously study techniques they used.

Also, it was clearly evident that mapping strategies were easily assimilated after using the software for a relatively short amount of time [34]. The use of a visual aid perhaps enables students to actively initiate an order association between the various terms mentioned in class and then helps them review and assimilate this information into their long-term memory in a more effective and personalized way.

Use of specialized technologies can be useful in the development and assimilation of mind mapping strategies in LD service centers in universities and colleges. They are therefore recommended for developing learning strategies in academic courses.

# References

1. Chambers, D., Rabren, K., Dunn, C.: A comparison of transition from high school to adult life of students with and without disabilities. Career Dev. Except. Individ. **32**(1), 42–52 (2009)
2. Heiman, T., Precel, K.: Students with learning disabilities in higher education: academic strategies profile. (postsecondary education). J. Learn. Disabil. **36**(3), 248–258 (2003)
3. Johnson, G., Zascavage, V., Gerber, S.: Junior college experience and students with learning disabilities: implications for success at the four-year university. Coll. Stud. J. **42**(4), 1162–1168 (2008)
4. Faraone, S.V., Biederman, J.: What is the prevalence of adult ADHD? results of a population screen of 966 adults. J. Atten. Disord. **9**(2), 384–391 (2005)
5. Proctor, B., Prevatt, F.: Confirming the factor structure of attention-deficit/hyperactivity disorder symptoms in college students using student and parent data. J. Learn. Disabil. **42**(3), 250–259 (2009)
6. Biederman, J., Monuteaux, M., Doyle, A., Seidman, L., Wilens, T., Ferrero, F., Morgan, C., Faraone, V.: Impact of executive function deficits and attention-deficit/hyperactivity disorder (ADHD) on academic outcomes in children. J. Consult. Clin. Psychol. **72**(5), 757–766 (2004)
7. Weyandt, L., DuPaul, G.J., Verdi, G., Rossi, J.S., Swentosky, A.J., Vilardo, B.S., Carson, K.S.: The performance of college students with and without ADHD: neuropsychological, academic, and psychosocial functioning. J. Psychopathol. Behav. Assess. **35**(4), 421–435 (2013)
8. Brown, T., Reichel, P., Quinlan, D.: Executive function impairments in high IQ adults with ADHD. J. Atten. Disord. **13**(2), 161–167 (2009)
9. Scholnick, R., Friedman, S., Wallner-allen, K.: What do they really measure? a comparative analysis of planning tasks. In: Friedman, S.L., Scholnick, E.K. (eds.) The Developmental Psychology of Planning: Why, How, and When Do We Plan?. Psychology Press, New York (2014)
10. Shrieber, B., Hetzroni, O.: The characteristics of learning planning functions and implementation among students with and without learning disabilities. J. Appl. Res. Intellect. Disabil. **23**(5), 443 (2010)
11. American Psychiatric Association: Diagnostic and statistical manual of mental disorders (DSM-5®). American Psychiatric Pub (2013)
12. Goldberg, R., Higgins, E., Raskind, H., Herman, K.: Predictors of success in individuals with learning disabilities: a qualitative analysis of a 20-year longitudinal study. Learn. Disabil. Res. Pract. **18**(4), 222–236 (2003)
13. Reiff, H., Gerber, P., Ginsberg, R.: Exceeding Expectations: Highly Successful Adults with LD. Pro-Ed, Austin (1997)
14. Pannucci, L., Walmsley, S.: Supporting learning-disabled adults in literacy. J. Adolesc. Adult Lit. **50**(7), 540–546 (2007)
15. Barkley, R.: ADHD and the Nature of Self-Control, pp. 203–207. Guilford Press, New York (1997)
16. Biederman, J., Petty, C., Fried, R., Fontanella, J., Doyle, A., Seidman, L., Faraone, S.: Can self-reported behavioral scales assess executive function deficits? J. Nerv. Mental Dis. **195**, 240–246 (2007)

17. Cutting, L., Denckla, M.: Attention: relationships between attention-deficit hyperactive disorder and learning disabilities. In: Swanson, H.L., Harris, K.R., Graham, S. (eds.) Handbook of Learning Disabilities, pp. 125–157. Guilford Press, New York (2006)
18. Lezak, M.: Neuropsychological Assessment, pp. 650–675. Oxford University Press, Oxford (1995)
19. Shrieber, B.: Planning Functions and Implementation, from a Learning Perspective, Among Postsecondary Students with Learning Disabilities, With and Without ADHD (Unpublished doctoral dissertation). University of Haifa, Israel, Hebrew (2010)
20. Meltzer, L., Pollica, L., Barzillai, M., Meltzer, L.: Executive function in the classroom: embedding strategy instruction into daily teaching practices. In: Executive Function in Education: From Theory to Practice, pp. 165–193 (2007)
21. Gioia, G., Ispuith, P., Guy, S., Kenwirthy, L.: BRIEF: Behavior Rating Inventory of Executive Function – Professional Manual. PAR - Psychological Assessment Resources Inc. (2002)
22. Klassen, R.M., Krawchuk, L.L., Lynch, S.L., Rajani, S.: Procrastination and motivation of undergraduates with learning disabilities: a mixed-methods inquiry. Learn. Disabil. Res. Pract. **23**(3), 137–147 (2008)
23. Gathercole, S., Alloway, T.: Working Memory & Learning: A Practical Guide for Teachers. Sage, London (2008)
24. Lezak, M., Howieson, D., Loring, D.: Neuropsychological Assessment, 4th edn. Oxford University Press, Oxford (2004)
25. Lang, R., Ramdoss, S., Sigafoos, J., Green, V.A., van der Meer, L., Tostanoski, A., Lee, A., O'Reilly, M.F.: Assistive technology for postsecondary students with disabilities. In: Assistive Technologies for People with Diverse Abilities, pp. 53–76. Springer, New York (2014)
26. Higgins, K., Boone, R.: Technology for Students with Learning Disabilities: Educational Applications. Pro-Ed, Austin (1997)
27. Mull, C.A., Sitlington, P.L.: The role of technology in the transition to postsecondary education of students with learning disabilities a review of the literature. J. Spec. Educ. **37**(1), 26–32 (2003)
28. Raskind, M., Higgins, E.: Assistive technology for postsecondary students with learning disabilities: an overview. In: Vogel, S., Vogel, G., Sharoni, V., Dahan, O., (eds.) Learning Disabilities in Higher Education and Beyond: An International Perspective, pp. 173–199. Baltimore, MD (2003)
29. Raskind, M., Higgins, E.L.: Assistive technology for postsecondary students with learning disabilities: an overview. J. Learn. Disabil. **31**(1), 27–40 (1998)
30. Davies, M.: Concept mapping, mind mapping and argument mapping: what are the differences and do they matter? High. Educ. **62**, 279–301 (2011)
31. Cook, A.M., Polgar, J.M.: Cook & Hussey's Assistive Technologies: Principles and Practice, 3rd edn. Mosby Elsevier, St. Louis (2012)
32. Draffan, E.A., Evans, D.G., Blenkhorn, P.: Use of assistive technology by students with dyslexia in post-secondary education. Disabil. Rehabil. Assist. Technol. **2**(2), 105–116 (2007)
33. Boon, R.T., Burke, M.D., Fore, C., Hagan-Burke, S.: Improving student content knowledge in inclusive social studies classrooms using technology-based cognitive organizers (CO): a systematic replication. Learn. Disabil.: A Contemp. J. **4**(1), 1–17 (2006)
34. Shrieber, B., Adato-Biran, I: Mind mapping technology for students with learning disabilities. In: Paper Presented at the 33rd YAI Network's International Conference on Developmental and Learning Disabilities, New York (2012)

# Data Quality as a Bottleneck in Developing a Social-Serious-Game-Based Multi-modal System for Early Screening for 'High Functioning' Cases of Autism Spectrum Condition

Miklos Gyori[1](✉), Zsófia Borsos[1], Krisztina Stefanik[2], and Judit Csákvári[1]

[1] Institute for the Psychology of Special Needs, ELTE University,
Budapest, Hungary
gyorimiklos@elte.hu, {zsofia.borsos,
judit.csakvari}@barczi.elte.hu
[2] Institute of Special Education for Atypical Cognition and Behavior,
ELTE University, Budapest, Hungary
krisztina.stefanik@barczi.elte.hu

**Abstract.** Our aim is to explore raw data quality in the first evaluation of the first fully playable prototype of a social-serious-game-based, multi-modal, interactive software system for screening for high functioning cases of autism spectrum condition at kindergarten age. Data were collected from 10 high functioning children with autism spectrum condition and 10 typically developing children. Mouse and eye-tracking data, and data from automated emotional facial expression recognition were analyzed quantitatively. Results show a sub-optimal level of raw data quality and suggest that it is a bottleneck in developing screening/diagnostic/assessment tools based on multi-mode behavioral data.

**Keywords:** Autism spectrum condition · Data quality · Emotional facial expression · Eye tracking · Screening · Serious game

## 1 Background

### 1.1 Autism Spectrum Conditions and Their Early Recognition

Autism spectrum conditions (ASC) are underlain by atypical neurocognitive development, resulting in atypical patterns of abilities and behaviors in social interactions, social communication, and the adaptive, flexible organization of one's own behaviors and interests. Medical diagnostic systems categorize affected individuals under the labels of pervasive developmental disorders [1] and autism spectrum disorders [2]. Important discussions are ongoing, however, whether it is appropriate to regard (all cases of) these conditions as cases of a disorder and/or a disability [3].

© Springer International Publishing Switzerland 2016
K. Miesenberger et al. (Eds.): ICCHP 2016, Part II, LNCS 9759, pp. 358–366, 2016.
DOI: 10.1007/978-3-319-41267-2_51

Regardless of these debates, early recognition of ASC is a key task, as most of the affected individuals benefit significantly from autism-specific interventions, especially if started early [4]. In developed countries, most of the more severe cases are diagnosed between 30 and 60 months of age. 'High functioning' (HF) cases – individuals with ASC but without impairments in intellectual and linguistic skills – tend to be identified significantly later, mostly at school-age [5]. Bringing this later wave to an earlier age remains an important goal, and is the motivation for our R+D project, described below.

To date, both screening and diagnosis of ASC are based on behavioral data. In line with this, established screening tools in use today are low-tech psychometric ones, relying on reports from human observation and the ratings of observed behaviors [6].

### 1.2 Current Trends in Developing Technology-Augmented Tools for the Recognition of ASC

There has been a strong trend over the last decades to attempt to develop technologically more advanced screening/diagnostic tools that may potentially enhance the precision of diagnostic decisions and/or bring the age of diagnosis earlier. A review of these works would exceed the scope of this paper; we briefly point to trends and examples.

Several projects have focused on enhancing well-established screening/diagnostic tools by technological means. Attempts have been made to use machine learning to redesign a diagnostic tool to enhance its efficiency [7]; to develop computerized rating procedures for existing observational diagnostic tool [8]; to develop technological solutions to assist data collecting and evaluating [9]; and to make the training of professionals in autism screening and diagnosis more effective [10].

Efforts have also been made to create essentially new diagnostic or screening tools. A part of them utilize data from the neural level, collected mainly by neuroimaging and/or electrophysiological methods [11]. Another set of projects, being most closely related to our goals, target the development of novel, essentially technology-based screening/diagnostic systems using behavioral data, often of multimodal nature. Some of these exploit robotic technology [12].

None of these systems has been developed to the stage of applicability in daily practice. Arguably, however, the technological approach has key potentials, and therefore this focus of R+D expectedly remains a key one.

## 2 Objectives

### 2.1 Project Objectives

The main objective of the R+D project in the focus of this paper is designing, implementing and evaluating a social-serious-game-based, multi-modal, interactive software system for screening for HF cases of ASC at kindergarten age, in an autonomous, robust and cost-efficient way [13]. The system is intended to collect *mouse state, gaze focus* and *emotional facial expression data* during the game sessions and assess the risk of the presence of ASC in the player on the basis of complex patterns of these data. What makes this project unique is primarily its focus on kindergarten-age HF children with ASC.

The first prototypes of the game component of the system were designed via an evidence-driven iterative process. A partial and then a full game prototype were created, with data recording functionality but without the decision making (risk evaluation) component yet. A user experience test was completed on the partial prototype [13]. A first sweep of evaluation was started with the full and playable game prototype.

## 2.2    Research Questions of this Paper

We see data quality as a key issue for at least two reasons. (1) Available mainstream technologies for collecting behavioral data (such as eye-tracking and automated emotional facial expression recognition) were developed with neurotypical (NT) users in the focus, and studies found that they are less effective when collecting data from neurocognitively atypical individuals [14]. (2) As there is no single behavioral bio-marker for ASC, expectedly, it is of decisive importance for successful screening to combine rich bodies of behavioral data of various kinds, in order to identify their specific combined patterns as predictive markers.

Data quality is a key and complex issue in eye-tracking methodologies [15]. In contrast to our goal to develop a screening game to be used in a playful and natural way (e.g., head movements being not constrained), the majority of the available studies seem to focus on data quality in laboratory-based use of the technique. The situation seems to be similar in the field of automated emotional facial expression recognition [16].

The objective of the present paper is to explore the quality of raw data, collected in the first evaluation study with the first full, playable prototype of our game. More specifically, we formulated an exploratory research question and a hypothesis:

1. Exploratory research question: What are the basic characteristics of the quality of our raw data, collected via mouse responses, automated facial expression recognition, and gaze tracking? We examine these via means and distributions, group differences (ASC vs. NT), temporal trends, and outliers.
2. Hypothesis: Since both automated emotional facial expression recognition and eye-tracking technologies are sensitive to head/face position and movements, we expect a positive relationship between the qualities of these two kinds of behavioral data.

# 3    Methods

**Subjects.** Results from the matched samples of 10 HF kindergarten-age children with ASC (mean age: 64.27 months; SD: 9.45; range: 49–78; mean IQ: 121.00; SD: 18.11; range: 91–147) and 10 NT children (mean age: 55.80 months; SD: 9.10; range: 41–70; mean IQ: 124.50; SD: 19.72; range: 100–161) are reported here. Independent samples t-tests indicate a difference between the two groups in age, on the margin of statistical significance (t(19) = 2.89; p = 0.05); and lack of difference in IQ. Diagnostic and assessment procedures and parental reports were used to ensure that none of the participants had any accompanying developmental or ophthalmological disorder, visual or motor impairment, or difficulty with using a computer mouse to control screen events.

All children participated with consents from them and their parents, and were informed adequately about the purpose of the study and that they could interrupt their participation at any time. Children received the individualized reward items which they collected in the game at the end of the game session; families received a shopping coupon of approx. 30 € value for their participation in the project.

**Game script and presentation.** The main theme of the game is based on scenarios from a developmental psychological study by Sodian and Frith [17]. This examined the ability to use deception and sabotage as social strategies in children with and without autism. Accordingly, there are 8 social micro-experiments (scenes) at the center of our game script, where the player can influence the behaviors of a competitor and a co-operator strategically, in order to maximize her/his own reward. Mostly these scenes contain 'presses' that are expected to evoke behavioral responses potentially relevant to making the screening estimates. The game has 4 further scenes: an additional micro-experiment scene to detect perceptual preferences, two introductory-instruction scenes, and a closing one. The scheme of the game script and the key functions of the scenes are shown in Table 1.

**Table 1.** The scheme of the game script

| | Scene theme | Scene function |
|---|---|---|
| 1 | 'perceptual preferences' | to evoke gaze and emotional responses |
| 2 | introduction and instruction, 1 | to familiarize the child with characters, task, controls |
| 3 | sabotage, co-operative context | to evoke behavioral, gaze and emotional responses |
| 4 | sabotage, competitive context | |
| 5 | sabotage, co-operative context | |
| 6 | sabotage, competitive context | |
| 7 | introduction and instruction, 2 | to familiarize the child with task and controls |
| 8 | deception, co-operative context | to evoke behavioral, gaze and emotional responses |
| 9 | deception, competitive context | |
| 10 | deception, co-operative context | |
| 11 | deception, competitive context | |
| 12 | closing | to close the game |

Visual elements of the game are presented on a 22-inch LCD monitor, auditory elements via desktop speakers. The competitor and the co-operator are represented as animated 2D cartoon figures of children, the narrator is a more adult-like 2D cartoon figure. The player can influence the actors' behaviors by manipulating two control surfaces on the screen by mouse clicks.

**Technological setting.** The game prototype was developed using the Unity game engine (Unity Technologies), and is running on a standard desktop-mounted, binocular eye-tracking PC (Eyefollower 2 by LC Technologies), with a 120 c/sec recording rate, in a Microsoft Windows 7 environment. The game software receives and records mouse positions and actions, and gains gaze focus coordinates from the eye-tracker software, in real time. These data were logged at a 590 c/sec mean rate in this study. A web-camera positioned below the monitor makes video recordings of the players' face. These are analyzed later, in an off-line way, by an emotional facial expression recognition software, the Noldus FaceReader (v5.1, by Noldus Information Technology). FaceReader attempted to assign emotional states at a 22.77 c/s mean rate, in the total sample.

**Procedure and additional means of data collecting.** In the recruitment phase, data were collected on children's use of, and experience with, ICT devices from their parents. Game sessions took place individually in a lab room, and were managed by the second author, having significant experience in working with children with ASC and using the equipment. If the child or the parent wished so, the parent was present at the game session; otherwise she/he was awaiting in a neighboring room. A short and simple game for warming up and practicing mouse-using skills was administered first, followed by the administration of the game prototype. After completing it, data were collected on children's experiences about the game via a questionnaire. The sessions lasted for 30–40 min; within that, playing with the prototype took 15–25 min.

**Analysis.** Log files from the game software – containing mouse coordinates, mouse actions, and gaze coordinates – and the FaceReader output files served as input for analysis. Quality of raw data was quantified as the ratio of data points with successful data acquisition ('valid data' in the followings) within the total amount of data points for which data acquisition was attempted. Data quality was analyzed in 3 time slots: in the first and last 5 min of the game (time slots 1 & 3), and in two consecutive scenes in between (time slot 2), lasting for 170–249 s. Statistics was done by the IBM SPSS Statistics software, version 23 (IBM Corp.).

# 4   Results

## 4.1   Background Variables

We explored subjects' performance in the game (the amount of correct mouse responses): it was close to ceiling (24) in the total sample (mean score = 22.6, range: 20–24); the Mann-Whitney test showed no group difference. We also explored the scores given by the children in the user experience questionnaire. It was, too, close to ceiling (33) in the total sample (mean score = 26.93; range: 16–33); the Mann-Whitney test did not show group difference. That is, completing the game successfully was well within the reach of the participants, in both groups; and they, overall, found the game attractive and engaging. This suggests that potential sub-optimal data quality is not an effect of frustration, non-effective efforts, or an overall dissatisfaction with the game.

## 4.2    Data Quality

Mouse response data were fully valid in both groups: at all data points, the game software was able to gain the mouse coordinates and the mouse state (action) from the operating system.

Emotional facial expression and eye-tracking data quality. Beyond the ratio of valid data points, we generated two further data quality indicators from FaceReader output: the ratio of data points where FaceReader was unable to find the face on the video frame ('find failed ratio'); and the ratio of data points where FaceReader was able to find the face, but was unable to fit an emotion pattern onto it ('fit failed ratio'). Table 2 below presents basic descriptive data quality indicators along these variables.

**Table 2.** Descriptive characteristics of indicators of raw data quality

|  | Time slot 1 | Time slot 2 | Time slot 3 | Aggregated |
|---|---|---|---|---|
| FaceReader find failed ratio | mean: 6.284 % | mean: 10.263 % | mean: 14.325 % | mean: 9.796 % SD: 9.441 % |
|  | SD: 9.013 % | SD: 13.204 % | SD: 14.704 % |  |
| FaceReader fit failed ratio | mean: 23.877 % | mean: 22.033 % | mean: 22.200 % | mean: 22.201 % |
|  | SD: 26.269 % | SD: 26.415 % | SD: 20.514 % | SD: 22.401 % |
| FaceReader valid data ratio | mean: 69.839 % | mean: 67.703 % | mean: 63.475 % | mean: 68.003 % |
|  | SD: 27.336 % | SD: 28.488 % | SD: 24.066 % | SD: 23.416 % |
| Eye-tracking valid data ratio | mean: 81.581 % | mean: 75.324 % | mean: 66.863 % | mean: 75.426 % |
|  | SD: 21.349 % | SD: 29.122 % | SD: 28.327 % | SD: 22.976 % |

No significant difference was found between the two subject groups by Mann-Whitney tests, in any of the raw data quality indicators. Data above are influenced by 3 significant outliers: one subject served with extremely low (7.52 %) valid FaceReader data ratio; two subjects with extremely low (14.502 % and 5.805 %) valid eye-tracking data ratio. Inspection of video recordings showed that all of them produced a lot of intensive head movements, largely towards their parents and/or the experimenter.

According to Wilcoxon Signed Rank tests on valid data ratios, FaceReader data quality did not change significantly across the 3 subsequent time slots; eye-tracking data quality, however, decreased significantly ($z = -2.668$, $p = 0.007$ between time slots 1 and 3; $z = -2.725$, $p = 0.006$ between time slots 2 and 3).

### 4.3   The Relationship Between Data Qualities

We calculated Spearman's rho for the relationships between the three FaceReader data quality indicators (described above), and the eye-tracking data quality variable, for the 3 time slots and for the aggregated data sets, separately. Using a Bonferroni correction, we set the threshold of statistical significance at $p = 0.008$. Significant and moderate/strong negative relationships were found between (FaceReader) find failed ratio and eye-tracking valid data ratio in the 1st time slot (rho = −0.688; $p = 0.001$), in the 2nd time slot (rho = −0.630; $p = 0.004$), and in the aggregated data set (rho = −0.602; $p = 0.005$).

This pattern of results confirms a *refined* form of our hypothesis about a relationship between data qualities. Head movements seem to influence both data qualities negatively: more head movements seem to lead to higher find failed ratio in the emotion recognition data set, and, correspondingly, to lower valid data ratio in eye-tracking data.

## 5   Conclusions and Perspectives

There does not exist any objective or consensual reference threshold for satisfying ratio of valid raw data in eye-tracking or in automated emotional facial expression recognition research. Some researchers suggest a 50 % critical threshold for eye-tracking data in research [18]. Although we found higher valid data ratio in all variables, we interpret our results as indicating a clearly sub-optimal level of data quality, for four reasons.

Firstly, inter-individual differences in raw data quality were remarkable, even in this relatively small sample, as indicated by high SD values. Secondly, a few outlier subjects produced 'dramatically' sparse valid data. Although they would be excluded from further analyses in standard lab-based research, their exclusion could decrease the sensitivity of the screening process in the present context. Thirdly, the positive relationship between emotional facial expression data and eye-tracking data qualities decreases the expected robustness of the screening system. Fourthly, it is important to emphasize that our sample has been 'optimized' for data quality already in the recruiting/inclusion phase, as we excluded subjects without enough experience with using a mouse, or with atypical motor development, or with eye or visual impairment, etc. These considerations suggest that data quality is a bottleneck and a key issue to be addressed in developing screening/diagnostic/assessment technologies based on multi-mode behavioral data, including automated emotional facial expression recognition and eye-tracking.

A few ways of addressing this issue plausibly arise. The decrease in eye-tracking data quality along game time raises the possibility that maintaining or increasing user engagement may reduce head movements. The finding that outlier subjects seemed to show a lot of interactions towards others present suggests that making the system more suitable for autonomous, independent use may reduce this source of data loss. Using wearable eye-tracker may fully eliminate data loss due to head movement, although it makes data processing and analysis more complex. Emotional facial expression raw data quality may potentially be enhanced by more than one recording cameras.

Finally, we wish to emphasize that this study is only a first step in exploring and understanding data quality issues in the context of our project objectives; its conclusions need further confirmation. Studies with significantly bigger samples and deeper analyses are clearly needed. Our intention is to continue research in this direction.

**Acknowledgements.** This research was approved by the Research Ethics Committee of the 'Bárczi Gusztáv' Faculty of Special Education, ELTE University. There is no conflict of interests. Some elements of the project were funded by a grant within the EIT ICT Labs Hungarian Node (PI: András Lőrincz), and via a TÁMOP grant (4.2.1./B-09/KMR-2010-0003). We thank András Lőrincz for his support in the preparatory phases of the project, and Tibor Gregorics for coordinating software development.

# References

1. World Health Organization: International Classification of Diseases and Disorders (ICD-10). World Health Organization, Geneva (1993)
2. APA [American Psychiatric Association]: Diagnostic and Statistical Manual of Mental Disorders (DSM-5). American Psychiatric Association, Washington DC (2013)
3. O'Reilly, M., Karim, K., Lester, J.N.: Should autism be classified as a mental illness/disability? evidence from empirical work. In: O'Reilly, M., Lester, J.N. (eds.) The Palgrave Handbook of Child Mental Health. Discourse and Conversation Studies, pp. 252–271. Palgrave Macmillan, UK (2015)
4. Eikeseth, S.: Intensive early intervention. In: Matson, J.L., Sturmey, P. (eds.) International Handbook of Autism and Pervasive Developmental Disorders, pp. 321–338. Springer, New York (2011)
5. Daniels, A.M., Mandell, D.S.: Explaining differences in age at autism spectrum disorder diagnosis: a critical review. Autism **18**, 583–597 (2014)
6. García-Primo, P., Hellendoorn, A., Charman, T., Roeyers, H., Dereu, M., Roge, B., et al.: Screening for autism spectrum disorders: state of the art in Europe. Eur. Child Adolesc. Psychiatry **23**, 1005–1021 (2014)
7. Wall, D.P., Kosmicki, J., Deluca, T.F., Harstad, E., Fusaro, V.A.: Use of machine learning to shorten observation-based screening and diagnosis of autism. Transl. Psychiatry. **2**, e100 (2012)
8. Rynkiewicz, A., Schuller, B., Marchi, E., Piana, S., Camurri, A., Lassalle, A., Baron-Cohen, S.: An investigation of the 'female camouflage effect' in autism using a computerized ADOS-2 and a test of sex/gender differences. Mol. Autism 7, 1–8 (2016)
9. Klein, T.J., Al-Ghasani, T., Al-Ghasani, M., Akbar, A., Tang, E., Al-Farsi, Y.: A mobile application to screen for autism in Arabic-speaking communities in Oman. Lancet Glob. Heal. **3**, S15 (2015)
10. Kobak, K.A., Stone, W.L., Ousley, O.Y., Swanson, A.: Web-based training in early autism screening: results from a pilot study. Telemed. e-Health **17**, 640–644 (2011)
11. Bölte, S., Bartl-Pokorny, K.D., Jonsson, U., Berggren, S., Zhang, D., Kostrzewa, E., et al.: How can clinicians detect and treat autism early? Methodological trends of technology use in research. Acta Paediatr. **105**(2), 137–144 (2016)

12. Dehkordi, P.S., Moradi, H., Mahmoudi, M., Pouretemad, H.R.: The design, development, and deployment of roboparrot for screening autistic children. Int. J. Soc. Robot. **7**(4), 513–522 (2015)

13. Gyori, M., Borsos, Z., Stefanik, K.: Evidence-based development and first usability testing of a social serious game based multi-modal system for early screening for atypical socio-cognitive development. In: Sik-Lányi, C., Hoogerwerf, E.-J., Miesenberger, K. (eds.) Assistive Technology: Building Bridges. Studies in Health Technology and Informatics, vol. 217, pp. 48–54. IOS Press, Amsterdam (2015)

14. Csákvári, J., Gyori, M.: Applicability of standard eye-tracking technique in people with intellectual disability: methodological conclusions from a series of studies. Stud. Health Technol. Inform. **217**, 63–70 (2015)

15. Nyström, M., Andersson, R., Holmqvist, K., Weijer, J., van de Weijer, J.: The influence of calibration method and eye physiology on eyetracking data quality. Behav. Res. Methods **45**, 272–288 (2012)

16. Dhall, A., Goecke, R., Joshi, J., Sikka, K., Gedeon, T.: Emotion recognition. In: The Wild Challenge 2014: Baseline, Data and Protocol. ICMI 2014 Proceedings of the 16th International Conference Multimodal Interact, pp. 461–466 (2014)

17. Sodian, B., Frith, U.: Deception and sabotage in autistic, retarded and normal children. J. Child Psychol. Psychiatry **33**, 591–605 (1992)

18. Sasson, N.J., Elison, J.T.: Eye tracking young children with autism. JoVE (J. Vis. Exp.), e3675 (2012)

# Interpersonal Distance and Face-to-face Behavior During Therapeutic Activities for Children with ASD

Airi Tsuji[⊠], Soichiro Matsuda, and Kenji Suzuki

Faculty of Engineering, Information and Systems, University of Tsukuba, Tennodai, Tsukuba 305-8573, Japan
{tsuji,matsuda}@ai.iit.tsukuba.ac.jp, kenji@ieee.org

**Abstract.** This study proposed a quantitative estimation method for interpersonal distance by using a prototype measurement system. With the aid of motion capture technology and marker caps, we estimated the body position and orientation of children with autism spectrum disorders (ASD) and their therapists. A prototype measurement system was introduced in practicing therapy rooms and captured behavior during ongoing therapy for children with ASD. This study confirmed that approaching behavior and, to a lesser extent, interpersonal distance can be effectively estimated using the proposed motion capture system. Additional system improvements are required to capture face-to-face behavior.

**Keywords:** Autism spectrum disorders · Interpersonal distance · Motion capture

## 1   Introduction

Interpersonal distance is an important factor in nonverbal communication. High demands exist for quantitative evaluation of nonverbal communication in social skills development training for children with autism spectrum disorders (ASD). In the field of psychology, researchers have evaluated personal space and interpersonal distance for children with ASD who have difficulties using nonverbal cues [1–3]. In these prior studies, interpersonal distance data were collected by human observers reviewing videos. Data captured using this human-based method was investment of time. Regarding intervention for children with ASD, an easy and quantitative understanding of children's behavior and dynamic response–such as approaching or avoiding in response to each therapeutic activity–is essential. This study proposes a technology-based method for the quantitative estimation of interpersonal distances and face-to-face behavior. The technology, Social Imaging [4], was used to identify and represent social behaviors. We designed a soft marker cap that can be easily worn by children and used with the motion capture technology to record changes in interpersonal distance between the child with ASD and their therapist. This prototype measurement system was introduced in a practicing therapy room and captured ongoing therapy for children

© Springer International Publishing Switzerland 2016
K. Miesenberger et al. (Eds.): ICCHP 2016, Part II, LNCS 9759, pp. 367–374, 2016.
DOI: 10.1007/978-3-319-41267-2_52

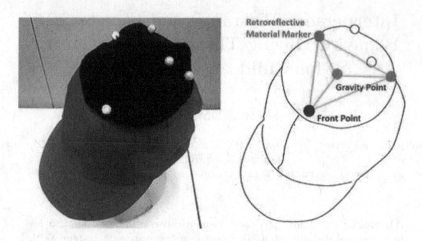

**Fig. 1.** Soft marker cap for motion capture (Color figure online)

with ASD. In this paper, we report the analysis results regarding the quantitative estimation of interpersonal distance from captured data.

## 2    Method

### 2.1    Measurement

The most common quantitative evaluation method for interpersonal distance is the stop-distance method [1]. This method requires two persons to approach one another until they feel discomfort or unpleasantness; the distance between their toe positions at this final point is measured. Although commonly used, this method presents an unnatural situation for measuring interpersonal distance. Motion capture systems, similar to the one proposed in this study, show promise for accurately measuring interpersonal distance in a natural environment without observation. However, many ASD children have hypersensitivity [5,6] that makes them resist multiple motion capture markers on their body. In Japan, children wear caps in school and during physical education. Most ASD children are also accustomed to wearing a cap without elastic straps. Based on these observations, Fig. 1 shows the marker cap developed in this study capable of measuring children's position and orientation.

Optitrack's Flex3 motion capture system and Motive software [7] were used in this study. When estimating interpersonal distance, close (approaching) and away (avoiding) motions for both children and therapists are important. Equations (1–3) describe these motions, where $C(t)$ is the position of the child and $T(t)$ is the position of the therapist, both at time t.

$$D(t) = \frac{\alpha(t)}{\beta(t)} \tag{1}$$

$$\alpha(t) = \Delta(C(t) - T(t)) \tag{2}$$

$$\beta(t) = \Delta(C(t) - C(t - \tau)) \tag{3}$$

If both the child and therapist remain stationary (do not move), $\alpha = 0 \cap \beta = 0$. If only the child moves, $\alpha \neq \beta \neq 0 \cap \alpha - \beta = 0$. If only the therapist moves, $\alpha > 0 \cap \beta = 0$. If both the child and therapist move, $\alpha(t) - \alpha(t - \tau) = 0 \cap \beta \neq 0$. If $D(t) > 0$, the subjects are approaching. If $D(t) < 0$, the subjects are avoiding. Motion capture technologies can also calculate position and orientation. Researchers in one prior study determined the field of view (FOV) for face-to-face communication to be 129 [8]. This study used this criterion when estimating interpersonal distances with and without face-to-face communication.

## 2.2   Experimentation

Figure 2 shows the experimental setup used in this study to quantitatively estimate interpersonal distance. Children with ASD and their therapists wore the marker cap (shown previously in Fig. 1) for motion capture during the one-hour therapy session. Four children with ASD participated in this experiment. Table 1 summarizes participant characteristics. All participants were male with chronological ages (CA) ranging from approximately 4 to 6 years old. Developmental ages (DA)-derived using the Kyoto Scale of Psychological Development [9]- ranged from approximately 2 to 4 years old. The Kyoto Scale scores various subcategories of physical motion, verbal-social skills, cognitive-adaptation skills, and total developmental age. Participants were also assessed using the Pervasive Development Disorders Autism Society Japan Rating Scale (PARS) [10] and the Childhood Autism Rating Scale (CARS) [11]. Both assessments are used to confirm ASD diagnosis. This experiment was approved by the Institutional Review Board, and participants joined in the experiment after providing informed consent.

Both two video cameras for human coder (professional psychologist) and the motion capture system recorded motion behavior of the child participants and their therapists during the standing therapy sessions. Physical motion under 0.5 m/s is considered stagnant movement in preschool-aged children [12]. The human coder observed and recorded (in ms) predefined behaviors during therapy activities. Table 2 lists the predefined behaviors captured by the human observer. The frame rate of motion capture for the technology was set to 60 fps.

## 3   Result

Figures 3, 4, 5 and 6 show the participating children's approach (value in Eqs. 1–3) and face-to-face behavior recorded by both the human coder and motion capture system. Table 3 shows the rate of agreement between the human coder and

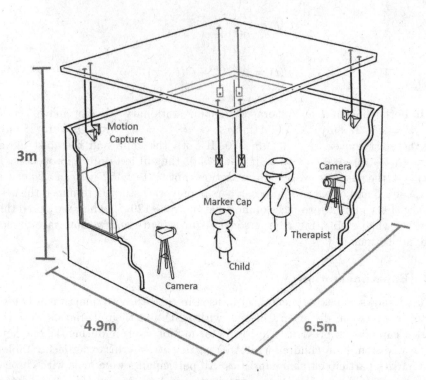

**Fig. 2.** Experimental setup in therapy room

**Table 1.** Participant characteristics

| Participant | Age | | Diagnosis | | Handedness |
|---|---|---|---|---|---|
| | CA | DA | PARS | CARS | |
| A | 4 y, 5 mo. | 1 y, 9 mo. | 21 | 36 | Lefty |
| B | 4 y, 7 mo. | 2 y, 0 mo. | 46 | 44 | Both (Unknown) |
| C | 5 y, 8 mo. | 4 y, 0 mo. | 26 | 32.5 | Righty |
| D | 3 y, 8 mo. | Unknown | 21 | Unknown | Both (Unknown) |

**Table 2.** Predefined behaviors observed by human coder

| Behavior | | Description |
|---|---|---|
| Approaching | Child | Participant approaching to the therapist |
| | Therapist | Therapist approaching to the participant |
| Avoidong | Child | Participant avoiding (away from) the therapist |
| | Therapist | Therapist avoiding (away from) the participant |
| Face-to-face | Both | Both of them looks each other |

**Table 3.** Agreement rate between human- and technology-based methods when recording approaching behavior

| Participant | Accuracy | Precision | Recall |
|---|---|---|---|
| A | 70 % | 48 % | 33 % |
| B | 59 % | 38 % | 51 % |
| C | 70 % | 50 % | 15 % |
| D | 85 % | 68 % | 63 % |

the motion capture system when recording approaching behavior. For each of the participants, behavior data captured by the human coder and technology were similar when recording approaching behavior with one exception–participant B (Fig. 4). Comparatively, the rate of agreement when recording face-to-face behaviors was not as high.

## 4    Discussion

This study confirmed that approaching behavior can be effectively captured using the proposed motion capture system. Additionally, we confirmed that the system can dynamically estimate changes in interpersonal distance, but the agreement rate is not as high likely because of the limited capture frame. More

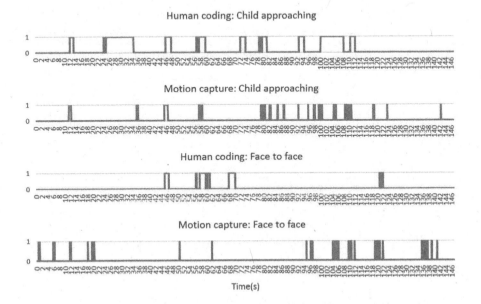

**Fig. 3.** Participant A results for approaching and face-to-face behavior

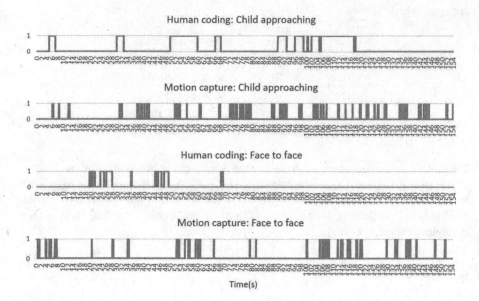

**Fig. 4.** Participant B results for approaching and face-to-face behavior

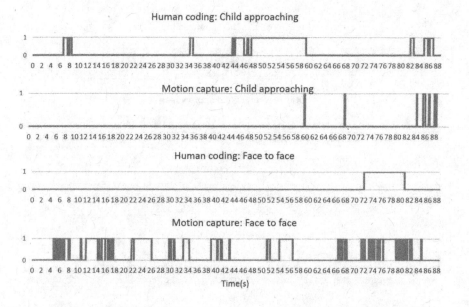

**Fig. 5.** Participant C results for approaching and face-to-face behavior

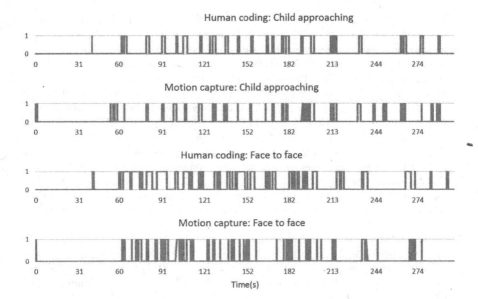

**Fig. 6.** Participant D results for approaching and face-to-face behavior

differences were observed between the human coder and technology when recording face-to-face behavior. The human observer considered face-to-face behavior for a shorter period of time compared with the motion capture system in many cases. The obtained motion data may be used to develop an advanced behavior model that improves face-to-face behavior recognition. In addition, the marker cap was occasionally out of alignment due to the actions of the children. Design enhancements are needed to reduce this occurrence.

## 5   Conclusion

In this study, a method and prototype system for quantitatively estimating interpersonal distance by using motion capture technology and a marker cap for children with ASD was proposed. Future work includes design improvements to the marker cap so that it remains in place and further analysis of the experimental data to improve upon estimation methods.

**Acknowledgments.** This study was supported by JST-CREST "Social Imaging for All Children's Education Supporting Creative Activities and Facilitating Social Interaction."

## References

1. Gessaroli, E., Santelli, E., di Pellegrino, G., Frassinetti, F.: Personal space regulation in childhood autism spectrum disorders. PloS One **8**(9), e74959 (2013)

2. Pedersen, J., Livoir-Petersen, M., Schelde, J.: An ethological approach to autism: an analysis of visual behaviour and interpersonal contact in a child versus adult interaction. Acta Psychiatr. Scand. **80**(4), 346–355 (1989)

3. Rogers, A.L., Fine, H.J.: Personal distance in play therapy with an autistic and a symbiotic psychotic child. Psychother. Theor. Res. Pract. **14**(1), 41 (1977)

4. Suzuki, K.: Social imaging technology to identify and represent social behaviors. In: Proceedings of the 2015 ACM International Joint Conference on Pervasive and Ubiquitous Computing and Proceedings of the 2015 ACM International Symposium on Wearable Computers, pp. 907–908. ACM (2015)

5. Rogers, S.J., Hepburn, S., Wehner, E.: Parent reports of sensory symptoms in toddlers with autism and those with other developmental disorders. J. Autism Dev. Disord. **33**(6), 631–642 (2003)

6. Tomchek, S.D., Dunn, W.: Sensory processing in children with and without autism: a comparative study using the short sensory profile. Am. J. Occup. Ther. **61**(2), 190–200 (2007)

7. Optitrack. http://www.optitrack.com/

8. Pan, Y., Hirokawa, M., Suzuki, K.: Measuring k-degree facial interaction between robot and children with autism spectrum disorders, Robot and Human Interactive Communication (RO-MAN). In: 2015 24th IEEE International Symposium on IEEE, pp. 48–53 (2015)

9. Ikuzawa, M., Matsushita, Y., Nakase, A.: Kyoto scale of psychological development 2001. Kyoto International Social Welfare Exchange Centre, Kyoto (2002)

10. Ito, H., Tani, I., Yukihiro, R., Adachi, J., Hara, K., Ogasawara, M., Inoue, M., Kamio, Y., Nakamura, K., Uchiyama, T., et al.: Validation of an interview-based rating scale developed in japan for pervasive developmental disorders. Res. Autism Spectr. Disord. **6**(4), 1265–1272 (2012)

11. Schopler, R.J.R.E., Renner, B.R.: The childhood autism rating scales (cars). Western Psychological Services, Los Angeles, Calif, USA (1988)

12. DeJaeger, D., Willems, P.A., Heglund, N.C.: The energy cost of walking in children. Pflügers Archiv **441**(4), 538–543 (2001)

# AT and Inclusion of Deaf and Hard of Hearing People

# Support System for Lecture Captioning Using Keyword Detection by Automatic Speech Recognition

Naofumi Ikeda[1]([✉]), Yoshinori Takeuchi[2], Tetsuya Matsumoto[1], Hiroaki Kudo[1], and Noboru Ohnishi[1]

[1] Graduate School of Information Science, Nagoya University, Furo-cho, Chikusa-ku, Nagoya 464-8603, Japan
ikeda@ohnishi.m.is.nagoya-u.ac.jp,
{matumoto,kudo,ohnishi}@is.nagoya-u.ac.jp
[2] Department of Information Systems, School of Informatics, Daido University, 10-3 Takiharu-cho, Minami-ku, Nagoya 457-8530, Japan
ytake@daido-it.ac.jp

**Abstract.** We propose a support system for lecture captioning. The system can detect the keywords of a lecture and present them to captionists. The captionists can understand what an instructor said even when they cannot understand the keywords, and can input keywords rapidly by pressing the corresponding function key. The system detects the keywords by automatic speech recognition (ASR). To improve the detection rate of keywords, we adapt the language model of ASR using web documents. We collect 2,700 web documents, which include 1.2 million words and 5,800 sentences. We conducted an experiment to detect keywords of a real lecture and showed that the system can achieve higher F-measure of 0.957 than that of a base language model (0.871).

**Keywords:** Speech recognition · Language model · Lectures · Keyword detection · Hearing-impaired

## 1 Introduction

Hearing-impaired students often need complementary technologies, such as sign-language interpretation and PC captioning, to enable them to fully understand college lectures. PC captioning is a method in which supporters transcribe an instructor's speech by typing on a keyboard in real time. Figure 1 shows the state of caption presentation by PC captioning in the lecture. The caption is displayed next to the lecture slide. In this lecture, captionists in a remote location type in real time while watching a lecture video sent from the classroom [1].

To enable high-speed input, captionists usually type captions in pairs. In addition, captionists obtain lecture materials such as presentation slide in advance, and prepared for captioning. For example, a predictive conversion of kana and kanji (Japanese characters) is trained by inputting texts in lecture

© Springer International Publishing Switzerland 2016
K. Miesenberger et al. (Eds.): ICCHP 2016, Part II, LNCS 9759, pp. 377–383, 2016.
DOI: 10.1007/978-3-319-41267-2_53

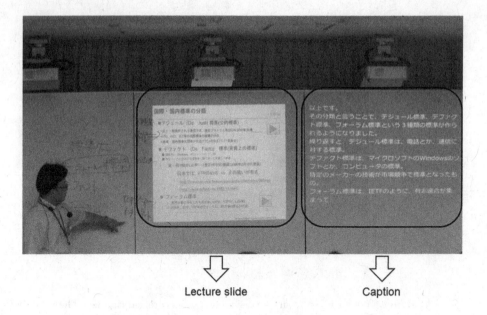

Fig. 1. State of caption presentation by PC captioning

materials. Such preparation is necessary for good PC captioning, which is already being used at several universities, and various groups have done work in this area. The lectures at university often deal with technical content, so it is desirable that captionists understand the lecture content. However, it is sometimes difficult to secure such captionists, and there are many cases in which out-of-field volunteers perform PC captioning. Such lectures are very difficult to listen to and then accurately input unfamiliar words such as technical terms or proper nouns. Kato *et al.* proposed a system for presenting keywords in a lecture [2]. They concluded that presenting such keywords to captionists is effective for improving captioning; however, this system requires supporters with technical knowledge to input keywords.

On the other hand, many studies on lecture captioning using automatic speech recognition (ASR) have been conducted. However, it is difficult to recognize spontaneous speech such as an instructor's speech, so the recognition rate is not sufficient for captioning. The recognition rate required for the captioning of lectures is said to be at least 75 %, but the real rate is 60 %–70 % [3]. Miyoshi *et al.* are developing a real-time captioning system that uses a "re-speak" method [4]. The re-speaker listens to the instructor's speech and then repeats clearly what the instructor said. The system is trained on the re-speaker's voice, and the recognition rate is high in the subsequent ASR step. Miyoshi *et al.* reported that by using a directional microphone and ASR software trained on a re-speaker's voice, a recognition rate of about 90 % was obtained [5]. However, it is not easy to "re-speak", so this method requires training of the re-speaker. In addition, the re-speaker must concentrate on a lecture intensely, which is difficult to do for a long time.

In this research, we propose a support system to detect keywords such as technical terms by ASR. The detected keywords are presented to the captionists. This system aims to assist captionists with no technical knowledge of a lecture.

## 2    Captioning System with Keyword Detection

We propose a system presenting keywords detected by ASR to captionists. As preprocessing, we adapt a language model to a lecture's topic. Figure 2 shows a flowchart of the system.

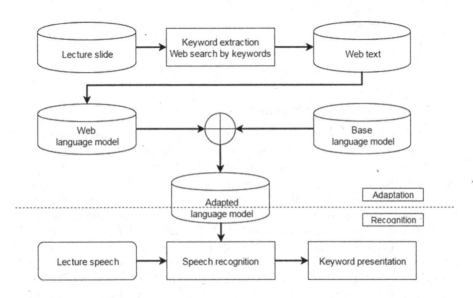

**Fig. 2.** System flowchart

### 2.1    Language Model Adaptation Using Web Documents

To improve the ASR rate for highly specialized university lectures, it is effective to generate a topic-dependent language model, and combine it with a general-purpose, large-vocabulary language model [6,7]. We collect web documents related to the lectures, and we use the text in the presentation slides of the lectures. First, we generate web search queries from the text, and collect the web documents. Next, we train a topic-dependent language model with the collected web documents. Finally, the model is interpolated with the existing general-purpose conversational model to generate a model appropriate for the style of the lectures. By this processing, the keyword detection rate is expected to be improved.

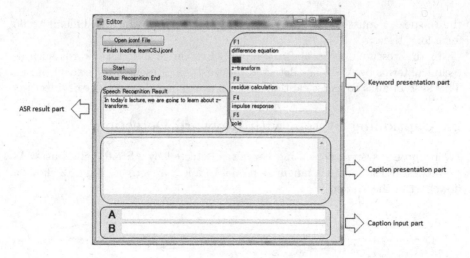

**Fig. 3.** Editor for lecture captioning

## 2.2   Editor for Lecture Captioning

Figure 3 shows a concept of an editor for captioning. The editor consists of a caption input part, caption presentation part, ASR result part and keyword presentation part. Two people usually perform PC captioning for Japanese lectures, so there are two caption input areas located at the bottom of the editor. When captionists input text, they are presented with a caption presentation part located above the caption input part. The texts in the caption presentation area are presented to hearing-impaired students. This system recognizes every utterance of an instructor's speech, and presents results in the ASR result part. If a keyword is included in the result, the keyword is presented in the keyword presentation area, which is located at the right of the editor. When the first keyword is detected, it is presented in the area labeled 'F1'. Then, the next keyword is presented in 'F2', and so on, through 'F5'. After a keyword is presented in 'F5', the process starts over with 'F1'. The color of the label with a newly presented keyword turns red. The captionists can insert the keyword into the sentence in the input by pressing the corresponding function key. This can shorten the time for inputting keywords.

## 3   Experimental Result and Discussion

We conducted an experiment to detect keywords from a lecture at Nagoya University. The course name of the lecture is "Signal processing", and the time length is about 60 min. In advance, we extracted 27 keywords from the lecture slides manually. The keywords are shown in Fig. 4. Original keywords are Japanese. Keywords were uttered 229 times in the lecture. In general, captionists input such keywords by keyboard before the lecture. This can train the predictive conversion of kana and kanji and make it easy to input keywords of the lecture.

| | |
|---|---|
| z-transfom | integral route |
| inverse z-transfom | closed integral route |
| partial fraction expansion | discrete-time system |
| pole | discrete-time signal |
| single pole | linear system |
| double pole | time invariant system |
| k-folds pole | linear time invariant system |
| m-folds pole | time variant system |
| residue | non-linear system |
| residue calculation | causal |
| impulse | convergent zone |
| impulse response | bounded |
| z-transfom pair | expansion into power-series |
| difference equation | |

**Fig. 4.** Extracted keywords

For the ASR decoder, we used Julius, an open-source real-time large vocabulary speech recognition engine. To generate the base language model, we used the Corpus of Spontaneous Japanese (CSJ) database [8], which consists of presentation speech from academic conferences. We trained a trigram language model with the CSJ (6.8 M words) as a base language model. We used only the words that appeared more than four times in the corpus. The lexicon size of the model was 25 K words, and we added 27 keywords.

Then, we collected web documents related to the lecture. In this experiment, we used keywords as the query of the web search, and 100 relevant web documents were collected per query. Collected web documents contained sentences that were not suitable for training of the language model, so only sentences satisfying the following conditions were extracted:

- contains more than 10 characters.
- the ratio of 'hiragana' characters is more than 5 %.

The web-based language model was trained with collected documents containing 1.2 M words, and 5.8 K sentences. We used Palmkit [9] for training. Finally, the web-based model was interpolated with the base model, and generated the adapted model. Language model interpolation was conducted by the following formula.

$$p_A(x|w_1, w_2) = \lambda p_B(x|w_1, w_2) + (1 - \lambda)p_W(x|w_1, w_2), \qquad (1)$$

where $p$ is the probability of observing word $x$ after the sequence of words $w_1 w_2$, and $\lambda$ is interpolation weight. We use the SRI Language Modeling (SRILM) toolkit [10] for interpolation. Figure 5 shows an example of interpolation of conditional probability. As the evaluation index of keyword detection rate, we used the following precision, recall, and F-measure.

$p_B(system \mid speech, synthesizer) = 0.1157$

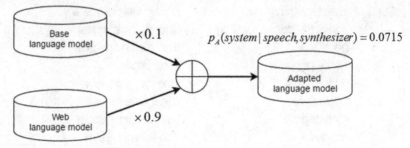

$p_A(system \mid speech, synthesizer) = 0.0715$

$p_W(system \mid speech, synthesizer) = 0.0666$

**Fig. 5.** Example of trigram interpolation in case of $\lambda = 0.1$

**Table 1.** Keyword detection results of base and adapted language models

|  | Precision | Recall | F-measure |
|---|---|---|---|
| Base | 0.890 | 0.852 | 0.871 |
| Adapted ($\lambda = 0.05$) | 0.934 | 0.983 | 0.957 |
| Adapted ($\lambda = 0.10$) | 0.940 | 0.965 | 0.953 |
| Adapted ($\lambda = 0.15$) | 0.921 | 0.969 | 0.945 |

$$Precision = \frac{TP}{TP + FP}. \tag{2}$$

$$Recall = \frac{TP}{TP + FN}. \tag{3}$$

$$F - measure = \frac{2 \cdot Precision \cdot Recall}{Recall + Precision}. \tag{4}$$

Every speech utterance is recognized, and the recognition result is obtained. $TP$, $FP$, and $FN$ are counted as follows.

- $TP$: Number of keywords detected by the system and uttered by the instructor.
- $FP$: Number of detected keywords not uttered by the instructor.
- $FN$: Number of uttered keywords not detected by the system.

Table 1 shows the keyword detection rate using base and adapted models. $\lambda$ is interpolation weight. By adaptation, keyword detection rate was improved.

## 4   Conclusion and Future Work

We proposed a captioning system with keyword detection by ASR. The captionists can understand what instructors said even when they could not understand the keywords, and can input keywords rapidly by pressing the corresponding function key. In addition, we showed that by adapting a language model using lecture slides, the keyword detection rate improved. We showed the result of keyword detection in only one lecture. Hence, we are going to conduct more experiments to detect keywords in different lectures.

We are now examining a technique to automatically extract keywords. The definition of the keywords to be extracted has to be decided while getting feedback from users. Furthermore, we expect to detect keywords that do not appear in a lecture slide, but may be spoken by the instructor. We are continuing to develop this captioning system. In future work, we plan to add keywords to the predictive conversion function to aid input and will conduct lecture captioning by using our proposed system.

# References

1. Miyoshi, S., Kawano, S., Nishioka, T., Kato, N., Shirasawa, M., Murakami, H., Minagawa, H., Ishihara, Y., Naito, I., Wakatsuki, D., Kuroki, H., Kobayashi, M.: A basic study on supplementary visual information for real-time captionists in the lecture of information science. IEICE Trans. Inf. Syst. (Japanese edition) $J91(D(9))$, 2236–2246 (2008)
2. Kato, N., Kawano, S., Kuroki, H., Murakami, H., Nishioka, T., Wakatsuki, D., Minagawa, H., Shionome, T., Miyoshi, S., Shirasawa, M., Ishihara, Y.: Basic Study of Keyword Presentation System for Hearing Impaired Students. IEICE Technical Report ET2007-81 107(462), pp. 71–76 (2008). (in Japanese)
3. Kawahara, T.: Recent progress of spontaneous speech recognition deployment in parliament and applications to lectures. J. Multimed. Educ. Res. $9(1)$, S1–S8 (2012). (in Japanese)
4. Miyoshi, S., Kuroki, H., Kawano, S., Shirasawa, M., Ishihara, Y., Kobayashi, M.: Support technique for real-time captionist to use speech recognition software. In: Miesenberger, K., Klaus, J., Zagler, W.L., Karshmer, A.I. (eds.) ICCHP 2008. LNCS, vol. 5105, pp. 647–650. Springer, Heidelberg (2008)
5. Miyoshi, S., Kuroki, H., Kawano, S., Shirasawa, M., Ishihara, Y., Kobayashi, M.: Support Technique for Real-Time Captionist to Use Speech Recognition Software. Tsukuba University of Technology Techno Report 14, pp. 145–151 (2007). (in Japanese)
6. Munteanu, C., Penn, G., Beacker, R.: Web-based language modelling for automatic lecture transcription. In: Proceedings of 8th Annual Conference of the International Speech Communication Association, no. ThD.P3a-2, pp. 2353–2356 (2007)
7. Kawahara, T., Nemoto, Y., Akita, Y.: Automatic lecture transcription by exploiting presentation slide information for language model adaptation. In: Proceedings of ICASSP, pp. 4929–4932 (2008). (in Japanese)
8. Furui, S.: Recent advances in spontaneous speech recognition and understanding. In: Proceedings of ISCA & IEEE Workshop on Spontaneous Speech Processing and Recognition, pp. 1–6 (2003). (in Japanese)
9. Ito, A.: Palmkit (2009). http://palmkit.sourceforge.net/
10. Stolcke, A.: SRILM – An extensible language modeling toolkit. In: Proceedings of ICSLP (2002)

# Compensating Cocktail Party Noise with Binaural Spatial Segregation on a Novel Device Targeting Partial Hearing Loss

Luca Giuliani[1], Sara Sansalone[2], Stefania Repetto[2], Federico Traverso[3], and Luca Brayda[1(✉)]

[1] Fondazione Istituto Italiano di Tecnologia, Genoa, Italy
luca.brayda@iit.it
[2] Linear s.r.l., Genoa, Italy
[3] DITEN - University of Genoa, Genoa, Italy

**Abstract.** The ability of focusing on a single conversation in the middle of a crowded environment is usually referred at as the cocktail party effect. This skill exploits binaural cues and spectral features of a target speaker. Unfortunately, traditional acoustic prostheses tend to modify these cues in ways that the brain cannot recover. Social isolation is an inevitable consequence. In this work we tested the Glassense, an intelligent pair of glasses. Binaural input from microphones arrays is processed to spatially segregate the soundscape surrounding the listener, so that frontal speech sources are preserved, while competing sources from the sides and the back are attenuated, just as an "acoustical lens". We report an increase in speech intelligibility by about 4 dB, measured as reception threshold, under severe noisy conditions. Our device can be a complementary input to existing acoustic prostheses, aimed at increasing spatial awareness of persons affected by partial hearing loss.

**Keywords:** Hearing aid · Disability · Microphone arrays · Beamforming · Binaural · Real time

## 1 Introduction

Over 5 % (360M people) of the world's population suffers from disabling hearing loss, that is hearing loss greater than 40 dB in the better hearing ear. It affects approximately one-third of people over 65 years of age. A significant percentage of patients treated with modern hearing aids pleads not satisfied with the results and so does not use them, specifically when speech must be understood in noisy environments. The brain usually processes binaural cues to locate and isolate possible disturbances [1], solving the so-called "cocktail party problem". Although visual cues help to point to acoustic sources of interest, hearing-impaired individuals are less efficient in doing so [2]. Wearing one microphone per ear has shown to be better than having one microphone only in the most damaged ear [3] and recent works show that binaural multi-microphone hearing

© Springer International Publishing Switzerland 2016
K. Miesenberger et al. (Eds.): ICCHP 2016, Part II, LNCS 9759, pp. 384–391, 2016.
DOI: 10.1007/978-3-319-41267-2_54

aids can decrease the effect of unwanted spatial sound sources [4]. Directional audio input is preferred by hearing impaired persons because head motion can act as a spatial selector [5]. However, very few setups are lightweight enough to become commercial prototypes [6,10].

## 1.1   State of the Art

In the last years, several beamforming techniques have been evaluated to increase hearing aids performance by mean of microphones arrays. Interesting results have been obtained by van Hoesel and Clark [7] using binaural microphones as two-elements arrays for beamforming in cochlear implants patients and again by Froehlich et al. [8] using the same approach with binaural hearing prostheses. Some beamforming techniques have been evaluated by Kates and Weiss [9] with an array of five microphones, 10 cm long, with the acoustic focus steered on the sides of the array (end-fire orientation). The results showed that super-directive and adaptive digital processing can increase the Signal to Noise Ratio (SNR, the ratio between the interesting audio signal and the unwanted noise that comes with it) up to 9 dB. An effective device was presented by Widrow in 2001 [10], based on a microphone array with the form factor of a necklace. The solution appeared able to dramatically increase words comprehension percentage in patients and it was able to communicate with hearing aids by means of a magnetic transductor. An interesting solution exploiting binaural microphones arrays mounted on a pair of glasses has been proposed by Boone [6] in 2006 (based on Merks preceding work [11]). This solution claims a directivity index of 7.2 dB and it treats head-masking effects related to the position of the microphones. Since 2000 the hearing glasses have been developed in collaboration with the Company Varibel and are currently available as market product. In 2011 Mens [12] published a performance analysis of the hearing glasses with different beamforming modalities on some hearing impaired subjects, also considering the effects of head shadowing. The results of this last work were expressed in terms of SRT (Speech Recognition Threshold, the SNR value at which the subjects guess 50 % of target speech words) improvement with respect to non-directional binaural hearing aids. In the best performing modality the Varibel hearing glasses is capable of a SRT improvement equal to 6.5 dB, i.e. a solid reinforcement in speech comprehension capabilities of hearing impaired subjects in cocktail parties noise.

However, this device acts as a substitute for a hearing prosthesis. Therefore, it requires to be configured on each subject's hearing loss profile. In this work, instead, we propose a generic system that can potentially be complementary, and not substitutive, to any existing - already personalized - acoustic hearing aid.

## 2   The Glassense System

In this work we propose and validate a wearable device which acts as an acoustical lens: we deliver spatial selectivity to binaural audio input by means of two

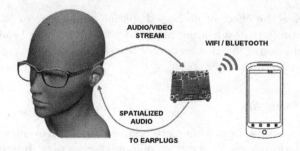

**Fig. 1.** The Glassense system. The audio captured by the microphones is sent to the relay device, which performs filtering and sends the resulting signal to the earplugs. The device con also be connected with a smartphone for configuration.

microphone arrays. The arrays attenuate sounds coming from the sides and the back of the listener, while preserving frontal sound sources. In principle, the listener can point at frontal target sound sources by means of head motion, therefore adding spatial selectivity to binaural audio inputs. The Glassense system, depicted in Fig. 1, is composed by two superdirective microphone arrays mounted on the left and right temples of a pair of glasses.

A relay device is used to acquire and process audio signals and two earplugs send the processed signals to the ears, therefore granting that binaural audio output is processed in quasi real-time. Each microphone arrays is made with 4 digital MEMS microphones. The relay device includes a ZedBoard, a low-cost Linux-based development board based on ARM processing system. A data-independent filter-and-sum beamforming has been used to design two specular end-fire linear microphone arrays [13]. The array has 4 equally spaced elements over 0.12 m and the beamformer structure is composed by 4 FIR filters of order 127. The working frequency band ranges from 400 Hz to 4 kHz. The sampling frequency is 16 kHz. In this work we adopted one frequency-invariant and one frequency-variant superdirective beam patterns, the latter having stronger spatial selectivity. In Fig. 2a we show a polar representation of the nominal Beam Power Pattern (BPP), measured in dB at 1 kHz, for the frequency-invariant filter. As one notes the array response has the main lobe steered at 90°, with aperture (i.e. −3 dB respect to the steering direction) of about 60°, and a single sidelobe at the opposite end-fire, i.e. 270°, about 10 dB lower. The designed array is superdirective for frequencies up to 2300 Hz (i.e. more than 2 octaves). The DI has a mean value of 5.51 dB over the array working frequency band. Moreover, in Fig. 2b also the white-noise gain (WNG) of the same array is shown. The WNG indicates the improvement in the SNR ratio provided by the array, for sensor self-noise. A WNG level higher than 0 dB generally ensures a sufficient robustness against array imperfections. The same array design and beamformer structure has been used for the microphone array pair. We tested the efficacy of the beamforming algorithms of Glassense with the speech understanding tests described in the following.

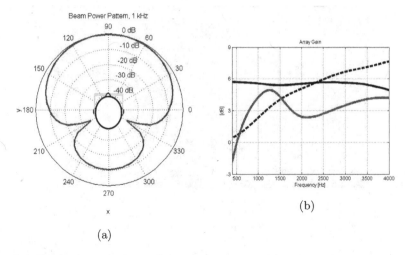

**Fig. 2.** (a) Beam power pattern at 1 kHz. The listener's head is depicted in the middle. (b) Directivity (black line) and white-noise gain (red line) of the end-fire array. The directivity of an uniformly weighted linear array (dashed black line) is shown for comparison (Color figure online)

## 3    Method

### 3.1    Participants

Seven subjects (mean age 41.37, range 33–50 yr) were recruited. Subjects had normal hearing, with pure tone thresholds below 20 dB HL at all standard audiometric frequencies between 250 Hz and 8000 Hz. All subjects spoke Italian as a first language. All gave written informed consent.

### 3.2    Experimental Setup

Subjects were seated in a sound attenuated audiometric booth (size= $3.2 \times 4.8 \times 2.73$ m), lined with 50 mm acoustic foam to create a semianechoic environment (T60 = 0.2 s). Four Behringer active loudspeakers were placed 1 m away from the subject at 0° (directly ahead), 180° (back) and ±90° on either side of the midline. All subjects were facing towards the loudspeaker at 0°, although their heads were not constrained.

### 3.3    Stimuli

Stimuli consisted of a target speech and of competing cocktail-party speech. They were part of a wide-band corpus 20 Hz–20 kHz in accordance with ISO 8253-3:2012 [14] which specifies the requirements for the composition, validation and evaluation of speech test materials. The target was taken from the Bocca Pellegrini elaborate corpus [15], which comprises 200 meaningful bisyllabic words

**Fig. 3.** The experimental setup, with a subject wearing the Glassense

spoken in Italian language. The cocktail party noise was presented by using a four-channel sound card, mixed with the target speech with a mixer. The target and competing noise were played at different combined sound pressure level (SPL), that is different Signal-to-Noise Ratio (SNR), obtained by altering the level of the competing noise while maintaining constant the target (Fig. 3).

## 3.4  Procedure

All subjects carried out a free ear diffuse-field speech audiometry test, in quiet conditions (i.e. without competing noise). In such a test, only the target was played at different levels from the loudspeaker at 0° (directly ahead) and the target speech level at which 100 % of the test words were correctly identified (Speech Intelligibility Threshold) was calibrated on each subject. We delivered stimuli in three conditions (randomized across subjects):

1. *Unfiltered microphones*: the device acquired sound with two microphones (one for each temple) and reproduced the sound into the subject's ears through headphones;
2. *Beamforming frequency invariant*: the device acquired using all the eight microphones and filtered the signals using a frequency invariant beam pattern;
3. *Beamforming frequency variant*: the device acquired using all the eight microphones and filtered the signals using a frequency variant beam pattern;

   The target speech was played from the loudspeaker located at 0° and cocktail party speech was played from each of the four loudspeakers at once. The task was to identify target words and to repeat them. Stimuli ranged at SNRs from −20 dB to 10 dB. An SNR equal to 0 means target level equal to noise level, where the target level was corresponding to the Speech Intelligibility Threshold. For each SNR we played a block of ten words. For each block we scored the guess rate, i.e. number of correctly repeated words.

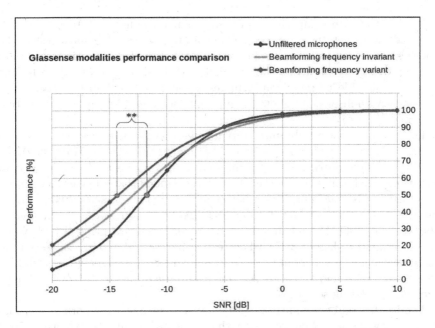

**Fig. 4.** Comparing average audiometric curves of all subjects in three conditions with different filtering methods. Stars indicate significantly different SNR values (Color figure online)

## 4   Data Analysis and Results

We evaluated the mean guess rate at each SNR in the three conditions. For each condition, each subject's guessing rate forms an audiometric curve, where performance grows as the SNR grows. Since comparisons are typically done at 50 % performance (i.e. the SRT, Speech Reception Threshold), we stored the SRT value for each subject and condition. The three SRT distributions (one per condition) resulted to be normal (Kolmogorov-Smirnov and Bartlett tests) for repeated analyses of variances (ANOVA). We considered the filtering condition as dependent variable and the SRT as the independent variable. Post-hoc analysis employed a t-test with Bonferroni correction. We found a significant improvement (3.8 dB) in the SRT for the frequency-variant beamforming over the unfiltered condition (p-value = 0.008). We also averaged all the audiometric curves of each condition. Figure 4 clearly shows the superiority of the beamforming algorithms of the Glassense.

## 5   Discussion and Conclusion

We proposed a novel device designed to compensate the typical limitations of modern hearing aids. We hypothesized that binaural audio feedback, filtered with superdirective microphone arrays mounted on the temples of a pair of glasses, is able to attenuate competing audio speech not facing the listener, while it preserves the target speech coming from frontal sources. We have tested the hypothesis in a controlled environment, where cocktail party noise from multiple sound sources disturbed the intelligibility of a frontal target speech. The Glassense was able to significantly increase speech intelligibility, especially in severe noise conditions. We show a significant increase of the Speech Reception Threshold of 3.8 dB.

The improvement we obtained during this experiment is lower than the one claimed by Mens [12] when assessing the Varibel hearing glasses. However, Mens tested the Varibel hearing glasses using phrases as target speech, while we used lists of unrelated words. Therefore we a priori excluded that a better recognition of isolated words had influence on better understanding of contextual information, something that is a natural but less directly measurable phenomenon. It is entirely possible that an improvement in SRT assessed using list of words may correspond to higher SRTs when testing phrases. Moreover, we tested the Glassense using a real cocktail party recording and a male target speech, while in [12] a female voice and a synthesized noise were used. Future tests will attempt to match the testing scenarios.

Admittedly, our experimental setup involved people with normal hearing; future steps will also include persons with hearing impairment, who however need careful inclusion criteria due to different factors affecting the disability (degree, type and kind of used aid). The earplugs used in our protocol could also have biased our results, but this will be anyway overcome in our next studies, where we will employ the Glassense as a complement to existing hearing aids, which already compensate for mismatch of acoustic feedback from the outer ear. The exposed test have been done in a low reverberation environment, while higher reverberation levels seems to decrease speech intelligibility [17] and previous findings indicate that microphone array devices can reduce reverberation effects on speech comprehension [9]. Thus, further investigation in this direction will be necessary in order to assess the performance of our device in places with reverberation characteristics typical of everyday life contexts.

Concluding, our spatially segregating device can potentially serve as complementary wearable tool for persons with ipoacusia in everyday contexts such as the working place and leisure. It can potentially act as an "acoustical lens". Interestingly, the form factor of a pair of glasses does not make the Glassense a new prosthesis, but a novel assistive aid, with no need of wearing it or switching it on all the time.

**Acknowledgments.** We would like to thank Francesco Diotalevi for his contribution on hardware development, Petra Bianchi for her help in performing the audiometric measures and all our volunteers. This work is partly supported by the Ligurian PAR-FAS grant Glassense (CUP G35C13001360001) and partly by the EU FP7 grant BLINDPAD (grant number 611621).

# References

1. Haykin, S., Chen, Z.: The cocktail party problem. Neural Comput. **17**(9), 1875–1902 (2005)
2. Brimijoin, W.O., McShefferty, D., Akeroyd, M.A.: Auditory and visual orienting responses in listeners with and without hearing-impairment. J. Acoust. Soc. Am. **127**(6), 3678–3688 (2010)
3. Feuerstein, J.F.: Monaural versus binaural hearing: ease of listening, word recognition, and attentional effort. Ear Hear. **13**(2), 80–86 (1992)
4. Bogaert, T., Doclo, S., Wouters, J., Moonen, M.: Speech enhancement with multichannel Wiener filter techniques in multimicrophone binaural hearing aids. J. Acoust. Soc. Am. **125**(1), 360–371 (2009)
5. Neher, T.: Relating hearing loss and executive functions to hearing aid users' preference for, and speech recognition with, different combinations of binaural noise reduction and microphone directionality. Front. Neurosci. **8**, 391 (2014)
6. Boone, M.M.: Directivity measurements on a highly directive hearing aid: the hearing glasses (2006)
7. van Hoesel, R.J., Clark, G.M.: Evaluation of a portable two-microphone adaptive beamforming speech processor with cochlear implant patients. J. Acoust. Soc. Am. **97**(4), 2498–2503 (1995)
8. Froehlich, P.M., Freels, K., Powers, T.A.: Speech recognition benefit obtained from binaural beamforming hearing aids: comparison to omnidirectional and individuals with normal hearing. Audiol. Online **14338**, 1–8 (2015)
9. Kates, J.M., Weiss, M.R.: A comparison of hearing-aid array-processing techniques. J. Acoust. Soc. Am. **99**(5), 3138–3148 (1996)
10. Widrow, B.: A microphone array for hearing aids. IEEE Trans. Circuits Syst. **1**(2), 26–32 (2001)
11. Merks, I.L.D.M.: Binaural application of microphone arrays for improved speech intelligibility in a noisy environment, Ph.D. Thesis (2000)
12. Mens, L.H.M.: Speech understanding in noise with an eyeglass hearing aid: asymmetric fitting and the head shadow benefit of anterior microphones. Int. J. Audiol. **50**(1), 27–33 (2011)
13. Trucco, A., Traverso, F., Crocco, M.: Maximum constrained directivity of oversteered end-fire sensor arrays. Sensors **15**(6), 13477–13502 (2015)
14. ISO 8253–3:2012: Acoustics - Audiometric test methods - Speech audiometry (2012)
15. Bocca, A., Pellegrini, E.: Studio statistico sulla composizione fonetica della lingua italiana e sua applicazione pratica all'audiometria con la parola. Arch. Ital. Otol. Rinol. Laringol. **56**(5), 116–141 (1950)
16. Kato, M., Uematsu, H., Kashino, M., Hirahara, T.: The effect of head motion on the accuracy of sound localization. Acoust. Sci. Technol. **24**(5), 315–317 (2003)
17. Moncur, J.P., Dirks, D.D.: Binaural and monaural speech intelligibility in reverberation. J. Speech Hear. Res. **10**(2), 186–95 (1967)

# CoUnSiL: Collaborative Universe for Remote Interpreting of Sign Language in Higher Education

Vít Rusňák[1,3], Pavel Troubil[1], Svatoslav Ondra[2(✉)], Tomáš Sklenák[2],
Desana Daxnerová[1], Eva Hladká[1], Pavel Kajaba[1], Jaromír Kala[1], Matej Minárik[1],
Peter Novák[1], and Christoph Damm[2]

[1] Faculty of Informatics, Masaryk University, Brno, Czech Republic
{rusnak,pavel}@ics.muni.cz, eva@fi.muni.cz,
{410301,409748,374283,396546,347550}@mail.muni.cz
[2] Support Centre for Students with Special Needs, Masaryk University, Brno, Czech Republic
{ondra,sklenak,damm}@teiresias.muni.cz
[3] Institute of Computer Science, Masaryk University, Brno, Czech Republic

**Abstract.** In this paper, we report on CoUnSiL (Collaborative Universe for Sign Language), our ongoing project on the videoconferencing environment for remote interpreting of sign language. Our work is motivated by the lack of qualified interpreters capable of interpreting highly specialized courses at universities. We present the tool that ensures low latency and sustainable framerate of multiple video and audio streams. We describe both the user interface of the CoUnSiL application followed by the background technologies. Next, we present the three evaluations with users.

**Keywords:** Collaborative environments · Remote interpreting · Sign language · Deaf · Higher Education · Video conference

## 1 Introduction

Masaryk University (hereinafter as MU) grants accessibility to all study branches accredited at the university for students with special needs and provides several types of service, including communication services – typically sign language interpreting, speech-to-text reporting, visualization of spoken language through articulation, etc. to ensure communication between deaf or hard-of-hearing and hearing people. The number of students and employees of MU who communicate primarily in sign language has grown in last decade much faster than a number of sign language interpreters effectively available to provide the interpreting service. Currently, more than 25 sign language speakers study almost at all 9 faculties of the university, plus approx. 10 are employees of the university; in contrary MU employs only 7 sign language interpreters, several others are short-time contracted.

In order to utilize free capacity of those interpreters who cannot be available on the spot of a tuition event which requires interpreting, a research of technological solution for remote sign language interpreting started. As deployment of such a system involves IT into teaching environment more extensively, we focused on finding a solution for

© Springer International Publishing Switzerland 2016
K. Miesenberger et al. (Eds.): ICCHP 2016, Part II, LNCS 9759, pp. 392–399, 2016.
DOI: 10.1007/978-3-319-41267-2_55

lessons of smaller groups (such as workshops, seminars) taking place in teaching rooms that are technically adjustable better.

## 2    Related Work

Our ambition is to have a system which will enable interpreting remotely to the same extent and quality as interpreting on-site. Therefore, we firstly analyzed prerequisites, facts, and needs of all parties of the lessons in which a sign language interpreter is present on-site: (a) the teacher speaks to students verbally, uses a presentation screen and/or interactive whiteboard, moderates a discussion (giving the floor to particular students), is able to hear the interpreter and is able to monitor the interpreter visually; (b) either signing students or verbally speaking students are able to perceive the interpreter visually and hear (if they can) the interpreter, they can "raise their hands" and they are able to recognize teacher's decisions of moderating; (c) interpreter is able to hear the teacher and all students that speak verbally, is able to see the teacher and his/her interaction with presentation screen and/or interactive whiteboard, is able to see all students (and recognize legibly the signing ones), is able to see content of the screen/whiteboard legibly, is able to secondarily moderate a discussion (can give the floor to particular students); (d) additionally, it is presumed that students and teacher have to use their computers for any educational purpose; (e) a teacher is able to see interpreter legibly and vice versa.

Our research of existing studies and reviews of videoconferencing technologies has proved that most of them consider deployment of the technologies only in terms of providing video remote interpreting of person-to-person communication (e.g. [4–6, 10]), i.e. they did not consider conditions given above at all. Much less of existing studies and analyses (e.g. [7–9]) are focused on technologies applicable to the extremely complex conditions of communication in teaching events (or any collaborative events) and are relevant for our research.

Studies and reviews [8, 9] have proved that employment of "personal" platforms for audio and video chat (e.g. TokBox, Vidyo, Skype, ooVoo, Camfrog) is not sufficient for legibility of signing speech due to their rate of latency, image quality (mainly framerate). In addition, their incapability to handle so many parallel audio and video streams were alleviated with running multiple instances on two or more platforms, but then the startup is very difficult and user demanding, and the connection unstable. H.323/SIP as well as other proprietary ("enterprise") video conferencing systems provide high quality of both video and audio in case of hardware clients but requirement of their availability on the spot diminishes flexibility. Software H.323/SIP clients have similar issues like the aforesaid tools.

Outcomes of the research have conducted to the project on the development of our own videoconferencing system for remote interpreting of sign language in the environment of university tuition events.

# 3    Requirements of the New System

When defining primary requirements on the new video conferencing application, we tried to minimize additional cognitive load on students and allow teachers to feel natural, ideally as in standard face-to-face class without any video conferencing enhancements. In summary, the requirements of the system have been defined as follows: (a) number of participants: 1 teacher, 1 interpreter, the maximum number of 8 students; (b) captured audio inputs and audio streams: teacher, interpreter, verbally speaking students – up to 10 streams in total; (c) captured video input and video streams: teacher (considering his/her possible motions), interpreter, all students, the content of presentation screen and/or interactive whiteboard – up to 12 streams in total; (d) the image resolution of video streams min. $240 \times 180$ and max. $640 \times 480$ pixels, min. 25 fps, low latency (estimated values, to be defined exactly during development based on survey); (e) user interface has to include a view of all participants, presentation screen and/or whiteboard (interpreter's view), window of currently signing participant is automatically enlarged; (f) a feature of ergonomic moderating (giving the floor by teacher and interpreter) to recognize who is currently speaking/signing; (g) setup and startup of the system clients have to be easy and user-friendly; (h) the system clients should run on commodity desktop computers and accessories, no additional high-performance hardware required.

# 4    CoUnSiL Client

In a pursuit to develop an application which fulfills the requirements, we developed the CoUnSiL environment, consisting of a server and a client application. The CoUnSiL Client is a desktop application providing the user interface for the videoconferencing environment. It is partially inspired by the GColl video conferencing environment, which was shown to improve collaboration and trust in comparison to standard video-conferences [1]. The application currently distinguishes three roles of users: student, teacher and interpreter. The window layout changes according to the selected role. Figure 1 shows the user interface for the student. CoUnSiL client interface is made of two types of components: the interaction menu and content windows. Basic options of the menu are Exit and About button. According to the role chosen at client initialization, the menu is more specified. Teacher and interpreter have additional buttons available: mute and volume control. Whereas student has the choice to indicate he/she wants to talk using Raise hand button. When pressed, a red frame around window of the student is displayed. Content windows are situated in three areas, each representing windows roles. Window of interpreter is shown in the area in the top right corner. Interpreter has also function of "giving floor" to a student by clicking on student window. On the top left corner there is area dedicated to teacher content. In this area video of teacher and presentation is displayed. The bottom area is dedicated to windows of students and the menu. The menu is situated at the right side of the screen. Windows in this area are automatically rearranging while students are arriving and initiating their application. One row of windows is formed when there are 1–3 student connected and two rows are formed when there are more students. The application centers automatically the whole set of windows on the screen. Each user – regardless his role – has self-view available, e.g. interpreter can monitor himself/herself in the interpreter area, etc.

**Fig. 1.** User interface of the CoUnSiL client – student view

The application is available for three major platforms (MS Windows, OS X, and OS Linux).

## 5   Technology in Background

One of the main requirements of the video conferencing environment is establishing low-latency transmission of the video content while ensuring minimal frame rate of 25 frames per second. Our system uses the UltraGrid[1] [2] for audio and video transmissions. It has been developed in cooperation of MU and the CESNET association for low-latency transmission of high-quality video. The UltraGrid is capable of transmitting video in extremely high resolution while compressing or decompressing it in real-time, using commodity "off-the-shelf" hardware. Its performance allowed us to expect that multiple video streams in relatively low resolution could be transmitted even by less expensive computers over IP network.

The UltraGrid provides unidirectional point-to-point transmission of single video and audio stream only. However, the aforementioned application requires concurrent transmission of multiple video and audio streams, hence multiple UltraGrid instances have to be configured and run. Thus, we employ CoUniverse middleware[2] [3], which has also been developed by MU and CESNET. Purpose of the CoUniverse is to orchestrate complex collaborative environments built upon numerous point-to-point multimedia transmissions.

The CoUniverse provides aforementioned collaborative environments with a set of general features required in virtually any networked multimedia application, particularly: (a) keeping account of participating network nodes (machines), their network capabilities, multimedia processing features and capacity; (b) maintaining records of

---

[1] http://ultragrid.cz.
[2] http://couniverse.sitola.cz.

data sources and corresponding requests; (c) dynamic response to changes in any knowledge above; (d) optimizing data distribution structure using including application-level multicast and multimedia transcoding options; (e) and configuring single-purpose point-to-point multimedia applications to cooperate in an advanced environment.

In order to achieve these goals, the CoUniverse builds a control plane independent from data transmissions. One of nodes in the environment, called Application Group Controller, plays a prominent role in this network: it centralizes information from the other nodes and decides on data distribution structure.

CoUnSiL is created on top of the CoUniverse. On each client of CoUnSiL always starts core of CoUniverse which gives access to all functionality of CoUniverse. While utilizing general features of the CoUniverse, the CoUnSiL client defines transmission requirements, operates the user interface and adds features like raising hand and giving the floor.

A listener of topology, which responds on any change, is used in CoUnSiL. If any node changes its state, leave or come, CoUnSiL client is performing appropriate action. In case of leaving, assigned media application is stopped and vice versa in case a new node is coming. CoUnSiL is also reacting when a student "raises hand" in CoUnSiL GUI – highlighting the student's window.

CoUnSiL client automatically distributes windows on desktop. First it calculates position where to place the windows; this calculation takes account of number of connected users and a layout scheme defined in a configuration file. This layout can be defined for each machine independently.

In case that an UltraGrid window crashes or stops refreshing the content, the window is closed and automatically reopened by CoUniverse with no impact on the rest of application. Because windows restored automatically are not placed back to their original position, CoUnSiL periodically checks position of all windows and reorganizes them when needed.

# 6  Evaluation

## 6.1  Prototype Evaluation

The first evaluation was rather informal. Our goals were: (a) to demonstrate the abilities of the UltraGrid and CoUniverse in a scenario close to the "real-world" settings; (b) test the prototype and our technologies in the seminar rooms of the Centre for Students with Special Needs. We performed a simulated seminar given by a university lecturer. Participants were questioned on usability and observed issues and asked for suggestions on future development from the user's point of view afterwards. The simulated lecture took 40 min, questioning further then 20 min.

Five students, a lecturer, and a sign language interpreter participated in this evaluation. We equipped the All-in-One computers HP Compaq Elite 8300 with Logitech QuickCam 9000 web camera. The teacher wore a wireless microphone; the interpreter used a headset. The interpreter operated in the room next to the seminar room occupied with other participants. As a CoUnSiL server, we used a computer with Intel Core i7, 16 GB RAM, NVidia GTX 960, Gigabit Ethernet LAN.

We collected multiple comments and suggestions on future improvements. The most crucial were: the need for the self-view, to ensure synchronization of audio and video streams between teacher and the interpreter, to implement a procedure for "raising the hand". Several minor comments addressed the window sizes, video quality and the area captured by the teacher's camera. All the remarks were taken into account in further development.

## 6.2 Window Size Evaluation

The second evaluation followed in November 2015. Its main purpose was to compare different window sizes. The evaluation was based on mockup static web pages with predefined layouts on a display with a native resolution of 1920 × 1080 px. The layouts consisted of two windows of the resolution 640 × 480 px which corresponded to the interpreter and teacher video streams. Resolutions and sizes of smaller windows (representing students) decreased with their growing number: 6 windows of 360 × 270 px, 8 windows of 300 × 225 px and 18 windows of 240 × 180 px. There was only one window containing the short video recording (2–4 min long). We refer them to as active window. The rest were static images taken as screenshots from videos. In case of the layout with 8 windows of students, we considered two alternatives: (a) the active window will remain the same size (300 × 225 px); (b) the size of the active window to be 400 × 300 px. All the videos were encoded in H.264. The reference video (640 × 480 px) has 30 frames per second (fps), the rest were 25 fps. Each video includes different message that was further questioned in the questionnaire. We questioned 6 males and 3 females on their subjective perception of video quality. The additional question regarding the content of signed message from video clip verified their comprehension. Table 1 summarizes acquired responses.

**Table 1.** Summary of the user evaluation. Values in the upper half of the table represent the average of 9 responses on four-point Likert scale (4 = definitely agree, 1 = definitely disagree).

| Video resolution | 640×480 | 400×300 | 300×225 | 240×180 |
|---|---|---|---|---|
| The video quality was sufficient enough to understand the content. | 3.4 | 3.6 | 3.6 | 3.0 |
| The video quality was comfortable for watching all the time. | 3.0 | 3.1 | 2.6 | 1.8 |
| The video would be comfortable for watching even in the longer period (10–20 minutes). | 2.6 | 2.4 | 1.7 | 1.3 |
| A number of correct answers to the complementary question. | 6 | 6 | 3 | 4 |
| A number of incorrect answers to the complementary question. | 1 | 1 | 3 | 3 |
| A number of "Do not know" answers. | 2 | 2 | 3 | 2 |

The lowest resolution is hardly usable even for a short period which corresponds with e.g. time for asking a question. Although the number of participants is not representative, the results suggested the need for further investigation of video resolution and the upper boundary on a number of participating students.

### 6.3  CoUnSiL 1.0 Evaluation

We held the third evaluation at the beginning of March 2016. Our goal was to test the CoUnSiL client version 1.0 (described above) likewise the prototype implementation. The evaluation was held at the same rooms as the previous one. Three students, a lecturer, and a sign language interpreter participated in this evaluation.

Opposed to the previous setup, we used the integrated webcams for students and Logitech CC3000e set and VGA-to-USB frame grabber for the teacher. The interpreter's computer was equipped with Philips SPC 1330 NC web camera and ClearOne Chat 150 speakerphone. The video streams were of $640 \times 480$ pixels for the teacher and the interpreter and $320 \times 240$ px for students with 30 fps. Presentation stream was $640 \times 480$ px at 15 fps.

The simulated lecture took 20 min, followed by the discussion. We structured the discussion into four main topics: quality of video streams, the audio quality between the interpreter and the seminar room, the size and the placement of the presentation window, utilization of the self-view window. Students and the interpreter complained about the low resolution of the presentation that made the text on the slide barely readable. Self-view was appreciated especially by the interpreter who was checking regularly whether he was captured properly. Further, we discussed the procedure of raising the hand and the opposite approach when the teacher asks a particular student to speak. Since the CoUnSiL 1.0 was unable to realize switching or selecting students from the teacher's interface, this will be one of our goals for the next version.

## 7  Conclusions

Our goal is to provide easy-to-use yet powerful tool which improves the quality of learning for students with special needs and support to effectively utilize the free capacity of sign language interpreters nationwide and possibly worldwide. During the development, we collaborate intensively with the target group of users – interpreters, deaf students, as well as lecturers who regularly teach lessons (workshops, seminars) in which deaf students participate. Besides further improvements of the application, we are going to run the pilot deployment of the CoUnSiL system for several seminars in Spring semester 2016. The system will be deployed and tested as a remote site of interpreters in collaboration with partners of the project.

**Acknowledgement.**  This work has been supported by Faculty of Informatics Dean's program and Development Fund of CESNET.

## References

1. Slovák, P., Troubil P., Holub P.: GColl: Enhancing trust in flexible group-to-group videoconferencing. Extended Abstracts of the 28th International Conference on Human factors in Computing Systems. ACM SIGCHI 2010, pp. 3607–3612 (2010)

2. Holub, P., et al.: High-definition multimedia for multiparty low-latency interactive communication. Future Gener. Comput. Syst. **22**(8), 856–861 (2006). Amsterdam, The Netherlands, Elsevier Science, ISSN 0167-739X

3. Liška, M., Holub, P.: CoUniverse: framework for building self-organizing collaborative environments using extreme-bandwidth media applications. In: César, E., Alexander, M., Streit, A., Träff, J.L., Cérin, C., Knüpfer, A., Kranzlmüller, D., Jha, S. (eds.) Euro-Par 2008 Workshops. LNCS, vol. 5415, pp. 339–351. Springer, Heidelberg (2009)

4. Ponsard, C., Sutera, J., Henin, M.: Video relay service for signing deaf - lessons learnt from a pilot study. In: Holzinger, A., Miesenberger, K. (eds.) USAB 2009. LNCS, vol. 5889, pp. 511–522. Springer, Heidelberg (2009). doi:10.1007/978-3-642-10308-7_38

5. Video Remote Interpreting. Standard Practise Paper. © 2010 Registry of Interpreters for the Deaf, Inc. Written by the Video Interpreting Task Force 2010. http://rid.org/about-interpreting/standard-practice-papers/

6. RIT Libraries: Interpreter Resources: Video Relay & Video Remote Interpreters. http://infoguides.rit.edu/c.php?g=441626&p=3013020

7. Vogler, C., Tucker, P., Williams, N.: Mixed local and remote participation in teleconferences from a deaf and hard of hearing perspective. In: ASSETS 2013 Proceedings of the 15th International ACM SIGACCESS Conference on Computers and Accessibility. ACM, New York (2013). doi:10.1145/2513383.2517035

8. King, C.M., Parks, E.: Bilingual web conferencing with multi-point videos. Paper Presented at International Symposium on Technology and Deaf Education, National Technical Institute of the Deaf, Rochester, NY, 21 June 2010

9. Sklenák, T.: Videokonference pro neslyšící. Videoconferencing for Deaf. Master's thesis. Masaryk University, Brno (2010)

10. GURIEC Video Interpreting Repository. Gallaudet University, Washington, DC. http://www.gallaudet.edu/guriec/programs-and-projects/video-interpreting-repository.html

# Classifiers in Arab Gloss Annotation System for Arabic Sign Language

Nadia Aouiti[✉] and Mohamed Jemni

Research Laboratory LaTICE, Tunis National Higher School of Engineering (ENSIT),
University of Tunis, 5, Avenue Taha Hussein, B.P. 56, Bab Mnara, 1008 Tunis, Tunisia
nadia.aouiti@gmail.com, mohamed.jemni@fst.rnu.tn

**Abstract.** As we know deaf people present about 70 million of the person in the word. 17 million of this community is only in Arabic word. Therefore this community of person require more and more attention from researchers and precisely SLMT (Sign Language Machine Translation) researchers to be able to practice their natural right which is communication with other person. In this context the research laboratory LaTICE of the University of Tunis lunched science many years the project WebSign [1] aiming to translate automatically a written text to sign language whatever the language as input (English, French, Arabic, etc.). WebSign is a Web application. It is based on the technology of avatar (animation in virtual world). The input of the system is a text in natural language. The output is a real-time and online interpretation in sign language. This interpretation is constructed thanks to a dictionary of word and signs. The creation of this dictionary can be made in an incremental way by users who propose signs corresponding to words [2]. Our work as a part of this project aims to develop a translation module from Arabic text to Sign Language to be integrated in the WebSign project. This module offers to Arab Deaf and hearing people a tool facilitating their communication. Anyone can use this tool to translate an Arabic written text to Arabic Sign Language (ArSL). In fact in this level, it's very useful to define a transcription system for Arabic Sign Language based on Arabic Gloss. This intermediate annotation system is a textual representation of sign language that covers the different parameters of the sign with a simplified representation to avoid the complexity of understanding [3].

**Keywords:** Arabic gloss annotation system · Machine translation · ArSL

## 1   Introduction

In Arabic world many Arabic sign language exist depending to the countries such as (Egyptian Sign Language, Tunisian Sign Language, Yamani Sign Language, etc.). Like spoken language ArSL differ from one country to another, that's due to the dialect and not to the mother tongue. But, if a Tunisian deaf and a Yemeni deaf met, they can resort to another sign language to understand each other. Some initiative had been lunched toward the unification of sign language in some Arabic countries, because it comes from the same spoken language which is Arabic [4]. Many papers and dictionary have been published aiming to unify ArSL (Arab dictionary Sign Language for deaf part 1 [5] and

© Springer International Publishing Switzerland 2016
K. Miesenberger et al. (Eds.): ICCHP 2016, Part II, LNCS 9759, pp. 400–406, 2016.
DOI: 10.1007/978-3-319-41267-2_56

part 2 [6], Arabic and Quatarian Sign Language Rules [7]) which are the initiative of the representatives of eighteen Arab country from governmental and civil entities. This community contains an important number of experts in ArSL and also members in different association for deaf person. Despite the important efforts focused on the problem of standardization of ArSL, unifying is still a challenge for many researchers. It's due to the absent of a transcription system to write Arabic text in a simplified text and forms. This annotation system covers hand shape, movement, location, facial expression, etc. of the sign. In this context our work aims to define an intermediate representation from Arabic text to ArSL basing on the construction of Arabic Gloss. This work is a part of a machine translation taking Arabic written text as an input and giving ArSL gesture as an output.

The paper is organized as follows: Sect. 2, is devoted to an enumeration of the existing works. In Sect. 3 we present an overview of our proposed ArSL gloss Annotation system for the two levels: Syntax and morphology function and Classifiers with some some illustrative examples.

## 2  Related Work

From the Eighties, researchers begin to analyze and process sign language. Next, they design and develop routines for communication intra-deaf and between hearing and deaf people. Starting from the design of automatic annotation system of the various components of sign language and coming to the 3D synthesis of signs through virtual avatars [8]. SL has gained increased attention by scientist, many studies was done in the field of MT (Machine Translation). However, the progression of each one depends on the language in input (Latin language or Arabic language). In fact we have two groups of works related to Sign Language MT as follows: systems for Non Arabic language and systems for Arabic language.

Multitude of MT exists for non-Arabic language such as: (Morrissey and Way 2005, 2006) and (Morrissey et al. 2007) proposed a system using example-based methodologies as part of a data-driven framework. (Stein et al. 2006) has proposed a statistical MT system which uses Hidden Markov Model and IBM models for training the data. (Chiu et al. 2007) also present a Statistical approach for their work with Chinese and Taiwanese Sign Language [9]. The European cultural Heritage Online (ECHO) built a corpus of Swedish, Britsh and Dutsh SLs (Morrissey 2008); It contains five children's stories signed in each SL. Approximately 500 signed sentences were collected in each language. The EUDICO Linguistic Annotator (ELAN) [10] was used to analyze the sentences [11].

However, as previously stated, existing research for Arabic language are rare. For instance, Almasoud and Al-Khalifa [12] proposed a translation system using ArSL translation rules and domain ontology to produce SignWriting notation (SW). The SW will be used as a final output of the system or as an intermediate level for future avatar animation. Mohandes [13] developed a system to translate Arabic text into Arabic SL. This system is one stage in the process of developing a system to translate Arabic speech to Arabic sign language. The system has a database, to store Arabic dictionary words with the corresponding signs and file names of the sign representation video. If the user enter a word that's available in the database, the recorded clip will be shown, otherwise if the word is not included then finger spelling is done. Similarly, Tawassol, is another Arabic system for translating Arabic text to Arabic SL. The system is used as an educational tool. It contains a translator, a dictionary of Arabic words for a set of categories, in addition to a finger spelling editor. The system uses Vcommunicator Gesture Builder 2.0 with Sign Smith Studio program to generate the animation output. Almohimed et al. [14] developed a translation system. They have adopted a chunk-based Example on Based Machine Translation (EBMT) system which produces output sign sentences by comparing the Arabic text input to matching text fragments, or 'chunks'. The corpus of this system has 203 signed sentences with content restricted to the domain of instructional language, typically used in deaf education. The system has two phases. Phase1 is run only once; it pre-compiles the chunks and their associated signs. Phase2 is the translation system, that converts Arabic input into ArSL output using Arabic Gloss annotation system only for facial expression (Mouth, Head, Eyes and Nose) [3].

# 3   Arabic Sign Language Gloss Annotation System

SL is a natural means of communication for deaf people based on facial expression and body movement. Therefore a MT from a written text to SL needs a lot of parameters to identify the appropriate sign. In this case, using an annotation system as an intermediate representation from a written text to SL is very useful. This gloss notation system is a textual representation used to describe a sequence of signs based on labels of spoken language. In gloss, we use a transcription symbols to express many types of linguistic information such as: topic of the sentence, type of the sentence, location of the sign, Hand-Shape, gesture sign, repeated sign, sign made with one, both and/or alternating hands, finger spelled sign, classifier sign, etc.

In this section, we will present a gloss notation system for Arabic language basing on Arabic and Quatarian Sign Language rules [7] and referring to all policies outlined in the agreements Liddell [15]. This work is composed by three main parts that define the system in whole which are: Syntax and Morphology Rules, Classifiers and Facial Expression.

In this paper, we will present a brief description of the syntax and morphology rules which are already defined with details in our last article [3], then we will present in details the classifiers part of the Arabic Gloss annotation proposed system.

## 3.1   Syntax and Morphology Rules

Each gloss is represented by an Arabic word. One Arabic word identifies on ArSL sign. To better introduce this section, we will present an illustrative example that cover a number of gloss used to transcribe an Arabic sentence to ArSL Gloss:

This figure presents a transcription of the sentence "Ahmed hates the foods of his sister". This transcription covers the annotation of:

Personal pronouns (1-ع-سلم /Possession for masculine absent pronoun). Pronouns are divided into three groups taking account the specificity of the Arabic Language as follows: (absent pronoun, addressee pronoun and speaker pronoun), in each category we have the first person (the signer in a conversation) and others (another person) (Fig. 1).

**Fig. 1.** Transcription of the sentence Ahmed hates the foods of his sister

Type of the sentence: sentence is classified into four different types such as: interrogative, negative, conditional and rhetorical form. Each type of the sentence is defined by a line above the sentence and marked by his appropriate symbols. In this sentence, we used the symbol "سلب" for negative form.

The symbol "#" before the word used to be finger spelled. In general it's used to spell the names.

All verbs in the annotation system are in infinitive form.

In addition to the annotation symbols used for the transcription of the sentence above. In Arabic gloss annotation system, we have defined a multitude of symbols to cover syntax and morphology rules such as: topic of the sentence, Action of the sign, reduplication, tenses, articulation for emphasis, location of the sign, etc. [3].

### 3.2 Classifiers

In this system, we transcribed not only syntax and morphological function of ArSL but also, movement, form and size of the objects. It's what we call Classifiers in ASL. The classifiers can be used to indicate the type, size, name, movement, or the extent of the information given. Signs containing a classifier are called "classifier predicates" [16] or "verbs of motion, orientation, and location" [17]. A predicate is the part of the sentence has been changed, the subject of the sentence or a name or other noun phrase in the sentence. Each classifier, present an additional information about subject (noun or object). It's a description information of the form, location, etc. In fact, in ASL many types of classifiers exist which have the same function (description of object, the object's moving, the relation of the object with other object or person, etc.), but they differ according to the characteristic of the classifier as follow:

- Semantic classifiers
- Body classifiers
- Hand shape classifiers
- Locative classifiers

– Instrument classifiers

In this section, we will present the hand shape classifier used for ArSL. By analogy to ASL, Classifiers are represented with the word "صنــف". Additional Arabic letters or numbers are added for each one to give descriptive information about a subject or predicate (verb) as follows:

"صنف أ, صنف س,صنف خ (مسطحة),صنف ن,صنف ن (مسطحة), صنف ن (مغير), صنف ل", etc.". For example the classifier "صنف ن" as the picture below, can means a small and around thing, the width or the height of one object, etc. Such as: button, disc, moon, small bottle, etc. If we use this classifier to describe the object button that's popped of, we can sign a jacket and use the classifier "صنف ن" then we throw it (Fig. 2).

صنف ح          صنف ن          صنف ن(مغير)

صنف خ          صنف س          صنف ن (مسطحة)

**Fig. 2.** Letters hand shape classifiers in ArSL

These different types of Classifiers are defined to represent the object itself, to describe the movement of the sign and to define haw the object is related to another object or people. The description of the meaning for each classifier is presented in the list below:

– "صنف-ن" Classifier « ن »:
  • round flat objects: a disc, a medal, piece of food, Crescent, moon, *Eyeglasses Sunglasses,* etc.
– "(صنف-ن (مغير)" Classifier « ن - مغير »:
  • Long cylindrical objects: hose, etc.
  • Viewing devices: *goggles, telescope,* camera, etc.
  • Short cylindrical objects: *cup, glass, bottle*, etc.
– "(صنف-ن (مسطحة)" Classifier « ن - مسطحة »:
  • Short object: small stack of papers, etc.
  • Flat object with squared edges: ruler, paper, etc.
  • Thin object
– "صنف-خ" Classifier « خ »:
  • Describing a flat object with position relative to the signer: roof, tunnel, street, etc.
– "صنف-ح" Classifier « ح »:
  • Curved objects: bowl, sink, basin or a digging device
– "صنف-س" Classifier « س »:
  • Smooth, flat surfaces: road, window, wall, door, land, mountain, table, etc.

- Smooth, flat surfaces: a long stretch of desert or sky, etc.
- Flat mobile surfaces: valley
- To give some description: person's height (tall or short), light, etc.
- The position of an object or a person: Distant, near, before or behind, above, next to, outside, etc.
- "صنّف-هـ" Classifier « هـ »:
  - Solid, spherical objects.
  - Handles conveyance: Motorcycle, bicycle, etc.

## 4 Conclusion

This paper presents a proposed annotation system for ArSL Gloss to limit the problem of standardization of ArSL. This annotation system does not cover only syntax and morphology function of ArSL, but also the movement and location of the sign called classifiers. Therefore as a future direction we will focus on the study of the grammar of the face to achieve the various components of our proposed system.

## References

1. Jemni, M., El Ghoul, O.: An avatar based approach for automatic interpretation of text to sign language. In: 9th European Conference for the Advancement of the Assistive Technologies in Europe, San Sebastián 3-5 October 2007
2. Jemni, M., Elghoul, O.: A system to make signs using collaborative approach. In: Miesenberger, K., Klaus, J., Zagler, W.L., Karshmer, A.I. (eds.) ICCHP 2008. LNCS, vol. 5105, pp. 670–677. Springer, Heidelberg (2008)
3. Aouiti, N., Jemni, M.: Arabic gloss anotation system for Arabic sign language. In: The fifth International Conference of Information and Communication Technology and Accessibility (2015)
4. Jemni, M., Samreen, S., Othmen, A., Tmar, Z., Aouiti, N.: Toward the creation arab gloss for Arabic sign language annotation. In: The fifth International Conference of Information and Communication Technology and Accessibility (2013)
5. The representative of eighteen Arab countries from governmental and civil entities, The Arabic Dictionary of Gesture for Deaf part 1
6. The representative of eighteen Arab countries from governmental and civil entities, The Arabic Dictionary of Gesture for Deaf part 2
7. Samreen, S., Albanali, M.: Arabic and Quatarian Sign Language Rules, Quatar (2009)
8. Othem, A., Jemni, M.: Statistical Sign Language machine translation: from English written to American Sign Language Gloss. In: IJCSI International Journal of Computer Science Issues, vol. 8, issue 5, no. 3, pp. 65–73 (2011)
9. Aouiti, N., Jemni, M.: For a translating system from Arabic Text to Sign Language. In: Proceedings of the Conference Universal Learning Design, Paris 2014. Masaryk University, Brno, pp. 33–38 (2014). ISBN 978–80-210-6882-7
10. Official ELAN website: http://www.lat-mpi.eu/tools/elan/
11. Almohimeed, A., Wald, M., Damper, R.: An Arabic Sign Language corpus for instructional language in school. In: LREC 2010: 4th Workshop on the Representation and Processing of

Sign Languages: Corpora and Sign Language Technologies, pp. 81–82. European Language Resources Association 17-22 May 2010

12. Almsoud, A., Al-Khalifa, H.: A proposed semantic machine translation system for translating Arabic text to Arabic Sign Language. In: Second Kuwait Conference on E-Services and E-Systems, pp. 79–84, 5-7 April 2011

13. Mohandes, M.: Automatic translation of arabic text to Arabic sign language. In: ICGST International Journal on Artificial Intelligence and Machine Learning AIML, vol. 6, pp. 15–19 (2006)

14. Almohimeed, A., Wald, M., Damper, R.I.: Arabic text to arabic sign language translation system for the deaf and hearing-impaired community. In: EMNLP The Second Workshop on Speech and Language Processing for Assistive Technologies (SLPAT), Edinburgh, pp. 101–109 (2011)

15. Liddell, S.K.: Grammar, Gesture and Meaning in American Sign Language. Cambridge University Press, NewYork (2003)

16. Liddel, S.K.: An Investigation into the Syntactic Structure of American Sign Language. University of California, Thèse de doctorat (1977)

17. Supalla, T.: Morphology of verbs of motion and location in American Sign Language. In: Proceedings of the Second National Symposium of Sign Language Research and Teaching, pp. 27–45 (1978)

# Image-Based Approach for Generating Facial Expressions

Ibtissem Talbi[(✉)], Oussama El Ghoul, and Mohamed Jemni

Research Laboratory of Technologies of Information and Communication and Electrical Engineering LaTICE, University of Tunis, Tunis, Tunisia
ibtissem.talbi@hotmail.fr, elghoul.oussama@gmail.com,
Mohamed.jemni@fst.rnu.tn

**Abstract.** In this paper we present a new approach to automatically generate realistic facial expressions by using image based techniques. The proposed approach aims to combine a deformation method with the Phong illumination model. We use real images of real person to generate 2D animations. However, we created an algorithm which consists of changing the color of a party of face in order to give a lot of realism to the deformation methods. The purpose is to propose methods to improve the process of creating realistic facial animations and to facilitate the communication between deaf and hearing impaired people.

**Keywords:** Deaf and hearing impaired people · Illumination model · Facial expressions · 2D animations · Image-based techniques

## 1 Introduction

Sign languages are the primary means of communication for people with hearing disabilities. These languages use two principal components which as the manual gestures and the non-manuals gestures. The manual gestures can involve simultaneously combining hand shapes, orientation and movement of the hands. The Non Manual gestures are an essential component to express phonology, morphology, and syntax of the signing sentences such as arms or body and facial expressions to fluidly express a speaker's thoughts [1].

The facial expressions play an important role in communication with sign language [2]. Facial expressions are used in sign languages to convey specific meanings. In a simple case, emotional facial expressions affect the meaning of a sentence. Many of them indicate specific grammatical information about sentences [3]. Some emotional states, such as happiness or sadness, are expressed through a smile or a frown.

The communication between Deaf and Hearing people has been very complicated and usually deaf people have to communicate through an interpreter or in written form with hearing people. Many applications and systems have been developed to facilitate communication and interaction between deaf people, hearing impaired people, and even between natural persons, but unfortunately these applications need more of realism [4]. Indeed, the problem of low realism of the signing characters can result limited legibility of animated signs and low appeal of virtual signers. The research presented in this article

© Springer International Publishing Switzerland 2016
K. Miesenberger et al. (Eds.): ICCHP 2016, Part II, LNCS 9759, pp. 407–414, 2016.
DOI: 10.1007/978-3-319-41267-2_57

in order to improve communication and access to information for deaf people who face many communication problems.

In this context, we propose a new solution to generate a realistic facial expression based on 2D images. This idea consists of creating intermediate frames from an input image to generate fluid signing gestures. Indeed, image-based rendering techniques are becoming increasingly popular, in recent years, because they can provide real scenes exclusively from a set of 2D images [9, 10]. Image-based rendering is one of the most interesting new research areas in computer graphics. The union between computer graphics and computer vision has created a lot of research in the structure of the scene modelling and the appearance of images [11]. It has built image-based models to re-record new points view and new images closer to the reality ([5, 6, 8]). For this reason, we have opted to use such techniques to produce the set of images needed to synthesize the video sequences.

The rest of the paper is organized as follows: Sect. 2 presents the deformation techniques. Section 3 describes our contribution. Section 4 provides a brief conclusion and discusses the future prospects of our proposed method.

## 2  Deformation Techniques

Several deformation techniques can be used to generate the intermediate images in the form of 2D curves, textured images, 3D models or projections. So, we review here some of the proposed approaches of deformation techniques including the Linear Interpolation, it is a first degree method that passes a straight line through every two consecutive points of the input image [12]. Another technique is named *Anchor Points Interpolation*, with which the user specifies the correspondence between points. It considers characterize the movement as well as the space-time path between each pair of anchors. *B-splines or NURBS Interpolation* is another deformation techniques used to interpolate the keys poses smoothly and thus generates smoother movement and more natural [15].

Burtnyk and Wein have proposed the skeletal deformation, it is a different method based on 2D skeletons. We draw only skeletons for the parts of the character to animate [16, 17].

The most important deformation technique is a free form deformation initially described by Sederberg and Parry, which based on the idea of enclosing an object within a cube or another hull object, and transforming the object within the hull as the hull is deformed [14].

Mesh deformation is based on the edge detection or the characteristic points in order to change their locations to create intermediate images.

These deformation techniques have been used in different approaches and have given good results, but they have some disadvantages in sign language. Indeed, there are some actions that we can't represent them if we use only one of the deformation techniques citing for example the suction and puffing of the cheeks. For this reason, we propose a new approach that allows representing the sign language gesture closer to the real. In the next part we will represent our contribution to remedy this problem.

## 3   Our Contribution

The proposed work forms a part of the WebSign project [18] which was developed within the Research Laboratory of Technologies of Information and Communication & Electrical Engineering LaTICE in Tunisia. The main objective of this project is to improve the deaf accessibility to information and this by offering a set of tools able to translate and synthesize any information, written in the form of text in oral language [17] or in the form of sign language notations [19, 20], to fluid signing.

The next objective of this project is to develop a new system able to generate 2D signing gestures in the form of video sequence from a single image. The process of generating animation includes two parts. Firstly, the system begins with the creation of intermediates images and this by transforming the main image using image based rendering techniques. An illumination model will be adopted here to correct the unde-sired effects. Secondly, the system will combine the obtained images which are created in the previous step to generate video sequences. The Fig. 1 shows an overview of the main architecture of the proposed system.

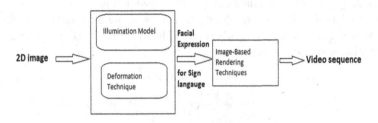

**Fig. 1.**  The architecture of the proposed approach

As known, sign languages (SL) are visual-gestural languages whose forms consist of sequences of movements and configurations of the hands and arms, face, and upper torso. Typically, the existing methods of animations cannot simulate precisely the correct signing gestures and this due to the complexity of such motions. To overcome this problem, we propose to apply an illumination model at the deformed regions in order to change the color nuances and therefore emulate the desired effects. For example,

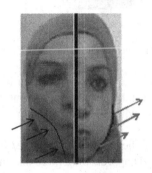

**Fig. 2.**  Suction and puffing of the cheeks

**Fig. 3.** Light's effect on small and large angle (Color figure online)

we can see in Fig. 2 that the image contrasts are modified after the puffing and sucking of cheeks. By applying animation techniques, some transformations could not lead to relevant results. For that, we propose that changing the colors of affected pixels via an illumination model could enhance the obtained results.

In the real world, we see objects because they reflect light, so their color is visible only if it receives light. In this part of our contribution we propose to compute the illumination of each pixel undergoes a transformation during an animation. When the angle is small, as at location B, a large amount of light will reflect back and the point will have a light color. Where the angle is large, as at location A, little light will reflect back and the point will have a dark color as we shown in Fig. 3.

Then, we based on the average color we seek the angle between the normal vector and the vector representing the light's source. The figure below (Fig. 4) represents the angle's variation for just the red frame.

**Fig. 4.** Color variation computing in a face (Color figure online)

The green curve represents the variations of green intensity in RGB mode in the above image. However, the red and blue curves represent the red and the blue intensity. We calculated the average color when the normal vector (surface orientation) is perpendicular to the light vector.

Modeling work was done in the context of virtual reality and this model has proven given the quality of rendered 3D approaching more and more of reality. Among these models found that Phong.

### 3.1 Phong Illumination Model

Illumination models are used to generate the color of an object's surface at a given point on that surface. Due to the relationship defined in the model between the surface of the objects and the lights affecting it, illumination models are also called shading models or lighting models. Surfaces in real world environments receive light in 3 ways:

- Directly from existing light source such as the sun or a lit candle.
- Light that passes and refracts through transparent objects such as water or a glass vase.
- Light reflected, bounced, or diffused from other existing surfaces in the environment.

The intensity in point is the sum of ambient reflection, diffuse reflection and specular reflection:

**Ambient Reflection.** The Ambient Reflection [7] is the most basic. It gives a uniform sort of color to an object, while the parts of the object that are protected from the light. There is normally a certain intensity and color involved. The result is a sort of matte looking object. The reflected intensity Ia of any point on the surface is:

$$Ia = Ka \cdot Isa \tag{1}$$

- Ia - ambient light intensity
- $Ka \in [0,1]$ - surface ambient reflectivity

**Diffuse Reflection.** Lambert said that the energy reflected off a surface from a light source is proportional to the cosine of the incident angle, i, between the light and the normal to the surface [15]. The reflected intensity Id of a point on the surface is:

$$Id = Isd \cdot Kd \cdot cos\,\theta \tag{2}$$

- Ip - the point light intensity.
- $Kd \in [0,1]$ - the surface diffuse reflectivity.

**Specular Reflection.** The light is reflected in the direction of perfect mirror reflection. It is the mirror-like reflection of light from a surface, in which light from a single incoming direction is reflected into a single outgoing direction [7]. An ideal specular surface (mirror) reflects light exclusively in one direction:

$$Is = Iss \cdot Ks \cdot (cos\,\alpha)^n \tag{3}$$

- Is: intensity of reflected specular light
- Iss: intensity of specular light from the source
- Ks: specular reflection coefficient of the material
- $\alpha$: the angle between the directions of reflection and views

In the RGB system, we add the intensities red, green and blue. Then you will see the three equations

$$I_R = IsaR \cdot KaR + IsdR \cdot KdR \cdot cos\,\theta + IssR \cdot KsR \cdot (cos\ \alpha)^n \qquad (4)$$

$$I_V = IsaV \cdot KaV + IsdV \cdot KdV \cdot cos\,\theta + IssV \cdot KsV \cdot (cos\ \alpha)^n \qquad (5)$$

$$I_B = IsaB \cdot KaB + IsdB \cdot KdB \cdot cos\,\theta + IssB \cdot KsB \cdot (cos\ \alpha)^n \qquad (6)$$

### 3.2 Our Algorithm

Using the illumination model, we proved that the color change can give a suction effect on the cheeks. Subsequently, we concluded that we can deform the cheeks by the color change without using deformation techniques.

The studies cited above show that the sucked cheeks pixels correspond generally to the pixels with lower intensity. Based on this scientific hypothesis, we could confirm that the simulation of the cheek actions such as sucking and puffing can be performed by changing the intensity values of pixels in the cheek region. In other words, we believe that an increase in the intensity values of pixels results the simulation of puffing action, while, the diminution of these ones results the simulation of sucking action. But, in order to prove the performance of the proposed method, we have developed an algorithm that allows browsing all the pixels of the image and changing their intensity values and this with a view to emulate the puffy cheeks. The main objective of the proposed algorithm is to increase the intensity values of the pixels which are located in the center of the cheek and reduce the intensity values of the pixels which are located in its extremities. For this idea, we have designed our algorithm like following:

- Step 1: divide the image into a grid, and representing the color of each cell in the grid, called a pixel, with a numeric value.
- Step 2: browse rows and columns that represent the right cheek
- Step 3: change the pixel intensity value, depending on the distance which separates the current pixel from the central pixel. The pixels which are concentrated close to the center of the cheeks will have higher intensity.

## 4   Conclusion and Future Work

The main goal of this paper is to give a basic understanding of the variety of techniques that can be used to simulate facial expressions near to the reality. But the more important goal is to help deaf people to communicate with each other easily without providing the feeling of being in communication with virtual person. To achieve this, an effort has been made to describe our approach to each of these steps starting with calculate the color in each pixel transformed.

We also talked in this article about our algorithm which considers the Phong theorem to simulate the puffing and the sucking effects of the cheeks. The next step of this work is to propose an algorithm able to generate deformed face. However, we see this idea as a simple beginning of an ambitious research to build a sign language gestures based on 2D images.

# References

1. Adamo-Villani, N., Hayward, K., Lestina, J., Wilbur, R.: Effective animation of sign language with prosodic elements for annotation of digital educational content. In: ACM SIGGRAPH 2010 Talks, p. 39 (2010)
2. Kacorri, H.: Models of linguistic facial expressions for American Sign Language animation. ACM SIGACCESS Accessibility Comput. (105) (2013)
3. Huenerfauth, M.; Lu, P., Rosenberg, A.: Evaluating importance of facial expression in American Sign Language and Pidgin Signed English animations. In: Proceedings of the 13th International ACM SIGACCESS Conference on Computers and Accessibility (ASSETS 2011), Dundee, Scotland. ACM Press, New York (2011)
4. Wallraven, C., Breidt, M., Cunningham, D.W., Bülthoff, H.H.: Evaluating perceptual realism of animated facial expressions. ACM Trans. Appl. Percept. **4**, 1–20 (2008)
5. Shum, H.Y., Kang, S.B.: A review of image-based rendering techniques. In: IEEE/SPIE Visual Communications and Image Processing (VCIP), pp. 2–13 (2000)
6. Liu, K., Ostermann, J.: An Image-based Talking Head System, LIPS 2009 Special Session in AVSP 2009. Norwich, UK (2009)
7. Debevec, P.: Rendering synthetic objects into real scenes: bridging traditional and image-based graphics with global illumination and high dynamic range photography, University of California at Berkeley, SIGGRAPH (1998)
8. Shum, H.Y., Kang, S.B., Chan, S.C.: Survey of image-based representations and compression techniques. IEEE Trans. Circuits Syst. Video Technol. **13**(11), 1020–1037 (2003)
9. Zhang, C., Chen, T.: A survey on image-based rendering: representation, sampling and compression. SP:IC **19**(1), 1–28 (2004)
10. Kang, S.B.: A survey of image-based rendering techniques, vol. 3641, San Jose, CA, 23–29 January 1999
11. Su, G.M., Lai, Y.C., Kwasinski, A., Wang, H.: 3D Visual Communications, 1st edn. Wiley, UK (2013)
12. Chen, S., Williams, L.: View interpolation for image synthesis. In: Computer Graphics (SIGGRAPH 1993), pp. 279–288, August 1993
13. Shum, H.-Y., Szeliski, R.: Construction of panoramic mosaics with global and local alignment. Int. J. Comput. Vis. **36**(2), 101–130 (2000)
14. Holzschuch, N.: "Modèles de matériaux", iMAGIS is a joint project of CNRS - INPG - INRIA – UJF, The University of Texas at Austin, Department of Computer Sciences, Graphics – Spring 2013
15. Triki Bchir, O.: Modelisation, reconstruction et animation de personnages virtuels 3D à partir de dessins manuels 2D", Computer Science. Universit_eRen_e Descartes - Paris V, French (2005)
16. Burtnyk, N., Wein, M.: Interactive skeleton techniques for enhancing motion dynamics in key frame animation. In: Procedings of the 2nd Annual Conference on Computer Graphics and Interactive Techniques, BowlingGreen, Ohio, June 1976, vol. 19, pp. 78–80 (1976)
17. Jemni, M., Elghoul, O.: A system to make signs using collaborative approach. In: Miesenberger, K., Klaus, J., Zagler, W.L., Karshmer, A.I. (eds.) ICCHP 2008. LNCS, vol. 5105, pp. 670–677. Springer, Heidelberg (2008)
18. ElGhoul, O., Jemni, M.: WebSign: a system to make and interpret signs using 3D Avatars. In: Proceedings of the Second International Workshop on Sign Language Translation and Avatar Technology (SLTAT), Dundee, UK (2011)

19. Bouzid, Y., Jemni, M.: An Avatar based approach for automatically interpreting a sign language notation. In: Proceedings of the 13th IEEE International Conference on Advanced Learning Technologies, pp. 92–94 (2013)
20. Bouzid, Y., Jemni, M.: A virtual signer to interpret SignWriting. In: Miesenberger, K., Fels, D., Archambault, D., Peňáz, P., Zagler, W. (eds.) ICCHP 2014, Part II. LNCS, vol. 8548, pp. 458–465. Springer, Heidelberg (2014)

# Developing eLecture Materials for Hearing Impaired Students and Researchers: Designing Multiple-Video Programs and Usability Assessment

Ritsuko Kikusawa[1,2(✉)], Motoko Okumoto[3], Takuya Kubo[4],
and Laura Rodrigo[5]

[1] National Museum of Ethnology, 10-1 Senri Expopark,
Suita-shi, Osaka 565-8511, Japan
ritsuko@minpaku.ac.jp
[2] The Graduate University for Advanced Studies,
Hayama, Kanagawa 240-0193, Japan
[3] University of Kyoto, Nihonmatsu-cho, Sakyo-ku, Kyoto-shi 606-8501, Japan
okumoto.motoko.3m@kyoto-u.ac.jp
[4] Hiroshima University, Kagamiyama,
Higashi-Hiroshima-shi, Hiroshima 739-8524, Japan
takuyak0625@gmail.com
[5] Autonomous University of Madrid,
Campus de Cantoblanco, 28049 Madrid, Spain
laurarodricr@gmail.com

**Abstract.** eLecture materials for deaf and hard-of-hearing scholars with sign language (SL) interpretation inevitably include multiple-video content. A usability assessment of such a program was conducted, contrasting presentations with 3 media and 6 media views. The preference of Deaf researchers for SL interpretation to subtitles was confirmed, and the need for different arrangements depending on the needs of users was discovered. A prototype system was developed based on the results.

**Keywords:** Electure · Multiple-Video program · Sign language · Hearing impaired

## 1 Introduction

This study investigates ways to best develop eLecture materials for deaf and hard-of-hearing (D/HH) students and researchers. Despite the claim by D/HH scholars that such materials should include sign language (SL) interpretation as well as subtitles, providing captions in written text is generally assumed enough by university instructors. eLecture materials with SL interpretation require multiple video footages running simultaneously, but the effect of such a program was not clear. A project was therefore established aimed at developing ways to archive sign language linguistics lectures at international symposia hosted by Kikusawa in 2012 through 2014. The assumed

© Springer International Publishing Switzerland 2016
K. Miesenberger et al. (Eds.): ICCHP 2016, Part II, LNCS 9759, pp. 415–418, 2016.
DOI: 10.1007/978-3-319-41267-2_58

audience of the final product consisted of students and researchers in Japan, both D/HH and hearing.

The following were recorded at the symposium on site and used (with minimum editing) for this purpose: video (and audio, when applicable) recording of the presenter, PPt, and American Sign Language (ASL) interpretation. When the language of presentation was either ASL or International Sign (IS), the audio of the English interpretation was also recorded on site. For English subtitles, edited caption transcriptions were used. Additional procedures after each event consisted of translations from English to Japanese, then from Japanese to JSL. The latter was done by professional Deaf interpreters. Table 1 shows the types of materials collected.

**Table 1.** Sample combinations of the materials used in this study. *Abbreviations: ASL: American Sign Language, Eng: English (written or spoken), IS: International Sign, Jap: Japanese (written or spoken), JSL: Japanese Sign Language, LP: Language of Presentation.

| Combination | | 1 | 2 | 3 | 4 | 5 |
|---|---|---|---|---|---|---|
| AUDIO | (original) | Eng [LP] | Eng [LP] | Eng | Jap [LP] | – |
| VIDEO 1 | ASL/IS | ASL | ASL | IS [LP] | – | – |
| VIDEO 2 | JSL | ✓ | ✓ | ✓ | ✓ | ✓ [LP] |
| VIDEO 3 | PPT | Eng | Eng | Eng | Jap | Jap |
| VIDEO 4 | PRESENTER | ✓ | ✓ | =VIDEO 2 | ✓ | =VIDEO 2 |
| TEXT 1 | ENGLISH SUBTITLES | Caption | Caption | Caption | – | – |
| TEXT 2 | JAPANESE SUBTITLES | Translation | – | Translation | Caption | Translation |
| TOTAL # OF MEDIA | | 6 | 5 | 6 | 4 | 3 |

Research on eLearning materials for D/HH has been limited to captioning technology and effective presentations of subtitles [3], and the use of a SL is limited to text material-narration [1]. In addition, multiple-video presentations are not typically included in the discussion of eLearning studies [2, 4]. The materials of each lecture were edited therefore in a cut-and-try manner from the scratch into a single video program following opinions and suggestions of Deaf members on our team. The results are posted on a website: http://www.minpaku.ac.jp/sokendai/ssll/lecture.html .

## 2  Usability Assessment and Results

One of our main interests was the positive and negative effects of a program containing multiple-media with multiple-videos. For this, a program with 3 windows (PPt, subtitles in Japanese, and JSL interpretation) and with 6 windows (PPt, presenter, subtitles in English and Japanese, JSL and ASL interpretation) were contrasted. The first 10 min of each was extracted and were viewed by 2 Deaf and 2 hearing academics. The qualitative experiment included (i) questionnaire, (ii) video viewing with eye tracking with a 5 min break between the two programs, (iii) an interview session, (iv) simulation of an "ideal" structure of a 6 media program using mock-ups (Fig. 1).

**Fig. 1.** The screen arrangement of the programs used for usability assessment

Results were found which require further investigation, such as: (1) Increasing the number of media provides D/HH with more options, and helps hearing audience concentrate on the program for a longer period. (2) Deaf researchers, although fluent in reading and writing Japanese and English, mostly viewed the SL interpretation. (3) The Deaf viewer's eyes were mostly fixed on the SL interpretation. Occasional quick references were made to PPt (but not to subtitles), for easier capturing of technical terms and points of the lecture. (4) The types of media needed and their arrangement differs from person to person. Reflecting such, a downloadable PC application in which the user can select and customize the combination of available media for each program has been developed (Fig. 2). Further investigation of how the system is actively used and utilized is planned for practical and experimental purposes.

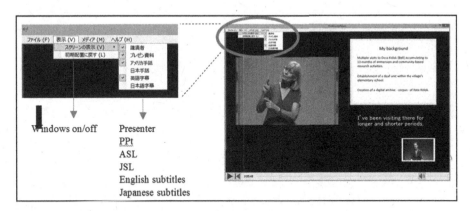

**Fig. 2.** A screen shot of the PC application with customisable windows (The position and size of each window can be adjusted by the user by using the drag-and-drop function.)

**Acknowledgements.** This research was funded by The Center for the Promotion of Integrated Sciences Research, The Graduate University for Advanced Studies [SOKENDAI] (2012–2015).

# References

1. Elhadj, Y., Huang, T., Zeng, Z., Li, C., Leung, C.-S.: Multimedia educational content for saudi deaf. In: Huang, T., Zeng, Z., Li, C., Leung, C.S. (eds.) ICONIP 2012, Part IV. LNCS, vol. 7666, pp. 164–171. Springer, Heidelberg (2012)
2. Mayer, R.: Introduction to multimedia learning. In: Mayer, R.E. (ed.) The Cambridge Handbook of Multimedia Learning, pp. 1–18. Cambridge University Press, Cambridge (2005)
3. Okura, T.: Universal design of learning environment using active captioning. J. Multimed. Educ. Res. 5(2), 45–54 (2008)
4. Stanisavljevic, Z., Nikolic, B., Tartalja, I., Milutinovic, V.: A classification of eLearning tools based on the applied multimedia. Multimed. Tools Appl. 74(11), 3843–3880 (2013)

# Effect of Vibration on Listening Sound
# for a Person with Hearing Loss

Junichi Kanebako[1][✉], Toshimasa Yamanaka[1], and Miki Namatame[2]

[1] Graduate School of Comprehensive Human Science,
University of Tsukuba, Tsukuba, Japan
kanebako@kansei.tsukuba.ac.jp,
tyam@geijutsu.tsukuba.ac.jp
[2] Tsukuba University of Technology, Tsukuba, Japan
miki@a.tsukuba-tech.ac.jp

**Abstract.** We examined the effect of tactile stimuli for rhythm discrimination and hearing impression with ABX methods. We used semantic differential scale composed of 10 impression word pairs. We set the experiment condition with Audio (A), Audio+Vibration (AV), and Vibration (V). In the rhythm discrimination test, the hearing loss group showed better performance in (AV) than (A). The without hearing loss group showed that (AV) differed non-significantly from (A). We focused to "Enjoyable - Not fun" in impression evaluation for the effect of tactile stimuli. As a result of "Enjoyable - Not fun" impression evaluation showed significant differences with hearing loss group and without hearing loss group in (AV) between (A).

**Keywords:** Tactile · Vibration · Rhythm · Music

## 1 Introduction

Studies of substitution for sense organs are conducted such as presenting pace information of the sound on the tip of finger like Braille patterns or transferring rhythms through vibrations [1–3]. Conventional studies frequently evaluate the accuracy of music actions by the presented information. This study aims to clarify rhythm discrimination results and the effects on evaluation when a person with hearing loss listens to music using a device to supplement sounds with vibrations. We will verify the following hypotheses by conducting the same experiment on persons without hearing loss. H1: When vibration stimuli are presented simultaneously with sounds, the rhythm discrimination improves more than when sound stimuli alone are presented. H2: Improvement of discrimination is more remarkable in the group with hearing loss than in the group without hearing loss. H3: When vibration stimuli are presented simultaneously with sounds, the enjoyable impression improves more than in the case of sound stimulation alone. H4: Improved evaluation of "Enjoyable" is more remarkable in the group with hearing loss than in the group without hearing loss.

Our study involves two participant groups: one without hearing losses and one with hearing losses. In the hearing loss group we have both hearing aid and cochlear implant

© Springer International Publishing Switzerland 2016
K. Miesenberger et al. (Eds.): ICCHP 2016, Part II, LNCS 9759, pp. 419–423, 2016.
DOI: 10.1007/978-3-319-41267-2_59

users with varying level of hearing impairment. In the following, for readability, we denote the participants with Hearing Loss and No Hearing Loss "HL" and "NHL", respectively.

## 2  Rhythm Discrimination Test and Result

A participant plan was established to provide groups divided by a combination of two-factors, i.e., whether the subject has hearing loss or not and the stimuli presenting condition with Audio(A), Audio+Vibration(AV), vibration(V). Twelve university students with moderate congenital sensorineural hearing loss and twelve university students without hearing loss participated in the experiment. Twenty rhythm patterns from Primary Measures of Music Audiation (PMMA) and 20 rhythm patterns from Intermediate Measures of Music Audiation (IMMA), both of which are rhythm patterns of the music ability test developed by Edwin E. Gordon [4], were used as stimuli for the experiment, and a 523.3 Hz (C5) square wave was used as the sound source.

The percentage of correct answers to the rhythm test (%) was measured as the index to measure rhythm discrimination ability. For impression evaluation from listening to music, 10 adjective pairs (7 point scale) were used. The experiment was conducted in a single room where it was hard to hear outside sounds. Stimuli were given from a computer through a speaker and a vibration device connected to it via an audio interface. The vibration device consisted of a wooden housing with piezoelectric elements fastened to it and can regenerate waves at frequencies from 100 Hz to 40 kHz. The subject holds the device with a single hand firmly so that he or she can feel vibrations at the finger tips. The ABX method was used for the rhythm discrimination test. A test session (Fig. 1) consisted of 40 cycles of bellow-mentioned trial, and a total of three test sessions were conducted, one under each presentation condition. The subject was record the impression of stimuli on the questionnaire at the end of each test session.

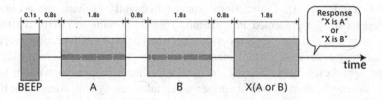

**Fig. 1.**  One trial example by ABX method

In the rhythm discrimination result, the average of the percentages of correct answers of persons without hearing loss was 89.58 % (SD = 6.01) under (A), 88.96 % (SD = 8.08) under (AV), and 73.96 % (SD = 8.62) under (V). The average of the percentages of correct answers of persons with hearing loss was 75.00 (SD = 9.47) under (A), 80.42 % (SD = 7.89) under (AV), and 77.5 % (SD = 8.79) under (V). In the percentages of correct answers, a two-way factorial analysis of variance was conducted using two factors (Table 1), i.e., presence or absence of hearing loss and the presentation condition. The results of simple verification of main effects and multiple comparisons are depicted in the Fig. 2.

**Table 1.** Analysis of variance table of a percentage of correct answers

| source of variation | Sum of squares | flexibility | mean square | F value |
|---|---|---|---|---|
| **between-subject** | | | | |
| NHL·HL | 767 | 1 | 767 | 6.4 p < .05 |
| Error | 2636.1 | 22 | | |
| **within-subject** | | | | |
| presentation condition | 1032.5 | 2 | 516.2 | 12.477 p < .01 |
| presentation condition×NHL·HL | 1022.1 | 2 | 511 | 12.351 p < .01 |
| error ( presentation condition ) | 1820.5 | 44 | 41.4 | |
| total | 7278.8 | 71 | | |

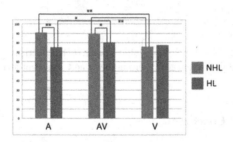

**Fig. 2.** Bar graph of a percentage of correct answers (The asterisks *, ** indicate that the coefficients are statistically different from zero at the 5, and 1 percent level, respectively). (Color figure online)

For the presence or absence of hearing loss and the presentation condition, we conducted a two-way factorial analysis of variance on 10 items of impression evaluation. Presence or absence of the main effect and interaction for each evaluation item are listed in the Table 2.

No interaction between presentation condition and presence or absence of hearing loss was observed in any evaluation item. Multiple comparisons on the 10th item "Enjoyable - Not fun" revealed differences in the results between (A) and (AV) in persons with hearing loss were significant at the 1 percent level and that for persons without hearing loss was observed between (A) and (AV) was significant at the 5 percent level (Fig. 3).

**Table 2.** List of each outcome measure, main effect and interaction

| Q # | Evaluation Adjectives 1 | Evaluation Adjectives 2 | Main effect of NHL / HL | Main effect of presentation condition | interaction |
|-----|-------------------------|-------------------------|-------------------------|----------------------------------------|-------------|
| 1 | Like | Dislike | p<.05 | p<.05 | NO |
| 2 | Kindle | Calm | NO | p<.05 | NO |
| 3 | Rhythmical | Not rhythmic | NO | NO | NO |
| 4 | Comfortable | Uncomfortable | NO | p<.05 | NO |
| 5 | Pleasant | Unpleasant | NO | p<.05 | NO |
| 6 | Fresh | Stale | NO | p<.05 | NO |
| 7 | Intense | Weak | NO | NO | NO |
| 8 | Severe | Friendly | NO | p<.05 | NO |
| 9 | Interesting | Boring | NO | p<.01 | NO |
| 10 | Enjoyable | Not fun | NO | p<.01 | NO |

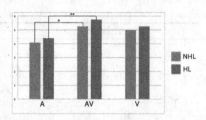

**Fig. 3.** Bar graph of a "Not fun – Enjoyable" point. (The asterisks *, ** indicate that the coefficients are statistically different from zero at the 5, and 1 percent level, respectively.) (Color figure online)

## 2.1 Discussion and Conclusion

The results of this test show that the rhythm discrimination of persons with hearing loss improves when vibration stimuli are presented simultaneously with sound stimuli as compared with sound stimuli alone being presented. In persons without hearing loss, no difference in the rhythm discrimination results was observed when vibration stimuli are presented simultaneously with sound stimuli.

Analysis of variance on each evaluation item using the presence or absence of hearing loss as the between-subjects factor and the presentation condition (A, AV, or V) as the within-subject factor revealed a significant difference in "Not fun – Enjoyable" between (A) and (AV) both in the persons without hearing losses and those with hearing loss. Because the difference between (A) and (AV) in the hearing loss group was significant at the 1 percent level and the difference between (A) and (AV) in the without hearing loss group was significant at the 5 percent level, the evaluation of "Enjoyable" is more remarkable in persons with hearing loss than in persons without hearing loss. This study revealed that simultaneous presentation of sound and vibration stimuli improves the rhythm discrimination of persons with hearing loss and also provides enjoyment for both groups of persons with and without hearing loss.

# References

1. Galvin, K.L., Ginis, J., Cowan, R.S.C., Blamey, P.J., Clark, G.M.: A comparison of a new prototype tickle talker with a tactaid 7. Aust. N. Z. J. Audiol. 23(1), 16–18 (2001)
2. Ifukube, T.: From sensory substitute technology to virtual reality research. Artif. Life Robot. 2(4), 145–150 (1998)
3. Sasaki, N., Ohtsuka, S., Ishii, K., Harakawa, T.: The development of a music presentation system by two vibrators. In: Miesenberger, K., Fels, D., Archambault, D., Peňáz, P., Zagler, W. (eds.) ICCHP 2014, Part I. LNCS, vol. 8547, pp. 602–605. Springer, Heidelberg (2014)
4. Gordon, E.E.: Primary Measures of Music Audiation, Intermediate Measures of Music Audiation. GIA Publications, Inc., Chicago (1979, 1986)

# Designing a Collaborative Interaction Experience for a Puppet Show System for Hearing-Impaired Children

Ryohei Egusa[1,2](✉), Tsugunosuke Sakai[3], Haruya Tamaki[3],
Fusako Kusunoki[4], Miki Namatame[5], Hiroshi Mizoguchi[3],
and Shigenori Inagaki[2]

[1] Japan Society for the Promotion of Science, Chiyoda-ku, Tokyo, Japan
126d103d@stu.kobe-u.ac.jp
[2] Kobe University, Tsurukabuto, Nada, Kobe, Hyogo, Japan
inagakis@kobe-u.ac.jp
[3] Tokyo University of Science, Yamazaki, Noda, Chiba, Japan
{7515624,7515636}@ed.tus.ac.jp, hm@rs.noda.tus.ac.jp
[4] Tama Art University, Yarimizu, Hachioji, Tokyo, Japan
kusunoki@tamabi.ac.jp
[5] Tsukuba University of Technology, Amakubo, Tsukuba, Ibaraki, Japan
miki@a.tsukuba-tech.ac.jp

**Abstract.** In this study we have developed a puppet shows system for hearing-impaired children. It is difficult for hearing-impaired children to experience a puppet show. One of the reasons that hearing-impaired children have difficulty experiencing a puppet show is because the performance is a collaborative interaction experience. Collaborative interaction experiences encourage immersive viewing toward an empathetic understanding of the characters. This paper aims to design a collaborative interaction experience function for hearing-impaired children. This function provides collaborative interaction for the audience to work with the characters to resolve issues in the story by using body motion. From the results of the evaluation experiment, we understood that the collaborative interaction experience function generally supported an immersive puppet show experience for the audience.

**Keywords:** Puppet show · Hearing-impaired children · Kinect sensor · Collaborative interaction experience

## 1 Background and Purpose of the Study

Puppet shows have taken root in the cultures of nations in the world [1]. In particular, puppet shows are a familiar cultural experience for children when the puppets are used as educational materials in preschools and elementary schools. A puppet show is an important experience that supports the development of children [2].

However, it is difficult for hearing-impaired children to experience a puppet show for two reasons. First, the dialogue of the story in the puppet show is important. Hearing-impaired children find it difficult to hear these sounds. An appropriate means

K. Miesenberger et al. (Eds.): ICCHP 2016, Part II, LNCS 9759, pp. 424–432, 2016.
DOI: 10.1007/978-3-319-41267-2_60

to secure such information is needed to resolve this problem. The second reason that hearing-impaired children have difficulty experiencing a puppet show is because the performance is an interactive experience. This means not just watching the puppet show but participating in the performance itself. For example, there are puppet shows in which the viewers and characters solve problems together during the story, or the viewers participate by helping create the puppets or the stage [3]. Such collaborative interaction experiences encourage immersive viewing toward an enjoyable experience, comprehension of the story, and an empathetic understanding of the characters. In many cases, however, these shows are not designed for hearing-impaired children. It would be difficult to say that there has been sufficient research on puppet shows for these young people.

We have conducted research and development on a puppet shows system for hearing-impaired children [4]. To provide information to the audience, the system has two functions: a dialogue projection and an interactive experience. The dialogue projection function shows the dialogue in the background as text information in a markup balloon. This enables the audience to obtain the sound information via the text. Using range image sensors, the story participation function uses body motion as a communication method. The puppet show system thereby offers an interactive experience without relying upon the spoken word. Past research has studied the effect on an audience of interactive experience and availability of the dialogue projection.

In this paper, we have developed a novel collaborative interaction experience function using body motion. This provides collaborative interaction for the audience to work with the characters to resolve issues in the story. We also conducted an evaluation of the puppet show system. The purpose of this experiment was to consider the effectiveness of the system and the functions as it supported the immersive viewing experience of the puppet show.

## 2  Related Research

There're many means to design amusements for special needs [5–7]. However, there is no research relating to amusement design for children with a hearing impairment in the ICCHP proceedings from 2010 till 2014. Also, in the field of technological development relating to the securing information as a right, research relating to puppet shows is rare, as far as we know. As mentioned in Sect. 1, puppets shows are an important cultural experience. The importance of research into puppet shows that are suitable for children with a hearing impairment can therefore be highlighted.

There are two main methods of communication for Hearing-Impaired Children. One is the use of the medium of text. In research that develops text-related technology to ensure universal information delivery, systems have been developed that convert vocal information in lectures and meetings into text [8]. The use of text is an effective method, particularly when there is more than one speaker. This is because the provision of markup balloons and annotation facilitates the linking of a speaker to what is being said [9]. This method is also considered effective for securing information about dialogues in puppet shows, where there are some performers.

Expression via the medium of body movement is the other main means of communication. Language using the body such as sign language and gesture is a familiar means of communication for many children with a hearing impairment. There has been a great deal of research in the field of video games with regard to sensing technology that measures body movement and the senses of immersion and presence [10]. With regard to the gaming experience, it has been pointed out that introducing an operation through body movement provides a social experience in which the screen and space are shared [11]. This social experience is also important in puppet shows because the audience shares a single stage and space. This helps to establish collaborative interaction without using the spoken word.

## 3    System

### 3.1    Framework

The system is based upon a paper puppet theater, where the stage consists of a screen, paper-puppets, projector, and a PC. An animation is projected onto the screen from the projector, as a backdrop.

**Fig. 1.**  Dialogue projection function

### 3.2    Dialogue Projection Function

The puppet show system, by converting the characters' dialogues into text for display, serves the function of securing delivery of information about spoken dialogues in the puppet show to people with a hearing impairment. All the dialogues in the puppet show are expressed visually, as they are said, in the backdrop animation. The reason for voice actors read the dialogues aloud is that these spoken dialogues are for hearing-impaired children who still possess some hearing ability. Figure 1 Shows the dialogue projection function. The dialogues are displayed in the form of markup balloons projected behind the puppet. Thus, the audience is able to obtain information about the puppet's behavior and spoken dialogues within the same field of vision. This function delivers to hearing-impaired children accurately and in real time.

### 3.3    Collaborative Interaction Experience Function

There are two games in the system's puppet show. Both of the games are presented as problems to the audience. The puppet show story progresses as the audience members collaborate to clear the game. The two types of games are an electricity generation game and a fill-in-the blank game.

**The Electricity Generation Game.** In the electricity generation game, the audience is asked to make the electricity that the character in the story needs. Electric power is made by two people energetically jumping on a pump at the same time (Fig. 2, Left). Next, the audience members form pairs to execute simultaneous jumping motions. Last, after each pair of audience members succeeds in simultaneously jumping a certain number of times, the game switches to the next pair. This game is designed to require collaborative play by the participants.

**Fig. 2.** Screen of the electricity generation (left), game playing the fill-in-blank game (right)

**The Fill-in-the-Blank Game.** In the fill-in-the-blank game, the audience members are asked to teach the character in the story how to use correct grammar. The audience members are shown a sentence without a Japanese positional particle, and options of particles to fill in the blank. The problems are shown on a screen, which enables all audience members to share information. These positional particles are parts of speech that play an important role in the Japanese language for defining subjects and objects. Hearing-impaired children in Japan—particularly those who use sign language on a daily basis—tend to struggle with the use of positional particles in writing because sign language sometimes omits this part of speech.

Next, one representative is chosen from the audience. The representative then chooses the option that he or she thinks is correct. When doing so, the audience jumps in front of the selection (Fig. 2, Right). If the choice is correct, the next problem is displayed. If the choice is incorrect, the audience can try to solve the same problem again. When they at last provide the correct answer, the character understands grammatically correct Japanese, and the story continues. Through the experience of teaching the character grammar, the audience can enjoy themselves while confirming and sharing their knowledge. This game is designed to promote collaborative learning as the whole audience consults one another and engages in discussion.

## 4   Evaluation Experiments

### 4.1   Methods

**Participants.** Participants are 18 hearing-impaired children in their $3^{rd}$ to $6^{th}$ year of elementary school (8 to 12 years of age).

**Tasks and Procedures.** The participants watched the puppet show system for 30 min and completed a paper questionnaire consisting of 20 items: four concerning viewing experience of puppet-show, eight concerning electricity generation, and eight character fill-in-the blank games. Four items concerning viewing experience of puppet-show is assessed enjoyment and understanding the puppet-show's story: "The puppet-show was fun", "I was able to understand the story of the puppet-show", "I concentrated on viewing the puppet-show from start to finish", "I was able to read each character's dialogues in the balloons".

The other items were created as follows: In the electricity generation game, based on the physical/emotional/narrative presence (PENS) scale, there were eight items concerning the subject: "The electricity generation game was emotionally engaging", "I experience feelings as deeply in the electricity generation game as I have in real life", "When playing the electricity generation game I feel as if I was part of the puppet-show's story", "I am not impacted emotionally by events in the electricity generation game", etc. "I am not impacted emotionally by events in the electricity generation game" was reverse scoring item.

In the fill-in-the-blank game, which was also based on the PENS scale, there were eight items concerning the subject: "the fill-in-the-blank game was emotionally engaging", "When I accomplished something in the fill-in-the-blank game I experienced genuine pride", "I am not impacted emotionally by events in the fill-in-the-blank game", "When playing the fill-in-the-blank game, I feel transported to the time and place of the puppet-show's story", etc. "I am not impacted emotionally by events in the fill-in-the-blank game" was reverse scoring item.

For each item the participants replied using a seven-stage Likert scale with *strongly agree* to *strongly disagree*.

**Study Date.** The study was conducted on November 30, 2015.

## 4.2   Results

Participant replies were classified into the positive responses of strongly agree, agree, and somewhat agree, and neutral or negative responses of no strong opinion, somewhat disagree, disagree, and strongly disagree. Reverse scoring is necessary so that lower scores indicate higher positive affectivity. We conducted an analysis of the differences in count between positive, neutral, and negative replies for each item using a 1 x 2 Fisher's exact test. There was difference in two population proportions.

Table 1 shows the responses from the participants about the questions about the viewing experience of the puppet-show. In the viewing experience of the puppet- show, in all of four items, there were significantly more positive answers than neutral or negative replies. These results suggest that the puppet-show system supported hearing-impaired children to view the puppet-show. Moreover, they were able to enjoy and understand the story of the puppet-show.

**Table 1.** Questions examining the viewing experience

| Items | SA | A | SWA | N | SWD | D | SD |
|---|---|---|---|---|---|---|---|
| 1. The puppet-show was fun[**] | 12 | 4 | 2 | 0 | 0 | 0 | 0 |
| 2. I was able to understand the story of the puppet-show[**] | 14 | 3 | 1 | 0 | 0 | 0 | 0 |
| 3. I concentrated on viewing the puppet-show from start to finish[**] | 7 | 6 | 4 | 0 | 0 | 0 | 1 |
| 4. I was able to read each character's dialogues in the balloons[**] | 10 | 6 | 0 | 1 | 0 | 1 | 0 |

$N = 18$, [**]$p < 0.01$, [*]$p < 0.05$, [n.s.]: not significant.
SA: Strongly Agree A: Agree SWA: Somewhat agree N: No strong option SWD: Somewhat disagree.
D: Disagree SD: Strongly disagree.

Table 2 shows the responses from the participants about the questions about the experience of the electricity generation game. In the electricity generation game, in six of eight items concerning PENS scale, there were significantly more positive answers than neutral or negative replies. For the two items concerning PENS scale, "When playing the electricity generation game, I feel transported to the time and place of the puppet-show's story" and "When moving through the electricity generation game, I feel as if I am in the world of the puppet-show actually", no significant difference was seen between positive replies and neutral or negative ones. These results suggest that the collaborative interaction experience in the electricity generation game prompted participation and absorption in the puppet-show for hearing-impaired children. However, there are difficult to reveal the effectiveness of the game from the aspect of promoting their immersion and feeling presence.

Table 3 shows the responses from the participants about the questions about the experience of the fill-in-the-blank game. In the fill-in-the-blank game, for seven of the eight items concerning physical/emotional/narrative presence, there were significantly more positive answers than neutral or negative replies. For the one item on the

**Table 2.** Questions examining the electricity generation game

| Items | SA | A | SWA | N | SWD | D | SD |
|---|---|---|---|---|---|---|---|
| 1. The electricity generation game was emotionally engaging [**] | 13 | 2 | 2 | 1 | 0 | 0 | 0 |
| 2. I experience feelings as deeply in the electricity generation game as I have in real life [**] | 8 | 5 | 3 | 1 | 0 | 0 | 1 |
| 3. When playing the electricity generation game I feel as if I was part of the puppet-show's story [**] | 10 | 1 | 3 | 3 | 0 | 1 | 0 |
| 4. When I accomplished something in the electricity generation game I experienced genuine pride [**] | 5 | 3 | 4 | 2 | 0 | 1 | 3 |
| 5. I had reactions to events and characters of the puppet-show in the electricity generation game as if they were real [*] | 3 | 1 | 2 | 0 | 1 | 3 | 8 |
| 6. I am not impacted emotionally by events in the electricity generation game (-) [*] | 6 | 1 | 1 | 5 | 0 | 3 | 2 |
| 7. When playing the electricity generation game, I feel transported to the time and place of the puppet-show's story [n.s] | 6 | 1 | 1 | 5 | 0 | 3 | 2 |
| 8. When moving through the electricity generation game, I feel as if I am in the world of the puppet-show actually [n.s] | 6 | 3 | 2 | 1 | 0 | 5 | 1 |

$N = 18$, [**] $p < .01$, [*] $p < .05$, [n.s]: not significant, (-): reverse scoring item
SA: Strongly Agree A: Agree SWA: Somewhat agree N: No strong option
SWD: Somewhat disagree D: Disagree SD: Strongly disagree

**Table 3.** Questions examining the fill-in-the-blank game

| Items | SA | A | SWA | N | SWD | D | SD |
|---|---|---|---|---|---|---|---|
| 9. The fill-in-the-blank game was emotionally engaging [*] | 9 | 3 | 3 | 1 | 0 | 1 | 1 |
| 10. I experience feelings as deeply in the fill-in-the-blank game as I have in real life [**] | 5 | 8 | 1 | 2 | 0 | 1 | 1 |
| 11. When playing the fill-in-the-blank game I feel as if I was part of the puppet-show's story [n.s] | 6 | 2 | 2 | 2 | 4 | 1 | 1 |
| 12. When I accomplished something in the fill-in-the-blank game I experienced genuine pride [**] | 9 | 2 | 4 | 2 | 0 | 0 | 1 |
| 13. I had reactions to events and characters of the puppet-show in the fill-in-the-blank game as if they were real [*] | 7 | 3 | 5 | 1 | 0 | 1 | 1 |
| 14. I am not impacted emotionally by events in the fill-in-the-blank game (-) [*] | 3 | 0 | 0 | 2 | 1 | 6 | 6 |
| 15. When playing the fill-in-the-blank game, I feel transported to the time and place of the puppet-show's story [*] | 3 | 5 | 4 | 4 | 1 | 0 | 1 |
| 16. When moving through the fill-in-the-blank game, I feel as if I am in the world of the puppet-show actually [*] | 8 | 0 | 5 | 3 | 0 | 1 | 1 |

$N = 18$, [**] $p < .01$, [*] $p < .05$, [n.s]: not significant, (-): reverse scoring item
SA: Strongly Agree A: Agree SWA: Somewhat agree N: No strong option
SWD: Somewhat disagree D: Disagree SD: Strongly disagree

physical/emotional/narrative presence scale, "When playing the fill-in-the-blank game I feel as if I was part of the puppet-show's story", no significant difference was seen between positive replies and neutral or negative ones. These results suggest that the effectiveness of the collaborative interaction experience in the fill-in-the-blank game was not revealed from the aspect of the participation. However, from the aspect of immersion and presence, these results proved the effectiveness of the fill-in-the-blank game for the hearing-impaired children.

# 5  Conclusion

From the results of the experiment, we understood that the system and the collaborative interaction experience function generally supported an immersive puppet show experience for the audience. The puppet-show system supported hearing-impaired children to view the puppet-show with enjoyment and understanding the story of the puppet-show. Moreover, results show the collaborative interaction experience prompted feeling presence, participation, absorption, or immersion in the puppet-show for hearing-impaired children. We expect that system we developed is the useful way to enrich puppet-show experience of them.

However, no significant differences were seen between positive and neutral or negative replies for a number of items related to physical/emotional/narrative presence. In the future, we'll further analyze the causes to improve the system.

**Acknowledgments.** This work was supported by Grant-in-Aid for JSPS Fellows Number 15J00608 and JSPS KAKENHI Grant Number 26282061.

# References

1. Zweers, J.U., Los Angeles County Museum: History of Puppetry. Los Angeles County Museum, Los Angeles (1959)
2. Hunt, T., Renfro, N.: Puppetry in Early Childhood Education. Nancy Renfro Studios, Austin (1982)
3. Kato, A.: Gulliver in Puppet Land - Study on Puppet Show in Czech Republic. Chuokoron-Shinsha Inc., Tokyo (1978)
4. Egusa, R., Nakayama, T., Nakadai, T., Kusunoki, F., Namatame, M., Mizoguchi, H., Inagaki, S.: Puppet show system for children with hearing disability: evaluation of story participation function with physical movement. In: Proceedings of Global Learn, pp. 482–487. AACE Press, Berlin (2015)
5. Kobayashi, M.: A basic inspection of wall-climbing support system for the visually challenged. In: Miesenberger, K., Klaus, J., Zagler, W., Karshmer, A. (eds.) ICCHP 2010, Part II. LNCS, vol. 6180, pp. 332–337. Springer, Heidelberg (2010)
6. Othman, A., El Ghoul, O., Jemni, M.: SportSign: A Service to Make Sports News Accessible to Deaf Persons in Sign Languages. In: Miesenberger, K., Klaus, J., Zagler, W., Karshmer, A. (eds.) ICCHP 2010, Part II. LNCS, vol. 6180, pp. 169–176. Springer, Heidelberg (2010)
7. Kobayashi, M.: Blind bowling support system which detects a number of remaining pins and a ball trajectory. In: Miesenberger, K., Fels, D., Archambault, D., Peňáz, P., Zagler, W. (eds.) ICCHP 2014, Part I. LNCS, vol. 8547, pp. 283–288. Springer, Heidelberg (2014)
8. Takeuchi, Y., Ohta, H., Ohnishi, N., Wakatsuki, D., Minagawa, H.: Extraction of displayed objects corresponding to demonstrative words for use in remote transcription. In: Miesenberger, K., Klaus, J., Zagler, W., Karshmer, A. (eds.) ICCHP 2010, Part II. LNCS, vol. 6180, pp. 152–159. Springer, Heidelberg (2010)
9. Wald, M.: Captioning multiple speakers using speech recognition to assist disabled people. In: Miesenberger, K., Klaus, J., Zagler, W.L., Karshmer, A.I. (eds.) ICCHP 2008. LNCS, vol. 5105, pp. 617–623. Springer, Heidelberg (2008)

10. McMahan, A.: Immersion, engaging, presence, a method for analyzing 3-D video games. In: Wolf, M.J.P., Perron, B. (eds.) The Video Game, Theory Reader, pp. 67–86. Routledge, Taylor & Francis Group, New York (2003)
11. Eisenberg, M., Pares, N.: Tangible and full-body interfaces in learning. In: Sawyer, R.K. (ed.) The Cambridge Handbook of the Learning Science, pp. 339–357. Cambridge University Press, New York (2014)

# SingleScreenFocus for Deaf and Hard of Hearing Students

Raja S. Kushalnagar[✉], Poorna Kushalnagar, and Fadi Haddad

Gallaudet University, Washington, DC, 20002, USA
raja.kushalnagar@gmail.com, poorna.kushalnagar@gmail.com,
fadi.haddad@gmail.com

**Abstract.** Deaf and hard of hearing (DHH) students who use sign language interpreters have to simultaneously watch both the slides and interpreter. In addition, it is difficult to scan, pick and watch new information, as the the teacher, interpreter and slides tend to be spatially distributed around the room. In addition, they become tired more quickly than their hearing peers as they have to track the movement of the teacher and interpreter. We developed and evaluated a system to address the simultaneous challenges of multiple distributed visuals (teacher, slides and interpreter), and the teacher or interpreter can move, which adds to the difficulty. Our SingleScreenFocus system has two parts: a viewing system, and a tracking and recording system. The tracking and recording system uses a iPad mounted on a tracking device to automatically track and record the teacher, and another similar system to track and record the interpreter. The recordings are then automatically streamed to the student's large viewing screen. Our evaluation indicated that deaf and hard of hearing students prefer this system over a regular view in large classrooms because it reduced their need to split the attention between visuals and to search for details in the visuals.

**Keywords:** Deaf · Hard of hearing · Visual management

## 1 Introduction

Deaf and hard of hearing students often utilize sign language interpreters or real-time captioners to access mainstream classroom lectures. Students have to divide their visual attention between these and other information sources such as presentation materials, instructor, personal notes, and other classmates, which are often spatially distributed. As a result, deaf and hard of hearing students are likely to miss important content in the classroom environment due to need to split their attention between simultaneous visuals [4]. DHH students continue to be under-represented compared to their hearing peers: the graduation rate is 16 % for DHH students as compared to 30 % for hearing students [1].

We discuss the development and evaluation of a SingleScreenFocus system which aims to reduce the need to split attention between widely dispersed visuals by bringing together them (slides, interpreter and teacher) on one single screen in the classroom.

The student's screen shows the slides in the center along with two smaller screens that show the interpreter and teacher. The two small screens display the tracking system video, which tracks the teacher and interpreter as they can move around without

© Springer International Publishing Switzerland 2016
K. Miesenberger et al. (Eds.): ICCHP 2016, Part II, LNCS 9759, pp. 433–437, 2016.
DOI: 10.1007/978-3-319-41267-2_61

restrictions in the classroom. The fixed location of each visual means that the student can easily monitor the visuals without having to turn and locate the widely separated locations of the teacher, interpreter and slides.

Traditional lecture capture systems seem like promising solutions, but typically use only one camera to capture video, and, unless dedicated staff are on hand to manage the system, the view from the camera does not change and results in a video that is boring to watch. With only a single view, users may lack the visual information required for adequate context [3]. Dedicated video production staff can improve video context and interest, but at a significant cost. Moreover, a camera operator operating a single video camera or even multiple video cameras may not be able to predict the learning needs of a deaf or hard of hearing student, let alone several deaf and hard of hearing students [5].

We address this need for high quality close up views through our SingleScreenFocus system. It consists of two subsystems: (1) a viewing system, and (2) a tracking and recording system. The tracking and recording system uses an iPad mounted on a tracking device to automatically track and record the teacher. It also uses a second iPad mounted on a tracking device to automatically track and record the interpreter.

The recordings are then automatically streamed to the student's large viewing screen at a fixed size and location. The fixed size and location makes it easy for students to switch between the slides and interpreter quickly and effortlessly. Our system also provides a mechanism for deaf and hard of hearing users to easily customize their learning focus in the classroom for their own needs, by enabling them to select, focus and customize their view.

## 2  Background

Our SingleScreenFocus system builds on another research project called ClassInFocus [2]. Both SingleScreenFocus and ClassInFocus systems utilize the same concept of having different video streams in one screen during the classroom sessions for organized visual attention. Both systems draw inspiration from findings in cognitive psychology, literature on the visual needs of deaf and hard of hearing students in learning environments, and our own experiences and observations.

The difference between the SingleScreenFocus and ClassInFocus systems is the tracking of the teacher or interpreter. The ClassInFocus system uses a standalone camera to capture a single area; the teacher cannot move from that location without being out of view. The ClassInFocus system also connects to a video stream of a live interpreter from another location into the camera. The interpreter also has to stay still, so as not to go out of view. Additionally, the interpreter may have a hard time capturing all aural information because they are not in the same room, and have to depend on the quality of the audio as captured by the microphone, which also cannot move. As the teacher moves away from the microphone, the audio quality will worsen. By contrast, the SingleScreenFocus system uses a tracking system to track and follow both teacher and interpreter. The camera can then capture a close up, high quality view and display it on student's screen.

## 3  Development

We evaluated a prototype with six components. The video capture and streaming components consist of iPads that are mounted on two tracking systems. The two tracking systems work by following a radio transmitter unit worn by the teacher and interpreter. In turn the iPads connect wirelessly to a laptop through a private wireless router. The sixth and final component is a tablet that connects to the computer to provide the teacher with the ability to change slides or to write new information on the PowerPoint from the tablet (Fig. 1).

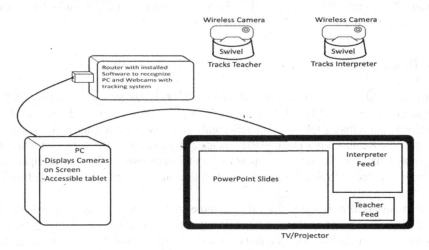

**Fig. 1.** SingleScreenFocus diagram

## 4  Evaluation

The SingleScreenFocus evaluation was carried out in a classroom with a teacher and interpreter. We had two equally long lectures on a historical topic that involved many slides and facts. Each lecture lasted for five minutes each so as to present a balanced, repeated measures evaluation. We recruited a total of 13 deaf and hard of hearing participants, ages 20–27 (5 female). All participants typically request accommodations such as sign language interpreters or captioners for classes or presentations.

We divided the participants into two groups, one with 6 students and the other with 7 students. After completing a short demographic questionnaire to determine eligibility for the test, the first group watched the lecture using SingleScreenFocus and then viewed the class without any video system. The second group watched the lecture without any video system, and then watched using SingleScreenFocus. The participants also viewed a 30 s introductory video to familiarize themselves. After each presentation, we collected surveys from each student regarding their experience in watching the lecture.

## 5  Results

We posed all questions with Likert scale answers. The participants rated their views of the classroom lecture by answering the questions. The first question (Q1) asked "What is your rating of the [Regular View/SingleScreenFocus] view lecture?" with answers ranging from 1 "Didn't like it at all" to 5-"Liked it a lot". The second question, (Q2), asked "Did the [Regular View/SingleScreenFocus] view help during the lecture?"

The third question, (Q3) asked "Is [Regular View/SingleScreenFocus] view easy to use?" The fourth question (Q4), asked "I am confident in using [Regular View/Single-ScreenFocus] view in class". The fifth and final question, (Q5), asked "I would recommend [Regular View/SingleScreenFocus] view for use by other deaf or hard of hearing students". Q2 through Q5 all had possible Likert responses ranging from 1-"Not at all" to 5-"Very much".

## 6  Discussion

Participants rated SingleScreenFocus much higher for Q1: the average rating for Single-ScreenFocus was 4.5 (SD = 0.5) whereas the regular view was only 3.7 (SD = 0.9). Similarly, participants felt that SingleScreenFocus was more helpful at 4.7 (0.5), as compared to Regular View at 4.0 (0.8) as indicated by their responses to Q2. Participants also noted that it was easier to use, as noted by their responses to Q3. For example, one participant noted, "[In SingleScreenFocus,] all information is easy to notice. [There is] less "empty space".

Participants also indicated that they felt more confident using SingleScreenFocus at 4.6 (0.5), as compared to Regular View at 3.9 (0.6) as indicated by their responses to Q4. Finally, participants indicated that they would be more likely to recommend Single-ScreenFocus at 4.8 (0.4), as compared to Regular View at 4.2 (0.7) to others as indicated by their responses to Q5.

## 7  Conclusion

We show that incorporating further technological innovations such as tracked views to reduce the need for switching views across widely spread visuals has benefits. The evaluation study with deaf and hard of hearing participants shows that they significantly prefer the SingleScreenFocus system over a regular view of a classroom lecture with an interpreter. The participants note that they are able to keep focus and not have to move their head while watching a single screen with SingleScreenFocus.

## 8  Future Work

Many more supporting features to collect or display additional visual information for deaf and hard of hearing students can be investigated in terms of usability and accessibility. One participant suggested "You could add a low light capable camera that is capable of accurately displaying the screen during low light situations when lights are dimmed for slide shows".

Based on this suggestion, a low light could be used as an add-on. The system could also be extended to seamlessly capture both teacher and interpreter's frontal pose and display it the participant and interpreter so that both share the same visual space. The system could also store preferences for each student's preferences.

**Acknowledgements.** This work is supported by the National Science Foundation Awards: IIS-1218056 and IIS-1460894.

# References

1. Aud, S., et al.: The Condition of Education 2011. NCES 2011-033. National Center for Education Statistics. ERIC (2011)
2. Cavender, A.C., et al.: ClassInFocus: enabling improved visual attention strategies for deaf and hard of hearing students. In: Proceedings of the 11th International ACM SIGACCESS Conference on Computers and Accessibility - ASSETS 2009, New York, USA, pp. 67–74 (2009)
3. Foote, J., et al.: Region of interest extraction and virtual camera control based on panoramic video capturing. IEEE Trans. Multimed. 7(5), 981–990 (2005)
4. Mayer, R.E., Moreno, R.: A split-attention effect in multimedia learning: evidence for dual processing systems in working memory. J. Educ. Psychol. 90(2), 312–320 (1998)
5. Ranjan, A., et al.: Improving meeting capture by applying television production principles with audio and motion detection. In: Proceedings of the 26th Annual CHI Conference on Human Factors in Computing Systems - CHI 2008, New York, USA, pp. 227–236 (2008)

# A Web Application for Geolocalized Signs in Synthesized Swiss German Sign Language

Anna Jancso, Xi Rao, Johannes Graën, and Sarah Ebling[✉]

Institute of Computational Linguistics, University of Zurich, Zurich, Switzerland
{anna.jancso,xi.rao}@uzh.ch, {graen,ebling}@cl.uzh.ch

**Abstract.** In this paper, we report on the development of a web application that displays Swiss German Sign Language (DSGS) signs for places with train stations in Switzerland in synthesized form, i.e., by means of a signing avatar. Ours is the first platform to make DSGS place name signs accessible in geolocalized form, i.e., by linking them to a map, and to use synthesized signing. The latter mode of display is advantageous over videos of human signers, since place name signs for any sign language are subject to language change. Our web application targets both deaf and hearing DSGS users. The underlying programming code is freely available. The application can be extended to display any kind of geolocalized data in any sign language.

**Keywords:** Avatar · Sign language · Geolocalized signs · Web platform

## 1 Introduction

Swiss German Sign Language (*Deutschschweizerische Gebärdensprache*, DSGS) is the sign language of the German-speaking area of Switzerland. In any sign language, names for geographical locations (such as city or country names) can be signed in different ways, of which the most common are [4]:

- Using a conventionalized *place name sign*, e.g., the sign for GENF ('GENEVA')[1] in DSGS as shown in Fig. 1;
- *Fingerspelling* the place name, i.e., using dedicated signs for the letters of the place name in the surrounding spoken language[2] (the *finger alphabet* of DSGS is shown in Fig. 2); or
- Pointing in the relative compass direction of a place and articulating with the mouth (i.e., *mouthing*) the spoken language place name.

Which of the three above devices is chosen depends, among other factors, on the prominence of the geographical location and the origin of the signer.

---

[1] "GENF" is an example of a *sign language gloss*, a label for the meaning of a sign. Glosses are commonly written in all caps.

[2] A *spoken language* is a language that is not signed, whether it is represented as speech or text.

© Springer International Publishing Switzerland 2016
K. Miesenberger et al. (Eds.): ICCHP 2016, Part II, LNCS 9759, pp. 438–445, 2016.
DOI: 10.1007/978-3-319-41267-2_62

**Fig. 1.** Sign GENF ('GENEVA') in DSGS [1]

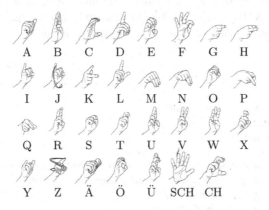

**Fig. 2.** Finger alphabet of DSGS [1]

For example, a DSGS signer from Zurich may not know the sign for the place Muttenz, a town outside of Basel. Hence, he is likely to sign the place name using fingerspelling or pointing and mouthing. However, using conventionalized signs for place names where possible is desirable. This makes an inventory of place name signs an indispensable resource for any sign language. Often, these inventories form part of a general sign language lexicon, as is the case for DSGS.[3]

In this paper, we report on the development of a web application that displays DSGS signs for places with train stations in Switzerland in synthesized form, i.e., by means of a *signing avatar*. Ours is the first platform to make DSGS place name signs accessible in geolocalized form, i.e., by linking them to a map, and to use synthesized signing. The latter mode of display is advantageous over videos of human signers, since place name signs for any sign language are subject to language change. As an example, the sign for the place *Winterthur* in DSGS has recently changed.

---

[3] http://signsuisse.sgb-fss.ch/ (last accessed: January 14, 2016).

Our web application targets both Deaf[4] and hearing DSGS users and is accessible at http://pub.cl.uzh.ch/purl/geosign. The source code of our web application (including database schema, SiGML codes, train station names and their coordinates, web frontend and backend scripts) is available at the same address.

## 2   Synthesized Signing

The Java Avatar Signing (JASigning) system [3] was used to synthesize the DSGS place names. Its main release is freely available for research purposes.[5] JASigning accepts input in the form of Signing Gesture Markup Language (SiGML) [2], an XML version of the form-based sign language notation system HamNoSys [6]. Figure 3 shows the SiGML code for GENF (cf. Fig. 1) in DSGS.

```xml
<sigml>
  <hamgestural_sign gloss="GENF">
    <sign_nonmanual>
    </sign_nonmanual>
    <sign_manual>
      <handconfig ceeopening="slack" handshape="cee12" mainbend="bent"
        second_handshape="finger2" second_thumbpos="out"/>
      <handconfig extfidir="ul"/>
      <handconfig palmor="l"/>
      <location_bodyarm contact="touch" location="chin"
        side="right_beside">
        <location_hand digits="1" location="nail" side="palmar"/>
      </location_bodyarm>
      <par_motion>
        <directedmotion direction="do"/>
        <tgt_motion>
          <changeposture/>
          <handconfig handshape="pinch12" mainbend="bent"/>
          <handconfig extfidir="uol" palmor="ul"/>
        </tgt_motion>
      </par_motion>
    </sign_manual>
  </hamgestural_sign>
</sigml>
```

**Fig. 3.** SiGML code for the place name sign GENF ('GENEVA') in DSGS

---

[4] It is a widely recognized convention to use the upper-cased word *Deaf* for describing members of the linguistic community of sign language users [5].

[5] http://vh.cmp.uea.ac.uk/index.php/JASigning (last accessed: January 14, 2016).

The names and positions (longitude, latitude) of all train stations of the Swiss Federal Railways (*Schweizerische Bundesbahnen*, SBB) are available online.[6] From this list, we extracted 1829 stations that we wanted to display in synthesized DSGS. For 232 of these stations, conventionalized DSGS signs (cf. Sect. 1) could be identified. For the remaining stations, the names are signed using fingerspelling (cf. Sect. 1).

The SiGML codes for fingerspelling signs were generated by first normalizing and segmenting the station names and finally concatenating the corresponding partial SiGML codes. Normalizing involved handling diacritics in French and Italian place names (e.g., converting *à* to *a*). For segmentation, recall from Fig. 2 that the DSGS finger alphabet features 31 signs. Segmenting the station names according to fingerspelling signs included identifying the letter combinations *sch* and *ch* as one segment. Successive vowels and consonants were also combined into a single segment: In DSGS, double vowels are signed by adding a horizontal movement (a *glide*) to the sign for the vowel, and for double consonants, a small stamping movement is appended after each consonant. Overall, this resulted in 56 partial SiGML codes.

## 3   Implementation

The SiGML documents for those train stations that have a place name sign (cf. Fig. 3) and the partial SiGML codes for the finger alphabet (cf. Fig. 2) are stored in a database, together with the station names, the coordinates of the stations (longitude and latitude), and a *category* parameter assigning every station to one of five categories (cf. Sect. 3.4).

A stored procedure returns valid SiGML code for any given word, defaulting to a fingerspelled realization if no SiGML code for a lexical sign is found.

### 3.1   Architecture

We chose Python as a server-side language for retrieving data from the database and delivering it to the web client. The web client can make two different requests: The first extracts all the information regarding the train stations needed for creating markers on a map (cf. Sect. 3.2) and is raised just before the initialization of the map. The second request is executed when the user clicks on a marker or issues a query for a specific train station. As a response, the corresponding SiGML code is returned and passed to the avatar. Both requests are asynchronously handled via *Ajax* on the client side to avoid "freezing" and reloading of the entire web page.

---

[6] http://www.bav.admin.ch/dokumentation/publikationen/00475/01497/index.html (last accessed: January 14, 2016).

```
<?xml version="1.0" encoding="UTF-8"?>
<sigml>
<player_settings>
  <camera_location cx="0.00" cy="0.40"
        r="2.20" theta="0.0" phi="10.0" fov="30.0"/>
  <ambient_motions body="ON" head="ON" blink="ON"/>
  <avatar name="bad"/>
</player_settings>

<hamgestural_sign gloss="TAESCH">
  <sign_manual>
    <sign_manual>
      <handconfig bend1="hooked" bend2="round" handshape="finger2"
↪   mainbend="round" thumbpos="out"/>
      <handconfig extfidir="u"/>
      <handconfig palmor="dl"/>
      <location_bodyarm location="shoulders" side="right_at"/>
    </sign_manual>
    <sign_manual>
      <handconfig handshape="fist" second_handshape="fist"
↪   thumbpos="out"/>
      <handconfig extfidir="u"/>
      <handconfig palmor="d"/>
      <location_bodyarm location="shoulders" side="right_at"/>
      <rpt_motion repetition="fromstart">
        <tgt_motion>
          <changeposture/>
          <handconfig handshape="fist"/>
        </tgt_motion>
      </rpt_motion>
    </sign_manual>
    <sign_manual>
      <handconfig handshape="finger2345" thumbpos="out"/>
      <handconfig extfidir="u"/>
      <handconfig palmor="d"/>
      <location_bodyarm location="shoulders" side="right_at"/>
    </sign_manual>
  </sign_manual>
</hamgestural_sign>

<hamgestural_sign>
</hamgestural_sign>
</sigml>
```

**Fig. 4.** Concatenated SiGML code for the fingerspelling sign TÄSCH in DSGS

## 3.2   The Map

Our aim was to visualize the train stations on a map by means of markers. Clicking on a marker or searching for a train station triggers a pop-up window containing the avatar, which subsequently signs the train station name in DSGS. We used Google Maps as map material and implemented its API to configure our map (cf. Sect. 3.5).

## 3.3   Coordinates

In the coordinate data described in Sect. 2, longitude and latitude information was available only in LV03 (*Landesvermessung 1903*) format. Since the Google Maps API only accepts coordinates in the WGS84 (*World Geodetic System 1984*) format, we converted the LV03 coordinates using a Python module.[7]

## 3.4   Clustering Markers

To avoid overload of markers on the map, the number of markers was set to increase with the zoom levels. The most intuitive criterion for selecting train stations for the different zoom levels is passenger frequency, i.e., the number of passengers getting on/off at a given train station (as obtained from a list provided by the SBB). However, this results in an uneven distribution of markers on the map in some cases: For example, *Zürich Stadelhofen* and *Zürich HB* are both ranked high (9 and 1, respectively) in the list of passenger frequencies. Since they are located close to each other, displaying the markers for both stations is not ideal. We therefore introduced proximity to other stations as an additional criterion. We then defined five categories, imposing a specific threshold value for the distances: *high* (0.15, 185 stations), *high-medium* (0.075, 235 stations), *medium* (0.0375, 434 stations), *medium-low* (0.01875, 473 stations), and *low* (0.009375, 502 stations).

## 3.5   Zooming

Once the web application is loaded, a map is initialized, centering on Switzerland at zoom level 8.[8] For every train station, a marker is generated by passing its coordinates and name to the constructor of a class called *Marker*. The avatar is integrated into a pop-up window. For this, an object of the class *InfoWindow* is created and associated with a specific marker. An event listener is then added to every marker to ensure that the appropriate info window opens upon clicking on a marker. Initially, i.e., when the page is loaded, only markers belonging to the highest category are shown on the map. Zooming in results in more markers

---

[7] http://www.swisstopo.admin.ch/internet/swisstopo/en/home/products/software/products/skripts.html (last accessed: January 14, 2016).

[8] Zoom level 0 is the most zoomed out (the entire world is shown), meaning that you need to zoom in eight times to get to zoom level 8 (Switzerland).

being placed on the map, while zooming out removes them again. To implement this behavior, we first added another event handler, which fires as soon as a change in the zoom level is detected. To recognize whether the user zooms in or out, the new zoom level and the previous zoom level are compared. Zoom levels 8 to 12 are then mapped (1) to the category where stations need to be put on the map (zooming in) and (2) to the category where stations need to be removed from the map (zooming out). Based on the old and new zoom levels and the mapping, the algorithm decides on the next action.

### 3.6 Searching for Stations

As an additional feature, we provide a search mask with autocompletion function.[9] This function renders the query for train stations easier and more precise because it prevents the user from typing and submitting any non-existing name. Since the stations are sorted by rank during retrieval from the database, the ones with higher frequency appear first in the list. Once a station name in the input field is submitted, the application looks up the corresponding marker. If found, the marker is set on the map (provided this has not yet been done), the corresponding SiGML code is retrieved, the info window is opened, and the signing avatar is triggered.

### 3.7 Embedding the Avatar Applet

HTML files with sample embeddings of the avatar using JavaScript are provided on the JASigning website (cf. Sect. 2). HTML code is passed to the constructor of the *InfoWindow* class. We modified a method in the original JavaScript code so that it now operates on the SiGML code extracted from the database instead of reading the content from a file. The method is invoked by the *Play* button below the avatar. Figure 5 shows a screenshot of our web application.

## 4 Outlook

DSGS is composed of five dialects that originated in former schools for the Deaf, resulting in Zurich, Berne, Basel, Lucerne, and St Gallen dialects. Currently, our application contains only signs from the Zurich dialect. As a next step, we intend to include all dialect variants of a place name sign. The display of the variants will be similar as that of the *Spread the Sign* web page.[10]

Our database can be extended to not only contain SiGML documents for train station names, but any word/gloss in DSGS, thus providing a resource for web applications based on signing avatars. If interchanged or extended with the finger alphabet SiGML codes of another sign language, the system will support that language instantly.

---

[9] https://api.jqueryui.com/autocomplete/ (last accessed: January 14, 2016).

[10] https://www.spreadthesign.com/de/map/ (last accessed: January 14, 2016).

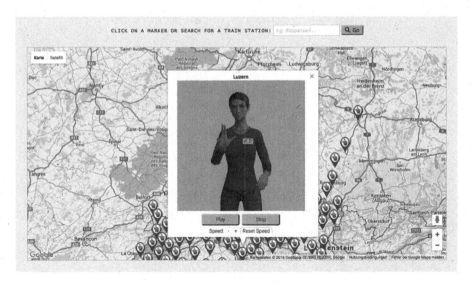

**Fig. 5.** Screenshot of our web application

**Acknowledgments.** Synthesized signing was produced with the JASigning software developed at the University of East Anglia, UK. We gratefully acknowledge the work of Prof John Glauert, Dr Ralph Elliott, Dr Richard Kennaway, and Mr Vincent Jennings on Animgen. Furthermore, our thanks go to the Bundesamt für Verkehr and Swisstopo, where we obtained the relevant data for the train stations of the SBB and a Python script to convert the coordinates.

# References

1. Boyes Braem, P.: A multimedia bilingual database for the lexicon of Swiss German Sign Language. Sign Lang. Linguist. **4**(1/2), 133–143 (2001)
2. Elliott, R., Glauert, J., Kennaway, R., Marshall, I.: The development of language processing support for the ViSiCAST project. In: Proceedings of the 4th International ACM SIGACCESS Conference on Computers and Accessibility (ASSETS), pp. 101–108. Arlington, VA (2000)
3. Jennings, V., Elliott, R., Kennaway, R., Glauert, J.: Requirements for a signing avatar. In: Proceedings of the 4th LREC Workshop on the Representation and Processing of Sign Languages, pp. 133–136. La Valetta, Malta (2010)
4. Matthews, P., McKee, R., McKee, D.: Signed languages, linguistic rights and the standardization of geographical names. In: Proceedings of the 23rd International Congress of Onomastic Sciences, pp. 721–732. Toronto, Canada (2008)
5. Morgan, G., Woll, B.: The development of complex sentences in British Sign Language. In: Directions in Sign Language Acquisition: Trends in Language Acquisition Research, pp. 255–276. John Benjamins, Amsterdam, Netherlands (2002)
6. Prillwitz, S., Leven, R., Zienert, H., Hanke, T., Henning, J.: HamNoSys: Version 2.0: An Introductory Guide. Signum, Hamburg (1989)

# Accessible Computer Input

# Evaluation of a Mobile Head-Tracker Interface for Accessibility

Maria Francesca Roig-Maimó[1]([⊠]), Cristina Manresa-Yee[1], Javier Varona[1], and I. Scott MacKenzie[2]

[1] Department of Mathematics and Computer Science, University of Balearic Islands, Palma, Spain
{xisca.roig,cristina.manresa,xavi.varona}@uib.es
[2] Department of Electrical Engineering and Computer Science, York University, Toronto, ON M3J 1P3, Canada
mack@cse.yorku.ca

**Abstract.** FaceMe is an accessible head-tracker vision-based interface for users who cannot use standard input methods for mobile devices. We present two user studies to evaluate FaceMe as an alternative to touch input. The first presents performance and satisfaction results for twelve able-bodied participants. We also describe a case study with four motor-impaired participants with multiple sclerosis. In addition, the operation details of the software are described.

**Keywords:** Mobile human-computer interaction · Assistive technology · Head-tracker interface · Alternative input · Multiple sclerosis

## 1 Introduction

Nowadays, mobile device usage is growing rapidly. But, users with special needs find challenges using these devices. To offer the same opportunities to all members of a society, users with the full spectrum of capabilities and limitations should be able to access all Information and Communication Technologies [20]. Users with motor impairments (mainly in the upper-body) may be unable to directly use mobile devices or they may experience difficulty interacting via touch [1,21]. So, how can users with motor impairments interact with mobile devices? Kane et al. [13] reported that people with disabilities rely on mass-market devices instead of using devices specially designed for them. One approach to accessibility is to utilize built-in sensors, for example, sensors which do not require touch input or an external switch. Not surprisingly, there is a higher adoption of tablets than smartphones for people with motor impairments since the larger format brings more possibilities for interaction [21].

The integration of cameras on mobile devices combined with greater processing capacity has motivated research on vision-based interfaces (VBI). Whereas in desktop computers, VBIs are widely used in assistive tools for motion-impaired users [14], in mobile contexts the use of VBIs is relatively new. VBIs detect and

© Springer International Publishing Switzerland 2016
K. Miesenberger et al. (Eds.): ICCHP 2016, Part II, LNCS 9759, pp. 449–456, 2016.
DOI: 10.1007/978-3-319-41267-2_63

use the voluntary movement of a body part to interact with the mobile device, achieving a non-invasive hands-free interface. FaceMe is a new head-tracker interface for mobile devices [18]. It works as a mouse replacement interface in desktop computers [23] and offers promise as a device for accessible computing [14]. The objective here is to explore, extend, and evaluate FaceMe as an assistive tool for mobile devices.

## 2   Related Work

While users with perceptual impairments (e.g., vision, hearing) may encounter problems with computer output, people with motor impairments face difficulties in computer input. This latter group cannot employ standard input devices, and instead use established solutions for desktop computing. The interfaces range from head wands or switches [16] to eye trackers [4] to head trackers [15].

There are fewer assistive tools for mobile devices than for desktop computers. Mobile accessible solutions typically arrive through third-party developers or via the operating system. Examples include screen magnifiers or screen readers (e.g., VoiceOver on iOS or Talkback on Android) which support users with sight loss.

For able-bodied users, touch gestures are widely used. So, accessible alternatives are required to perform standard gestures. An example is AssistiveTouch on iOS which uses a single, moveable touch point to access the device's physical buttons.

An alternative to touch input is voice-control (e.g., SIRI on iOS or Google Now on Android) which is beneficial for users with vision or motor impairments. But, these methods do not offer total control of the system, as they are usually for specific tasks such as opening an app or placing a call.

Other mobile input mechanisms involve external devices such as switches to detect and incorporate the user's body motion. Detecting body motion can be done by processing data from various sensors, such as the gyroscope or the front camera. In this research, we focus on processing images provided by the device's front camera. The data are used for vision-based control and interaction. Commercial applications, such as the Smart Screen on Samsung's Galaxy S4, use camera data to detect the position of the face and eyes to perform functions like scrolling within documents, screen rotation, or pausing video playback. However, additional research is needed to explore the detection of body motion as an input means for users with physical impairments. Notably, there are some related projects [8,9] or apps [7,11,19,22] and some research on vision-based interfaces integrated in specific applications, such as gaming or 3D interaction [6,10].

## 3   System Description

FaceMe is a head-tracker for mobile devices (developed in iOS 8.0) that uses front-camera data to detect features in the nose region, to track a set of points, and to return the average point as the nose position (i.e., the head position of the user).

The nose position is then translated to the mobile screen by a pre-defined transfer function based on differential positioning. The interface reports the change in coordinates, with each location reported relative to the previous location, rather than to a fixed location. To perform a selection, we use a dwell-time criterion.

FaceMe is stable and robust for different users, light conditions, and backgrounds [17]. Earlier work established the method's viability in a target-selection task with able-bodied users [18].

## 4   Evaluation

Two user studies were conducted to evaluate FaceMe as an alternative input system for mobile devices. The studies aim at determining if *all* regions of the device screen (an iPad) are accessible for users.

The first user study involved simple pointing tasks that spanned all the regions of the device screen. The task was a picture-revealing puzzle game. A picture was covered with an $m \times n$ grid of tiles (with three different tile sizes); participants had to move over all the tiles to remove them and to uncover the image (see top row Fig. 1). A tile was selected and removed immediately when movement of the user's head/nose produced a coordinate inside the tile. This selection mode is equivalent to a 0-ms dwell-time criterion.

The second study used a point-select task with a 1000 ms dwell-time criterion for selection. The task simulated the iOS home screen on an iPad (see Fig. 1a) with three icon sizes (see Fig. 1b–d). Participants were asked to select all the icons, which were distributed across the screen.

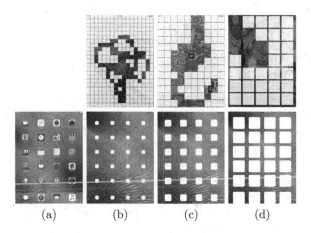

(a)        (b)        (c)        (d)

**Fig. 1.** Top row: screenshots of the picture reveal puzzle game with three different tile sizes. Bottom row: (a) iOS home screen on an iPad. (b–d) Screenshots of the simulated iOS home screen with three different icon sizes.

### 4.1   Participants and Apparatus

Twelve able-bodied unpaid participants (4 females) were recruited from the local town and university from an age group of 20 to 71 (mean = 34.8, SD = 18.3). None had previous experience with head-tracker interfaces.

Four participants with multiple sclerosis (two female) participated in the user study. Ages ranged between 46 and 67 years. They all need assistance in basic daily activities due to their motor and sensory impairments. They possess some control of their heads, although the range of movement is limited. They all use wheelchairs and lack trunk control. Three have vision disturbances.

The tests used a iPad Air (2048 × 1536 resolution, 264 dpi)[1]. which was placed on a stand over a table (see Fig. 2).

**Fig. 2.** Two of the motor-impaired participants performing the user studies.

### 4.2   Procedure and Design

We followed a within-subjects design with one independent variable for both user studies. The levels for the target size were the same for both studies: 44 px, 76 px, and 132 px. According to the iOS Human Interface Guidelines [2], the optimal sizes are 44 × 44 px for a UI element and 76 × 76 px for an App icon. The third level (132 × 132 px) was chosen to simulate a zoom or screen magnifier operation.

For the first user study (picture-revealing puzzle), we had 391 tasks for the 44 px level, 130 tasks for the 76 px level, and 35 tasks for the 132 px level. For the second user study (home screen icon selection), we had 24 tasks for each level of the target size independent variable.

Each able-bodied participant completed two blocks of three conditions presented randomly; each motor-impaired participant completed only one block. Thus, there were (12 participants x (391 tasks + 130 tasks + 35 tasks) x 2 blocks)

---

[1] That means a resolution of 1024-by-768 Apple points. From now on, we refer to the Apple point as px and assume a 1024-by-768 px resolution.

+ (4 par x (391 tasks + 130 tasks + 35 tasks) x 1 block) = 15,568 tasks for the first user study, and (12 par x 24 tasks x 3 conditions x 2 blocks) + (4 par x 24 tasks x 3 conditions x 1 block) = 2016 tasks for the second user study.

The dependent variables for both studies were task completion time (efficiency) and whether or not all regions of the screen were reachable (effectiveness).

Participants also assessed the usability of FaceMe using the System Usability Scale (SUS) questionnaire [5] and a comfort assessment based on ISO 9241-411 [12].

### 4.3   Results and Discussion

**First User Study: Picture-Revealing Puzzle.** All able-bodied participants were able to uncover all the tiles of the puzzle in all the size conditions.

The mean completion time was lower for the 132 px condition (20.4 s) compared to 76 px (58.0 s) and 44 px (579.5 s). The differences were statistically significant ($F_{2,22} = 220.1, p < .001$). Pairwise comparisons with Bonferroni corrections revealed significant differences between all pairs ($p < .05$). See Fig. 3a.

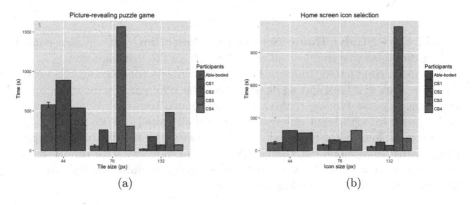

**Fig. 3.** Completion time by participant group for (a) the *picture-revealing puzzle* user study and (b) the *home screen icon selection* user study. (Color figure online)

Two of the four motor-impaired participants were able to uncover all the tiles of the puzzle in all the size conditions but the other two had difficulty with the smallest tile size (44 px). Figure 4 shows the evolution of the uncovered tiles for the motor-impaired participants: most started uncovering the tiles in the center of the screen and left the tiles placed in the edges of the screen for the end.

These observations suggest that FaceMe is a viable accessible input method that enables users to access all the screen regions as long as the interactive elements have a minimum size of 76 px. As far as possible, those elements should be placed toward the center of the screen.

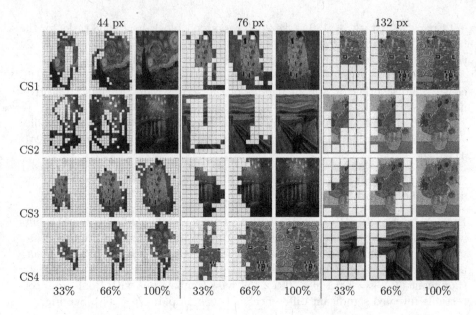

**Fig. 4.** Time evolution of the uncovered tiles for the motor-impaired participants.

**Second User Study: Home Screen Icon Selection.** All the able-bodied participants were able to select all the targets in all the size conditions.

The mean completion time was lower for the 132 px condition (34.5 s) compared to 76 px (50.1 s) and 44 px (73.0 s). The differences were statistically significant ($F_{2,22} = 178.5, p < .001$). Pairwise comparisons with Bonferroni corrections revealed significant differences between all pairs ($p < .05$). See Fig. 3b.

Two of the four motor-impaired participants were able to select all the targets in all the size conditions but participant CS4 had difficulty with the 44 px tile size and participant CS3 felt tired and was not abled to finish the test with the 44 px and 76 px tile sizes (see Fig. 5).

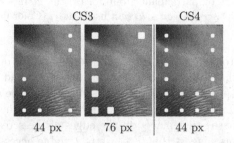

**Fig. 5.** Targets that could not be selected by the participants CS3 and CS4.

Observing the results obtained, we can argue that FaceMe can be used for selecting targets as long as they have a minimum size of 76 px. Considering the targets that could not be selected by participants CS3 and CS4, targets should be placed toward the center of the screen to the extent possible.

**Usability.** The overall average SUS score was 87.1 (SD = 10.3). According to Bangor et al. [3], scores higher than 70 are in the acceptable range. Our score (87.1) is above Excellent in the *adjective ratings* scale. Figure 6 gives the results for the questionnaire of assessment of comfort. Overall, FaceMe received a positive rating, even in the question about neck fatigue.

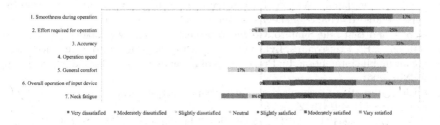

**Fig. 6.** Assessment of comfort questionnaire results. (Color figure online)

## 5   Conclusion

In this work, FaceMe, a touch-alternative head-tracker vision-based interface for users with physical limitations was presented and evaluated through two user studies with twelve able-bodied participants and four motor-impaired users with multiple sclerosis. The results indicate that FaceMe can be used as an alternative input method for motor-impaired users to interact with mobile devices, allowing them to perform point-select tasks across all the regions of the device display. The study with the motor-impaired participants highlights the importance of the size of interactive elements (recommended minimum is 76 px) and their location on the screen (preferably toward the center).

**Acknowledgments.** This work has been partially supported by grant BES-2013-064652 (FPI) and project TIN2012-35427 by the Spanish MINECO, FEDER funding.

## References

1. Anthony, L., Kim, Y., Findlater, L.: Analyzing user-generated YouTube videos to understand touchscreen use by people with motor impairments. In: Proceedings of CHI, CHI 2013, pp. 1223–1232. ACM (2013)

2. Apple Inc.: iOS Human Interface Guidelines: Designing for iOS. https://developer. apple.com/library/ios/documentation/userexperience/conceptual/mobilehig/
3. Bangor, A., Kortum, P.T., Miller, J.T.: An empirical evaluation of the system usability scale. Int. J. Hum. Comput. Int. **24**(6), 574–594 (2008)
4. Biswas, P., Langdon, P.: A new input system for disabled users involving eye gaze tracker and scanning interface. J. Assistive Technol. **5**(2), 58–66 (2011)
5. Brooke, J.: SUS-A quick and dirty usability scale. Usability Eval. Ind. **189**(194), 4–7 (1996)
6. Cuaresma, J., MacKenzie, I.S.: A comparison between tilt-input and facial tracking as input methods for mobile games. In: Proceedings of IEEE-GEM, pp. 70–76. IEEE (2014)
7. Electronic rescue service: Games Sokoban Head Labyrinth. https://play.google. com/store/apps/details?id=ua.ers.headMoveGames
8. Fundación Vodafone España: EVA facial mouse. https://play.google.com/store/ apps/details?id=com.crea_si.eviacam.service
9. Google and Beit Issie Shapiro: Go ahead project. http://www.hakol-barosh.org.il/
10. Hansen, T.R., Eriksson, E., Lykke-Olesen, A.: Use your head: exploring face tracking for mobile interaction. In: Proceedings of Extended Abstracts CHI, pp. 845–850. ACM (2006)
11. Inisle Interactive Technologies: Face Scape. https://itunes.apple.com/es/app/ face-scape/id1019147652?mt=8
12. ISO: ISO/TS 9241–411:2012 - Ergonomics of human-system interaction - Part 411: Evaluation methods for the design of physical input devices. http://www.iso.org/ iso/catalogue_detail.htm?csnumber=54106
13. Kane, S.K., Jayant, C., Wobbrock, J.O., Ladner, R.E.: Freedom to roam: a study of mobile device adoption and accessibility for people with visual and motor disabilities. In: Proceedings of SIGACCESS, Assets 2009, pp. 115–122. ACM (2009)
14. Manresa-Yee, C., Ponsa, P., Varona, J., Perales, F.J.: User experience to improve the usability of a vision-based interface. Interact. Comput. **22**(6), 594–605 (2010)
15. Manresa-Yee, C., Varona, J., Perales, F.J., Salinas, I.: Design recommendations for camera-based head-controlled interfaces that replace the mouse for motion-impaired users. Univers. Access Inf. Soc. **13**(4), 471–482 (2014)
16. Ntoa, S., Margetis, G., Antona, M., Stephanidis, C.: Scanning-based interaction techniques for motor impaired users. In: Kouroupetroglou, G. (ed.) Assistive Technologies and Computer Access for Motor Disabilities. IGI Global (2013)
17. Roig-Maimó, M.F., Manresa-Yee, C., Varona, J.: A robust camera-based interface for mobile entertainment. Sensors **16**(2), 254 (2016)
18. Roig-Maimó, M.F., Varona Gómez, J., Manresa-Yee, C.: Face me! head-tracker interface evaluation on mobile devices. In: Proceedings of Extended Abstracts CHI, pp. 1573–1578. ACM Press (2015)
19. Shtick Studios: HeadStart. https://play.google.com/store/apps/details?id=com. yair.cars
20. Stephanidis, C.: The Universal Access Handbook. CRC Press, New York (2009)
21. Trewin, S., Swart, C., Pettick, D.: Physical accessibility of touchscreen smartphones. In: Proceedings of SIGACCESS, ASSETS 2013, pp. 19:1–19:8. ACM (2013)
22. Umoove Ltd.: Umoove experience: the 3D face & eye tracking flying game. https:// itunes.apple.com/es/app/umoove-experience-3d-face/id731389410?mt=8
23. Varona, J., Manresa-Yee, C., Perales, F.J.: Hands-free vision-based interface for computer accessibility. J. Newt. Comput. Appl. **31**(4), 357–374 (2008)

# Replacement of the Standard Computer Keyboard and Mouse by Eye Blinks

Muhammad Bilal Saif$^{(\boxtimes)}$ and Torsten Felzer

Institute for Mechatronic Systems,
Technische Universität Darmstadt, Darmstadt, Germany
Bilalsaif03f@gmail.com

**Abstract.** In this work, a system is presented, replacing the standard computer keyboard and mouse with a headband carrying piezoelectric sensors. The novel system allows the user to enter text and select on-screen objects (mouse function) by just using eye blinks. It has been tested by one disable and five able-bodied volunteers. Combined they have shown an average typing speed of 9.1 characters per minutes (CPM).

**Keywords:** Head-Band · Piezoelectric sensors · Readout circuitry · OnScreenDualScribe (OSDS) · VirtualKeypad (VK)

## 1 Introduction

Now-a-days, computers are helping humans in every domain of life. Their application field spreads from solving complex problem to organizing day-to-day human activities. Individuals with physical disabilities often find it difficult to get full benefits of this modern tool. To reduce this barrier for physically disabled persons, Felzer et al. [1] have developed a software tool named as OnScreenDualScribe (OSDS). In addition to text typing, this tool also allows the user to select and click on-screen objects. OSDS is usually controlled by 18 physical keys which are located on a small number-pad. In this work, another software VirtualKeypad (VK) has been developed. VK responds to the user's eye signals, i.e., blinks and closing both eyes. In response to these signals, VK generates virtual keystrokes. These keystrokes are picked by OSDS, which does not know if these keystrokes are generated by an actual keypad or by VK. This connectivity of VK and OSDS, allows the user to perform the functionalities of the standard keyboard and mouse by eye signals.

To capture the eye signals, two piezoelectric sensors have been used (Fig. 3). These sensors are attached to a readout circuit, which constantly monitors them and sends their raw data to the computer. Inside computer this data is received and processed by VK.

The remainder of the paper is organized as follows. In the next section, the state-of-the-art (literature review) is described. Section 3 presents the proposed system. Results and comparison with other publications is discussed in Sect. 4 and Sect. 5 concludes the paper.

© Springer International Publishing Switzerland 2016
K. Miesenberger et al. (Eds.): ICCHP 2016, Part II, LNCS 9759, pp. 457–463, 2016.
DOI: 10.1007/978-3-319-41267-2_64

## 2  Related Work

In the past years, a number of attempts have been made to enter text by using the eyes. All of these techniques have two things in common. First, they have a sensor monitoring the eyes, and second, they have a software receiving raw data from the sensors and processing it. The eye sensors can be categorized into three main categories. The first category sensors work on the principle of electrooculography (EOG). In the second category, cameras are used to observe eye blinks and sometimes eye gaze, whereas the third category consists of piezoelectric sensors.

Electrooculography-based systems are presented in [2–4]. Borghetti et al. [2] have used 7 electrodes and have achieved a typing speed of 7.1 CPM. Soltani et al. [3] have developed a small PCB which monitors five electrodes and sends their data to the computer. Their system has shown a typing speed of 5.9 CPM. Tangusksant et al. [4] have used six electrodes and have achieved a typing speed of 2.4 CPM. Electrooculography needs many electrodes, which should be precisely placed for accurate detection. For a physically disabled person, such sensor placement is cumbersome or even impossible without help.

Królak and Strumiłło [5] have used a camera to detect eye blinks and have reported a typing speed of 5.0 CPM. Benefit of using a camera, is the elimination of facial sensors, whereas its drawback is the significant increases in required computational power. Several images per second has to be acquired and processed by the computer for successful operation of this technique. The complexity of this approach further increases if the user is wearing spectacles or suffering from gaze jitter problem.

Related to the last category of sensors, Felzer et al. [6] have used a single piezoelectric sensor, reporting a typing speed of 4.3 CPM. With a single sensor it is not possible to find which eye has been blinked. This problem makes the system less efficient and also reduces the typing speed.

## 3  Proposed System

A novel system is proposed in this work which requires less sensors as compared to EOG based systems and requires less computational power as compared to camera based systems. In this work two piezoelectric sensors have been used so that "right eye blink", "left eye blink", and the "both eyes closed" can be effectively distinguished. Proposed system is pictorially illustrated in Fig. 1. Sensor placement, sensor readout circuitry, and the VirtualKeypad (VK) software are described in the following subsections.

### 3.1  Sensors Placement

To find appropriate spots for the sensor placement, anatomy and physiology of the fascial muscles have been studied.

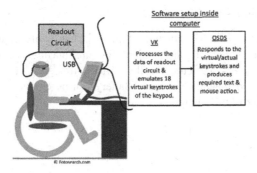

**Fig. 1.** System Setup (©Fotosearch.com)

Eye blinks are caused by Orbicularis Oculi muscular rings. Placing sensors directly on these muscular rings would restrict the eyelashes movement and would cause discomfort.

Both sensors can also be placed on forehead because the movement of the Orbicularis Oculi muscle also sends vibrations in the forehead skin and the Frontalis muscle. Placing sensors on the forehead make it easier to detect the eye blinks however the determination of signal type (i.e. "right eye blink", "left eye blink" or "both eyes are closed") becomes very difficult. Main reason for this problem is the close proximity of sensors, resulting in almost same readings on both sensors when any eye is blinked.

To solve these problems the sensors are placed on the bone between Temporal and Orbicularis muscles on each side of the skull. These spots are shown in Fig. 2 (see also [7]). Each spot shows significant movement, when the eye on its side is blinked. Being on separate sides of the skull, each sensor receives minimum interference from the blink of other eye. The headband with piezoelectric sensor is shown in Fig. 3.

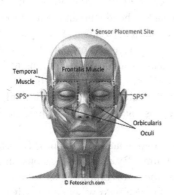

**Fig. 2.** Facial Muscles (©Fotosearch.com)

**Fig. 3.** Headband with readout circuitry

## 3.2   Sensor Readout Circuitry

Sensor readout circuit is also shown in Fig. 3. It has cable connections with the headband and the computer. Readout board contains biasing circuit of piezoelectric sensors, analog amplifiers, a microcontroller (Atmel Atmega 329P), a 600 mAH LIPO battery and a battery management circuit. Battery can be charged either by computer USB port or by micro USB charger.

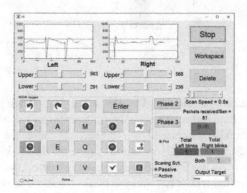

**Fig. 4.** VirtualKepad (VK)

## 3.3   VirtualKeypad (VK)

This software is developed in Matlab® and its user interface is shown in Fig. 4. It receives the raw data from the sensor readout circuitry and processes it to determine the type of eye signal which can be "Right eye blink", "Left eye blink", and "Both eyes closed".

At the start, the user needs to calibrate the VK. The calibration process has three phases. In the first phase, the user is required to wear the headband and relax. Once the user is calm and stationary, the second phase can be started. In this phase, VK monitors the background noise. In the third phase, the user is required to provide at least three right and three left eye blinks. By evaluating background noise and intensity of deliberate signals, VK computes the detection envelopes for both sensors which are shown by dotted lines in Fig. 3. The calculation of the detection envelopes is explained in more detail in [8]. To determine the type of eye signal VK follows the algorithm shown in Fig. 5.

To scan the virtual number-pad keys, VK has two scanning schemes. In passive scanning, the system automatically scans rows/columns. By default, VK stops on each selected element for 800 ms before incrementing the row/column. This time can be adjusted from 500 ms to 4 s. A "Left eye blink" starts/stops row scanning, whereas a "Right eye blink" starts/stops column scanning. Whenever both eyes are closed, the selected key is "virtually" pressed, which means that its keycode is generated. This keycode is intercepted by OSDS.

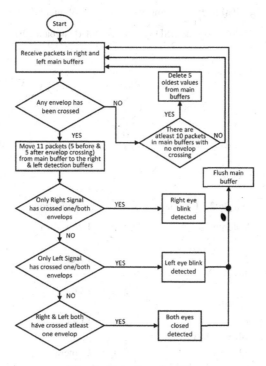

**Fig. 5.** Detection algorithm

In active scanning, the user has more control. The system waits for the user signal. "Left eye blink" results in row increment, "Right eye blink" increments the column, and "Both eyes closed" virtually presses the selected key.

## 4    Results and Comparison

To measure the accuracy and typing speed, an evaluation software called "Writing" is used, which is a part of the OSDS software. This software generates a random sentences on the screen and asks the user to type it. After completion of five sentences, the software writes required time and accuracy report to the computer's hard disk.

The presented system has been tested on five able-bodied and one disable volunteer. To make the results comparable, all the volunteers have used ambiguous mode in OSDS and passive scanning in VK (in early pilot testing, this has been found to yield the higher entry rates, and active scanning is much less comfortable).

The test was divided into three parts. In the first part, volunteers were given some practice time. When they had become comfortable with the new system, the remaining two parts were performed. During the second part, volunteers were asked to enter five phrases using a physical number-pad, and in the last part, they have used the headband and the VK software to enter the test phrases. Results are summarized in Table 1. The average entry rate shown by six volunteers is 9.1 characters per minute (CPM). In Table. 2, this speed is compared with other publications.

**Table 1.** Showing the result of volunteers

| Sr. # | Avg. CPM (keypad, & OSDS) | Avg. CPM (headband, VK, & OSDS) |
|-------|---------------------------|----------------------------------|
| 1 | 18.6 | 8.6 |
| 2 | 23.5 | 9.6 |
| 3 | 22.7 | 9.1 |
| 4 | 20.8 | 9.8 |
| 5 | 21.4 | 8.8 |
| 6 | 25.1 | 8.9 |
| **Avg.** | **22** | **9.1** |

**Table 2.** Comparison with other publications.

| Sr. # | Publication | Volunteers | CPM | Eye sensor | Mouse function |
|-------|-------------|------------|-----|------------|----------------|
| 1 | [2] | 20 (all healthy) | 7.1 | EOG | No |
| 2 | [3] | 1 (healthy) | 5.9 | EOG | No |
| 3 | [4] | 10 (all healthy) | 2.4 | EOG | No |
| 4 | [5] | 49 (37 healthy & 12 disabled) | 5.0 | Camera | Yes |
| 5 | [6] | 1 (disabled) | 4.3 | One Piezoelectric sensor | Yes |
| 6 | [9] | 20 (all healthy) | 12.0 | EOG | No |
| 7 | This work | 6 (5 healthy & 1 disabled) | 9.1 | Two Piezoelectric sensors | Yes |

The disable volunteer in this work is a 45 years old male who was diagnosed with Friedreich's Ataxia in 1985. Same volunteer had also participated in [6], where a single piezoelectric sensor was used. There he had achieved a typing speed of 4.3 CPM. It is interesting to note that with this novel system he was able to type at the speed of 8.9 CPM which is more than double of his previous speed.

From Table 2, it can be seen that the typing speed achieved in this work is better than all other approaches except the one reported in [9]. However, in [9], the speed test has been performed by entering a five character word. This test approach is inadequate, because the sample consisting of just one word of five letters is simply too small. Other than this, [9] does not have any mechanism to control the mouse.

# 5   Conclusion

In this work, a novel system is presented; which – with the help of the OnScreen-DualScribe (OSDS) software – replaces computer keyboard and mouse. The presented system consists of a headband fitted with two piezoelectric sensors, a readout circuit, and software called "VirtualKeypad (VK)". With this new system, the user can click and type by using only three eye signals: "Left eye blink", "Right eye blink", and "Both eyes closed". During tests, it has allowed users to enter text at an average speed of 9.1 characters per minute (CPM).

# References

1. Felzer, T., MacKenzie, I., Rinderknecht, S.: OnScreenDualScribe: a computer operation tool for users with a neuromuscular disease. In: Stephanidis, C., Antona, M. (eds.) UAHCI 2013, Part I. LNCS, vol. 8009, pp. 474–483. Springer, Heidelberg (2013)
2. Borghetti, D., Bruni, A., Fabbrini, M., Murri, L., Sartucci, F.: A low-cost interface for control of computer functions by means of eye movements. Comput. Biol. Med. **37**(12), 1765–1770 (2007)
3. Soltani S. Mahnam A.: Design of a novel wearable human computer interface based on electrooculograghy. In: Proceedings of the ICEE 2013. IEEE, pp 1–5 (2013)
4. Tangsuksant W., Aekmunkhongpaisal C., Cambua P., Charoenpong T. Chanwimalueang T.: Directional eye movement detection system for virtual keyboard controller. In: Proceedings of the BMEiCON 2012. IEEE, pp 1–5 (2012)
5. Królak, A., Strumiłło, P.: Eye-blink detection system for human–computer interaction. Univ. Access Inf. Soc. **11**(4), 409–419 (2012)
6. Felzer T., Nordmann R.: Speeding up hands-free text entry. In: Proceedings of the CWUAAT 2006. Cambridge University Press, pp. 27–36 (2006)
7. Marieb, E.N.: Essentials of Human Anatomy & Physiology, Eleventh edn. Pearson Education (2014). ISBN 978-0-321-91900-7
8. Saif M. B., Neubert M., Spengler S., Beckerle P., Felzer T., Rinderknecht S.: Multi-signal virtual keyboard (MSVK) use of various sensors to replace the standard keyboard – first steps. In: Proceedings of the MIDI 2014 (2014)
9. Usakli, A.B., Gurkan, S.: Design of a novel efficient human–computer interface: an electrooculagram based virtual keyboard. IEEE Trans. Instrum Measur. **59**(8), 2099–2108 (2010)

# SWIFT: A Short Word Solution for Fast Typing

Philippe Roussille and Mathieu Raynal[✉]

University of Toulouse - IRIT, Toulouse, France
{Philippe.Roussille,Mathieu.Raynal}@irit.fr

**Abstract.** In this paper, we study one specic problem linked to text input techniques based on prediction and deduction lists; namely, short-word problems. Indeed, while prediction is fast and can be easily made effective for long words (e.g. more than 4 characters), short words take longer to be typed with prediction: the time spent browsing a list-based interaction slows the user down. The present study compares two possible approaches where the user selects inside a prediction list of short words versus tactile exploration (native Voive Over for Apple). Results of our comparative study reveal that our technique reduces the overall typing time and the error rate by 38 % compared to tactile exploration.

**Keywords:** Text input · Visual impairment · Touchscreen · Mobile device · Short words · Word prediction

## 1 Introduction

Touch screens rapidly and significantly replace physical keyboards on mobile devices. Hence, text entry is now dependent on software (or virtual) keyboards that are widely used by sighted people, but raise accessibility issues for visually impaired users. These users rely on tactile exploration with vocal feedback of the whole screen for entering text, which is time consuming.

In order to solve this problem, different prediction-based techniques or deduction system exist. However, if these systems are generally enhance the speed of text-entry for users, they are inappropriate for entering short words. For example, within the DUCK [6] system, the use of the deduction system increases the input speed for words comprised of 5 characters or more. For shorter words, the use of the deduction system is too costly in time compared to the low number of characters to enter. This is even more a problem that some short words are very frequently used.

In this article, we therefore focus on entering short words. Our study aims to improve the typing of such words for use with the DUCK system. The proposed interactions have therefore been designed to be easily integrated and in tune with the rest of the interactions already proposed on this system. Both proposals interactions were evaluated and compared with the text input system traditionally used (like VoiceOver entry system).

© Springer International Publishing Switzerland 2016
K. Miesenberger et al. (Eds.): ICCHP 2016, Part II, LNCS 9759, pp. 464–471, 2016.
DOI: 10.1007/978-3-319-41267-2_65

## 2    Related Works

### 2.1    Adaptation of the Traditional Keyboard

Text to speech (TTS) synthesis is the most used method to assist text entry on a mobile device coupled with a standard keyboard layout (e.g. QWERTY or AZERTY, depending on the culture). The underlying principle is simple: the user moves his finger onto the keyboard or hits a key, and the keys he hits or he moves across are spoken (see e.g. Apple VoiceOver). When he releases his finger, the corresponding character is inputted. Additional gestures can be used as well. One big problem with that comes from the fact that the keys of a virtual keyboard on a mobile device are very small. Thus, the risk of mistyping a letter is quite high. The second hindrance of such a solution resides in the need for users to go through most of the keys before finding the one they seek which has been reported as a "painful exploration" by the users because it usually takes some time. The offered sets of gestures might also be too complex to perform in mobility.

### 2.2    Specific Text Input System

More specific text-input system exist. They are often based on a character encoding which allows to limit the number of keys and thus help visually impaired people to find their location onscreen. The most known encoding for visually impaired people is the Braille alphabet. BrailleType [5] or TypeInBraille [4] adapted this encoding on touchscreens. In order to do so, such keyboards mimic a 6-dots Braille cell onto the phone screen. The characters are entered by successively activating the dots of the cell. Unlike the QWERTY standard keyboard, these keyboards have a much easier learning phase, due to the similarity with the Braille alphabet. On the other hand, the user must fill-in the dot matrix for each character, which leads to a quite high Keystroke Per Character (KSPC), hence drastically reducing text-entry speed.

Other methods, like NavTouch [2] & NavTap [3] allow the user to dynamically select a letter with a specific gesture performed anywhere on the screen, drawing a pattern on the device. These techniques are very efficient for quickly targeting one letter. However, they generate high cognitive load to simultaneously remember the correct gesture, as well as the position of the typed letter in the word.

The No-Look-Notes [1] text-entry method uses multiple fingers, relying on the multi-touch capacities of the device. The screen is divided in different zones, with a set of characters associated for each. The user can search for a character among a group of letters with one finger, and confirms the selection via a split-tapping. This method provides a fast and easy access to letters, but drastically increases the number of taps, which slows word typing down, and may cause muscular fatigue.

## 3   DUCK Keyboard

### 3.1   Principle

DUCK (deDUCtive Keyboard) [6] is based on typical existing keyboard layouts, so layouts are the most used ones, meaning that most people are acquainted with them. We decided, however, to simplify the user interaction to type letters. The main objective was to get rid of the accurate search of each character on the layout. Besides, we aimed to compensate for the lack of precision related to small and mobile keyboards.

The user initially explores the keyboard to find the first letter of the intended word. Each finger motion provides a vocal feedback, allowing the user to locate a letter on the layout. Once he releases the key, the corresponding character is selected. For typing the remaining letters of the word, the user doesn't have to explore the keyboard again. He just needs to press the location where he believes the keys are according to the memorized representation of the AZERTY or QWERTY layout.

The problem of such a solution relates to words shorter than four characters. Indeed, the interaction offered in the DUCK keyboard to confirm words is compensated for words that are long enough (words that contains more than five characters), but is inefficient when used for shorter words.

### 3.2   Short-Word Problems

Zhai and Kristensson [7] indirectly studied the short-words problem by using shorthand gestures for the most frequent short words of the English language. However, these gestures are based on the keyboard layout. A novice user can therefore use the visual keyboard representation to draw his gesture. This is not applicable for visually impaired people since they can't access that visual representation. Besides, it would be too hard for the user to memorize all the gestures.

This article aims to explore various interaction techniques in order to improve short-word typing by visually impaired people.

## 4   Proposed Interactions

As we saw, the DUCK keyboard is efficient to type words longer than five character. We are thus looking for an interaction technique which would be usable on the DUCK keyboard while allowing to type words shorter than 4 character faster than the used one.

In order to make such a technique easily integrable with DUCK, we kept the same interaction paradigms that DUCK typing uses:

– the user select the first character of the word he wants to type through a keyboard exploration;

– then, in order to access the most frequently used short words, he needs no additional key hits.

He just has to validate the first character of the word to access a list (of at most seven words) of the most frequently used short words starting with that character.

er diffrentes techniques d'interaction pour passer d'un mode l'autre: Our study is thus focusing on the choice of the best interaction to switch from classical input mode of a word with DUCK to typing a short word. As such, we chose to compare different interaction techniques to switch from one mode to another: In the first technique, which we called "dual-tap" validation, the user browses the keyboard by dragging his finger to locate the letter he looks for. He then releases his finger from the screen to select the character. The user then taps on the screen with two fingers to validate his choice and switch to the list mode. In the second technique, called "split-tap" validation, the character is selected the same way, but the user has to press a second finger without releasing the first finger. When he releases both fingers, the keyboard switch to the list.

### 4.1    Display and Feedback

In order to maximize the easiness of use for the user, we displayed the list in the same way as selecting a word with the system DUCK: over the whole screen, and each item is evenly taking the same size. They are contiguously aligned along the width of the screen, while taking the full height. When the user browses the list, he has to keep his finger pressed onto the screen, and the underlying elements are read at the same time. Releasing his finger validates the word underneath. Furthermore, in order to facilitate memorization, words are always displayed in the same order.

## 5    Method

### 5.1    Comparison Technique and Hypothesis

In order to correctly assess our techniques, we chose to compare both of these techniques to a third one, which keeps the tactile exploration principle: the user maintains his pressure as he slides his finger onto the next letters, and performs a split-tapping gesture by pressing a second finger on the screen in order to add a letter to the word hes typing. Such an approach also allow the user to increase his knowledge of the keyboard, while not being intrusive in the proper functioning of the device. We named that technique the "slide-typing" approach.

We selected this method as a basis for our comparison due to the fact that the study we made for DUCK [6], this technique was better than DUCK for words shorter than four characters.

Our main hypothesis is that by reducing the number of actions needed to type a short word, our interaction techniques will take less typing time; and will thus be faster than the currently used technique. Interactions are more precise than DUCK.

## 5.2  Participants

12 participants (4 women and 8 men, mean age = 24.7) with normal or corrected-to-normal vision participated in our study. They were all blindfolded to ensure they couldn't see the screen at all. They had a familiar use (from a daily use) of smart phones and mobile devices. Among them, six claimed to have a good knowledge of the AZERTY layout due to heavy gaming experience. Our choice of recruiting non-visually impaired participants is justified to verify the evaluated techniques as a proof of concept.

## 5.3  Apparatus

Participants used a Samsung Galaxy SIII smartphone. The device has a resolution of 306 ppp for a 136.6 mm × 70.6 mm screen, a ARM Cortex-A9 MPCore Quad core set at 1.4 GHz and uses Android 4.3. They used their finger to navigate through the items. The items were synthesized from text using the Google Translate service. The audio was trimmed to provide feedback as fast as possible, reducing any possible delay. Nothing was displayed onto the screen during the experiment, making the grids and items invisible to the users.

## 5.4  Procedure

The task was to type a short word (a word comprised of less than four letters) as fast as possible. The task went as follow: first, the participant was read the instruction, he was then given the word to search, then he had to type it. If he answered a different word, we considered his answer to be wrong. Once a session was completed, the participant was asked to answer a SUS test for each technique, and state his preference among the interactions he went through by ranking them in the order of preference.

## 5.5  Design

Each participant had to go through three sessions, one for each interaction: dual-tap validation, split-tap validation, slide-typing. All three sessions were run one after the other. The twelve participants were then split at random into three even groups. The groups were then assigned interactions according to a balanced Latin square. For every session, the participant had to go through 44 tasks. For each task, the word to select was picked at random. However, in each series, every initial letter is checked with two different words.

This leads us to a total of 1,584 trials.

## 5.6  Collected Data

In order to study the different presentations, we collected various data during the experiment: we collected the number of items seen by the user, the time taken for the participant to make his selection, the errors he made and the answers he gave to the SUS questionnaire.

# 6    Results

## 6.1    Time Spent

We decided to measure the time taken by the user by counting between the moment he entered the first letter of the word, and the moment he validated his word.

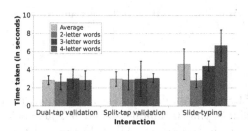

**Fig. 1.** Time taken to type a word by technique and by word length (Color figure online)

As we see on Fig. 1, for both list-based techniques, there is no significant ($p > 0.05$) influence on the word length: the dual-tap validation takes on average 2.85 s compared to the 2.99 s for the split-tap validation.

The time taken to type a word using the slide-typing is dependent on the word length ($p < 0.04$), and it increases along the length of the word (2.82 s for two letter words versus 6.66 s for four letter words).

Nevertheless, it is quite apparent that both list-based techniques are significantly faster ($p < 0.05$) than the slide-typing technique (2.85 s and 2.99 s versus 4.63 s on average). The list-based techniques have no significantly different typing speed. They are also operating in near constant time. In comparison, the DUCK keyboard requires 7 s on average to type words under five characters, which is longer than our techniques here. This validates our main hypotheses.

## 6.2    Error Rate

We then computed the error rate for each technique. It corresponds to the percentage of the wrongly selected words during the input over the total of these words.

As seen on Fig. 2, the two techniques based on the lists offer a good accuracy with 13 % for dual-tap validation and 11 % for split-tap validation, without any significant effect due to the while the slide-typing technique offers a 21 % error rate. DUCK itself offers 20 % error rate.

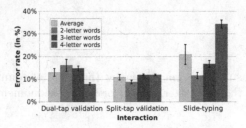

**Fig. 2.** Error rate when typing a word by technique and by word length (Color figure online)

## 6.3   User Feedback

We computed the SUS score obtained for each technique given the users' replies to the test. The slide-typing technique scored 86, just before the dual-letter validation technique which scored 85. The split-tap technique scored last with 79. When asked to rank the techniques, the users followed what they thought on the SUS assessment: the dual-tap validation technique was ranked first (5 our users), while the slide-typing approach came second; the split-tap validation technique being the most disliked interaction.

## 7   Discussion

Given our results, we can safely affirm that word lists are really effective when used in a short-word typing context. Such techniques are more efficient than the existing method built-in DUCK.

As we found in the experiment, the lists are really effective in a short word typing context. They turned to be faster than the slide-typing method, as well as being more resilient to errors. The lists work in near constant time. When it comes to accuracy, lists retrieve the words with less errors. This can be explained by the fact that both of the lists offers the possible word without any mistake in its spelling. As such, the only possible error in the validation is selecting a completely different word; while such errors are possible at each letter if the user is entering a word letter by letter (by using the slide-typing technique).

Besides, as the users knowledge of the list increases with its use, he spends less time browsing the list seeking the item he wants, and could validate his answer directly.

However, lists are very static. Indeed, the users can't choose other words than the words that have been elected to be in the list.

Therefore, our technique is very effective on the most commonly used short words, but is useless for other short words. However, with a maximum of 7 words starting with the same letter, our system allows the use of 124 most used words short, representing 74 % of the short words used in the French language.

Finally, word lists are static, we believe that the performance obtained in this study without learning can be improved gradually as the user will type words using these lists. Indeed, the more he will use them, the more he will know the position of the words in the list and will lose less and less time to browse through the list to find the desired word. On the other hand, he will also know if the word is in the list of suggested words, and therefore may or may not use this interaction to quickly enter a short word.

## 8  Conclusion

The list-based solution we offer is faster and more accurate than a technique based on tactile exploration, or the technique offered in DUCK. Even if this solution is limited to a restricted number of short words, it will improve the overall typing speed as these words are the most frequently used ones.

## References

1. Bonner, M.N., Brudvik, J.T., Abowd, G.D., Edwards, W.K.: No-look notes: accessible eyes-free multi-touch text entry. In: Floréen, P., Krüger, A., Spasojevic, M. (eds.) Pervasive 2010. LNCS, vol. 6030, pp. 409–426. Springer, Heidelberg (2010)
2. Guerreiro, T., Lagoá, P., Nicolau, H., Gonçalves, D., Jorge, J.A.: From tapping to touching: making touch screens accessible to blind users. IEEE MultiMed. **15**(4), 0048–0050 (2008)
3. Guerreiro, T., Nicolau, H., Jorge, J., Gonçalves, D.: Navtap: a long term study with excluded blind users. In: Proceedings of the 11th International ACM SIGACCESS Conference on Computers and Accessibility, Assets 2009, pp. 99–106. ACM, New York (2009)
4. Mascetti, S., Bernareggi, C., Belotti, M.: TypeInBraille: quick eyes-free typing on smartphones. In: Miesenberger, K., Karshmer, A., Penaz, P., Zagler, W. (eds.) ICCHP 2012, Part II. LNCS, vol. 7383, pp. 615–622. Springer, Heidelberg (2012)
5. Oliveira, J., Guerreiro, T., Nicolau, H., Jorge, J., Gonçalves, D.: BrailleType: unleashing braille over touch screen mobile phones. In: Campos, P., Graham, N., Jorge, J., Nunes, N., Palanque, P., Winckler, M. (eds.) INTERACT 2011, Part I. LNCS, vol. 6946, pp. 100–107. Springer, Heidelberg (2011)
6. Roussille, P., Raynal, M., Jouffrais, C.: Duck: a deductive soft keyboard for visually impaired users. In: Proceedings of the 27th Conference on L'Interaction Homme-Machine, IHM 2015, pp. 19:1–19:8. ACM, New York (2015)
7. Zhai, S., Kristensson, P.: Shorthand writing on stylus keyboard. In: Proceedings of the SIGCHI Conference on Human Factors in Computing Systems, CHI 2003, pp. 97–104. ACM, New York (2003)

# An Empirical Evaluation of MoonTouch: A Soft Keyboard for Visually Impaired People

Saber Heni[1,2(✉)], Wajih Abdallah[2], Dominique Archambault[1], Gérard Uzan[1], and Mohamed Salim Bouhlel[2]

[1] Laboratoire Technologies, Handicaps, Interfaces et Multimodalités (THIM), EA 4004 CHART, Université Paris 8, Saint-Denis, France
heni.saber@gmail.com

[2] Unité de recherche Sciences Et Technologies de l'Image et des Télécommunications (SETIT), Université de Sfax, Sfax, Tunisia

**Abstract.** This article presents a new text entry method for Visually Impaired people called MoonTouch. This method uses an enhanced version of the Moon system to help and assist visually impaired people to enter text into their touchscreen devices using simple gestures. A clinical tests of the method with a population of visually impaired participants showed that MoonTouch was perceived well by the users and presented a good learning curve.

**Keywords:** Universal access · Text entry · Gesture based · Blind · Visually impaired people · Smartphone · Multimodal interaction

## 1 Introduction

In this era where the use of touchscreen based mobile phones is commonly increasing, some visually impaired people can feel excluded because of the absence of the tactile cues in these devices which privileges the visual mode. Nevertheless, there are a lot of visually impaired people who uses these smartphones regularly.

Entering text is a basic and fundamental task, but using the soft keyboard is a challenge for most visually impaired people, particularly for blind users [1]. The accessibility features incorporated into these mobile phones to overcome these issues are mainly based on voice interaction like screen readers and speech synthesis.

In this paper, we present the design of a new text input method for touchscreens named MoonTouch basically aiming visually impaired people but it could interest sighted persons also. Our method is a gesture-based text input technique that uses an enhanced version of the moon alphabet.

## 2 Related Works

A large number of researches have presented solutions to enhance the non-visual text entry on touchscreens based mobile phones. In this article, we mention only uni-gestures solutions and their performances. These methods are evaluated using metrics specific to text entry. To quantify the performance of such methods, in the

© Springer International Publishing Switzerland 2016
K. Miesenberger et al. (Eds.): ICCHP 2016, Part II, LNCS 9759, pp. 472–478, 2016.
DOI: 10.1007/978-3-319-41267-2_66

literature we found many metrics. The most used ones are those related to the typing speed in Word Per Minute (WPM) [2], the error rate using the MSD (Minimum String Distance) and KSPC (KeyStrokes Per Character) [3]. These two latter metrics are used to quantify the error rate by localizing the committed typing errors and counting the corrected ones, which can be considered as an additional effort.

Unistrockes is a gesture-based system. Its name refer to the original alphabet (Fig. 1) that appeared in 1993 [4], Unistrokes symbols bare little resemblance to Roman letters [5]. Each letter is associated to a short gesture. The most frequent letters are represented with strait lines. An empirical comparison with Graffity-stroke gave 15.8 WPM with an MSD error rate of 16.8 % after 20 sessions.

**Fig. 1.** Unistrokes alphabet above and Graffity alphabet below

Graffity-stroke (11.4 wpm after 20 sessions and an MSD of 26.2 %) [5] is a text entry system that uses strokes resembles its assigned Roman letters (Fig. 1). This is intended to facilitate learning. Support for this was found in a previous study [6], where users demonstrated 97 % accuracy after only five minutes of practice.

EdgeBraille is a new Braille-based text input method, which allows entering Braille characters by swiping one finger along the edges of the touchscreen to activate the cells composing the letter in Braille [7]. The empirical evaluation result showed an average speed of 7.17 WPM and an MSD of 8.43 %.

## 3   Prototype and Design

MoonTouch is a technique based on an enhanced version of the Moon alphabet. This system was invented by Dr. William MOON. It consists of a set of simple symbols made as similar as possible to the Roman alphabet. In order to use this system as a text entry method, we chose to change some symbols to reduce the similarity between some of them. We changed the symbols of the "P" and the "Q" and the "T" letters. We chose, also, to add a starting point to every symbol which means from where to where the users should perform the gesture and allow us to use the same symbol to produce many characters.

MoonTouch provide gestures for spaces and backspaces. A natural gesture for the space character is an horizontal line performed from the left to the right and from the right to the left for the backspace. MoonTouch provide also a gesture to switch between

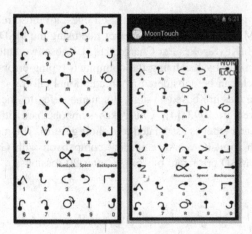

**Fig. 2.** MoonTouch alphabet on the left and MoonTouch Android application on the right

the "Letter mode" and the "Numerical mode". In the first mode, all the gestures produce the Roman letters from "A" to "Z". In the second, the same gestures produce numbers from 0 to 9.

MoonTouch provide a multimodal feedback to its users in order to compensate the visual modality. It assists users all along the text entry task with audio and vocal and vibro-tactile feedbacks. MoonTouch use the phone incorporated speech synthesis to pronounce every character entered by the user. It pronounces also the last written word when a space is entered. If the user delete a character, it pronounces it flowed by the word "deleted". It informs the user by saying the words "Num Locked" or "Num unlocked" if the user switch from the letter mode to the numerical mode and vice versa (Table 1).

**Table 1.** MoonTouch Multimodal assistance

| User Action | MoonTouch reaction |
| --- | --- |
| Enter a character | Pronounce the character |
| Enter a space | Pronounce the last entered word |
| Delete a character | Pronounce the character followed by "deleted" |
| Switch to Numerical mode | Pronounce "Num locked" |
| Switch to Letter mode | Pronounce "Num unlocked" |
| Perform unrecognized gesture | Produce a short beep and a 0.2 ms vibration |

Other than the speech feedbacks, MoonTouch, produces vibrations and sounds signals as a reaction to some usage errors. The phone produces a vibration of 0.2 ms and a short beep, every time the user performs an unrecognized gesture (Table 1).

## 4   Evaluation

The most used metrics mentioned in the literature are WPM, KSPC and MSD. WPM is calculated based on CPS (Character Per Second). This latter unit measures the entry speed and it's calculated simply by dividing the total number of characters entered by the time to enter them.

In text entry, the most used metric to deduce the writing speed is WPM. It's deduced from CPS by multiplying the CPS figure by 60 s/minute and dividing by 5 characters/word. Prior to about 1924, typing rates were reported using actual words per minute. Since then, rates have been reported using 5-stroke words per minute [8].

$$\text{WPM} = \frac{|S| \times 60}{T \times 5} = \text{CPS} \times \frac{60}{5} \tag{1}$$

KSPC measures a combination of two quantities, without providing a means to separate them. It is interpreted as the cost of committing errors and fixing them. A large KSPC value indicates that many errors were committed and correction took few keystrokes or that few errors were committed but correcting them required many keystrokes [3].

In order to evaluate MoonTouch, we created an Android application (Fig. 2) that calculate the writing speed and measure the effort made by the user using a metric called GPC (Gesture Per Character) [9]. GPC is an extension of KSPC and it denotes how many gestures it took on average to input a letter. As most unistroke methods have dedicated gestures for all the used alphabet letters, a flawless system will require a GPC of one, providing there was no human error. This was calculated to provide an overall picture of the input process, and to check whether the more faulty letters yield higher GPCs compared to less faulty ones, as one might expect. GPC, is calculated as follow:

$$\text{GPC} = \frac{|IS|}{|T|} \tag{2}$$

Where |IS| is the length of the input stream, including unrecognized gesture, the spaces, backspaces and other actions. |T| is the length of the presented text.

In the beginning of the evaluation, participants (Table 2) started to learn the MoonTouch alphabet. Moreover, learning the system and interacting with it during a time interval of at least 15 min and at most 20 min. During the training session, participants were encouraged to ask questions if they have doubts.

After the learning sessions, we conducted a weekly evaluation sessions. During these sessions, participants were asked to write a set of phrases as quickly and accurately as possible, without the need of any accent or punctuation. Each trial consisted of entering three randomly selected sentences out of a corpus of 105 (Statistics in Table 3).

The evaluation consisted in five sessions. At each session, participants were asked to copy the presented sentences, as fast and accurately as possible.

**Table 2.** Participant's characterization

| Participant | Gender | Age | Blind (B) /Partially Sighted (PS) |
|---|---|---|---|
| PR 01 | Female | 34 | B |
| PR 02 | Male | 32 | B |
| PR 03 | Male | 39 | B |
| PR 04 | Female | 43 | B |
| PR 05 | Male | 51 | B |
| PR 06 | Female | 41 | PS |

**Table 3.** Phrase's corpus statistics

| | |
|---|---|
| Characters count (Without blanks) | 3123 |
| Characters count | 3865 |
| Words count | 743 |
| Phrases count | 105 |
| Characters per word | 4.203 |
| Words per phrase | 7.076 |
| Correlation with French | 0.979 |

# 5 Results

During 5 sessions, the participants have entered text using MoonTouch. We measured WPM and GPC for every participant in all sessions.

As shown in the Fig. 3, participants have remarkably progressed as the evaluation progress. They succeeded to attain a speed going from 8.26 to 12.70 WPM in the last session. The participant PR06, the only partially sighted person, has scored the top speed of 12.70 WPM in the last session.

The lower WPM scored in the last session was 8.26. It was the entry speed of the participant PR2. But, if we look closely we can see that this participant has made an enormous progress. He began the evaluation with a speed of 2.37 WPM and in the last session he succeeded to enter text at 8.26 WPM.

MoonTouch has demonstrated that it has a great potential in term of speed and learning curve for blind people and especially for partially sighted people. In average during the last session, participants have entered text at a speed of 10.14 WPM.

Either the entering speed, we measured the GPC in order to see the errors committed by the user during the evaluation. As we can see above (Fig. 4), the curve of the average GPC rapidly converges to 1 without reaching it. The best GPC recorded by a participant is 1.06 in the fifth session. A perfect text entry means the participant perform 1 gesture per character. The average for all users in the fifth session is 1.22 GPC.

In general, participants have made a quick progress, which means that MoonTouch is an easy to use and learn text entry method for touchscreen mobile phones and this is thanks to the limited number of symbols used. MoonTouch uses 6 different symbols

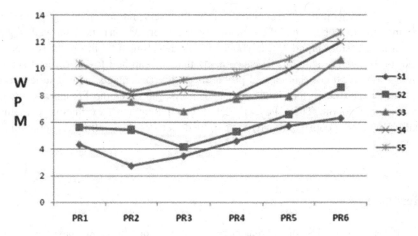

**Fig. 3.** WPM Text entering speed evolution during the 5 sessions

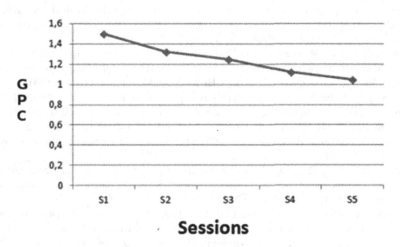

**Fig. 4.** Average GPC by session

flipped every time horizontally and/or vertically to produce a new letter. In the beginning we thought that this will create a lot of confusion to the participants but the evaluation results showed, in average, that users make mistakes in general every 5 characters entered. One of the participants has only made in the last session a mistake every 16 characters.

## 6 Conclusion

In this paper we presented a new text entry method called MoonTouch that uses an enhanced version of the ancient moon alphabet and discussed different approaches of text entry for visually impaired people on touchscreen devices.

Overall MoonTouch was perceived well by the users and presented a good learning curve in term of speed and effort made by the user. MoonTouch showed a good potential as a gesture based soft keyboard for visually impaired in only 5 sessions.

Currently, we are studying enhancements that we can add to the method such as changing some gestures that caused problems to the participants, adding a new mode called the special characters mode in which users can enter the French accentuated characters and so on. Then we consider doing a long term evaluation with more visually impaired people and why not sighted persons to confirm the potential of MoonTouch.

# References

1. Vanderheiden, G.C.: Use of audio-haptic interface techniques to allow nonvisual access to touchscreen appliances. In: 40th Annual Meeting of the Human Factors and Ergonomics Society (1996)
2. Heni, S., Archambault, D.,Uzan, G., Bouhlel, M.S. :MorseTouch : Méthode de saisie non visuelle pour les téléphones tactiles. In: Congrès Handicap 2014 : Les technologies d'assistance : de la compensation à l'autonomie, Paris, pp. 211–217 (2014)
3. Soukoreff, R.W. et MacKenzie, I.S.: Metrics for text entry research: an evaluation of MSD and KSPC, and a new unified error metric. In: Proceedings of the SIGCHI Conference on Human Factors in Computing Systems. CHI 2003. ACM, NY, pp. 113–120 (2003)
4. Goldberg, D. Richardson, C.: Touch-typing with a stylus. In: Proceedings of the INTERACT 1993 and CHI 1993 Human Factors in Computing Systems, ACM, pp. 80–87 (1993)
5. Castellucci, S.J., MacKenzie, I.S.: Graffiti vs. unistrokes: an empirical comparison. In: Proceedings of the SIGCHI Conference on Human Factors in Computing Systems, ACM, pp. 305–308 (2008)
6. Wigdor, D., Balakrishnan, R.: A comparison of consecutive and concurrent input text entry techniques for mobile phones. In: Proceedings of the SIGCHI Conference on Human Factors in Computing Systems, ACM, pp. 81–88 (2004)
7. Mattheiss, E., Regal, G., Schrammel, J., Garschall, M., Tscheligi, M.: Dots and letters: accessible braille-based text input for visually impaired people on mobile touchscreen devices. In: Miesenberger, K., Fels, D., Archambault, D., Peňáz, P., Zagler, W. (eds.) ICCHP 2014, Part I. LNCS, vol. 8547, pp. 650–657. Springer, Heidelberg (2014)
8. Yamada, H.: A historical study of typewriters and typing methods: from the position of planning Japanese parallels. J. Inf. Process. 2(4), 175–202 (1980)
9. Wobbrock, J.O., Myers, B.A. Kembel, J.A. EdgeWrite: stylus-based text entry method designed for high accuracy and stability of motion. In: Proceedings of the ACM Symposium on UIST 2003. New York: ACM Press, pp. 61–70 (2003)

# Zoning-Based Gesture Recognition to Enable a Mobile Lorm Trainer

Michael Schmidt, Cathleen Bank, and Gerhard Weber[(⊠)]

Technische Universität Dresden, Institute for Applied Computer Science,
Human-Computer Interaction, Nöthnitzer Straße 46, 01062 Dresden, Germany
{Michael.Schmidt1,Gerhard.Weber}@tu-dresden.de, Cathleen.Bank@gmail.com

**Abstract.** In this work, a mobile learning tool for the Lorm-alphabet is developed. A person who is deaf-blind is lorming by finger spelling on another person's palm and fingers. We aim to provide an easy and anywhere to use Lorm trainer for caregivers, companions, and the general public. A robust gesture recognition utilizing zoning techniques and matching of symbol sequences has been developed for touch sensitive mobile devices. Tests with three users of the target group were conducted and qualitative evaluation of three experts was obtained. Overall, our development got positive feedback and a broad demand for the application was communicated. It is promising not only to support students of Lorm in their training process, but to widen the application of Lorm, therefore, diminishing social isolation of deaf-blind.

**Keywords:** Lorm-alphabet · Deaf-blind · Gestures · Zoning · Multitouch · Recognition

## 1 Introduction and Motivation

Without the possibility to communicate with other persons, deaf-blind face social, emotional, and intellectual degeneration [11]. Though there are some rudimentary approaches to construe speech information by (vibro)tactile stimulation [15], elaborate communication for deaf-blind typically is realized by tactile signing or fingerspelling (dactylology), print on palm methods (i.e., block letters, Lorm, Braille signing), or - rarely - reading facial gestures (Tadoma). Preconditions of requiring both communication partners to be familiar with special alphabets, often leave deaf-blind persons within isolation [6]. Lorming (i.e., entering letters of the Lorm-alphabet) is a communication strategy for deaf-blind persons which consists of writing strokes, taps, and simple signs by hand into the palm and fingers of another person (see Fig. 1 left). A similar approach is followed by the Malossi alphabet where letters consist of taps or pinches onto the counterpart's hand (see Fig. 1 right).

© Springer International Publishing Switzerland 2016
K. Miesenberger et al. (Eds.): ICCHP 2016, Part II, LNCS 9759, pp. 479–486, 2016.
DOI: 10.1007/978-3-319-41267-2_67

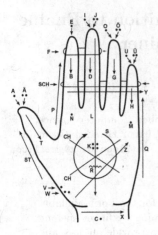 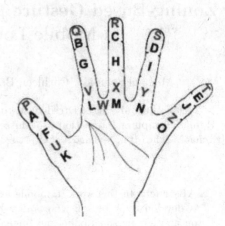

**Fig. 1.** Left: Lorm alphabet letters, consisting of (possibly multi-touch) taps, pinches, (multi-)strokes, and circles. Right: Malossi alphabet with black letters being pressed or tapped and red letters pinched [3]. (Color figure online)

## 2    State of the Art in Assistive Technologies for Deaf-Blind

Assistive technology for deaf-blind to receive text in remote communication is investigated, for instance, in terms of Morse codes [2] or - since the 1970 s and with various results - for tactile fingerspelling [1]. Starting with efforts by the Southwest Research Institute (SWRI) in 1977, several mechanical hands for fingerspelling were realized - Dexter (three versions since 1985), Gallaudet hand (1993), RALPH (1994) [10]. However, by Caporusso [3], the most effective available assistive technology for this purpose is still based on Braille systems. Bidirectional communication is supported, for instance, by the DB-HAND [3], a glove enabling utilization of the Malossi alphabet by pressure sensors and tactile actuators. It also provides keyboard input as well as visual and audio output to allow communication with hearing and sighted people. Similarly, the Mobile Lorm Glove [6] is a mobile communication device which translates between text and Lorm. Tactile feedback is given by vibrating motors on the back of the glove. Examples of these developments are illustrated in Fig. 2.

In talks with experts and caregivers we learned that practicing lorming typically means 'talking' to oneself and utilizing instructional information sheets (see Fig. 1 left) only. Also, errors are seldom communicated as deaf-blind tend to be rather tolerant in this aspect. They even trade time for accuracy and recognize incomplete words by their context. In fact, the authors did not find any application - besides prototypical realizations as the Mobile Lorm Glove [6] - to support learning of Lorm other than to present templates of the alphabet. Misinterpretations (e.g., the gesture for 'R' in left side of Fig. 1 is depicted as a wavy line, but is to be interpreted as a sequence of taps) are handled by further textual infor-

**Fig. 2.** From left to right: Dexter II [10]; DB-HAND [3]; Mobile Lorm Glove [6]

mation or instructions by a teacher. The possibility of individually learning and practicing lorming in a motivating way and to encourage broader use are main objectives of our work. Therefore, an educational tool for teaching the Lorm-alphabet to sighted persons (caregivers or companions) on mobile devices and on the basis of a virtual hand is presented. As communication is hard to distinguish from other interactions, a robust input recognition is mandatory. Having in mind not only mobile learning, but a transfer of the concepts to a - maybe 3D-printed - touch sensitive dummy hand, input differing from signs occurring in the alphabet is to be filtered out as best as possible. This particularity of unintentional input was - in analogy to the Creek parable - named 'Midas Touch Effect' in the context of interaction based on eye movements [9]. For this reason, the virtualized hand is divided into zones and an generic and easy to implement recognition routine based on template-matching of symbol sequences is realized. Extensions for other alphabets, e.g., Malossi, are easily possible.

## 3    Zoning-Based Gesture Recognition

Zonings or regions are commonly applied in character recognition [5,7,12,14] and quantize contours or trajectories by traversed areas within an applied planar separation. Specific feature retrieval within zones (in manifold variations [8]) can achieve smoothing effects (to suppress noise), data reduction, or a focus on prominent areas. As a template-matching method for on-line recognition, sequences of zones may be represented by strings of symbols and matched on the basis on Levenshtein distances [4]. For our application, we have to distinguish between the following gestures (see left side of Fig. 1):

- taps: a, c, e, i, m, n, o, u, v
- double taps: j, w, ä, ö, ü
- multiple taps: r
- multi-touch taps or pinches: f, k, sch
- lines: b, d, g, h, l, p, q, t, x, y, z, st

- multi-stroke lines (cross): ch
- circle: s

To realize robust gesture recognition and, by the same time, aspire to ignore unintended input, we choose a zoning-based approach. Underneath our presentation of a virtual hand, we use an invisible layer of zones in different colors (see Fig. 3 b). These zones not only define regions where input is enabled, but due to their color scheme, allow in spite of arbitrary - not necessarily uniform - (manual) divisions, efficient indexing for determination of those areas that are traversed during input.    Each gesture of the Lorm alphabet is represented by a unique

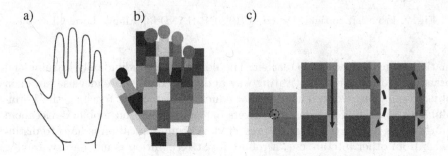

**Fig. 3.** Interactive virtual hand (a) and the invisible colored zoning (b) for input interpretation. Illustration of our utilization of an area cursor (c) - potentially hitting multiple zones. Intended input (black arrow) is included in list of possible interpretations even if correct zones are not hit directly. (Color figure online)

sequence of colors (determined by all traversed zones). Templates in terms of such color sequences are specified in advance and unambiguously matched with input. However, for ease of use, we tolerate flexible input by applying an area cursor (see Fig. 3 c). Therefore, multiple interpretations have to be handled within the matching procedure. During input, the area cursor's center point defines a list with entries for each of its traversed zones in temporal order. Each entry is a set of zones touched by a fixed range around the cursor while its center passes through the zone representative. Though this zoning based approach is robust to ambiguous interpretations when applied to the Lorm alphabet, a bigram analysis is implemented to resolve few existing multiple interpretations.[1]

## 4    Requirements and Realization

Considering requirements and context of our application, the conceptual design of 'LeLorm'[2] incorporates the following aspects (see Fig. 4 for snapshots illustrating some of the concepts):

---

[1] An analysis of pixel density may lead to further improvements of classification accuracy.

[2] The app's acronym works in English and German and means LEarning LORM.

- In its context of mobile learning on the basis of a normal sized virtual hand, target platform are Android tablets with screen size of at least 10".
- LeLorm realizes components for learning, guided (exercises) or free practicing of Lorm, and tests[3]. Similar to concepts for teaching Braille [13], learning content is separated into lectures. Information and error reporting is provided in terms of detailed description of the alphabet's subset used in a lecture, illustration and animation of correct input.
- For motivation, gamification concept 'easy fun' - in terms of free practicing (additional gestures for ease of use provide space and delete) - and 'serious fun' - in terms of earnable badges - are embedded. Users can win medals for (partially) completing lectures, on the basis of time spent using the app, reading instructions, or perfect success rates in tests. A trophy earned for collecting all medals activates a bonus game were the user has to enter Lorm signs that are falling down from top of the screen before they reach the bottom.
- In tests with professionals, lorming was done up to 141 signs per minute. This leads to a requirement of recognizing 2,5 gestures per second which is fulfilled by our classification routine. Additionally, we use this value to determine a 200ms delay needed to enter umlauts by double taps on the vowels' locations.
- Input requiring pinching of several fingers, i.e., 'F' or 'SCH', is not possible on a 2D Hand. It is realized slightly modified and most similar by pinch gestures next to or over the fingers involved.

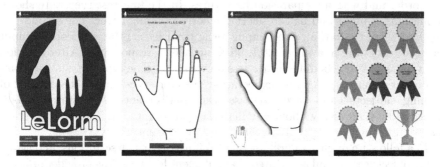

**Fig. 4.** From left to right: start screen of LeLorm, introductory screen for a lecture, error reporting by animation of correct input, and overview on collectable badges.

## 5   Evaluation

Besides a preliminary technical evaluation by the authors, LeLorm was evaluated with three subjects. Additionally, we gathered feedback of three experts in lorming - two caregivers and one deaf person.

---

[3] Letter frequencies of phrases designed for tests - and used in evaluation - correlate at $r = 0.96$ with that in German language.

## 5.1   Technical Inspection

To set success rates and results of input's classification into perspective, we determined the responsiveness of the device[4] used in all evaluations.

The device itself detected 1-finger taps with 100 % accuracy (at 100 randomized repeated trials with different positions and time-differences), but misses a large fraction when multiple-finger taps are used (up to 13 % of 3-finger taps were reported of being 1 finger only and 50 % were not detected at all). Thus the touch screen's resolution forces to split fingers on multi-touch input which may be not always possible when input, e.g., the letter 'k', is to be placed onto the virtualized hand. Most letters of Lorm, however, should not be affected by this issue and entering each letter 100 times by on of the authors achieved a recognition rate of 97.1 %. Similarly, the German pangram 'Franz jagt im komplett verwahrlosten Taxi quer durch Bayern' plus signs for 'Ä', 'Ö', 'Ü', 'ST', and 'SCH' were recognized with an accuracy of 97.8 %.

## 5.2   User Study

After short instructions, three users (female, aged 24–30, no restrictions to sight or hearing abilities, no knowledge of Lorm) successfully completed all lectures without further help by the supervisor. After each lecture, time and error rates were logged. Users required 17.5, 21.39, and 25.25 min, respectively. Finally, users had to complete two tests consisting of entering the complete alphabet in random order and without separation in lectures. In the first test they were shown animations of input and had to select the corresponding letter. The second test required them to do the correct input for a given letter. Rates of correct input for both tests were in average 99 %, 96 %, and 96 %, respectively. After a period of seven days, subjects did another session with the same type of tests (randomized order of letters). Against expectation of lower success rates due to lack of training, subjects 2 and 3 even increased their performance. They stated to have practiced by their own without any materials out of interest. This time, average success rates per user were 97 %, 99 %, and 97 %, respectively.

In a follow-up questionnaire, users rated illustrations, descriptions, and structuring of lectures helpful and stated that sufficient feedback was provided. Recognition of gestures was commented as being satisfying and badges motivating. One user criticized the awkward input with artificial fingernails. Another user had trouble with entering the second stroke for signing 'CH' within the implemented timeout which resulted in a recognition of 'Z'. He also asked for acoustic feedback.

## 5.3   Inspection by Experts

Three experts who use Lorm regularly inspected the Lorm application. Subsequently they rated (3-scale: negative, neutral, positive) items of a questionnaire

---

[4] An Asus Transformer Pad TF300TG (NVIDIA Tegra 3, 1,3 GHz, 1 GB RAM, Android 4.2.1) with 10,1" screen with capacitive 10 finger multi-touch.

regarding practicality and correctness of content, usefulness of structure and lectures, motivation by badges, intuitivity and recognition rates of gestures, design and measurements, general practicality and willingness to use. The first expert - a caregiver to a deaf-blind person - rated all questions positive, but mentioned that one has to get familiar with the slightly modified pinch gestures. She also sees the possibility of using LeLorm within education of assistance for deaf-blind.

The second expert is deaf (since age 14) and works since more than ten years with deaf-blind persons. She rated all questions positive and gave hints how the software can be modified to be used by deaf persons or people with low vision.

Within the context of a professional meeting, several persons with sight or hearing impairments tested our tool and gave positive feedback with a request for publication. Additionally, one of the caregivers for deaf-blind could be acquired for another expert feedback. He rated the tool intuitive and easy to use. It was stated that there is nothing comparable available.

## 6   Conclusion and Outlook

All experts confronted with our system as well as several interest groups requested the unique tool to be distributed. Utilization for teaching purposes, e.g., education for assistance of deaf-blind was recommended, too. Currently we are in the process of publishing the LeLorm app on the Google play store to make it available for free. Furthermore, we plan modifications for accessibility to people with hearing loss or eye disorder which would aid users affected by Usher syndrome in learning Lorm. Possibly - with concepts of audioguidance for gesture training - accessibility to blind persons might be achieved. Another future work, besides general internationalization, are extensions by other alphabets, for instance, Malossi.

**Acknowledgments.** The authors kindly thank all participants of our tests for their help, constructive input, and valuable feedback. We thank Michael Jobst for final modifications to the software for publishing it on the app store.

## References

1. Andersson, C., Campbell, D., Farquharson, A., Furner, S., Gill, J., Jackson, A., Lucker, J., Nolde, K., Werner, E., Whybray, M., et al.: Assistive technology for the hearing-impaired, deaf and deafblind. Springer Science & Business Media, London (2006)
2. Arato, A., Markus, N., Juhasz, Z.: Teaching morse language to a deaf-blind person for reading and writing SMS on an ordinary vibrating smartphone. In: Miesenberger, K., Fels, D., Archambault, D., Peňáz, P., Zagler, W. (eds.) ICCHP 2014, Part II. LNCS, vol. 8548, pp. 393–396. Springer, Heidelberg (2014)
3. Caporusso, N.: A wearable malossi alphabet interface for deafblind people. In: Proceedings of the Working Conference on Advanced Visual Interfaces, AVI 2008, pp. 445–448. ACM, New York (2008)

4. Coyette, A., Schimke, S., Jean, V., Vielhauer, C.: An algorithm for pen-based gesture recognition based on levenshtein distance. Working paper 07/05, Louvain School of Management, Universität catholique de Louvain (2007)
5. de Almendra Freitas, C.O., Oliveira, L.S., Aires, S.B.K., Bortolozzi, F.: Zoning and metaclasses for character recognition. In: Proceedings of the ACM Symposium on Applied Computing, SAC 2007, pp. 632–636. ACM, New York (2007)
6. Gollner, U., Bieling, T., Joost, G.: Mobile lorm glove: introducing a communication device for deaf-blind people. In: Proceedings of the Sixth International Conference on Tangible, Embedded and Embodied Interaction, TEI 2012, pp. 127–130. ACM, New York (2012)
7. Hussain, A.B.S., Toussaint, G.T., Donaldson, R.W.: Results obtained using a simple character recognition procedure on munson's handprinted. IEEE Trans. Comput. C–21(2), 201–205 (1972)
8. Impedovo, D., Pirlo, G.: Zoning methods for handwritten character recognition. Pattern Recogn. 47(3), 969–981 (2014)
9. Jacob, R.J.K.: The use of eye movements in human-computer interaction techniques: what you look at is what you get. ACM Trans. Inf. Syst. (TOIS) 9(2), 152–169 (1991)
10. Jaffe, D.L.: Evolution of mechanical fingerspelling hands for people who are deaf-blind. J. Rehabil. Res. Dev. 31(3), 236–244 (1994)
11. Lemke-Werner, G., für Blinden, V., Sehbehindertenpädagogik.: Taubblindheit, Hörsehbehinderung-ein Überblick. Ed. Bentheim (2009)
12. Li, X., Plamondon, R., Parizeau, M.: Model-based on-line handwritten digit recognition. In: International Conference on Pattern Recognition 2, 1134 (1998)
13. Scheithauer, M.C., Tiger, J.H.: A computer-based program to teach braille reading to sighted individuals. J. Appl. Behav. Anal. 45(2), 315–327 (2012)
14. Soraluze, I., Rodriguez, C., Boto, F., Perez, A.: Multidimensional multistage k-nn classifiers for handwritten digit recognition. In: Proceedings of Eighth International Workshop on Frontiers in Handwriting Recognition, pp. 19–23 (2002)
15. Szeto, A.Y.J., Christensen, K.M.: Technological devices for deaf-blind children: needs and potential impact. Eng. Med. Biol. Mag., IEEE 7(3), 25–29 (1988)

# HandiMathKey: Mathematical Keyboard for Disabled Person

Elodie Bertrand[1], Damien Sauzin[1,3(✉)], Frédéric Vella[1,3(✉)],
Nathalie Dubus[2,3(✉)], and Nadine Vigouroux[1,3(✉)]

[1] IRIT-UPS, 118 Route de Narbonne,
31062 Toulouse Cedex 9, France
{sauzin, vella, vigouroux}@irit.fr
[2] ASEI, 1 Avenue Tolosane,
31520 Ramonville St Agne, France
nathalie.dubus@asei.asso.fr
[3] Hand'Innov Agreement (IRIT and ASEI), Toulouse, France

**Abstract.** To type mathematical formula is a tedious task for all of us with the usual applications. Moreover, this task is very tiring for motor impairment. This paper describes the user centred methodology used to design the HandiMathKey virtual keyboard to type more easily the mathematical formula. Then we present a case study that compares the entry time between HandiMathKey and Word office for the mathematic formulas typing. This study shows that the Handi-Mathkey is easier to use and more efficient.

**Keywords:** Mathematical virtual keyboard · Accessibility · User centred approach

## 1 Introduction

In recent years, many research have focused on text entry assistive tools [1] – prediction system and layout of virtual keyboard – and on web browsing tool adapted to the disabled. These researches led to design appropriate devices or interfaces for disabled persons with motor impairment of upper limbs: for instance, the AVANTI web browser [2] and the INPH virtual keyboard [3] for navigation through as well as many virtual keyboards for text input [4]. Most of these disabled people use their virtual keyboard with an appropriate pointing device adapted to their abilities. The displacement carried out by the pointer of the pointing device on the screen causes motor fatigue [3]. Mackenzie [5] presented some metrics to measure the efficiency of keyboards. Scanning keyboard [6] is an alternative solution. Although many studies have been conducted (1) to increase the speed of text input and (2) to reduce the motor fatigue [4] there are few works about the design of a mathematical keyboard for all, but mainly for disabled with a motor impairment in upper limbs.

© Springer International Publishing Switzerland 2016
K. Miesenberger et al. (Eds.): ICCHP 2016, Part II, LNCS 9759, pp. 487–494, 2016.
DOI: 10.1007/978-3-319-41267-2_68

Within the context of Hand'Innov between IRIT and ASEI, the occupational therapists of the Jean Lagarde Centre for Specialized Secondary Education (CSSE) of ASEI[1] (http://www.asei.asso.fr/) have formulated a demand to design a mathematical keyboard to facilitate the typing of mathematical formula. Indeed, lot of students present important difficulties to type mathematical formula, because of their weak motor abilities and/or memory, or also their visual difficulties. So we are interested here in the entry of mathematical formulas. In fact, the main used text processing – Word Office and Writer Open Office – include menus with mathematical symbol buttons and a "sheet" in order to enter mathematical formulas and visualize them (see Fig. 1).

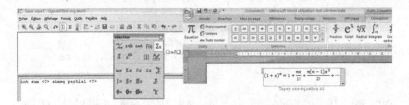

**Fig. 1.** Interfaces of OpenOffice Writer (left) and Word Office 2007 (right).

Typing these formulas remains therefore complicated and tiring for several reasons:

- Each mathematical symbol corresponds to a key not always easy to find in all the bars (a button displayed can match more symbols of the same category for example "fraction symbol");
- Many "round trips" between the entry sheet and interface buttons are needed; these "round trips" could generate attentional and motor fatigue for person with a motor impairment because there are many cursor movements;
- Typing with a physical keyboard needs "short cuts" knowledge and memory that increase the cognitive load.

The consequences are a waste of time and energy for students.

In this paper we describe the user centred methodology used to design our solution, named HandiMathKey. Then we present a case study that compares the performance and the usability between HandiMathKey and Word Office for formula typing.

## 2   Design Methodology

### 2.1   User Centred Design

We conducted four meetings with five members of the Jean Lagarde CSSE: 3 occupational therapists; 2 teachers: one in mathematics and one in physics and chemistry. The aim of these meetings was to define the list of mathematical symbols and functions

---

[1] ASEI welcomes children with motor, visual, hearing impairment and dysphasia. The ASEI concerns the overall care, support, education and the integration of people with disabilities and dependent or vulnerable persons.

needed for two levels of education: college and high school. These virtual interfaces must be used with both two text editors (Word Office and OpenOffice Writer). Firstly, we conduct a cognitive introspection on main applications allowing to the typing mathematical formula. Secondly, sketches of graphical user interface have been drawn. Finally, a first prototype was designed.

### 2.2 Cognitive Introspection of Existing Solutions

The aim of this cognitive introspection is to list the main applications allowing to type mathematical formula. This allowed us to identify advantages and disadvantages of each application.

10 tools have been studied. A classification in three classes of tools for typing mathematical formulas is proposed:

- The first ones are included in the Word Office and OpenOffice Writer as Dmaths [9], MathType [10], MathMagic [11], Rapid Pi [12];
- The second ones are online specific editors like Wiris Editor [13], ShareMath [14], Daum Equation Editor [15];
- The third types are desktop applications like GeoGebra [16], MathCast [17], Math-o-mir [18].

The main advantage of these interfaces is the presence of tabs that permits the displaying of several symbols at the same location on the screen.

The inconvenient are: (1) too small keys; (2) too large size of virtual interface and (3) none of these solutions allows writing directly in Word Office and OpenOffice Writer document.

This last inconvenient is a high source of fatigue and cognitive overload. Moreover, some symbols requested by the teachers are not available in the studied solutions.

### 2.3 Design of Graphical User Interface Sketches

After the cognitive introspection, brainstorming and meetings with two occupational therapists and one mathematics teacher from ASEI, a paper prototype was designed (see Fig. 2a). Then we held several focus groups, which have generated several keyboard modifications during the iterative design cycle.

The layout of mathematics keyboards (see Fig. 2) consists of numbers, Latin letters and some Greek letters, symbols of sixty functions for the college level and fifteen more for the high school level.

A system of tabs was designed to allow the user to choose the symbols available within a specific tab. This choice of selection was retained both to reduce the size of the virtual mathematics keyboard and to facilitate the choice of the symbol. All symbols don't appear simultaneously on the keyboard interface, but they are all accessible through the selection of the corresponding tab. Symbols and functions matching with the topic of a tab are grouped under the same tab. When a student will do an exercise in geometry, for example, all the geometric symbols are available under the geometric tab. Therefore, he will not have to change between tabs. This design choice was retained to

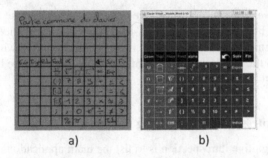

a)    b)

**Fig. 2.** (a) Paper prototype and (b) High-fidelity prototype

facilitate the key choice and so, reduce the selection time. Six themes have been defined after search of mathematics major themes studied in college and high school on the internet. These are Arithmetic, Geometry, Trigonometry, Probability/Statistics and functions. After that, we categorized the symbols and functions of the specifications in these themes.

Then, several high-fidelity prototypes (see Fig. 2b) were designed with the SoKeyTo platform [4]. This platform allows designing the morphology, the semantic and the interaction of each key of a virtual keyboard. Furthermore, the spatial layout could be also defined according class of functions for instance. Following the expression of needs we start the design with the keyboard those students already known.

## 2.4   Design of the HandiMathKey

We have designed two final virtual keyboards: one for College (see Fig. 3) and another one for high school. The reason for designing two versions is to not complicate the college keyboard with the high school symbols. Then the mathematical formulas requested by teachers have been added (see Fig. 3). Three types of keys have been defined: the blue keys correspond to mathematical symbols that will be used for all themes (geometry, trigonometry, probability and functions).

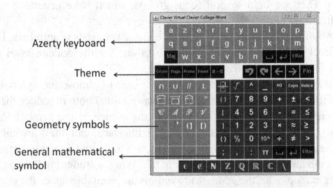

Azerty keyboard ←

Theme ←

Geometry symbols ←

General mathematical ←
symbol

**Fig. 3.**   College level HandiMathKey

The orange keys are associated to a single theme, here geometry symbol. Azerty keyboard and Greek keyboard were added to facilitate the text input of the Greek symbol. A button allows switching between these two keyboards. We have chosen to put these keyboards in the field of vision.

## 2.5 Case Study

This case study aims to compare the duration of input mathematical formulas with two tools: the HandiMathKey, designed for the College and the mathematical formula tools of Word Office. It was carried out by a person suffering from Myopathy. This person uses daily a virtual keyboard with a trackball as pointing device. The interaction technique is single pointing. Usually, he does not type mathematical formula. The corpora test consist of five text documents containing all symbols and mathematical functions, representative of the five mathematical categories defined by mathematic teachers: general, geometry, trigonometry, probability and functions. The corpora consist in 166 mathematical symbols, 486 numerical digits and 147 functions. After the input mathematical formula, the person has completed a satisfaction survey.

# 3   Results and Discussion

As results, classical metrics [7] to measure the efficiency of a keyboard are reported — time, distance and the number of keys—. The Fig. 4 reports the total time that was necessary to type all the mathematical formulas respectively with the Word Office tools and with the HandiMathKey College. Note that the time input with the HandiMathKey College is more than two times lower than that achieved with the Word tools. This result is independent of the formula theme.

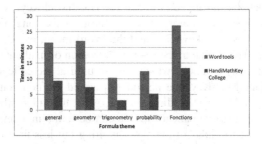

**Fig. 4.** Time of formula typing between HandiMathKey College and Word tools. (Color figure online)

The travel distance (see Fig. 5a) of device cursor is more important for Word tools than HandiMathKey. Indeed, when the participant uses the Word tools, the distance is over ten times higher for the "General" and almost seven times higher for the "probabilities" compared to those of HandiMathKey.

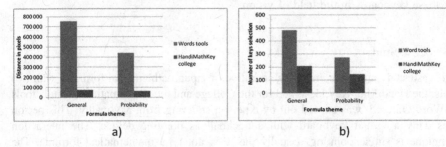

a)                                                                b)

**Fig. 5.** (a) Distance of formula typing between HandiMathKey College and Word Office tools and (b) Number of keys selection of formula typing between HandiMathKey College and Word tools.

Moreover, the number of keys for typing a formula (See Fig. 5b) — key of HandiMathKey and buttons of Word Office tools— is two times more high with the Word tools than HandiMathKey. This difference can be explained by a lot of pointing to be performed between the mathematical formula components, the entry sheet and the interface buttons of the Word. The design choice of structuring the HandiMathKey layout in several sub-keyboards corresponding to a specific theme is relevant. However other tests should be pursued.

Thanks to the questionnaire the person has issued opinions on the use of Word Office and HandiMathKey. A likert scale was used in four points: 1: Not at all agree, 2: Disagree, 3: Somewhat agree, 4: Strongly agree.

The Table 1 shows that the HandiMathKey is easy to use and to learn compared to Word Office tools. The use of HandiMathKey reduces the fatigue and the mobilized attention. The participant has loved so much the HandiMathKey.

Using Word tools causes motor fatigue because of the long distances of travel, between the Windows virtual keyboard and the Word menu, and the large number of manipulations to do. This is due to the poor organization of mathematical symbols and the presence of too many symbols, which are not used at the college level.

When using HandiMathKey, the person has issued opinions on the writing of a formula is naturally, just as the reading thereof. Also, that all symbols and functions necessary for entering a mathematical formula can be found in a single interface. And finally, the seizure last formulas of the study is tiring but less than using Word tools.

The disabled person produces rich verbatim during the experiment: For the HandiMathKey keyboard "The keyboard allows natural writing just like to read the formula" and for the Word tool: "Every time I must click again on insert key, I hate, it tires me because there are too many movements to do".

**Table 1.** Likert scale in four points.

|    | Questions on tools used | Word Office Tools | HandiMathKey |
|----|-------------------------|-------------------|--------------|
| 1  | The learning of the tool is easy | 2 | 4 |
| 2  | The tool is easy to use | 2 | 4 |
| 3  | The use of the tool seems intuitive | 2 | 4 |
| 4  | The use is tiring | 4 | 2 |
| 5  | The tool is attractive | 3 | 4 |
| 6  | The organization of the keys/buttons seems logical to you | 3 | 3 |
| 7  | The colored blocks are useful for the choice of the function | 4 | 4 |
| 8  | The images on the keys well represent the key functions | 4 | 4 |
| 9  | Memorizing keyboard commands is easy | 2 | 3 |
| 10 | The visual feedback seems useful | 3 | 4 |
| 11 | Using the keyboard/tool has mobilized attention/concentration | 4 | 1 |
| 12 | You have achieved the task in an acceptable time you see when using the tool | 1 | 4 |
| 13 | You enjoyed using the tool | 1 | 4 |

## 4 Conclusion and Future Work

The HandiMathKey is currently used at the CSSE by students with motor impairment and dysphasia. The feedback of mathematics teacher and occupational therapist is very positive. A usability survey will be conducted among students and teachers in mathematics after six month of use. Another deployment is currently done at the university library of the University Paul Sabatier on free computer for disabled students.

**Acknowledgments.** This work is developed in the framework of the Hand'Innov agreement. We thank Christine Gallard for his involvement in the project.

## References

1. Gara-Vitoria, N., Abascal, J.: Text prediction systems: a survey. Univ. Access Inf. Soc. **4**, 188–203 (2006)
2. Stephanidis, C., Paramythis, A., Karagiannidis, C., Savidis, A.: Supporting interface adaptation: the AVANTI web-browser. In: 3rd ERCIM Workshop on User Interfaces for All (UI4ALL 1997), Strasbourg, France (1997)
3. Dieudonné, V., Mahieu, Ph., Machgeels, Cl.: INPH interface de navigation pour personnes handicapées moteurs. In: IHM 2003, pp. 202–205 (2003)

4. Vella, F., Vigouroux, N.: Layout keyboard and motor fatigue: first experimental results. AMSE J. **67**, 22–31 (2007)
5. MacKenzie, I.: Modeling text input for single-switch scanning. In: Miesenberger, K., Karshmer, A., Penaz, P., Zagler, W. (eds.) ICCHP 2012, Part II. LNCS, vol. 7383, pp. 423–430. Springer, Heidelberg (2012)
6. Swiffin, A.L., Arnott, J.L., Pickering, J.A., Newell, A.F.: Adaptive and predictive techniques in communication prosthesis. Augmentative Altern. Commun. **3**, 181–191 (1987)
7. Sauzin, D., Vella, F., Vigouroux, N.: SoKeyTo: a tool to design universal accessible interfaces. In: International Conference on Applied Human Factors and Ergonomics (AHFE 2014), Pologne, pp. 659–670 (2014)
8. Anthony, L., Yang, J., Koedinger, KR.: Evaluation of multimodal input for entering mathematical equations on the computer. In: Proceedings CHI 2005 Extended Abstracts on Human Factors in Computing Proceeding, pp. 1184–1187 (2005)
9. https://www.dmaths.org/
10. http://www.dessci.com/en/products/mathtype/
11. http://www.mathmagic.com/
12. http://trident-software-pty-ltd.software.informer.com/
13. http://www.wiris.com/editor
14. http://sharemath.com/
15. http://s1.daumcdn.net/editor/fp/service_nc/pencil/Pencil_chromestore.html
16. https://www.geogebra.org/?lang=fr
17. http://mathcast.sourceforge.net/home.html
18. http://gorupec.awardspace.com/mathomir.html

# A Study of an Intention Communication Assisting System Using Eye Movement

Shogo Matsuno[✉], Yuta Ito, Naoaki Itakura, Tota Mizuno, and Kazuyuki Mito

Graduate School of Informatics and Engineering, The University of Electro-Communications,
Tokyo, Japan
m1440004@edu.cc.uec.ac.jp

**Abstract.** In this paper, we propose a new intention communication assisting system that uses eye movement. The proposed method solves the problems associated with a conventional eye gaze input method. A hands-free input method that uses the behavior of the eye, including blinking and line of sight, has been used for assisting the intention communication of people with severe physical disabilities. In particular, a line-of-sight input device that uses eye gazes has been used extensively because of its intuitive operation. In addition, this device can be used by any patient, except those with weak eye. However, the eye gaze method has disadvantages such as a certain level of input time is required for determining the eye gaze input, or it is necessary to present the information for fixation when performing input. In order to solve these problems, we propose a new line-of-sight input method, eye glance input method. Eye glance input can be performed in four directions by detecting reciprocating movement (eye glance) in the oblique direction. Using the proposed method, it is possible to perform rapid environmental control with simple measurements. In addition, we developed an evaluation system using electrooculogram based on the proposed method. The evaluation system experimentally evaluated the input accuracy of 10 subjects. As a result, an average accuracy of approximately 84.82 % was determined, which confirms the effectiveness of the proposed method. In addition, we examined the application of the proposed method to actual intention communication assisting systems.

**Keywords:** Eye movement · Eye blink · Human interface · Eye gaze input

## 1 Introduction

Hands-free intention communication methods are sought by people having severe physical disabilities, such as amyotrophic lateral sclerosis (ALS) patients. There are conventional one-switch methods that use eye blinks [1–3] and line-of-sight input methods [4–10], which are used by ALS patients for performing intent transmission by using remaining physical functions. The one-switch method determines an input by performing an eye blink when it becomes the desired state by shifting the operating screen at regular intervals. This structure of the method is simple, and it is easy to operate and set. However, the disadvantage of this method is that it increases the operation load on the user as more time is required for input or correction. In contrast, the line-of-sight method inputs characters to a computer by capturing the line-of-sight of a user, using a

© Springer International Publishing Switzerland 2016
K. Miesenberger et al. (Eds.): ICCHP 2016, Part II, LNCS 9759, pp. 495–502, 2016.
DOI: 10.1007/978-3-319-41267-2_69

recording instrument such as a video camera. The line-of-sight input method only requires the motion of the eyeball or eyelids. Therefore, it can be used in patients with limited motor function such as ALS patients. Moreover, the eye gaze input method, which is a type of line-of-sight input method, is possible for intuitive operation as the position of the eye gaze is directly used as input value. Therefore, several line-of-sight input devices have been developed as input method for hands-free intended communication. The eye gaze input method has a high degree of accuracy, as has been established by previous studies. However, the eye gaze input method has the following disadvantages

1. The positional relationship between the user's head and the measuring instrument needs to be fixed in order to precisely identify the position of the eye gaze position from a moving angle.
2. A certain level of input time is required for determining eye gaze input.
3. It is necessary to present the information for fixation when performing input.
4. The size of the equipment required for performing high-precision measurement is large.

In previous research, we proposed an eye gesture input method in order to solve these problems [11]. The eye gesture input method focuses on the direction of movement of the line-of-sight rather than the position of the eye gaze. This method does not require the head to be restrained as it focuses only on the direction of movement of the line of sight. In addition, it is possible to reduce the variation of input accuracy in each direction by using the input of the line-of-sight movement in the oblique direction because measurement of the oblique direction can avoid to the point in a vertical direction of the line-of-sight is difficult to measure as compared to a horizontal direction. However, the eye gesture input method cannot automatically distinguish between the input intention as it cannot clearly determine whether the eye movement was intended or not. This problem in conjunction with the problem 2 of the eye gaze input method is known as Midas Touch problems [12, 13]. We examined the eye glance input method [14] for limiting the input conditions of the eye gesture input method in order to solve this problem. The eye glance input method uses the reciprocating movement in the oblique direction of the line-of-sight (Eye Glance) for entering inputs. Reciprocating movement of the line-of-sight is generated hardly work unless done with the intention for routine. Thus, the method solves the Midas Touch problem by to start the input when observe the reciprocating movement. In addition, previous intention communication assisting systems based on the eye gaze input method required an information display. In addition, the eye gaze input method requires more measurement accuracy to specify the eye gaze fixation position when the information display area is narrowed. On the contrary, the accuracy of the eye glance input method is not dependent on the size of the information display because it measures only the direction of movement. In other words, a user does not require an information display if the user is able to ascertain even input values. Therefore, the proposed method can be expected to resolve problem 4 by miniaturization of the system equipment.

In this paper, we consider an intention communication assisting method using the eye glance input method. We were examined the input of the few options that assumes a case of performing predetermined simple intention communication by experiment. In addition, we investigate how to enter many alternatives in order to perform various intention communication assisting.

## 2   Eye Glance Input Interface Using Amplitude by AC-EOG

An electrooculogram (EOG) generally uses a DC amplifier, including a DC component, for amplifying a signal (DC-EOG). DC-EOG is known to show a linear relationship with respect to eye angle. Therefore, there are many studies on line-of-sight input systems using DC-EOG. However, a user must adjust the offset of the signal in DC-EOG. In addition, change in potential is slow as changes in the contact resistance of the electrode leads to the so-called drift phenomenon, which is a problem. It is necessary to stabilize the contact resistance between an electrode and skin by performing the experiment after sufficient time has passed since pasting the electrode in order to avoid drift phenomenon. The proposed system uses an AC amplifier for amplifying the signal by cutting the low-frequency components (AC-EOG). Thus, the use of an AC-EOG can be helpful in avoiding these problems. The potential of the AC-EOG is attenuated by being influenced by the time constant. The time constant is set even when there is no eye movement. As a result, the eye gaze fixation position cannot be determined from the potential variation because the potential and the eyeball angle disappears in a linear relationship. The advantages of using AC-EOG are that the drift phenomenon is avoided and it is possible to adjust the offset. Figure 1 shows an example of a horizontal exchange EOG when subjected to fixation after the eye moves in the left direction. When the eye moves, potential waveform returns to the baseline after a large potential fluctuation occurs. The movement of the eye is emphasized by calculating the difference value. From these characteristics, detecting eye movement is possible by setting a threshold value. In addition, the amount of line-of-sight movement can be estimated from the integrated value of zero-crossing waveforms during eye movement. Therefore, the movement of eyes can be measured.

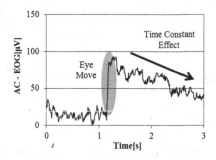

**Fig. 1.**   Sample data waveform of AC-EOG.

The eye glance input method dealing with eye movement observes the (glance) the four corners of an information display area as an input signal. The system must detect the reciprocating eye movement in the diagonal direction. This is indicated by the arrow shown in Fig. 2. The arrow represents the reciprocal line-of-sight movement in a diagonal direction to the base point of the center. This eye movement is hardly in normal times. Therefore, it is possible to suppress an unintended input by assuming it at the start of the input process. Figure 3 shows an example of a difference EOG waveform when the eyes glanced in an upper right direction. Positive values of the horizontal component represent the left direction, while negative values represent the right direction of eye movement. Further, positive values in the vertical component represent the upward direction, while negative values represent the downward direction of a line-of-sight. The region near point 'a' of Fig. 3 shows the movement of the eye from the center to the upper right direction. The region near point d shows the difference waveforms of the EOG generated by moving the eye from the upper right direction to the center. Thus, the eye glance input method distinguishes between four directions by using a combination of two eye movements.

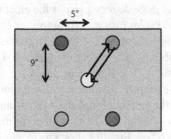

**Fig. 2.**   Experiment screen of Eye Glance.

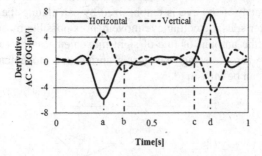

**Fig. 3.**   AC-EOG difference of Eye Glance.

## 3   Detection Algorithm

The features of EOG waveform of the eye glance input timing include large individual difference. Therefore, accuracy is improved by performing a calibration. Calibration is performed to determine the detection threshold and the input waiting time between two reciprocating eye movements. In addition, calibration is performed to measure the eye glance once in the upper right and lower left directions. The detection threshold is determined by averaging the smallest value of the difference peak value during eye movement and the value of RMS before eye movement. The input waiting time is used as long latency between two Eye Glances.

The first step in the detection algorithm involves determining the difference between the horizontal and vertical components of an AC-EOG. Next, the algorithm searches for a part which crosses a detection threshold is a horizontal difference value, after then, detecting a continuous waveform twice in horizontal direction. Moreover, it is judged whether two waveforms detected reverse, whether both waveforms are continuous at short intervals. This is checked between point a to point d of Fig. 3. Next, the direction of the vertical component is determined. The vertical component is measured upward or downward at the peak time of the horizontal component. Finally, detecting waveform is determined the blinking or not. An eye blink is assumed to occur when the vertical component is greater. An eye blink determines the maximum value of the vertical component as compared with the component of time of calibration.

## 4   Experiment

The detection experiment for the eye glance input method proposed in Sects. 2 and 3 were carried out for 10 subjects.

### 4.1   Experiment Environment

Electrode in the horizontal direction component 1ch, the average of 2ch and 3ch a vertical component. A small device that consists of a signal acquisition section, which corresponds to the signal amplifier, and an A/D converter, which corresponds to the biological amplifier for capturing EOG signals. The device has a low cut frequency of 0.1 Hz, a high cut frequency of 10 Hz, a horizontal gain of 66 dB, and a vertical gain of 72 dB. The device is connected to the computer through a USB connection with a sampling frequency of 100 Hz. In addition, to perform noise reduction at a high cut frequency of 10 Hz even during data acquisition, it is necessary to remove noise components at the high frequency even for a difference value.

A PC monitor was used in this experiment. The subject sat in front of the monitor. The subject performed an input operation in accordance with the input instruction and the output was obtained from the monitor. The resultant signals were forwarded to the PC through the device mentioned above. After that, the system will return feedback the result performs detection processing in real time to subject.

### 4.2   Experiment Procedure

In order to evaluate the detection precision of the eye glance input system, the detection algorithm described in Sect. 3 was used. The experiment was carried out by instructing the subject to perform the input process through displaying indications shown in Fig. 2 to the PC monitor. The subject provided 40 eye glance inputs, including 10 inputs in each of the four oblique directions, and the discrimination rate was calculated. The direction of the input instruction was random every time. The input instruction is displayed as soon as the subject uses the input keyboard of the experimental PC. After then, subject act Eye Glance. The system output in the background was decided in each direction when the input signal was detected. The detection results are to the subject. Eye Glance waveform of two.

### 4.3    Evaluation of the Experimental Results

Table 1 shows the experimental results. The average detection success rate was 84.82 % for all subjects. The results show that the detection algorithm does not limit a user. Subjects I and J showed a lower success rate than other subjects. We examined the eye glance waveform of the two subjects individually. It was observed that the waveform in the horizontal and vertical components were displaced in the peak time of the wave-form. We believe that the eye glance could not be detected as the peak of the vertical component is was overlooked. This problem can be addressed by expanding the search range of the peak of the vertical component in the time direction. Another cause for the decrease in detection rate was that the eye glance waveform was not recorded for some subjects after the input instruction. As a reason, too much to be aware of the input, it is thought that it has become an awkward operation.

**Table 1.**    Result of evaluation experiment.

| Subjects | Success rate [%] |
|----------|------------------|
| A        | 92.5             |
| B        | 97.5             |
| C        | 100.0            |
| D        | 87.5             |
| E        | 87.5             |
| F        | 97.5             |
| G        | 80.0             |
| H        | 82.5             |
| I        | 65.0             |
| J        | 60.0             |
| Average  | 84.82            |

### 4.4    Application to Intention Communication Assisting System

As a result, it was possible to confirm that the four choices input is possible to determine with about 85 % accuracy at present. We attempted to determine the causes of the errors in this experiment. All errors were oversight detection. There were no false positives. Detection oversight may be dealt with by prompting the system to re-enter the user at considering the application to the input interface. Therefore, although improvements in accuracy are necessary, the results of applying the input interface of the proposed detec-tion algorithm can be considered sufficient. In this experiment, we used a computer monitor owing to the requirements of the evaluations; however, in real operations, a monitor would not be necessary. That is, the user can input information even while watching a paper or board, if the system can measure the EOG signal, assuming that the user understands the execution result corresponding to the input direction.

The proposed method allows four choices of input operation. This is for severely physically disabled persons, which means that it is possible to operate in various ways just using the simple motion of eye movement. For example, operations such as calling for a nurse and start-up of other communication assisting systems, configured in advance, can be performed. In addition, it is possible to increase the number of options by combining the plurality of eye glances. For example, two eye glances mean $4 \times 4 = 16$ choices, while three glances mean 64 choices, which is high enough that complex inputs such as character input can be performed in the system. Moreover, an increasing number of choices does not change the required accuracy of the measuring instrument because it does not require an information display area. In addition, we believe that this method is also applicable to non-handicapped persons because there is no need for fixation of the head and the input response time is faster. This method can work when both hands are occupied, such as operating equipment with the hands and feet, environmental controls, and operation of wearable devices.

## 5   Conclusion

In this paper, we proposed the Eye Glance input method as a hands-free input interface. We evaluated the input accuracy of an AC-EOG system based on the proposed method. We found that an average determination accuracy of 84.82 % is obtained with four choices of input. This result indicates that it is possible to construct a decision algorithm that does not limit the user. Additionally, we investigated multi-choice for the application method and the input interface for the purpose of communication assisting systems based on the proposed method.

In the future, we aim to improve the input accuracy of multi-choices. In addition, we want to build a real intention-communication assisting system and assess its operational performance.

## References

1. Baljko, M., Tam, A.: Indirect text entry using one or two keys. In: Proceedings of 8th International ACM SIGACCESS Conference on Computer and Accessibility, pp. 18–25, October 2006
2. Machkenzie, I.S.: The one-key challenge: searching for a fast one-key text entry method. In: Proceedings of 11th International ACM SIGACCESS Conference on Computers and Accessibility, pp. 91–98, October 2009
3. Yamada, M., Fukuda, T.: Eye word processor (EWP) and peripheral controller for the ALS patient. Phys. Sci. Measur. Instrum. Manag. Educ. IEEE Proc. A **134**(4), 328–330 (2008)
4. Mollenbach, E., Hansen, J.P., Lillholm, M., Gale, A.G.: Single stroke gaze gestures. In: CHI 2009 Extended Abstracts on Human Factors in Computing Systems, pp. 4555–4560, April 2009

5. Abe, K., Sato, H., Matsuno, S., Ohi, S., Ohyama, M.: Input interface using eye-gaze and blink information. In: Tino, A., Stephanidis, C. (eds.) HCII 2015 Posters. CCIS, vol. 528, pp. 463–467. Springer, Heidelberg (2015). doi:10.1007/978-3-319-21380-4_78

6. Pedrosa, D., Pimentel, M.D.G., Wright, A., Truong, K.N.: Filteryedping: design challenges and user performance of dwell-free eye typing. ACM Trans. Accessible Comput. 6(1), 1–37 (2015)

7. Kherlopian, A.R., Gerrein, J.P., Yue, M., Kim, K.R., Kim, J.W., Sukumaran, M., Sajda, P.: Electrooculogram based system for computer control using a multiple feature classification model. In: Proceedings of the 28th IEEE EMBS Annual International Conference, pp. 1295–1298, August 2006

8. Mondal, C., Azam, Md.K., Ahmad, M., Hasan, S.M.K., Islam, Md.R.: Design and implementation of a prototype electrooculography based data acquisition system. In: Proceedings of International Conference on Electrical Engineering and Information Communication Technology, pp. 1–6, May 2015

9. Yagi, T.: Eye-gaze interfaces using electro-oculography (EOG). In: Proceedings of the 2010 Workshop on Eye Gaze in Intelligent Human Machine Interaction, pp. 28–32, February 2010

10. Taher, F.B., Amor, N.B., Jalloulo, M.: A multimodal wheelchair control system based on EEG signals and Eye tracking fusion. In: Proceedings of International Symposium on Innovations in Intelligent SysTems and Applications, pp. 2–4, September 2015

11. Gao, D., Itakura, N., Mizuno, T., Mito, K.: Improvement of eye gesture interface. J. Adv. Comput. Intell. Intell. Inf. 17(6), 843–850 (2013)

12. Velichkovsky, B., Sprenger, A., Unema, P.: Towards gaze-mediated interaction: collecting solutions of the "Midas touch problem". In: Proceedings of IFIP TC13 International Conference on Human-Computer Interaction, 14–18 July, pp. 509–516, September 1997

13. Vrzakova, H., Bednarik, R.: That's not norma(n/l): a detailed analysis of midas touch in gaze-based problem-solving. In: CHI 2013 Extended Abstracts on Human Factors in Computing Systems, pp. 85–90, April 2013

14. Matsuno, S., Akehi, K., Itakura, N., Mizuno, T., Mito, K.: Computer input system using eye glances. In: Yamamoto, S., Abbott, A.A. (eds.) HIMI 2015. LNCS, vol. 9172, pp. 425–432. Springer, Heidelberg (2015). doi:10.1007/978-3-319-20612-7_41

# A Review of Computer-Based Gesture Interaction Methods for Supporting Disabled People with Special Needs

Chutisant Kerdvibulvech[✉]

Graduate School of Communication Arts and Management Innovation,
National Institute of Development Administration, Bangkok, Thailand
chutisant.ker@nida.ac.th

**Abstract.** Gesture interaction is currently a very emerging field in computer science and engineering. This is since it is able to allow humans to communicate interactively with the machine via numerical linear algebra and mathematical techniques. In this paper, we discuss various modern state-of-the-art techniques the academic researchers including the author have attempted in recent years in order to achieve the gesture recognition and interaction in a robust way interactively. This paper is divided into three main parts. First, we introduce hand gesture recognition and body gesture recognition for general purposes using computer vision technology. These include a fast learning mechanism from an accurate six-degrees-of-freedom pose tracker, a real-time extended distance transform for the hand model, and a robust integration of support vector machine and superpixels. Second, recent gesture interaction methods, more specifically, for helping disabled people with special needs are reviewed using human-computer interaction and sensor technology. These methods include combinatorial approach recognizer (CAR), hand skeleton recognizer (HSR) and Viewpoint Feature Histogram (VFH). Third, we discuss the advantages and disadvantages of the aforementioned gesture interaction methods. By understanding the state-of-the-art approaches for computer-based gesture interaction presented recently by leading researchers, this would advance beneficially the interactions that persons with disabilities would conveniently, practically and easily have with modern recognition technology.

**Keywords:** Gesture recognition · Gesture interaction · Physical disabled people · Computer vision · Interface · Wearable computing · Sensor technology

## 1 Gesture Recognition

In recent years, gesture recognition is popularly one of the most interesting subjects in related-computer science, computer engineering and language technology. Generally, the main aim of gesture recognition is to interpret human gestures, such as hand and body, using numerical linear algebra and mathematical techniques for human-computer interaction. We divide into two main groups. The first group is hand gesture recognition. There are some significant methods about hand gesture recognition presented recently.

© Springer International Publishing Switzerland 2016
K. Miesenberger et al. (Eds.): ICCHP 2016, Part II, LNCS 9759, pp. 503–506, 2016.
DOI: 10.1007/978-3-319-41267-2_70

For example, Kiliboz and Gudukbay [1], in 2015, introduced a real-time robust gesture recognition algorithm for hand using a quick learning mechanism and a six-degrees-of-freedom pose tracker interactively. By collecting gesture data and learning process, it is able to help adaptively increasing new gestures to the recognized gesture set. However, the number of hand recognized gestures is still limited due to hand gesture space dimensions. In addition in 2015, a hand gesture recognition technique was presented in [2] by extending distance transform and utilizing the hand model interactively. The algorithm is also computed and performed in real-time with accurate and promising results. The work of [2] also shows several representative examples for hand gesture tracking. Nevertheless, this method has the limitation about self-occlusion. The second group is body gesture recognition. There are several important methods proposed in recent years for body gesture recognition. For instance, a human pose gesture recognition method was built by Kim et al. [3] in 2015 using SVM (support vector machine). Superpixels are then used for reducing the processing time. It uses just depth information and operating with just a CPU (Central Processing Unit). Therefore, the mobile platform of this method, e.g., embedded surveillance boards, is not expensive, but it is quite practical. Nonetheless, this method has the limitation about the estimation of body orientation in the human pose estimation process. Next, a human-computer interaction technique for continuous body gesture recognition from an unsegmented input stream was created by Song and Davis [4] from Massachusetts Institute of Technology (MIT) in 2015. With a temporal sliding window, three dimensional coordinates of body joints are estimated using a multimodal filtering method continuously. Thus, it is able to recognize and track body gesture from an unbounded input stream. Moreover in 2014, a technique for analyzing structural human shape was presented in [5]. It use 3D gait signatures computed from 3D data for modeling and gesture recognition. However, this technique has the limitation about the database for collecting a large number of human subjects. With advances in recognition technology robustly from the modern developments in the 21st century, gesture recognition both hand and body plays a significant role for assisting disabled people with special needs. The next section will discuss about the gesture recognition methods for enhancing people with disabilities.

## 2   Recent Gesture Interaction Methods for Disabled People

Gesture interaction is one of the possibly practical and interactive ways to help people with disabilities, including hand gesture recognition. For example, gesture interaction for hand is able to be utilized for interpreting sign language for impaired people with special needs. In 2015, Luo et al. [6] presented a gesture interaction technique for hand by integrating two recognizers to determine the sign language of hand. Combinatorial approach recognizer (CAR) equation and hand skeleton recognizer (HSR) are utilized for gesture interaction. This human-computer interaction research output is purposely used for assisting disabled people and robot to recognize automatically what message they need to interpret and convey for deaf community. Also in 2015, Sempere et al. [7] developed a small robotic system for monitoring activities of disabled people with special needs in the home using Viewpoint Feature Histogram (VFH) and sensor technology. This system is composed of an adaptive interface with a motorized webcam and a cheap RGBD sensor for recognizing hand gestures. After that, it is programmed and ordered by hand gesture interaction in three dimensions to control this low-cost robot. Their experiment has revealed that the system is beneficial for assisting people with physical disabilities and elderly persons, such as moving from one place to another inside their house for observing what is happening remotely. However, this mini-robot has some limitation about how to define the behaviors and tasks of the robotic system. In addition, Premaratne [8] in 2014 suggested a good overview of hand gesture interaction methods for interpreting and deciphering from American Sign Language (ASL) and Australian Sign Language (Auslan). This work also gave a good explanation about several main challenges of the hand gesture recognition from both static hand posture and dynamic hand movement when using computer vision technology for sign languages. Moreover in 2014, a wearable activity recognition research was introduced by Kirkham [9] for assisting people with disabilities by ameliorating a range of disability related symptoms prosthetically using sensor technology. It is somewhat similar to assistive technology equipment. This system has a suite of sensors for wearable computing platforms. The work of [9] also displays some good examples of accessibility of the wearable activity recognition system. Representative accessibility of the wearable activity recognition system is utilized for helping physical disabled people using sensor technology by ameliorating a range of disability related symptoms. The aim of this research is to combine the domains of wearable computing for activity recognition and disability discrimination law in the mutual benefit scheme. Furthermore, Gomez-Donoso and Cazorla [10] in 2015 built a human-computer interaction prototype for recognizing Schaeffer's gestures, a reduced set of gestures developed to support disabled people, using computer vision. By applying this recognition technique, it helps people with cognitive impairment by capturing body gesture, and then sends alarms to a disability caregiver. Nevertheless, although the system is quite reliable and beneficial for people with physical disabilities, it has the limitation since it is able to recognize just a small subset of different gesture classes (i.e., 11 gesture classes in this work).

## 3    Advantages and Disadvantages

According to the mentioned works, it is obvious that there are many advantages of the aforementioned methods for gesture recognition for supporting physical disabled people with special needs. Beneficially, those advantages are such as [6] for assisting deaf people robotically to recognize their message for interpreting, [7] for observing elderly persons with special needs remotely, [8] for interpreting from sign languages and [9] for ameliorating a range of disability related symptoms. Still, there are several advantages of the aforementioned works, such as the system requirement for training in [8] and the requirement of a subset for gesture classes in [10]. In conclusion, we believe that by understanding the recent robust gesture interaction methods, it would advance practically the interactions between disabled people with special needs and modern recognition tools, and also would technologically improve the life chances of people with impairments in more convenient ways.

# References

1. Kılıboz, N.Ç., Güdükbay, U.: A hand gesture recognition technique for human–computer interaction. J. Vis. Commun. Image Represent. **28**, 97–104 (2015). Academic Press, Inc., Orlando, FL, USA
2. Kerdvibulvech, C.: Hand tracking by extending distance transform and hand model in real-time. Pattern Recogn. Image Anal. **25**(3), 437–441 (2015). Springer Publisher
3. Kim, H., Lee, S., Lee, D., Choi, S., Ju, J., Myung, H.: Real-time human pose estimation and gesture recognition from depth images using superpixels and SVM classifier. Sensors **15**(6), 12410–12427 (2015). Multidisciplinary Digital Publishing Institute (MDPI)
4. Song, Y., Davis, R.: Continuous body and hand gesture recognition for natural human-computer interaction. In: International Joint Conference on Artificial Intelligence (IJCAI), Buenos Aires, Argentina, vol. 4212. AAAI Press (2015)
5. Kerdvibulvech, C., Yamauchi, K.: Structural human shape analysis for modeling and recognition. In: Fränti, P., Brown, G., Loog, M., Escolano, F., Pelillo, M. (eds.) S + SSPR 2014. LNCS, vol. 8621, pp. 282–290. Springer, Heidelberg (2014)
6. Luo, R.C., Wu, Y.-C., Lin, P.H.: Multimodal information fusion for human-robot interaction. In: Proceeding of IEEE 10th Jubilee International Symposium on Applied Computational Intelligence and Informatics (SACI), Timisoara, Romania, pp. 535–540. IEEE Computer Society (2015)
7. Sempere, A.D., Serna-Leon, A., Gil, P., Puente, S., Torres, F.: Control and guidance of low-cost robots via gesture perception for monitoring activities in the home. Sensors **15**(12), 31268–31292 (2015)
8. Premaratne, P.: Sign languages of the world. In: Human Computer Interaction Using Hand Gestures. Cognitive Science and Technology. Springer, Singapore, 174 pages, March 2014
9. Kirkham, R.: Forays into disability discrimination legislation and wearable computing. In: Proceeding of ACM International Symposium on Wearable Computers (ISWC), Seattle, WA, USA, 13–17 September, pp. 119–124. ACM (2014)
10. Gomez-Donoso, F., Cazorla, M.: Recognizing Schaeffer's gestures for robot interaction. In: Puerta, J.M., Gomez, J.A., Dorronsoro, B., Barrenechea, E., Troncoso, A., Baruque, B., Galar, M. (eds.) Advances in Artificial Intelligence, CAEPIA'15. LNAI, vol. 9422, pp. 1045–1054. Springer (2015)

# Optimizing Vocabulary Modeling
# for Dysarthric Speech Recognition

Minsoo Na[1] and Minhwa Chung[2(✉)]

[1] Interdisciplinary Program in Cognitive Science, Seoul National University,
Seoul, South Korea
dix39@snu.ac.kr
[2] Department of Linguistics, Seoul National University, Seoul, South Korea
mchung@snu.ac.kr

**Abstract.** Imperfection in articulation of dysarthric speech results in the deterioration on the performance of speech recognition. In this paper, the effect of the articulating class of phonemes in the dysarthric speech recognition results is analyzed using generalized linear mixed models (GLMMs). The model with the features categorized according to the manner of articulation and the place of tongue is selected as the best one by the analysis. Recognition accuracy score for each word is predicted based on its pronunciation and the GLMM. The vocabulary optimized by selecting words with the maximum score shows a 16.4 % relative error reduction in dysarthric speech recognition.

**Keywords:** Dysarthria · Vocabulary modeling · Speech recognition

## 1 Introduction

Dysarthria is a motor speech disorder caused by damage to the central or peripheral nervous system. As the error rate of recognition is significantly higher when dysarthric speakers use an ASR system developed for non-dysarthric speakers, researchers have focused on improving the models for recognition. The speech recognizer is composed of models such as acoustic model, pronunciation model, vocabulary and language model. The acoustic characteristic of dysarthric speech is analyzed and dysarthric speech is converted to be heard as normal speech [1]. The acoustic model is improved by using speaker adaptation or by using DNN [2]. Confusions in pronunciation are modeled as pronunciation variants or embedded to the search network [3]. In ASR-based applications developed for dysarthric speakers, recognition errors are reduced not only by improving the models but also by defining problems in the application of ASR with small vocabulary and simple-patterned utterances for lowering perplexity [4–6]. The voice keyboard [5] is an interface for inputting the mapped key by recognizing an isolated word utterance, which is a method for text input using small vocabulary isolated word recognition. A phonetic alphabet is set as the default vocabulary for the interface [5, 6]. Customizing the vocabulary leads to a decrease in the errors in recognition [6], however, the customization is performed by trial and error. One of the characteristics of dysarthric speech is imperfection in articulation. The frequencies of articulation errors of phoneme and of class of phoneme are observed in

K. Miesenberger et al. (Eds.): ICCHP 2016, Part II, LNCS 9759, pp. 507–510, 2016.
DOI: 10.1007/978-3-319-41267-2_71

dysarthric speech [7, 8]. For consonants, fricatives and affricates show higher error rates when classified by manner of articulation and alveolars show higher rates when classified by place of articulation and the error rate for monophthongs at extreme positions such as /i, ae, a/ is higher [7]. The difference between recognition accuracy by ASR system and score of intelligibility test by human rater is observed [9].

From previous researches, we assume that error rates in recognition depend on the class of the phoneme and the effect of the articulating the classes in recognition result rather than in the judgement of human raters is analyzed in order to estimate the recognition performance of each word based on its phoneme-level pronunciation. We analyze the effect of the articulating class of phoneme in dysarthric speech recognition result using the generalized linear mixed model (GLMM) and define the recognition score based on the analysis of optimizing the vocabulary for improving the ASR performance.

## 2   Method

In our voice keyboard, users enter text into the application by repeatedly uttering a recognition word for a target alphabet. Korean graphemes are composed of 19 consonants, 8 monophthongs, and 13 diphthongs. We exclude 5 consonants for fortis and 9 less frequent diphthongs from arrangement of the keys in the voice keyboard due to lack of data, which results in the keyboard having a total of 47 keys for 14 consonantal graphemes, 12 vowel graphemes and 21 control functions.

Two sets of isolated word corpus of Korean dysarthric speakers are used for analysis and evaluation [10]. The vocabulary of one corpus is composed of 173 words and the other is 500 words. Recording the word utterances is repeated at least twice for 13 speakers. One set among two sets of the utterance is used for the acoustic model adaptation, and the other is used for recognition test. The GMM-HMM models are trained and adapted by applying fMLLR and MAP methods [11]. The isolated word grammar for a total of 47 words in a vocabulary is made to define the search network. The number of phonemes for each class in the canonical pronunciation of the word for an utterance in the speech corpus is counted. Severity of the speaker and four types of counts according to criteria of classification of consonants and vowels are written to form the fixed effects of the generalized linear mixed model (GLMM). Speaker ID and word ID are also included as the random effects in the model. As a result, four GLMMs are built to predict the recognition accuracy: Place-Frontness model, Place-Height model, Manner-Frontness model and Manner-Height model. Among the models, the Manner-Frontness model minimizes the negative of log likelihood and the model size. The estimates of the model are shown in Table 1.

Fricative, Nasal, Front, Central, Back and Severity are significant ($p < 0.05$). Accuracy decreases as Severity and the number of Fricative and Lateral increases. Accuracy increases as the number of Nasal, Plosive, Affricate, Diphthongs and monophthongs increases.

The word set of the speech corpus includes three types of alphabet word lists whose words are selected based on their ease of articulation. Words in each alphabet word lists and 1-best words among control candidate set are combined to yield three kinds of

**Table 1.** Estimate of the Manner-Frontness model.

| Effects | Intercept | Plosive | Fricative | Affricate | Nasal | Lateral |
|---------|-----------|---------|-----------|-----------|-------|---------|
| Estimate | 3.96 | 0.04 | −0.26 | 0.03 | 0.20 | −0.04 |
| Sign. | *** | | * | | * | |
| Effects | Front | Central | Back | Severity | Diphthong | |
| Estimate | 0.36 | 0.80 | 0.44 | −1.57 | 0.08 | |
| Sign. | *** | *** | *** | *** | | |

*** p<0.001,
* p<0.05

baseline word lists. The recognition score of each word is defined as a weighted sum of the number of phonemes in each phoneme class counted from canonical pronunciation and the estimates of the Manner-Frontness model. The word error rate (WER) is the rate of the number of substitution and deletion errors from the total recognition number.

As shown in Table 2, the average WER of 100 trials of the random selection is 17.2 %. WERs using three alphabet word lists are $16.5 \sim 18.2$ %. Using the maximum of the number of phonemes as criterion for selecting words shows a 16.8 % rate and using the minimum criterion shows a 21.1 % rate. The differences between the WERs of baselines are not significant.

**Table 2.** Recognition results

| WER, % | Baseline | | | | | | Recognition Score |
|--------|----------|---|---|---------|---------|----------------|-------------------|
| | Phonetic Alphabet | | | Minimum | Maximum | RandomSelection | |
| | Set 1 | Set 2 | Set 3 | | | | |
| | 18.2 | 16.5 | 17.8 | 21.1 | 16.8 | 17.2 | 13.8 |

Using the word list with the highest recognition score, a 13.8 % WER is obtained, which is a 16.4 % relative improvement compared to the baseline. The improvement is statistically significant ($p < 0.05$).

## 3   Conclusions

In this paper, four sets of the articulation features for each word are defined and the relationship between the features and WERs is analyzed using a GLMM. Among the models, the Manner-Frontness model is selected as the best one by the analysis. Estimates of the GLMM are observed and applied to calculate the recognition score. The results from Table 1 that increasing the number of Fricative increases the recognition error rates and the number of Nasal increases the accuracy are consistent with the analysis of the articulation errors of the English dysarthric speech. The difference between monophthong and diphthong is also consistent. The fortis phonemes which are complex to articulate seem to lower the estimate of Plosive. The vocabulary is optimized with words having the maximum recognition score for voice keyboard interface and, as a result, the WER decreases by 16.4 %, relatively. The results would be extended to other language by the mapping between the class of the phoneme in Korean and other language.

**Acknowledgements.** This work has been supported by the R&D Program of MKE/KEIT (10036461, Development of an embedded key-word spotting speech recognition system individually customized for disabled persons with dysarthria).

# References

1. Rudzicz, F.: Adjusting dysarthric speech signals to be more intelligible. Comput. Speech Language **27**(6), 1163–1177 (2013)
2. Christensen, H., Aniol, M.B., Bell, P., Green, P., Hain, T., King, S., Swietojanski, P.: Combining in-domain and out-of-domain speech data for automatic recognition of disor-dered speech. In: Proceedings of INTERSPEECH 2013, pp. 3642–3645 (2013)
3. Morales, S.O.C., Cox, S.J.: Modelling errors in automatic speech recognition for dy-sarthric speakers. EURASIP J. Adv. Signal Process. **2009**, 308–340 (2009)
4. Hawley, M.S., Cunningham, S.P., Green, P.D., Enderby, P., Palmer, R., Sehgal, S., O'neill, P.: A voice-input voice-output communication aid for people with severe speech im-pairment. IEEE Trans. Neural Syst. Rehabil. Eng. **21**(1), 23–31 (2013)
5. Kim, S., Hwang, Y., Shin, D., Yang, C.-Y., Lee, S.-Y., Kim, J., Kong, B., Chung, J., Cho, N., Kim, J.-H., Chung, M.: VUI development for Korean people with dysarthria. J. Assistive Technol. **7**(3), 188–200 (2013)
6. Hamidi, F., Baljko, M., Livingston, N., Spalteholz, L.: CanSpeak: a customizable speech interface for people with dysarthric speech. In: Miesenberger, K., Klaus, J., Zagler, W., Karshmer, A. (eds.) ICCHP 2010, Part 1. LNCS, vol. 6179, pp. 605–612. Springer, Heidelberg (2010)
7. Platt, L.J., Andrews, G., Howie, P.M.: Dysarthria of adult cerebral palsy: II. phonemic analysis of articulation errors. J. Speech Language Hear. Res. **23**, 41–55 (1980)
8. Whitehill, T.L., Ciocca, V.: Speech errors in Cantonese speaking adults with cerebral palsy. Clin. Linguist. Phonetics **14**(2), 111–130 (2000)
9. Mengistu, K.T., Rudzicz, F.: Comparing humans and automatic speech recognition sys-tems in recognizing dysarthric speech. In: Advances in Artificial Intelligence, pp. 291–300 (2011)
10. Choi, D-L., Kim, B-W., Lee, Y-J., Um, Y., Chung, M.: Design and creation of dysarthric speech database for development of QoLT software technology. In: Proceedings of International Conference on Speech Database and Assessments 2011, pp. 47–50 (2011)
11. Povey, D., Ghoshal, A., Boulianne, G., Burget, L., Glembek, O., Goel, N., Hannemann, M., Motlicek, P., Qian, Y., Schwarz, P., Silovsky, J., Stemmer, G., Vesely, K: The kaldi speech recognition toolkit. In: Proceedings of ASRU 2011 (2011)

# Comparison of Two Methods to Control the Mouse Using a Keypad

Torsten Felzer[1], Ian Scott MacKenzie[2(✉)], and John Magee[3]

[1] Institute for Mechatronic Systems, Technische Universität Darmstadt, Darmstadt, Germany
felzer@ims.tu-darmstadt.de
[2] Department of Electrical Engineering and Computer Science, York University, Toronto, Canada
mack@cse.yorku.ca
[3] Math and Computer Science Department, Clark University, Worcester, MA 01610, USA
jmagee@clarku.edu

**Abstract.** This paper presents a user study comparing two methods for keyboard-driven mouse replacement: CKM, an active Conventional Keyboard Mouse, and DualMouse, an innovative keyboard technique allowing stepwise, recursive target acquisition. Both strategies are implemented in the pointing component of OnScreenDualScribe, a comprehensive assistive software system that turns a compact keypad into a universal input device. The study involves eight non-disabled participants and a single user with Friedreich Ataxia. The results reveal that CKM yields about 60 % higher throughput that DualMouse. However, the DualMouse technique is preferable for certain specific tasks. Our intention with this research is to gain new insights into OnScreenDualScribe and to inspire future developers of mouse-replacement interfaces for persons with physical disabilities.

**Keywords:** Assistive technology · Neuro-muscular diseases · Keyboard replacement · Mouse replacement · Fitts' law · Real-world use

## 1 Introduction

Computer users with a motor disability often rely on alternative input interfaces, since standard entry devices (e.g., a keyboard and mouse) might be cumbersome, error-prone, inefficient, effortful, or impossible to use. One example for an alternative interface is OSDS (OnScreenDualScribe) [5] which was designed for persons with certain neuro-muscular diseases. OSDS receives input from a modified numeric keypad called DualPad (Fig. 1).

The main problem with full-size keyboards is the need to frequently reposition the hands between keys [13]. DualPad avoids this, since it is securely grabbed with both hands with every key reached from the same hand position. However, computer interaction also relies on mouse control. Switching between multiple devices would eliminate DualPad's advantage. Such was the drawback of the initial version of OSDS [3], which only replaced the keyboard. The current version implements three methods to control

© Springer International Publishing Switzerland 2016
K. Miesenberger et al. (Eds.): ICCHP 2016, Part II, LNCS 9759, pp. 511–518, 2016.
DOI: 10.1007/978-3-319-41267-2_72

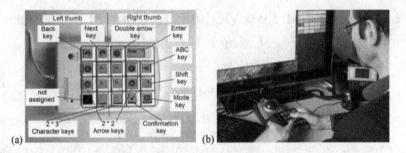

**Fig. 1.** Input device used in the study: (a) key labels (b) in action

the mouse. The methods are implemented internally and do not require an extra pointing device. Two of those methods are compared in this paper.

## 2   Related Work

The first author is the creator of OnScreenDualScribe and has previously presented details of its development, evaluation, and related work [3, 6]. The authors previously employed an evaluation technique similar that presented in this paper for mouse selection modalities with a camera-based interface [10]. The evaluation used Fitts' law, which is widely used for pointing device evaluation [9, 14]. Mouse pointing and selection tasks could also be modeled as a Keystroke-Level-Model using the Goals, Objects, Methods, Selection (GOMS) model [2, 8].

A Fitts' law evaluation on the AngleMouse [16] showed improved throughput for users with motor impairments while showing no significant differences for non-disabled users. Similar evaluation techniques were used to compare head orientation against neck muscle EMG signals in a pointer interface [15].

Evaluations of Alternative and Augmentative Communication (AAC) methods in the rehabilitation and speech pathology communities often focus on functional and outcome-based metrics (e.g., [1]). In the HCI and Computer Science communities, participatory design and user satisfaction metrics are often employed (e.g., [11]).

Other relevant point-select evaluations measure both qualitative user feedback and quantitative performance. For example, the Manual and Gaze Input Cascaded (MAGIC) [17] technique warps the mouse pointer to an intended area of the screen for further refinement. A user study found reduced physical effort and fatigue as compared to traditional manual pointing, greater accuracy and naturalness than traditional gaze pointing, and comparable or faster speed than manual pointing.

## 3   Implementation

To interact with a computer, persons who rely on a compact, tangible interface may use OSDS which serves as a driver for the keypad depicted in Fig. 1. The program computes virtual input events sent to the active window based on physical input from the user.

In this way, it fully emulates a standard keyboard and a two-button mouse (complying to [7] in the context of "real-world" applications).

For mouse emulation, the user chooses among three methods [6]. The first method is a simple active keyboard mouse (also called Continuous Keyboard Mouse or CKM) with certain keys for moving the mouse pointer in cardinal directions and other keys for issuing clicks at the current position. It is "active" because mouse movement continues while the user actively presses a key.

The second method (DKM for Discrete Keyboard Mouse) is similar, but the user only initiates a mouse movement in a certain direction, and then passively waits – while the pointer moves in that direction – before stopping the pointer by pressing a key. Both techniques have the disadvantage of requiring physical input events at specific points in time (so that the movement does not overshoot). This might be problematic for users with deficient fine-motor control. The third strategy, DualMouse, does not rely on mouse movement at all, but directly clicks at a destination location selected by the user following a step-by-step locating process.

The example in Fig. 2 gives an explanation of DualMouse. Suppose, the goal is to click on the little white circle below "Johannes Kepler Universität" in a web browser showing the ICCHP map. Initially, the screen is divided into 24 rectangles or cells (Fig. 2a). The user then selects the row and column of the cell containing the target. This is recursively repeated (Fig. 2b, c and d), meaning the cell is sub-divided and the user selects the appropriate sub-cell. Recursion can terminate (resulting in a click) if the target lies in the center of the current sub-cell (in the example, Fig. 2d). Left-clicking at this destination accesses details on the university hosting ICCHP (Fig. 2e).

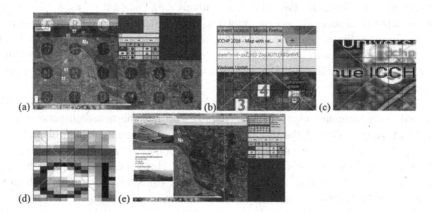

**Fig. 2.** Stepwise mouse control: (a) screen overlaid with 4 × 6 grid (b) recursion on cell B (c) enlarged sub-cell (d) last necessary refinement (e) screen after click (see text for explanation)

## 4  Evaluation

This section and the next describe a user study and a case study. First, we describe a user study with eight non-disabled participants (mean age 25 years, 2 female).

The results serve as a baseline for the input methods under test and for comparison with a case study with a representative user.

Two of the input methods described in Sect. 3 were chosen for evaluation: CKM and DualMouse. The evaluation uses FittsTaskTwo which implements the ISO 9241 Part 9 protocol for evaluating pointing devices (see [10] for related work using the same software). The task involves selecting circular targets of a specified width ($W$) at a specified amplitude ($A$) in a certain order. Thirteen target circles are arranged in a layout circle, as shown in Fig. 3.

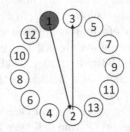

**Fig. 3.** FittsTaskTwo evaluation software (explanation in text)

Selecting all thirteen targets constitutes a sequence of trials. The diameter of the layout circle sets the amplitude of movement. Two amplitudes were used: 300 pixels and 500 pixels. Two target widths were used: 30 pixels and 60 pixels. Thus, there were 8 participants × 2 input methods × 4 blocks × 2 amplitudes × 2 widths × 13 selections per sequence = 3328 total trials. This is a relatively small amount of testing; however, this was a practical necessity as early pilot tests revealed that the time for each selection is 10 to 20 times longer than the time to do the same task using a regular mouse (with non-disabled users). Each input method was tested in a separate session, which lasted about one hour per participant. The two input methods were counterbalanced (4 participants per group) to offset learning effects.

The case study engaged a user from the target community. The participant is a 45-year-old male computer user, the first author, who has the neuromuscular disease Friedreich Ataxia. Due to the disease, he has deteriorating motor control problems keeping him from efficiently utilizing a full-size keyboard. His voice is dysarthric, so he cannot use speech recognition as an alternative. However, he (presently) has the manual control ability to hold the keypad in both hands and press keys with the thumbs, and thus uses OSDS daily to interact with a computer.

## 5    Results and Discussion

Although data for several dependent variables were collected, due to space limitations we focus primarily on the results for throughput. Throughput is a composite measure computed from the speed and accuracy in selecting targets [14].

In the user study with non-disabled participants ($n = 8$), the grand mean for throughput was 0.41 bits/s. This value is low – about $1/10^{th}$ the value typically obtained in mouse studies (see [14] for examples).[1] Clearly, the methods evaluated herein are not competitive with mouse input for non-disabled users. The main limitation is the movement time (*MT*) to select targets. *MTs* were typically in the range of 5 to 20 s per trial. This is compared to *MTs* typically under 1 s for similar tasks performed with a mouse.

The results for throughput by input method are seen in Fig. 4a. Throughputs were 0.31 bits/s for DualMouse and 0.52 bits/for CKM, representing a performance advantage of 68 % for CKM. The difference was statistically significant ($F_{1,6} = 115.4, p < .0001$). The results were consistent by participant, with throughputs ranging from 0.41 bits/s (P03) to 0.64 bits/s (P07) for CKM and from 0.19 bits/s (P03) to 0.60 bits/s (P07) for DualMouse. See Fig. 4b. Although not shown, there was a statistically significant improvement over the four blocks of trials ($F_{3,18} = 23.7, p < 0001$).

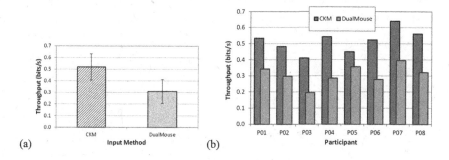

**Fig. 4.** User study results for throughput (bits/s) (a) by input method and (b) by participant (Color figure online)

In the case study with a user from the target community (n = 1), the grand mean for throughput was 0.17 bit/s. By input method, the means were 0.21 bits/s for CKM and 0.13 bits/s for DualMouse. See Fig. 5. This reflects a performance advantage of 63 % for the CKM. Interestingly, this performance advantage for CKM, as a percent, was similar to the 68 % advantage for CKM in the user study with non-disabled participants.

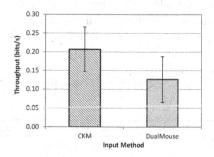

**Fig. 5.** Case study results for throughput (bits/s) by input method

---

[1] Each participant also did one post-experiment block of trials using a mouse. The mean throughput for the mouse trials was 4.26 bits/s.

Some examples of pointer traces are seen in Fig. 6. The remarkably different patterns are due entirely to the unique ways of repositioning the pointer in the CKM (left) and DualMouse (right) input methods. With the CKM input method, each selection is at a location differing from the last selection only in the x-coordinate (lateral movements) or y-coordinate (vertical movements). Hence, movement appears as lateral or vertical jumps in the cursor position. By contrast, with the DualMouse input method, recursively sub-dividing and zooming in to a location causes each selection to differ from the preceding selection by both the x- and y-coordinate. Hence, there is an apparent pattern of diagonal movement in the cursor position. Importantly, there is cognitive agreement between how the user feels the cursor is moving and the patterns shown in the figure.

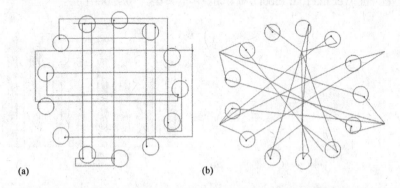

(a)                                        (b)

**Fig. 6.** Pointer trace examples in the case study for (a) the CKM input method and (b) the DualMouse input method. For both examples, $A = 500$ pixels and $W = 60$ pixels

We noted above that, as a percent, the performance advantage in throughput for CKM over DualMouse was similar ($\approx 60\%$) in the user study and the case study. The same percent difference is apparent when contrasting the results between the user study and the case study. See Table 1. The shaded cells contrast the results "by study" for movement time (s), error rates (%) and throughput (bits/s). The throughput for the participant in the case study was about 60 % lower than the mean throughput for the participants in the user study. This is true both for the CKM input method and the DualMouse input method. This result reflects an overall performance disadvantage for the user in the target community compared to non-disabled users.

**Table 1.** Comparison of results for user study and case study. Shaded cells show the difference (%) between studies

| Input Method | Study | Movement Time (s) | | Error Rate (%) | | Throughput (bits/s) | |
|---|---|---|---|---|---|---|---|
| | | Mean | diff | Mean | diff | Mean | diff |
| CKM | User study (n = 8) | 6.9 | | 2.42 | | 0.52 | |
| | Case study (n = 1) | 7.83 | +13.5% | 5.77 | +138.4% | 0.21 | -60.2% |
| DualMouse | User study (n = 8) | 12.1 | | 2.88 | | 0.31 | |
| | Case study (n = 1) | 11.78 | -2.7% | 1.92 | -33.2% | 0.13 | -59.0% |

For movement time (s), the user study and case study results were similar. For error rate (%), the case study participant had a lower error rate with the DualMouse input method, but a substantially higher rate for the CKM input method.

## 6   Conclusion

The objective of this paper is not to introduce OSDS nor its mouse modes, as both have been introduced elsewhere. Rather, the contribution is in the evaluation. This is the first time the innovative stepwise mouse control method implemented in OSDS is compared to the well-known keyboard mouse technique involving a Fitts' law task.

The results of this comparison are not only relevant for the development process of OSDS (and thus prospective future users). In addition, the results have a direct impact on research on mouse-replacement interfaces as a whole. Potential beneficiaries are users who are unable to use a standard mouse.

Despite multiple promising attempts to evaluate the software involving a larger group of members of the target population (e.g., [12]), the developer of OSDS himself so far remains the only truly committed test subject. However, it is hoped that this research will assist in motivating new users. In short, the time to get familiar with the tool is ultimately repaid. The more successful users have already expressed positive experiences.

This paper together with the text entry study involving non-disabled participants presented two years ago [4] mark the start of a series of user tests. The overall goal is to evaluate the entirety of OSDS features, positioning it as a useful assistant for persons with certain physical disabilities.

**Acknowledgments.** This work is partially supported by DFG grant FE 936/6-2 "EFFENDI – EFficient and Fast text ENtry for persons with motor Disabilities of neuromuscular orIgin".

## References

1. Branson, D., Demchak, M.: The use of augmentative and alternative communication methods with infants and toddlers with disabilities: a research review. Augmentative Altern. Commun. **25**(4), 274–286 (2009)
2. Card, S.K., Newell, A., Moran, T.P.: The Psychology of Human-Computer Interaction. L. Erlbaum Associates Inc., Hillsdale (1983)
3. Felzer, T., MacKenzie, I., Rinderknecht, S.: DualScribe: a keyboard replacement for those with Friedreich's ataxia and related diseases. In: Miesenberger, K., Karshmer, A., Penaz, P., Zagler, W. (eds.) ICCHP 2012, Part II. LNCS, vol. 7383, pp. 431–438. Springer, Heidelberg (2012)
4. Felzer, T., MacKenzie, I., Rinderknecht, S.: Applying small-keyboard computer control to the real world. In: Miesenberger, K., Fels, D., Archambault, D., Peňáz, P., Zagler, W. (eds.) ICCHP 2014, Part II. LNCS, vol. 8548, pp. 180–187. Springer, Heidelberg (2014)
5. Felzer, T., MacKenzie, I.S., Rinderknecht, S.: Efficient computer operation for users with a neuromuscular disease with OnScreenDualScribe. J. Interact. Sci. **2**(2) (2014)

6. Felzer, T., Rinderknecht, S.: Mouse mode of OnScreenDualScribe: three types of keyboard-driven mouse replacement. In: CHI EA, pp. 1593–1598. ACM (2013)

7. Jansen, A., Findlater, L., Wobbrock, J.O.: From the lab to the world: lessons from extending a pointing technique for real-world use. In: CHI EA,. pp. 1867–1872. ACM (2011)

8. John, B.E., Kieras, D.E.: Using GOMS for user interface design and evaluation: Which technique? ACM Trans. Comput.-Hum. Interact. (TOCHI) 3(4), 287–319 (1996)

9. MacKenzie, I.S.: Human-Computer Interaction: An Empirical Research Perspective. Elsevier, Amsterdam (2013)

10. Magee, J., Felzer, T., MacKenzie, I.S.: Camera Mouse + ClickerAID: Dwell vs. single-muscle click actuation in mouse-replacement interfaces. In: Antona, M., Stephanidis, C. (eds.) Universal Access in HCI. LNCS, vol. 9175, pp. 74–84. Springer, Heidelberg (2011)

11. Newell, A.F., Gregor, P., Alm, N.: HCI for older and disabled people in the Queen Mother Research Centre at Dundee University, Scotland. In: CHI EA, pp. 299–302. ACM (2006)

12. Saulynas, S., Albar, L., Kuber, R., Felzer, T.: Using OnScreenDualScribe to support text entry and targeting among individuals with physical disabilities. In: Proceedings of ASSETS, pp. 303–304. ACM (2015)

13. Soni, D.M.: A review on Friedreich Ataxia, a neurodegenerative disorder. J. Drug Deliv. Ther. 4(6), 45–52 (2014)

14. Soukoreff, R.W., MacKenzie, I.S.: Towards a standard for pointing device evaluation, perspectives on 27 years of Fitts' law research in HCI. Int. J. Hum.-Comput. Stud. 61(6), 751–789 (2004)

15. Williams, M.R., Kirsch, R.F.: Evaluation of head orientation and neck muscle EMG signals as command inputs to a human-computer interface for individuals with high tetraplegia. IEEE Trans. Neural Syst. Rehabil. Eng. 16(5), 485–496 (2008)

16. Wobbrock, J.O., Fogarty, J., Liu, S., Kimuro, S., Harada, S.: The angle mouse: target-agnostic dynamic gain adjustment based on angular deviation. In: CHI, pp. 1401–1410. ACM (2009)

17. Zhai, S., Morimoto, C., Ihde, S.: Manual and gaze input cascaded (MAGIC) pointing. In: Proceedings of the CHI, pp. 246–253. ACM (1999)

# AT and Rehabilitation for People with Motor and Mobility Disabilities

# Kalman-Based Approach to Bladder Volume Estimation for People with Neurogenic Dysfunction of the Urinary Bladder

Alessandro Palla[1](✉), Claudio Crema[2], Luca Fanucci[1], and Paolo Bellagente[2]

[1] University of Pisa, Pisa, Italy
alessandro.palla@for.unipi.it, luca.fanucci@unipi.it
[2] University of Brescia, Brescia, Italy
{c.crema001,p.bellagente}@unibs.it

**Abstract.** People with neurogenic dysfunction of urinary bladder often require daily catheterism because of their impairment. This issue is particularly critical for those that have not the urinary stimulus, because they have not the ability to understand when the bladder is full or not. From user's point of view, the absence of a urinary conscious stimulus can cause refluxes, damaging patient's health and his psychological status. For such necessities, most patients require professional nursing, increasing the work of the staff and the overall medical costs. Furthermore, catheterism itself applied every day for a long period can cause infection in the urinary tract. The authors propose a non-invasive bladder monitoring system based on real-time bioimpedance measurement. A Klaman filter was developed in order to estimate the bladder volume due to the intrinsic-uncertainty of the model itself and to remove the artifacts due to patient's movements by using accelerometer by monitoring it's activity. Theoretical analysis, in-system measurements and experimentations prove the effectiveness of the proposed solution.

**Keywords:** Bioimpedance · Bladder · Disability · Kalman filter · Neurogenic dysfunction · Wearable device · Bluetooth · Real time

## 1 Introduction

Some patient groups (for example, paraplegics) have an impaired bladder volume sensation due to damaged neural structures, often associated with the inability to urinate properly. A common therapy is regular intermittent self-catheterization [1,2] following a fixed time schedule. However, the emptying interval has to be chosen properly: a too short interval will unnecessarily interfere with quality of life and increase the risk of urethral damage or urinary infections, whereas a too long interval will increase the risk of complications due to an overfull bladder, e.g. over-distention of the bladder wall, reflux, hydronephrosis or autonomic dysreflexia [3]. Therefore, a demand-driven emptying scheme would be preferable for some patients. To achieve this, a promising concept is non-invasive continuous

© Springer International Publishing Switzerland 2016
K. Miesenberger et al. (Eds.): ICCHP 2016, Part II, LNCS 9759, pp. 521–528, 2016.
DOI: 10.1007/978-3-319-41267-2_73

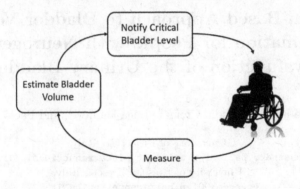

**Fig. 1.** System conceptual block diagram

impedance-based volume monitoring to estimate the appropriate moment for catheterization.

In this paper, authors propose a non-invasive and wearable bladder monitoring system based on bioimpedance measurement, as shown in Fig. 1. The systems exploit the difference in conductivity between urine and the tissue surrounding the bladder. Urine conductivity is mainly influenced by its saline concentration [4] and is usually in the impedance range of 526. In contrast, the tissues surrounding the bladder (muscles, connective tissue and fat) are in the impedance range of 0.24 [5]. To overcome the limitation due to electronic noise, external disturbances and model uncertainly, a Kalman Filter (KF) has been designed in order to estimate the bladder volume from noise bioimpedance measurements.

## 2    State of the Art Analysis

From literature and medical machinery, ultrasound measurements [6,7] and tomography [8] are the classical ways to measure bladder volume, due to their high reliability and well-known medical procedure. The work presented in [7] aims to create a low-cost wearable ultrasound bladder volume measurement and alarm system, based on ARM9 and DSP. To estimate bladder volume, this system uses a volume computing method based on the ultrasound echo obtained by one phased-array ultrasonic transducer. The signal processing of ultrasound echo is performed using a DSP chip; afterwards, the estimated value of bladder volume is transmitted to an alarm system based on ZigBee radio link. The bladder volume measurement and alarm system contains two parts. One is the wearable ultrasound measurements unit; the function of this part is to produce and receive ultrasonic pulse echo, processing it and estimating the bladder volume. After these operations are performed, the estimated volume is transmitted by means of a ZigBee wireless communication module to the second part, the alarm unit. Alarm unit's task are to receive the volume data, to set the personal bladder volume threshold and to trigger the warning when the threshold is exceeded.

In [8] two different approaches are presented: tomography algorithms, which rely on the reconstruction of a tomographic image and then extract a volume estimation, and parametric algorithms, which directly map the raw data to a volume estimate.

Electrical impedance tomography (EIT) is a medical imaging technique, which estimates an impedance distribution in the body volume by non-invasive measurements using electrodes attached to the skin. A small fixed current (e.g. 5 at 50 in accordance with IEC 60601-1) is applied to the body and the resulting voltage potential distribution is recorded. To generate one EIT frame, successive measurements with varying injecting electrodes are required, and for each injection, the voltage potentials of all remaining electrodes are recorded. In the two tomographic approaches, an image is reconstructed from the EIT raw data using a linear reconstruction matrix. These EIT frames are used to estimate the bioimpedance of the bladder, and thus its fill level, or they can be simply used in an image-processing algorithms, using the area of bladder pixels in the tomogram is used for estimation of the volume. Parametric approach can be used for volume estimation from EIT. Instead of mapping 208 EIT raw data to 1024 image pixels and extracting one volume estimate, a direct mapping of 208 EIT raw data to one volume estimate is proposed. This procedure is expected to reduce the influence of noise and numerical instabilities, which usually require regularization in image reconstruction. The proposed approach uses a feed-forward Neural Network: 208 input nodes and one single output node are used to represent the mapping from EIT raw data to the volume estimate, in addition to three hidden layers.

It appears clear that these techniques are best suited for high-cost medical equipment rather than wearable devices, due to the complexity and power consumption constraints of embedded devices.

Bioimpedance measurement can be used to estimate the bladder volume level, as proved in [9–11]. The idea behind this approach is quite simple: finding a correlation between the fill level of the bladder and its bioimpedance. This approach is well known, since one of the first works exploiting it has been published in 1971 [9]. The feasibility of using an oscillator, whose frequency is controlled by the bladder bioimpedance, to provide an electrical signal proportional to bladder volume for use in connection with an electronic bladder stimulator is presented. In this work, the frequency of an oscillator depends on the value of the bladder bioimpedance. Experiments were conducted on adult dogs; with electrodes attached directly to the bladder. To calibrate the electronic system, a urethral catheter was inserted to permit filling and emptying of the bladder with known amounts of warm normal saline. Most of the experiments were conducted with the electrodes placed on opposing lateral aspects of the bladder, approximately halfway from base to dome. Other tests involving anterior-posterior and base-dome electrode placement gave similar results, the most important factor being distance between electrodes. As the bladder fills, the bioimpedance increases in a manner roughly linearly proportional to bladder volume. This increase in resistance causes a corresponding decrease in oscillator frequency. Another work

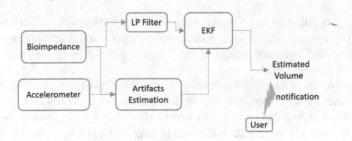

**Fig. 2.** System block diagram

which exploits this approach has been presented in [10]; the main difference is that the electrodes here are put on the abdomen of the dogs used for the experiment, and not inside their body, decreasing dramatically the invasiveness of this approach. The results obtained are similar, even if the relation is inverse: as the fill level increases, the bioimpedance value decreases with an almost linear relation. The work presented in [11] is an evolution of the aforementioned works: The system uses a four-electrode structure, which is composed of a pair of excitation electrodes and a pair of measurement electrodes. The Direct Digital Frequency Synthesis (DDS) is applied to generate a 50 kHz sine current excitation source. The impedance information extracted from phase sensibility demodulation technology is transferred to a computer through ZigBee wireless technology for real-time monitoring. These results show the feasibility of the bioimpedance measurement approach. However, this technique is still under study, and a commercial device for real-time bladder level monitoring is not yet available.

A feasibility study for real time bioimpedance measurements was performed recently in [12] using STMicroelectronics BodyGateWay (BGW) [13]. The BGW is a device that records a 1-lead electrocardiographic track and the bioimpedance of the subject by mean of 4 electrodes placed in a disposable patch, attached to the chest of the subject, plus his movements with a tri-axial accelerometer. Authors discovered a clear correlation between bladder volume and measured bioimpedance, but the data was afflicted by noise and uncertainly due to the patient movements.

## 3   System Description

Figure 2 shows the block diagram of the entire system. As previously mentioned, the sensing unit consists of a disposable patch and the BGW, which records the bioimpedance signal of the surface of the subject's skin (sampled at 32 Hz) and his tri-axial acceleration (sampled at 50), and stream them to a PC via a Bluetooth interface. Figure 3 shows BGW alone, on the left, and together with its patch, on the right. During these preliminary tests, four medical electrodes have been used, instead of the patch, because they can be placed anywhere, thus increasing the flexibility of the system and permitting to find the best configuration.

**Fig. 3.** BodyGateWay device and patch

**Fig. 4.** BodyGateWay device with medical electrodes

The medical electrodes are here attached in the lower part of the subject's abdomen, as shown in Fig. 4, in correspondence to his urinary bladder. This electrodes configuration was chosen, after several tests, in order to maximize the sensitivity of measurement regarding bladder filling and to reduce artifact due to movements. Figure 4 shows as well an example of bioimpedance measurement (Fig. 5).

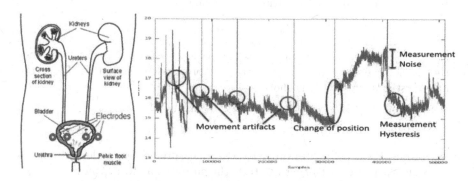

**Fig. 5.** BodyGateWay device with medical electrodes

A trend is clearly visible in the bioimpedacne during the bladder filling process, but artifacts due to the movements and random noise decrease the reliability of the measurement. To reduce the influence of these disturbances a Kalman Filter (KF) [14] has been designed based on the constant velocity model, as shown in Fig. 6. The state variables of the filter are the bladder volume $V_x$ and the urinary flux that fills the bladder $f_x = \dot{V}_x$.

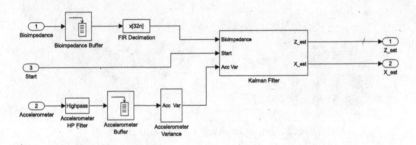

**Fig. 6.** Kalman filter model for bladder volume estimation

However the urinary flux is not observable from bioimpedance measurements. In order to take into account the flux variability, we can assume that urinary flux can be modeled as a constant flux plus a Brownian motion

$$f_x(t) = f_0 + B(t) \tag{1}$$

Due to the properties of Brownian motion [15,16], Eq. 1 can be rewritten as

$$\dot{f}_x(t) = q(t) \tag{2}$$

where $q(t) \sim \mathcal{N}(0, \sigma_q)$ is a Gaussian random variable with zero mean and standard deviation $\sigma_q$. The relation between bioimpedance and bladder volume, the mean urinary flux and the process noise covariance matrix were fitted by the acquired measurements.

To take into account the non-stationarity and impulsivity of movements disturbances, the measurement covariance is calculated as

$$q_m(k) = q_{m0} + \alpha * q_{acc} \tag{3}$$

where $q_{m0}$ is the noise covariance when the patient rests, $q_{acc}$ is the covariance of the accelerometers and $\alpha$ is a constant appropriately chosen. In Fig. 6 the complete estimation system is shown.

## 4    Results

A test protocol was defined in order to make measurement reliable and repeatable, as shown if Fig. 7. During the test, the subject has to lie, moving as less as possible in order to not generate artifacts, voiding his bladder when he feels the urge to do it, annotating the time and the quantity of expelled urine. In this first evaluation phase the measurement taken from the patients was used to fit the model parameters. In particular the parameter $f_0$ was estimated by

$$f_0 \simeq \mathbb{E}\{\frac{\Delta V_x}{\Delta T}\} \tag{4}$$

where $\Delta V_x$ and $\Delta T$ are measured urinary volume and time after each void and the operator $\mathbb{E}\{\cdot\}$ is the expectation.

**Fig. 7.** Test protocol

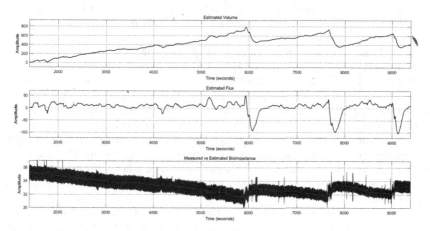

**Fig. 8.** Bladder volume estimation

Figure 8 shows an example of the estimation of the bladder volume, the urinary flux and the bioimpedance. In particular, it can be observed that in the three void phases the estimated urinary flux became negative, decreasing in such way the bladder volume. It can be shown as well that the system is capable to estimate the bladder volume even in the case of high measurement noise.

## 5   Conclusion

In this paper we proposed a wearable system capable to estimate the bladder volume from evaluating patient's skin bioimpedance. System tests and evaluations prove the validity and the effectiveness of the proposed solution in a real-word scenario. However a more extensive evaluation involving more users in order to validate and refine the model has been planned and will be carried out in the next future.

# References

1. Hald, T.: Neurogenic dysfunction of the urinary bladder. Ph.D. thesis, Coster (1969)
2. Madersbacher, H.G.: Neurogenic bladder dysfunction. Curr. Opin. Urol. 9(4), 303–307 (1999)
3. Warren, J.W.: Catheter-associated urinary tract infections. Infect. Dis. Clin. North Am. 11(3), 609–622 (1997)
4. Gazinski, E., et al.: Die elektrische leitfähigkeit als maß für die konzentriertheit des menschlichen urins, Bayerische Julius-Maximilians-Universität zu Würzburg (2004)
5. Martinsen, O.G., Grimnes, S.: Bioimpedance and Bioelectricity Basics. Academic press, London (2011)
6. Holmes, J.: Ultrasonic studies of the bladder. J. Urol. 97(4), 654–663 (1967)
7. Niu, H., Yang, S., Liu, C., Yan, Y., Li, L., Ma, F., Wang, X., Pu, F., Li, D., Fan, Y.: Design of an ultrasound bladder volume measurement and alarm system. In: 5th International Conference on Bioinformatics and Biomedical Engineering, (iCBBE), pp. 1–4. IEEE (2011)
8. Schlebusch, T., Nienke, S., Leonhardt, S., Walter, M.: Bladder volume estimation from electrical impedance tomography. Physiol. Meas. 35(9), 1813 (2014)
9. Waltz, F.M., Timm, G.W., Bradley, W.: Bladder volume sensing by resistance measurement. IEEE Trans. Biomed. Eng. 1, 42–46 (1971)
10. Denniston, J., Baker, L.: Measurement of urinary bladder emptying using electrical impedance. Med. Biol. Eng. Comput. 13(2), 305–306 (1975)
11. Li, R., Gao, J., Wang, H., Jiang, Q.: Design of a noninvasive bladder urinary volume monitoring system based on bio-impedance. Engineering 5(10), 321 (2013)
12. Palla, A., Rossi, S., Fanucci, L.: Bioimpedance based monitoring system for people with neurogenic dysfunction of the urinary bladder. Stud. Health Technol. Inf. 217, 892–896 (2014)
13. Rossi, S., Pessione, M., Radicioni, V., Baglione, G., Vatteroni, M., Dario, P., Torre, L.D.: A low power bioimpedance module for wearable systems. Sens. Actuators A Phys. 232, 359–367 (2015)
14. Kalman, R.E.: A new approach to linear filtering and prediction problems. J. Basic Eng. 82(1), 35–45 (1960)
15. Einstein, A.: The theory of the Brownian movement. Ann. der Physik 17, 549 (1905)
16. Hida, T.: Brownian Motion. Springer, New York (1980)

# Sound Feedback Assessment for Upper Limb Rehabilitation Using a Multimodal Guidance System

Mario Covarrubias Rodriguez[1]([✉]), Mauro Rossini[2], Giandomenico Caruso[1],
Gianluca Samali[2], Chiara Giovanzana[2], Franco Molteni[2],
and Monica Bordegoni[1]

[1] Dipartimento di Meccanica, Politecnico di Milano, Milan, Italy
mario.covarrubias@polimji.it
[2] Valduce Hospital, Villa Beretta, Rehabilitation Centre, Costa Masnaga, Italy

**Abstract.** This paper describes the implementation of a Multimodal Guidance System (MGS) for upper limb rehabilitation through vision, haptic and sound. The system consists of a haptic device that physically renders virtual path of 2D shapes through the point-based approach, while sound technology provides audio feedback inputs about patient's actions while performing a manual task as for example: starting and/or finishing an sketch; different sounds related to the hand's velocity while sketching. The goal of this sonification approach is to strengthen the patient's understanding of the virtual shape which is used in the rehabilitation process, and to inform the patient about some attributes that could otherwise remain unseen. Our results provide conclusive evidence that the effect of using the sound as additional feedback increases the accuracy in the tasks operations.

**Keywords:** Haptic guidance · Upper-limb rehabilitation · Sound interaction

## 1 Introduction

Haptic guidance tasks are common in several applications and have been widely analyzed. Trajectory assisted task has a significant value in many applications such as medical training, handwriting learning, and in applications requiring precise manipulations. In order to evaluate the effectiveness of the multimodal guidance device, several tests have been performed. Firstly by using a group of healthy people in order to get knowledge about the precision and limits of the device, then the haptic guidance device has been tested by patients with specific disorders such as post-stroke patients. This group of patients has been selected due the fact that they lack in many of the fundamental skills related to precision of movement, coordination of force, speed and reduced efficiency in performance as compared with healthy people. One of the hypotheses suggests that the source

© Springer International Publishing Switzerland 2016
K. Miesenberger et al. (Eds.): ICCHP 2016, Part II, LNCS 9759, pp. 529–536, 2016.
DOI: 10.1007/978-3-319-41267-2_74

of motor difficulties originates in deficit of the central representation of actions
[1], whereas other evidence suggest a peripheral impairments related to hypotonic
conditions.

As suggested by the literature [1,4] practice can have positive influence on
the motor skill. In previous work several solutions have been developed and
evaluated with people affected by Down syndrome [2]. By combining visual,
haptic and sound stimuli in order to obtain a multimodal system, which enables
three perceptive channels to works together, thus increasing the effectiveness of
the treatment.

## 2   Concept

Figure 1-a shows the virtual concept of the MGS. The Desktop Phantom haptic
device (1) is linked to a 2 Degrees of Freedom (DOF) mechanism (2) in order to
allow the planar motion required to perform the 2D tasks by handling the stylus
(4). In this way, the base component (3) is used as a support element while (5)
shows the sound system hardware. Figure 1-b shows a different position of the
stylus.

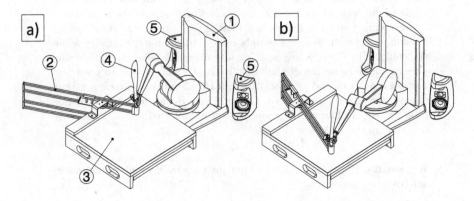

**Fig. 1.** The concept of the Multimodal Guidance System

Figure 2 provides the Computer Aided Design (CAD) concept of the sketching functionality. Figure 2-a shows an isometric view of the sketching approach
concept with a 3D shape (2), which is intersected by a plane (1). At the intersection is created the 2D haptic trajectory (4), which is used by the MGS to
provide the haptic guidance to the patient. The 3D model is necessary in order
to assign the Magnetic Surface constraint, which is a technique used to render
force on the haptic device based on a given distance from a virtual surface (3).
From the sketching initial point (5) up to the haptic trajectory (4) the Magnetic
Surface constraint is disabled, allowing free-motion to the patients hand (6).
Figure 2-b represents the geometry from the patients point of view, and Fig. 2-c
shows several basic geometries that have been designed for testing.

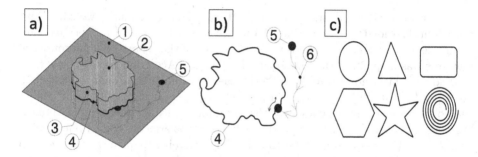

**Fig. 2.** The concept of sketching

The stylus of the Phantom desktop is driven under the operator's movement and assisted by the Magnetic Geometry Effect (MGE). When this option is activated, a spring force tries to pull the sphere of the stylus of the haptic device towards the virtual trajectory that is used as a virtual guide. In fact, this effect is used in order to assist the user's hand.

The patient hand's movement has been measured using the Phantom device as input. The operations have been performed by tracking the stylus of the Phantom device through the DeviceLog command provided by the H3D API platform. The tracked sample rate is 25 Hz.

## 3   Geometry Sonification

The main objective of a sonification application is to provide information using non-speech audio, as discussed in [3,6]. There are several related studies about sonification of geometrical data of surfaces in scientific and engineering applications. For example, in [5] it is presented a synthesizer for mapping surface data to frequency, timbre, volume and tempo using the Musical Instrument Digital Interface (MIDI) protocol.

The geometry sonification proposed in our research aims at using sound metaphors to expose patients to perceive some attributes that would otherwise remain 'unseen', Such unseen attributes may either be a result of limitations in the visual and haptic devices, or a result of limitations in human perception.

### 3.1   Assistance Interaction Through Sound

An important consideration in the design of the sonification strategy is the way by which the user interacts with the haptic device. For the sonification strategy described in this work, one mode of haptic interaction is considered. This mode tries to mimic a real pen/pencil while sketching on a sheet of paper. Note that the sonification is only triggered when the Phantom stylus is touching the virtual surface of the 3D shapes and at the same time the haptic feedback is enabled. If there is no contact with the virtual surfaces, no sound and no force feedback are produced.

A group of 12 students (age range 21–25, eight men and 4 woman) have been enrolled for this experiment. After experimenting with a number of map-pings, users preferred the sounds where the value of the geometrical parameter of interest was mapped to the fundamental frequency. According to the users, they considered this kind of sounds to be the easiest to understand and represents a real pen/pencil while sketching on a sheet of paper. In fact, this result comes as no surprise since frequency is a very common choice for this type of applica-tion and it is considered to be particularly strong as a means to sonify changing values [7]. The reason might be that humans perceive frequency changes with a relatively high resolution. Typically, frequency changes of pure tones can be determined with an accuracy of up to 0.3 % [8]. In practice, we implemented the mapping in such a way that the minimum absolute value of the velocity para-meter is mapped to a minimum frequency of 10 Hz and the maximum absolute value found in the dataset is mapped to a maximum frequency of 200 Hz and dynamically is modified according to the velocity parameter. These parameters are used to create the metaphoric sound A. The sound A has been set to force the subject to move slowly the pen on the shape. This choice is motivated by the evidence that a slower action in drawing and copying task is usually associated to a better performance, and then this sound could be considered as an indirect feedback about subject performance.

## 4    Validation of the Multimodal Guidance Device

This section presents the methodology for the validation of the MGD whose aim is to reach rigorous, useful and practical conclusions about the designed device. The proposed methodology is based on an iterative and continuous process of data collection, analysis and interpretation. In order to obtain more information about the various aspects of the device functioning, the methodology plans to test the device with two different kinds of population. The contribution of each population to the development of the device will be extensively exposed in the two phases of the methodology.

First we consider healthy people in order to validate the accuracy of the system (Phase 1). Then, we have considered post-stroke patients as subject of the research; this means thinking of them as active subjects (Phase 2).

### 4.1    Outputs of the System and Report Creation

The data stored by the MGS can provide the rehabilitation therapist with an objective and quantitative view of the patient's progress and the effect of the therapy. The report of the patient's activity includes a qualitative picture of the 2D tasks while using the haptic trajectories, a quantitative error and a force diagram. Basically, these are the graphics that show weather or not the patient is making progresses. Performances are computed after each trial is finished, and are stored in the personal patient's database.

Figure 3 shows the tracking results while sketching a circle. During the first trial the time required to sketch the circle was 1.45 s with a maximal force of about 7.8 N (Median Force = 3.01 N, Median Error = 6.5 mm).

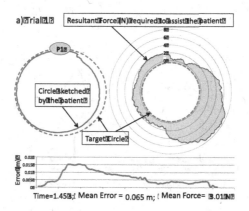

**Fig. 3.** Report of the patient's activity while sketching a circle

Figure 4 shows the tracking results while sketching a triangle. The force data values have been developed along the circular trajectory (polar coordinate system). In this task the time required to sketch the triangle was 2.84 s with a maximal force of about 7.2 N (Median Force = 1.67 N, Median Error = 4.5 mm).

## 4.2 Sketching Task by Healthy People

In this task, three basic 2D sketches (circle, triangle and rectangle) have been provided. Twelve healthy participants (age range 21–25, eight men and 4 woman). have been enrolled in the experiment. We request to the users to perform several sketches. The sketches have been randomly selected (free, force feedback and force feedback + audio) in order to analyse the improvements of additional feedback. In order to systematically assess the contribution of the haptic guidance we computed the error between the radius of the circles as previously described and reported on Fig. 5.

In fact, without the haptic guidance the mean error is 2.166 mm, while by using the haptic guidance the error is 1.95 mm. Wilcoxon rank sum test showed a significant difference between the error with and without haptic guidance (p = 0.045). Similar analysis is used to compare the free and the haptic-sound feedback. Also in this case Wilcoxon rank sum test showed a significant difference between the two modalities, e.g. free and audio-haptic feedback (p = 0.012). The authors are aware of the fact that the number of trials are not statistically significant, but the aim of the test was to check the effectiveness of the approach and to verify if the system requires further improvements.

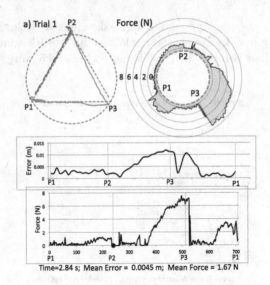

**Fig. 4.** Report of the patient's activity while sketching a triangle

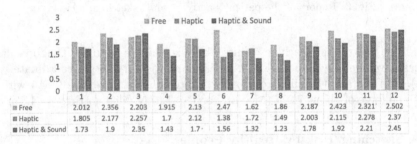

**Fig. 5.** Error reported by Healthy people

# 5    Motor Task and Treatment Protocol

## 5.1    Population

A preliminary test has been performed involving 8 subjects (5 females) aged 22 to 65 years as can be seen from Tables 1 and 2. Five post-stroke, and three patients with parkinson, consecutively admitted to the Rehabilitation Center of Villa Beretta, Valduce Hospital. In the case of post-stroke patients, their diagnosis of stroke was based on clinical assessment (presence of motor and possibly sensory deficits).

## 5.2    Intervention

The 8 patients received the protocol treatment for 10 sessions. The experimental procedure was the same than in the healthy users. The sketches have been randomly selected in order to analyse the improvements of additional feedback.

**Table 1.** Clinical data of post-stroke subjects.

| Subject | Patient | Gender | Age | Side | Onset (months) |
|---|---|---|---|---|---|
| 1 | Post-stroke | M | 63 | D | 28 |
| 2 | Post-stroke | F | 49 | D | 15 |
| 3 | Post-stroke | M | 57 | D | 22 |
| 4 | Post-stroke | M | 53 | D | 54 |
| 5 | Post-stroke | M | 22 | D | 69 |
| 6 | Parkinson | F | 65 | D | 108 |
| 7 | Parkinson | F | 63 | D | 36 |
| 8 | Parkinson | M | 62 | D | 60 |

**Table 2.** Mean error reduction in post-stroke patients %.

| Patient | Shape | Free | Haptic | Haptic and Sound |
|---|---|---|---|---|
| Post-stroke | Circle | 31 | 4 | 9 |
| Post-stroke | Triangle | 28 | 30 | 30 |
| Post-stroke | Rectangle | 20 | 30 | 30 |
| Parkinson | Circle | 40 | 10 | 12 |
| Parkinson | Triangle | 44 | 32 | 23 |
| Parkinson | Rectangle | 44 | 25 | 19 |

In this experiment a brief familiarization has been offered to the participants and it has been asked to all participants to perform a task that involved a combination of visual and haptic functions in order to trace out a circle, a triangle and a rectangle during two minutes by using the paretic upper limb. Then the same procedure has been performed by using the healthy upper limb. All the geometries are inscribed in a circle with 100 mm of radius. In order to systematically assess the contribution of the haptic guidance we computed the error between the ideal shapes and the patient's shapes (circle, triangle and rectangle).

## 6    Results

All patients enrolled in this study successfully completed the ten-sessions training protocol and the therapy was well accepted. Between initial and final phase of the protocol the sketching mean error has been reduced as can be seen from Table 2. Considering free-hand sketching, the values from the mean error significantly decreases for both, post-stroke and parkinson patients.

## 7    Conclusion

The results of our study showed that the sound feedback help patients during manual tasks by means of using the MGS as a rehabilitation tool. The main outcome of this pilot study is that the patients significantly reduce the mean error while sketching when the haptic trajectories are enabled, which indicates that each patient learned to use the device. In addition, we have compared the sketching data obtained by using the device in three modalities: free, haptic feedback and haptic & sound feedbacks. The comparison shows considerable difference in the accuracy of the operation. Further research, however, is still needed to improve the performance of the Multimodal Guidance System by increasing the working volume of the device to meet more demanding rehabilitation applications.

# References

1. Blank, R., Heizer, W., von Voss, H.: Externally guided control of static grip forces by visual feedback age and task effects in 3–6 old children and adults. Neurosc. Lett. **271**, 41–44 (1999)
2. Covarrubias, M., Gatti, E., Bordegoni, M., Cugini, U., Mansutti, A.: Improving manual skills in persons with disabilities (pwd) through a multimodal assistance system. Disabil. Rehabil. Assistive Technol. **9**(4), 335–343 (2014). pMID: 23692410
3. Hermann, T.: Sonification for exploratory data analysis. Ph.D. thesis, Bielefeld University, Germany (2002)
4. Kurillo, G., Gregorič, M., Goljar, N., Bajd, T.: Grip force tracking system for assessment and rehabilitation of hand function. Technol. Health Care **13**, 137–149 (2005)
5. Minghim, R., Forrest, A.R.: An illustrated analysis of sonification for scientific visualisation. In: Proceedings of the 6th Conference on Visualization 1995, VIS 1995, p. 110. IEEE Computer Society, Washington, DC (1995)
6. Scaletti, C.: Sound synthesis algorithms for auditory data representations. In: Auditory Display: Sonification, Audification, and Auditory Interfaces. SFI Studies in the Sciences of Complexity Proceedings, vol. XVIII, pp. 223–251. Addison-Wesley (1994)
7. Stockman, T., Nickerson, L.V., Hind, G.: Auditory graphs: a summary of current experience and towards a research agenda. In: Proceedings of the International Conference on Auditory Display (ICAD 2005) Limerick, Ireland (2005)
8. Wier, C.C., Jesteadt, W., Green, D.M.: Frequency discrimination as a function of frequency and sensation level. J. Acoust. Soc. Am. **61**, 178183 (1977)

# Personal Mobility Vehicle for Assisting Short-Range Transportation

Yoshiyuki Takahashi[✉]

Department of Human Environment Design, Faculty of Human Life Design,
Toyo University, Oka 48-1, Asaka-shi, Saitama 351-8510, Japan
y-takahashi@toyo.jp

**Abstract.** Personal mobility vehicle (PMV) for the people with limited mobility has been developed. This PMV is propelled by kicking off the ground by foot and electric motor assist the gliding. It aims to assist short distance transportation in urban area e.g. moving from a home to a train station. Folding mechanism makes it possible to carry PMV on public transportations and will help to extend the area of the user's activities. In this paper, the overview of our developed PMV, simulation model and the validation according to the results of preliminary experiments are mentioned.

**Keywords:** Personal mobility · Limited mobility · Transportation

## 1 Introduction

Recent years, personal mobility vehicle (PMV), is paid attention e.g. for commuting and delivery [1]. It is the one of the technological solution for saving energy and envi-ronment friendly to the sustainable future society by effective transportation. And also, it will be an application for assisting people with difficulty on transportation. Fully assisted vehicle e.g. electrical wheel chair and scooter will be suitable for the people who have severe problems on transportation. However, the people with weak muscle strength on lower limb e.g. elderly people should walk and move their body to maintain their physical strength and reduce the risk of disuse syndrome.

Therefore, a new concept of portable PMV have been developed for the people with moving difficulty. Our proposed PMV is a three-wheeled vehicle. It is propelled by kicking off the ground and electric motor assist the gliding. It aims to support short distance transportation in urban area or inside of facilities. Folding mechanism makes it possible to carry the vehicle on public transportations. It helps to extend the area of the user's activities. In this paper, outline of our developed PMV, a simulation model, preliminary experiment and validation of simulation are mentioned.

## 2 Personal Mobility Vehicle

Developed PMV is propelled by kicking off the ground and power-assisted by the motor on the rear wheel (Fig. 1). Power assist system consists of a servomotor, a rotary encoder, a micro controller and a motor driver. Rotary encoder is attached on the rear

© Springer International Publishing Switzerland 2016
K. Miesenberger et al. (Eds.): ICCHP 2016, Part II, LNCS 9759, pp. 537–540, 2016.
DOI: 10.1007/978-3-319-41267-2_75

wheel and measures the wheel rotation. If angular acceleration of the rear wheel excess the threshold, micro controller estimate that the user kicked off the ground. Therefore, the servomotor starts to rotate and assist the rotation of the rear wheel to reduce the deceleration.

**Fig. 1.** PMV

## 3 Modeling and Simulation

The layout of wheels of PMV is two in front and one in rear. The simulation model which we used is associated with simple two wheel bicycle model [2]. Each wheel has suspension and damper element. Euler equations are integrated in this rigid body model. The motion of PMV is described in an inertial XYZ coordination system that is fixed on the ground. PMV body is introduced xyz coordinate system. The origin of coordinate system is attached on the center of the mass of PMV. Velocities of the PMV body u, v and w are along to x, y and z axis as well as its rotational velocity around axes are p, q and r. Euler angles are used to describe the orientation of the PMV body. Force and Moment are based on Newton's equation for rigid body. Force F is to accelerate the center of mass. External forces on each axis are as follows. Dot notation for differentiation.

$$\begin{bmatrix} F_x \\ F_y \\ F_z \end{bmatrix} = m \begin{bmatrix} \dot{u} + qw - rv \\ \dot{v} + ru - pw \\ \dot{w} + pv - qu \end{bmatrix} \tag{1}$$

Longitudinal and lateral friction forces $F_x$, $F_y$ on the wheel contact point are calculated by friction coefficient $\mu_x$, $\mu_y$ and normal force on each wheel $F_n$.

$\mu_x$ and $\mu_y$ are calculated based on a magic formula [3]. Arguments of functions are wheel slip ratio s and wheel sideslip angle β of each wheel. Slip ratio s is calculated by wheel rotational speed rω and velocity of body u. where r is radius of the wheel. Side slip angle β is calculated by velocities of wheel u and v, in longitudinal and in lateral.

Moment M is calculated based on angular acceleration and angular velocity of the body coordinate system and also moment of inertia $I_{xx}$, $I_{yy}$ and $I_{zz}$. These forces and moments are transformed to inertial axis.

$$M_x = \dot{p}I_{xx} - (I_{yy} - I_{zz})qr$$
$$M_y = \dot{q}I_{yy} - (I_{zz} - I_{xx})pr \tag{2}$$
$$M_z = \dot{r}I_{zz} - (I_{xx} - I_{yy})pq.$$

## 4   Results and Validation

To confirm the simulation model, step steering input simulation with constant velocity was evaluated. Figure 2 shows steering input angle, yaw rate, yaw angle and position of the vehicle. It was confirmed that yaw angle and yaw rate were changed according to the steering angle.

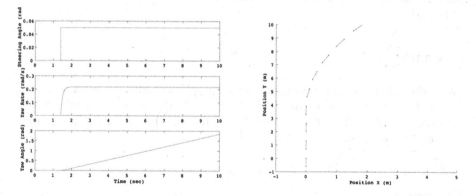

**Fig. 2.** Simulation result of step steering input

Preliminary experiments were carried out to confirm the functions of the developed PMV. Two young participants (age 24 female and male), three elderly participants (age 60 female and age 72 male) were enrolled in the experiments. The results of experiments with young participants were compared with simulation results. The participants kicked off the ground only once as much as they can and moved straight. Figure 3 shows the comparison of the results of velocity between simulation result (solid line) and experimental result (dashed line). On the simulation, propulsion force by kicking off the ground was provided as a longitudinal external force $F_x$ on the center of gravity. Propulsion force was estimated according to the level of acceleration and acceleration time in the experiment. It was provided constantly 0.8 s on the simulation. After accelerating, the velocity of PMV was reduced according to rolling resistance. The maximum gliding velocity on the simulation was 1.198 m/s and 1.1931 m/s in the experiment. It is confirmed that the similarity of velocity profile in accelerating and decelerating.

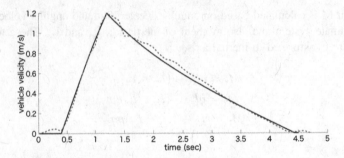

**Fig. 3.** Velocity profile of single kick-off. Sold line: Simulation, Dashed line: Experimental

## 5 Discussions

It is confirmed that simulation result and experimental result are approximately same in case of acceleration and deceleration. The simulation model was validated. Furthermore experiment including lateral motion will be held and evaluate in the next step. And also, mathematical model of propulsion assistance system will be integrated and tested.

## 6 Conclusions

Three-wheeled personal mobility vehicle for the people with difficulty on transportation was proposed. 6 DOF mathematical model was also developed and simulation results and experimental results were compared. As a result, the similarities of the results were confirmed and simulation model was validated.

## References

1. Segway. http://www.segway.com/
2. Huston, J., Graves, B., and Johnson, D.: Three Wheeled Vehicle Dynamics. SAE Technical Paper 820139, pp. 45–49 (1982)
3. Pacejka, H.B., Bakker, E.: The magic formula tyre model. In: Proceedings of the 1st International Colloquium on Tyre Models for Vehicle Dynamics Analysis, Supplement to Vehicle System Dynamics, vol. 21, pp. 1–18 (1991)

# Multimodal Sequential Modeling and Recognition of Human Activities

Mouna Selmi[1] and Mounîm A. El-Yacoubi[2(✉)]

[1] UR: SAGE - Systèmes Avancés en Génie Electrique, Université de Sousse, Sousse, Tunisia
selmi.mouna@gmail.com
[2] SAMOVAR, Telecom SudParis, CNRS, University Paris Saclay, Palaiseau, France
Mounim.El_Yacoubi@telecom-sudparis.eu

**Abstract.** Video-based recognition of activities of daily living (ADLs) is being used in ambient assisted living systems in order to support independent living of old people. In this work, we propose a new multimodal ADL recognition method by modeling the correlation between motion and object information. We encode motion using dense interest point trajectories which are robust to occlusion and speed variability. We formulate the learning problem using a two-layer SVM hidden conditional random field (HCRF) recognition model that is particularly relevant for multimodal sequence recognition. This hierarchical classifier optimally combines the discriminative power of SVM and the long-range feature dependencies modeling by the HCRF.

**Keywords:** Ambient assisted living system · Activities of daily living · Multimodal representation · Interest points · SVM-HCRF

## 1 Introduction

According to the World Health Organization, the number of elderly people is going to reach 2 billion by 2050. On the other hand, 89 % of seniors prefer to stay in their own homes. Such a demographic and social context brings significant challenges for health care systems and society in terms of increased costs of nursing home care and lack of resources. As an alternative to current care models, ambient assisted living (AAL) systems can offer the possibility for many old and vulnerable people to live independently and safely at home. One of the most important components in AAL systems is the activity of daily living (ADL) recognition component. ADL recognition helps evaluating the degree of dependency of the elderly by detecting changes in their behavior patterns, identifying early signs of dementia [1] and detecting their critical situations such as falls, which can enable early elderly assistance. ADLs that affect the independence of elders include taking medications, eating, bathing, dressing, cleaning, and socializing.

A wide-range of ADL recognition systems in the context of AAL applications use sensors either embedded in the environment or body worn. Recently, a growing popularity has been noted towards video sensors based monitoring of ADLs in AAL systems [2, 3] as they provide richer sensory information than traditional sensors. These sensors have relatively a low cost compared to systems based on environment sensors which

© Springer International Publishing Switzerland 2016
K. Miesenberger et al. (Eds.): ICCHP 2016, Part II, LNCS 9759, pp. 541–548, 2016.
DOI: 10.1007/978-3-319-41267-2_76

require generally a large network of sensors, which makes them relatively obtrusive and costly to maintain. However, video based AALs systems have several obstacles including users' acceptance and the risk of loss of privacy.

In spite of advances on vision techniques, recognizing ADLs in natural and unconstrained videos is a challenging task because of the degree of intra-class variability and inter-class ambiguity. As an example, consider activity *answering phone*. Dialing and answering phone differs slightly in terms of hand movements, which is an example of inter-class ambiguity. Intra-class variations, on the other hand, are ubiquitous, as the same activity is usually performed in many different ways according to the subject's ethnicity, appearance, mood, environment and recording settings like viewpoint changes, dynamic backgrounds and occlusions.

To tackle the ambiguity and variability issues, a robust solution is to combine activity multimodality aspects such as motion, contextual information and voice [15]. In this paper, we propose to leverage the interdependence between motion and contextual information consisting of the manipulated objects' nature, to help distinguish between similar activities. Object information modality is an important cue to discriminate between activities that draw part of their meaning from context. For example, activities *answer phone* and *drink* entail a similar motion at the beginning which is the elementary action *raise hands*. Identifying whether the manipulated object is a glass or phone is a strong cue for the activity disambiguation. Moreover, the temporal order of appearance of objects across frames is also of crucial importance for activity recognition.

A number of different approaches have been considered for multimodal object-motion fusion to perform ADL recognition over the last few years. Fathi et al. [4] concatenate features of segmented objects and hands to construct a feature vector used as input of an AdaBoost classifier. In their work, the authors record activities from a wearable camera which alleviates the occlusion problem; user compliance with wearable systems, however, is generally poor. Kjellstrom et al. [5] used a factorial CRF to simultaneously segment and classify human hand actions, as well as to classify the object affordances involved in the activity. Gupta et al. [6] use a Bayesian approach to analyze human-object interactions with a likelihood model based on hand trajectories. These approaches, however, have focused only on hand activities. Similar to our setting, Koppula et al. [7] model the mutual context between human poses and objects information to recognize full-body ADLs. In their work, human motion is represented using skeleton dynamics obtained through 3D video. The skeleton is nevertheless sensitive to occlusion and fast motion.

In fact, at the motion/action recognition level, approaches can generally be classified into holistic approaches [8] and local approaches [9]. The first category employs explicit body representation, by extracting features from the silhouette using 2D image features or 3D features. These approaches, however, require background subtraction and/or body tracking, which are unreliable for real-life scenes where adverse conditions such as complex backgrounds, fast non-linear motions and occlusions come into play. The second category uses local interest points (IPs) and can provide a concise representation of motion events while avoiding preprocessing related to foreground/background segmentation and tracking. The main issue with local IPs is that they cannot be extracted in a well-defined spatio-temporal order for each frame that would make extraction of an

IP-based feature vector of fixed dimension feasible for each time step. A bag-of-words (BOW) representation has been usually adopted since it overlooks this order and treats all the IPs on equal footing irrespective of their location in space and time. A BOW per video is obtained and used as input to a static, usually a Support Vector Machine (SVM), classifier [10]. Nonetheless, static classifiers neglect the temporal structures across activity frames, which are important for activity recognition. Sequential classifiers based principally on graphical models are better suited for activity recognition. These approaches have been introduced to model the sophisticated temporal structure of temporal sequences and exploit the temporal relationships between the local characteristics. As these models require a fixed size vector at each instant, this type of classification models was generally used with holistic features. This is because the number of the IPs extracted at each frame is variable, hence the impossibility of having fixed features' size at each instant. In this paper, we propose a new approach that combines the robustness of IPs in real scenes with the capacity of sequential classifiers to model the temporal dynamics of the activity in a discriminative way. For this purpose, we use a Hidden Conditional Random Field (HCRF) [12] classifier which is a powerful discriminative sequential model.

To summarize, we propose a new sequential approach that optimally combines different sources of information characterizing activities by modeling the multimodal temporal dynamics of the activity in a discriminative way. This method is based on a two-layer Support Vector Machine – Hidden Conditional Random Field (SVM-HCRF) model: (1) At the first layer, a static SVM classifier extracts from temporal local segments high-level discriminative features; (2) At the second layer, the discriminant classifier, HCRF, infers the most likely activity from the multimodal activity sequence.

Our main contributions can be summarized as follows: (1) Our SVM-HCRF model is highly flexible to incorporate different sources of information, such as motion and object IDs in a sequential way for a fine activity modeling and recognition. (2) We show how our hierarchical SVM-HCRF model combines two different sources characterizing motion activities: the temporally local segment discriminative power, represented by object information and motion semantic information inferred by SVM, and the temporal long rang motion and object features dependencies modeled by HCRF at a higher level. (3) Our classification architecture permits the use of IPs-based descriptors as input to the sequential classifier HCRF, thanks to the sliding window scheme.

The remainder of this paper is organized as follows. Section 2 describes our multimodal model. In Sect. 3, we compare the results we obtain with current state of the art on the CAD-120 dataset. Finally, in Sect. 4, we conclude and sketch some future directions of our work.

## 2   Multimodal Modeling and Recognition of Activities of Daily Living

The architecture of our multimodal ADL recognition model is depicted in Fig. 1. We first uniformly split the video into segments of fixed size $L$ (say 30 frames) with an overlapping rate of 50 % to take into account correlation. Thus, the number of segments is proportional to the video sequence length. From each segment, we extract the relative multimodal features: motion features and contextual features. Motion features are converted into high-level features by a SVM classifier. We then use a HCRF model as a high level sequential classifier to model the multimodal temporal correlation within a segment between motion-based features and contextual features. HCRF learns also the dependencies between the elementary parts of the ADL in a discriminative way.

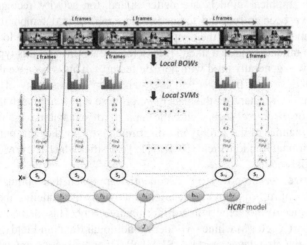

**Fig. 1.** The architecture of our recognition system of daily living activities

## 2.1 Motion Encoding by Dense Trajectories

From each segment, we extract motion features based on local IPs. Our model can be applied to variety of detectors [9, 11] for extracting IP features from videos. We opt to use Dense Trajectory IPs [11] as they deal better with realist conditions. Dense Interest Points are uniformly sampled by considering 8 spatial scales. Within each scale, IPs are tracked over 15 frames by a median filtering kernel. To describe these IP features, we use Motion Boundary Histogram (MBH) descriptors generated from a 3D Spatio-temporal volume surrounding each trajectory. MBH has shown optimal performance and stability when used with dense points on various action and activity datasets [11].

Given that dense points are geometrically and temporally disordered, we represent each local segment by a BOW vector of fixed size. For high-level feature extraction, SVM takes for each local segment the associated raw BOW as input and converts it into a vector of conditional class probabilities. Thus, each local segment conveys information about the label of the action/activity it belongs to. The amount of information differs from one segment to another depending on motion content. This permits to infer motion semantic information and allows also for a drastic feature dimensionality reduction which increases processing speed and prevents overfitting thus enhancing recognition accuracy. In our work, we consider a one-vs.-all SVM with an exponential $\chi^2$ kernel [16] to convert each segment into a class-conditional probability vector.

## 2.2   Context Modeling

To model the contextual information, we encode the occurrence frequency of each object. As shown in Fig. 2, each temporal segment $s_t$ of the video sequence $S = (s_1; s_2; ...; s_i; ...; s_T)$ is represented by the vector $\mathbf{S}_t = (P(a_1); P(a_2); ...; P(a_i); ...; P(a_A); F(o_1); F(o_2); ...; F(o_j); ...; F(o_N))$; where $A$ is the number of activities, $N$ is the number of objects, $P(a_i)$ is the probability of activity i conditionally on BOW of local segment t and $F(o_j)$ is the occurrence frequency of object $j$ in a given segment $t$.

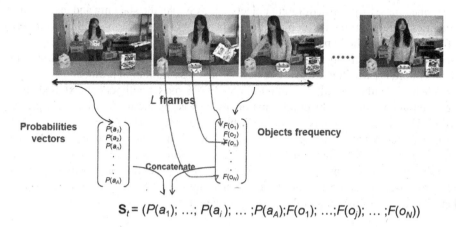

$$S_t = (P(a_1); ...; P(a_i); ... ;P(a_A);F(o_1); ...;F(o_j); ... ;F(o_N))$$

**Fig. 2.** Overview of the context integration method in SVM-HCRF model

## 2.3   Activity Modeling and Recognition Through SVM-HCRF Model

HCRFs [12] are an extension of CRFs initially used for natural language processing by Laferty et al. [13], which were recently proposed for sequence recognition purposes, by augmenting the CRF with hidden states in order to model the underlying latent structures in temporal sequences, such as the sub-events in ADLs.

In our model, the sequence of the motion-based activities probability vectors and objects occurrence frequency associated with the sequence of segments serve as the input observation sequence to the HCRF model. Using HCRF as a high level sequential classifier permits the modeling of the long-range feature dependencies. In addition, it models the temporal correlation within a segment between motion-based features and contextual features and it explicitly exploits the temporal order of objects' occurrence, which can be relevant for ADL recognition. It is important to note that the HCRF model harnesses the relationship between the partial high-level information conveyed by each segment through the SVM output probability vector, by learning dependencies between the elementary parts of the ADL motion in a discriminative way. Thus, HCRF does not spend its modeling efforts on learning the raw features, but rather on characterizing the semantic information that each segment conveys about the classes, i.e., the SVM output class probabilities. HCRF then integrates the sequence of semantic information from motion and objects in a discriminative way to make a decision at the sequential level.

## 3   Experiments

Given that there is no public video dataset of ADLs performed by elders, we compared our model, with most recent state-of-the-art ADL recognition methods, on the public Cornell Activity Dataset- 120 [7] (CAD-120), that contains 120 3D videos of four different subjects performing 10 high-level activities: making cereal, taking medicine, stacking objects, un-stacking objects, microwaving food, picking objects, cleaning objects, taking food, arranging objects and having a meal. Each high-level activity was performed three times with different objects; for example, the stacking and un-stacking activities were performed with pizza boxes, plates and bowls. Some of the challenges of this dataset are the important variations of camera-view angles, and recording locations within each activity class. We use the same experimental protocol that is used in the literature [7] which is a leave-one-person-out cross validation protocol.

We begin with an evaluation of our SVM- HCRF model without context modeling, i.e. without considering object information, by comparing the works using only primitives related to movement. As shown in Table 1, we get a much higher recognition rate than that obtained by [7] using primitives extracted from skeletons obtained by Kinect and a structural SVM for classification. Although Kinect's skeletons provide a rich description of movements, they are not very robust to occlusions, contrary to our motion features based on dense IP trajectories. In addition, our SVM-HCRF model enables better modeling of the temporal aspect of the activities.

**Table 1.** Comparison of performance on CAD-120 dataset without context (object) modeling

| Method | Recognition rate |
|---|---|
| Skeleton features + Structural SVM [7] | 27.4 % |
| SVM-HCRF | 73.4 % |

Table 2 shows the results achieved by exploiting the objects' occurrence frequency. As an activity is a temporal sequence of sub-activities (e.g. *cleaning an object* is an activity composed of sub-activities *reaching object*, *open* and *wash*), some works assume that temporal segmentation ground-truth of sub-activities is given, for each temporal segment. This is not realistic as the boundaries of activities within a continuous video stream are usually unknown. We thus report only the results of current state of the art of the approaches that perform conjoint segmentation and recognition of the activities.

**Table 2.** Comparison of performance on the CAD-120 dataset

| Method | Recognition rate |
|---|---|
| Koppula et al., [7] | 80.6 % |
| Koppula, Saxena, [14] | 83.1 % |
| SVM-HCRF + occurrence objects frequency | 90.3 % |

As can be seen from the Tables 1 and 2, by combining objects' information with motion features within the SVM-HCRF framework, we improve the accuracy by a high margin of 16.9 % (73.4 % vs. 90.3 %) w.r.t exploiting motion only. This shows the complementarity of motion and object information for identifying activities.

The best approach reported on the CAD-120 ADL dataset so far, is that of Koppula et al. [14], based on CRF to model the temporal aspect of activities, and using the primitives extracted from skeletons given by Kinect. Our multimodal SVM-HCRF outperforms [14] by a significant margin of 7.2 %. Unlike the approach in [14], our model allows modeling the latent activity substructures and relies on dense IP trajectories which are less prone to occlusion issues than the Kinect skeleton joins. Besides, our model elegantly combines the multimodal information of activities in a sequential way.

## 4 Conclusion

In this paper, we proposed a new two-layer SVM-HCRF model that explicitly learns the underlying temporal sub-structures of an activity and their interrelationships. This model allows combining in a fluid manner the multimodal aspect of ADLs which, in our case, is motion and object information. As the segments are described by high-level low-dimensional feature information, i.e. the conditional class probability vectors, and the objects' frequency vectors, and not by huge BOW representations, the HCRF is guided towards a better parameter space solution for sequence modeling while raw data parameter estimation is dealt with locally through SVMs.

Improving activity substructure modeling can be achieved by better characterizing each unimodal information source. For instance, we can cluster the activity class labels into sub-labels for a finer description of the activity classes depending on the underlying segment motion substructure and its temporal occurrence within the video sequence. Object information can be enhanced by considering not only the occurrence frequency of objects within the segment, but by tracking over time their location w.r.t the silhouette, and encoding them accordingly. Considering classes of sub-activities as SVM outputs and encoding objects by their IDs along with their location, means a richer and more discriminative description of the segments, and subsequently a more powerful high sequential model inference by HCRF.

Our experiments have allowed us to favorably benchmark our approach with current state of the art. Our goal now is to run experiments of recognition of ADLs performed by elders and fragile people in order to assess our approach in terms of accuracy, user-acceptability, and in order to adapt it to serve as real-life assistive technology.

## References

1. Suzuki, T., Murase, S., Tanaka, T., Okazawa, T.: New approach for the early detection of dementia by recording in-house activities. Telemed. J. E Health 13, 41–44 (2007)
2. Cardinaux, F., Bhowmik, D., Abhayaratne, C., Hawley, M.S.: Video based technology for ambient assisted living: a review of the literature. J. Ambient Intell. Smart Environ. 3, 253–269 (2011)
3. Chaaraoui, A.A., Padilla-López, J.R., Ferrández-Pastor, F.J., Nieto-Hidalgo, M., Flórez-Revuelta, F.: A vision-based system for intelligent monitoring: human behaviour analysis and privacy by context. Sensors 14, 8895–8925 (2014)

4. Fathi, A., Farhadi, A., Rehg, J.M.: Understanding egocentric activities. In: ICCV, Barcelona, pp. 407–414, 6–13 November 2011
5. Kjellström, H., Romero, J., Kragic, D.: Visual object-action recognition: inferring object affordances from human demonstration. CVIU **115**(1), 81–90 (2011)
6. Gupta, A., Kembhavi, A., Davis, L.: Observing human-object interactions: using spatial and functional compatibility for recognition. IEEE T-PAMI **31**(10), 1775–1789 (2009)
7. Koppula, H., Gupta, R., Saxena, A.: Learning human activities and object affordances from RGB-D videos. IJRR **32**(8), 951–970 (2013)
8. Blank, M., Gorelick, L., Schechtman, E., Irani, M., Basri, R.: Actions as space-time shapes. In: ICCV, pp. 1395–1402 (2005)
9. Laptev, I.: On space-time interest points. Int. J. Comput. Vis. **64**(2/3), 107–123 (2005)
10. Schuldt, C., Laptev, I., Caputo, B.: Recognizing human actions: a local SVM approach. In: ICPR (2004)
11. Wang, H., Klaser, A., Schmid, C., Liu, C.-L.: Action recognition by dense trajectories. In: CVPR (2011)
12. Quattoni, A., Wang, S., Morency, L.-P., Collins, M., Darrell, T.: Hidden conditional random fields. In: TPAMI (2007)
13. Lafferty, J., McCallum, A., Pereira, F.: Conditional random fields: probabilistic models for segmenting and labeling sequence data. In: ICML, pp. 282–289 (2001)
14. Koppula, H., Saxena, A.: Learning spatio-temporal structure from RGB-D videos for human activity detection and anticipation. ICML **28**, 792–800 (2013)
15. Fleury, A., Vacher, M., Portet, F., Chahuara, P., et Noury N.: A multimodal corpus recorded in a health smart home. In: Proceedings of the Workshop on Multimodal Corpora: Advances in Capturing, Coding and Analyzing Multimodality in conjunction with LREC 2010, Valetta, pp. 99–105, 17–23 May 2010
16. Boucenna, S., Anzalone, S., Tilmont, E., Cohen, D., Chetouani, M.: Learning of social signatures through imitation game between a robot and a human partner. IEEE Trans. Auton. Mental Dev. **6**(3), 213–225 (2014)

# Android Games for Developing Fine Coordination of Movement Skills

Tibor Guzsvinecz, Veronika Szücs, Szilvia Paxian, and Cecilia Sik Lanyi[✉]

University of Pannonia, Egyetem Street 10, Veszprem, 8200, Hungary
dzsiti@hotmail.com, {szucs,paxian}@virt.uni-pannon.hu,
lanyi@almos.uni-pannon.hu

**Abstract.** This paper introduces two serious games, "Cars Racing" and "Labyrinth" game. These games are planned to use and test within the "Intelligent Serious Games for Social and Cognitive Competence" project. The aim of these games are to teach youth with disabilities on creativity.

**Keywords:** Serious game · Stroke patients · Rehabilitation

## 1 Introduction

The main goal of our project was to design and implement Android based applications for children with learning disabilities. These games help the development of fine coordination of movements. Under the umbrella of the "Intelligent Serious Games for Social and Cognitive Competence" (isg4competence) project [1], two serious games were developed: Cars racing, a Labyrinth game. Each game has additional built-in mini-games.

## 2 The State of the Art

The mobile games are becoming more and more popular nowadays. Android is by far the best in the market, the development also shows that over a year the market share has risen by 8 %, which is unique in comparison with the competitors. The main advantage of Android system is an open source operating system and basically anyone can develop their own applications. Mobile learning is gaining its popularity as it is accepted to be an effective technique of delivering lessons and acquiring knowledge as its main strengths are that they are available anytime and anyplace. It can be utilized in many ways in the education industry [2]. A number of researchers' opinion is that mobile technologies should be seen as the extension rather than the replacement of the existing teaching and learning tools [2]. Mobile learning using serious games could be used for almost every learning object. Students, who need special education, have difficulties to develop cognitive abilities and acquire new knowledge. Fernández-Lopez and co-authors [3] have devised a mobile platform (based on iPad and iPod touch devices), called Picaa and designed it to cover the main phases of the learning process: preparation, use and evaluation. It includes four kinds of educational activities (Exploration,

© Springer International Publishing Switzerland 2016
K. Miesenberger et al. (Eds.): ICCHP 2016, Part II, LNCS 9759, pp. 549–552, 2016.
DOI: 10.1007/978-3-319-41267-2_77

Association, Puzzle and Sorting), which can be personalized by educators at content and user interface levels through a design mainly centered on student requirements, whose user profiles can also be adapted. Given the potential benefits, we focused on developing a mobile application which could foster learning and help children improve some of their fundamental skills, such as reading comprehension, orthographic coding, short-term memory and mathematical problem solving. Skiada and co-workers attempted to design a stimulating and interactive experience for children, which could encourage the learning process [4].

More advanced multimedia applications and tools in both research and in practice are limited to the human senses of hearing and vision. To truly exploit Multimedia, other human senses must be added. The new media deals with the human sense of touch [5]. Design for All is one of the main approaches in mobile applications too [6].

## 3 The Methodology Used

First the target groups' needs were explored by personal interviews. People with disabilities were asked what type of games they would like to play. After the assessment of user requirements began the development process which included the motion and the touch sensors of the mobile devices due to the needs of the users. The Labyrinth game was developed for Android operation system, in Eclipse integrated development environment and using Java programming language. The Cars Racing game was developed for Android platform using AndEngine and its plug-ins in Eclipse ADT environment. To test the games we used several Android devices and the Android Virtual Device. The game was tested by children and parents too.

### 3.1 The R&D Work and Results

The car in the Cars Racing game originates from the Walt Disney's Cars animated movie because the first users of the application loved this movie, though its graphics have been changed since then to avoid copyright issues. With regard for children and youth with disabilities the game was designed without using display controllers, this way the users can play the game with touching the whole screen and the left- or right-handed or the disabled children can easily control the car, as the application can be played with one hand. In the game, the car develops by collecting points (Fig. 1) and the bonus tracks can also be tried out. The bonus game is a memory card game, where games with more cards will appear after completing a level. The future plans include selecting the type of the car and also inserting extra levels or maps.

The Labyrinth game contains 2 types of games: the first one is the labyrinth itself, where the user has to collect the gems, which contain letters in it (Fig. 2 left); and in the second game the user has to find out which word you can put together from the letters collected from the gems (Fig. 2 right). The application uses the motion detectors of the device of the user to guide the player character. The game is set up of 10 levels with 2 levels of difficulty. The user can check the time of completion of each level and on each level of difficulty. The game had been tested with different hardware and software based

**Fig. 1.** Cars Racing game

mobile devices, which were successful. The feedback of both users with and without disabilities was also positive both regarding the concept and difficulty of the game as the first few levels are relatively easy and the difficulty slowly increases with every stage.

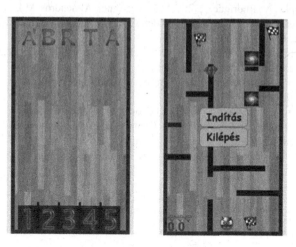

**Fig. 2.** Labyrinth game

### 3.2 The Scientific and Practical Impact or Contributions to the Field

The scientific and practical impact or contributions to the field of the games are multiple:

- Games designed for children and youth with disabilities (mild learning disabilities, sensory impairments, low level social skills, specific learning difficulties -dyslexia, dyspraxia, autism spectrum disorder, ADHD).
- Encourage progression by improving sensorimotor skills in an entertaining way.

# 4    Conclusion and Planned Activities

We developed two serious games: Cars racing and Labyrinth games. The games are easy to use and the main goal of the games is helping the development of fine coordination of movement skills. Our future plan is testing not only the user interface but making pedagogical testing too.

**Acknowledgement.** The research was partially funded by the "Intelligent Serious Games for Social and Cognitive Competence" project - 2015-1-TR01-KA201-022247). This paper and the participation in the conference have been supported by "Stiftung Aktion Österreich-Ungarn", project number: 91öu6 (Conference participation AAATE2015-ICCHP2016). The authors are grateful for the support of Mr. Norbert Szalay and Mr. Csaba Deák.

# References

1. isg4competence: Intelligent Serious Games for Social and Cognitive Competence (ERASMUS + 2015-1-TR01-KA201-022247). http://www.isg4competence.eu/
2. Bidin, S., Ziden, A.A.: Adoption and application of mobile learning in the education industry. Procedia – Soc. Behav. Sci. **90**, 720–729 (2013)
3. Fernández-López, Á., Rodríguez-Fórtiz, M.J., Rodríguez-Almendros, M.L., Martínez-Segura, M.J.: Mobile learning technology based on iOS devices to support students with special needs. Comput. Educ. **61**, 77–90 (2013)
4. Skiada, R., Soroniati, E., Gardeli, A., Zissis, D.: EasyLexia: a mobile application for children with learning difficulties. Procedia Comput. Sci. **27**, 218–228 (2014)
5. Saddik, A., El Shirmohammadi, S.: Touching beyond audio and video. Multimedia Tools Appl. **37**(1), 1–4 (2008)
6. Azpiroz, J., Arroyo, A., van Isacker, K., del Grosso, G., Cabrera-Umpierrez, M.F.: Designing Mobile Applications for All: Accessible Contact Manager, Interactive Technologies and Games: Education, Health and Disability conference, Nottingham Conference Centre, at Nottingham Trent University, Nottingham, UK, 26–27 October 2010

# HCI, AT and ICT for Blind
# and Partially Sighted People

# Extending the Technology Enhanced Accessible Interaction Framework Method for Thai Visually Impaired People

Kewalin Angkananon[1] and Mike Wald[2(⊠)]

[1] Suratthani Rajabhat University Thailand, Surat Thani, Thailand
pla_u@hotmail.com
[2] ECS, University of Southampton, Southampton, UK
m.wald@soton.ac.uk

**Abstract.** This paper focuses on extending the Technology Enhanced Accessible Interaction Framework Method for visual impairment based on interviews with people with visual impairment to help developers develop accessible technology solutions to help people with visual impairment to interact with people, technologies and objects.

**Keywords:** Accessible interaction · Visual impairment · Thailand

## 1 Introduction

No method helps developers with gathering or evaluating requirements and designing or evaluating of technology solutions to accessible interactions between people, technology, and objects in face-to-face situations involving visually impaired people in Thailand. Nearly 11 % of Thailand's registered disabled population had a visual impairment in 1996 and the National Statistics Office 2007 data estimating nearly two million women and men in Thailand, or approximately 3 per cent of the population, had a disability would suggest 220,000 people had a registered visual impairment[1]. There are 20 visually impaired students at Suratthani Rajabhat University Thailand with problems accessing information presented visually (e.g. difficulty reading from a board or screen and understanding what is being pointed at). To reduce discrimination in access requires accessible technology solutions, an accessible learning environment, accessible documents and teaching accessibly.

## 2 Literature Review

Quek and Oliveira [2] trained blind students to use a haptic glove with a raised line diagram and computer-vision-based tracking to provide awareness of deictic gestures to inform the user where on the diagram on the board the teacher was pointing as they spoke. The tactile diagrams was pre-prepared however tactile touch screens could be

---

[1] http://www.ilo.org/wcmsp5/groups/public/—ed_emp/—ifp_skills/documents/publication/wcms_112307.pdf.

© Springer International Publishing Switzerland 2016
K. Miesenberger et al. (Eds.): ICCHP 2016, Part II, LNCS 9759, pp. 555–559, 2016.
DOI: 10.1007/978-3-319-41267-2_78

used in real-time. Freire et al. [3] used a mediator to add screen reader accessible text annotations to the electronic images transmitted from teacher interactive whiteboard drawings. Technologies can assist disabled people and support some interactions between people (e.g. [4, 5]) however, until Angkananon et al.'s [6] Technology Enhanced Interaction Framework (TEIF) and Method there had been no consideration of all interactions occuring at the same time and in the same place and no method to guide the development of technology solutions for complex face-to-face situations for people with disabilities. The TEIF Method was only developed and evaluated for hearing impairment because of time limitations and this paper explains extending the TEIF Method for visual impairment. The TEIF and TEIF Method were developed by analysing, adapting and extending Dix's framework for Computer Supported Cooperative Work [6]. Table 1 shows the five TEIF sub-components for the interactions and communication main component.

**Table 1.** Interactions and Communication in the technology enhanced interaction framework

| Main component | Sub-component | Explanation and example |
|---|---|---|
| Interactions and Communi-cation | People-People (P-P) | People communicate verbally (speak, listen, ask, answer) and non-verbally (lip-read, smile, touch, sign, gesture, nod). When communicating, people may refer (speak or point) to particular objects or technology – this is known as 'deixis' |
| | People-Objects (P-O) | People interact with objects for two main purposes: controlling (e.g. touch, hold or move), and retrieving information (e.g. look, listen, read, in order to get information or construct personal understanding, and knowledge) |
| | People-Technology (P-T) | People control technology, (e.g. hold, move, use, type, scan, make image, press, swipe) transmit and store information (e.g. send, save, store, search, retrieve) |
| | People-Technology-People (P-T-P) | People use technology to transmit information to assist communication with (e.g. send sms, mms, email, chat, instant message) other people |
| | People-Technology-Objects (P-T-O) | People use technology (e.g. point, move, hold, scan QR codes, scan AR tag, use camera, use compass) to transmit, store, and retrieve information (send, save, store, search, retrieve) to, in, and from objects |

The TEIF Method was successfully validated by developer and accessibility experts, and an HCI professor and supports other methods by providing multiple-choice questions to help identify requirements, the answers to which help provide technology suggestions that support the design stage. An experiment with 36 developers showed that the 18 developers using the TEIF Method evaluated requirements for technology solutions to problems involving interaction with hearing impaired people better than the 18 developers using their preferred Other Methods. The TEIF Method also helped the developers select a best solution significantly more often and rate the best solution significantly closer to expert ratings.

# 3   Research Methodology

Requirement questions and answers and technology suggestions and example scenarios for visually impaired people have been extended and developed based on a literature review and interviews with visually impaired people in Thailand e.g.:

> "Golf is a blind student in the law faculty. In the class, when the teacher write or draws on a blackboard Golf needs the teacher or another student to read it aloud or explain it to him. Also when the teacher refers to material by pointing at the board he does not know what the teacher is pointing at."

The following relevant questions help elicit requirements and the corresponding answers for this scenario aspect are given:

1. Question: What media is used to provide information? Answer: (a) Non-text image, (b) Printed text, (c) Handwritten text
2. Question: What live in-class support is available? Answer: (a) None
3. Question: What interaction types take place? Answer: (a) People to People (i.e. speech) (b) People to Technology to People (i.e. writing/drawing on board)
4. Question: Is there Deixis? Answer: (a) Yes

Table 2 describes a few suggested technologies (some at prototype stage) with a tick indicating whether it could address the identified requirements.

**Table 2.** Technology Suggestions

| Technology Suggestions | Technology Description | 1a Non-text Image | 1b Printed text | 1c Handwritten text | 2a No in class | 3b P-T-p support | 4a Deixis |
|---|---|---|---|---|---|---|---|
| Screen Reading Technology (SRT) | Automatically reads displayed text aloud and allows blind user to navigate screen | x | ✓ | x | ✓ | ✓ | x |
| Optical Character Recognition (OCR) | Converts a text image into text that can be read by a screen reader | x | ✓ | x | ✓ | ✓ | x |
| Handwriting recognition (HWR) | Converts a handwritten image into text that can be read by a screen reader | x | ✓ | ✓ | ✓ | ✓ | x |
| Diagram mediated text annotation | Adds text to a diagram | ✓ | x | x | ✓ | ✓ | x |
| Camera focused on board with OCR/HWR to read text & SRT | Enables text on a non electronic board in class to be read by a screen reader | x | ✓ | ✓ | ✓ | ✓ | x |
| Electronic whiteboard with OCR/HWR to read text & SRT | Enables text on an electronic board in class to be read by a screen reader | x | ✓ | ✓ | ✓ | ✓ | x |
| Pre-prepared paper tactile diagram | Static 3D representation of a diagram that can be explored by touch by a blind person | ✓ | ✓ | ✓ | ✓ | ✓ | x |
| Live electronic tactile display | Dynamic 3D representation of a diagram that can be explored by touch by a blind person | ✓ | ✓ | ✓ | ✓ | ✓ | x |
| Camera and haptic glove tracking of teacher's pointing used with tactile diagram/display | Information is provided about what the teacher is pointing at using vibration in an electronic glove | ✓ | ✓ | ✓ | ✓ | ✓ | ✓ |

## 4   Conclusion and Planned Activities

Through interviews with visually impaired people the TEIF Method has been extended to help developers develop technology solutions to help people with visual impairment to interact with people, technologies and objects. Future work is planned to evaluate its use with developers and visually impaired students.

# References

1. Petrie, H., Fisher, W., Langer, I., Weber, G., Gladstone, K., Rundle, C., Pyfers, L.: Universal interfaces to multimedia documents. In: Fourth IEEE International Conference on Multimodal Interfaces (ICMI 2002), pp. 319–324 (2002)
2. Quek, F., Oliveira, F.: Enabling the blind to see gestures. ACM Trans. Comput.-Hum. Interact. **20**(1), Article 4 (2013)
3. Freire, A.P., Linhalis, F., Bianchini, S.L., Fortes, R.P., Pimentel, M.C.: Revealing the whiteboard to blind students: an inclusive approach to provide mediation in synchronous e-learning activities. Comput. Edu. **54**(4), 866–876 (2010)
4. Dix, A.: Computer supported cooperative work - a framework. In: Rosenburg, C., Hutchison, C. (eds.) Design Issues in CSCW, pp. 23–37. Springer, London (1994)
5. Rukzio, E., Broll, G., Wetzstein, S.: The Physical Mobile Interaction Framework (PMIF). Technical report LMU-MI-2008-2 (2008)
6. Angkananon, K., Wald, M., Gilbert, L.: Developing and evaluating a technology enhanced interaction framework and method that can enhance the accessibility of mobile learning. Themes Sci. Technol. Edu. **7**(2), 99–118 (2014)

# Types of Problems Elicited by Verbal Protocols for Blind and Sighted Participants

Andreas Savva[✉], Helen Petrie, and Christopher Power

Human-Computer Interaction Research Group, Department of Computer Science,
University of York, York, YO10 5GH, UK
{as1517,helen.petrie,christopher.power}@york.ac.uk

**Abstract.** Verbal protocols are often used in user-based studies of interactive technologies. This study investigated whether different types of problems are revealed by concurrent and retrospective verbal protocols (CVP and RVP) for blind and sighted participants. Eight blind and eight sighted participants undertook both CVP and RVP on four websites. Overall, interactivity problems were significantly more frequent in comparison to content or information architecture problems. In addition, RVP revealed significantly more interactivity problems than CVP for both user groups. Finally, blind participants encountered significantly more interactivity problems than sighted participants. The findings have implications for which protocol is appropriate, depending on the purpose of a particular study and the user groups involved.

**Keywords:** User-based studies · Concurrent verbal protocol · Retrospective verbal protocol · Usability · Accessibility · Blind users

## 1 Introduction

User-based studies are regarded as the gold standard for assessing the usability and accessibility of interactive systems. Typically, users perform a verbal protocol while they undertake tasks with the system. The verbal protocol was first introduced in human computer interaction studies by Lewis [9], but its origins can be traced back to the work of Ericsson and Simon [4, 5] in cognitive psychology. Verbal protocols can offer insight into the users' thought processes, their problem solving strategies [10] and it can be an effective method for detecting the problems users encounter with an interactive system [7, 20]. Many usability textbooks have established the verbal protocol as a core component of usability testing practice [3, 10, 14].

A key aspect of the approach proposed by Ericsson and Simon [4, 5] is the passive role of the evaluator during the study. The only intervention by the evaluator is to remind participants to think aloud if they become silent. Nevertheless, some evaluators do not follow this approach and take a more active role [1, 11]. Boren and Ramey [1] proposed an approach to verbal protocols that is based on the speech-communication theory. The evaluator provides acknowledgement tokens such as "mm hm" or "uh-huh" to keep participants verbalizing their thoughts.

© Springer International Publishing Switzerland 2016
K. Miesenberger et al. (Eds.): ICCHP 2016, Part II, LNCS 9759, pp. 560–567, 2016.
DOI: 10.1007/978-3-319-41267-2_79

The verbal protocol can be performed either concurrently, concurrent verbal protocol (CVP), or retrospectively, retrospective verbal protocol (RVP). In CVP participants think out loud while doing the task, whereas in RVP participants first perform the tasks in silence and then they perform the verbal protocol, usually prompted by a video of themselves performing the tasks [10, 13]. Blind participants can also perform RVP by listening to an audio of their interaction with their screen reader.

Numerous studies have compared the two protocols in terms of the participants' task success or the number of problems revealed [2, 15–19]. However, there is little research into the differences in the types of problems that the two protocols reveal [16–19] and these studies have been conducted only with sighted participants. A limitation of these studies is that a single website was used in each one and inconsistencies in the classification of usability problems that were used to categorize the problems across studies. In addition, some studies showed that RVP reveals more problems of a specific type but the results were not consistent across studies. Moreover, the results of these studies cannot be generalized to all people as the participant's ages in all studies were between 18 and 25.

Even though these studies provide a better understanding of the different problem types that the two protocols reveal, more comprehensive studies with a wider variety of websites need to be conducted. As far as blind participants are concerned, no work could be found comparing the two verbal protocols in terms of the problem types they reveal and how they differ from the problems sighted participants encounter. It is important to investigate the research methods assessing usability and accessibility of websites, as we can get more insights into which method can be considered a better option for studies with either blind or sighted users. This paper investigates whether there is difference in the problem types revealed by CVP and RVP and between blind and sighted users.

## 2   Method

### 2.1   Participants

Sixteen participants, eight blind and eight sighted, undertook the study. The two groups of participants were matched as closely as possible in terms of age, gender, operating system used, web experience and web expertise. The blind participants were six men and two women with a median age of 43 years (range 23–64); the sighted participants also comprised six men and two women with median age of 40 years (range 22–55). Five blind and five sighted participants were Windows users and three blind and three sighted participants were Mac OSX users. Participants rated their web experience using a five-point Likert item (1 = very low to 5 = very good). Blind participants' average rating was 4.0 (SD = 0.9), whereas for sighted participants it was 4.5 (SD = 0.5). Participants also rated their web expertise in the same way. Blind participants' average rating was 3.8 (SD = 0.9), whereas for sighted participants it was 3.6 (SD = 0.9).

All blind participants used screen readers to navigate the web. The five participants who used Windows used JAWS as their screen reader and the three participants who used Mac OSX used VoiceOver as their screen reader.

## 2.2  Websites and Tasks

Four websites from different domains were used in the study: a government website (www.gov.uk), a real estate website (www.rightmove.co.uk), an online shop (www.boots.com) and a news website (www.channel4.com). The websites included a range of different web design aspects such as headings, forms, tables, and links. The tasks included both navigation and data input. Each participant undertook one task on each website. The tasks were:

- Gov.uk: Find how much it is going to cost to arrange a meeting to apply for a National Insurance Number from your mobile phone number.
- Rightmove: Find a house to rent with a minimum of two bedrooms and a rent of no more than £1200 per month, near to a secondary school (a postcode was provided).
- Boots: Find the cheapest, five-star rated car seat for a two-year old child who weights 24 kg.
- Channel4: Find which movie will be on Film4 at 9 pm the day after tomorrow.

## 2.3  Procedure

The study was conducted in the Interaction Laboratory at the Department of Computer Science of the University of York and at the National Council for the Blind of Ireland (NCBI). Participants were briefed about the study and then signed an informed consent form. Participants used their preferred operating system and browser in order to avoid any problems related to lack of familiarity with the technology. Blind participants also used their preferred screen reader and the appropriate version. With their permission, all the sessions were recorded using Morae 3.1 on Windows and ScreenFlow 4.0.3 on Mac OSX.

For each protocol, the researcher gave a standard demonstration of the protocol that the participant was about to perform. The participants then tried out the protocol for themselves on a practice website. The verbal protocol procedure was based on the Boren and Ramey [1] approach. For CVP, participants thought out loud as they performed the tasks. If they were quiet for more than 20 seconds, they were prompted with a general question such as "What are you thinking about?". However, there were cases when the prompts relied on the evaluator's discretion, particularly for the blind participants. There were occasions when participants were silent for extended period because they were listening to the screen reader. For example, participants were searching for a specific link in a list of links, which may have included more than one hundred links, thus the 20 seconds time interval would not be appropriate on such an occasion. For RVP, participants first performed the tasks in silence, then reviewed them on the video (or audio for the blind participants) which was played back to them after the completion of each task.

Each time participants encountered what they considered to be a problem (be it with the website, the browser or the operating system), they were asked to describe it.

After completing both protocols, participants were asked to complete a demographic questionnaire and were debriefed about the study and any questions they had were answered.

The order of the tasks and the verbal protocols were counter-balanced within each user group, to minimize practice and fatigue effects.

## 2.4    Data Analysis

The video recordings were reviewed and problems were categorized using the classification of usability problems developed by Petrie and Power [12]. This involves four main types of problem: physical presentation, content, information architecture and interactivity. An additional type was added to deal with the problems encountered by blind participants, for problems involving incompatibilities between the browser and the screen reader, we named this category technology problems. We used the classification of problems by Petrie and Power [12], as it was more explicit but a similar categorization of problems to that used by van den Haak et al. [16–19]. To distinguish the differences between the content, information architecture and interactivity, we considered interactivity problems those that break the interaction of the user with the website, information architecture those that are related with the organization and the structure of the information between and within the pages and content problems those that are associated with the information in the pages. Table 1 shows examples of each problem type from blind and sighted participants.

**Table 1.**  Examples of each problem type from blind and sighted participants

|  | Blind participants | Sighted participants |
|---|---|---|
| Content | There is nothing about schools in the description of the house (P8) | The product description is limited. There is nothing about weight (P16) |
| Information architecture | The structure of the movies is confusing. I cannot understand which of the two times is the correct one for the movie (P5) | The option to filter by schools is very deep in the site (P13) |
| Interactivity | The input of the maximum number of bedrooms does not have a label (P1) | The group weight options in the filtering are not very clear (P15) |

Inter-coder reliability on the identification of problems was calculated on 10 % of the video sessions. An additional evaluator, not involved in the study, independently extracted the problems from the videos. The reliability was calculated using the any-two agreement by Hertzum and Jacobsen [6]:

$$\frac{|Pi \cap Pj|}{|Pi \cup Pj|} \tag{1}$$

The any-two agreement is based on the number of problems the two evaluators have in common divided by the total number of problems they identified. P refers to number of problems identified and i and j refers to the two evaluators. The conservative approach we followed in terms of the definition a problem resulted in 100 % agreement on the identification of user problems.

Inter-coder reliability on the categorization of problems was calculated on 10 % of the problems. Cohen's Kappa (K) [8] was calculated between one of the authors and a additional coder who was not involved in the study. Inter-coder reliability showed satisfactory levels of agreement for the categorisation of the problems with K = 0.883 for the main types of problems and K = 0.836 for the sub-type of problems.

For the main analysis of data, we compared only the problems that were encountered by both user groups. Thus, we included only the content, information architecture and interactivity problems, as blind participants did not encounter any physical presentation problems and sighted participants did not encounter any technology problems.

## 3   Results

A total of 260 instances of problems were reported across both protocols and all websites. To investigate whether there is difference between problem types that the two protocol reveal and whether there were differences between the problem types reported by the two user groups, an analysis of the instances of problems of each type was conducted. A 3-way ANOVA (verbal protocol x user group x type of problems) did not reveal any significant main effect for user group (F = 3.19, df = 1,14, n.s.). Thus, blind and sighted participants did not differ in the overall number of problems encountered. The analysis revealed a significant main effect for verbal protocol (F = 5.30, df = 1, 14, p < 0.05). The mean number of problem instances in CVP was 5.94 (SD = 2.02) per participant, whereas in RVP it was 8.50 (SD = 4.00). The analysis also revealed main effect of problem type (F = 41.07, df = 1.46, 20.42, p < 0.001, with Greenhouse-Geisser correction). Post-hoc comparison using t-tests with Bonferroni correction indicated that the mean number of interactivity problems (M = 9.06, SD = 4.43) per participant was significantly higher than the mean number of content problems (M = 2.50, SD = 2.00) and the mean number of information architecture problems (M = 2.88, SD = 1.75).

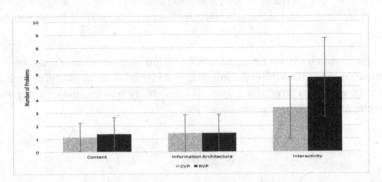

**Fig. 1.**  Mean number of problems for the three problem types, for CVP and RVP.

There was a significant interaction between verbal protocol and the problem type (F = 4.29, df = 2, 28, p < 0.05). Figure 1 shows the mean number of problems for the three problem types, for CVP and RVP, per participant. Post hoc paired sample t-tests showed there was there was a significant difference between protocols for the interactivity problems (t = −2.79, df = 15, p < 0.05). The mean number of interactivity problems identified using CVP was 3.38 (SD = 2.36), whereas in RVP it was 5.69 (SD = 3.05). None of the other comparisons were significantly different.

There was also a significant interaction between user group and problem type (F = 12.34, df = 1.46, 20.42, p < 0.001, with Greenhouse-Geisser correction). Figure 2 shows the mean number of problems per problem type and user group. Post hoc sample-t-tests showed that there was a significant difference between blind and sighted participants on interactivity problems (t = 3.47, df = 7, p < 0.05). The mean number of interactivity problems encountered by blind participants was 12.00 (SD = 3.82), whereas for sighted participants it was 6.13 (SD = 2.42).

Further examination of the interactivity problems showed that there were interactivity problems that encountered only by blind participants and not by sighted participants. These problems included lack of feedback on user actions, labels missing on interactive elements, links that lead to external sites without warning, interactive elements not grouped clearly, lack of consistency between the interactive elements used, and input formats not clear. In addition, there were interactivity problems that were encountered more frequently by blind participants than by sighted participants. These included instructions on interactive elements not clear, options not complete, and elements not clearly identified as interactive or not.

There was no interaction between user group and verbal protocol (F = 0.03, df = 1, 14, n.s.). Finally, there was no significant three way interaction between problem type, verbal protocol and user group (F = 1.13, df = 2, 28, n.s.).

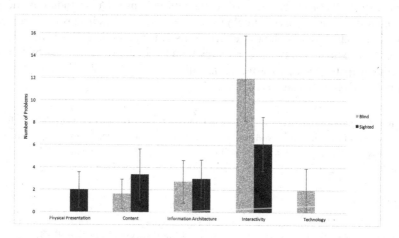

**Fig. 2.** Mean number of problems per problem type for blind and sighted participants.

## 4   Discussion and Conclusions

This paper compared two verbal protocols, CVP and RVP, on whether they identify different types of problems. In addition, a comparison of the problem types revealed by blind and sighted users was conducted. The results indicate that RVP produced significantly more problems overall. There was also a significant difference between frequency of problem types. Interactivity problems were encountered significantly more often than content and information architecture problems. In addition, there was a significant interaction between protocol and the problem type: RVP revealed significantly more interactivity problems compared with CVP, with no differences in the other problem types. Finally there was a significant interaction between user group and problem type: blind participants significantly reported more interactivity problems than sighted participants, with no significant differences between the groups in the other problem types.

The difference in frequency in interactivity between blind and sighted participants comes from several sources. There were interactivity problems that only encountered by blind participants, for instance the lack of feedback on user actions and system progress, missing labels on interactive elements, and links that lead to external sites without warnings. There were also types of problems that were encountered by both user groups but which blind participants encountered more frequently than sighted participants. These included instructions on interactive elements not clear, and options not complete.

The study has provided a better understanding of the differences between the two verbal protocols in terms of the problem types the two protocols reveal. The results indicate that RVP may be considered a better option in user-based studies, particularly if the interest is in interactivity problems. However for studies interested in content or information architecture problems, either protocol is appropriate. We believe it is the first study to compare the type of problems found with the two protocols by blind and sighted participants and it has provided insights into the differences in terms of problem types between blind and sighted users.

**Acknowledgements.**   We thank the National Council for the Blind of Ireland (NCBI) for their assistance in running this study, and all the participants for their time. Andreas Savva thanks the Engineering and Physical Science Research Council of the UK and the Cyprus State Scholarship Foundation for his PhD funding.

## References

1. Boren, T., Ramey, J.: Thinking aloud: reconciling theory and practice. IEEE Trans. Prof. Commun. **43**(3), 261–278 (2000)
2. Bowers, V.A., Snyder, H.L.: Concurrent versus retrospective verbal protocol for comparing window usability. Hum. Factors Ergon. Soc. Annu. Meet. **34**(17), 1270–1274 (1990)
3. Dumas, J.S., Redish, J.: A Practical Guide to Usability Testing. Intellect Books, London (1999)
4. Ericsson, K.A., Simon, H.A.: Protocol Analysis. MIT Press, Cambridge (1993)

5. Ericsson, K.A., Simon, H.A.: Verbal reports as data. Psychol. Rev. **87**(3), 215–253 (1980)
6. Hertzum, M., Jacobsen, N.E.: The evaluator effect: a chilling fact about usability evaluation methods. Int. J. Hum. Comput. Inter. **13**(4), 421–443 (2001)
7. Jørgensen, A.H.: Thinking-aloud in user interface design: a method promoting cognitive ergonomics. Ergonomics **33**(4), 501–507 (1990)
8. Landis, J.R., Koch, G.G.: The measurement of observer agreement for categorical data. Biometrics **33**(1), 159–174 (1977)
9. Lewis, C.: Using the "thinking-aloud" method in cognitive interface design. Research report RC9265, IBM TJ Watson Research Center, Yorktown Heights, NY (1982)
10. Nielsen, J.: Usability Engineering. Elsevier, New York (1994)
11. Nørgaard, M., Hornbæk, K.: What do usability evaluators do in practice?: an explorative study of think-aloud testing. In: 6th Conference on Designing Interactive Systems, pp. 209–218 (2006)
12. Petrie, H., Power, C.: What do users really care about?: a comparison of usability problems found by users and experts on highly interactive websites. In: SIGCHI Conference on Human Factors in Computing Systems, pp. 2107–2116 (2012)
13. Preece, J., Sharp, H., Rogers, Y.: Interaction Design: Beyond Human-Computer Interaction. Wiley, Chichester (2015)
14. Rubin, J.: Handbook of Usability Testing. Wiley, New York (1994)
15. Savva, A., Petrie, H., Power, C.: Comparing concurrent and retrospective verbal protocols for blind and sighted users. In: Abascal, J., Barbosa, S., Fetter, M., Gross, T., Palanque, P., Winckler, M. (eds.) INTERACT 2015. LNCS, vol. 9296, pp. 55–71. Springer, Heidelberg (2015)
16. van den Haak, M.J., De Jong, M.D.T., Schellens, P.J.: Employing think-aloud protocols and constructive interaction to test the usability of online library catalogues: a methodological comparison. Interact. Comput. **16**(6), 1153–1170 (2004)
17. van den Haak, M.J., De Jong, M.D.T., Schellens, P.J.: Evaluation of an informational web site: three variants of the think-aloud method compared. Tech. Commun. **54**(1), 58–71 (2007)
18. van den Haak, M.J., De Jong, M.D.T., Schellens, P.J.: Evaluating municipal websites: a methodological comparison of three think-aloud variants. Gov. Inf. Q. **26**(1), 193–202 (2009)
19. van den Haak, M.J., De Jong, M.D.T., Schellens, P.J.: Retrospective vs concurrent think-aloud protocols: testing the usability of an online library catalogue. Behav. Inf. Technol. **22**(5), 339–351 (2003)
20. Wright, P.C., Monk, A.F.: The use of think-aloud evaluation method in design. ACM SIGCHI Bull. **23**(1), 55–57 (1991)

# Multimodal Attention Stimulator

Andrzej Czyzewski[✉], Bozena Kostek, and Lukasz Kosikowski

ETI Faculty, Multimedia Systems Department, Gdansk University of Technology,
Gdansk, Poland
{andcz,kosiq}@sound.eti.pg.gda.pl

**Abstract.** Multimodal attention stimulator was proposed and tested for improving auditory and visual attention, including pupils with developmental dyslexia. Results of the conducted experiments shown that the designed stimulator can be used in order to improve comprehension during reading tasks. The changes in the visual attention, observed in reading test results, translate into the overall reading performance.

**Keywords:** Multimodal · Attention · Stimulator · Cross-dominance · Dyslexia

## 1 Introduction

The lateralization of brain function stems from some specific neural or cognitive processes that are more dominant in one brain hemisphere than the other. One of the most popular approaches of the lateralization training is the Tomatis Method based on the listening therapy of the audio processed employing some specific rules of signal processing. Those consist of high and low-pass filtration controlled by the level of the input signal, e.g. to obtain correct lateralization, sound level for the left ear is reduced, in order to force the usage of the right ear. As a result, the sound is routed directly to the left hemisphere, where the speech center is located. The widely known Tomatis Method is also the base of such methods as: Berard method, SPS-S method [1], and other. Those methods differ from each other in the hardware configuration, the type of music used during the training and sound processing algorithms.

The proposed multimodal attention stimulator uses speech modification performed in two domains: time scale modification (TSM) and signal amplitude modification. TSM is obtained using non-uniform real-time speech stretching algorithm [1, 2]. The main assumption of the TSM algorithm is to modify in a real-time the duration of the different speech units using various time scaling factors.

Visual attention consists of many sub-systems and mechanisms, often with different functional characteristics [3, 4]. Nevertheless, visual attention is one of ways of information processing that does not necessarily involve higher mental functions. It is known [3] that visual attention is directed to certain areas of the visual field (space based attention), attention is directed to the object or group of objects located in the visual field (object based attention), whereas functioning of the attention may be flexible, and the selection is made due to the locations or objects.

© Springer International Publishing Switzerland 2016
K. Miesenberger et al. (Eds.): ICCHP 2016, Part II, LNCS 9759, pp. 568–571, 2016.
DOI: 10.1007/978-3-319-41267-2_80

According to Treisman theory [5], attention acts in the same manner as a spotlight for the brain. It scans the environment and obtains features like shape, color, and then links them together to form a comprehensive whole. The visual part of the developed stimulator was based on this theory. Highlighting the word forces the user to look at a specific area (emulates the spotlight function for the brain). By excluding the words before or after the selected word the number of distractors in the central field of view is reduced. This should allow for improving perceptions and, consequently, for increasing the visual attention.

The main idea underlying the proposed stimulator is to perform parallel stimulation of the sight and hearing senses employing digital signal processing techniques. The modification of the visual and hearing stimuli is performed in order to force the perception through those senses by the appropriate hemisphere. The proposed method of stimulation was implemented as a dedicated software. The image was modified in the same way for both eyes i.e. currently heard words were highlighted through the changes of the font color from black to red (font size was invariable). The speech signal was time-expanded for both ears, however its amplitude was left unchanged. Vowels were stretched up using higher values of scale factor than consonants. This time-expansion strategy is similar to the typical human behavior in the situation when a person starts to speak slower. There are several scenarios in which the stimulator could be used. In the main scenario, an ordinary PC with headphones and an LCD computer monitor is utilized which can be extended optionally with an eye-tracking system (Fig. 1).

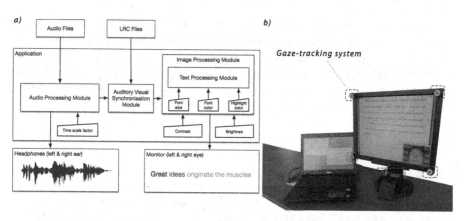

**Fig. 1.** Developed attention stimulator: (a) block diagram; (b) training stand: visual auditory attention stimulator extended by an optional gaze-tracking system.

## 2    Research Tools and Results

The experiment employed 40 children with difficulties in learning of reading, diagnosed with developmental dyslexia, at the age of 8–13 years. In the experimental group (named E) were 20 children (11 boys, 9 girls). In the control group (named C) there were 20 children (15 boys and 5 girls). Persons were examined using a battery of different attention tests. The study included children with normal peripheral hearing, normal vision, revealing intelligence quotient within normal limits.

The examined group was subjected to standard pedagogical therapy. In the experimental group (E), therapy with reading and writing exercises was supplemented with exercises using the multimodal attention stimulator. The training time lasted one hour per week, whereas exercises with the developed system occupied a 20 %–30 % of the whole time. The children were sited 60 cm from the monitor screen. The tests were conducted in a quiet room, during daylight. The text material was edited from simple stories, adequate to the children's age.

The control group was treated only with standard pedagogical therapy. Both groups were distinguished only by using or not the multimodal attention stimulator.

## 2.1  D2 Test

In this research the Polish adaptation of the test procedure, made by Dajek E, was used [6]. The test requires concentration on the external visual stimuli. Test d2 based on the definition of attention, according to which a series of selections related to concentration is required. Consequently a person's ability to work without interruption is verified, and their ability to analyze quickly and properly the relevant internal or external stimuli in a selective manner is checked. Based on the test results, three indicators were calculated: total number of analyzed letters; percentage of mistakes and overall ability of perception indicator.

Subjects in the group E experienced a bigger improvement both in terms of the number of scanned characters and smaller amount of errors. In e.g. the total number of analyzed letters (raw value) changed for the control group (C): from 350 to 399, and for the experimental group (E): from 330 to 398. The observed changes are related to the improvement of the speed and accuracy of the visual search and to the increase of the visual attention, which has a direct impact on reading literacy.

## 2.2  Reading Aloud Test

Reading speed reading technique and the number of mistakes during reading process ware examined using two different reading aloud tests: Test developed by Straburzynska T., Sliwinska T., which is used for examination disciples from the first to the third class; Test developed by Sobolewska M. and Matuszewski A., which is used for examination of older children.

An improvement was observed in both: the experimental group E and the control group C, so the results are comparable in both groups. At the same time, this improvement was greater in the experimental group E in terms of the number of properly read syllables. After excluding from counting the subjects able to read entire words, prior to therapy, the median value of the parameter: "the number of syllables read correctly" changed for the experimental group (E): from 75 to 100, and for the control group (C): from 105 to 112. This result is to be associated with the use of visual attention stimulator, exclusively.

### 2.3 Auditory Processing Tests

The hearing functioning was examined by using: tonal audiometry; impedance audiometry; central auditory processing tests: Speech understanding in noise test (aSPN); Pitch differentiation test (FPT); Assessment of interhemispheric integration mechanisms test (DDT).

Statistically significant improvements were observed in both experimental and control group in the results of the following tests: DDT (left ear), FPT, and aSPN. In the experimental (E) and in the control (C) group there were no statistically significant changes only for DDT test for the right ear. Greater improvements of the auditory processing tests results were observed in the experimental group (E).

## 3  Conclusions

Improvements in all hearing test results in the experimental group (E) and in the control group (C) may be associated with both: the positive effects of typical, pedagogical therapy, and results of using the auditory visual attention stimulator.

The attention test used is precisely focused on examining functions that the multimodal attention stimulator trains, therefore the observed differences between the experimental group (E) and the control group (C) demonstrated the effectiveness of the proposed therapeutic approach.

**Acknowledgments.** The project is partially funded by the National Science Centre of Poland on the basis of the decision DEC-2014/15/B/ST7/04724. Authors wish to acknowledge the work with children done by Dr. Andrzej Senderski employed by the Children's Memorial Health Institute, Warsaw, Poland.

## References

1. Czyzewski, A., Skarzynski, H., Kostek, B., Skarzynski P.: New technology for hearing stimulation employing the SPS-S method. In: 127th AES Convention 09–12.10.2009, preprint No. 7919, New York (2009)
2. Kupryjanow, A., Czyzewski, A.: Real-time speech signal segmentation methods. J. Audio Eng. Soc. **61**(7/8), 1–14 (2013)
3. Eysenck, M.W., Keane, M.: Cognitive Psychology. A Student's Handbook. Psychology Press, Hove (2005)
4. Styrkowiec, P., Nęcka, E.: O dwóch systemach uwagi wzrokowej, (On two systems of visual attention). Przegląd Psychologiczny **51**(2), 113–133 (2008). (in Polish)
5. Tresiman, A.M., Gelade, G.: A feature-integration theory of attention. Cogn. Psychol. **12**, 97–136 (1980)
6. Brickenkamp, R.: Auferksamkeits-Belastungs-Test (Test d2). Hogrefe, Gottingen (1962)

# Assessing Braille Input Efficiency on Mobile Devices

Norbert Márkus[✉], Szabolcs Malik, and András Arató

Rehabilitation-Technology Laboratory, Wigner Research Centre for Physics,
Institute for Particle and Nuclear Physics, Hungarian Academy of Sciences,
Budapest, Hungary
{markus.norbert, szabolcs.malik,
andras.arato}@wigner.mta.hu

**Abstract.** Our team has conducted a research on how today's Braille input methods suit the needs of blind smartphone users. Hungarian blind volunteers (all active Braille users) were invited to participate. The research consisted of a survey on the participants' relation to Braille and a series of input tests based on short Hungarian and multilingual texts both in grade 1 and 2 Braille using different devices and methods. Results showed that experienced Braille users can achieve remarkably high speeds and accuracy and that the use of contracted Braille further increases input efficiency. This paper also discusses the characteristics of typos occuring and their manual or automated correction during Braille input on mobile devices. Adding adequate automated correction mechanisms optimized for Braille typos may further increase the input speed nearing or even surpassing the speed of sighted people using ordinary on-screen input methods.

**Keywords:** Assessment and profiling · Accessibility · Blindness · Assistive technology · Braille · HCI and Non-classical interfaces · eLiteracy · Usability and Ergonomics · Mobility · Input methods · Efficiency

## 1 Introduction

In Hungary, assistive technology based on speech synthesis has gradually supplanted Braille in its traditional forms over the last two decades. Before long, scools and educators followed suit, especially after the introduction of integrated schooling. Their focus shifted from Braille literacy to computer skills mostly ignoring modern Braille technologies.

Hungaryan contracted Braille is much simpler and hence less efficient than English or German grade 2, and the number of its readers is on the decline. Sweeping new reforms have been stepped up and recently been introduced in official publications and lately in textbooks. These reforms left teachers and students in confusion and discouraged many Braille enthusiasts (the number of subscribers to Hungarian Braille periodicals dropped dramatically).

Writing Braille already fell into disuse in the early 1990s, with ten-finger typing on standard computer keyboards taking precedence. However, a new shift is witnessed as

K. Miesenberger et al. (Eds.): ICCHP 2016, Part II, LNCS 9759, pp. 572–578, 2016.
DOI: 10.1007/978-3-319-41267-2_81

entering text on the small touch screens of today's smartphones poses a challenge for the blind. Surprisingly or not, On-screen input methods based on Braille just appear to be the most effective. Dormant skills of those who learnt Braille at school were quickly recovered and adapted to this new interface. Others face the challenge of learning it from scratch on their own as no formal training is available in Hungary for chorded braille entry on touch screens.

We aimed our research at the assessment of the current state of Braille, in particular at its usage on smart devices in Hungary. Our paper will discuss the findings of a survey combined with a series of Braille input efficiency measurements conducted with active Braille users.

## 2  Research Idea

In the first round, ten Hungarian regular Braille users of different backgrounds were invited to participate in our research. The idea was to let them go through the same set of Braille writing related tasks all based on the same short Hungarian text. These tasks included Braille entering tests performed on their own smartphones, and using other less familiar devices made available for the occasion, a single-finger dot-after-dot entry and a so-called chorded entry, entering on the sheer touch screen and on a screen covered by a Braille mask then on a connected keyboard, with one hand and with two hands, using uncontracted (grade 1) and contracted (grade 2) Braille.

In the second round, five regular Braille users (also from Hungary) were involved, practically going through the same set of tests but this time based on multiple texts in various different languages including English, German, Esperanto and Russian. In another bilingual set of texts, these foreign languages were combined with Hungarian (i.e., Hungarian + English, Hungarian + German, etc.). Where possible, grade 2 Braille was also tested with these texts. The idea behind these tests were to assess the differences in efficiency of the Braille systems involved and the subjects' adaptation to them, plus the difficulty of changing the input language on the fly.

Furthermore, a joint survey was conducted with the aim of getting a full picture on Braille used in Hungary on mobile devices. Our goal is to summarize in this paper the results and issues encountered during these tests and in the survey, with the hope that raising awareness may help find solutions and so the status of Braille on smart devices would be consolidated in our region.

## 3  State of the Art

- MObile SlateTalker (MOST) [1–3]: A self-voiced Android app that is a package of useful applications for the visually impaired. A special mask assists in using the on-screen Braille input surface either in a dot-after-dot or in a chorded manner. The app's unique feature is a comprehensive haptic feedback system for the deaf-blind.
- mBraille [4]: A versatile app suite with full-screen Braille input for iOs and Android devices with proprietary gestures and dot-commands. Important: a simultaneous use

of both hands and up to six fingers is required for the operation of the screen surface dedicated to Braille input, plus, on Android the app is functional only with the screen reader being suspended.

- BrailleTouch [5]: A mobile app providing a proprietary multitouch braille input method on touch screen powered iOs devices. It only supports the major languages and braille systems. References to publications of related research on input efficiency and other materials can be found on the project's website [6]. There is an Android app with the same name on the Google Play Store, but it may be an unrelated project with French support.

## 4    Methodology

Fifteen select blind Braille users were invited to participate in the research on a voluntary basis (ten for the first round and five more for the second round). The first group consisted of four females and six males, their ages ranging between 14 and 71 with an average of 49, while the second group consisted of all males. Four of them were teachers. Programmers, musicians, a lawier and other professions were also represented, plus a young blind student.

A short text was composed in Hungarian to be embossed both in grade1 and grade 2 braille. It served as a basis for the first round of our efficiency tests. This text consists of three sentences of medium complexity. Each test subject was given a leaflet with this text to study and memorise. Participants were then made to perform a series of Braille writing tests based on the text. The second group was given multiple texts in English, German, Esperanto, Russian and also in combination with Hungarian.

Three input devices were involved: a Mobile Slate Talker [2] powered Android phone with a braille mask placed over its touch screen, a wireless keyboard serving as an electronic brailler, and an iPhone offering a third-party on-screen chorded braille input method [4]. Subjects were called on to enter the text on each input device using the modalities relevant to their physical abilities and the device currently in use.

An app installed on the Android device allowed for a sequential single-finger (dot-after-dot) entry, plus a chorded (simultaneous multifinger) entry, in contracted or uncontracted braille assisted with a mask placed over the touch screen. The same Android app made it possible to enter the text on a connected wireless keyboard providing two-hand and single-hand layouts for braille input. The mBraille app installed on an iPhone provided an input method limited to an on-screen chorded input and to uncontracted braille on the naked screen.

Thus in total, nine different kinds of measurement could be performed by a single participant based on one of the texts provided. Subjects had the choice to skip or repeat any of the measurements. At each test stage, the times required for entering the text were measured and associated with the particular kinds of input. An audio footage was also made during many of the sessions to facilitate later in-depth analysis. When requested, the relevant bit of the text was read aloud for support during the tests. Subjects were instructed to produce a flawless output (i.e., containing the right capitalization if relevant and no typos undealt with).

**Table 1.** Properties of the sample texts in contracted and uncontracted Braille.

| | | Grade 1 | Grade 2 |
|---|---|---|---|
| Length (cells) | | $163^H$; $155^E$; $159^{HE}$; $153^G$; $151^{HG}$; $158^{Eo}$; $197^{HEo}$; $175^R$; $164^{HR}$ | $117^H$; $116^E$; $128^{HE}$; $106^G$; $118^{HG}$ |
| Compared to print | Saved (characters): | $2^H$; $-4^E$; $2^{HE}$; $12^G$; $9^{HG}$; $-2^{Eo}$; $-1^{HEo}$; $-5^R$; $2^{HR}$ | $48^H$; $35^E$; $33^{HE}$; $59^G$; $42^{HG}$ |
| | Shrink factor (%): | $1.2^H$; $-2.6^E$; $1.2^{HE}$; $7.3^G$; $5.6^{HG}$; $-1.3^{Eo}$; $-0.5^{HEo}$; $-2;9^R$; $1.2^{HR}$ | $29.1^H$; $23.2^E$; $20.5^{HE}$; $35.8^G$; $26.3^{HG}$ |
| Compared to grade 1 | Saved (characters): | – | $46^H$; $39^E$; $31^{HE}$; $47^G$; $33^{HG}$ |
| | Shrink factor (%): | – | $28.2^H$; $25.2^E$; $19.5^{HE}$; $30.7^G$; $21.9^{HG}$ |
| Sequential entry | Total dots: | $568^H$; $533^E$; $537^{HE}$; $518^G$; $512^{HG}$; $518^{Eo}$; $664^{HEo}$; $630^R$; $575^{HR}$ | $387^H$; $378^E$; $433^{HE}$; $358^G$; $399^{HG}$ |
| | Text dots: | $405^H$; $378^E$; $378^{HE}$; $365^G$; $361^{HG}$; $360^{Eo}$; $467^{HEo}$; $455^R$; $411^{HR}$ | $270^H$; $262^E$; $305^{HE}$; $252^G$; $281^{HG}$ |
| | Spaces: | $23^H$; $26^E$; $25^{HE}$; $26^G$; $24^{HG}$; $24^{Eo}$; $29^{HEo}$; $29^R$; $26^{HR}$ | $19^H$; $26^E$; $20^{HE}$; $26^G$; $21^{HG}$ |
| | Auxiliary dots: | $140^H$; $129^E$; $134^{HE}$; $127^G$; $127^{HG}$; $134^{Eo}$; $168^{HEo}$; $146^R$; $138^{HR}$ | $98^H$; $90^E$; $108^{HE}$; $80^G$; $97^{HG}$ |
| | Average dots/cells: | $3.5^H$; $3.4^E$; $3.4^{HE}$; $3.4^G$; $3.4^{HG}$; $3.3^{Eo}$; $3.4^{HEo}$; $3.6^R$; $3.5^{HR}$ | $3.3^H$; $3.3^E$; $3.4^{HE}$; $3.4^G$; $3.4^{HG}$ |
| Chorded entry | Total dots: | $428^H$; $404^E$; $403^{HE}$; $391^G$; $385^{HG}$; $384^{Eo}$; $496^{HEo}$; $484^R$; $437^{HR}$ | $289^H$; $288^E$; $325^{HE}$; $278^G$; $302^{HG}$ |
| | Text dots: | $405^H$; $378^E$; $378^{HE}$; $365^G$; $361^{HG}$; $360^{Eo}$; $467^{HEo}$; $455^R$; $411^{HR}$ | $270^H$; $262^E$; $305^{HE}$; $252^G$; $281^{HG}$ |
| | Spaces: | $23^H$; $26^E$; $25^{HE}$; $26^G$; $24^{HG}$; $24^{Eo}$; $29^{HEo}$; $29^R$; $26^{HR}$ | $19^H$; $26^E$; $20^{HE}$; $26^G$; $21^{HG}$ |
| | Average dots/cells: | $2.6^H$; $2.6^E$; $2.5^{HE}$; $2.6^G$; $2.5^{HG}$; $2.4^{Eo}$; $2.5^{HEo}$; $2.8^R$; $2.7^{HR}$ | $2.5^H$; $2.5^E$; $2.5^{HE}$; $2.6^G$; $2.6^{HG}$ |

# 5 Results

## 5.1 About the Text

Grade 2's shrink factor varies by text and language. Respecting the number of Braille dots entered, chorded entry is more efficient because the auxiliary dots (corresponding to the "cell completed" function in sequential entry) are out of the play. This is why auxiliary dots are not shown for chorded entry. Sequential dot entry aided by a mask is chosen by those who prefer or are only able to use one hand.

Superscript letters next to the numeric values refer to the language(s) of the text related to that value (i.e., H: Hungarian, E: English, G: German, Es: Esperanto, R: Russian, HE: Hungarian + English, etc.).

**Table 2.** Entry speeds summarized for the test subjects using different input methods

| One-hand entry: $8^H$; $5^E$; $5^{HE}$; $5^G$; $5^{HG}$ | | Grade 1 | Grade 2 |
|---|---|---|---|
| On masked screen | People | $8^H$; $5^E$; $5^{HE}$; $5^G$; $5^{HG}$ | $8^H$; $3^E$; $3^{HE}$; $3^G$; $3^{HG}$ |
| Newbie: $4^H$; $3^E$; $3^{HE}$ Skipped: $1^H$; $0^E$; $0^{HE}$ | Fastest: | $20.2^H$; $20.1^E$; $22.5^{HE}$; $23^G$; $24.3^{HG}$ | $30.9^H$; $22.7^E$; $24.8^{HE}$; $30^G$; $28.2^{HG}$ |
| | Mean: | $9.4^H$; $10.7^E$; $13.8^{HE}$; $13^G$; $13.8^{HG}$ | $12.8^H$; $18.4^E$; $18.7^{HE}$; $21.6^G$; $20.7^{HG}$ |
| | Slowest: | $3.8^H$; $3.3^E$; $5.1^{HE}$; $4.3^G$; $5.1^{HG}$ | $4.5^H$; $9.9^E$; $9.1^{HE}$; $9.6^G$; $9.3^{HG}$ |
| On keyboard | People: | $3^H$; $2^E$; $2^{HE}$; $2^G$; $2^{HG}$ | $3^H$; $2^E$; $2^{HE}$; $2^G$; $2^{HG}$ |
| Newbie: $8^H$; $4^E$; $4^{HE}$ Skipped: $7^H$; $3^E$; $3^{HE}$ | Fastest: | $44^H$; $39.4^E$; $42^{HE}$; $42.1^G$; $45.7^{HG}$ | $58.2^H$; $44.2^E$; $44.9^{HE}$; $52.1^G$; $48^{HG}$ |
| | Mean: | $24.2^H$; $37.8^E$; $39.9^{HE}$; $41.3^G$; $44.2^{HG}$ | $35.6^H$; $43.3^E$; $43^{HE}$; $50.8^G$; $45.8^{HG}$ |
| | Slowest: | $9.8^H$; $36.2^E$; $37.9^{HE}$; $40.4^G$; $42.7^{HG}$ | $15.5^H$; $40.3^E$; $41.1^{HE}$; $49.5^G$; $43.6^{HG}$ |
| Two-hand entry: $9^H$; $5^E$; $5^{HE}$; $4^G$; $4^{HG}$ | | | |
| On masked screen | People: | $5^H$; $5^E$; $5^{HE}$; $4^G$; $4^{HG}$ | $5^H$; $3^E$; $3^{HE}$; $3^G$; $3^{HG}$ |
| Newbie: $9^H$; $3^E$; $3^{HE}$ Skipped: $5^H$; $0^E$; $0^{HE}$ | Fastest: | $34.1^H$; $27^E$; $33.3^{HE}$; $34.7^G$; $36.2^{HG}$ | $48.3^H$; $34.8^E$; $37.9^{HE}$; $41.3^G$; $45.7^{HG}$ |
| | Mean: | $20.1^H$; $17.3^E$; $21.4^{HE}$; $26.2^G$; $27.1^{HG}$ | $29.7^H$; $28.5^E$; $29.8^{HE}$; $32.7^G$; $35.5^{HG}$ |
| | Slowest: | $12.1^H$; $3.6^E$; $7.5^{HE}$; $18.9^G$; $19^{HG}$ | $17.7^H$; $17.1^E$; $15.7^{HE}$; $18.2^G$; $20^{HG}$ |
| On naked screen | People: | $7^H$; $4^E$; $4^{HE}$; $4^G$; $4^{HG}$ | |
| Newbie: $5^H$; $2^E$; $2^{HE}$; $2^G$; $2^{HG}$ Skipped: $3^H$; $0^E$; $0^{HE}$; $0^G$; $0^{HG}$ | Fastest: | $36.7^H$; $27.9^E$; $36.5^{HE}$; $34.1^G$; $40.9^{HG}$ | |
| | Mean: | $24.9^H$; $22.6^E$; $28.9^{HE}$; $26.6^G$; $28.8^{HG}$ | |
| | Slowest: | $7.9^H$; $15.8^E$; $16.4^{HE}$; $18.9^G$; $16.4^{HG}$ | |
| On keyboard | People: | $9^H$; $4^E$; $4^{HE}$; $4^G$; $4^{HG}$ | $8^H$; $3^E$; $3^{HE}$; $3^G$; $3^{HG}$ |
| Newbie: $4^H$; $4^E$; $4^{HE}$; $4^G$; $4^{HG}$ Skipped: $1^H$; $1^E$; $1^{HE}$; $1^G$; $1^{HG}$ | Fastest: | $47.1^H$; $41.2^E$; $48.3^{HE}$; $55^G$; $53.3^{HG}$ | $58.2^H$; $45.3^E$; $53.7^{HE}$; $52.1^G$; $51.9^{HG}$ |
| | Mean: | $26.3^H$; $31.9^E$; $42.2^{HE}$; $46.1^G$; $46.7^{HG}$ | $34.8^H$; $38.6^E$; $44.9^{HE}$; $45.1^G$; $45.8^{HG}$ |
| | Slowest: | $9.2^H$; $20.8^E$; $29.7^{HE}$; $30.5^G$; $34.9^{HG}$ | $14.9^H$; $29.2^E$; $32.7^{HE}$; $32.5^G$; $36.2^{HG}$ |

## 5.2 Speed Tests

In Table 2, integer numbers represent participants, decimals indicate typing rates expressed in words per minute (wpm). "Newbie" shows the number of participants new to a particular method or device, "Skipped" refers to newbies unwilling or unable to complete the test in question. Superscript letters indicate the language(s) of the sample text used for the test yielding the value (see the explanation for Table 1).

In capable hands, certain types of Braille input can be fairly fast. For reference, an experienced blind person typing on a PC keyboard with ten fingers can enter our short Hungarian text flawlessly within 24 s i.e., 82.5 words per minute. On a Braille enabled PC keyboard, the fastest rate measured with one of the test subjects was 32 s (58.2 wpm) typed in grade 2. A mask assisted chorded input yielded 41 s (48.3 wpm) in grade 2. Input efficiency also relies on the way typos can be avoided or removed when entering text on a touch-screen.

## 5.3  About Hungarian Contracted Braille

Tests revealed that the subjects were rather inexperienced in writing grade 2 as it was mostly encountered so far when reading Braille. For some, it was the first time to actually write any text using this contraction system. After spending some time with this feature, all iPhone using participants regretted that Hungarian grade 2 Braille was not available for them. This issue may be dealt with by coordinated contributions to the open-source LibLouis project.

According to our survey, most participants keep the spell checker and autocorrection features disabled for Braille input because they find it cumbersome to tackle with the offered suggestions. Writing in Hungarian contracted Braille reduces the typo rate. This is not only because grade 2 reduces the number of Braille cells to be entered, but by the contractions themselves, also the number of dots to be entered is reduced (see Table 3).

Dot patterns consisting of 4–6 Braille dots are more prone to typos. Therefore grade 2 applied over our Hungarian text comes with numerous benefits. Hungarian grade 2 not only reduces the number of cells to be entered but also reduces the number of the so-called heavy cells (consisting of 4–6 dots) and often introduces light cells (having

**Table 3.** Comparative table on dot pattern statistics.

| Pattern type | Instances in grade 1 | Instances in grade 2 | Reduction (%) |
|---|---|---|---|
| 1-dot cells | $16^H$; $9^E$; $19^{HE}$; $9^G$; $13^{HG}$; $20^{Eo}$; $19^{HEo}$; $7^R$; $12^{HR}$ | $16^H$; $12^E$; $19^{HE}$; $6^G$; $12^{HG}$ | $0^H$; $-33.3^E$; $0^{HE}$; $33.3^G$; $7.7^{HG}$ |
| 2-dot cells | $36^H$; $29^E$; $29^{HE}$; $40^G$; $37^{HG}$; $33^{Eo}$; $50^{HEo}$; $36^R$; $33^{HR}$ | $26^H$; $20^E$; $20^{HE}$; $21^G$; $26^{HG}$ | $27.8^H$; $31^E$; $31^{HE}$; $47.5^G$; $29.7^{HG}$ |
| 3-dot cells | $42^H$; $59^E$; $49^{HE}$; $37^G$; $38^{HG}$; $50^{Eo}$; $52^{HEo}$; $42^R$; $45^{HR}$ | $26^H$; $31^E$; $36^{HE}$; $23^G$; $28^{HG}$ | $38.1^H$; $47.5^E$; $26.5^{HE}$; $37.8^G$; $26.3^{HG}$ |
| 4-dot cells | $39^H$; $26^E$; $31^{HE}$; $40^G$; $35^{HG}$; $31^{Eo}$; $43^{HEo}$; $55^R$; $42^{HR}$ | $26^H$; $19^E$; $27^{HE}$; $19^G$; $24^{HG}$ | $33.3^H$; $26.9^E$; $12.9^{HE}$; $52.5^G$; $31.4^{HG}$ |
| 5-dot cells | $7^H$; $6^E$; $6^{HE}$; $1^G$; $4^{HG}$; $4^{HEo}$; $6^R$; $6^{HR}$ | $4^H$; $7^E$; $6^{HE}$; $7^G$; $5^{HG}$ | $42.9^H$; $-16.7^E$; $0^{HE}$; $-600^G$; $-25^{HG}$ |
| 6-dot cells | $0^E$; $0^G$; $0^{HG}$ | $1^E$; $4^G$; $2^{HG}$ | |

1–3 dots). The reduction of the total number of dots entered directly translates to benefits for sequential entry and comes with indirect benefits for chorded entry, since heavy cells have the potential to produce more typos.

## 6  Impact and Contributions to the Field

Our findings may help app developers and AT designers better profile their Braille related solutions, especially in handling contractions and typos in mobile environments. Extension of the Grade 2 support to further languages including Hungarian may be stimulated by our paper raising the awareness of those contributing to the open-source LibLouis project.

Data collected during our research may serve as the base of further studies e.g. on how best to reduce stress caused by the acoustic and mental overload on the users being forced to maintain multilevel concentration and exposed to an increased amount of artificial and often polyphonic speech while using Braille input methods on mobile devices.

40 % of our test subjects in the first group are teachers at a special school for the blind and active Braille users. By their help, the methodology for a new training scheme for writing Braille on the touch screen may be worked out for the benefit of many blind smartphone users.

## 7  Conclusion

Courtesy to the Budapest School and Methodology Centre for the Blind, Our Rehabilitation-Technology Laboratory has successfully conducted tests and a joint survey with select Hungarian blind Braille users. The research has produced a great wealth of data about Braille input efficiency on mobile devices and helped identify and address important issues. The same data may be used for further research in this field.

## References

1. Markus, N., Malik, S., Juhasz, Z., Arató, A.: Accessibility for the blind on an open-source mobile platform. In: Miesenberger, K., Karshmer, A., Penaz, P., Zagler, W. (eds.) ICCHP 2012, Part II. LNCS, vol. 7383, pp. 599–606. Springer, Heidelberg (2012)
2. Mobile Slate Talker (MOST). http://rehab.wigner.mta.hu/?q=en/node/34
3. Juhasz, Z., et al.: Usability evaluation of the MOST mobile assistant (SlatTalker). In: Miesenberger, K., Klaus, J., Zagler, W.L., Karshmer, A.I. (eds.) ICCHP 2006. LNCS, vol. 4061, pp. 1055–1062. Springer, Heidelberg (2006)
4. Pasanenm, H.: mBraille. http://mpaja.com/mbraille
5. Romero, M.: BrailleTouch, Georgia Institute of Technology (USA). http://www.cc.gatech. edu/~mromero/brailletouch/
6. Southern, C., Clawson, J., Frey, B., Abowd, G., Romero, M., An evaluation of BrailleTouch: mobile touchscreen text entry for the visually impaired. In: MobileHCI 2012, (Full Paper), San Francisco, September 2012

# Smart Glasses for the Visually Impaired People

Esra Ali Hassan and Tong Boon Tang[✉]

Department of Electrical and Electronic Engineering,
Universiti Teknologi PETRONAS, 32610 Bandar Seri Iskandar, Perak, Malaysia
alnow93@gmail.com, tongboon.tang@petronas.com.my

**Abstract.** People with visual impairment face various problems in their daily life as the modern assistive devices are often not meeting the consumer requirements in term of price and level of assistance. This paper presents a new design of assistive smart glasses for visually impaired students. The objective is to assist in multiple daily tasks using the advantage of wearable design format. As a proof of concept, this paper only presents one example application, i.e. text recognition technology that can help reading from hardcopy materials. The building cost is kept low by using single board computer raspberry pi 2 as the heart of processing and the raspberry pi 2 camera for image capturing. Experiment results demonstrate that the prototype is working as intended.

**Keywords:** Visually impaired · Text recognition · OCR · Raspberry pi 2

## 1 Introduction

The number of visually impaired people is growing over the past decades. As reported by the world health organization (WHO), about 285 million people worldwide are estimated to be visually impaired [1]. However, until now many schools and jobs cannot accommodate them mainly due to lack of assistive technologies and economic barriers [2]. As a result, 90 % of them still live in low level of income [1]. Even when the new aids or technologies become available, they are either too expensive ($3000 and above), or affordable ($200) but with single or limited task functions only [3].

Among all assistive devices, wearable devices are found to be the most useful because they are hand free or require minimum use of hands [4]. The most popular type is head mounted device. Their main advantage is that the device points naturally at the viewing direction, thus eliminates the need of additional direction instructions, unlike other devices [5]. This paper presents a new design of smart glasses that can provide assistance in multiple tasks while maintaining at a low building cost. The design uses the new raspberry pi 2 single board computer, a camera, and an earpiece to convey information to the user. Due to page limit, we only demonstrate reading task only. The experiment results and how additional tasks may be added are discussed.

© Springer International Publishing Switzerland 2016
K. Miesenberger et al. (Eds.): ICCHP 2016, Part II, LNCS 9759, pp. 579–582, 2016.
DOI: 10.1007/978-3-319-41267-2_82

## 2    Related Works

The most popular reading device is Braille reader which can read and/or write using an arrangement of dots to form different letters [4]. Another device is the audio book which read books or newspaper saved in audio format by certain suppliers [6]. Screen reader and e-book readers read digital content from computer screen, and convert the text to an audio format using a text-to-speech synthesizer [6].

Eyewear devices are the most recent technology. OrCam is a commercially released glasses that use an embedded computer with a gesture (a point of finger) recognition system to perform different tasks includes reading and convey them to the user in an audio format [7]. Esight is another eyewear technology for people with low vision. It captures and processes live scenes, and displays them back on a specialized screen in front of the user's eyes [8] (Table 1).

**Table 1.** Comparison between proposed design and available assistive devices

| Device | Functionality & No. of tasks | Price | Remarks |
|---|---|---|---|
| Braille readers [4] | Reading and writing (two tasks) | $1000–$3000 | Only support tactile materials |
| Audio books [6] | Reading (one task) | $25 per month | Only for certain available books |
| Screen reader [6] | Reading digital format (one task) | $150–$1000 | Only for digital content |
| OrCam [7] | Multitask - includes reading | $2,500 | Non affordable price |
| Esight [8] | Re-display the live scenes for visually impaired to see (multitask) | $15,000 | Non affordable price and only for people with low vision, but not total blindness |
| **Proposed design** | Proposed as reading. Has the capacity to be multitask | $100–$150 | Limited by performance and accuracy of hardware |

## 3    Proposed Smart Glasses Design and Implementation

Smart eyewear design depends mainly on the processing unit, which is the raspberry pi 2, in this case. The main hardware is a Linux based ARM processor that accepts a micro SD card and thus allows us to increase the number of task functions as we wish. A raspberry pi camera was used for image acquisition. It was connected to the raspberry pi using a flex cable, and was fixed on the top middle of the glasses for optimal image capturing. The raspberry pi has an audio port which connects to earpiece. The raspberry pi GPIO port was configured to receive input from push button switches. To identify the text easier, the reading material is placed within a customly-designed frame with red borders.

The general principle of operation for such glasses is by giving instructions via switches and listening to the output through an earpiece. Similarly in this case, the user starts the task mode by a push of the button. For text recognition mode, the glasses will first confirm if the text area is correctly positioned and readable. Otherwise, it will ask the user to change the orientation of the material. After confirmation, the view is processed in real time to get the image sent to an optical character recognition (OCR) software for text extraction and subsequently forwarded to a text-to-speech synthesizer. The text is then read through the audio output port.

The image processing adopted in this work were implemented by using Simulink (Mathworks, Natick, MA). In the reading mode, the main challenge is the image quality, text position and orientation in the image. Therefore, the first step is to detect the red borders and the frame orientation. To simplify subsequent image processing, we propose an indicator to inform user if the image is skewed significantly or part of the frame is cropped. Once the text area is localized and cropped, image is enhanced by noise filtering, contrast enhancement (histogram matching technique) and morphological operations. Tesseract OCR engine [9] is used in the last step to extract the text before converting into audio output.

## 4 Results

Several sample texts were prepared and tested. Figure 1 shows an example reading text and the experiment results with the proposed smart glasses. Admittedly the text is relatively simple, but it proves the basic concept of our design. Future works include

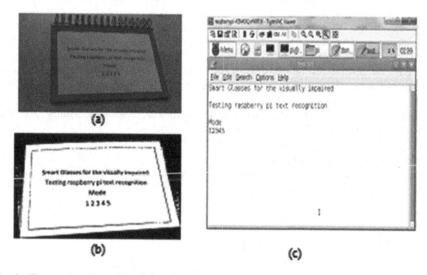

**Fig. 1.** Text recognition: (a) original image, (b) image after enhancement, (c) Tesseract OCR result of reading material. (Color figure online)

implementing additional image processing and more robust text recognition technique to compensate for the low quality images from the raspberry pi camera.

## 5   Conclusion and Future Work

This paper presents a new concept of smart glasses designed for visually impaired people using low cost single board computer raspberry pi 2 and its camera. For the demonstration purpose, the glasses are designed to perform text recognition. The system capability however can be easily extended to multiple tasks by adding more models to the core program, albeit restricted by the size of the raspberry pi SD card. Each model represents a specific task or mode. The user can have the desired task run independently from the other tasks. The system design, working mechanism and principles were discussed along with some experiment results. This new concept is expected to improve the visually impaired students' lives despite their economic situations. Immediate future work includes assessing the user-friendliness and optimizing the power management of the computing unit.

## References

1. WHO|Visual impairment and blindness. WHO, 7 April 1948. http://www.who.int/mediacentre/factsheets/fs282/en/. Accessed Oct 2015
2. Unisco. Modern Stage of SNE Development: Implementation of Inclusive Education. In: Icts in Education for People with Special Needs, Moscow, Kedrova: Institute For Information Technologies in Education UNESCO, pp. 12–14 (2006)
3. Low vision assistance. EnableMart (1957). https://www.enablemart.com/vision/low-vision-assistance. Accessed Oct 2015
4. Velázquez, R.: Wearable assistive devices for the blind. In: Lay-Ekuakille, A., Mukhopadhyay, S.C. (eds.) Wearable and Autonomous Systems. LNEE, vol. 75, pp. 331–349. Springer, Heidelberg (2010)
5. Jafri, R., Ali, S.A.: Exploring the potential of eyewear-based wearable display devices for use by the visually impaired. In: International Conference on User Science and Engineering, Shah Alam, 2–5 September 2014
6. The Macular Degeneration Foundation, Low Vision Aids & Technology, Sydney, Australia: The Macular Degeneration Foundation, July 2012
7. OrCam, OrCam. http://www.orcam.com. Accessed Dec 2015
8. Esight. http://esighteyewear.com/
9. Smith, R.: An overview of the Tesseract OCR engine. In: ICDAR 2007, pp. 629–633 (2007). doi:10.1109/ICDAR.2007.56

# EasyTrans: Accessible Translation System for Blind Translators

Dina Al-Bassam[1], Hessah Alotaibi[1], Samira Alotaibi[2], and Hend S. Al-Khalifa[1(✉)]

[1] College of Computer and Information Sciences, King Saud University, Riyadh, Saudi Arabia
hendk@ksu.edu.sa
[2] College of Languages and Translation, King Saud University, Riyadh, Saudi Arabia

**Abstract.** This paper presents the design and implementation of EasyTrans, an accessible translation web application system for Blind Translators (BT). Easy-Trans runs entirely on a web server and utilizes many web services, allowing BT users to perform their translation tasks online, thus relieving them from installing any software. EasyTrans has a simple and intuitive user interface with several dictionaries to support BT in their translation tasks. Usability evaluation of Easy-Trans showed that BT were satisfied by its performance and provided further suggestion for enhancement.

**Keywords:** Accessibility · Translation accessibility · Visual impairment · Blind translators

## 1 Introduction

Blind translators who use technology do more than sighted people could ever imagine, as they can translate with technology anywhere and anytime. Nevertheless, fully understanding this issue is reflected in the growth of facing many challenges regarding their techniques of translating texts. One of these challenges is that blind people start scanning and skimming texts without having a highlighting tool. They pick every difficult word and look for it in electronic dictionaries and websites on the Internet, which of course, adds a heightened degree of difficulty during translation. In addition, blind translators have to check many different online pages at the same time in order to locate the suitable equivalent word, therefore, repeating this process frequently can make blind translators, for certain, feel frustrated and tired.

When the methods blind people use are compared to the methods sighted people use, it is clear that blind people tend to consume more time, need more focus, and exert more effort as a result of not having paper dictionaries or a reachable comprehensive website for all their translation needs. Furthermore, if they must use paper dictionaries as sighted people do, they have to look for a worthy and qualified person to read to them, which no doubt decreases their independence. Also, existing commercial translation tools such as SDL Trados Studio has been reported inaccessible (http://goo.gl/aFKaDV).

Therefore, taking the previous issues into consideration, a translation system, which is user-friendly and easily accessible, is needed and vital to the process of translation for people facing visual impairment and blindness. In this paper, we present the design

© Springer International Publishing Switzerland 2016
K. Miesenberger et al. (Eds.): ICCHP 2016, Part II, LNCS 9759, pp. 583–586, 2016.
DOI: 10.1007/978-3-319-41267-2_83

and implementation of EasyTrans, an accessible web translation system targeting Blind Translators (BT). EasyTrans runs entirely on a web server and utilizes many web services, allowing BT users to perform their translation tasks online, thus relieving them from installing any software.

## 2   EasyTrans System

EasyTrans system is based on User Centered Design (UCD) approach. We relied on the participation of a blind translator in all phases of our system design. The blind translator was involved in the first phase of the project by helping eliciting the system's functional requirements. After that, the blind translator was involved in testing each component in the system and providing the proper feedback in terms of usability and accessibility. Furthermore, the blind translator suggested many modifications that we fixed accordingly. Finally, the complete system was tested and evaluated again by another set of blind translators to verify that the system works as expected. Next, we explain in details the different system components.

### 2.1   Interface Design

EasyTrans interface (http://trans.computing.edu.sa) applied WCAG 2.0 guidelines provided by W3C [1] as follows:

1. **Text alternatives:** Each image has an alternative name that describes it.
2. **Ordering content in a meaningful sequence:** HTML elements and the system's contents are structured in a meaningful sequence that makes the blind user grasp the content quickly and easily.
3. **Use headings:** each system page uses headers to simplify the navigation between contents.
4. **Keyboard accessibility:** each element can be accessed by an access key.
5. **Bypass blocks:** each error message used in the system is a skip link; to let the blind user read it and navigate directly to the area that has the error.
6. **Focusing on content:** the system will automatically focus the blind user to the result of the fired action by using JavaScript focus function (i.e. if the blind user translates a word, the system will focus on the translation result area to immediately read it).
7. **Mobile compatible:** the system is designed using web responsive design approach to be compatible with any mobile device.

### 2.2   Used Dictionaries

As part of the system requirements, we asked the blind translator to recommend a list of online dictionaries that are used during the translation task. Lists of seven dictionaries were recommended. However, while inspecting if the recommended dictionaries provide proper REST APIs to integrate with our system, we found that only some of them can support this feature. Therefore, as a first phase of the project, we used "Glosbe" and "Google Translate" dictionaries. The system currently only supports Arabic/English languages. However, it can be expanded in the future to include more languages.

### 2.3   System Functionality

EasyTrans targets two types of users (registered and unregistered). Both users can set the translation language, display dictionaries that support the selected translation language, highlight difficult words or sentences in the original text and export the translated text. However, the only added function for registered users is the ability to save the translation text for later editing. Thus, EasyTrans provides three main services as follows:

1. **Translator:** as a first step in the translation process, the blind user will set the translation language (e.g. From: English To: Arabic). Then, (s)he will select the dictionaries from a list which supports the chosen translation languages. Finally, the user is ready to translate and whenever (s)he translates a text, the system will focus on the translation result area by using the JavaScript focus function to allow the screen reader to immediately read it.
2. **The highlighter function:** provides an accessible way for the blind translators to highlight any text. First, they paste the whole text to be translated into the original text area. Then, they skim the text using their screen readers and highlight difficult words by adding the following symbols "@" and "*" before and after the designated word and click on highlight. The system will loop over the text and fetch all the words that are between the @ and * symbols. Then, the highlighted words will be displayed as a list beside the original text area.
3. **Editor:** While the user is highlighting and translating difficult words, (s)he can use the editor to write the translated text. The editor allows the user to export the translated text as a pdf or txt file where the user can save the whole work for later editing (if (s)he is logged into the system).

## 3   EasyTrans Evaluation

In EasyTrans system, we used two approaches for evaluation. The first approach is by using the AChecker tool (http://achecker.ca) to check the system accessibility. Also, it displays recommendations and observations to reach the proper accessibility level. When using the AChecker tool it did not detect any accessibility issues on EasyTrans system, which indicates that it is accessible.

The second approach is by conducting a usability study on blind translators who had no previous knowledge of the system. Four blind translators participated in the evaluation; they were female undergraduates, between the ages of 21 and 24 years old. Voice-over was used to read the system content.

After accomplishing the tasks, we asked them to fill out a System Usability Scale (SUS) questionnaire [2]. The obtained average score results of SUS for all participants was 87.5 %; this indicates that EasyTrans system gained participant satisfaction.

Summarizing the results of the usability evaluation, users mentioned a handful of small changes in regards to the user interface; in fact we received the same comments from the evaluators regarding the different text areas in the translation step. The areas were not labeled for easy identification. Also, one of them suggested having an instant translation for highlighted words. In addition, they suggested having a mobile application for the system.

## 4 Conclusion and Future Work

EasyTrans is a system that targets blind translators by providing the necessary tools needed for a translator to accomplish his/her task easily. The system guarantees the accessibility and the usability for the blind translators by integrating and providing all the needed translation dictionaries in one accessible system.

Evaluation of the EasyTrans system showed that it has a simple and user-friendly interface that supports BT in their translation tasks. However, EasyTrans system is still in its early stages of development; in the upcoming version we will search for ways to integrate dictionaries which have no APIs with it to enrich the dictionary support. We will also expand the functionality of the system to include grammar and spell checkers, translation memory and collaboration features. Furthermore, we will assert the usability of EasyTrans by conducting more extensive user study. The study will target a larger number of blind translators with varying previous knowledge of translation.

## References

1. Caldwell, B., Cooper, M., et al.: Web Content Accessibility Guidelines 2.0. W3C Recommendation (2008). https://www.w3.org/TR/WCAG20/
2. Brooke, J.: SUS-A quick and dirty usability scale. Usability Eval. Ind. **189**(194), 4–7 (1996)

# An Accessible Environment to Integrate Blind Participants into Brainstorming Sessions

## User Studies

Stephan Pölzer[1](✉), Andreas Kunz[2], Ali Alavi[2], and Klaus Miesenberger[1]

[1] Institut Integriert Studieren, Johannes Kepler University, Linz, Austria
{Stephan.Poelzer,Klaus.Miesenberger}@jku.at
[2] Swiss Federal Institute of Technology, Zürich, Switzerland
{kunz,alavi}@iwf.mavt.ethz.ch

**Abstract.** This paper presents user studies done for a system supporting blind people to take part in co-located brainstorming meetings. For supporting blind people, visual information exchange has to be made accessible to them. This visual information exchange takes place in two ways (a) by using artefacts to hold and share visual information (e.g. text on blackboards, content of mind-map nodes) (b) by non-verbal communication exchange (e.g. nodding to agree to someone's arguments, pointing to highlight some important artefacts). The presented prototype uses Leap Motion to detect pointing gestures as a representative example for non-verbal communication elements, while for the artefact layer a mind-map is used. A so-called "blind user interface" serializes the star structure of this min-map and allows accessing it by the blind user through a regular screen reader.

**Keywords:** Co-located meeting · Brainstorming session · Mind–map · Blind user · User studies

## 1 Introduction

Co-located meetings play an important role in our professional lives. To overcome barriers and to establish a better integration of blind people in such meetings, visual information exchange has to be made accessible to blind meeting participants. Two main layers of visual information exchange were identified: (a) artefacts like text on a blackboard, nodes on a mind-map, etc. (b) non-verbal communication elements like for instance pointing gestures to highlight an artifact during an ongoing discussion, or nodding to agree to someone's arguments.

Ongoing research shows a high effort to make the artefacts layer accessible to blind meeting participants. Accessibility issues of artefacts are for instance researched in many fields. In the fields of mathematics for example, Archambault et al. [1] developed a mathematical conversion library for a better accessibility of equations. For making graphical elements accessible to blind users, Ramloll et al. [2] developed a sonification

K. Miesenberger et al. (Eds.): ICCHP 2016, Part II, LNCS 9759, pp. 587–593, 2016.
DOI: 10.1007/978-3-319-41267-2_84

for haptic line graphs. For representing more complex diagrams such as UML to the blind user, King et al. [3] developed the TeDUB system.

However, the possibilities to improve information accessibility in co-located meetings, the difficulties in tracking and representation of non-verbal communication to the blind user, as well as the helpfulness for blind people to follow an ongoing discussion by considering the layer of non-verbal communication are not well studied so far. First aspects are researched by Pölzer and Miesenberger [4], who developed a user interface for the serialized representation of the mind-map's content and giving the possibility to blind user to also edit and enter nodes to the mind-map. This work was then combined with a prototype for a co-located team meeting, which was developed by Kunz et al. [10]. Within this prototype, the pointing gesture was taken as a representative example of a non-verbal communication element. It allowed including blind meeting participants into co-located brainstorming sessions, using a mind-map and pointing gestures. The used mind-map application was not based on a large sheet of paper, but in digital form on an interactive table, which is a fundamental requirement to allow blind-meeting participants to interact with it. In the following, the paper summarizes the conducted user studies.

## 2   System Design

The concept of the overall system architecture and different user interfaces were already presented earlier. Pölzer & Miesenberger discussed various user interfaces for the mind-map presentation [5], while a virtual Braille keyboard on an interactive surface was described by Zaim et al. [6]. Finally, the software design for the prototype was described by Pölzer et al. [7]. The implemented prototype for the user tests consists of a user interface for the sighted meeting participant, a separate user interface for the blind meeting participant (displayed on an interactive table Microsoft Pixelsense), and a LEAP-based tracking system to track the occurring pointing gestures (the non-verbal communication elements).

### 2.1   User Interface for Sighted Meeting Participants

The mind-map for the sighted users was displayed on a Microsoft Pixelsense interactive table, which allowed the sighted users to modify and edit the mind-map by using touch gestures and a virtual keyboard. Since mind-map software typically is not de-signed for collaborative multiuser interaction, it offers only a correct perspective view to one of the users around the table, while the other sighted users only can see nodes from the sides or even upside-down. Since this would significantly impact the efficiency of a brainstorming session, a new software "CoME" was developed which allows editing nodes in any orientation and later correct alignment with the rest of the mind-map. Further functionalities of the software are adding, deleting, cutting, copying and pasting nodes as well as to modifying their content (see Fig. 1). The software can be found on sourceforge.net [11].

**Fig. 1.** Overview on the system

## 2.2  User Interface for Blind Meeting Participants

A detailed description of the user interface for the blind meeting participant is given by Pölzer et al. [7]. This blind user interface mainly consists of a tree-view representation of the mind-map on the Pixelsense table, which is presented to the blind user on a separate PC (see Fig. 1). The blind user interface, which allows manipulating of and navigating through the mind-map, can be managed by the blind user by the help of standard AT (Braille Displays, speech output). The blind user interface's functionality for basic operations (e.g. adding, deleting or modifying a bubble) is identical with the functionalities of the user interface of the sighted users.

## 2.3  Tracking System

To track the occurring pointing gestures of a sighted user, the Leap Motion sensor is used. It is placed on the Pixelsense's edge, directly in front of the user. During the user tests, each person was tracked by his/her "own" Leap Motion (see Fig. 1), since the tracking range of one sensor is too small to cover the whole space above the table. A detailed description of the tracking system is given by Alavi & Kunz [8].

## 3   User Tests and Feedback

The whole design of the user study was based on the main aspects of usability engineering, as described by Nielsen [9]. During the usability engineering cycle, important aspects are: (i) analysis of user needs and user benefits from such systems through experts and target group representatives; (ii) an iterative user centered design process; and (iii) an evaluation process. The evaluation process (test scenario) and the corresponding tasks were clearly defined (see Sect. 3.1). The usability assessment methods were mainly based on the methods of observations, questionnaires and interviews (see Sect. 3.3).

## 3.1  Experimental Setup

The setup was designed for two sighted and one blind meeting participant. The working space for the blind user, including the required AT (Braille Display) was placed next to the short side of the Microsoft PixelSense on a small table (see Fig. 1). Thus, the blind user was able to acoustically follow the discussion directly without any additional means. The Leap sensors for tracking the pointing gestures of the sighted users were placed in a way so that the one sighted person was standing on a long side of the table and the other one at a short side of the table, each with his own LEAP sensor in front of him. During the design of the experimental setup, special attention was paid on the close integration of the blind participant.

The topics for the brainstorming sessions were defined for each meeting separately within the present group. The following topics were discussed: 'study' ("Studium"), 'holiday' ("Urlaub"), 'restaurant delivery service' ("Lieferservice") and 'Organization of the Institute's 25 Year Anniversary' ("Organisation der 25-jährigen Institutsfeier"). The topics were chosen in such a way that they did not require any previous knowledge or skills to fully participate in the brainstorming session. Within a 15 min brainstorming session, participants were asked to develop ideas to those topics and to integrate these ideas in the mind-map tool to trigger a further discussion.

## 3.2  User and User Instruction

Four different user studies with four different blind participants were conducted. All four blind participants were already familiar with Braille displays. Two of them were involved in the ongoing user centered design process of the blind user interface. For the other two blind users, the concept and the user interface were totally new. For the blind users not involved in the development process, an extended introduction time was used to get familiar with the concept of mind-maps and the functionalities of the designed user interface.

One sighted participant, who was familiar with the whole experimental setup and therefore able to answer occurring questions, took part in all four sessions. The second sighted participant was different in 3 out of 4 meetings (in one case only one sighted and one blind participant took part in the meeting).

Sighted users are normally familiar with the concept of mind-maps and the user interface was not too complex, which allowed the sighted users directly to start the meeting. Each of the four user tests took around 15 min without introduction time.

## 3.3  Evaluation and User Feedback

Any tool to improve the accessibility of co-located meetings without imposing additional effort to the blind users can be seen as a progress in accessibility, since such tools are rare or even do not exist. As discussed in the above, this is mainly due to the difficulties in acquiring non-verbal communication elements of the sighted users. Thus, it was decided to develop a questionnaire for the blind participants to evaluate the system based on their personal impression. Special attention was paid to the following aspects:

- General idea and concept of information representation,
- Understanding of the mind-map's content and possibility to follow occurring mind-map changes,
- Importance of non-verbal communication elements (pointing gestures),
- Suggestions for improvements.

**General Idea.** All blind users evaluated the idea and the system architecture (including the use of synchronized different views for sighted- and blind meeting participant) as suitable. The fact that all blind meeting participants started to add nodes directly after the start of the test scenario showed that they liked and understood the concept. The blind users appreciated that this new interface is not just to output data, but can also be used to modify the content of the mind-map and to active take part in the discussion. For them, it was important that the new tools allow them to participate in the discussion in "real time", thus removing the impression that they slow down the whole team process.

**Understanding of the Mind-Map.** The generated mind-maps were not perceived as too complex by the sighted users, but also all blind participants stated that they can follow the changes in the mind-map and that they have an understanding of the mind-map's structure. The understanding of the mind-map by the blind participant can also be supported by the fact that they interact and manipulated the mind-map during the ongoing meeting, and that they were fully integrated in the generation of the mind-map's layout.

**Importance of Pointing Gestures.** All blind participants agreed that the presentation of the pointing gestures and highlighting the related content of the nodes can help them to follow the ongoing discussion. Since the blind users know that non-verbal communication elements such as pointing are an important communication means by the sighted users, they appreciated to have access also to this important communication layer. Having access to this layer allowed the blind users to understand the focus of the discussion much easier, since they do not have to extrapolate this from the spoken word only.

**Suggestions for Improvements.** An idea came up to show the available elements in a fast way without the structure by presenting only the first letters of each node's content in one line. The blind user normally is involved in the generation of the mind-map and knows the nodes. Based on the presentation of the first letters, the blind user has than a fast way to find and select a node of the mind-map. The fact that letters could appear twice or even more frequently in such a line representation of the mind-map's tree structure was regarded as less disturbing, since the position of the letter in the line gives another important hint on which node is actually meant.

# 4  Summary and Outlook

The user tests showed us that such a system was accepted by all meeting participants. It did not impose an additional overhead to the sighted users, since they interact with the mind-map in a convenient way. On the other hand, the system allowed the blind users to easily follow the discussion and the actively take part within without decelerating the whole process. Thus, the active participation of all persons showed that such a system can reduce the information gap between sighted- and blind meeting participants. As we have seen in the user studies, not only the accessibility of artefacts can help blind meeting participants to follow an ongoing discussion, but also the presentation of non-verbal communication elements such as pointing gestures. Besides the well-known complexity of tracking and reasoning issues, a deep understanding of the importance for non-verbal communication elements for blind user has to be gained to achieve an adequate, non-overloading and non-disturbing presentation of such elements.

Future work will focus on different state of the art and new presentation techniques which have to be analyzed to find a proper way of presentation. Moreover, the additional filtering algorithms should be further improved by e.g. reasoning procedures to further increase the stability of the system and to better avoid false alerts to the blind user. In addition, future work will also address the fact that information is spatially distributed not only on a tabletop, but also in multiple dimensions in the complete meeting room. This will impose a higher level of complexity to the blind user interface, which have to be mastered in the future.

**Acknowledgements.** This work has been partially supported by the FWF (Austrian Science Fund) with the regional project number I867-N25 and was done in a D-A-CH project. It was a joint project between TU Darmstadt, ETH Zurich and JKU Linz with the respective funding organizations DFG (German Research Foundation), SNF (Swiss National Science Foundation) and FWF (Austrian Science Fund).

# References

1. Archambault, D., Fitzpatrick, D., Gupta, G., Karshmer, A.I., Miesenberger, K., Pontelli, E.: Towards a universal maths conversion library. In: Miesenberger, K., Klaus, J., Zagler, W.L., Burger, D. (eds.) ICCHP 2004. LNCS, vol. 3118, pp. 664–669. Springer, Heidelberg (2004)
2. Ramloll, R., Yu, W., Brewster, S., Riedel, B., Burton, M., Dimigen, G.: Constructing sonified haptic line graphs for the blind student: first steps. In: Proceedings of the 4th International ACM Conference on Assistive Technologies (Assets 2000), pp. 17–25 (2000)
3. King, A., Blenkhorn, P., Crombie, D., Dijkstra, S., Evans, G., Wood, J.: Presenting UML software engineering diagrams to blind people. In: Miesenberger, K., Klaus, J., Zagler, W.L., Burger, D. (eds.) ICCHP 2004. LNCS, vol. 3118, pp. 522–529. Springer, Heidelberg (2004)
4. Pölzer, S., Miesenberger, K.: Presenting non-verbal communication to blind users in brainstorming sessions. In: Proceedings of the 14th International Conference on Computers Helping People with Special Needs, pp. 220–225 (2014)
5. Pölzer, S., Miesenberger, K.: 2D presentation techniques of mindmaps for blind meeting participants. In: Proceedings of the 13th AAATE Conference, pp. 533–538 (2015)
6. Zaim, E., Gruber, M., Gaisbauer, G., Heumader, P., Pölzer, S., Miesenberger, K.: Virtual braille-keyboard in co-located meetings. In: Miesenberger, K., Fels, D., Archambault, D., Peňáz, P., Zagler, W. (eds.) ICCHP 2014, Part I. LNCS, vol. 8547, pp. 231–236. Springer, Heidelberg (2014)

7. Pölzer, S., Schnelle-Walka, D., Pöll, D., Heumader, P., Miesenberger, K.: Making brainstorming meetings accessible for blind users. In: Proceedings of the 12th European AAATE Conference, pp. 653–658 (2013)
8. Alavi, A., Kunz, A.: Tracking deictic gestures over large interactive surfaces. J. Comput. Support. Coop. Work (JCSCW) **24**, 109–119 (2015)
9. Nielsen, J.: Usability Engineering. Elsevier, Amsterdam (1994)
10. Kunz, A., Miesenberger, K., Mühlhäuser, M., Alavi, A., Pölzer, S., Pöll, D., Heumader, P., Schnelle-Walka, D.: Accessibility of brainstorming sessions for blind people. In: Miesenberger, K., Fels, D., Archambault, D., Peňáz, P., Zagler, W. (eds.) ICCHP 2014, Part I. LNCS, vol. 8547, pp. 237–244. Springer, Heidelberg (2014)
11. Sourceforge.net, March 2016. http://sourceforge.net/p/come/wiki/CoME%20-%20Collaborative%20Mindmap%20Editor/

# Elements of Adaptation in Ambient User Interfaces

Laura Burzagli[✉], Fabio Gori, Paolo Baronti, Marco Billi, and Pier Luigi Emiliani

IFAC CNR, Institute for Applied Physics "Nello Carrara", National Research Council of Italy,
Florence, Italy
{l.burzagli,fgori,p.baronti,m.billi,p.l.emiliani}@ifac.cnr.it

**Abstract.** In the "Design4All" project, a hardware and software architecture is under development for the implementation of adaptable and adaptive applications aimed to support all people in carrying out an independent life at home. In this paper, the problems of interactions with applications implemented in the Android platform, chosen for the experiments of interaction with the developed applications, are discussed with main emphasis on two main aspects: (i) the use of facilities supporting accessibility available in the most commonly used operating systems (mainstreaming) and (ii) the portability of solutions across different platforms.

**Keywords:** Design for all · Ambient intelligence · Accessibility · Mainstreaming

## 1 Introduction

A change in the paradigm of interaction with ICT systems and services is taking place, due to the ongoing development of the information society as an ambient intelligent environment. Until recently, the user was normally interacting with a specific device or service. Now s/he is increasingly interacting with the entire environment, e.g. the classroom, the hospital ward, the office, the house, up to the emerging smart city [1, 2]. In every context, a set of smart objects is available. These objects are connected in a local and/or an external network and offer users a set of functionalities. The communication between objects and the possibility of access to information and interpersonal communication enable the design of structured and complex services, where environmental control, access to information, and interpersonal communication can coexist and contribute to meet user's objectives. This may extend and increase the value of services, but also increases their complexity.

## 2 The Project "Design4All"

The reported activity is carried out in the project "Design4All", "Software integration and advanced Human Machine Interfaces in design for Ambient Assisted Living"[1],

---

[1] http://www.d4all.eu/.

© Springer International Publishing Switzerland 2016
K. Miesenberger et al. (Eds.): ICCHP 2016, Part II, LNCS 9759, pp. 594–601, 2016.
DOI: 10.1007/978-3-319-41267-2_85

funded by the Italian Ministry of Education, Universities and Research. The project consortium includes 13 partners, from both research and industry.

Its main objective is to favour the design of home environments that are also suitable for elderly and disabled people. Using a design for all approach, it is supposed to implement a hardware and software architecture able to integrate in the intelligent environment applications whose adaptability and adaptivity allow the use of the available functionalities to all users. From the accessibility perspective, the main emphasis is not on the accessibility of single devices and functionalities, but on the design of the interface between users and the entire living environment.

As a demonstration environment, the kitchen has been selected, since it contains several different devices, as the fridge and the oven, for storing or cooking food, or the dish washing machine. They can also provide complex services, if equipped with electronic controls and networked. For example, the oven cooking cycle can be selected in connection with the description of a recipe, its ingredient and the procedure for cooking the food. This implies the needs of appropriate interfaces to manage the different levels of interaction, with objects (the oven), information (the recipe) and communication (the friends). However, it must be emphasized that the main goal is not to give access to the oven or the washing machine, but to allow the inhabitants, any inhabitant irrespective of individual abilities, the use of all facilities in the kitchen to feed themselves.

## 3 Design Approach and Aims of the Paper

As already mentioned, the project adopted the Design for All approach (Design4All is also the acronym of the project), aiming to the design and implementation of a hardware and software architecture able, in principle, to manage every kind of adaptations of equipment controls and services and their interfaces [3]. However, in order to implement a first prototype of the system with selected services in the kitchen environment and the corresponding interactions and to test the adaptation capabilities, a restricted number of user groups has been considered. According to the interests of the rehabilitation centre in the consortium, in addition to people without any limitation elderly people without major disabilities have been considered, i.e. people with low vision, problems of dexterity and light cognitive problems, such as memory loss.

The present paper is not concerned with the description of the problems and developments connected to the implementation of the general architecture for the deployment of adaptable and adaptive environments. It mainly concerns the interaction with services necessary to support people with problems related to food, including how to operate necessary equipment, what to eat (recipes), how to identify necessary ingredients (shopping list), how to acquire them (e.g. remote shopping) and how to interact with other people (for example to acquire new recipes and getting support).

## 4 Technical Implementation – General Principles

One of the reason why the kitchen has been chosen as an interesting environment, in addition to the complexity of the environment and the (potentially intelligent) technology present, is that some of the partners were active in earlier projects dealing with this environment, as the AAL "FOOD"[2] and the Italian Industria 2015 "eKitchen"[3]. The cited projects carried out an in-depth analysis of the activities to be carried out in the kitchen for feeding and the support that can be offered by the technology in the environment and/or remote and by networked people. In addition, the necessity of generalizing approaches to increase usability and grant accessibility to all people with adaptivity and adaptability was clearly pointed out [4–6].

So far, in ICT the general approach was to make available systems and services (e.g. a word processor, a browser, etc.) whose functionalities and interactions were decided by the designer. The users had to learn how to use them and if they had problems, normally in interact with them, special interfaces were added (assistive technology) or adaptability and adaptivity was introduced in the interaction. The main emphasis was in coping with sensory and motor problems and in transduction between different modalities. More recently, some activity was devoted to mental problems, mainly with reference to old people.

What came out from the analyses in the cited projects is that the technology available or proposed in the intelligent environments is such that it is possible and necessary to consider adaptability and adaptivity not only at the level of interaction but also in terms of functionalities to make available to the different users. For example, if only paper and pen or a word processor are available, the shopping list is only a list of items to be bought. Anyway, if one is living in a kitchen that is an environment of interconnected equipment and a node of a social network, the shopping list may be a complex multimedia document. It is constructed in cooperation with an agent that, if requested, suggests a possible menu as a function of the health situation of the user, with the fridge and the pantry that know what is already available at home, with the market that controls if what is needed is available on the shelves, with friends who can advise. Each user must be offered the functionalities that she feels necessary, organized in the way she likes and made available through suitable interactions. Therefore, it is necessary to carry out a complete analysis of all activities that a person consciously or unconsciously (because part of the default habitual activities) carry out to construct the shopping list in order to decide what are the functionalities and their adaptable and adaptive, if any, combinations to make available.

From the perspective of interaction, it became evident that the emerging technological platforms (e.g. operating systems) are offering by default many facilities to favour accessibility. It may be convenient to use them before the integration of special purpose technology.

The paper describes the accessibility features of an application for the preparation of the shopping list whose functionalities (services) can be (re)organized to meet the needs and preferences of users. Even if in the future, the interaction with the environment and with objects in it will probably be based on different paradigms and technologies (Voice interaction? Gesture recognition? Elements of virtual reality?), in order to test ideas about adaptability and adaptivity of service functionalities, it was decided to

---

[2] http://www.food-aal.eu/.

[3] http://www.cucinelube.it/en/lube-plus/research-and-innovation/e-kitchen/.

implement the interface using a tablet, considered a good compromise between several different options. Tablets are portable, well known and used by a large portion of population, due to the large number of application already available on them. Moreover, the operating systems available on tablets have built in facilities for accessibility. Therefore, it is possible, at least in this environment that is supposed to stay with us for some time in the future, to test possible advantages or disadvantages of using these "general purpose" facilities. A specific App(lication) is being designed, whose more innovative part is in its adaptation features, which have to take into account the specific characteristics of selected users' profiles. The Android platform has been chosen for the wide availability of devices running on this platform and the large diffusion that the operating system has worldwide.

## 5    Technical Implementation – Mainstreaming Accessibility

The first step of the App design was an accurate analysis of the accessibility problems. Several guidelines produced by W3C have been considered: WCAG 2.0[4], WCAH2ICT[5] and the document on Mobile Accessibility. In particular, the document "How WCAG 2.0 and Other W3C/WAI Guidelines Apply to Mobile"[6] has been analysed in order to adopt the basic rules of accessibility. On Android several adaptation characteristics are available (Fig. 1).

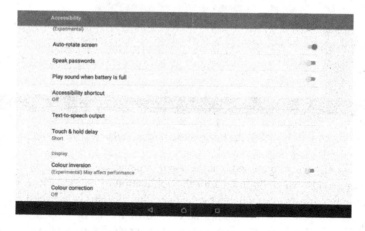

**Fig. 1.** Android accessibility settings

Among Android accessibility features (Android 5.x and 6.01), some elements have been identified of interest for the adaptations necessary for the already mentioned user groups considered in the experiments: Colour inversion, Colour Setting, Large Text, Magnification Gestures, Text to Speech and Speech to Text.

---

[4] https://www.w3.org/TR/WCAG20/.
[5] https://www.w3.org/TR/wcag2ict/.
[6] https://www.w3.org/TR/mobile-accessibility-mapping/.

The availability of such features on the App enables a set of adaptation properties on the interface. For people with problems of sight the inversion of colour is set by default when the user logs in. Moreover, some checks by voice are available, for example to be sure about time and temperature settings for the appliances. For people with dexterity problems, it is possible to introduce the same values by voice, avoiding problems with the graphic interface. Anyway, every user who considers useful a specific accessibility feature can activate or remove it very easily. At present, a system to manage this function also in a dynamical way, according to the behaviour of the user, is under development. Figure 2 shows how all this accessibility features are available in the App (accessibility icons), and can be activated or deactivate by pressing the specific icon.

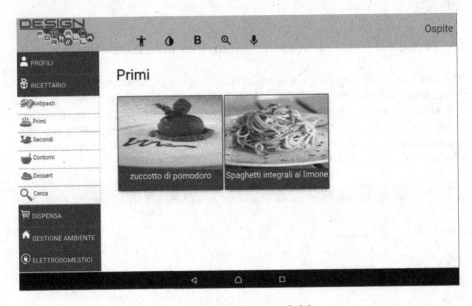

**Fig. 2.**  Recipes list: normal sight

It can obviously be maintained that the use of adaptations particularly designed for specific user groups can be optimized for the application of interest. However, the use of adaptation features made available by the operating systems has several advantages: (i) they offer the possibility of taking advantage of the technological changes and improvement of the operating system, provided by a team of expert developers, rather than the limited group that implements the App; (ii) the adaptation features are evaluated by a large number of users, thus ensuring that the resulting solutions is more robust than a specific solution. On the other side, an "a priori" activation of these characteristics (this means at the level of the device and not inside the App) does not represent an appropriate solution for the accessibility problem in complex environments. Indeed, the house interface on the tablet is thought to be utilized by different users with different configurations or directly by the home system in a dynamic way, when the system automatically recognize difficulties experienced by the user in working with the App. Therefore, the adaptation features even if made available by the operating system, must be controlled by the interface of the App.

## 6    Technical Implementation – Portability

One obvious disadvantage of working in a specific platform is that the developed application may be usable only on systems based on it. This is particularly disturbing, because in reality the available platforms offer similar accessibility supports. Therefore, the portability across different platforms of the developed application has been carefully analysed.

For the technical implementation of the App, three different approaches can be followed. A first approach is the development of a mobile web app, which is based on the use of the Internet technology and on the browser as the layout engine of the interface graphical widgets. A second option is the implementation of a native app, i.e. an application program that has been developed for use on a specific platform or device. The third possibility is the use of a hybrid App, which, as a mobile web app, is built with a combination of web technologies like HTML, CSS, and JavaScript, but is hosted inside a native application that utilizes a mobile platform's WebView[7] (it allows Android apps to display content from the web directly inside an application).

If these options are compared from the accessibility perspective or, more in general, from an adaptation perspective, a web implementation may appear the most appropriate, because the WCAG 2.0 can be adopted as a guide to accessibility. Anyway, several accessibility features, even if available at the operating system level, are not available at the browser level because for security reason all system functionalities are not natively accessible from code executed inside a browser. They can be used only with the development of a number of specific plugins. What is worse is that different plugins are necessary for different browsers (i.e. Firefox, Chrome, Opera, Safari, etc.), thus multiplying the necessary effort if different users are comfortable with different browsers.

A native application may simplify the use of the specific accessibility features of the platform but requires a completely new development if a different platforms become of interest.

This is the reason why the solution of a hybrid App has been considered appropriate, and has been developed using the Apache Cordova framework[8]. With Apache Cordova, apps are built using CSS3 and HTML for rendering and JavaScript for logic. Specific tools for every supported platform[9] (i.e. Android, iOS, Windows Mobile, etc.), enable apps to be compiled and packaged for the specific environment. JavaScript code, HTML tagsets and CSS3 style sheets are managed by WebKit, which is specific for each platform and represents the layout engine software component for rendering page in a web browser. Moreover, access to specific hardware like GPS or camera and system

---

[7] http://searchsecurity.techtarget.com/definition/Android-Webview .
[8] https://en.wikipedia.org/wiki/Apache_Cordova .
[9] https://cordova.apache.org/#supported_platforms_section .

functionalities like accessibility functions is granted by a standard API. This interface exposes a set of commands, which is common to all platforms and maps them to the specific instruction sets of every single platform.

In order to use these features, a hybrid app has been developed (Fig. 2), where the activation of accessibility functions is made available inside the App itself. While some features are made available with the installation of a specific plugin for the API management on the Cordova framework (text-to-speech and speech-to-text) (org.apache.cordova.speech.speechrecognition and cordova-plugin-tts), for the colour inversion and for magnification gestures a specific plugin has been developed, called it.cnr.ifac.eilab.securesettings.

The main positive feature is that the App can be designed without reference to a specific platform and then compiled on the platform of interest, thus allowing an easier migration on different equipment. Obviously, this is not true for the activation and use from inside the applications of all accessibility features of the different platform. As in the case of the application described in the paper for the Android system, it will be necessary to develop some plugins for interfacing the application with some of the facilities of the operating system not integrated in the Cordova framework. This is the only additional effort for the portability of the application (Fig. 3).

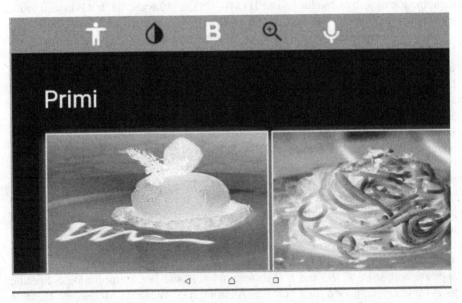

**Fig. 3.** Recipes list: color inversion and magnification gestures activated

## 7   Conclusions

The described system is still under development. From the functionality perspective, the application, at the moment, is able: (i) to control the equipment in the kitchen (oven, fridge, refrigerator and dish washing machine); (ii) to get, organize and present information about what is available in the fridge, refrigerator and pantry; (iii) to show people recipes and cooperate with them in the preparation of the shopping list; (iv) to guide the user in the execution of the recipe, with a control of the features of the user and identification of necessary problem she can encounter (e.g. cutting if she has manipulation problems).

The integration of the accessibility facilities, which is the main concern in the present paper, has been carried out, showing that it is possible to give a complete control of the available functionalities from inside the application, first to the developers and then to the users. The accessibility facilities can be adopted by any user for the services that the system makes available in the kitchen environment. Moreover, user needs and preferences can be monitored by the system through its adaptation system.

Evaluation tests with users are not yet available. Anyway, since the project consortium include also an Institute of Rehabilitation, a first evaluation by experts has been carried out with positive reactions. A structured process of evaluation is foreseen at the end of the year, when the development of the prototype will be completed.

# References

1. Bibri, S.E.: The Human Face of Ambient Intelligent. Atlantis Press, Amsterdam (2015)
2. Geissbühler, A., Demongeot, J., Mokhtari, M., Abdulrazak, B., Aloulou, H. (eds.): Inclusive Smart Cities and e-Health. LNCS, vol. 9102. Springer, Heidelberg (2015). doi: 10.1007/978-3-319-19312-0
3. Nakashima, H., Aghajan, H., Augusto, J.C.: Handbook of Ambient Intelligent and Smart Environment. Springer, Heidelberg (2010)
4. Burzagli, L., Emiliani, P.L., Gabbanini, F.: An innovative framework to support multi-modal interaction with Smart Enviroments. Expert Syst. Appl. **39**, 2239–2246 (2012)
5. Burzagli, L., Emliani, P.L.: Open ambient intelligence environments. In: 13th European Conference on the Advancement of Assistive Technology, pp. 159–166. IOS, Amsterdam (2015)
6. Burzagli, L., Di Fonzo, L., Emiliani, P.L.: Services and applications in an Ambient Assisted Living (AAL) environment. In: Stephanidis, C., Antona, M. (eds.) UAHCI 2014, Part III. LNCS, vol. 8515, pp. 475–482. Springer, Heidelberg (2014)

# Erratum to: Experimenting with Tactile Sense and Kinesthetic Sense Assisting System for Blind Education

Junji Onishi[1]([✉]), Tadahiro Sakai[2], Msatsugu Sakajiri[1],
Akihiro Ogata[1], Takahiro Miura[3], Takuya Handa[4],
Nobuyuki Hiruma[4], Toshihiro Shimizu[4], and Tsukasa Ono[1]

[1] Tsukuba University of Technology, Ibaraki, Japan
ohnishi@g.tsukuba-tech.ac.jp,
sakajiri@cs.k.tsukuba-tech.ac.jp
[2] NHK Engineering System, Tokyo, Japan
sakai.tadahiro@nes.or.jp
[3] The University of Tokyo, Tokyo, Japan
[4] NHK Science and Technology Research Laboratories, Tokyo 157-8510, Japan

**Erratum to:
Chapter 13 in: K. Miesenberger et al. (Eds.)
Computers Helping People with Special Needs
DOI: 10.1007/978-3-319-41267-2_13**

In an earlier version of this paper, the following reference was omitted: Jafri, R., Ali, S. A.: Utilizing 3D printing to assist the blind. In: Proceedings of the 2015 International Conference on Health Informatics and Medical Systems (HIMS 2015), July 27–30, Las Vegas, Nevada, USA, pp. 55–61 (2015). This has now been updated.

The updated original online version for this Chapter can be found at 10.1007/978-3-319-41267-2_13

# Author Index

Printed in the United States
By Bookmasters